The Parliamentary Register
by Great Britain. Parliament

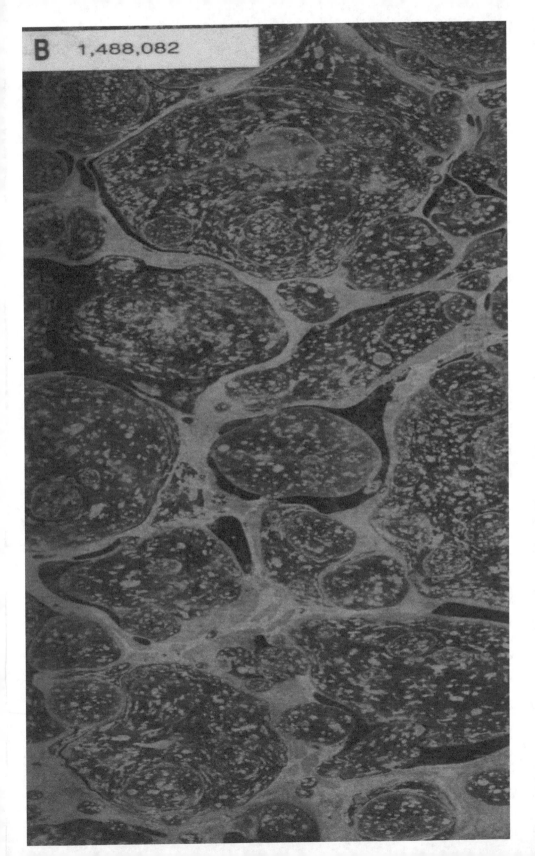

George Purling.

THE
Parliamentary Regifter;

OR

HISTORY

OF THE

PROCEEDINGS AND DEBATES

OF THE

HOUSE OF COMMONS;

CONTAINING AN ACCOUNT OF

The moft interefting SPEECHES and MOTIONS; accurate
Copies of the moft remarkable LETTERS and PAPERS;
of the moft material EVIDENCE, PETITIONS, &c.
laid before and offered to the HOUSE,

DURING THE

THIRD SESSION of the SIXTEENTH PARLIAMENT

OF

GREAT BRITAIN.

VOL. XIX.

LONDON:

Printed for J. DEBRETT, oppofite BURLINGTON HOUSE,
PICCADILLY.

M DCC.LXXXVII.

CONTENTS

of

VOLUME the NINETEENTH.

A 2

Speech

INDEX.

INDEX.

I N D E X.

THE

THE
HISTORY
OF THE
PROCEEDINGS AND DEBATES
OF THE
HOUSE of COMMONS,

In the THIRD SESSION of the

Sixteenth Parliament of GREAT BRITAIN,

Appointed to be holden at WESTMINSTER

On TUESDAY the 18th of MAY, 1784.

24th *January*, 1786.

ON the twenty-fourth of January, 1786, the King went, at three o'clock, in the usual state, to the House of Lords, when Sir Francis Molyneux, Knight, (Gentleman Usher of the Black Rod), was ordered to signify to the Commons the royal command that they should attend at the bar. The Commons accordingly appearing, His Majesty made the following speech :

" My Lords and Gentlemen,

" Since I last met you in Parliament, the disputes which
" appeared to threaten an interruption to the tranquillity
" of Europe have been brought to an amicable conclusion ;
" and I continue to receive from foreign powers the strong-
" est assurances of their friendly disposition towards this
" country.
" At home, my subjects experience the growing blessings
" of peace, in the extension of trade, the improvement of
" the revenue, and increase of the public credit of the na-
" tion.

VOL. XIX.   B   " For

" For the farther advancement of thofe important objects,
" I rely on the continuance of that zeal and induftry which
" you manifefted in the laft feffion of Parliament.

" The refolutions which you laid before me, as the bafis
" of an adjuftment of the commercial intercourfe between
" Great Britain and Ireland, have been, by my direction, re-
" commended to the Parliament of that kingdom; but no
" effectual ftep has hitherto been taken thereupon, which
" can enable you to make any farther progrefs in that falu-
" tary work."

" Gentlemen of the Houfe of Commons.

" I have ordered the eftimates for the prefent year to be
" laid before you: it is my earneft wifh to enforce œconomy
" in every department, and you will, I am perfuaded, be
" equally ready to make fuch provifion as may be neceffary
" for the public fervice, and particularly for maintaining our
" naval ftrength on the moft fecure and refpectable footing.
" —Above all, let me recommend to you the eftablifhment
" of a fixed plan for the reduction of the national debt. The
" flourifhing ftate of the revenue will, I truft, enable you
" to effect this important meafure, with little addition to
" the public burdens."

" My Lords and Gentlemen,

" The vigour and refources of the country, fo fully ma-
" nifefted in its prefent fituation, will encourage you in con-
" tinuing to give your utmoft attention to every object of
" national concern; particularly to the confideration of fuch
" meafures as may be neceffary in order to give farther fecu-
" rity to the revenue, and to promote and extend, as far as
" poffible, the trade and general induftry of my fubjects."
The Speaker and the Members having returned to their
own Houfe, the former begged leave to acquaint them that,
in purfuance of the Act of Parliament, vefting him with
certain powers, he had, during the recefs, iffued his warrants
to the Clerk of the Crown to make out new writs for the
election of reprefentatives for feats vacated in Parliament,
either by deceafe or other caufes.

Several new Members now took the ufual oaths.

The *Speaker* next read (as a matter of form, and, in proof
of the long-eftablifhed right of the Commons to difcufs
what points they chofe to introduce, even previoufly to their
confideration of the fpeech from the throne), the title of a
bill for the more effectual prevention of clandeftine out-
lawries.

At

At length, the King's Speech having been read from the chair,

Mr. *John Smyth* (the Member for Pontefract) said, that the pleasure with which he rose for the purpose of moving an address of thanks to His Majesty, for the gracious speech which he had been pleased to deliver from the throne, was enhanced by the conviction that it stood, in every passage, so totally secure from all justifiable objections, as to establish the fullest claim to the unanimous approbation of the House. Under this idea, he should have felt it highly proper to leave the address, which he designed to take the liberty of proposing, standing upon the firm basis of its own merits, did not the respect due to those in the presence of whom he had the honour of speaking, call upon him, in some measure, to describe the motive for his rising. He should have felt a difficulty in remaining silent, while impressed with the opinion that the sentiments delivered from the throne must deeply affect the feelings of all Englishmen, who, placing a right value upon their mutual enjoyments and advantages, as fellow-subjects, were anxious for the most extended increase of the happiness and the glory of the British empire. Nor could he, upon this occasion, suppose that every Member of the House was not eager to participate with him in his joy at hearing the confirmation of the calmest existence of peace throughout the states of Europe; and of the amicable disposition with which the foreign powers seemed glad to turn their general attention to Great Britain. Attachments of this valuable kind from the surrounding nations, might be considered as the forerunners of blessings yet to issue from the introduction of peace; as the promisers of a still more extended and rapidly-accumulating commerce; as the earnest of the invigorated state and augmentation of the revenue; and as the harbinger of the firm establishment and affluent increase of public credit. Even in the example wherein success had not totally kept pace with natural expectations, though the commercial intercourse with Ireland was not yet settled upon the liberal and equitable plan which was completed in the last session, the majority of the House were not destitute of the comforting recollection that they had followed up all possible expedients to demonstrate the affectionate liberality of their attachment to a sister-country, and their anxious desire to throw open to her an unequivocal participation of every commercial benefit with Great Britain; a participation of which the leading object was to preserve inviolate the rights of either kingdom. Sensible that, from our naval strength, the first and most irresistible palladium of our country would certainly arise, he could not avoid turning with the most heart felt satisfaction to that

passage

paſſage in the ſpeech from the throne which ſo expreſſively recommended the maintenance of a powerful marine eſtabliſhment, becauſe he conſidered it (and he was ſure that the Houſe would coincide with him in this opinion) as a circumſtance which muſt occaſion rival nations to feel a proper awe, and to offer us, for their own ſake, every due tribute of reſpect. He ſcarcely felt it needful to declare that the fixed plan for the reduction of the national debt was thoroughly intitled to an immediate, ſtrenuous, and effectual adoption; and the rather as the moſt flattering proſpects of lowering it to a ſum much leſs conſiderable were now in view, whilſt commerce, vigorous in its revival, was ſeen to flouriſh through a variety of highly profitable and extenſive channels. Under theſe circumſtances, the Miniſter who could ſummon up the virtuous and truly politic intrepidity to conceive and fully execute a plan for leſſening, in a great degree, the amount of thoſe millions which the country owed, muſt deſerve, and ought, certainly, to receive the countenance and approbation of his Sovereign and of his fellow-ſubjects. His chief aids, in this important, this patriotic meaſure, muſt unavoidably connect themſelves with the ſinking-fund: and, ſurely, the People would never murmur at the ſlightly-increaſing impoſitions of ſome moderate and equitable taxes, when they diſcovered that it led, unerringly and rapidly, to the attainment of ſo deſirable an object.

Mr. Smyth now concluded with obſerving that he ſhould no longer treſpaſs upon the patience of the Houſe than by moving,

"That an humble addreſs be preſented to His Majeſty, "to return His Majeſty our moſt humble thanks for his "moſt gracious ſpeech from the throne:

"To expreſs our ſatisfaction that the diſputes which ap- "peared to threaten an interruption to the tranquillity of "Europe have been brought to an amicable concluſion; "and, that His Majeſty continues to receive from foreign "powers the ſtrongeſt aſſurances of their friendly diſpoſi- "tion toward this country:

"To aſſure His Majeſty, that we are deeply ſenſible of "the bleſſings which we experience from the enjoyment of "peace, in the extenſion of trade, the improvement of the "revenue, and the increaſe of the public credit of the na- "tion; and that His Majeſty may rely on the utmoſt exer- "tion of our zeal and induſtry for the farther advancement "of theſe important objects.

"That, in order to promote, as far as in us lie, the com- "mon intereſts of all His Majeſty's ſubjects, we humbly "laid before His Majeſty, in the laſt ſeſſion of Parliament, "ſeveral reſolutions, as the baſis of an adjuſtment of the
"commercial

" commercial intercourfe between Great Britain and Ire-
" land; but that, as no effectual ftep has hitherto been taken
" thereupon by the Parliament of that kingdom, we do not
" find ourfelves at prefent enabled to make any farther pro-
" grefs in that falutary work :

" To exprefs our gratitude for His Majefty's gracious af-
" furances of His earneft wifh to enforce œconomy in every
" department; and our readinefs, at all times, to make fuch
" provifion as may be neceffary for every branch of the
" public fervice, particularly for maintaining the naval
" ftrength of thefe kingdoms on the moft fecure and re-
" fpectable footing: That, as we are fully impreffed with
" the neceffity of eftablifhing a fixed plan for the reduction
" of the national debt, we fhall lofe no time in entering
" on that important confideration; and that it will afford
" us the moft folid fatisfaction to find that this moft de-
" firable object may be attained with little addition to the
" public burdens :

" That the vigour and refources of the country fo happily
" manifefted in our prefent fituation muft give encourage-
" ment and confidence to all His Majefty's fubjects; and can-
" not fail to animate our exertions in endeavouring, by a
" continued attention to the fecurity of the revenue, and
" the extenfion of trade, to confirm and improve the in-
" creafing profperity of the empire."

Mr. *Addington*, feconding the addrefs, remarked, that he did Mr. Ad-
not entertain a doubt but that the Houfe would unanimoufly dington.
receive the motion of his honourable friend; aware of the
impropriety of objecting to return their moft grateful thanks
for a fpeech in which His Majefty had been gracioufly pleafed
to affure them of the continuance of their enjoyment of
peace, and its attendant bleffings, and in which he afked for
little more than œconomy and regulation. That the felicities of
peace were already in our poffeffion, appeared from the extenfion of trade, the improvement of the revenue, and the increafe
of the public credit. And furely the Houfe muft feel the neceffity of paying the moft zealous attention to the furtherance
of objects, fo immediately conducive to interefts fo powerfully
interwoven with their own. Yet, certainly, although feeling
juft caufe for exultation in the enjoyment of thefe happy
confequences of the peace, they all lamented the unfortunate
jealoufies and ill-founded alarms which occafioned the fifter
kingdom to reject a plan of commercial intercourfe calculated to have admitted her to a participation of the fame
advantages. He trufted, however, that the time was not far
diftant, when the arrow of prejudice would have fpent its
force, and the mifconceived idea of any defign in the Britifh
Parliament to refume the legiflative rights of Ireland, or in
any

any degree trench upon its independence or conftitution; would
exift no longer. While he confidered the prefent prosperous
fituation of public affairs in its moft pleafing ftate of con-
traft to their former alarming condition ; he trufted that even
the innocent inftruments of incurring thofe burdens, with
which the country had been loaded by the heavy expences
of the late unfortunate war, would join in the general joy at
the happy change of circumftances, and chearfully co-operate
in endeavouring to alleviate the public burdens by every
means which either œconomy could dictate, or the wifeft
management effect. The great points recommended in the
fpeech, all went to the neceffary and invigorating revival of
that conftitution, the fabric of which had not long fince tot-
tered, and experienced the danger of being fhaken to its
foundation. He was perfuaded, therefore, that every gentleman would feel it to be a common caufe, and not hefitate, on
the prefent occafion, to give his unanimous fupport to the
addrefs. For his own part, he did not confider it in the leaft
requifite to place a watch upon the emotions of private friendfhip, becaufe the commendation which it behoved him to
beftow was due to the public conduct of the Minifter, and
confequently ftood diftinct and feparate from his partialities
for the man.

The Earl of   The addrefs having been read from the chair, the Earl of
Surry.   *Surrey* obferved, that he could not fubfcribe to the extravagance of the panegyrics pronounced by the two honourable
gentleman who opened the debate. He could, by no means,
concur in the opinion of either the honourable gentleman
who had fpoken firft, or that of the honourable gentleman
who had fince, with fo much eloquence, difcuffed the few
topics which compofed the fpeech from the throne; much
lefs could he join in complimenting the right honourable
gentleman now at the head of the national affairs. He had
declared, when the Adminiftration firft came into his hands,
he had no confidence in either him or his coadjutors in office.
His opinion had not been in the leaft altered by recent circumftances, but, on the contrary, confirmed and eftablifhed.
So far from thinking him deferving of his confidence, or that
of the honourable gentlemen with whom he acted, he had
every reafon to conclude that the confidence of thofe gentlemen, who had hitherto fupported the Minifter, ought now to
be withdrawn. Thofe meafures which the right honourable
gentleman had too fuccefsfully brought forward, were bad meafures in themfelves, and ought never to have been propofed :
while fuch of his meafures as were deferving of fuccefs, had
uniformly failed, which was, to *his* mind, an unanfwerable
proof of his incapability as a Minifter, and of his loft claims
to the confidence of that Houfe. The right honourable gentleman

man's firſt meaſure, had been his India Bill, which inſtead of ſecuring peace and order in India, had produced the oppoſite effect, and excited the moſt violent and clamorous diſcontents. The ſecond meaſure of the right honourable gentleman had been as wiſe a one as ever was brought forward by any Miniſter, and in which he had himſelf joined and endeavoured to ſupport him moſt heartily; the attempt to effect a reform in the repreſentation of the People. The right honourable gentleman's failure in that meaſure, and his want of power to carry it, convinced him that he was unfit for his ſituation. The other meaſures of the right honourable gentleman had been, in his opinion, unwiſe and miſchevious in their tendency, as well the oppreſſive taxes he had impoſed, as the reſolutions for the adjuſtment of a commercial intercourſe with Ireland, brought forward in ſo ſtrange a manner, and giving ſo much diſguſt to both countries. It appeared extraordinary, that an alluſion to thoſe reſolutions made any part of the addreſs. What neceſſity exiſted for mentioning them at all, after the declaration from the Throne, that they could not do any thing reſpecting them? It ſeemed by no means proper for the Houſe to ſay any thing upon the ſubject, and therefore, he ſhould move, by way of amendment to leave out the whole paragraph of the addreſs alluding to the reſolutions in queſtion. With regard to the ſurplus of the revenue, he could not, for one, admit that Miniſters deſerved the credit of it; and, though ready to acknowledge, that œconomy was a proper object of attention, he did not think that the meaſures of the Miniſter were equal even to aſſurances that he honoured it with his attachment. Was the maintaining an Ambaſſador to Madrid at a large expence for two years together, during all which time he had never once been in Spain, a proof of the œconomy of Adminiſtration? Or was the having two Ambaſſadors upon ſeparate eſtabliſhments at Paris to be conſidered as its teſt? Poſſibly, the right honourable gentleman who was appointed the new Ambaſſador, with new powers, and whom he did not then ſee in his place, [A loud laugh, Mr. Eden ſitting upon an *oppoſite* bench.] could convince him that he was in an error, in thinking that two Ambaſſadors to one Court were neither neceſſary nor œconomical; and perhaps the ſame right honourable gentleman would ſtate, that he had been furniſhed with reaſons to induce him to give his confidence to that very Adminiſtration; or for withholding his confidence from him whom he had at different times ſupplied with ſo many reaſons. Not finding the right honourable gentleman, his late political friend, upon the bench where he *once* ſat, and from whence he had declaimed ſo ably againſt the meaſures of the Miniſter, he could ſcarcely believe, in ſpite of recent circum-

ſtances,

ftances, that he had changed his place. Lord Surrey now expreffed his fuppofition, that the part of the fpeech which recommended the maintaining the naval ftrength of the empire, on the moft fecure and refpectable footing, went to an increafe of the navy.

(Mr. Pitt rofe and faid, " fuch words were not in the fpeech." The Speaker then read the paragraph in queftion.)

By maintaining our naval ftrength, he hoped it was not meant, the confining our navy to its prefent eftablifhment, or governing it by what it was in 1748, or at the end of the war before the laft; but that keeping in view the number and ftrength of the navy of the Houfe of Bourbon, we fhould take care to make our marine prove at leaft equal to theirs; fince upon that circumftance alone depended our fecurity. If this was to be underftood, he fhould not object to that part of the addrefs, though he owned he fhould have been far better pleafed, if the recommendation of maintaining our naval ftrength on a refpectable footing, had been accompanied with a declaration that the ftanding army was to be reduced. He faw no occafion whatever for keeping up as large a military force during a ftate of difmembered and diminifhed empire, as before fuch diminution took place. He did not mean to object to any part of the addrefs, except the paragraph which mentioned the Irifh propofitions, the whole of which he moved by way of amendment, to omit.

Mr. Minchin, (but without a fpeech) feconded the motion.

Mr. *Fox* declared that of all the fpeeches from the throne which he ever remembered to have heard delivered at the opening of a feffion of Parliament, of all the fpeeches of that kind which he had ever heard of by relation, or read of in hiftory, he did not recollect to have met with an inftance of one fo cautioufly worded, or that afforded fuch little ground for objection of any kind. He rofe therefore to fpeak to what was out of it, rather than what was in it; to that which perhaps ought to have been there, rather than to what was there. The propriety of a Minifter's contenting himfelf with addreffing a Britifh Parliament from the Throne, with general ideas of the political fituation of a country inftead of fpecifically adverting to facts and circumftances, which deeply and materially concerned its firft and deareft interefts, relatively confidered with thofe of other ftates, would be for others to judge and to decide upon. It was enough for him to fay, that there were fo many matters pending, and fo much had been lately done by foreign powers, the confequences of which might more or lefs critically affect Great Britain in proportion to the meafures that His Majefty's Minifters had purfued; and, indeed, upon the ground of thefe tranfactions, he had looked for fomething more than vague affurances of

the

Mr. Fox.

the tranquillity of Europe, and had expected His Majesty's
speech would have given that House a variety of great and
important subjects, intimately connected with the future
prosperity or ill fortune of the empire; upon all of which
the speech left the House in utter and impenetrable darkness.
With regard to the extension of trade, the increase of the
public credit of the nation, and the growing surplus of the
revenue; those were circumstances in which every man must
rejoice; and at which no party, no political faction, no set
of persons of any name and description whatever could suppress their exultation, because they went to prove, what
must be to all ranks of men and all political parties, a matter
of solid satisfaction and unrestrained triumph, the returning
vigour of our resources! But, were these matters of surprise,
were these circumstances to cause astonishment? Undoubtedly
they were not. Almost every man knew there would be
some surplus; almost every man expected it; they only differed about the amount of that surplus, one gentleman alone
excepted, who had certainly contended, and had endeavoured
to prove, that there would be no surplus; but that gentleman
had probably been since convinced of his error, had retracted
it, and as every man of candour would do, he had no doubt
he was ready publicly to acknowledge that retraction. That
there would be some surplus, he had always admitted; what
that surplus was, he would not then attempt to bring into
discussion. Indeed it was not possible till he knew it, till he
had it stated to him, and its amount was fairly before him,
and capable of argument and of investigation. He would
not assert to what the signs of returning vigour were ascribe-
able; that might be matter of much useless difference of
opinion; several of them might be owing to the success of
some of the measures of the present Administration; he would
not be so uncandid as to deny that they were; but more, far
more, he believed, were owing to the failure of others of their
measures, which, had they succeeded, must have been attended
with consequences, the most fatal to the revenue, and to
the national credit and prosperity, that could possibly be
imagined. Nothing but the alarm and disgust created by the
agitation of those bad measures could have so long kept back
the returning trade of the country, the natural consequence
of peace, and which ever had been the case at the end of
every war before the last. Those alarms and disgust had
been done away, in a great degree, by the failure of the measure to which he alluded, and the tide of trade was now returning to its old and natural channel. For his part, he
certainly should not object to the address in general, though
he might probably vote with his noble friend for his amendment; but there were two matters of considerable import-

ance which, in one instance, arose out of the wording of the
speech, in its first paragraph, and in another, was mentioned
in a subsequent part of it upon both of which he must say
a few words, and expect to receive some answer; whether satisfactory or not the event would prove. What he meant was,
to inquire what sort of construction, whether broad or narrow, was to be put upon that part of the speech which related
to the tranquillity of Europe, and stated, that His Majesty
continued to receive the strongest assurances from foreign
powers of their friendly disposition towards this country? He
wished also to know what was meant by the manner in which
the resolutions relative to an intended adjustment of a commercial intercourse with Ireland was mentioned, and whether
they were to understand, by being told from the Throne, that
they were incapable of making any farther progress in the work,
that the resolutions were completely abandoned and given
up, or that they were to be revived, and endeavoured to be
carried into effect at any future period of time? On both of
these points it was exceedingly material that such information should be given, that each might be clearly and precisely
understood. With regard to the first, if the mention of the
tranquillity of Europe alluded only to the end put to the
threatened war between the Emperor and the United States
of Holland, in that case the construction was too narrow,
and His Majesty's Ministers greatly undervalued the information of that House, and not of that House only, but of every
man who read or attended to the political transactions of
Europe, and who was at all aware of what passed on the
Continent, the different treaties lately entered into by different
foreign powers, and the conduct which ought to have been
pursued with a view to counteract the operation of those
treaties, and transactions, as far as it was likely to prove or
capable of proving prejudicial to the interests of Great Britain. He was aware, that being no Minister, he had it in
his power to speak in a style, in which it would be highly
imprudent for His Majesty's Ministers to express themselves,
and as the matters that he should have occasion to treat of,
were of infinite consideration, he should endeavour to make
himself as well understood as possible. With respect to the
naval force of this country, and what ought to be the criterion of its number and strength, a noble Earl (of Surrey) had
mentioned only the naval force of France, forgetting that
France was but one branch of the powerful confederacy of
maritime powers, entered into with a professed hostility to
Great Britain; for though all treaties were avowedly treaties
of a defensive nature, and entered into upon a pretence of
mutual defence, every man who knew any thing of the
meaning of treaties, knew that their true intent and purpose
was

was offensive to all who, in the opinion of the contracting
parties, took any measure, considered as inimical to the interests of either of them. The treaty, therefore, which the
House of Bourbon had persuaded the United States to enter
into with them, and which effectually secured Holland in
their hands, was to be considered as a treaty hostile to this
country, inasmuch as it combined three of the most powerful
maritime powers of Europe in a confederacy against Great
Britain. That it was unadviseable and impolitic for the
United States to enter into any such treaty, he verily believed; but, as the treaty was made and executed, it behoved
our Minister to be vigilant and assiduous in engaging in some
alliances with other European maritime powers, whose connection and support might enable us to counteract the mischievous tendency and effect of the operation of the confederacy in case of a war with either of the contracting powers.
In explanation of the consequences to be dreaded from this
confederacy, he should beg leave to remind the House, that
our late war with France had been purely a maritime war,
as we had carried on no military operations by land, excepting only against our own subjects in America; and this,
surely, afforded arguments to shew the extreme and urgent
necessity for our forming a close and intimate alliance with
the Court of Petersburgh; and doubtless, if the two Cabinets
properly understood the relative interests of Great Britain and
Russia, and how much they were by the character, commerce,
and situation of each mutually involved, and naturally combined, they would lose no time in the negociation of such a
treaty. Two years ago a crisis was formed, of which this
country ought to have taken advantage, and which he had,
at the precise moment, pointed out in that House. Many
gentlemen might recollect the moment to which he alluded,
was that, when the Empress of Russia had settled her differences with the Porte, on the subject of the Crimea. Though
it had been admitted on all hands, that the settlement of
those differences about the Crimea had formed the crisis he
talked of, and that the most glorious opportunity had been
afforded for Great Britain to help herself, had the circumstance been managed with dexterity, nothing had yet been
done. The recent advantage France had acquired as a maritime power, by obtaining possession of a port in the Baltic,
should,- if possible, have been prevented. In one situation of
affairs, the possession of Gottenburgh, it was true, France could
make but little use of it; but, in case of a war, the advantage
must be prodigious to her. Let gentlemen recollect, that in
all her wars, France had been most embarrassed by her continental situation, and the dread of an attack from the neighbouring powers; the whole of her policy therefore had been

directed

directed to engage them in such a manner, as to add to her security, and hence it was, that during her last war, she had been able to render her maritime force so respectable and so powerful, because she had no occasion to give her attention to the strengtening of her frontier towns, the adding to her internal fortifications, the recruiting her garrisons, and all those variety of considerations necessary kept alive, while it appeared possible for her continental neighbours to seize the opportunity of profiting of her being engaged in hostilities at sea. Nay, she was even able to aid her resources by a reduction of her army in time of war, and apply the saving to the increase of her maritime strength. What was the case at present? France was safe by her family compact, as to any fear from Spain; and she had by the late treaty quieted all possibility of dread from Holland, which indeed had never been very powerful by land. Her only cause of alarm, therefore, was the court of Vienna, and that, notwithstanding all former assurances of good fellowship, and notwithstanding the still more endearing bonds of connection cemented by family union, was a constant and serious source of alarm; but that cause of terror we had put to rest, having given His Imperial Majesty great disgust, and rendered his feelings adverse to Great Britain. All this had arisen from the part which the Elector of Hanover had taken in joining the Elector of Saxony, and other Germanic Princes in the league founded on the plea of preserving the liberties of the empire. The safety of France by land was effectually secured by the effect of that league on the mind of the Emperor, and we should find her hands strengthened considerably in any future war in which we might be engaged with her. France had nothing to wish for before that league was made, but that some circumstance or other should happen to create a jealousy and dislike of Great Britain in the Emperor. That circumstance we had ourselves provided, and provided gratis, at a moment when France would have paid us any price for it, far more than she had expended in bringing about the peace between the United States of Holland and the Emperor. The most sanguine dreamer of national good fortune could not have pictured to himself the possibility of such a prosperous event in favour of France.

One circumstance looked propitious to this country, which he had heard from such authority as he could rely on, and therefore he would mention it. At the same time he did not doubt but the right honourable gentleman, as a Minister, was aware of it; but as it was a favourable omen for Great Britain, he was glad to be the person to announce it in that House, and that was, that there now offered a good opportunity for renewing a treaty of commerce with Russia, and that
it

it was in a fair way to be renewed with fuccefs. He well knew the fafhionable mode of calling treaties commercial and treaties political diftinct and feparate forts of treaties; but he was not to be blinded by any fuch new-fangled and ill-founded diftinctions; treaties of commerce entered into between two countries always had influenced their politics in a very great degree, and he had not a doubt but a treaty of commerce, entered into between the Court of London and the Court of Peterfburgh would have its due and falutary effect politically as well as commercially; he was, therefore, extremely glad of a circumftance fo promifing to the interefts of both countries. To the mention, however, that the treaty was likely to go on between Ruffia and Great Britain, he thought it fair to add, that he had heard Ruffia would, at the fame time, enter into a commercial treaty with France; of that, he had received his information from a very different quarter, from an authority not equally good, as that from which he had heard the other, and therefore he hoped, and believed, that the information was ill founded. He had no opinion of good refulting to this country from a commercial treaty between Great Britain and France, and his reafon for not thinking that fuch would be its effect, was, that the experience of paft times proved, that this country had grown great, profperous, and flourifhing, from the moment that fhe quitted all her commercial connections with France. He expreffed his ftrong difapprobation of the idea of putting the country to the expence of two different eftablifhments for two different Plenipotentiaries to Paris, and contended that it was idle and unneceffary. There were two ways of doing the bufinefs of this commercial treaty, and finifhing the negociation of it. Either the noble Duke (of Dorfet) now there might do it, or a perfon like Mr. Crawford, who had been employed already, might act under him. At any rate, he declared he faw no reafon for fending out a gentleman, whofe rank in life rendered it improper for him to act in a fubordinate capacity. The right honourable gentleman at the head of the Treafury, had undoubtedly chofen a gentleman (Mr. Eden) for the office of extra Plenipotentiary, who knew fomewhat more of the details of trade and commerce than he did himfelf. That the right honourable gentleman was better acquainted with commercial concerns, the laft feffion had well convinced the Minifter on more than one occafion; but ftill he faw no reafon for employing even that right honourable gentleman's talents on the fubject, and he feared the appointment had rather been made out of refpect to the perfon, than from any neceffity for the exercife of the right honourable gentleman's abilities in the way in which they were to be employed. The New
Board

Board of Trade, which was undoubtedly compofed of men of great abilities and confideration, and men of higher rank than the members of the Old Board of Trade, were the moft extraordinary timeifts, if he might fo call them, that ever exifted. Laft year, after the propofitions had come over from Ireland, and juft as the Britifh Parliament was called upon to vote them, the New Board of Trade proceeded to inquire whether the propofitions were fuch as were fit for either country. In the cafe of the commercial treaty, they were equally fingular in the time of their fending out a perfon with proper powers to negociate it. By the treaties of 1782, a treaty of commerce was to be negotiated between this country and France, on or before the 1ft of January, 1786, and from that day all negociation was to be at an end. Now, therefore, when the time of negotiation was paft, the New Board of trade were bufy with the fubject, and they were about to fend out a negotiator. He fuppofed no ftep had been taken, nor fcarely any progrefs made within the time prefcribed by treaty. A fecond proof of the bad timing of our political proceedings was, that Sir James Harris had prefented a memorial to the States upon the fubject, but unfortunately not till after the treaty was concluded. When he read the memorial, he pitied the fituation of Sir James, as he could from his own knowledge declare, that Great Britain never had a more refpectable, a more able, or a more active and accomplifhed Ambaffador at any foreign Court whatever. As to affairs in India, ever fince the Board of Control had been eftablifhed, a dark veil had been carefully drawn over all which had paffed in that diftant part of our dominions, and he verily believed not without good and fufficient reafon; fecrecy, he was perfuaded, was the only fafeguard for the conduct of the Commiffioners, whofe orders had added to the confufion of our affairs in India, rather than produced any one falutary effect in the Britifh poffeffions in that quarter of the globe. Let the Minifter declare, whether after all that had happened, he ftill would venture to talk of his Eaft-India Bill in his ufual tone of triumph? Every man was pardonable for entertaining a fpeculative opinion of the probable good effect of any meafure of his own before it came to be tried; but no man ought to be allowed to indulge himfelf in expreffions of felf-praife, which experience had proved that he by no means merited. His India Bill had been attacked on the ground of its taking away the charter of the Eaft-India Company, after proof of its having been grofsly abufed; but the right honourable gentleman's bill did what was ten thoufand times worfe; it took away the unalienable rights of individuals, and deprived Britifh fubjects of their birth-right, the right to trial by jury, and of trial by their Peers; a right fecured of every

English-

Englishman by the great charter of our liberties. The clause, obliging all the servants of the Company who came from India, after a certain period to give an account of their fortunes on oath, was most unjust and delusive. It held out protection and security to the rich, while it obliged the poor to submit to its severest operation; it gave all that wished not to submit to it three years to return home in; this the opulent, and the opulent alone could take advantage of. As to the boasted accounts of the promising state of the revenues of India, instead of only 1,400,000 pounds deficiency, they would now, he believed, find not mere errors of fractions, but errors of millions. Lord Macartney had acted throughout the whole of his stay in India upon the most upright principles, and had come home with hands perfectly unsullied. His Lordship, from a conviction of the necessity of the measure, had taken the collection and management of the revenues of the Carnatic out of the hands, not of the Nabob, but of his agents and usurers, who plundered the natives and robbed him, and had vested both in the hands of the Company. This measure the Board of Control had overthrown by their orders, and directed the collection and management of the Nabob's revenues to be restored to him. The fatal effects of the order had spread alarm and terror through the Carnatic, and impressed the Council at Fort St. George with so strong an idea of its impropriety, that Lord Macartney went himself to Calcutta, to remonstrate with Mr. Hastings, and to deprecate the consequences. Let the House guess the surprise of his Lordship, on finding Mr. Hastings departed for Europe, and a commission there appointing him Governor General, a situation it was impossible for him to accept, while the order to restore the collection and management of the Carnatic revenues to the Nabob continued in force. How absurd to remove the Governor General, who recommended the measure Lord Macartney had reprobated, and appoint his Lordship to the post of Governor General with orders to do, what he himself had found to be equally unwise and mischievous to the interest of the Company and the interest of the Nabob, and had condemned? As to the Irish propositions, it was highly necessary that Parliament and the Public should clearly know what was intended. When the subject was first started the right honourable gentleman, (Mr. Pitt) in some of the most vehement strains of his all-powerful eloquence, had condemned the noble Lord (North) in the blue ribband for giving Ireland certain grants, without having first asked her whether they would be acceptable, and for leaving matters as they stood, when the propositions were first taken up, the right honourable gentleman having again and again told the House it was impossible they could remain as they were. He
desired

defired to know what was the true conftruction and meaning
of that part of His Majefty's fpeech then under confideration,
that mentioned the refolutions, but a declaration to that
Houfe, that matters muft remain as they were? He urged
the flat contradiction that the event of the bufinefs had given
to all their predictions refpecting its fuccefs, and ftated in
ftrong terms the mifchief that he conceived the agitating the
matter at all had done, by difgufting the manufacturers of
Great Britain, teaching them that the Houfe of Commons
would difregard their petitions, ftating their dread of the
mifchievous confequences to their feveral branches of manufacture, were the intended fyftem carried into execution; and
as the beft means of checking the evil, and preventing the effect
of having entered into a difcuffion of points, which he was
convinced ought never to have been difturbed or brought before the public, he advifed the Minifter explicitly and unre-
fervedly to declare his determination to abandon all farther
thought of attempting to carry a meafure fo deteftable in the
eyes of the manufacturers and merchants of Great Britain
and Ireland. While mentioning the manufacturers, he fhould
declare that he was fatisfied that to their ingenuity and induftry, and to their fpirit and perfeverance, the country
owed its exaltation to the ftate of refpect, character, confideration, and profperity, to which its trade, manufactures, and
commerce had been raifed in the eyes of all mankind. As
to the reafoning ufed by the Secretary of State for Ireland, in
his celebrated letter to his conftituents, in recommendation
of the propofitions on the ground that, as the Britifh manufacturers confidered the grant of the propofitions to Ireland
to be highly injurious to their interefts, they muft neceffarily
be advantageous in an equal proportion to the interefts of the
Irifh manufacturers, it was an argument perfectly found and
forcible in itfelf; but extremely humiliating to the Britifh
Minifters, and placing them in a very contemptible light. Mr.
Fox expreffed his readinefs to grant that his remarks formed
rather a feries of reafoning againft what was out of the fpeech
than againft what was in it; yet, thefe ferved more to ftrengthen than invalidate his right to an explanation of the two
main points of the fpeech on which he had defcanted. The explanation once given, he fhould, for the prefent, ceafe to
trouble the Houfe, though moft of the topics which he had
touched upon would, hereafter, need a full difcuffion.

Mr. Pitt.   A fhort interval of filence having taken place, Mr Pitt
rofe and faid, he had refrained, during fome moments, from
troubling the Houfe, expecting, but in vain, to hear (what
certainly had not fallen from the right honourable gentleman who fpoke laft) objections againft the addrefs. He
could not avoid bearing teftimony to that peculiar, and almoft
in-

inftinctive, dexterity, with which the right honourable gentleman was enabled, on all occafions, to leave out of the difcuffion fuch parts of the fubject as were unfavourable to him;
and he enjoyed at the prefent juncture, equally an opportunity of admiring a fimilar talent of introducing, however
foreign and unconnected, fuch matter as he expected would
be favourable.   Thus did he entirely abandon the various
fubjects of the fpeech, in order to difcufs fome that were, as
he complained, omitted.   The right honourable gentleman's
fentiments, with refpect to the fituation of the country, being
rather of a defponding caft, he had, no doubt, an expectation
of finding fomething in the King's Speech prefenting him
with an opportunity of indulging his melancholy feelings on
the ftate of public affairs; but perceiving every part of the
fpeech filled with the happeft intelligence, he had been
obliged to travel into foreign countries in purfuit of his
object. He had traverfed the empires of Germany and Ruffia;
he had vifited Turkey and the Crimea for this purpofe; but,
confidering, like other modern difcoverers, Europe as too
narrow for his inquiries, he had carried his fpeculations to
the remoteft parts of the globe, and ranfacked the Indies for
fources of complaint and of defpair.   Although he by no
means intended to follow the right honourable gentleman in
his deviations from the fubject as largely as he had fet him the
example, he fhould yet make fome anfwer to each part of the
right honourable gentleman's fpeech, allowing himfelf however a latitude of avoiding to give any opinion whatfoever
concerning particular parts of it, though on all fuch as he
thought he could with propriety animadvert, he would freely
deliver his fentiments.   The right honourable gentleman had
acknowledged that he confidered himfelf at liberty, in his prefent fituation, to fpeak of foreign Courts, and their views and
interefts, in a manner, to which His Majefty's Minifters were,
by a fenfe of duty, prevented from recurring.   For his own
part, although ready to admit, that there was a ftronger and
more facred reftraint on thofe who were in the immediate
confidence of His Majefty than upon other gentlemen, yet
he muft alfo obferve, that the duty of members of Parliament, although in fome, from their additional character of
Minifters, it might differ in degree, was, in general, of the
fame nature with refpect to all; and that part of his duty,
which enjoined a delicacy and caution, when fpeaking of
foreign States, was one from which he would not fuffer
himfelf to be diverted by the right honourable gentleman.
The right honourable gentleman had defired to be informed
to what particular part of continental politics that part of
His Majefty's fpeech alluded, which announced the project of
of a general peace.   He could take upon him to fay that it

solely related to that particular transaction, which had taken place since the conclusion of the last session, the treaty of peace between the Emperor of Germany and the States General of the United Provinces, by which a dispute was terminated that, until then seemed to threaten the peace of Europe, and had been described in that light by the speech from the Throne, at the opening of the last session.——As to the question the right honourable gentleman had thought proper to ask, whether there did not exist between any other Princes or States of Europe such seeds of disagreement and ill-humour, as might probably break out into future animosities and wars; that was a subject on which he thought proper to decline giving any opinion whatsoever. The right honourable gentleman had signified his apprehensions of a hostile disposition towards *Great Britain* in certain Courts of *Europe*; and to this he could answer (in terms similar to those contained in the speech,) that there was every assurance of the most friendly intentions from them all. With respect to the treaty with the Empress of Russia, it was in a state of forwardness, and (he had every ground to hope) would be completed in such a manner as should give general satisfaction. The German confederacy, to which His Majesty, in his capacity of Elector of Hanover, had acceded, had also been mentioned, and Ministers were loudly told that they must step forward as the vindicators of it propriety. He should by no means take upon him to make such a defence; as he was ready to confess, that whatever might prove either the merit or demerit of that measure, he and his colleagues in office were by no means entitled to pride themselves on the former, or reduced to the necessity of taking shame to themselves in consequence of the latter. As to the connection with Hanover, however accident had placed the sovereignty of that country and of this, in the same hands, it by no means followed that the interests of each must necessarily be the same; though he was willing to admit, that from the circumstance of their having one and the same Sovereign, it was likely that their interests might sometimes be parallel, when without that circumstance they might prove different, and perhaps it might advance their mutual advantage to make their interests as reconcileable to each other as possible. Yet he desired to have it understood, that Great Britain was by no means committed or bound by any league lately entered into by the Elector of Hanover; nor did he look upon it as incumbent on the Ministers of this country to lay before Parliament, except in cases of necessity, such arrangements as may have been made for Hanover, by the advice of the Ministers of that Electorate. What could equal the inconsistency of the right honourable gentleman's (Mr. Fox) ap-

pre-

prehenfion of our being involved in difficulties through the means of His Majefty's German territories; and yet his expecting, that the Adminiftration of thofe territories fhould be fubordinate to, and regulated by the Minifter of Great Britain, as if that very circumftance would not of itfelf render it abfolutely neceffary that this country fhould on all occafions confider itfelf as bound to protect and affift the electorate! Whereas the only way for Great Britain to avoid embroiling herfelf in quarrels for Hanover, was by our Adminiftration ftanding as much as poffible independent of Hanoverian politics. With refpect to the fituation of India not being touched upon in the fpeech, he apprehended that the right honourable gentlemen might as well have objected to a fimilar omiffion concerning any other of the foreign poffeffions of the empire. The complaint was that our Indian affairs had not been mentioned, as in former fpeeches, ever fince the appointment of the Board of Control. The reafon of this was perfectly obvious, and had been explained on the firft day of the preceding feffion. It was, that fo many errors and mifcarriages arofe formerly out of the Government of that country, that His Majefty for many feffions had been induced to call upon his Parliament to adopt fome mode of effectual regulation, by which a ftop might be put to the enormities complained of; that Parliament had at laft taken up the bufinefs, and applied an effectual remedy; and therefore the neceffity for the Crown to remind them of it no more exifted. The right honourable gentleman had been carried away by his warmth on this fubject fo far as to introduce a topic, which formerly he was extremely averfe to hear mentioned—the violation of charters. On this head the right honourable gentlemen had gone great lengths; for, he had ftigmatized the mode of trial appointed for Eaft-Indian delinquents as an infringement on the Great Charter, by fetting afide the trial by Jury. He chofe, indeed, with a degree of liberality, to applaud that mode of trial, but contended, that there might be tribunals in certain particular cafes that would be found adequate to all the purpofes of public juftice in a like degree; and he particularly inftanced the prefent mode of trial as entitled to equal approbation, and very nearly refembling in its conftitution the beft fort of fpecial jury.—But furely when the right honourable gentleman reflected that no man became fubject to this new judicature, except by his own choice, and at the fame time compared the fituation of the Company's fervants with that of the men on whofe bravery the independence and fafety of our country depended, (our land and naval forces) many of whom were forced into the fervice againft their will, and detained there contrary to their wifhes, he could not pretend to fay,

that

that if it were juft to govern fuch men by martial law, and to fubftitute in their trials a Court Martial inftead of a jury, it was any hardfhip on the fervants of the Eaft-India Company, who had the option to go there or remain at home, and return as they pleafed, that a mode of trial fhould be inftituted for them, different from that which was generally ufed, and which they might entirely avoid, unlefs the profits and advantages of the Eaft-India employment appeared to them a fufficient compenfation. The right honourable gentleman had entered largely into the ftate of the revenue of the Company's fettlements, and had calculated, that the only increafe which he expected to hear of, was an annual deficiency of 13,000, and errors not of fmall fums and fractions, but of millions. He would not for the prefent attempt an exact ftatement of the furplus of the revenues of the Eaft Indies; but he would only fay, that he expected and believed that they would appear, and fome regulations and retrenchments had taken place, to exceed, in a ten-fold proportion to the incumbrances under which they laboured, any furplus that might be hoped for in this country. His warmeft wifhes would indeed be gratified, and the moft fanguine dreams at any moment formed of the profperity of Great Britain would prove more than realized, if it could be found that our refources for diminifhing our debt bore any comparifon to thofe of the Eaft-India Company. With refpect to the fuppofed inconfiftency of Lord Macartney's appointment to the prefidency over the general affairs of the Company, at the fame time that his conduct in the affignment of the revenues of the Carnatic was not approved of, he defired it to be recollected, that although he and Mr. Haftings had differed upon more points than one, yet that affair alone excepted, he had acted in fuch a manner as entitled him to the higheft applaufe which words could poffibly beftow. Such were the talents of Lord Macartney, that, from the whole of his Adminiftration of the Government of Madras, he appeared perfectly eligible to that of Bengal, and particularly as the fole object, in which his conduct at *Madras* had been fuppofed objectionable, was one in which the policy of the meafure was with Lord Macartney, though the good faith and credit of the nation rendered it neceffary to make a facrifice; befides that particular object would no longer have refted under Lord Macartney's department, after his removal to Bengal.

He was happy to find the right honourable gentleman entertained fo high an opinion of the noble Lord, becaufe it would tend, perhaps, to reconcile him to a part of the Eaft-India bill, of which he fo violently complained, to find that a nobleman of fuch great reputation and diftinguifhed virtue had borne in the moft pointed manner the teftimony of his

appro-

approbation to the fyftem of calling all perfons returning from the Company's fervice to account on oath for their acquifitions. For, though that reftriction did not extend itfelf to him, yet fo much did he approve the fpirit and principle of it, nay fo neceffary did it appear to him, for his own honour, that he voluntarily came forward and complied with the claufe, even before its operation commenced. And he hoped, that after fo illuftrious an example no man would take upon him to depreciate the good policy and juftice of the reftriction. This action of Lord Macartney's was in itfelf fo noble, fo difinterefted, and fhewed fo pointedly the greatnefs of his fentiments, that even if his opinion of that nobleman's character were inferior to the ideas formed of it by the right honourable gentleman; nay, had he even difapproved of his general conduct in his government, yet this action alone would have been fufficient to atone for all former mifcarriages, and to have entitled him to the higheft glory and the moft marked encomiums and applaufe. He had been called upon by the right honourable gentleman to declare, whether the event had juftified the confident affurances that had been given by him and his friends, that his bill would be received with joy and gratitude in India? He faid, that if fuch affurances had at any time been made, it would then become fair to expect their ratification to be fullfilled. But, in fact, nothing of that fort had dropt from him at any moment whatfoever. The bill was a reftrictive bill, and, as fuch, no perfon could reafonably conclude that it would be received with any fanguine marks of approbation by thofe on whom its reftrictions were to operate. But this laft-recited inftance proved, that, however inquiry and fcrutiny may militate againft the inclinations of the unjuft and difhonourable, the man of true virtue and integrity will be always ambitious to meet them. So far, Mr. Pitt remarked, he had followed the right honourable gentleman in fuch parts of his fpeech as were entirely foreign to the fubject. He fhould now return to paffages more immediately within the compafs of the queftion. He was glad to find that the right honourable gentleman had changed his fentiments fo completely on the fubject of the finances fince the conclufion of the preceding feffion. He remembered that, then the right honourable gentleman declared it as his firm and fixed opinion, that the revenue would be found to fall fhort by, at leaft, 1,400,000l. either of the annual expenditure of the kingdom, or of that fum which was to leave 1,000,000l. furplus for the diminifhing of the national debt; for which of the two, the right honourable gentleman had declared himfelf at a lofs to determine; however in either cafe there muft have been a confiderable

deficiency;

deficiency; and yet now the right honourable gentleman declared, that no person could have ever doubted but there must be some surplus. The right honourable gentleman had thought proper to observe, that there was scarcely any part of the speech worthy of consideration, and when he made mention of the increase of the revenue, he only expressed himself by the trival term—some surplus. Absurdity must, doubtless, strongly mark the singular idea, that proposals for diminishing the burdens of the country, establishing her credit, and strengthening her resources, were subjects scarce worthy of consideration; and all this in the eye of a gentleman who had thought the leagues and views of almost every other state in Europe worthy of the attention of Parliament. The surplus of the revenue might soon appear considerable and important, and prove to the right honourable gentleman, that the contemptuous expression of which he had made use was highly inapplicable. Upon the question, through what means this surplus had accrued, and whether the honour resulting from it belonged to His Majesty's Ministers, he found himself very little inclined to enter, because it was enough for him that the surplus did exist, and the satisfaction which he felt at the comfortable prospect afforded by it to his country was sufficient to absorb and overpower every idea of a personal nature to which it possibly could give occasion. He felt it difficult to restain his indignation, and astonishment that the right honourable gentleman should have expatiated upon a subject of such delicacy as the Irish arrangement, in so unguarded and inflammatory a manner. He must, however, notwithstanding his own disapprobation of such language, do the right honourable gentleman the justice to acknowledge, that he was convinced he must have had some public good in view in what he uttered, for he could not possibly conceive any personal motive for introducing certain topics which had been made use of; he had accordingly delivered his sentiments fully and clearly, notwithstanding the disagreeable feelings to which they must have given rise and in defiance of that sharpest of all stings, his own invective. He had in the plainest and most unequivocal manner declared, that no enemy to the British empire could possibly accomplish his malicious designs against it in so effectual a manner as by impressing the sister kingdoms with an idea that their interests were incompatible, and that the advantage of one must naturally imply the detriment of the other. He must, on the present occasion, beg leave to bring back the recollection of the House to the origin of such a doctrine, and to point out, that during the discussion of the whole of the Irish business, while he and his friends uniformly endeavoured to argue on the grounds of mutual
and

and reciprocal advantage to each kingdom, they were answered from the other side of the House by arguments which had for their backs nothing else but this now reprobated idea of the incompatibility of English and Irish interests, from whence it was inferred that an arrangement to benefit one country must proportionably injure the other. The right honourable gentleman (Mr. Fox) had ventured reprehensibly far, indeed, by saying that the two countries were in a situation similar to that which precedes the commencement of war—one having made demands with which the other had refused to comply. What would the right honourable gentleman think, were two friends, proceeding to settle an account, to find themselves suddenly interrupted by some good-natured friend suggesting the danger of any proposal being made by one until there was a certainty the other would agree to it—for, in that case, exclaims the mediator, you must go to war!—Mr. Pitt concluded by remarking, that no person could have lamented more sincerely than himself over the failure of the Irish negociation; expressing, at the same time, how fervently he had hoped that Great Britain might, upon the broad basis of mutual advantages have transmitted to the sister kingdom a full share of her commercial felicities.

Mr. *Fox* replied, that he felt it difficult to avoid smiling at the absurdity of the right honourable gentleman's arguments respecting the accession of Hanover to the Germanic league, as it was obvious that the Regency of Hanover ought neither to form laws nor enter into any treaties which might prove injurious to Great Britain, consequently it behoved the Ministers of this country to have prevented their entering into any alliances which might involve serious consequences to the interests of England. If Hanover, through this mistaken policy, should sustain a detriment, it naturally followed that Great Britain must become her guarantee. Such was the drift of his argument; and he only had contended that Ministers were not warranted, by any plea or pretended exigency whatsoever, to disable Great Britain from acting subsequently with the Emperor, provided that a co-operation of this nature should appear the most likely to advance the interests of the former. And, surely, the right honourable gentleman (Mr. Pitt) would not presume to run lengths to which no former Ministers had daringly proceeded, and disavow the fullest responsibility for all the counsels which he might give his royal Master in his character of Elector of Hanover. The right honourable gentleman seemed eager (Mr. Fox observed) to meet his arguments with unjustifiable misrepresentation; and therefore he must desire him to bear in mind, that when he said that he could speak more freely concerning our particular connections

Mr. Fox.

nections with foreign powers than if he were a Minister, he did not (in fact, he could not) mean, even in the most distant manner, to drop the slightest intimation that he was more entitled than the right honourable gentleman to utter words, including an unpardonable tendency to wound the interests of his country. The fullest scope of his allusion was, that he felt himself warranted to mention France as the natural enemy of Great Britain, in terms more open and unguarded than those consistent with the reserve which, upon principles of decent policy, a Minister either is, or ought to be, under the necessity of maintaining. The right honourable gentleman had been pleased to exercise his wonted ingenuity, by putting the case of two private men engaged upon the settlement of an account, and tracing out the supposed absurdity of contending that they ought to be excluded from all power of giving it a previous discussion. Be the absurdity what it might, he would, with chearfulness, monopolize the whole, and still stedfastly and inviolably embrace his former argument, that in great questions requiring a settlement between two princes, two Parliaments, or two powers, considerations and objects would arise of which the discussion could never prove allowable, except under the firmest assurances that both parties were ultimately determined to receive them with unequivocal assent.

Mr. Pitt. Mr. *Pitt* replied, that whenever the right honourable gentleman should chuse in a proper way to take up the ground of the supposed responsibility of Ministers for the part which their Sovereign might take, respecting his territories and concerns in the Electorate of Hanover, he would meet him and investigate the subject. Nor had he contended against the responsibility, but only urged the needlessness of informing the Parliament, at the present juncture, what steps the Crown had taken with regard to the Electorate of Hanover.

Mr. Francis. Mr. *Francis* said, that when he came into the House, he had no thoughts of taking part in any debate which might arise upon that day: that he seldom troubled the House, and never long; that some things, which had fallen from Mr. Pitt, compelled him now to rise, and to request their attention for a few minutes. That Mr. Pitt, in speaking of our affairs in India, had given a very flattering description of them, and had advanced many favourable assertions concerning them, which he could assure the House were utterly groundless: that the reverse of every thing which Mr. Pitt had affirmed was the truth, and that he would prove it to be so from authority; which he was sure that Mr. Dundas at least, who ought to know something of the matter, would not controvert. That the House had often heard the same sort of language from Mr. Pitt: that, in former times, he might

might have been excusable in holding out hopes and promises, on which it was possible he himself might have depended; but that now, with the certain knowledge that all his professed hopes had been disappointed, and with the experience of two years before him, in which his promises had completely failed, his continuing to hold the same language was unpardonable. That Mr. Pitt had joined with the Directors in deceiving the Public, or at least had given them countenance in endeavouring to deceive. With respect to the state of the Company's finances in India, Mr. Francis said, that so far from their being in that flourishing condition represented by Mr. Pitt, they were in as great, or greater distress than ever. That at Bombay they had no revenue at all proportioned to their current expence: that the bonded debt there now amounted to 3,000,000l. sterling, which bore an interest of nine per cent. per ann. and was continually increasing by half-yearly conversions of the interest into capital. That he did not know what the amount of the debt at Madras might be, but he knew it was confiderable, and that that presidency was finking under its distresses. In proof of this affertion he read part of a letter from Mr. Macpherson to the Court of Directors, dated 30th of July, 1785, as follows:—" In the Carnatic your late orders had been carried into some effect; the general ruin which that country has undergone from the devastation of war, will keep your affairs in that quarter a long time in distress."

He then reminded the House of the error, of which he had already convicted the Directors in their calculation and promises exhibited to the House above two years ago. That he had convicted them of promising a surplus of above 1,500,000l. sterling in the Bengal revenues on the 1st of May, 1785, which they were to apply to the discharge of their debts, but which, in effect, turned out a deficiency to more than that amount; so that their estimates had imposed upon Parliament to the amount of more than 3,000,000l. sterling in the revenues of one year. But the language then holden in defence of that error, was, that their estimate did not include some expences which could not be foreseen; that it relied on savings, which, as it happened, could not be made in that specific year, and that it provided for all the arrears of the army, and all the outstanding charges of the war; but that in the ensuing year, no similar causes of expence would exist; that wonderful reforms would take place, and manifold savings arise out of them; that the revenues of Bengal would exhibit a surplus beyond all doubt and contradiction, sufficient to make a confiderable diminution of their debt: that Mr. Pitt even now continued to hold the same fort of language, and talked of surplusses in the Indian revenues, under the inftant application of which all their debts and incumbrances would fpeedily be annihilated.

Mr. Francis faid, he hoped that the right honourable gentleman when he talked of the actual exiftance of means to conftitute a powerful finking fund at home, fpoke with better knowledge and information of the fubject than he appeared to poffefs concerning the Indian revenues: that, fo far from having a furplus in Bengal, even in this third year of peace, when fo much oeconomy had been promifed, the balance of the eftimate of refources and difburfements for the year ending May 1, 1785, was againft the Company to the amount of 1,200,000l. sterling: that their bonded debt and unfatisfied demands on the Treafury, by the laft accounts, amounted to 3,000,000l. sterling, and that this debt was evidently in a courfe of increafe rather than diminution, and muft continue fo, as long as their current expences exceeded, as they ftill did, their current refources. With refpect to the boafted reform which had been fo much and fo often fpoken of, he faid, it had yet produced no material effect; and in fupport of this, read another paffage from the letter from Mr. Macpherfon as follows: " The great and fnoft important work " of a reform in the expences of this government, which " was refolved upon, and in fome degree begun before the " departure of Mr. Haftings, has been carried through under " every influence that I could exert, and every effort of the " abilities of your prefent Adminiftration. I muft, at the " fame time, regret that the progrefs made in this falutary " meafure is not equal to my wifhes, nor has it in any very " alleviating degree relieved your diftreffes."

With refpect to the late India bill, the merits and good effects of which Mr. Pitt had exalted in high terms, Mr. Francis begged leave to remind the Houfe, that he had oppofed it in every ftage, without knowing or confidering how it was likely to be received in India. That he had oppofed it on what he thought the true principles of this conftitution, becaufe it invaded the original and unalienable rights of a confiderable part of his fellow fubjects, which they had not acquired by their virtues, and, if they were ever fo criminal, could not forfeit by their crimes; that is, to be tried by a jury of their peers, however enormous the magnitude of their offences might be. That it was plain he acted on this principle alone, fince it was well known, that his connections with the gentlemen of India were not very intimate or extenfive; confequently, that there was no perfonal reafon why he fhould be particularly forward in their defence. That he knew many of them to be worthy men; but, if he had thought otherwife, his conduct would have been the fame. That it was very remarkable, that, while he had done

his

his utmost to oppose the bill, the persons who supported it most strenuously, and who in effect carried it into a law, were the friends, the relations, and the companions of those against whom the law was to operate; that it was shameful to see the same persons, who, if wealth implied guilt, were the most guilty, who had returned from India loaded with fortune, and now sat in Parliament secure against all inquiry —to see these very persons making laws to restrain and punish, with unheard-of severity, others, at least as meritorious as themselves, and certainly more innocent, that is, as far as poverty implies innocence. That the only persons upon whom the law would bear, and against whom it would operate, were those who had not acquired fortune enough to leave India before the time limited by the act for the commencement of the inquisition; whereas to all those who had already acquired fortune enough to be able to come to England before January 1787, this boasted law held out indulgence, security, and protection; that is, it deferred the exertion and application of all its rigour, until those who ought to be the objects of its severity had put themselves under shelter, and out of the reach of inquiry.—Mr. Francis said, that while the bill was depending, he had spoken of it with a detestation and abhorrence which it might not be decent to apply to an existing law: but he hoped, that before the end of the present session, he should see some attempt made to repeal this law entirely, or, if that could not be obtained, at least to repeal that part of it which invaded the rights and attacked the freedom of the nation at large: that he stood upon the *vitæ antiquæ* of the constitution, the unalienable right of every Englishman to a trial by his peers; that Mr. Pitt had endeavoured to abolish the trial by jury in one instance, and defend it by arguments which would equally apply to other cases and other classes of men. That these were the steps by which the worst principles were gradually established, and the best political institutions sooner or later subverted. That the fact of itself was dangerous, and the doctrines by which it was supported equally weak and profligate: first, that Mr. Pitt had declared, that military men, that our soldiers and sailors, had voluntary renounced that privilege, of which the East-India Company's servants were deprived by this law; and that at all events it was no hardship to those persons, since they were at liberty to choose whether they would continue in the Company's service or not, and had sufficient time allowed them to make their option. That, in the first place, the conclusion drawn from the state and circumstances of military men to the other members of the community was false and absurd. That if any army was admitted to be necessary, it followed that mi-

E 2   litary

litary men muſt be governed by the ſtrict rules of military diſcipline; and that as to themſelves they ſuffered no injuſtice, ſince they previouſly knew what they had to truſt to. But that if ſuch a concluſion could fairly be drawn from the diſcipline of the army to deprive the reſt of the community of their civil rights, it was a reaſon ſtronger than any we had ever had for curſing the introduction of a ſtanding army into the conſtitution of this country. That it was abſolutely falſe that an option was given to the Company's ſervants. The perſons in queſtion were already engaged in that ſervice; they had ſerved in it many years; they had acquired no fortune; their ſole dependance reſted on the occupation in which they were engaged, and all their proſpects in life were confined to it. Was it an opinion to ſuch perſons to tell them, that if they did not accept of the terms newly impoſed upon them, they were at liberty to come home? That is, if they did not ſubmit to give up their birthright by ſtaying in India, they might preſerve their birthright by a ſurrender of all their claims and merits in the India-Company's ſervice, and return to ſtarve in England.

Mr. Francis ſaid, that he objected to the law as ſubverſive of the principles of the conſtitution, and not to be juſtified by any precedents oppoſed to principles. That he never would admit that the King, Lords, and Commons had a right to take the trial by jury out of the Engliſh conſtitution. That Mr. Pitt's telling the people in India what they were to expect if they continued there, was no anſwer to the objection. That on the ſame principle he might have introduced the rack and the torture, and, provided he gave them timely notice of his intention, the parties concerned would have no right to object to it; for that, if they were unwilling to ſubmit to the rack and the torture, it depended on themſelves to leave the country before the law began to operate.

Mr. Francis cautioned the perſons who had the management of India affairs, to act with prudence and circumſpection in the preſent criſis; but, that this was a ſubject on which he thought it right to ſpeak with great reſerve, wiſhing them only to remember, that Bengal was utterly unaſſailable by the power of Great Britain. He concluded with ſaying, that he lamented the precedent unneceſſarily eſtabliſhed by this law of depriving Britiſh ſubjects of the trial by jury, for many reaſons: firſt, for the injury which it did to the community at large, as a dangerous example; ſecondly for the ſake of the perſons immediately affected by it; and finally, for a reaſon, which, though of much leſs importance he confeſſed was particularly painful to himſelf, from th reſpect he bore to the memory of a noble relation to M Pit

Pitt; that he was forry to fee that two ideas which he never thought could come under any poffible fuppofition, were united, —that of the name of the right honourable gentleman, and of the deftruction of the trial by jury, fhould belong to one another, and be delivered down to pofterity together.

Mr. *Dundas* remarked that, feeling it his duty to rife in vindication of the laft Eaft-India bill, he fhould ftate what moft certainly was the meaning of his right honourable friend (Mr. Pitt) when he mentioned the comparative ftate of the finances of the Eaft-India Company and this country. The tendency of his argument was to prove, that, confidering the debt owing by the India Company, the ftate of her revenue being fo much greater than her difburfements, fhe might entertain the moft flattering profpect not only of paying the debt, but of acquiring great wealth; and, therefore, undoubtedly, her fituation was, by a multitude of degrees, preferable to that of this country, of which the revenue, however great, could not bear any proportion in point of the profpect of getting rid of the debt it owed, which had increafed in equal meafure and rapidity with the diminution of its power. Whatever accounts the honourable gentleman (Mr. Francis) might have received from letter extracts, from two fcraps of paper, in his mind they ought to have no weight with the Houfe, as the one was mere matter of private opinion, and the other apparently the fentiments of perfons who thought the bill would prevent them from making fortunes, in the way which had excited fuch a violence of complaint. As to the notice of moving for a repeal of the bill, he fhould at prefent only fay, that whenfoever it fhould be brought forward, either for a repeal of the whole, or part, he would freely deliver his fentiments, and defend the fteps which his right honourable friend and he had taken; a defence capable (he had the vanity to believe) of refcuing the Company from the hurt it had received, more by the infinuations of the honourable gentleman, than from the eloquence of the right honourable member (Mr. Fox) who fpoke before him. Even the moft powerful difplay of the brilliant oratory of the latter could not operate with fo deep and dangerous an impreffion as the dark, yet apparently ingenuous, infinuations of the former, to whom he fhould chearfully pledge himfelf to enter, at a proper time, into a difcuffion of the ftate of the Bengal revenues, and of other points relating to the Eaft Indies, not doubting but that he could prove the fallibility of his affertions.

Mr. *Francis* anfwered, that he was glad Mr. Dundas had promifed to enter into a difcuffion of the revenue accounts, becaufe he concluded, from that promife, that the papers neceffary for going into that difcuffion would not be refufed

when

Mr. Dundas.

Mr. Francis.

when they fhould be called for; and he thanked Mr. Dundas for giving him that fatisfaction.

Mr. Dundas.

Mr. *Dundas* rose, and declared, that he muft refufe thofe thanks; nor would he promife to produce papers until he knew the object.

Mr. Francis.

Mr. *Francis* faid, there could be but one paper immediately in queftion, viz. the eftimate of refources and difburfements for the year ending the rft of May, 1786.

Major Scott.

Major *Scott* obferved, that far from admitting the juftice of the colouring of an honourable member (Mr. Francis) when he painted the *fuppofed* deplorable fituation of Afiatic affairs, he was totally of a different opinion, and could not conceive why he or any other gentleman fhould attempt to inculcate principles deftitute of any foundation. But, the honourable gentleman was refolved to feize on every opportunity of throwing an odium on the prefent fyftem; and defpifed all ideas of impartiality, provided that he fucceeded in his favourite object. He likewife had received letters from India, which militated very much againft the honourable gentleman's affertions; and as he flattered himfelf they were founded in truth and equal refpectability, he was of opinion, that his information would totally fubvert that of the honourable gentleman. With refpect to the account which Lord Macartney had given in, concerning his fortune acquired in India, it comprehended only an eftimate of the riches which he had acquired for thefe laft two years, and not during the whole period of his abfence from Europe.—He did not, by any means, wifh to detract from his Lordfhip's well-known principles of juftice and integrity, but he apprehended that it was an obfervation worthy of notice.—With regard to Mr. Haftings, he was ready at any time to give the Houfe or nation ample fatisfaction relative to the riches which he had accumulated in India. All this had he long fince offered; and the Directors well knew that his fortune was inconfiderable. Like others, he only wifhed to have the account voluntary and not compulfive. When a candid inveftigation took place, he was fully perfuaded that many gentlemen who had been particularly active in their condemnation of this great character would alter their opinions, and blufh over the violence of their rancour and their prejudice.

Mr. Martin.

Mr. *Martin*, defiring permiffion to trefpafs for a few moments, upon the patience of the Houfe, faid that he flattered himfelf that his requeft would not be rejected, as it was well known how feldom he deviated from an habitual filence. He lamented, that there was on the oppofite fide of the Houfe a fpirit of illiberal oppofition to the prefent government, whofe exertions certainly deferved more indulgence and candour. But he applauded that fpirit of national œconomy which

thofe

thofe gentlemen profeſſed; and, proceeding on this idea, he muſt expreſs his ſorrow for the charge of profuſion which had been brought againſt the right honourable gentleman (Mr. Pitt), whoſe patriotiſm and integrity deſerved, and ought to gain, the tribute of unanimous approbation. As this was an accuſation of a ſerious nature, and contrary to the right honourable gentleman's acknowledged principles of integrity, he confeſſed, that it would give him and the Houſe confiderable ſatisfaction if his right honourable friend would enter into an explanation of the reaſon for allowing a ſalary to a Spaniſh Ambaſſador, who had not performed any of the duties incumbent upon him, and who had not ſo much as reſided in the country for which he was appointed. With regard to India, he wiſhed that ſuch an aſylum had never been thrown open to adventurers; but, if gentlemen were reſolved to go thither, in his opinion it followed, that their claim to the protection of a Britiſh legiſlation ſhould die away, and heartily did he wiſh that they never might reviſit their native country.

Mr. *Pitt* replied, that he conſidered it as barely an act of juſtice to ſhew the moſt reſpectul attention to any member, virtuous and independent like the honourable gentleman who ſpoke laſt. Anxious to deſerve his good opinion, he ſhould truly anſwer, that with regard to allowing a ſalary to an Ambaſſador for the court of Spain, it had been agreed to from a principle of policy; becauſe at the time when the noble Earl (of Cheſterfield) was appointed, an Ambaſſador was expected from thence to this Court. The noble Earl who had accepted the appointment, certainly, from his knowledge and ability, had every claim to ſuch a diſtinction. He now, however, roſe to inform the Houſe and his honourable friend, that His Majeſty, after conſidering the circumſtance alluded to, had been graciouſly pleaſed to approve of his Lordſhip's conduct; but, at the ſame time, to order his immediate return to this country. This communication he hoped would ſatisfy the Houſe, and convince every unprejudiced mind, that His Majeſty's Miniſters were reſolved to adopt the moſt rigorous plans of œconomy. He truſted that this explanation would remove all exceptions; and convince all diſpoſed to look on miniſterial meaſures with an eye of candour, that œconomy was ſtill their favourite object.

Mr. *Burke* now entering the Houſe,

Major *Scott* begged leave to remind a right honourable gentleman, whom he, at length, ſaw in his place, that, at the concluſion of the preceding ſeſſion, he had pledged himſelf to bring forward a motion in the courſe of the preſent, reſpecting a gentleman but lately returned from Bengal (Mr. Haſtings.) He ſhould now take the liberty to bring the circumftance to the recollection of the right honourable gentleman, and to requeft that he would have the candour and fairnefs to fay when he meant to proceed, if he did mean to proceed at all; that he embraced this firft opportunity to call upon him, and trufted that, if he had any thing to offer refpecting the conduct of Mr. Haftings, he would fubmit it to the Houfe with all poffible expedition.

Mr Fox.

Mr. *Fox* replied, if his right honourable friend defigned, (but this he did not believe) fo far to neglect his duty, as to forget to fulfil his promife, the honourable gentleman might reft affured, that other members would make the point an object of inveftigation.

Mr. Burke.

Mr. *Burke* faid, that he fhould anfwer the honourable gentleman with a fhort anecdote of Henry the Fourth and the Duke of Parma, who came from Amiens to fight him at Paris, when the former urging him to meet him on a certain day, the Duke replied, that he had not travelled fo far as from Amiens to Paris, to learn from his enemy the propereft time and place for meeting him in a duel.

The queftion was now put on the amendment, and negatived; after which the refolution was read and agreed to; and, next referred to a Committee, who formed it into an addrefs, to be, on the morrow, reported and read a firft and fecond time.

Wednefday, 25th January.

Mr. Smyth brought up the Report of the Committee, to whom the refolution agreed to by the Houfe on Tuefday was referred, for the purpofe of forming it into an addrefs, in anfwer to His Majefty's moft gracious fpeech from the throne, and the fame having been read a firft time,

The Earl of Surrey.

The Earl of *Surrey* expreffed his wifhes for an elucidation of a particular paffage in the fpeech from the Throne, in which the Commons being addreffed, mention was made of fome little addition to the public burdens. If by this was meant merely the modification of fuch taxes as experience had proved to require fome little alteration in the mode of impofition, he fhould have no objection; but if it was to be underftood from it that new and additional taxes were propofed to be laid on the fubject, he fhould in that cafe ftrenuoufly object to it; and, under this idea, he judged it candid to deliver his opinion at an early period, and the rather, becaufe the words had not merely excited an alarm, but affected the public funds with fome degree of detriment.

Mr. Fox.

Mr. *Fox* faid that, as the obfervations which he fhould beg leave to make, bore an affinity to his remarks, on the preceding day, they would lie all within a narrow compafs. Recent in the memory of the Houfe were his two
quef-

questions to a right honourable gentleman, (Mr. Pitt). To one of these he had given a precise and clear answer; to the other he had not spoken in terms equally unambiguous; and as that was a question of infinite importance to the interests of the country, it was his duty to endeavour, if possible, to obtain such an answer as should remove all doubt and difficulty. What he alluded to was, the particular degree in which Ministers held Great Britain to be committed, as to any future consequences that might arise from the effect of the league entered into by the Elector of Hanover with the Elector of Saxony, the King of Prussia and other Germanic Princes. He was aware, that the right honourable gentleman at the head of His Majesty's councils had disclaimed all responsibility for the wisdom and policy of the measure, had stated it to be a separate and distinct transaction from any British concern, and had declared that Great Britain was not committed as to her future conduct, should the league be productive of disturbances in the empire, in which her interests might call her into action. If this was really and truly the case, and Great Britain was not effected at all by the league, the more clearly it was known in that House, to the Public, and to all Europe, the better; because however well we understood the distinction between Great Britain and the Electorate of Hanover, as separate States, it was not a very easy matter to teach foreign powers to understand the same discrimination. A variety of possible cases existed in which it would be almost out of the power of this country to adhere to any such distinction in practice, however clearly it might be defined in theory. It might, hereafter, happen that circumstances would make it an essential policy in Great Britain to join the Court of Vienna, and to proceed in counteraction of the league. In that case, as all treaties were offensive in their effect, though nominally defensive, a war between the parties to the league and its opponents might probably arise. Granting the likelihood of such a war, could the British troops act against those of Hanover? Or, to make the case stronger, and yet to put a *possible* case, suppose the Elector of Hanover were to head his troops in person, (and they were all aware that it was not a new thing for an Elector of Hanover to take the command in the field) who would say that the British army could be directed to act hostilely against troops led by their Sovereign in the character of Elector of Hanover? The supposition teemed with the most gross absurdity, and it was to shew the extraordinary predicament into which the Elector of Hanover's becoming a party to a league of the nature in question, and without the advice of a Minister responsible for his conduct to that House, might draw Great Britain, and involve its interests, that he brought forward such unaccountable cases. One historical example would strengthened the argument which he had used, and prove beyond all doubt the mischiefs to which this country was liable to become exposed, by considering herself as wholly independent of the interests of Hanover. The case to which he alluded, was that of George the First, who, by his treaty with Denmark for the sale of Bremen and Verden, drew down upon him the vengeance of Sweden; and the consequence was, this country had been threatened with an invasion, the most alarming, and the most dangerous to the liberties of Englishmen of any it ever had occasion to expect. General Stanhope, at that time the Minister of the Crown, had, when the treaty was first heard of, come down to that House, and used precisely the same sort of language as that uttered by the right honourable gentleman, (Mr. Pitt) on the preceding day. He had talked of the separate and distinct interests of Great Britain and Hanover, and had said that the British Parliament had nothing to do with the conduct of His Majesty respecting his Electoral dominions; but what was the consequence? The very next year, General Stanhope, who held this language, came down to the House, and urged the expences which His Majesty had incurred on account of his purchase as a plea for calling for additional supplies. If the matter were not now fully and clearly ascertained, so that foreign powers, as well as that House, might be certain that Great Britain was not committed as to any part which her policy might dictate to her as most advisable to pursue hereafter, in the case of a war in Germany, the right honourable gentleman, who had on the foregoing day disclaimed all responsibility for the wisdom and policy of the measure in question, might come down to the House, on a subsequent occasion, and make that very measure, respecting which the British Parliament was excluded from all inquiry and control, the ground of an application for additional supplies. Mr. Fox concluded, by observing, that he never spoke concerning a point of state with less reluctance, persuaded that, on the present occasion, he neither divulged a secret, nor gave the slightest wound to the security and interests of the nation.

Mr. Pitt.   Mr. *Pitt* replied, that if he felt astonishment, on the preceding day, in discovering that the right honourable gentleman had used no arguments which he could have wished to coincide with, he was now overwhelmed by surprise to find his reasoning still more unworthy of an imitation. The right honourable gentleman had himself admitted that there wer subjects on which His Majesty's Ministers could not with propriety be so explicit as indifferent members of the House. For *his part*, he conceived that, although a cautious delicacy

in

in fpeaking on the fubjects of foreign politics was one part of the duty of His Majefty's Minifters, yet it was a duty which alfo belonged to every member of Parliament, nay, to every good citizen; however in each it might differ in degree, its nature was the fame in all.——It was, notwithftanding, as he apprehended, peculiarly improper for a gentleman, who had poffeffed a high official fituation, and by whom the foreign concerns of this country had been adminiftered—a gentleman who had generally affected to hold himfelf out as a perfon of fingular weight and authority, to indulge in fuch a latitude. In the debate of the preceding day the right honourable gentleman had gone, in his opinion, to moft improper lengths; but on this day he had difcovered, (he fuppofed from better judgement, and from more mature reflection, perhaps, from *diplomatic* information) that he had not gone far enough, and had therefore refumed the fubject, in order, that as he had before difplayed his ingenuity and acutenefs, he might now prove equally diftinguifhed for his information and his judgement. He had accordingly methodized his argument, and had brought it to a fpecific and certain point. He had firft laid it down that it would be a prejudice to this country, fhould the Princes of Europe confider her as bound by the treaty to which Hanover had acceded, and yet he had exercifed the whole ftrength of his abilities to perplex the argument, and to prove that fhe was in fact thus abfolutely bound. How he could juftify his intentions in this acknowledgment, and in this endeavour, he could not forefee; for, furely if it were, indeed, prejudicial to this country, that it fhould be underftood fhe was concluded by the act of the Miniftry of Hanover, that very circumftance ought to be a fufficient reafon for every friend to Great Britain to endeavour, as much as poffible, to enforce and uphold the doctrine, that fhe was not fo concluded. It was difficult to reconcile the caution of the right honourable gentleman to prevent this country being on any occafion embroiled for Hanover, with his attempt to make the Minifters of Great Britain refponfible for the Government and politics of that country. If that were done, it would become a limb and member of the Britifh empire, and as fuch would be entitled to demand protection. Should the Minifters of England interfere to prevent thofe of Hanover from forming fuch alliances and confederacies as they faw neceffary for her fafety, would they not have every right to demand, in cafe of future wars or dangers, the affiftance of that country who had prevented them from arming themfelves with allies and with friends, and would not this country be bound to affift them with, and even to the effufion of, the laft drop? and what could be more ridiculous than the idea of the right honourable

gentle-

gentleman, that the method of securing the friendship of the Imperial court, was by putting ourselves into the necessity of interfering in German politics, and abandoning that option of neutrality, which, standing as we do now, detached from the government of Hanover, it was in our power to make?——Mr. Pitt closed his remarks by declaring, that he had now discussed the subject as far as he felt himself warranted to examine it upon public ground; that perhaps, even a greater degree of reserve would have become him better; and that, here, he dropped the point, resolved no more to suffer the right honourable gentleman to bring him to its investigation.

Mr. Fox.

Mr. *Fox* reprobated (what he described as) the uncandid misrepresentation which the right honourable gentleman had put upon his arguments, striving to prove (what did not exist) his deviation from the character of a good citizen. Did the right honourable gentleman imagine, that the facts upon which he had reasoned were any secret, or that any of the European powers needed to send here for information respecting their nature? The contrary was notoriously true; the circumstances to which he alluded in argument were well known. Let the right honourable gentleman recollect the style of the different letters sent from the Courts of London, Versailles, and Petersburgh, to the King of Prussia, on the subject of the league, stating that the Court of Versailles had sent a letter, couched in terms of civility, and implying something like an approbation of the league, and that the Court of Petersburg had sent one, full of civility, but expressing extreme regret that any such league had been entered into in consequence of groundless doubts and ill-founded jealousies. Into how strange a situation must Great Britain fall, should a war in Germany be the consequence, and should she find it her interest to connect herself with the two imperial courts. Could she, with any decency, charge the Elector of Hanover with having joined in a league formed upon groundless doubts and ill-founded jealousies? The right honourable gentleman was pleased to indulge his talent for ridicule, upon the supposition that he had since the preceding day enjoyed the advantage of a *diplomatique* information. He knew the respectable character to whom the expression alluded; and although he was not so young as the right honourable gentleman, he did not consider it as disgraceful to seek for instruction, nor was it congenial with his nature to hold himself up as a man superior to those with whom he acted, however such extremes of vanity might actuate persons of a certain temper. Let such, however, steer at a proper distance from the ridiculous and dangerous supposition that they could deceive the bulk of individuals; nor venture to imagine that, although daring to lull the manufacturers of Great Britain into

the

the falfe conclufion that the Irifh propofitions were not hoftile to their interefts, and to palm upon the fifter kingdom the fame fcandalous idea, they might with impunity deceive all men by what they faid; or, becaufe they had confidently prefumed to perfuade the manufacturers of this country, that the Irifh propofitions contained nothing detrimental to their interefts, and to tell the people of Ireland that——

Mr. Fox was called to order by the Chair, the Irifh propofitions not being under confideration.

Mr. Pitt now, exclaimed: " Go on !" Mr. Fox replied, " No; we fhall both have opportunities enow to difcufs the fubject in the courfe of the feffion." After this, bowing to the Chair, he fat down, and clofed his fpeech.

When that part of the addrefs was read which related to the refolutions to be made the bafis of an adjuftment of the commercial intercourfe between Great Britain and Ireland,

Mr. *Sheridan* obferved, that he had felt no little curiofity on the foregoing day, to know the nature of the reply which the Minifter defigned to make to the inquiries of his right honourable friend concerning the Irifh propofitions; and whether it was his intention to bring them forward by a motion. The right honourable gentleman, although entrufted to prepare the bill brought in upon the twenty refolutions, did in that very bill totally depart from the refolutions as they had been voted. This was a grofs infult to the Houfe, and as ftrong a breach of faith with Parliament, as an indi- vidual could poffibly commit. He was indeed, aware that the right honourable gentleman had moved merely " that " leave be given to bring in a bill upon the fubject of the " refolutions," and not that " the refolutions be put into " the fhape and form of a bill;" but ftill the meaning of that Houfe clearly was, that the whole of the refolutions fhould be ftrictly adhered to in the bill. He would not, now, take up the time of the Houfe, by going at large into proofs of his accufation; but he would remind them of one ftriking circumftance, and that would fufficiently fhew that he was founded in his charge. The right honourable gentleman (they muft all recollect) had repeatedly blamed his right ho- nourable friend for making his grants in favour of Ireland matters of perpetual option, and had contended, that it was neceffary to enter into a treaty with Ireland, that fhould be final and conclufive; hence his conftant argument in defence of the propofitions had been, that *they* were to be final and con- clufive. Under that idea, he believed it would be generally agreed, that the majority of that Houfe had voted for the propofitions. What then were they to think of the conduct of the right honourable gentleman, when, upon examining his bill they fhould find, that fo materially had he departed

from

from the spirit of the propositions, that, instead of the condition of the bill being final and conclusive, it left the point open, and a matter of perpetual option. What miserable changes had not that business perpetually experienced ! Mr. Pitt's bill was different from the twenty resolutions, and Mr. Orde's bill again had been different from Mr. Pitt's. In corroboration of the assertion that the bill of Mr. Orde differed materially from Mr. Pitt's bill, he might quote the Irish debates which had been reported with singular accuracy, but he would cite an authority not to be questioned—the printed letter of the Secretary of State for Ireland to his constituents. He then read a passage to the House from the forty-second page of the Secretary of State's letter. Before he dropped the subject of the propositions, Mr. Sheridan compared them to buildings much too visible in many parts of the kingdom, and called Mr. Such-a-ones folly, for the absurdity of their architecture and a multitude of inconveniences which render it almost impossibe that they should continue long inhabited.

Attorney General. · The *Attorney General* replied to Mr. Sheridan, and read the following paragraph from the address of both Houses of Parliament during the last session, to prove that he was mistaken :

" We therefore deem it indispensable that these points should be secured, as conditions necessary to the existence and duration of the agreement between the two countries. They can only be carried into effect by laws to be passed in the Parliament of Ireland, which is alone competent to bind Your Majesty's subjects in that kingdom, and whose legislative rights we shall ever hold as sacred as our own."

Mr. Sheridan. Mr. *Sheridan* replied, and persisted in making a positive and peremptory charge against the Chancellor of the Exchequer, of having brought in a bill materially different from the resolution on which the House had expressed it to be founded.

The House then adjourned.

Thursday, 26th *January.*

The Earl of Courtown reported to the House, that His Majesty, having been waited upon (pursuant to the order of yesterday) humbly to know His Majesty's pleasure when he would be pleased to be attended by this House, had been pleased to appoint this day, at three of the clock, at his Palace of Saint James.

The order of the day being read, the House proceeded to take into consideration His Majesty's most gracious speech to both Houses of Parliament.

And the same was again read by Mr. Speaker.

Mr. Rose

Mr. Rofe having made a motion, that a fupply be granted to His Majefty; it was refolved, that the Houfe fhould, on the morrow morning, refolve itfelf into a Committee of the whole Houfe, to confider of that motion. The Houfe having adjourned, afterwards, went to Saint James's with the following addrefs:

The humble addrefs of the Houfe of Commons to the King.

"Moft Gracious Sovereign,

"We, Your Majefty's moft dutiful and loyal fubjects the Commons of Great Britain, in Parliament affembled, beg leave to return Your Majefty our humble thanks, for your moft gracious fpeech from the Throne.

"We learn, with great fatisfaction, that the difputes which appeared to threaten an interruption to the tranquillity of Europe have been brought to an amicable conclufion, and that Your Majefty continues to receive from foreign powers the ftrongeft affurances of their friendly difpofition towards this country.

"We are deeply fenfible of the bleffings which we experience from the enjoyment of peace, in the extenfion of trade, the improvement of the revenue, and the increafe of the public credit of the nation: and Your Majefty may rely on the utmoft exertion of our zeal and induftry for the farther advancement of thefe important objects.

"In order to promote, as far as in us lay, the common interefts of all Your Majefty's fubjects, we humbly laid before Your Majefty, in the laft feffion of Parliament, feveral refolutions, as the bafis of an adjuftment of the commercial intercoufe between Great Britain and Ireland; but, as no effectual ftep has been hitherto taken thereupon by the Parliament of that kingdom, we do not find ourfelves at prefent enabled to make any farther progrefs in that falutary work.

"We cannot refrain from offering the warmeft expreffions of our gratitude for Your Majefty's gracious affurances of your earneft wifh to enforce œconomy in every department: we fhall be equally ready, at all times, to make fuch provifion as may be neceffary for every branch of the public fervice, particularly for maintaining the naval ftrength of thefe kingdoms on the moft fecure and refpectbale footing. Fully impreffed with the neceffity of eftablifhing a fixed plan for the reduction of the national debt, we fhall lofe no time in entering on that important confideration; and it will afford us the moft folid fatisfaction to find that this moft defirable object may be attained with little addition to the public burdens.

"The vigour and refources fo happily manifefted in our prefent fituation muft give encouragement and confidence to all

Your

Your Majesty's subjects, and cannot fail to animate our exertions in endeavouring, by a continued attention to the security of the revenue, and the extension of trade, to confirm and improve the increasing prosperity of the empire.

Friday, 28th. January.

The Speaker, as soon as he had taken the chair, rose up and reported His Majesty's answer to the address of that House of Tuesday last, which was as follows:

" Gentlemen,

" I thank you for this very loyal address. I receive with great satisfaction the assurances of your disposition to enter with zeal and industry into the consideration of those important and salutary objects which I have recommended to your attention."

Mr. Rose.

The House resolved itself into a Committee of the whole House.

Mr. *Rose* moved, that His Majesty's speech be read, which was read accordingly; and then he moved, that a supply be granted to His Majesty, which being put and carried, the Chairman left the chair and reported the same.

Mr. Sheriff Saunderson, attending at the door, he was ordered to the bar, where he presented a petition from the Lord Mayor, Aldermen and Common Council of the city of London, praying a repeal of the shop tax. It was ordered to be laid on the table.

Sir Watkin Lewis.

Sir *Watkin Lewis* signified his intentions of embracing the earliest opportunity to move for leave to bring in a bill to repeal the act passed in the last session of Parliament, for laying a duty upon shops. He trusted that an occasion would present itself soon after the delivery of petitions upon the subject; and when he could foresee it to a certainty, he would give a week's notice of his design.

Mr. Jenkinson.

Mr. *Jenkinson*, begged leave to remind the House of the necessity of embracing some immediate measures, as a farther relief to Newfoundland. The wisdom of the legislature limited, in the course of the last year, the duration of the Bill which allowed bread, flour, biscuit, &c. to be exported from the United States of America to Newfoundland during twelve months, which term being nearly expired, His Majesty's Ministers meant to adopt a similar bill for two years longer, by which time Newfoundland would probably, become fully supplied, and render farther aid from that quarter needless.

Mr. M. A. Taylor.

Mr. *M. A. Taylor* observed, that although the bill would particularly affect his constituents (the merchants of Poole). yet

yet he was so convinced of the necessity of the measure, that he should give it no opposition.

The *Speaker* having reminded Mr. Jenkinson, that the regular way was to let the bill originate in a Committee, the House resolved itself into a Committee, Mr. Gilbert in the chair.

Mr. *Jenkinson* then moved for leave to bring in a bill to allow the importation of bread, flour, biscuit, &c. from the United States of America into Newfoundland; which being agreed to, the Committee broke up, and Mr. Gilbert reported the same to the House.

Adjourned, until

Mr. Jenkinson.

Tuesday, 31st January.

The Honourable *Charles Marsham* moved for leave to bring in "a bill for amending and reducing all the laws relative " to the militia of that part of Great Britain called Eng- " land, into one act of Parliament;" and begged permission briefly to explain the motives which induced him to solicit the attention of the House to points of such particular importance. He flattered himself that it was scarcely necessary to declare how much he deemed the militia the natural and most constitutional defence of the kingdom. A friend to it in the strictest sense of the expression, he wished to find it equally the favourite of the whole House, and was persuaded that nothing could prove so prejudicial to the service as treating it with indifference. A set of gentlemen, who, like himself, had served in the militia, and were persuaded of its great consequence, had, with him, directed their attention closely to the subject, and exerted their endeavours towards discovering the best possible means of preserving it upon a respectable and useful footing; and with such views, and under such circumstances, should he bring forward the motion of which he had already given notice. On this occasion, candour obliged him to declare, that he did not believe it possible to find any Minister who would receive a proposal for improving the situation in which the militia stood, in a more fair, open, and proper manner, than the right honourable gentleman, who presided over the Administration of the national affairs. This was the genuine sentiment of his heart, or he would not have uttered it; and no man, he flattered himself, could charge him with having pursued a conduct in that House, upon any one occasion whatsoever, that was not direct and sincere. Gentlemen would please to recollect the origin of the militia, the manner in which its services were received, not only at the end of the war before the last, but at the conclusion of the last war; and he would leave it to them to draw the in-

Honourable Charles Marsham.

ferences from the facts which he should state, and submit it to their consideration, whether it was not absolutely necessary, that some measures should be immediately taken respecting the militia, unless it was meant that the use and advantage of having such a constitutional defence should be entirely done away. In the year 1756 or 1757, when the war before the last broke out, a body of Hanoverians and Hessians were brought into this kingdom for its internal security. This introduction, at once impolitic and unconstitutional, occasioned some disturbance; Englishmen revolted at the unmerited idea of their not being capable of defending themselves and their country, and the militia began to be set on foot. So agreeable did the circumstance prove to that House, and so well did they think of the plan, when reduced to practice, that in the course of one and the same session they recognized, countenanced, and established the scheme into a national measure; and such were the benefits which the country derived from the militia, that, at the conclusion of the war, the officers who had served in it received the especial thanks of His Majesty, and of that House. What rendered the thanks of the House of Commons doubly dear to the officers was, that these were voted at the very same moment when an address to the King, thanking His Majesty for having put an end to the calamities of war was voted. This was, to his knowledge, a matter extremely pleasing to all who had served in it; and as a proof that it was so considered, he begged leave to state that the colonel of the corps in which he had since had the honour to serve (the Kentish militia) ordered a copy of the vote of thanks of the House of Commons to be made out and sent to each individual officer, that he might take it home with him, when the militia was disbanded, and preserve it as an honourable testimonial of the sense which the representatives of the people entertained of the service he had done his country. After the peace of Paris, the militia was called out, embodied, and trained, once a year; a circumstance from which the kingdom had derived essential advantage, as the House would see upon reverting to facts within all their knowledge. At the commencement of the session, during which hostilities between Great Britain and France took place, His Majesty, in his speech from the Throne, assured them that he had received the most pacific assurances from all the European powers, and yet, in the month of March of the same session, news arrived of the French having concluded a treaty of amity and commerce with the United States of America, then at war with us, and an authentic paper upon the subject was laid before both Houses of Parliament. The militia were, in consequence, called out; and it was remarkable that a militia camp was formed as early, that year, as in any one year during the war. The

practi-

practicability of this could only be imputed to the difcipline and the habits of duty, in which the militia was kept from being fo conftantly trained and exercifed. How different had been the conduct of Government at the end of the laft war? He had predicted what would follow; nor had he the good fortune to find himfelf (as, upon this occafion he could have wifhed to prove) a falfe prophet. Notwithftanding that the militia acted as well during the laft war as during the war preceeding it; and, although many gentlemen had dedicated their whole attention to the fervice, it was not thought that the militia deferved thanks for their accomplifhment of their duty. He meant not to give offence; and, perhaps, he had ufed too harfh an expreffion; but the fact was, that no thanks were given to the militia by the Crown, no thanks had been voted by that Houfe, and for three years together the militia had never been even once called out. The confequence was, that gentlemen grew indifferent to the fervice, and were difgufted at the neglect with which it had been treated. He begged leave to affure the Houfe that, making this remark, he did not intend to caft the leaft reflection on any fet of men in particular; but the fact ftood as he had ftated it; and it was with a view to preferve the militia from being loft altogether, that he had given himfelf the trouble to turn his thoughts to the fubject. He would take up no more of the time of the Houfe, than fhortly to mention fome of the views with which the bill, he fhould move for leave to bring in, had been prepared. The gentlemen, who affifted him, were unanimoufly of opinion that one mode was, to reduce all the various laws into one, and that another material object of it was, to change the time of the duration of the fervice, and to alter it from three years to five. Three objections were generally made to the militia. One, the great expence to the kingdom: another, the prejudice it did to the recruiting fervice of the amry; and a third, the heavy burden which it entailed upon the country. The alteration which he had ftated met all thefe three objections; becaufe, if the men were drawn for five years inftead of three, and their cloathing fo regulated, it would not only put the kingdom to an expence confiderably fhort of what it had hirtherto coft; but, alfo prove infinitely lefs prejudicial to the recruiting fervice, inafmuch as frefh men for the militia would not fo foon be wanted as before; and laftly, as fubftitutes were only to be provided once in five years inftead of three, the individuals drawn, and confequently the country in general, would not experience burdens of fuch enormous weight. Another alteration propofed by the bill, was reducing the number of ferjeants and drums, by having

in

in future only two drums for the flank companies, and only one for thofe of the battalion inftead of the prefent number.

Having added, that, as a fimilar reduction of ferjeants would, if introduced, occafion no inconfiderable retrenchment in the national expenditure, Mr. Marfham clofed his remarks by moving, " For leave to bring in a bill for amending " and reducing into one act all the militia laws in that part of Great Britain called England."

Mr. *Pye* feconded the motion.

Mr. Pitt.   Mr. *Pitt* obferved that, upon the prefent occafion, when the majority of the Houfe were, doubtlefs, ready to meet the motion of the honourable gentleman with their concurrence, little remained for him but to exprefs his fatisfaction at perceiving a moft important fubject fo properly brought under their confideration. The interval of peace was, undoubtedly, the fitteft moment poffible for them to unite in endeavouring to put the great and moft conftitutional defence of the kingdom upon a refpectable and ufeful footing; and much as he profeffed himfelf to be the friend of œconomy in that, as in every other branch of the public fervice, from a conviction of its extreme and indifpenfable neceffity, he was not fo much the flave of his opinion as to wifh to carry his efforts to introduce a rigid and univerfal adherence to œconomy fo far, as by any means to leffen the advantages which the country had ever felt, and he hoped ever would feel, from the eftablifhment of a well-difciplined and effectual militia. How far the means fuggefted by the honourable gentleman for attaining a purpofe equally defirable to him, and, he trufted, to all who heard him, might be thought the beft means poffible to be adopted, was a matter for future confideration, and would regularly fall under difcuffion when the bill fhould come before them, and its contents be fpecified. If it fhould appear poffible to preferve the militia on a refpectable footing without putting the public to the heavy expence attendant on calling that force out every year, he owned, he fhould be glad to adopt fuch means as might be fuggefted for that purpofe. Waiting for the pleafure of hearing fome future, ample, judicious and impartial inveftigation of the fubject; he fhould, now, content himfelf with defiring that honourable mover, and thofe gentlemen who had enjoyed the happinefs of affifting him in tracing out and bringing into one point of view the moft falutary amendments for laws which, by the magnitude of their conftitutional importance, demanded the attention of every member of the legiflature in particular, and of every friend to his country in general, would accept of his fincereft and moft warm acknowledgements.

Mr. *Mar-*

Mr. *Marſham* begged leave once more to intrude himſelf upon the patience of the Houſe, merely to obſerve, that the calling out the militia regularly every year was, in his opinion, ſo indiſpenſably neceſſary to the preſervation of that force on a reſpectable and uſeful footing, that if the right honourable gentleman, (Mr. Pitt) had determined to oppoſe it, he ſhould ſcarcely think it worth his while to bring the ſubject forward to the inveſtigation of the Houſe. Every gentleman preſent, who had ſerved in the militia, muſt certainly feel the moſt irreſiſtible conviction, that nothing could tend ſo much towards making the militia capable of entering, at a moment's notice, into action, as the accuſtoming the men to be trained and exerciſed once a year, and if they were not called out, but upon the ſpur of the occaſion, it would become almoſt an abſurdity to expect any great benefit from their military operations, ſhould either invaſions, or any other circumſtances require their preſence in the field.

The Speaker having put the queſtion, the Houſe gave it their unanimous concurrence, and then adjourned.

Wedneſday, February 20.

The Earl of *Courtown* acquainted the Houſe that His Majeſty had been waited upon with their addreſs of Tueſday laſt, and that His Majeſty had been graciouſly pleaſed to ſay, he would give directions accordingly. The Earl of Courtown

Mr. *Pitt* gave notice, that he ſhould very ſhortly bring forward the ſtate of the revenue, and that preparatory to that purpoſe, he muſt move for ſeveral papers. He moved, accordingly, for Mr. Pitt.

" An account of the quantity of rum imported into North
" America for ſix years previous to the year 1784."

" An account of the quantity of rum imported into England for the laſt ten years." Alſo the ſame account of rum imported into Scotland."

" Three accounts of Exchequer bills."

" An account of the ſums of money ariſing from duties
" on houſes paid over."

" An account of the total of all ſums of money aſſeſſed
" on houſes, carriages, and ſervants."

" An account of the total of all ſums impoſed in 1785,
" and which have been paid into the Exchequer."

" An account of the amount of money on carriages and
" male ſervants under the direction of the Commiſſioners of
" Excise."

" An account of all ſums ariſing from the duties on waggons and other carriages.

" An account of all duties on carriages and male ſervants
" paid by the Commiſſioners of exciſe.

" An

" An account of all fums due from the Eaft-India Com-
" pany, previous to the year 1785."

" An account of all fums arifing from the land and malt
" for the laft ten years." And alfo,

" An account of the public debt."

The Houfe adjourned.

Thurfday, 2d February.

Sir George Yonge.   Sir *George Yonge*, as Secretary of war, prefented the army eftimates, and begged leave to apprife the Houfe of his intention to move for referring them to the confideration of a Committee of Supply on the enfuing Wednefday.

The Speaker.   She *Speaker* defired to bring back to the recollection of the Houfe the cuftom of fuffering the army eftimates to remain, during the fpace of a week, upon the table, for the information of the members, previous to their being taken into confideration. Although, confiftently with his duty, he mentioned this circumftance, refpect for the Houfe obliged him to obferve, that either the adoption or the rejection of the mode lay in their own breafts.

The Earl of Surrey.   The Earl of *Surrey* expreffed his wifhes that, as no particular bufinefs ftood for Wednefday, the Houfe would take that day, and that all the public affairs and political concerns might be brought on early, and not (as too frequently had proved the cafe) defer it until an extremely advanced period of the feffion.

The notice was taken for Wednefday.

Mr. Cruger prefented a petition from the fhopkeepers of Briftol, praying a repeal of the act, impofing a tax on retail fhopkeepers.

The petition was read at the table.

Mr. Cruger.   Mr. *Cruger* remarked, that fuch of his conftituents whofe fignatures were at the bottom of the petition complained of the tax as partial, oppreffive, and confequently unjuft. But, he did not entertain a doubt that they would fubmit to it without a murmur, were it altered to a general tax upon all houfekeepers.

The petition was, upon motion, ordered to lie on the table.

Mr. Rolle.   Mr. *Rolle* requefted the Chancellor of the Exchequer (Mr. Pitt) to bring forward fome meafure, in the courfe of the feffion, relative to the fale of wafte lands. An anfwer in the negative (Mr. Rolle added) would confirm him in his yet wavering refolution fhortly to trouble the Houfe with a motion upon the fubject.

Mr. Pitt.   Mr. *Pitt* replied that, in all likelihood, the prefent feffion would not clofe without an inveftigation of many interefting particulars relative to the wafte lands.

Mr. *Rolle*

Mr. *Rolle* said, that he could wish the right honourable gentleman would please to favour him with a more decisive answer. Mr. Rolle.

Mr. Pitt remaining silent, the Speaker put the question, and the House adjourned.

Friday, 3d February,

No debate.

Monday, 6th February.

Petitions against the shop tax were presented to the House from the tradesmen, inhabitants of Middlesex, Westminster, Southwark, the city of London, and the towns of Birmingham, Leeds, and Cirencester, which, after they were read by the clerk, were ordered to lie on the table.

Lord *Hood* having presented a petition from the shopkeepers of Westminster, it was read at the table; and, immediately afterwards, Lord Hood.

Mr. *Fox* expressed his wishes, that such a number of petitions, from the most respectable multitudes, amidst the great constituent body of the people, might excite the attention of their representatives, and induce them to meet such powerfully-enforced requests with unreserved compliance. He did not then see the worthy Alderman in the house who had pledged himself to make a motion on the subject, and therefore he would not say more respecting it for the present, except to intimate, that as the petition presented by his noble colleague had received the signature of more than 4000 persons, all of whom were, to his knowledge, real shopkeepers; this striking circumstance must unavoidably convince the House that, whatever differences of opinion there might have prevailed in Westminster, with respect to politics, the complaints against the shop tax were not the partial, but the general voice of the whole mass of the electors. Mr. Fox.

Mr. *Thornton* now delivering the Southwark petition, observed that it bore equal marks of unanimity with that from Westminster, being signed by 1300 shopkeepers; a proportion of nearly three parts of his constituents. Mr. Thornton.

No sooner had the Speaker put the question, "That the petition should lie on the table," than

The Earl of *Surrey* rose, and said he hoped that the honourable member who gave notice of his intention to move for leave to bring in a bill for the repeal of the shop tax, would fix on an early day for that purpose, or that, if this were not the case, Government would follow up the business to an effectual and serviceable length. A tax on shops had been imposed on the subject by the authority of Parliament; yet, far from having been collected, stood at this day a disgrace- The Earl of Surrey.

ful

ful proof of the inefficiency of Administration. Government ought, therefore, to propose such regulations as should enforce the collection of the tax, or to repeal it. On the present occasion, he could not sit down without remarking, as a singular circumstance, that since the commencement of the session the House had met generally about three, and the Minister came down to move the question of adjournment at about twenty minutes before four o'clock; a most improper mode of conducting the national concerns, which, from their nature, required that more should have been brought forward for the consideration of that House, than hitherto became submitted to their discussion. For his own part, he intended to have addressed his observations to the right honourable gentleman at the head of His Majesty's councils, had he been present, and he hoped that some of those who were immediately connected with him, would inform him of what had been thrown out, as in all probability the question of adjournment would that day be moved, and carried, before the appearance of the right honourable gentleman in his place.

Mr. Rose.

Mr. *Rose* replied, that whatever Government might think it adviseable to do, with regard to either the shop tax, or any other measure of public concern, it would be a fitter subject for discussion when his right honourable friend was present; and he could assure the noble Lord that he might expect his entrance every moment. With regard to the public business being delayed, there was not the smallest foundation for the complaint. The supplies of the year had been brought forward in regular gradations as early as during the preceding session of Parliament; nor could one be instanced, considering the period of time since the House met, in which the public business was more accelerated and attended in its progress. As to what the noble Lord had been pleased to say in respect to the shop tax not being collected, as far as facts had reached his knowledge, the contrary was the fact. Regular instalments, as in the case of every other tax, had been made, and he had not heard of any obstruction to the collection. And all this (he must beg leave to assert) was a proof of the present fallibility of the arguments of the noble Lord.

The Southwark petition was ordered to lie on the table.

Mr. Alderman Sawbridge.

Mr. Alderman *Sawbridge* signified his intention to defer making any motion as to that part of the Petition of the retail shopkeepers of the city of London, which prayed to be heard by themselves or council against the tax, till the motion which an honourable member had pledged himself to make, should fall under consideration, together with every petition relating to the subject.

Mr. *Brett*

Mr. *Brett* begged leave to inform the House of his design to move the number of seamen for the service of the current year in the Committee of Supply, on the ensuing Friday.

The Chancellor of the Exchequer having entered and taken his seat, Mr. *Marsham* intreated the attention of the House to some necessary observations respecting the militia. Several honourable gentlemen, who had served in that constitutional body of force, investigated the subject with an anxious wish to be able, by fit and salutary regulations, to put the militia on a respectable and useful footing; and, with this view they prepared a bill, in which they introduced several alterations, which they should not have judged worthy of adoption, but, under the conviction, that an adherence to the strictest œconomy was absolutely necessary, all the circumstances of the country considered. Finding, however, that Administration differed from them respecting a point which in their minds was the most essential of any towards restoring the militia to the degree of respect and utility which every friend to his country must wish it to enjoy, being no less than the necessity of embodying and training them regularly every year, and as the right honourable gentleman who presided over the affairs of Government had not been able to make up his mind upon that point, without the enforcement of which, many, if not all, of the gentlemen with whom he had consulted upon the subject, were of opinion it would be better to have no militia at all, he thought it right to take no farther step in the business, but to let the matter rest upon its usual ground. Of this, however, he was persuaded, that another year could not pass over without some material change, a positive act of Parliament being at that time in full force, which expressly ordered, that the militia should be called out every year, whereas they had not been once called out for two years together.

Mr. Marsham.

Mr. *Pitt* replied, that he perceived, with no inconsiderable concern, how unjustly attempts were made to mark *him* out as the person through whom the public was to be deprived of the advantages, which several officers of rank and character in the militia expected would result from a plan on which they had bestowed so much pains and attention. He confessed that there could be nothing more desirable than an arrangement that should reconcile the national defence by a militia to the principles and practice of œconomy; but though he had not made up his mind upon the question, whether the present proposal would have that effect; he saw no reason why the circumstance of one individual member of Parliament, wishing to withhold his opinion until after a subject

Mr. Pitt.

of fuch importance could be debated and argued, fhould be a means of preventing its coming forward at all. It was certainly the duty of every member of Parliament to fuggeft and propofe fuch plans as appeared to him likely to promote the public welfare; yet the honourable gentleman, (unlefs he greatly miftook the point) was particularly pledged to the country to bring forward his plan, having given notice that he had methodifed and arranged it; nor ought it to be any objection to his fo doing, that he (Mr. Pitt) had not yet fufficiently confidered it to venture to give any decifive fentiment on the propriety of one particular part of it (the calling out the militia annually) and efpecially as he had not yet heard even the arguments of the honourable gentleman himfelf, he muft of courfe want confiderable helps towards forming his judgement upon it. On the prefent occafion, he muft beg leave to appeal to the candour of the honourable gentleman, and call upon him as a refpectable and wellmeaning member of Parliament, and as a zealous friend to the inftitution of the militia, to fay, whether it was confiftent with his duty to the Public and the Houfe, to withhold from them a plan which he thought of fuch confequence, merely becaufe one member wifhed to have the advantage of hearing the fubject fully difcuffed before he would venture to decide upon a moft effential point of it; or whether it was fair to prefs him to give an opinion before he was fufficiently mafter of the fubject. As to the idea ftarted by the honourable gentleman, that the not having called out the militia for the laft two years, might fubject any particular defcription of perfons to blame, he felt it more than difficult to give it a concurrence; becaufe, it was well known, that although the act of Parliament authorifed and enjoined an annual embodying of the militia, yet it lay with the Houfe to provide the means, by voting the fupply for defraying the expence attendant on it; and when that Houfe did not provide the means, the act of Parliament was (as the right honourable gentleman in the chair would certainly admit,) a dormant ftatute. It would prove highly improper, except in cafes of the greateft neceffity, to call out the militia, when no provifion had been made for the charges incident to it; nor could a meafure of this impolitic nature fail to load the country with an expence for which Parliament did not afford the leaft fanction.

Mr. *Marfham* anfwered, that the manner in which the right honourable gentleman had ftated the facts in queftion between them was not candid.—And, in proof of this affertion, he muft beg leave to appeal to the Houfe, whether a matter of fuch important national concern as the militia, was not more fit for Government to fuperintend and regulate,

gulate, by the propofing of fuch meafures refpecting it as fhould from time to time appear neceffary, than to be left to the fuggeftions of private perfons, or members of Parliament? He had, certainly, in conjuction with other gentlemen, endeavoured to prepare a bill, calculated as far as their judgements went, towards the eftablifhment of the militia upon a refpectable footing; and he had ftated feveral of the particular regulations it contained, to the Houfe, at an early day after their meeting; but finding that the fenfe of a right honourable member—of the Minifter of the country—oppofed to him upon that point, which he and thofe who had with him turned their thoughts to the fubject, confidered as the moft effential of all, in effecting the wifhed-for purpofe, he had not loft a moment in declaring, that if the right honourable gentleman could not make up his mind to the idea of calling out the militia once a year, (a meafure without which, in his opinion, and that of the beft-informed men concerning the fubject, the militia would become not merely an ufelefs, but a burdenfome incumbrance on the country, he fhould think it right to fave the Houfe and himfelf from all farther trouble refpecting it, and let the matter reft as it was. A friend to the militia he certainly was; and he trufted that he endeavoured faithfully to difcharge his duty to his conftituents and to his country as a member of Parliament; but he could not conceive that he acted improperly, if finding that the right honourable gentleman had not yet decided concerning the moft effential of all thofe propofed by his intended bill, he chofe to ftop where he was, and to proceed no farther with a propofition, the main point of which was not likely to meet with the countenance and fupport of Adminiftration. With regard to what the right honourable gentleman faid, in refpect to the exifting ftatute, which enacted, that the militia fhould be regularly embodied once a year, being a dormant law, and in no force, unlefs the Houfe provided the means of putting it in force, not only he, but a great many very refpectable perfons differed from the right honourable gentleman. That the purfe of the nation was in that Houfe could not be controverted; yet, he conceived that an unrepealed, pofitive ftatute was, and ought to be, in full force, and that it was the duty of that Houfe to vote in the courfe of every feffion the fum which the embodying of the militia would coft. If they neglected this point, they took upon themfelves to difpenfe with the law of the land, and render the authority of the whole legiflature a matter of actual infignificance.

The Earl of *Surrey* now rofe a fecond time, renewing his complaint againft the neglect of Adminftration to open the feffion with more bufinefs. The Houfe, he obferved, had

The Earl of Surrey.

ufually

usually met about three o'clock, and adjourned before four.
An honourable gentleman (Mr. Rose) in office had, that
day, declared, that the business of supply had gone on as
quick and as regularly as ever; but was there no other public business than the business of supply? If the question
respecting the shop tax had been brought forward, it might
then have undergone a full discussion; and if it was meant
to try to enforce that unpopular tax by a variety of minute
regulations, in all probability the bill, when it should be
brought in, would take up the time of the Committee for many
days together. If so, would it not prove better to introduce
it early, and thus prevent it from becoming the means of
keeping the House sitting so late in the year as the end of
August, to which period they had been obliged to spin out
the session? The principal matter which then detained them,
had failed; on which account, he would not say, but possibly
that was one reason among others, why they had not been
sooner called together. At any rate, the great questions (and
surely, there were some respecting the finances and the revenue of that kingdom which required investigation) had
better be brought on early. A great part of the delay arose
from the circumstance of the House having within its walls
but one responsible Minister. A Secretary of State should
always sit among them; nor indeed was it right for the
office of Chancellor of the Exchequer and the office of Minister to be united in one and the same person. The business of finance was supposed chiefly to occupy the mind of
a Chancellor of the Exchequer, and that alone was sufficient
to employ any one's whole time, without his attention being
diverted and engaged by the various objects that required the
application of a Minister. In conclusion, the Earl of Surrey
observed, that he could not sit down without once more alluding to (what indeed had given alarm) the passage in the
speech from the throne, concerning little additional burdens.
That matter called for explanation; the Public ought to know
whether more taxes were shortly to increase the load beneath
the violence of which they languished.

No answer was given, and the House adjourned.

Tuesday, 7th February.

Mr. Rose signified his intention of moving, upon the
morrow, for the land tax for the current year in the Committee of ways and means.

Mr. Francis   Mr. *Francis* remarked that, conceiving it necessary for the
House to pay the earliest and strictest attention to the affairs of
the East-India Company, so far as they respected their revenue,
disbursement, and debt in India, he should beg leave to move
for

for papers fimilar to thofe granted to him during the courfe
of the preceding feffion; and as gentleman would fee, that
it was abfolutely impoffible to enter upon any difcuffion
of the ftate of the Company's affairs, without having the
neceffary papers before them, he trufted that he fhould find
no oppofition to his motion,

" That there be laid before this Houfe an eftimate of the
" probable refources and difburfements of the Bengal go-
" vernment, from the 30th of April, 1785, to the 1ft of
" May, 1786."

" That there be laid before this Houfe a ftate of the
" bonded debt due by the Eaft-India Company of the pre-
" fidencies of Fort William, Fort St George, and Bombay
" refpectively."

" That there be laid before this Houfe a ftate of the ar-
" rears due in the feveral departments of government, and of
" the orders on the feveral treafuries iffued and remaining
" unpaid at the prefidencies of Fort William, Fort St.
" George, and Bombay refpectively."

The motions were all carried.

Mr. *Baftard* obferved that, not wifhing to intrude himfelf Mr. Baf-
upon the patience of the Houfe by needlefs motions, he tard.
fhould, for the prefent, only requeft an information from
fome honourable gentleman in the confidence of government,
whether it was intended to enforce the fentence for the
tranfportion of convicts, and carry into effectual execution,
by any meafure to be propofed to that Houfe, on the part of
Adiminiftration during the period of the prefent fittings.

Mr. *Pitt* begged leave to affure the right honourable gen- Mr. Pitt.
tleman, that the matter to which he interrogatively referred,
had long been, and was at that time, under the confideration of Government; that a great variety of propofals had
been prefented to them upon the fubject, and that every
reafon exifted for believing that when they had been able
maturely to weigh the tendency of each, and to compare
their practicability, propriety, and policy, the refult would
prove an application to Parliament, accompanied by a defcription of the leaft unexceptionable plan, which would of
courfe be fubmitted to the inveftigation and final decifion
of the Houfe.

Mr. *Mainwaring* intimated his wifhes to have heard a Mr. Main-
more particular reply; to have been affured that it was in the waring.
comtemplation of Government pofitively to carry into literal
effect the act for the tranfportation of convicts fentenced to
tranfportation, and not to commute the punifhment, by fub-
ftituting imprifonment or hard labour, either on fhore or
fhipboard. Experience had convinced him, that it was owing
entirely to the having abondoned the execution of fentences of
tranfpor-

transportation, that such numerous, such daring, and such dangerous gangs of villiains assembled, to the great annoyance of the Public. It was the substitution of a different mode of punishment, which did not effectually remove from the kingdom gangs of the description to which he had alluded, which had peopled the metropolis with the most outrageous and abandoned robbers. As he knew this to be the fact, he was anxious in his wishes, that the attention of Government should rather be directed to the enforcing the transportation, than to the providing any means of punishment in its place; and therefore was he desirous of receiving information whether the length of the imprisonment of the convicts at hard labour, either on shore or shipboard, was to be considered as a portion of that period of time, throughout which they had been sentenced to continue in a state of transportation.

Mr. Chancellor Pitt.

Mr. *Pitt* observed, that as an honourable gentleman (Mr. Bastard) had received no vague answer to his close question, he should have imagined any lengthened agitation of the matter at present needless. The honourable gentleman had asked whether any measure was meant to be proposed to that House in the course of the session, with a view to enforce sentences of transportation on convicts, and to carry them into effect? In reply, he stated that the matter was under the consideration of His Majesty's Ministers, and that a variety of proposals for the purpose were now before them. Gentlemen were, undoubtedly, no strangers to the difficulties which lay in the way of carrying into execution the act for transporting convicts sentenced to transportation, and they perfectly well knew, that the difficulty had grown out of the change of situation which the country had experienced within the course of a very few years. It must be evident to all impartial examiners of the subject, that it was much easier for gentlemen to state, and to complain of the grievance, than for Government to find out and to apply an adequate remedy. He wished, therefore, when gentlemen were desirous of pointing out the one, that they would have the goodness to come prepared to suggest the other; for this, he could assure the House, that every possible attention should be shewn on the part of Government to all suggestions which carried with it the smallest appearance of practicability, and that no pains should be spared to push them to their full effect. At present, a variety of proposals were under the consideration of Government, and the great difficulty lay in fixing upon a fit place for the transportation of convicts; and, until this difficulty could be surmounted, it necessarily became incumbent on Government to dispose of the convicts in such a manner, as should at once serve to free the jails of their company, and to

keep

keep the felons employed in a way moft likely to be felt by them as a punifhment, and to conduce, in fome degree, to the public fervice. Inconveniencies unavoidably would refult from the convicts being fo employed rather than fent out of the country; but to fuch, let their magnitude prove what it might, it were found policy to agree until Adminiftration (determined in this cafe to lofe no time) fhould have devifed inevitable modes for carrying into complete force the fentences againft the tranfports.

This fubject being concluded,

The *Chancellor of the Exchequer* next begged leave, in fome meafure, to prepare the Houfe for the early difcuffion of a fubject which had excited a confiderable degree of attention on the part of the public, and were very naturally looked for with impatience by many honourable members of that affembly. Thefe important points were the ftate of the revenue and of the finances of the country, both of which he conceived, and he flattered himfelf gentlemen would perceive, muft of neceffity be divided under two diftinct heads, and form two feparate objects of inquiry and confideration. The firft of the two would form an afcertainment of the actual ftate of the revenue, which could only be derived from a comparative ftatement of our annual national income with our annual difburfement; and the other would lead to a fure difcovery of the beft and wifeft means of appropriating the furplus of our revenue, compared with our expenditure, fo as to form a permanent fund for a conftant and invariable application to the diminution of the public debt. Gentleman might fee that the firft of thefe two objects would require the firft inveftigation, and that it muft become entirely difpofed of, previous to any difcuffion of the fecond. Under this impreffion it was, that he had moved, fome days fince, for a variety of papers, containing public accounts under a variety of heads, all of which accounts were neceffary for the infpection of the Houfe, in order to enable them to mark and trace the order and progrefs of the increafe of the revenue, and to fee what was, on the one hand, to be added to the annual difburfements upon grounds of fair and accurate calculation, and what, on the other hand, was to be deducted from the income, as matters for which credit ought nor to be taken in refpect to the increafe of the annual revenue. To tranfcribe and arrange thefe papers, would neceffary employ no inconfiderable fpace of time. Several were before the Houfe already, others were accounts to be made up to particular periods, and though not all concluded, were daily haftening to a completion. As foon however as they fhould be upon the table, after allowing a reafonable time for gentleman to infpect them, he

would

would take the liberty to move for a Committee to examine them, and report their amount. The appointment of such a Committee would scarely have any thing to do, except to sum up the amounts of the different accounts, and to report the total to the House, compared with the total of the other side, which necessarily give an accurate statement of the surplus, whatever it might be. He should hope that the occupation of the Committee would not prove lasting, and that, in consequence, no great delay could possibly take place. The whole having, by means of the report of the Committee, been brought fully and fairly before the House, he would give notice of an early day, on which he should state the nature of the measures in contemplation; measures most likely to conduce to an advantageous appropriation of a permanent fund to be invariably applied in diminution of the national debt. On the present occasion, he had briefly thrown out these few remarks, from a respectful wish to convince the House what unavoidable causes had existed, (and did *still* exist) to retard the discussion of a subject of such singular importance.

The question of adjournment was then put, and carried.

Wednesday, 8th *February.*

The order of the day was read for the House to resolve itself into a Committee of ways and means. The Speaker then left the chair, and the House went into a Committee; and after some time Mr. Gilbert reported that the Committee had come to two resolutions, viz.

" That a sum not exceeding four shillings in the pound be raised by a land tax for the year 1786."

" That the duties on malt, mum, perry, and cyder be continued."

The said resolutions were ordered to be reported on the ensuing Friday.

After a long and uninterrupted pause,

Mr. Sheridan.

Mr. *Sheridan* remarked that he concluded the House were now waiting, in silent suspense, for the appearance of the Secretary at War, with his proposal of a vote in favour of the army estimates. But surely the House would act with more propriety if, instead of listening at so early a period to the discussion of this important subject, they were to adjourn immediately, and thus allow themselves more time for the investigation of the army estimates.

Mr. Rose.

Mr. *Rose* answered that, in his opinion, the honourable Gentleman had introduced his proposition with rather too considerable a degree of precipitation; and the more so, because, as the presence of the Secretary at War was every moment expected, a fitter time would then arrive for determitermining whether the army eftimates ought directly to fall under the confideration of the Houfe.

The *Secretary at War* now entered, and moved, " That " the Houfe fhould refolve itfelf into a Committee of fup- " ply for the purpofe of taking the army eftimates into " confideration."

When the Speaker had put the queftion whether he fhould then quit the chair,

Mr. *Minchin* declared that he felt himfelf under the pain- ful neceffity of oppofing the motion that the Speaker fhould leave the chair, becaufe he could not confent to a vote for the army when the militia had been fo much neglected. The militia, undoubtedly, were much preferable to a ftanding army. They were the interior guardians of the country, and ought to be fupported agreeably to the principles of our conftitution, and therefore muft, of courfe, attract the jealoufy of all who felt a laudable anxiety for its welfare. He very much apprehended, at leaft it had been infinuated without doors, that the militia was to be abolifhed, and a proportional number of ftanding troops fubftituted in its place. He could not, without alarm, give credit to the report, becaufe a ftanding army had always been confidered as dangerous to the liberties of Englifhmen. The corps of militia, during the whole period of the laft war, proved exceedingly ufeful to the defence of the country. They had acted as became good foldiers and patriotic citizens, and, upon all occafions, difplayed confiderable zeal in the fervice. It had been faid, that they were local troops, and could on no emergency be fent abroad. But, did that circumftance leffen their value or utility? Far from it. For while the militia were employed in guarding the interior parts of our dominions, the regular troops might be fent on foreign fervice. It gave him concern to remark that, notwithftanding the truth of thefe pofitions, it now appeared, that they were very much leffened in point of eftimation and importance. It had been cuftomary, fince the eftablifhment of this corps, to call them out once every year, in order to keep them in proper difcipline. The expence was trifling in comparifon of the magnitude of the meafure. It had only amounted to about forty thoufand pounds when the whole corps performed duty for the limited period of twenty-eight days. If, however, it was intended to reduce them in proportion to the reduction of the army, and to limit the number in time of peace to 17000 men, the expence of training and exercifing them for twenty-eight days would amount only to the fum of 20,000l. If any reduction was intended, why not reduce the ftanding army, and continue the militia in that important point of view to which they certainly were entitled?

They were the local and stationary troops of the country, and from every consideration, deserved more confidence than a standing army. Besides, it was now absolutely necessary to retain a defensive corps at home, in case of a sudden rupture with our enemies abroad. Formerly, our navy was found adequate to our national defence, and considered sufficient for that purpose, both internally and externally. The times were, very unfortunately for Great Britain, altered; and our navy, which had been in later periods, considered as the bulwark and pride of the nation, had experienced a diminution of its importance in the eyes of all Europe, by the formidable exertions of the House of Bourbon. France and Spain were now equal to us in a naval arrangement; nay, he believed, by the accession of the navy of the United Provinces, greatly superior. He could not avoid supposing that, on the commencement of another war, our navy would prove inferior to such a formidable confederacy. If therefore we neglected this navy, it was necessary that we should invigorate our internal defence; and, consequently, the regular training and exercising of the militia was the primary object. The right honourable gentleman (Mr. Pitt) had, on a former occasion, spoken in strong terms concerning œconomy in the expenditure of the public money.—He approved very much of the right honourable gentleman's ideas of œconomy; but he did not like to see any œconomical plan carried to such a length as to infringe upon general systems of necessity. A judicious plan of œconomy he conceived to be a proper application of the money voted for the particular service for which it was appropriated; but when the sum voted was misapplied, he considered that the object for which it was intended was entirely defeated. He wished to know whether the right honourable gentleman designed to support the bill intended to be introduced by several honourable friends. He believed it was very well calculated to regulate any defect in the militia laws. If the right honourable gentleman agreed to support the bill alluded to, he would consent to the House going into a committee on the army estimates, although he apprehended that it was acting with too great precipitation; for the estimates had not lain a sufficient time upon the table of the House for the inspection of the members. But, if he might take the freedom to draw inferences from the part which the right honourable gentleman pursued, on the preceding day, he could not venture to flatter himself with the hope of finding him friendly to the bill; and therefore for the purpose of delaying the matter until he should become acquainted with the result of the militia bill, he would move, " That the " House should now adjourn."

Mr. *Steele*

Mr. *Steele* declared that he opposed the motion from a consciousness of its impropriety, and added, that if gentlemen were resolved to cavil on every occasion, and stand forward merely for the sake of opposition, there would be an endless contest, because on every trifling occasion opportunities would always present themselves for objecting to a measure, however salutary in its consequence. With regard to the militia bill, if gentlemen were determined to wait till it passed before they consented to vote the estimates for the army, they would probably retard that event till the conclusion of the session; because, as the adjustment of that question depended upon the passing of the militia bill, no man could tell when that event would become accomplished. Concerning the short notice given respecting the business now in dispute, he differed in opinion from the honourable gentleman who had preceded him. He might pretend that he had not received sufficient notice; but he was firmly persuaded that the House would not agree with him. The estimates had during a length of time, remained upon the table open to a general examination; a circumstance which certainly operated irresistibly against all arguments in favour of a procrastination of the business.

Mr. *Minchin* begged leave to tell the honourable gentleman that he had totally misrepresented his observations. He had never contended, that the militia bill ought to pass before the army was voted; but, on the contrary, only intimated that it behoved ministers to acquaint the House whether they intended to establish the militia upon a respectable footing previous to any application to the House in favour of the army estimates.

Mr. *Sheridan* said that he also must resist the motion for the Speaker's leaving the chair; yet upon an important principle, in some measure dissimilar from that of his honourable friend, and for the sake of preserving a strict and invariable adherence to the established rules and forms of proceeding in that House. On the present occasion, he felt it right to urge the necessity of preserving such an adherence, and therefore, must beg leave to remind the right honourable gentleman in the chair that he rested on his authority for the validity and justness of his argument as applicable to the present instance. It had been the well-known and established rule of proceeding with the army estimates, to have them lay upon the table eight days prior to any motion's being made for referring them to the consideration of a Committee. This rule had, he believed, been invariably adhered to in every former instance, but in the present the estimates had not been upon the table more than five days, and now it was attempted to go into a Committee for the purpose of voting them, although at the

time that they had been prefented, when Wednefday was nominated, as the day on which they fhould be taken into confideration, they had heard from the firft authority in that
Houfe, that the practice had been in all preceding times not
to move for their being referred to the Committee of Supply
until they had been upon the table eight days. With fuch
indecency did Adminiftration fly in the face of the Chair; and
fatal would prove the confequences if a bad precedent were
once fuffered to be eftablifhed. He did not mean to infinuate
that any improper intention operated upon the right honourable gentleman at the head of the War Office in thus urging
the Houfe to break through their eftablifhed rules; but if he
was to be indulged in every eccentric flight of genius that
he might choofe to take, there was no knowing into what
ftrange extravagances he might not lead them. For his part,
he wondered from whom he had learnt the idea of breaking
through the eftablifhed rules and forms of the Houfe; his
predeceffors in office had been content to adhere invariably to
thofe rules, and in fo doing they had acted wifely. If the
rule was once broken through, it might be abolifhed altogether. If it was right to vote the army eftimates after they
had been upon the table only five days, why not vote them
after being there only four, three, or two days: or why not
bring them down, prefent them, and call upon the Houfe to
vote them the next day or the very day on which they were
prefented? The fame reafon which would juftify the violation of the rule in one inftance, would juftify it in all. Befides, in all former feffions the conftant ufage had been to
vote the navy before the army eftimates; and, as the ftrength
of our marine was to be the guide what fort of an army might
be neceffary, the vote of the navy ought always to precede
the vote of the army. This infringement of the ufual practice was highly reprehenfible; and though he could not
agree that it was not improper to vote the army before the
militia, or think that there required any argument whatever
to prove the extreme impropriety of going into a Committee,
befides that very ferious one which he had already urged, the
abfolute neceffity of a ftrict adherence to the eftablifhed rules
and forms of proceeding in that Houfe, yet certainly the
matter in which the right honourable gentleman had expreffed
himself on the fubject of the militia, afforded ftrong ground
of objection to voting the army eftimates at prefent. The
right honourable gentleman had contended that an honourable and refpectable friend of his ought not to fhrink from
his intention of bringing in the bill for regulating the militia,
becaufe he, a fingle individual in that Houfe, had declared he
had not made up his mind to one particular point. For his
part, he was of the fame opinion; and he hoped, notwithstanding

standing what had paffed, that the worthy and refpectable member would bring in his bill; and, furely, the Public were already under infinite obligations to him for what he had done, and his introducing the bill, even if it were to fall, from that part of it being objected to and overcome that enacted the meafure, which the honourable gentleman and thofe who had with him taken the trouble of digefting the fyftem, (and who were confequently the beft able to judge of every part of it) deemed the moft effential point of all, would be attended with this good confequence, that it would not only bring the fubject fairly under difcuffion, but open the eyes of the Public, and convince them who were and who were not the friends of the militia, and whether there was or was not any defigns to annihilate the inftitution. With regard to the right honourable gentleman's calling himfelf, as he had thought proper to do in refpect to the militia, a fingle individual, it might fairly be obferved that the right honourable gentleman paffed under various characters in that Houfe; at one time he called himfelf a Member of Adminiftration, at another the Minifter, then again the Minifter of the Crown, nay he had even once affumed the felf-created character of Reprefentative of the Reprefentatives of the People, and fent his own will in a dictatorial manner to the Irifh Parliament, inftead of the refolutions of that Houfe; but when the fit of humility was on him, he bent to the more fubmiffive character of a fimple individual. It was not a little remarkable that the effect and fuccefs of his meafures for the moft part depended on the character which he thought fit to affume. When the right honourable gentleman chofe to ftand up as a fingle individual, he generally failed of achieving his purpofe. On the grand queftion of reform in the reprefentation of the People in Parliament, the right honourable gentleman profeffed he was acting as a fingle individual, and there he did not fucceed. In this fcrutiny, in like manner, acting as a fingle individual, he failed; and had he been no more than a fingle individual in the cafe of his India bill, he verily believed the right honourable gentleman would have failed likewife. He hoped and believed that the militia bill, if brought in and gone on with, would fucceed, as the right honourable gentleman chofe, on the prefent occafion, to call himfelf a fingle individual, however much the gentlemen who had waited upon him refpecting the militia, might have found him the Minifter at his Houfe in Downing ftreet. On the whole it appeared that the Houfe could not immediately go into a Committee upon the army eftimates without violating an eftablifhed practice, and thereby introducing a precedent which might lead to moft mifchievous and alarming confequences. He felt it difficult to conclude without

obfer-

observing, that the half-ftifled laughter with which the Minifter and his friends met fome of his remarks were indecently.
mifapplied to a fubject of fuch particular importance.

The Secretary at War. The *Secretary at War* faid that he flattered himfelf that the
defence of his own conduct would reft firmly upon a plain
ftatement of facts, and therefore he fhould leave it to the
Houfe to judge from them and draw the natural conclufions.
There was not in that Houfe, he believed, a member who
had fhewn more refpect and reverence to their forms of proceedings than he had uniformly done for the thirty years,
during which he fat in Parliament, and he trufted that he had
not in the prefent inftance acted fo as to violate any one of
them. The papers had now been feven days upon the table
[Mr. Sheridan cried out, No! no! only five] The Secretary.
at War added that he fhould perfift in his affertion; they
were prefented on the preceding Thurfday, and he fhould contend, that Thurfday was one day, Friday two, Saturday
three, Sunday four, [The oppofite fide of the Houfe laughed.]
Monday five, Tuefday fix, and Wednefday feven; that was
a complete week, for he knew of no rule that the whole of
the feven fhould be fitting days. Saturdays and Sundays
would ferve as well for the infpection of papers as any other
days; and therefore let the Houfe judge whether the papers
had not been before them a full week, and whether he was
chargeable with any attempt either to proceed precipitately,
or to violate any eftablifhed form of proceeding. Indeed he
fhould have imagined that the honourable gentleman who had
juft fat down, knew his character as a member of Parliament
too well to have fuppofed him capable of fuch a defign, and
as to eccentric flights of genius, he could only fay, he was
at that moment [tortured by the gout] lefs qualified than ever
to attempt flights than at any other time, had he been fo inclined. As a proof that his arguments were far from incon-
clufive, he begged leave to remind the Houfe, that when he
gave notice of the day on which he fhould move to refer the
eftimates to the Committee of Supply, a noble Earl (of Surrey)
expreffed his fatisfaction that the time of inveftigation was fo
little diftant.

Mr. Sheri-dan. Mr. *Sheridan* anfwered that the right honourable gentleman had contended himfelf with attempting to prove that
the papers had been upon the tab'e a week or feven days, but
even if that could be made out (which he muft beg leave to
deny) this was not meeting his argument, which was, that
the papers had not been on the table the ufual time, and in
that argument he had been fupported by the firft authority in
that Houfe. When he alluded to the eccentric flights of
the right honourable gentleman, he certainly did not mean
to infinuate that the right honourable gentleman had taken a
flight

flight of such altitude as that of a right honourable friend of his (Colonel Fitzpatrick) during the course of the preceding year.—[The House laughed].

Ld. North.

Lord *North* having expressed the pleasure which he always felt at coinciding in opinion with the noble Earl (of Surrey) who sat near him, begged leave to add, that although the noble Earl, from his zeal for the dispatch of the public business, and perhaps from thinking that matters went on too slowly, had on the day when the estimates were presented, declared his approbation of the proposal then to take them into consideration, notwithstanding that it was at the time stated from the Chair, that it had been a constant practice to allow them to be upon the table a longer while, he *must* say that it appeared to him to be highly improper, and pregnant with the most serious consequences, to violate an ancient, and hitherto an invariable, rule of proceeding. It had been always usual, soon after the commencement of the session, to present the army estimates, and in a day or two afterwards, notice was given, that the seamen for the service of the year, would be voted on a particular day, and the vote on the navy always took place of the vote for the army, and preceded it, most probably, because the seamen and marines were voted without estimate. With regard to the estimates of the army, they had constantly lain upon the table eight or ten days before it had been attempted to move to refer them to a Committee of Supply, nor did he ever know, that the day on which they were presented, was counted as one of the number of days on which they were before the House. He trusted that before the House departed from their ancient rule and usage, a precedent of such a departure might be pointed out, or that some public ground of necessity might be stated. The practice had clearly obtained to prevent the House from being taken by surprise. In the present case most probably surprise was not intended; yet it behoved the House to guard against the introduction of an exceptionable precedent.

The Chancellor of the Exchequer.

The *Chancellor of the Exchequer* remarked that he should find himself exceedingly puzzled perfectly to understand the conversation to which the gentlemen on the other side of the House had given rise, were it not for a complaint made a few days ago by a noble Earl (of Surry), of the House meeting at three o'clock, and regularly adjourning before four.—This mode of creating a warm debate, and calling forth all the powers of a most vigorous opposition on an ordinary question like the present, was, he must confess, a very effectual method of remedying the evil complained of: but at the same time he dreaded lest an adherence to it should prove the means of increasing another cause of uneasiness finefs which had alfo been fuggefted, but which, as of lefs importance, he fuppofed gentlemen were willing to facrifice to the former; and this was the flow progrefs which the public bufinefs was making in the Houfe. The noble Lord, and the honourable gentlemen who had preceded him, endeavoured to eftablifh it as a certain and conclufive ground of objection to the motion before the Houfe, that it was contrary to the eftablifhed order of parliamentary proceeding to go into a committee of fupply on the army eftimates, until they had lain on the table during feven or eight days, (for the noble Lord, in particular, could not venture to fay which, and not being able to produce any written document to prove that fuch an order exifted) he had argued it on the principle that it was neceffary to prevent the Houfe being taken by furprife on a fubject of fuch confiderable importance. Now, certainly, however found and judicious this principle might in general prove, it could by no means apply to the prefent cafe; for he believed that not one member who faw how well the Houfe was attended, and obferved the degree of preparation which fome gentlemen had made, as well in point of argument as in wit and pleafantry (which none, ignorant of the peculiar talents of one of the honourable gentlemen oppofite (Mr. Sheridan) would have thought could have found a place in a debate on fo dry a fubject as the prefent) would pretend to fay, that there was any danger of the Houfe being taken by furprife. In aid of this fact, of the Houfe being fufficiently awake and upon their guard, gentlemen had moreover difclaimed any fufpicion of the Minifter having meditated fuch a furprife. How unfair was it in gentlemen to fit by and hear notice of a motion given to the Houfe, particularly of a motion in the ordinary and regular courfe of bufinefs, without imparting even one fingle hint of their intention to oppofe it, nay to fuffer fo many days to pafs over without any fuch intimation, and then to come forward (as they now did) with arguments drawn from a fuppofed eftablifhed practice, which no man could take upon himfelf to prove and fubftantiate! The noble Lord, after begging the queftion, as to the exiftence of the point of order which became the chief bafis of oppofition, had taken fome pains to afcertain the number of days during which the eftimates had lain upon the table; but furely his time was fpent to no great purpofe, for it would afford but little room for ingenuity and argument to prove, that if the papers were laid on the table on Thurfday, then Thurfday was one of the days on which they were on the table; and yet this difficulty, it feemed, was one which the noble Lord thought it no degradation to his talents and underftanding to attempt to folve. An argument had been

used

ufed by an honourable gentleman to prove that it would be improper to vote the army eftimates until after the feamen, for the fervice of the current year, fhould have been previoufly voted: and this undoubtedly fhewed, in the cleareft point of view, that he and his friends had no very great anxiety to forward and expedite the public bufinefs; for they would certainly, in fuch a cafe, have given notice of their intended oppofition, and fo have induced Minifters to move for the feamen on this day, and poftpone the army till Friday. But, in fact the whole of the oppofition to the queftion feemed to him to originate in the honourable gentleman's well-known difpofition to mirth and derifion, and appeared to proceed from a defign to laugh at the Houfe; and inftead of permitting them to enter upon a bufinefs for which they were prepared by proper notice, to tell them in plain terms, " Well, gentlemen, I fee you are all come down to vote the " army, but I promife you you fhall do no fuch thing, for " I have fpecial reafons to put it off for a day or two " longer, and I have found out a number of gentlemen to " vouch for me, that there either is, or ought to be, a " ftanding order to that effect." And thus was the humorous vein of the honourable gentleman to be gratified at the expence of the time of the members, and the dignity of the Houfe. However, left the intention of the honourable gentleman might appear too plainly, and fo defeat the object in view, he had taken care to keep himfelf back in the debate until an honourable gentleman of a graver caft, whofe eloquence was of a more ferious complection, and who had argued the queftion upon more folemn grounds, fhould precede him, and fo cover his main defign. As to himfelf, Mr. Pitt faid that he trufted that the Houfe would indulge him with a few words upon the fubject, which however foreign to the purpofe, had been drawn into the debate, and made confiderable ufe of by the gentlemen on the other fide of the Houfe, in hopes to create a prejudice againft him in the minds of his fellow fubjects. He had, on a former occafion, been called upon by an honourable member to deliver an opinion on a matter of the greateft confequence, and which comprehended in it the two moft effential objects of the attention of that Houfe, and of government, namely œconomy, and that conftitutional defence of the kingdom, the militia. He had begged leave to withhold his opinion on the fubject, until a public difcuffion fhould have enabled him to avail himfelf of the information which he expected to receive from thofe very refpectable members of Parliament and officers of the militia who had fo meritoriously applied themfelves to the bufinefs—advantages had been taken of this hefitation to raife a fuggeftion that he was in general hoftile to the inftitution of the militia, and that in confequence of his being fo, it would be to no purpofe to bring forward any meafures for its improvement—this conclufion was the more abfurd, becaufe the very gentlemen who endeavoured to ftigmatize him as an enemy to the militia, merely becaufe he had not yet clearly made up his mind on a certain particular queftion relating to it, had themfelves determined to withhold from the Houfe a plan methodically and induftrioufly arranged, and on the propriety and ufefulnefs of which, in all its parts, their judgements were agreed, merely in hopes of throwing an odium upon him. He profeffed himfelf to be as much as any man could poffibly prove, a friend (he might indeed fay an hereditary friend) to the militia, and fortified as he was in the confcioufnefs of that difpofition, he fhould look down with contempt on every illiberal infinuation calculated to injure his reputation and mifreprefent his principles; though were he not fo happy as to feel that confcioufnefs, he fhould certainly fmart feverely under the cenfures which he had undergone—and having not come to any fixed and determined judgement on the fubject alluded to, he fhould not be provoked either by the wit or the anger of the honourable gentleman (Mr. Sheridan) nor by his defire to create, or his inability to bear a laugh, to hazard an opinion without fufficient inveftigation, and which of courfe it was not improbable but he might afterwards find it neceffary to alter. He challenged any gentleman on the other fide of the Houfe, excepting thofe who had employed themfelves fo long in an inveftigation of the fubject, to ftand up and avow whether he had himfelf formed any fuch decifive opinion on the neceffity of bringing out the mititia annually, as he would venture to abide by; and if he had, to declare what were the arguments and reafons on which fuch opinion was eftablifhed.— If no gentleman was ready to commit himfelf in fuch a manner, why then fhould they expect or defire him to do fo? If his expreffing a doubt upon that fubject, and requefting time and information, was to be conftrued as an omen of the ill fuccefs of the whole arrangement propofed by the framers of the bill, though at the fame time declaring that he was not determined againft the principle, how dangerous muft it be (fince the gentlemen were pleafed to afcribe fuch weight to his opinion,) to force him to give one before it was fufficiently matured and digefted; and he defired the honourable gentleman to reflect how inconfiftent it was with his boafted zeal for the militia, on conftitutional grounds, to make himfelf inftrumental in propagating a doctrine, that it was juftifiable for any gentleman in poffeffion of a plan calculated

culated to ferve the Public, to withhold it from the Houfe until they fhould have procured the concurrence of the executive fervants of the Crown.

Mr. *Marfham* declared that he could not avoid regarding the verbal attack made *apparently* upon *him* by the right honourable gentleman as a kind of perfonal abufe. He had accufed him of abandoning, for frivolous reafons, a meafure of general utility. Of thefe reafons, however, the right honourable gentleman could not plead ignorance when he reflected upon the fteps which he had taken in the bufinefs; he was confcious that he had acted from the pureft motives; he had not deferted the caufe of the militia, or of the Public, by any meafure whatfoever; he wanted to fecure both, and he had been averfe from bringing forward his bill on this very account. He was aware, that in the prefent fituation of affairs, there exifted a ftatute, which might be called into execution, and which, in its execution, might, with the concurrence of the Houfe, give efficacy to that very regulation which he wifhed to eftablifh, as effential to the proper difcipline of the militia. He meant their being called out once a year. Were he, however, in the prefent circumftances of the cafe, to attempt, by any bill which he might bring in, to put matters on a better eftablifhment, he was fufpicious of endangering the very exiftence of that object which he chiefly felt an ambition to preferve. The right honourable gentleman's concurrence in the plan propofed, not as a fimple individual, but as the Minifter of the country, he confidered as abfolutely neceffary to the creation of the fyftem. He was not fingular in this opinion. There were two other gentlemen from whom he believed that the right honourable gentleman would not differ, but with reluctance, who were connected with the militia, who entertained the fame fentiments of the bufinefs as he did, and with whom the right honourable gentleman might commune if he faw fit, on this important fubject. If he was ferious in his intentions to adopt any fcheme which might render the militia more ufeful; if he was anxious to profit by the labours of thofe who had attended, perhaps more than he had done, to the fubject, he had it now fairly in his power. He now poffeffed every intelligence which could have been imparted by gentlemen, attentively and unremittedly engaged upon the inveftigation of the fubject, and it refted with him either to flight fuch refources, or turn them to a public benefit.

Mr. *Pitt* replied that it was not poffible to defcribe his aftonifhment at difcovering that the honourable member had fuppofed him capable of affailing him with invectives. Nothing could be more remote from his intention: the arguments he had employed would not fupport the conclufion.

K 2   It

It had become the favourite object with the other side of the House, to exhibit him as unfriendly to the militia, because he had not declared his intention to concur with respect to one regulation contained in the bill, before it should be discussed in the House. There was surely no ground for the allegation. If it belonged to any persons to bring forward measures of this nature, it was surely the province of those who, from a devotion of mind to a particular subject, were possessed of the most extensive knowledge of it. In the ostensible character in which he stood, various plans of operation were constantly pressing themselves on his notice. It was impossible for him to bestow that attention to each, to which a single individual or a body of men might find themselves absolutely equal. This was precisely the case in the present instance. Communications had, no doubt, been made by those who employed themselves in digesting a new system of militia law, against whom the honourable gentleman was one; but would any person venture to say, that though possessed of such communications, he was equally well qualified to bring forward a measure of this nature with those who had made it an object of study, and dedicated a large portion of their time to the consideration of it? Amongst the number of these, he was convinced the honourable gentleman was most conspicuous: it belonged, therefore, to him more properly to bring it forward; and if he considered the disapprobation of his intended desertion of duty as a personal attack, he had every allowance from him to take it up in that light.

North.　　Lord *North* said that he rose in vindication of himself and of his friends. The right honourable gentleman had charged them with a defect of duty, in not opposing the order of the House at an earlier period. Why, says the gentleman, did you not come down on Friday, and object to it? Why did you not oppose it before this time? If you had, the navy might have been voted in the mean-while, and all objections to precipitancy removed. This, indeed, may be a species of argument to the men, but not to the rule. As for his own part, his absence admitted of some sort of vindication. On the Friday and Saturday it was impossible for him to attend. On the Monday he went to the country. He had remained there till the present day. But supposing that he and his friends might not have been doing duty, as the Secretary at War, or the right honourable gentleman; yet surely this conduct had not escaped the observation of one, to whom particular attention was due in all matters of form: the observation he meant of the right honourable member who so deservedly filled the chair. He had declared his sentiments relative to this matter, when it was first proposed, and had

ex-

explained the uniform practice of the House. His observations at that period were perfectly coincident with his ideas on the subject, whatever it might be with those of the other side of the House. Sill however, every remark advanced was considered by the right honourable gentleman, as the language and argument of what he had denominated a "*vigorous opposition.*" Whether the opposition was vigorous or not, he would not pretend to say; but surely the present question was not a point of opposition, but a mere question of form. It was simply this: whether the House would agree, for no plausible reason whatever, to depart from a mode of procedure, which had been uniformly adopted by it, or not? For his own part, he must contend that there was no deviation from this practice, and that there ought to be none, unless upon the most critical occasions, or for the most urgent reasons. If none of these existed in the present case, why wander from the ordinary course? If then there were precedents, those precedents should be produced; and they should be more especially produced by those who were attempting a new and extraordinary mode of conduct. The obligation rested with them: not with those to whom an attachment to the invariable practice of the House was a point of anxious and undeviating attention.

Mr. *Pownie* wondered that the time of the House should be engrossed by the discussion of a matter, relative to the militia, which he conceived it by no means difficult to adjust. The honourable gentleman opposite to him (Mr. Marsham) had informed them, that he gave his bill on this subject to the right honourable gentleman. The right honourable gentleman, on the other hand, contended, that it was his duty to bring it forward. Why not, then, gratify the House with a sight of it? There could be no harm in this—and it was most probable that the House would, in its wisdom, dispose of it according to its deserts.

Mr. *Taylor* reprobated what he termed the unbecoming treatment which his right honourable friend (the Chancellor of the Exchequer) experienced respecting the militia business. He avowed himself a sincere friend to the militia. From the knowledge, however, which he had acquired on this subject, he entertained some doubts whether the regulation which was intended would be productive of any good effect. He hoped that the matter would be brought into discussion, and that every person would obtain that information which was absolutely necessary for a just decision on the point.

Mr. *Fox* said that he felt it impossible to permit the observations of the right honourable gentleman respecting the militia to pass unnoticed. The militia formed part of the defence of the nation. Did the right honourable gentleman, then,

Mr. Pownie

Mr. Taylor.

Mr. Fox.

then, affect a greater ignorance on this subject than any other person? Was it not his duty to inform himself of all its circumstances? He was the minister of the country, and, as such, it became him to be better informed on this point than any other person. This, therefore, was no ground of excuse why he should not bring forward any measure which might be judged necessary for putting the country into a better state of defence. It was his duty to know, and to do this beyond that of every other member of the House; and to decline this task on pretences of want of sufficient information, was no argument at all in his favour. He hoped such subterfuges would not be allowed as precedents in the House, nor received by the country at large. As to the point of form under more immediate discussion, he saw no reason why the uniform usage of the House should be departed from on the present occasion. His honourable friend near him (Mr. Sheridan) had contended that the estimates should have lain on the table, agreeable to practice, eight days. The right honourable Secretary at War had acknowledged, that they had lain there only seven. Why then transgress the ordinary usage of the House, or give birth to a precedent which might afterwards be employed as a dangerous instrument of surprize? He knew of no instance occurring on the face of the Journals, which justified the step; and he was of opinion that the gentleman on the opposite side of the table should either shew some authority for adopting this new line of conduct, or relinquish it altogether. He was strengthened in his opinion, that there was no precedent on the Journals of the House which justified their going into a Committee on the army estimates before they had lain eight days on the table, as this idea had been countenanced by an authority to which he had uniformly paid an implicit defference—the Chair. As to the plan of voting the army, contrary to custom, before the navy, he could easily conceive a reason for it. The navy was recommended warmly in his Majesty's Speech as an object of attention. If, however, it should be voted prior to the army when the latter came under subsequent consideration, various arguments of objection might be stated, which by the intended manœuvre would be entirely cut off. In consequence of the present reprehensible deviation, the army would be rendered the leading object, although the navy must experience the greatest need of aid and augmentation.

Rose.

Mr. *Rose* requested that the Journals of the 12th and 16th of December 1774, might be read. This being done, he from thence argued that it clearly appeared that Lord Barrington, then Secretary at War, had laid the estimates of the army on the table on the first of these periods; and that they

had

had been fubmitted to a Committee of the Houfe, and voted the following one; not after eight days confideration, as contended for, but only four. Mr. Rofe hoped that this precedent would not be objected to, or be in the leaft offenfive to the noble Lord (Lord North) on the oppofite fide of the Houfe, or his friends.

Lord *North* declared, that it had been produced for that Ld. North. very purpofe. [The Houfe laughed.] He obferved, that though he had uniformly contended for a ftrict adherence to the practice of the Houfe, yet he had never been abfurd enough to affert, that there was no fuppofable occafion on which it might be difpenfed with. He was perfuaded that there muft have been fomething fingular to have given rife to the precedent quoted, though it ought not to be urged as a general rule, as one fwallow does not make a fummer. The American war was then about to commence, at leaft the feeds of it had become apparent, and precipitancy in voting the army eftimates, might, on fuch an occafion, be juftifiable. The new Parliament had, at the period alluded to, met for the firft feffion; it was in the month of December; on account of the holidays, they muft adjourn about the 24th; there might, therefore, be no impropriety in a new Parliament, on the apparent approach of a war, giving a proof, by even tranfgreffing an eftablifhed rule, of their confidence in His Majefty's Minifters, by voting the army in the expeditious manner they had done.

The Honourable Mr. *Grenville* faid that he felt it more The Hon. than difficult to regard the argument of the noble Lord with- Mr Gren- out furprife and indignation. He and his friends had con- ville. tended, with unexampled confidence, that there was no precedent to countenance the propofed meafures. Yet what had appeared on the Journals of the Houfe, and during the noble Lord's own adminiftration alfo, but a precedent exactly in point, and a precedent which ought not to have efcaped the recollection of the noble Lord, or of his friends. The noble Lord afferted that the war with America was then in view, and that this circumftance might account for the Houfe going out of its common form for the purpofe of giving proof of its confidence in Miniftry. But for what purpofe was that confidence to be beftowed, but for the adopting a train of meafures which he hoped his right honourable friend was incapable even of conceiving, as they had been fo fatally prejudicial to the interefts of the country. He could not fufficiently reprobate the conduct of thofe in oppofition, who, with a ftrange effrontery, had called for precedents, and with an unexampled confidence had afferted, that there was no ground for continuing a meafure which feemed fully juftified by the Journals of the Houfe.

Lord

Ld. North. Lord *North* anfwered that the ingenuity of the honourable gentleman, who found it neceffary, on all occafions, to have recourfe to the American war, was entitled to admiration. The American war was a uniform topic to him and his friends. All its difafters were charged on him. In fhort, the American war was his great *cheval de bataille*; it was his favourite hobby-horfe, he was fond of mounting him on all occafions. He would remind him, however, as well as his right honourable friend, in what the American war originated—it was the ftamp act. Hereditary virtue, and hereditary merit, had been talked of, and he believed, that if there was any thing in fuch ideas, they were as applicable to the honourable gentleman, and his right honourable friend, in the view of the American war, as to him.

Mr. Courtenay. Mr. *Courtenay* remarked that the right honourable gentleman combated, in all his arguments, the authority of the Chair; that fuch an act of repugnancy was difrefpectful in the extreme; that —

Mr. Grenville. Mr. *Grenville* called him to order, contended that the honourable gentleman had tortured his arguments, with a view to make them appear to the Houfe calculated to convey a cenfure upon the Chair, than which nothing could be more diftant from his intention, as no one entertained a higher refpect for the opinion of the Chair than himfelf.

Mr. Courtenay. Mr. *Courtenay* replied, that the right honourable member had given a ftriking proof of his fagacity, in having been able to difcover, nor what he (Mr Courtenay) *had* faid, but what he was *going* to fay. It was impoffible, for two very fubftantial reafons, that he *could have* tortured the arguments of the right honourable gentleman: in the firft place, he had fcarcely uttered a fentence, when the right honourable gentleman thought proper to interrupt him. And in the next place, it was impoffible that he could have tortured his arguments; for, in truth, the right honourable gentleman had not ufed any arguments at all; but, inftead of fpeaking to the queftion, had deviated into extraneous matter, not at all applicable to the bufinefs then under confideration; fuch was his digreffion relative to the American war; in which the right honourable gentleman had ufed language the moft unexpected that could have fallen from any man of delicacy; for when he firft mentioned the American war, he thought he was moft certainly going to defend it, from a principle of *filial* piety; and that he was about to follow the example of the Chancellor of the Exchequer, who had boafted, this day, that he had an *hereditary* right to like the eftablifhment of a militia: fo might the right honourable gentleman have boafted that he had an *hereditary* right to approve, fupport, and defend the American war:—But it would feem, from what both

gentle-

gentlemen had said, that they claimed a right also to condemn and overturn those things for which they professed to entertain the greatest respect; and that tho' they agreed in principles with the Public, they were always liable to avoid being obliged to admit all the consequences that would flow from them, by riding away upon a distinction. The American war had, in truth, been the work of the right honourable gentleman's father; but he never failed to abuse it, when, by so doing, he found an opportunity of attacking the noble lord in the blue ribband. So the Chancellor of the Exchequer expressed his veneration for the militia, the establishment of which had been the work of his father, but his veneration appeared only in his words; for when the worthy and respectable country gentlemen, who had digested a system for rendering the militia efficient, waited upon him with their plan, he gave great praise to them for their patriotic labours, and approved of every part of the bill except one, which was precisely the most essential part of the whole, the *sine quâ non* of the plan, without which they did not think they ought to proceed in it, as the rejection of this one part, which was the calling out and training the militia every year, would completely defeat the great object of it. So that in truth the Chancellor of the Exchequer appeared now most clearly to be an enemy to the militia in effect, though he did not dare to avow it publicly in so many words; for he knew that, as it was a favourite service with the Public, he would be deserted by the most independent men, who now supported him. This was not an idle or a light suspicion on his part; he was sorry to see but too much reason for entertaining it. It was remarkable, that on all former occasions, the navy had been voted before the army: but this year there was a deviation from that practice, which was not a little surprizing; nay, it was alarming when coupled with another circumstance, of which he had heard something, and which he believed would soon be known to the House at large; and that was, that on the next supply day a reduction of *two thousand* seamen would be proposed. He would put it to the feelings of gentlemen, how far it was consistent with the spirit and genius of the constitution, to keep up a standing army to a great extent, which was only tolerated from year to year in this country; and to reduce the marine strength by the reduction of 2000 seamen while the constitutional land defence, the militia, was wholly neglected, and suffered to crumble away. This, he observed, was a subject worthy the most serious attention, but on which he would say no more at present. With respect to points of order, there was an authority to which it was usual to appeal in matters of that nature: the authority of the chair. The right honourable gentleman who presided in it would, therefore, please to declare his opinion on the subject, and his decision should determine his vote.

The House cried out " *Chair, Chair!*" upon which the *Speaker* rose, and observed that he trusted it would prove sufficient to repeat what he had said on the subject a few days ago, when the Secretary at War gave notice that he would move that the army estimates should on the present day be referred to the Committee of supply.—On that occasion, he had thought it his duty to state, that it was the practice of the House to let the army estimates lie eight days upon the table, before they suffered them to be referred to the Committee of Supply. He found, on that occasion (when he delivered his opinion), that the sense of the House seemed not to be in favour of that practice; upon which he observed that the House was certainly at liberty to change the order of its proceedings; but that he thought it his duty to state the practice, leaving it to the House to determine, whether it should be still followed.

Mr. *Dundas* having signified his veneration for the Chair, added, that in dissenting from it at present, he was countenanced by those who were ultimately to decide in such a point—the House at large. The honourable gentleman who had spoken immediately before the opinion was given from the Chair, had not used any new arguments, but merely repeated, in coarse and clumsy language, the preceding arguments of others. He had also indulged himself in licentiously attacking his right honourable friend, (the Chancellor of the Exchequer) endeavouring to represent him as an enemy to the militia; but should his right honourable friend think proper to make any reply to what had been urged against him on that head, he must have a much higher opinion of the arguments of that honourable gentleman than either he or (he believed) the House could possibly entertain. The honourable gentleman thought proper to observe, that his two right honourable friends (Mr. Pitt, and Mr. Grenville,) appeared constantly to agree with the Public upon all those principles, which were regarded sacred by the country; but that by riding off upon a distinction, they never failed to find a pretence for defeating the wishes of the People, and avoiding an agreement in the conclusion which might be deduced from the principles. But this was not the case; and it was only by misrepresentation that any colour could be given for such an assertion: for in no part of what the Chancellor of the Exchequer had said, could there be found the least reason for concluding that he was an enemy to the militia. Indeed the very reverse appeared; and all that could be said against him on that head was, that he remained as yet unprepared to give as decided an opinion upon one particu-

The Speaker.

Mr. Dundas.

lar

lar point as other gentlemen were who had made it the fubject of their ftudy for many months paft. Mr. Dundas faid,
that he muft now beg leave to take notice of a fophifm,
ufed by a right honourable gentleman, (Mr. Fox) who obferved, that he could not believe that his right honourable
friend had not yet formed a decided opinion relative to the
calling out the militia annually, and for this reafon, that, as
a Minifter, be muft long fince have determined what was to
be the plan of national defence for the prefent year; and
hence he inferred, that however the Chancellor of the Exchequer might wifh to deny it, he had actually made up
his mind on the queftion of calling out the militia, though
he would not venture to ftate his opinion to the Houfe.
He agreed with the right honourable gentleman in his premifes; that his right honourable friend, as a Minifter, muft
have made up his mind refpecting the national defence for
the prefent year; but it by no means followed from this,
that he had formed a decided opinion on the propriety of
calling out the militia annually; for certainly, a very great
difference exifted between the general plan of defence, and a
particular regulation, becaufe the calling out of the militia
was no more than a regulation of a part of the exifting defence of the country. On this occafion he muft remark,
that the very right honourable gentleman, who was fore-
moft in attacking his right honourable friend, for not having
already made up his mind upon that point, did not, even at
the prefent moment, poffefs a decided opinion on the fubject—and he was not an ordinary man—for although out of
office, he had been twice a Minifter— He fhould, therefore, beg leave to afk him, not as a Minifter, (and heaven
forbid that he were at this moment!) but as a gentleman who
had been a Minifter, why he did not make up his mind on
the fubject at either of the two periods when he had a fhare
in the direction of His Majefty's Counfels, as during neither
he had called out the militia. As to the point of order, and
with refpect to himfelf, it was a matter of indifference
whether the army was voted on the prefent day, or on the
enfuing Friday; but he was very much furprifed indeed,
that gentlemen fhould affume what they were not able to
prove; and his furprife was heightened, when he faw them
perfevere in defending a pofition, in defiance of evidence.
They had been pleafed to affert, that it was the invariable
practice of the Houfe not to vote the army eftimates, until
they had lain upon the table eight days; but, unfortunately
for them, an honourable gentleman (Mr. Rofe), who had
not been in the Houfe when the debate began, but who
hearing upon what it ran, opened the Journals, and the very
firft paffage which catched his eye, afforded the moft complete

refu-

refutation of their doctrine, it appearing that in the year 1774, the estimates of the army had been voted in four days after they had been laid upon the table. He made no doubt but that the Journals contained hundreds of similar precedents to beat down the doctrine so confidently assumed by the gentlemen on the other side of the House. It was rather singular that his noble friend in the blue ribband, should have forgotten, the case which had been quoted from the Journals, as it happened during his own Administration. In order to overturn the consequence that was fairly deducible from it, his noble friend ought to shew that the case happened either during a war, or upon some pressing emergency, that would warrant a departure from a general rule: but this he could not do; for, in the first place the matter had happened in time of peace, and in the next, the military establishment voted at that period was a peace establishment. This precedent, therefore, not having been founded on any extraordinary occurrence or event, was not to be deemed a departure from the rule, as some had asserted; and by being an exception to it, it was a proof of the existence of the rule. The natural and unanswerable conclusion was that it merited admission, as a proof that such practices were never in existence.

Fox.

Mr. *Fox* said, that he must now yield to the necessity of rising in his own defence, because the right honourable and learned gentleman had applied to him to know, why he, when in office, had not made up his mind, or called out the militia. This question was put to him as a man, and not as a Minister; and though the right honourable and learned gentleman had exclaimed, heaven forbid that he (Mr. Fox) should be a Minister, he made little doubt but that, were he one, he might have many questions and much business to do with him, if he pleased. His answer to the question was short; he had been twice a Minister, it was true; but the first time was a period of war, and consequently nothing could be drawn from his conduct at that time, applicable to a question about calling out the militia in time of peace; the second time he was in office, he remained there about nine months only, so that he had not had time to shew what his plan respecting the militia might have been; but, had he remained three months longer in office, possibly he might have thought it proper to call out the militia; and as it might have been done within the year, there was no ground for saying to a certainty that he would not have done it had he continued during a year in office. But thus much was certain, that he would have depended greatly upon the opinion of professional men, in the forming a decided opinion on that head; nor would he have been so *inops consilii*, as not to have been able to find men of proper talents to advise with; and

after

after having taken their counfels, he would foon have become empowered to make up his mind; but the right honourable gentleman had already received the beft advice from fome of the ableft militia officers, and the beft difpofed towards this country; and yet he faid he had not yet made up his mind on the fubject. When the American war became again the threadbare fubject, he was really furprifed that gentlemen on the other fide of the Houfe fhould be fo imprudent as not to fuffer that bufinefs to fleep; for if any one of them touched upon it, and ventured to condemn that war, he was fure to find at his elbow another ready to defend it. The enemies of that war would find in council, at dinner, at all the Public Boards, among their friends and affociates, perfons who would ftand forward ftrenuoufly to defend the juftice of that war; and, among others, a right honourable gentleman (Mr. Jenkinfon) high in the confidence of the Minifter, who was ftill a member of that Houfe, but who, if reports could be depended upon, would fhortly leave it, in order to grace another affembly. It had formerly been the practice of the other fide of the Houfe not to let any opportunity flip to attack him (Mr. Fox) upon a meafure (his Eaft-India bill) as much condemned as the American war; but he perceived, that of late, that bill had the good fortune to pafs unnoticed; probably on account of the amazing fuccefs which accompanied the other bill of the right honourable gentleman, which was to have removed all the objections that were urged againft his profcribed bill. He wondered that the gentlemen on the other fide of the Houfe did not act as wifely with refpect to the American war, and confign it to oblivion, equally with a bill which was once as much an object of cenfure as the American war. Prudence fhould have taught them to do the one, as well as the other. He had only one more obfervation to make, and that was, that the learned gentleman could have had no objection whatever to poftpone the confideration of the eftimates to Friday next, as he had faid he was perfectly indifferent on the fubject, until he had feen by whom the point of order was fupported; and then he oppofed the order; not becaufe he thought it bad, or difliked it, but becaufe he difliked thofe who argued for it. For fuch a proceeding the Houfe would, doubtlefs, not refufe the learned and right honourable gentleman his proper fhare of credit.

Mr. *Courtenay* begged leave to remind the right honourable and learned gentleman that when he (Mr. Courtenay) repeated, in coarfe and clumfy language, the arguments of others who had preceded him, he meant fo to tranflate them that the learned and right honourable gentleman might find them intelligible and congenial with his manners.

Mr. Courtenay.

Mr.

Mr. Drake.   Mr. *Drake*, junior, wondered that those honourable gentlemen who, not long before, signified their dissatisfaction at discovering that the public business was not sufficiently expedited, were now the foremost to retard its progress; and that those who pretended to be the greatest œconomists of time, were so injudicious, or inconsistent, as to shew themselves the greatest spendthrifts of it, if the expression was allowable.

At length the gallery was cleared of strangers, but the question was given up without a division, and the House resolved itself into a Committee, when the following resolutions were moved and voted:

First, " that it is the opinion of this Committee, that a " sum of money not exceeding 647,005 l. 0 s. 8 d. be granted " to His Majesty for maintaining guards and garrisons."

Second, " 234,160 l. 5 s. 11 d. for maintaining the forces " in the plantations and Gibraltar."

Third, " 6,358 l. 3 s. 0 d. for the difference between the " charge of the British and Irish establishment of six regi- " ments of foot."

Fourth, " 6,409 l. 8 s. for the pay of general and staff " officers in Great Britain."

Fifth, " 24,378 l. 7 s. 8 d. 1-half, for defraying the ex- " pence of full pay to reduced or supernumerary officers."

Sixth, " 81,230 l. 8 s. 7 d. 1-fourth, for the pay necessary " to be advanced for the troops in India."

Seventh, " 59,320 l, 13 s. 5 d. to the Paymaster General " and Secretary at War, &c. &c. for Exchequer fees and " poundage to be returned to the infantry."

Eighth, " 11,409 l. 7 s. 6 d. for pensions to widows of " commissioned officers."

These resolutions were ordered to be reported on the ensuing Friday.

The House being resumed,

Mr. Dundas.   Mr. *Dundas* gave notice, that in obedience to an act of Parliament, that the House should in thirty days after its meeting proceed to ballot for the members who were to compose the court of judicature for the trial of East-India delinquents, he would on Tuesday next propose a ballot on that subject; and therefore, did he wish that gentlemen would turn the matter in their minds, and come prepared to give in the names of such persons as they should think best qualified to be judges in that Court. Being informed that Tuesday was fixed for a ballot for an election committee, Mr. Dundas then named Wednesday.

Mr. Sheridan.   Mr. *Sheridan* desired to know what measure the learned and right honourable gentleman would pursue, if two hundred

dred members, the number prescribed by law, should not happen to attend.

Mr. *Dundas* replied, that the first time he should see two *Mr. Dundas.* hundred members in the House, he would abruptly move for a ballot, at the moment; but he still hoped that the majority of the House would attend voluntarily to carry into effect a salutary regulation in a salutary law.

Mr. *Sheridan* conceived that Government, knowing the *Mr. Sheridan.* inefficacy of the India bill and judicature, wished to get rid of the latter, by giving notice of a ballot, in the hope that a notice for attendance would prevent attendance. For his part he thought, that if none should attend but those who regarded the regulation and the law as salutary, there would never be two hundred members present to ballot for that tribunal. He therefore supposed that the learned and right honourable gentleman would propose some coercive measure, either by a short bill, or a call of the House at a short notice, to procure a sufficient attendance. At all events the sense of the House ought soon to be taken on that subject, as petitions were on their way from India, praying a repeal of the act, as far as it related to the judicature; and if a question were not soon proposed upon that point by the learned and right honourable gentleman, he himself would bring on one very shortly.

Mr. *Chancellor Pitt* remarked, that as the honourable mem- *Mr. Chancellor Pitt.* ber who spoke last, wished ardently to defeat the election of members to compose that judicature, he hoped he would attend, with all his friends, in order to defeat it, which must necessarily be the case if the majority of the House was against it, and did not think it a salutary regulation.

Mr. *Courtenay* expressed his concern at having cause to *Mr. Courtenay.* think Ministers were in earnest when they talked of the ballot, for he really conceived a hope that the learned and right honourable gentlemen had given notice of it, in order that he might deter members from attending, that thus a regulation which all thought absurd, might fall to the ground of itself; and that he might thus avoid the mortification of being obliged to repeat what he and his right honourable friend at the head of His Majesty's counsels, had so often declared to be a salutary and an essential part of their plan for governing India, but upon which point they had since had reason to alter their opinion.

The House now adjourned to

Friday, 10th *February.*

Mr. *Gilbert* having brought up the report from the Committee of Supply, of the vote of the army; it was read the first time, and, a motion being made for its second reading,

Mr.

Mr. Steele.   Mr. *Steele*, observing that he believed no person would consider he was hostile to the motion, added that his only reason for rising was to rescue his right honourable friend (Mr. Pitt) from the imputation thrown out upon him on the preceding Wednesday, that he despised and trampled upon the orders and forms of the House, in proposing to have the army voted before the estimate had lain a week upon the table. A noble Lord (North) whose opinion always carried with it great weight, had said that the week should be taken exclusive of the day on which the estimate was produced. But having since looked into the Journals, he found, that the precedent quoted on Wednesday last by an honourable friend, (Mr. Rose) was not the only one which might have been produced; it was not, what it had been called, " a single swallow;" for he could follow it up with a whole flight of swallows, and shew that, during a period of twenty years, there were four or five precedents where the army had been voted precisely within the same distance of time after the presenting of the estimate which had elapsed this year; and *seven*, where it had been voted within a much shorter distance, as he had committed these precedents to writing, he should beg leave to read them; and, *then*, it would appear that—

Mr. Sheridan.   Mr. *Sheridan* declared, that he must take the liberty immediately to interrupt the honourable member, because he had violated order in speaking from the question, which was, for the second reading of the report; and in alluding to a former debate. His precedents would have been very proper on Wednesday, had he been apprized on that day of their existence: they would have been properly urged on that day to prove, that there was no deviation from the practice of the House: but, surely they came too late *now*, to prove that the right honourable gentleman acted right on Wednesday last, when, in defiance of the opinion of the Chair, and when he did not know that these precedents had ever existed, he moved to have the army estimate voted. The gentlemen on the other side, he supposed, had enjoyed the good fortune to be assisted since Wednesday by an industrious searcher (Mr. Eden) of the Journals, whom he had seen on the first day of the session in a new place in that House; but whom he had not seen since, who divided his principles and affection between both sides, giving his support to the one, and his good wishes to the other. The precedents however availed but little; for, it had not been denied, but that occasions might occur, which would warrant a departure from the general practice, but then it was urged that the reason of such departure ought to be stated and made appear, which no one had attempted on Wednesday last. Then it was that numbers of his honourable friends, as controversialists, enjoyed the pleasure of finding themselves under the crouded standard of the Chair,

chair, in feeble oppofition to which but one folitary precedent had arifen,

Mr. *Steele* anfwered, that he did not mean, either on Wednefday laft, or at prefent, to juftify a departure from a practice or order of the Houfe, but to maintain that no fuch practice or order exifted. He then read the dates and years of the different precedents, and referred to the Journals for the authenticity.

Mr. Steele.

The *Speaker* begged leave to remind the Houfe of the facts as they have occurred; he then recapitulated what he had faid when it was firft moved to refer the eftimates to the Committee on Wednefday, and obferved that it refted with the Houfe at the time to decide whether Wednefday was too early a day, and that the Houfe had determined in the negative.

The Speaker.

The *Secretary at War* defired permiffion, as a member of fome ftanding, to give his opinion as to the practice, or rather the principle of the practice, of the Houfe in refpect to the time of having the eftimates upon their table for fome days previous to their voting them, and that undoubtedly was to prevent furprife. In the cafe in queftion, the Speaker had reminded the Houfe of their right, and they had exercifed it in agreeing to Wednefday when propofed; if in fo determining the Houfe had done wrong, the Secertary at War faid, it would have been the Speaker's duty on any one of the intervening days between the nomination of the day of reference and the day itfelf, to have again ftated, that the Houfe had violated their practice, and have defired that a day fubfequent to Wednefday might be chofen; this he had not done, and therefore it confirmed him in his opinion, that the whole lay in the difcretion of the Houfe.

Secretary at War.

Mr. *Courtenay* remarked, that he could not avoid expreffing his aftonifhment that the ingenuity of an honourable gentleman (Mr. Steele) did not fuggeft to him, that the ftring of precedents he had fo exultingly produced that day from the Journals, did not militate againft his own argument; as it was evident that the honourable gentleman and his friends were ignorant laft Wednefday that any fuch precedents exifted, when they had actually innovated on the eftablifhed practice of the Houfe, and flighted the authority of the Chair. Yet now, the honourable gentleman attempted to juftify their former conduct. They refted the defence of their proceedings on Wednefday laft, on precedents which they had difcovered after infinite refearch upon the Friday following. This was entirely a new fpecies of minifterial logic or fagacity. However, he would not prefs this point farther, left he fhould repeat, in *coarfe* or *clumfy* language, the arguments of his honourable friend (Mr. Sheridan)

Mr. Courtenay.

and again incur the invidious farcafm of a right honourable gentleman, (Mr. Dundas) who was perhaps juftly
jealous of his attempting to imitate his ftyle, and of transferring to himfelf that characteriftic of it, by which the
right honourable gentleman was fo fingularly diftinguifhed.
He was aware, if he fucceeded, how much the right honourable gentleman's reputation might be diminifhed—and his
intereft hurt in any future political arrangement that might
eventually take place between him and the noble Lord in the
blue ribband, or another right honourable gentleman, (Mr.
Fox.) However, he would candidly confefs, that the
learned gentleman had fufficient reafon to be alarmed, and
had great authority to apologize for the impatience and apprehenfion which he expreffed at the attempt. He was in a
fimilar predicament with the celebrated irritable critic, Den-
nis, who (like the learned gentleman) had invented a new
fpecies of play-houfe thunder; and appeared fo jealous of
his exclufive property, that one night hearing a *coarfe, clumfy*
grumbling in the theatric fky, he exclaimed in a rage. " By
" Heavens that's my thunder!" The gentleman's fagacity
would make the application.

Mr. Dun-das. Mr. *Dundas* replied, that it could not be expected that he
was ready with a cut and dry anfwer; but when it was the
intention of that honourable gentleman to ftudy a piece of
wit at his expence, he begged he would be fo good as to give
him notice of it, that he might make preparation of a piece
of wit likewife. Mr. Courtenay was on the point of anfwering, when

Mr. Wil-berforce. Mr. *Wilberforce* expreffed his wifhes that the Houfe would
confider themfelves as affembled for more ferious purpofes
than to crack jokes.

Mr. Courtenay, rifing a third time, was immediately called
to order by

Mr. W. W. Grenville. The right honourable *W. W. Grenville*; who obferved,
that the honourable gentleman could not poffibly rife to
explain, as the right honourable gentleman who had fpoke
before him (Mr. Dundas) had not taken any notice whatever of any part of his fpeech; Mr. Grenville then proceeded to reafon on the exceptions which had been produced,
and commended his honourable friend, for having in fo proper a manner refcued his right honourable friend from the
imputation that had been endeavoured to be caft on him by
the other fide of the Houfe. Mr. Grenville faid that it was
now clear that the practice which had been affumed by thofe
gentlemen, and afferted by them with fo much confidence to
have been the uniform, invariable practice of the Houfe, in
fact never had been the practice of the Houfe, but that the
Houfe had at all times, and on all occafions, exercifed their
own

own difcretion, as they had done in the late inftance of the
army eftimates.

Mr. *Vyner* declaring that *he*, alfo, rofe to order, added *Mr. Vyner.*
that the laft honourable gentleman could not be confidered as
defending it fince he had interrupted another honourable gentleman who had a right to be heard firft.

The *Speaker* obferved that he regarded the honourable gen- *The
tleman alluded to, as having waved his right of priority. Speaker.*

Mr. *Courtenay* declared that he had not, but all he meant *Mr. Courte-
to have faid, was, that his piece of wit fhould hereafter lie nay.*
eight days on the table, to give the right honourable gentleman time enough to make a preparation of wit in reply, and
then the Houfe would be able to judge whether the reply
was wit or no.

Mr. *W. Grenville* anfwered that if the honourable gentle- *Mr. W.
man had been fo long interrupted as not to have been able to Grenville*
have found any opportunity of faying what they had juft
heard, the Houfe would have fuftained no lofs. With refpect to the practice of the Houfe in regard to eftimates of any
kind laying upon the table, he fhould ftill contend that it lay
wholly in the difcretion of the Houfe to declare during what
time papers fhould be there, prior to their being referred to
a Committee of Supply. As a proof that the fact was fo,
Mr. Grenville read one of the ftanding orders, the purport
of which was, " that all eftimates for aids to be levied on the
fubject fhould not be voted, prefently after they were introduced and laid on the table, but that the Houfe fhould order
them to be confidered and voted on another day." This ftanding order, Mr. Grenville faid, was a clear written rule of
proceeding, on which the Houfe might rely with fafety, which
it was impoffible for them to do, on any affumed practice of
the Houfe, however confidently afferted.

The refolutions were read a fecond time, and the queftion
put upon each feparately. They were all agreed to, and the
Secretary at War ordered to bring in a bill grounded upon
them.

The Surveyor General of the Ordnance (Mr. Luttrell)
brought up the ordnance eftimates, which were ordered to be
printed.

The *Chancellor of the Exchequer* next brought up the efti- *Mr Chan-
mate of the expence of erecting fortifications for the protec- cellor Pitt.*
tion and fecurity of the dock-yards, which was likewife ordered to be printed. On this occafion, he obferved that he
confidered it as requifite to give notice to the Houfe of fuch
circumftances, relating to the paper which he had laid upon
the table, as would affift them more clearly to comprehend
and be prepared for the queftion which would arife upon it
on Monday fe'nnight; at the fame time, however, he fhould

for the prefent decline entering into any argument whatfoever concerning it. The year before laft the fum of 50,000l.
had been voted to the ordnance fervice for the purpofe of
fortifications;—that fum had been fuffered to lie dormant
without applying it to the purpofe for which it was intended,
and, confequently, during the courfe of the preceding feffion
when the ordnance eftimates were moved, intimation was
given to that Houfe that that fum continuing in the hands
of the Board of Ordnance rendered it unneceffary for any application to be then made to Parliament for money to carry
on the fortifications already begun, as they intended to apply
the fum voted for this purpofe. Hereupon fome diffatisfaction arifing in the minds of a part of the Houfe, from an idea
that the plan of fortifications was ufelefs and objectionable,
he had, to prove how anxious he was on all occafions to do
his duty as guardian of the national purfe, undertaken to
wave, for that time, any farther proceeding in the bufinefs,
until a board of inquiry fhould have been appointed, confifting of feveral officers of diftinguifhed character in both the
naval and military fervices, and the whole plan fhould have
been referred to them for their opinion and advice. That
accordingly fuch a board had been appointed, and his majefty had commiffioned them to proceed in the moft effectual
manner, as well by actual furvey upon the fpot, as by all
other modes of inveftigation to inform themfelves on the fubject, and to make a report of their opinions concerning it.
This Board, he faid, confifted of officers whofe reputations,
when their names were heard, would prove the fincerity
of the intentions of government with regard to the bufinefs.
Several fpecific fubjects were propofed to this board for their
inquiry, among which it was particularly referred to them, to
afcertain, whether our dock yards at Plymouth and Portfmouth could be thought fafe and defenfible, in the event of a
war, by a naval force alone, by a military force alone, or by
a naval and military force combined?—To this their anfwer
was, that neither a naval nor a military force, nor even a union
of both, were by any means a fufficient fecurity for the dock
yards, independent of fortification. They were farther directed to examine whether the plans of fortification propofed
by the Mafter General of the Ordnance, were fufficiently
calculated for the purpofe, and fuch as were eligible to be
adopted. To this they had reported, that on the moft mature deliberation and moft diligent inquiry, the plan alluded
to was thought perfectly adequate to the defence intended,
and that it was the moft eligible of any other that could be
fuggefted; not only as being leaft expenfive in regard to erection, but alfo as requiring a fmaller force to man than any
other that could be propofed. They likewife received inftructions

ftructions to report to His Majesty such farther matter as
might occur independent of the particular points referred to
them, and they might think conducive to the public advantage within the whole department,——and they had confequently given many useful hints of a miscellaneous and general nature, which, he hoped, would turn out to considerable
advantage.   After their report had been completed, the plans
which they recommended had been laid before the board of
engineers, with directions to estimate the expence of carrying
them into execution ; and this estimate he had now brought
up for the information of the members ; but they must see
how imprudent it would be for him to lay before the public a
matter of so serious and delicate a nature as the report of the
naval and military officers, concerning so important and so
serious a subject as the defence of our dock yards.   To proceed in carrying into execution the subject matter of the report of these officers, 50,000l. would for the present be necef-
sary ; but as that sum had already been voted for the service
of the Ordnance, with a view to apply it in the manner now
under consideration, there was no necessity of recurring to
Parliament for a second vote ; and the mode intended to be
adopted was to move for 300,000l. the estimates of the services of the current year, and if gentlemen thought proper to
oppose the carrying on of the fortifications, the method in
which they could with the greatest propriety argue that queftion, would be by moving that 250,000l. only, instead of
300,000l. should be voted for the Ordnance, that thus the
board might become obliged to apply the 50,000l. in hand to
the current service, and by that means the business of the fortifications must of necessity drop.   He trusted, and must beg
leave to express his earnest wishes that gentlemen would come
down to the House free from every prejudice on the present
occasion, without regarding it as a mere question of ordnance
service, or fortification, but to meet it as what, in truth, it
was, a naval question, the present measure being intended to
protect the seeds of the vital sources of our navy at home,
and to enable us in cases of necessity to go upon distant services, without an apprehension of being crushed at home by
a successful attack of an enemy upon those dock yards, in
which were deposited the stamina of our future vigour and
existence.   Nor could he, at this juncture, deem himself juftified, were he to neglect cautioning the House against the
danger of taking up the business as the suggestion of any one
man, however great and respectable, or avoid declaring, that
they were not to consider it as a mere assertion of an individual, or of a single minister, but as a matter resting on the
authority of a number of the ablest and most experienced men
in the two professions of arms ; rendered still more competent

to

to the task by a long and most minute investigation and research.

General Burgoyne.

General Burgoyne remarked that the occasion of his rising was, in some measure, to avoid a debate in that stage of the business, which was extremely delicate in its nature, and in some measure, to take care, lest in consequence of a reprehensible silence, he should be considered as admitting the suggestions of the right honourable gentleman in their utmost extent, as a correct representation of the report of the board of naval and military officers appointed to inspect the proposed plans of fortifying the dock yards. He hoped, and trusted, the minister would lay before the House so much of the report as might be submitted to public perusal without violation of discretion or danger to the state. In the report, undoubtedly there were parts which it would be extremely indiscreet to make a matter of notoriety; and those he neither wished nor expected to see.

Mr. Chancellor Pitt.

The *Chancellor of the Exchequer* answered that he had not stated any thing lightly, but from a collected and attentive consideration; that it would appear that what he had said upon the subject was perfectly true and candid; and that however closely and minutely he had already examined the report, he would still farther study it before the day appointed for the debate.

Mr. Sheridan.

Mr. *Sheridan* observed that unless the House were to be shewn such parts of the report of the Board of inspection as called for their discussion, they were exactly in the same situation in which they stood before that Board was appointed, and instead of having the whole of the question fully before them as the right honourable gentleman had said they would have it, viz. not on the assertion of an individual, of a single minister, nor of any man in office, but on the authority of a board consisting of naval and military officers of known character, experience and integrity, they would have nothing but the bare assertion of the minister, as a guidance for their judgement. For his own part he would not entertain a doubt but that the right honourable gentleman meant to be accurate in the statement which he had just made, as a statement of the outlines of the report in question, and that he had delivered what he himself conceived to be a correct statement of those outlines; but the House had heard that statement contradicted by the honourable general behind him, who had himself been a member of that board. In order therefore to enable the House to judge fairly between the right honourable gentleman and the honourable general, they ought to see such parts of the report at least as might be submitted to their perusal with safety to the state.

Mr.

Mr. *Dempster* contended that, under the idea of a determination to apply the surplus of the revenue to a sinking fund for the diminution of the national debt, it must naturally follow that to sacrifice any part of it to a speculative object like the present, would prove excessively improper. For his own part, he pretended to know little about fortifications, but unless they were found to be indispensably necessary for the defence of our dock yards, he hoped and trusted that Parliament would not squander away any of that money upon them, which might be laid out to such advantage as diminishing the national debt, and of course reviving the public credit, which he thought preferable, even for the preservation of the navy itself, and the strongest means of defence in case of a war, as it would enable us to make such exertions as in our present oppressed state we must despair of doing.

Mr. *Pitt* replied, that the sentiments of the honourable gentleman were perfectly coincident with his own, as far as they could relate to the impropriety of the House consenting to the fortifications, unless they appeared absolutely indispensable, for, he by no means thought that, on the present question, the House should be governed in their determination by the *quantum* of the surplus of the revenue, but solely by the necessity of the measure towards the defence of the navy. Let the surplus prove ever so great, it ought not to operate as a motive, nor could it be any excuse for laying out any part of it on an useless project, but though there were no surplus at all, if a measure appeared necessary for the security of that great bulwark of our glory and strength, the navy, the expence of carrying it into execution, should, on no account, stand as an obstacle, for, in that case, however difficult and distressing it might be, it would behove Parliament to provide the means.—Our being rich was no reason why we should grow profuse and prodigal, nor though we were poor should we therefore abandon our necessary defence. If we were rich, let us increase our riches; and if we were poor, let us endeavour to diminish our poverty by every saving which did not militate against the real safety of our dominions; but let us not, on any occasion, suffer ourselves to be betrayed by prosperity into extravagance, nor led by adversity into despondence:—yet, ill would it become us, whatsoever occasion might arise, to permit either prosperity to seduce us into wanton extravagancies, or misfortune to plunge us in unavailing despondence.

Mr. *Vyner* observed, that it would have given him pleasure to have discovered a tolerably certain prospect, that the estimates of the ordnance for the current service of the year, would become voted regularly on Monday se'nnight, and the question relative to the estimate of the fortifications reserved

Mr. Dempster.

Mr. Chancellor Pitt.

Mr. Vyner.

served

served for a future and distinct consideration. This would not retard the dispatch of the public business, but, on the contrary, give gentlemen an opportunity of properly and maturely deliberating upon a subject so new even in idea, that, for one, he could not persuade himself that he should ever agree to it. The navy of England had hitherto been constantly regarded as a sufficient security for our dock yards, and as they continued safe for such a long course of years without fortifications, he must look for the most convincing proofs of the absolute necessity for the measure, before he should consent to vote any of the public money for such a purpose; and, under this consideration, he flattered himself that the right honourable gentleman would not deny the House any part of the Report which merited examination, and the perusal of which was not forbidden by discretion.

Mr. Courtenay.   Mr. Courtenay said, that he did not mean, at present to argue on the propriety or impropriety of the proposed fortification. He rose, in the first place, to thank the Chancellor of the Exchequer for the very clear, explicit, accurate, and satisfactory detail which he had entered into, on the principal thing on which a Board of naval and land officers, to examine and report the plan proposed to the noble Duke at the head of the Ordnance, had been established. He should only observe, that it appeared to him, that such a military judicature was instituted for the express purpose of putting the noble Duke's office into commission, and to report their opinion on the judgement, and the military or engineering capacity of the noble Duke, who had submitted a plan of defence for the protection of the dock yards to the representatives of the people; but they, from a well-intended, but groundless suspicion perhaps of the noble Duke's experience or abilities for such an extensive plan (attended with an enormous expence) required, and almost compelled the Minister, to acquiesce in their sentiments, and to suspend the execution of the proposed works, till a Board of naval and land officers had made plausible, at least, such a system, by their approbation and authority. The Chancellor of the Exchequer seemingly submitted to the strong reasons, strong numbers, and forcible objections, of numbers of men, respectable country gentlemen, who might always, if they exerted themselves, command the attention, and restrain the excesses, of any Minister. However, when the commission was made out, the public was surprised that the noble Duke was appointed president of a tribunal, whose duty it was, and who were probably instructed, to investigate the noble Duke's system of expence, and report to the King their opinions concerning both the practicability of the plan, and the judgement and capacity of the projector.

Mr. Cour-

Mr. Courtenay therefore faid he meant, if the Chancellor of the Exchequer had no objection, to move for the Commiffioners' inftructions, which were given to the noble Duke on his being appointed prefident of that Board. At the fame time, Mr. Courtenay farther obferved upon the difference of opinion between the Chancellor of the Exchequer and the honourable General, the firft having declared that no part whatever of the Report made by the military Board, could with any degree of fafety be laid before the public; but the honourable General had, on the contrary, declared, that much ufeful information might be collected by the Houfe from that Report, without the fmalleft rifque or hazard of divulging any thing that could endanger the public fafety. Mr. Courtenay expreffed the admiration in which he held the abilities of the Chancellor of the Exchequer; but, on this particular point, (being not only a military point, but a point with which he was particularly converfant, from having been an officer of that Board) Mr. Courtenay faid he could not help deciding in favour of the honourable General, againft the opinion of the Chancellor of the Exchequer. He, therefore, could not help wifhing, that fuch parts of the Report might be felected, under the check and control of the Minifters, as might be ufeful to the members of the Houfe, without being detrimental to the public; and he urged the neceffity of this, from the nature of the fubject on which the Houfe was called upon to form their judgement, the matter being out of the common courfe of parliamentary proceeding, and not only entitled them, but made it their duty, to call for every degree of information refpecting it.

Mr. *Luttrell* obferved, that he confidered the conduct of the honourable gentleman who fpoke laft as reprehenfible, becaufe it bore the appearance of an attempt to miflead the Houfe, by an infinuation that fome of the queftions at the Board of Officers were carried by a majority of one fingle voice, and that the Prefident's. For his part, he had been himfelf a member of that Board, and he would venture to ftake his own knowledge againft the fpeculation of the honourable gentleman—he could fafely affirm that there was not a fingle queftion carried by a fmaller majority than that of twenty to three.

Mr. *Holdfworth* remarked that, having, during the courfe of the preceding feffion, given his voice againft fuffering the fortifications to proceed, without obtaining fome farther proof of their being neceffary befides the mere claim of the money by the Board of Ordnance, he muft now hold himfelf perfectly at liberty to act as might appear to him beft, after the Houfe fhould have become apprifed of the opinion of the Board of Naval and Military Officers upon the fubject, and

Mr. Luttrell.

Mr. Holdfworth.

the matter have fallen under their immediate, regular, and deliberate investigation.

Mr. Courtenay.

Mr. *Courtenay* said, that he by no means intended to affert as a fact, that any question had been carried at the Board by the cafting voice of the Prefident; he had only fuppofed fuch a fact to ftrengthen his argument, which was, that the Houfe could by no means judge, purely from the Report, of the juftice and propriety of it, unlefs it was alfo accompanied with the minute, that fo they might fee the ground on which the Report had been made; but at prefent, deprived as they were of thofe minutes, they might, for all that appeared to them, be determining on a point which at the Board had been carried by a majority of one only. Mr. Courtenay repeated, that it was his intention to move for a copy of the Commiffion and inftructions.

The Chancellor of the Exchequer.

The *Chancellor of the Exchequer* obferved, that if the honourable gentleman perfifted in his defign, the proper method would be for him to move for an addrefs to His Majefty to lay before the Houfe the papers of which he appeared defirous; and thus the fenfe of the Houfe would be known as to the propriety of making public a matter of fo delicate a nature.

Mr. Courtenay.

Mr. *Courtenay* moved for the Commiffion appointing the Mafter General of the Ordnance Prefident of the Board of Inquiry.

The Chancellor of the Exchequer.

The *Chancellor of the Exchequer* wifhed to be informed how the honourable gentleman had been induced to change his mind, and, contrary to the notice which he had juft given, of making a motion on Thurfday next, to make it on that day. This was an inconfiftency to which the honourable gentleman had proceeded, he fuppofed, on very good grounds, and by very found advice; yet candour feemed to call upon him for an explanation of his reafons.

Mr. Courtenay.

Mr. *Courtenay* said, that furely there could be no fort of objection to producing the commiffion by which the Mafter General of the Ordnance had been appointed Prefident of a Board, which he again defcribed as one inftituted as a control upon himfelf.

Mr. Sheridan.

Mr. *Sheridan* contended, that no danger whatever could poffibly arife from the circumftance of laying the inftructions and commiffion before the Houfe, but admitted that inconveniencies might follow the publication of the report of the officers.

The Chancellor of the Exchequer.

The *Chancellor of the Exchequer* expreffed his furprife at the change which appeared to him to have taken place in the minds of the honourable gentlemen; they had appeared grievoufly offended but two days ago to find the army eftimates taken into confideration before the navy, and yet now they were defirous of entering into a long debate on the ordnance and fortifications; a much lefs favourite fubject, though by

fo doing, they were poftponing that fervice which, on all
occafions, they feemed to have at heart; and which was no
lefs than the fervice of the navy appointed for difcuffion upon that day:——to prevent, therefore, an abufe of time in
a long and ufelefs converfation, he fhould move the order of
the day.

Mr. *Courtenay* made his motion, but the order of the day   Mr. Cour-
was carried.   tenay.

Monday, 13th *February.*

Mr. *Jenkinfon* gave notice, that on the enfuing Friday   Mr. Jen-
he fhould move for leave to revive a Bill to regulate the   kinfon.
intercourfe between the States of America and the Britifh
dominions.

Mr. *Burke* faid, that he had conceived the defign of giving   Mr. Burke.
notice of a motion for that day, which related to a fubject
of the higheft confequence that could poffibly fall under the
examination of the Parliament. It was for the production
of certain papers which he thought neceffary to fubftantiate
a charge which he had long intended to bring forward, and,
indeed, which the Houfe had long expected, and which the
party againft whom it was to be made, or, at leaft, a perfon
nearly connected with him, had called on him to haften.
He looked upon the bufinefs as the greateft and moft important criminal profecution that ever had engaged the attention of any human tribunal. The Houfe was prepared to
receive it; the party was prepared to meet it, and he was
prepared to introduce it;—he therefore wifhed to make no
delay, and was forry that the right honourable gentleman
had occupied the next open day, becaufe that might prove
the means of poftponing his motion, if a debate fhould arife
on the bill to be moved for on Friday, according to the
notice juft given.

Mr. *Jenkinfon* apprehended that there could be no debate   Mr. Jen-
of any length on his motion; and it was agreed that Mr.   kinfon.
Burke's motion fhould be expected on Friday next; or if a
debate fhould arife on the Intercourfe Bill, that then it fhould
be underftood as to come on the next fubfequent open day.

The *Chancellor of the Exchequer* obferved, that as the   The Chan-
right honourable gentleman had given notice of his motion in   cellor of the
fo folemn a manner, as a prelude to a charge of the higheft   Exchequer.
criminality that ever occupied the attention of a human judicature, he thought it would be more confiftent with its importance, if he were to mention particularly what papers he
intended to move for, becaufe otherwife his notice would
prove ineffectual towards preparing gentlemen for the debate.
He urged this to the right honourable gentleman on the
grounds of that fairnefs, candour and impartiality, by which

N 2   every

every thing relating to a judicial procefs ought to be diftinguifhed.

Mr. Burke.

Mr. *Burke* replied, that he did not mean to bring forward
any criminal charge on Friday, but only to move for preliminary papers neceffary to ground that charge upon, the nature of which the Houfe fhould be informed of on the enfuing Friday.

Major
Scott.

Major *Scott* obferved, that the right honourable gentleman
had undoubtedly pledged himfelf to proceed againft Mr.
Haftings three years ago ; he had repeated the pledge during
the courfe of the two following feffions, and particularly at
the clofe of the laft, when he declared his intention of proceeding as foon as the Parliament fhould have re-affembled.
The Major added, that he was not verfed in the mode of
proceeding in that Houfe; but he conceived, that after what
the right honourable gentleman had faid, of his readinefs to
proceed, he might as well then mention what papers he
wanted, as poftpone fuch a motion till Friday, by which
means all farther delay would become avoided : a point the
more to be wifhed for, becaufe now, four years had elapfed
fince the right honourable gentleman's firft pledge.

Mr. Vyner.

Mr. *Vyner* defired that he might be permitted to trefpafs,
during a fhort time, upon the attention of the Houfe, whilft
he briefly ftated his reafons for a motion which he flattered
himfelf would efcape all objection, as it was merely calculated to oblige them to do their duty as members of Parliament. Previous to his putting any motion into the hands
of the Speaker, he would ftate the reafons which induced him
to bring it forward, and he hoped that thofe reafons would
imprefs the minds of all prefent as forcibly as they had
ftricken him. The right honourable gentleman oppofite to
him had, with a degree of candour and fairnefs which did him
great honour, and for which, in his mind, the Houfe was
highly indebted to him, given as fpecific a notice as ever was
given by a Minifter, that when the ordnance eftimates were
to be taken into confideration, it was intended that they
fhould at the fame time determine upon the great queftion
of dock-yard fortification. The queftion Mr. Vyner declared to be, in his opinion, a queftion of infinite magnitude
and importance; it led to confiderations of the moft ferious
confequence, and, perhaps, might go the extreme length of
effecting a change in the government of the country; it was
in all regards neceffary, therefore, that the difcuffion of fuch
a fubject fhould come on before as full a Houfe as could
poffibly be convened. The regular way of obtaining a full
attendance, was by moving a call of the Houfe, and as he
meant to move a call with a view to the procuring a full
attendance, he hoped the right honourable gentleman, with
the

the fame candour which prompted him to give fo ample
and fair a notice of the queſtion, connected with the ordnance
eſtimates, would agree to feparate that queſtion from the
other, and let it lie over for the confideration of the Houfe
after the call had operated effectually. He had no wiſh, he
declared, to delay the public bufineſs an hour, but was ready
to vote the ordnance eſtimates forthwith. All he aſked was,
that before a queſtion of the magnitude of that, reſpecting the
fortifications intended to be erected for the defence of the
dock yards, ſhould fall under confideration, and become decided upon, the call might be allowed to take place, becauſe,
in his mind, it was due to their conſtituents, and due to the
nation, that they ſhould have the fulleſt opportunity of informing themfelves upon the fubject, before they paſſed a vote
that would authorife a fyſtem of national defence extremely
novel and extremely expenſive. In conclufion Mr. Vyner
moved, "That the Houfe be called on Tuefday three weeks."

Mr. *Chancellor Pitt* anfwered, that it was not poſſible for
him, upon any account whatfoever, much lefs on one of fo
important a nature as the ordnance eſtimates, and the queftion of fortifications, with which it was united, to harbour
even the moſt diſtant objection againſt the ufe of all methods
to enforce a complete attendance of the Houfe; but he could
not aſſent to the procraſtination of that bufineſs during the
length of time defired by the honourable gentleman. It was
difficult to account for the inconfiſtence with which gentlemen on the other fide of the Houfe endeavoured, on all occafions, to delay the bufineſs of the nation, after their complaining that the Houfe had not made fufficient progreſs. As
to the term novel, which the honourable gentleman had
applied to the bufineſs of the fortifications, he certainly
could not mean to defcribe it as fuch, with refpect to the degree of notoriety and expectancy with which it was attended;
for, furely no object had ever come before Parliament with
more preparation than it would appear, having now, been
depending during the courfe of three feffions, and a Board of
Naval and Land officers having been appointed to examine
and report the propriety of the meafure. So that evidently
the Houfe and the Public muſt be fufficiently apprifed of the
nature and extent of the bufineſs; nor could there arife any
neceffity whatfoever for putting off the final confideration of
it to a more diſtant period than that already appointed.
With thefe impreffions it was impoſſible for him to avoid
confidering the motion of the honourable gentleman, as a
meafure of procraſtination, and therefore ſhould he meet it
with an oppofition.

Mr. *Fox* expreſſed his aſtoniſhment that the right honourable gentleman ſhould have refiſted the motion, becaufe, in his

Mr. Chan-
cellor Pitt.

Mr. Fox.

opinion,

opinion, it was perfectly easy so to arrange the matter as not to lose a moment, in regard to the necessary dispatch of the public business, and at the same time to accommodate the wishes of the honourable gentleman who had made the motion, and of all who thought with him (as he had no doubt numbers did) that the question whether the fortifications of the dock yards should be adopted or not, was a question of the most serious importance. The right honourable gentleman had himself, in his speech on a former occasion, declared that those who were adverse to the proposed system of fortification, would naturally vote, that the sum to be granted to the ordnance for the estimates of the year should be 250,000l. instead of 300,000l. The case standing upon this ground, what objection could the right honourable gentleman entertain against their voting at once, next Monday, that 250,000l. be granted for the ordnance, and leaving it to be understood, that when a fit opportunity for a full and fair discussion of the fortification question offered, if it was then determined that the fortification system should be proceeded in, that an additional 50,000l. should be voted for the estimates of the ordnance? This would settle the point at once, and not check the necessary dispatch of business; but, taking the case another way, why not postpone the whole consideration, if it were true that the one question was inseparably implicated and involved in the other? This was but the month of February, and the ordnance estimates stood at present for Monday next. Was it possible for any sort of inconvenience to arise, if the consideration of these estimates and the vote of the money were to be delayed for a single fortnight? Mr. Fox declared it appeared to him to be absurd and fallacious to maintain that any inconveniency whatever would arise from so trifling a delay; and when the infinite importance of the vote they were to be called upon to give was duly considered, he hardly believed there was a man in the kingdom to be found who would not hold himself obliged to the House for its deliberation, and think they did their duty best, by not rashly and precipitately agreeing to a vote that was to entail on future Parliaments and on future constituents an expence, the size and extent of which he must suppose that no man living would take upon himself to define and describe. He reminded the House of the extreme and wide difference between the vote in question and all other votes. They were not to be called on to vote a stated sum, and by that vote to close the account; but they were to begin a series of votes which might entail upon the nation, and upon posterity, an endless system of charge, and an unlimited extent of expence. If a system, so far novel that few had made up their minds upon it, and upon which, for one, he had not made up his mind, was to be adopted blindly
and

and percipitately, what infinite mifchiefs might not enfue to
the country? Several of thofe mifchiefs the honourable gentleman who made the motion had glanced at, and, as it was
undoubtedly poffible that fuch might be the confequence,
why would not the right honourable gentleman meet the motion fairly? The honourable mover, with a degree of candour
which reflected much credit upon his conduct, had explained
the purpofes of his motion. This confideration, when added
to the received opinion of its great importance, intitled him
to the fupport of the Houfe.

Mr. *Martin* faid he had a great refpect for the noble Duke Mr. Mar-
at the head of the ordnance, and was inclined to think well of tin.
him on many accounts, but he believed that it would be extremely difficult for that noble perfon to perfuade him to
change his mind, or to bring him to the opinion, that fuch a
fyftem of fortification as that propofed was actually neceffary.
Perhaps, when the matter came to be difcuffed, he fhould
hear as an anfwer to the objections which might be ftated
againft the plan, that although we had hitherto relied on our
navy for the defence of our dock yards, yet at prefent our
navy, compared with the naval force of the other powers of
Europe, was not fufficiently fuperior to be trufted to folely.
In that cafe, he fhould think it would be wifer to vote the
50,000l. in queftion towards increafing and ftrengthening
our navy, than towards commencing the fyftem of fortification propofed. With regard to the call, Mr. Martin faid, he
certainly would vote for the motion, but if it fhould be carried, he hoped it would be effectually enforced, becaufe calls
of the Houfe, as generally executed, were, in his mind, the
greateft farces imaginable.

Mr. *Vyner* begged leave to affure the Houfe that he would Mr. Vyner
not have made the motion, except from the fulleft conviction, that the matter was of the firft moment, and that it
could not be too deliberately confidered. He hoped, therefore, that the motion would be agreed to, and that the right
honourable gentleman would confent to poftpone the queftion
of fortification till the call fhould have been made. As to himfelf he could declare, that no circumftance upon earth but a
fenfe of his duty to his conftituents and the nation fhould
have induced him either to make the motion, or propofe the
delay. He had not the honour to be known to the noble
Duke at this time at the head of the ordnance board; but if
the noble Lord who had preceded him in office, to whom he
was well known, and with whom he had lived on terms of
intimacy all his life, had propofed the plan in queftion, he
fhould have acted exactly in the fame manner.

The queftion was at length put, and the Houfe divided,

Ayes   -   -   -   -   54
Noes   -   -   -   -   100

The

The Houfe being refumed,

Mr. Fox.   Mr. *Fox* rofe and fignified his intention of making his motion on the election for Weftminfter. He remarked that thofe
who had fo often propagated opinions that he had not the fair
and legal majority of votes for Weftminfter, and affected to
doubt of his being fuffered to remain its reprefentative in the
prefent Parliament, retained no longer the right to inculcate
fuch doctrines or circulate any doubts concerning thofe points;
becaufe the perfons to whom he alluded having abandoned the
caufe, of which they had been proud to avow themfelves the
champions, it was demonftrable that they knew all along,
that they ftood upon rotten ground, and that it was impoffible
for them to make good their infinuations before that tribunal
legally conftituted, and undoubtedly the beft adapted to the difcovery of the truth in matters of the nature in queftion. Had
it been poffible for them to ftand at all before that tribunal,
they would not thus have deferted the means of doing fo.
Nothing furely of animofity, nothing of chicane, nothing of
fallacy, or of art, had been wanting on the part of his political
enemies, and therefore it was not to be fuppofed that any
thing fhort of a firm conviction arifing from the experience
derived from a fcrutiny, continued in different veftry rooms
of the city of Weftminfter, for fo many months together,
could have induced them to drop the purfuit, and abandon all
pretenfions to carry it on any longer. Mr. Fox obferved that
he thought it neceffary to fay thus much on that occafion;
and he had only to add, that though he fhould ever entertain
an equal degree of refpect and of gratitude for the electors of
both the places which had done him the honour to return him,
he fhould make his election for Weftminfter; he therefore
moved, " That the Speaker do iffue his warrant for the elec-
" tion of a reprefentative to ferve in Parliament for the Bo-
" rough of Kirkwall."

Lord Hood.   Lord *Hood* faid that he could not, without violence to his
gratefully-refpectful feelings for his conftituents, avoid expreffing his opinion that it reflected upon their conduct the
higheft credit that they had foreborne to prefent petitions
againft either his right honourable colleague or himfelf. A
contrary procedure (but this, doubtlefs, their liberality and
good fenfe difcovered and avoided) would have rekindled ani-
mofities which ought, henceforward, to remain not merely
extinguifhed, but buried in oblivion. Nor, perhaps, were a
petition brought to the bar of the Houfe, could any committee, howfoever judicioufly chofen, acquire, by the utmoft
affiduity, difcernment, unbiafled candour and activity, the
power of fo afcertaining the merits of the election, as to decide
upon it with the ftricteft and moft unequivocal juftice.

Mr.

Mr. *Baſtard* now roſe, and remarked, that no matter ſtood Mr.Baſtard
more in need of regulation and reform, than the practice of
the Eccleſiaſtical Courts, in a variety of different ſpecies of
legal proceſs and proſecution. On the preſent occaſion, however, he did not mean to take up the time of the Houſe by
entering into a detail of all the arbitrary, ſevere, and unjuſt effects which had ariſen, in conſequence of the practices in
queſtion; becauſe, he not only knew his own limited abilities, but would not wiſh to ſhock the feelings of the Houſe,
as a legiſlative body, by ſtating to them the degree of oppreſſion which they had, for a ſeries of years, ſuffered to exiſt in
the country. He would content himſelf with moving for
leave to bring in a Bill, and barely hint the objects to which
that Bill would be directed. The firſt went to the abolition
of the practice of proſecuting for anti-nuptial fornication as it
ſtood at preſent. In order to prove that this point required
immediate regulation, Mr. Baſtard ſtated two or three caſes,
in which the parties had been proſecuted with great appearance of oppreſſion; one in particular, the caſe of a man who
had a ſuit commenced againſt him in the Eccleſiaſtical Court
for anti-nuptial fornication ſix or ſeven years after his wife
had been dead. Mr. Baſtard ſaid another object of this Bill,
was to put a ſtop to all proſecutions for ſmall tithes in the
Eccleſiaſtical Court, and in the Court of Exchequer, and to
put them on a footing more fit to be adopted. He had, he
ſaid, intended to have put into his Bill an extenſion of what
was called the Lords act to debtors, to a limited amount; but
as there was a bill, he underſtood, now pending in the other
Houſe, in which that very purpoſe was achieved, and as it
was more proper for it to originate in that Houſe, he had
not interfered with it. In concluſion, he moved, "For leave
"to bring in a bill to prevent frivolous and vexatious ſuits in
"the Eccleſiaſtical Court, and for the more ſpeedy recovery
"of ſmall tithes."

Leave was given to bring in a Bill.

Lord *Mahon* next roſe, and ſaid that he was confident that Ld.Mahon.
he ſhould not be contradicted by any member of that Houſe,
when he laid it down as a fundamental principle of liberty in
this country, that it is neceſſary to ſupport the conſequence
of the Houſe of Commons; and, in order to preſerve the freedom of the people, and to ſecure their intereſts, that it is eſſential to maintain the full weight of that aſſembly in the ſcale
of the conſtitution. But it is poſſible that there may exiſt
out of that Houſe ſome extraordinary character who may act
on very different principles.

Every man of ſenſe muſt know and feel, that it is the Houſe
of Commons that conſtitutes the chief bulwark of the people,
and that forms the ſtrong barrier againſt the power of the

Crown; and it is for that reason, that the House of Commons is so much disliked by some people.

Lord Mahon said, that he must confess that he was not one of those who wished to see the House of Commons degraded. He was not one of those who wished to see destroyed, in this country, every barrier against prerogative. That he did not wish to see every formidable fortress of the People pulled down; or to see prerogative and tory principles established on the ruin of the constitution. [The House exclaimed, hear! hear! hear!] Lord Mahon then said, pulling out a paper, that he was not of opinion that, " A proposition, by receiving the approbation of the House of Commons, acquires no authority or weight whatever." Lord Mahon said, that, after a proposition had received the approbation of the House of Commons, he was not of opinion that, " it remains in the precise light of a perfect new proposition; with this only difference, that, as this proposition is a measure in which the House of Common is personally interested, it ought to be viewed with the more jealousy! He said he would appeal to the fairness and to the candour of every gentleman present, whether such principles were to be endured in a free country. [Again the House generally and loudly repeated the cry of Hear! hear! hear!] What! said Lord Mahon, is it to be endured in a free country, that it should be laid down as a maxim, when a public bill has received the most full and the most fair discussion, in that part of the legislature which represents the people, and has received the approbation of those whom the country has elected, and of those who have the best means of knowing the sense of their constituents upon the subject; that a bill so circumstanced, should, nevertheless be said to remain in the precise light of any visionary project, or perfect new proposition? The degrading the House of Commons, the taking every opportunity to abuse it, and the making that assembly a mere cypher in the constitution, one should have thought was quite sufficient to gratify the most bitter Tory spleen. But it is extraordinary indeed, that the approbation of the representatives of the People should be assigned as a reason for opposition to a measure which they demanded, and that that approbation should be urged as a motive for resistance, and should be held forth to mankind, as an object of "jealousy." Lord Mahon said, that there might be those, in this country, who wished to raise jealousies against the House of Commons, and to create ill-grounded jealousies against the People. That there might be those, who thought that their power would be increased, by decreasing the constitutional consequence of that assembly. That there might be those, whose maxim it was to endeavour to divide those parts of the legislature, which, for the public good,

ought

ought to remain united. That there might be those, whose motto it was, " to divide, in order to govern," and who wished to govern in order the better to endeavour to divide. Lord Mahon said, that a very honourable member (Mr. Bastard) had on that day obtained leave to bring in a bill upon a very interesting subject. The honourable gentleman might imagine, for his bill has been discussed for many months in that House, after it has been rendered as perfect as the wisest men in that House could make it, and after it has been highly approved of, (with only twenty dissenting voices) in the House of Commons; the honourable gentleman might imagine that he has made, at least, some progress; but, he might find, that after he has carried his bill through the House of Commons, that he is just as far advanced, as he was in the beginning. If he should have the misfortune to propose a measure, which is unexceptionable in its principle, which is well considered in its detail, and to which no rational objection can be made; the measure may be rejected without any rational objection whatever. It may be totally misrepresented from the first line of it to the last. If there is nothing objectionable in the bill, then the bill may be abused for what it does not contain; and the bill may likewise be abused for not containing that, which it actually does contain. And for fear such scandalous mis-statements should be detected, upon farther investigation of the subject, and for fear that such injurious misrepresentations should be finally done away, the bill may be rejected, with contempt, without a hearing; and without its being permitted even to go to a Committee, in order to be discussed. Lord Mahon said he knew that such things as these were possible. That he had, last year, brought in a bill himself, to prevent delays, uncertainty, and expence, in country elections. That the object was a great one, that the mode of obtaining it had been highly approved of, in that House, to whose elections it entirely related; and that that bill had, at the end of the last session of Parliament, been rejected in the House of Lords in a very thin House; and that it had been, there, treated (on the part of one person) with all the candour, with all the decency and decorum, and with all the respect to the House of Commons, which that assembly unquestionably deserved. Lord Mahon then moved, " That leave be given to bring in a bill for better se-
" curing the rights of voters at county elections."

Mr. Wilberforce seconded the motion, and leave was given for the bill to be brought in.

Lord *Mahon* said, that as soon as he had brought in the bill, he should move to have it printed. Lord Mahon, Mr. Wilbeforce, and Mr. Duncombe, were appointed a Committee to prepare and bring in the bill.

Ld. Mahon.

O 2

Thursday,

Thursday, 14th February.

This being the day appointed to ballot for a Committee to try the merits of a petition complaining of an undue election for the borough of Ilchester, the Speaker came down at half past two o'clock; but as the ballot could not take place without the attendance of two hundred members, and that number was not present, the House adjourned at four o'clock, without doing any business.

Wednesday, 15th February.

The House proceeded to ballot for a Committee to try the merits of Honiton election petition, and, after the usual ceremonies observed upon such occasions, the following members were returned as a jury:

Sir Edward Astley, Bart. Chairman.

Sir Joseph Mawbey
Hon. Wm. Mortimer
Henry Addington, Esq.
Wm. Pochin, Esq.
Sir Wm. Mansell, Bart.
Sir John Wodehouse, Bart.
John Cable, Esq.
John Hill, Esq.
Hon. Wm. Grimston
Robert Nicholas, Esq.
Clement Tudway, Esq.

Nominees,

T. Burney Bramston, Esq.   Sir Wm. Dolben.

The land-tax bill and the malt bill were read a second time, and committed for the morrow.

The marine mutiny bill was presented, and read a third time.

The House proceed afterwards to ballot for a Committee to appoint commissioners from different lists delivered in at the table for executing certain parts of the East-India judicature bill; and after the usual forms observed by the said act, the following members were returned:

Francis Annesley, Esq.
Sir Edw. Astley, Bart.
Henry Banks, Esq.
John Barrington, Esq.
John Pollexfen Bastard, Esq.
Henry Beaufoy, Esq.
Tho. Berney Bramston, Esq.
Charles Brandling, Esq.
Isaac Hawkins Browne, Esq.
John Blackburne, Esq.
Lord Fred. Campbell
Sir Rob. S. Cotton, Bart.
Sir Wm. Dolben, Bart.
Sir Rob. Lawley, Bart.
Sir Wm. Lemon, Bart.
Sir Ja. Langham, Bart.
Sir Edw. Littleton, Bart.
Thomas Masters, Esq.
Wm. M'Dowall, Esq.
Rich. Slater Milnes, Esq.
Lord Muncaster
Wm. Mainwairing, Esq.
Henry Pierse, Esq.
Wm. Praed, Esq.
Henry James Pye, Esq.
Edward Phelips, Esq.

Wm.

Wm. Drake, jun. Efq.
Hen. Duncombe, Efq.
Sir Archibald Edmonstone, Bart.
William Egerton, Efq.
Sir Adam Fergufon, Bart.
Joshua Grigby, Efq.
Ambrofe Goddard, Efq.
Lord V. Grimston
Sir Richard Hill
Sir Harbord Harbord, Bart.
Sir Henry Hoghton, Bart.
John James Hamilton, Efq.
Arth. Holdfworth, Efq.
Jn. Galley Knight, Efq.
Wm. Lygon, Efq.

William Pulteney, Efq.
Wm. Morton Pitt, Efq.
John Rolle, Efq.
Sir John Rous, Bart.
Hon. Fred. Robinfon
Hon. Dudley Ryder.
Sir. G. Aug. Shuckburgh, Bart.
Walter Sneyd, Efq.
Charles Lorain Smith, Efq.
John Smith, Efq.
John Sinclair, Efq.
Sir Rob. Smyth, Bart.
Henry Thornton, Efq.
Brook Watfon, Efq.
Sir John Wodehoufe, Bart.
Philip Yorke, Efq.

Mr. Sheridan complained, that fome of the above lifts had been delivered to the Houfe by the door-keeper.

Several petitions for private bills were prefented to the Houfe, and referred to a Committee to report.

Mr. Brett prefented to the the Houfe, purfuant to order, " a lift of the officers of ten and eight fhillings," &c. The title was read, and the lift ordered to lie on the table.

-Mr. Jenkinfon prefented " His Majefty's order in council " for regulating the trade and commerce between Great Bri- " tain and the united States of America, and between the " States and the Weft-Indies." The fame being read, was ordered to lie on the table.

The Coalmeters bill and the Tewkefbury road bill, were read a fecond time and committed.

The Houfe adjourned.

Thurfday, 16th February.

Sir *Robert Smyth* remarked that he had contemplated with pleafure the falutary effects which, during the courfe of the preceding year, had accompanied the operations of the bill for the prohibition of the exportation of hay. So fcanty had proved the crops of the laft feafon, and fo uncertain (as a point of courfe, within a climate perpetually fubject to va- rious and to oppofite changes) was the profpect of the enfu- ing fummer harvefts, that, for his part, he could not avoid entertaining an opinion that it would become neceffary to continue the prohibition until the expiration of a farther length of time. To effect all this was not poffible without the introduction of a new bill to take place inftantly upon the expiration of the old bill; a circumftance which muft happen upon the enfuing Tuefday. Thefe reafons, of neceffity, in- duced

Sir Robert Smyth.

duced him to move for leave to bring in " a bill for leave to
" continue the act of the laſt ſeſſion of Parliament, relative
" to the exportation of hay for a limited time."

Mr. Drake,
Junior.

Mr. *Drake*, junior, obſerved that he ſhould ſecond the motion of his honourable friend with particular pleaſure, from
the fulleſt ſenſe that the continuance of the prohibition was
indiſpenſably requiſite. In the capital, the price of hay had
ariſen to the enormous price of five pounds and ten ſhillings
for each load: but, ſuch a ſum, not confined to London, had
lately been received for hay at Saliſbury. And, doubtleſs,
were ſeveral honourable gentlemen preſent to favour the
Houſe with a communication of the reſult of their experience
upon the ſubject, it would be diſcovered that, in *their* ſeveral
neighbourhoods, the prices of hay had proved equally extravagant. Upon this ground, it was not needful to preſs for a
more extended prohibition of the exportation. Moſt places
on the continent had ſeverely ſuffered from the dearth of hay;
they had felt the diſtreſsful neceſſity of ſubmiting to the payment of prices ſtill more exorbitant than thoſe with which we
had not leſs inevitably complied; a ſtriking inſtance how
much the Parliament muſt become actuated by a moſt dangerous impolicy, were they, forgetful of the precept from
the proverb (wiſe and ſalutary, at leaſt, in the preſent inſtance) not to take care that *charity ſhould begin at home*, and
meet the motion with their unanimous conſent. He greatly
feared that the committee appointed to inquire into the number of the expiring laws, and to report the reſult of their inveſtigations to the Houſe, were little better than a mere
name; and whether they were now ſitting, or had aſſembled
at any prior period, was a matter altogether inſignificant,
becauſe, ſurely, a more reprehenſible impropriety could not
ariſe, than the tacit acquieſcence of the Houſe to the baneful act of amuſing the public with falſe lights, and affecting
a parade of buſineſs executed, when, in fact, no meaſure
whatſoever had been carried to a completion. Under theſe
circumſtances, it followed that, not harm, but great benefit
muſt attend the renewal and continuance of the prohibition.
The bill would ceaſe to operate at the return of plenteous
ſeaſons, becauſe it veſted the diſcretionary power of anull-
ing it in a quarter where he could not ſuppoſe that ſuch an
exertion would take place without the wiſeſt and matureſt
deliberation in the Crown, aſſiſted by the judgement and re-
commendations of its council.

Sir Joſeph
Mawbey.

Sir *Joſeph Mawbey* ſaid that, ſenſible of the *general* merits
of the motion, he was reſolved to give it his ſupport; and he
felt that it came forward *particularly* entitled to the concurrence of the Houſe, becauſe the late crops of grain, in all
likelihood, would prove exceedingly deficient, and the chances

ses of a more abundant produce in the enfuing feafons were as yet precarious. The barley, in his country·neighbourhood, made a moſt unpromiſing appearance; and, as he had reaſon to believe that other parts might not exhibit its uſual inſtances of fertility, he felt himſelf juſtified in earneſtly requeſting the Houſe to ſecure within the nation as much of the growth of its paſture and arable lands as poſſible.

The *Attorney General* begged leave (from the conſideration that the preſent bill would expire upon the next Tueſday, and that the Houſe appeared heartily inclined to countenance and eſtabliſh its renewal) to adviſe the honourable baronet (Sir R. Smyth) to follow up the precedent, dictated·by the exigencies of the ſtate, during the courſe of the foregoing year, and *inſtantly* to procure the firſt and ſecond reading of his bill; next, to have it as rapidly committed, read a third time, and paſſed upon the morrow; and thus, with equal facility and expedition, might it complete its progreſs through the Houſe of Lords on the enſuing Monday. *[margin: The Attorney General.]*

The Earl of *Surrey*, contending againſt the neceſſity of a new bill, added that, in *his* opinion, the price of hay was not in the leaſt beyond what *naturally* might be expected at this particular ſeaſon of the year; and therefore he, for this reaſon, could not approve of hurrying the bill through the Houſe in the manner recommended by the honourable and learned gentleman who ſpoke laſt. *[margin: The Earl of Surrey.]*

Sir *Edward Aſtley* ſaid, that, yielding to the juſtice of the arguments of thoſe honourable gentlemen who countenanced the motion, he ſhould declare himſelf an advocate for the utmoſt poſſible expedition in the paſſing of ſo ſalutary a bill. *[margin: Sir Edward Aſtley.]*

The motion being carried, the bill was brought in, read a firſt time, and ordered to be committed on the morrow.

Mr. *Sheridan*, riſing next, begged leave to aſſure the Houſe that it was very far from his intentions to treſpaſs upon their patience with ſome remarks which, *now*, he deemed it neceſſary to make, if, on the preceding day, ſome honourable gentlemen, in the ſervice of adminiſtration, had not inſinuated, with an air of triumph over him for his ſuppoſed defection, that, with reproachful inconſiſtency, he had firſt ſtated a motion to the Houſe, and then ſuddenly deſerted it, without having previouſly purſued it to any opening whatſoever. If gentlemen would pleaſe to honour him, upon the preſent occaſion, with their attention, he felt himſelf perſuaded that he ſhould totally exonerate himſelf from all charges of inconſiſtency. When upon the Wedneſday he came down to the Houſe, he perceived, and not without aſtoniſhment, the doorkeeper putting into the hands of every member a paper containing a written liſt of the names of gentlemen by way of a balloting liſt; and having the ſtrongeſt grounds for belief that theſe *[margin: Mr. Sheridan.]*

papers

papers were prepared at the treasury, and that it was by their
direction the door keeper delivered them, and feeling that
such conduct was a direct and scandalous attack upon the privileges of that House, and conceiving, likewise, that it was
most shamefully indecent on the part of Administration, and
that it flatly contradicted the affectation of impartiality with
which the bill was fraught, in respect to the mode of consti-
tuting the court of judicature, he had risen and stated his
intention of proving the fact by moving " that the doorkeeper be called to the bar of the House," which motion he
was proceeding to ground upon argument, when he had been
called down from the Chair, (very properly called down, he
was ready to admit, on the part of the Speaker, who had been
reminded that two hundred members were present, and desired to lock the door and proceed to the ballot, in compliance with the act of Parliament, which authorised the institution of the Court of Judicature.)   This having proved the
case, and the ballot having been actually proceeded upon,
was there any inconsistency in his not afterwards attempting to make his motion ?   One reason upon which he meant
to have rested it, and one object to which he intended to
have pointed it, tending to shew the necessity and propriety
of postponing the ballot to another day.   Mr. Sheridan
strenuously contended, that it would have been most absurd
in him to have attempted to have made his motion, when so
essential an end aimed at by it as the getting the ballot postponed was determined and over by the ballot's having taking
place.   That was an explanation of his conduct of the preceding day, and he left it to the House to decide whether it
was at all inconsistent or contradictory.   He complained of
the Minister's having taken an unfair advantage of the letter
of the act of Parliament in calling to the Speaker to shut the
doors when he did.   He admitted that, according to the letter of the act, such conduct was warranted, but under such
a strict enforcement of the letter of the act, the Minister
might, when the House were in a division, and one hundred
members (those in the opposition) out in the lobby, and two
hundred (all the friends of the Minister) within the House,
call to the Chair to lock the doors, and proceed to ballot with
a complete certainty of carrying the election his own way.
     What could be more gross and preposterous than the Mi-
nister's conduct of the preceding day, when he prevented
him from opening his motion, by calling to the Chair to have
the doors shut while he was on his legs ?   What he meant
now to move, would be that part of his yesterday's purpose,
which might be usefully accomplished, and this was " That
the doorkeeper be called to the bar of the house," there to
state from whom he received the written lists, and by whose
                                                  autho-

authority he delivered them to the members as they entered. The fact was an infringement of the privileges of the House, and an indecent and direct attempt to influence their members in their capacity of electors of the new Court of Judicature, by Treasury interference. He flattered himself that he should not again hear the ridiculous argument of the preceding day, that there was no compulsion used, and that the papers left the minds of the members as free and unbiassed as they were before they saw them. [Mr. Pitt said, across the house, so they did.] Mr. Sheridan declared his extreme surprise at the right honourable gentleman's still contending for so palpable an absurdity; he said, he had imagined even the shortest time for recollection would have convinced the right honourable gentleman, that the position was truly ridiculous; and, that although Mr. Pearson had not taken the members individually by the shoulders, and forced them by manual strength to ballot for the list which he had put into their hands, yet, certainly by thrusting the Treasury list into their hands, he had not left their minds as completely free and uninfluenced as they had been before. The bill affected great impartiality on the part of the Minister; and it had been argued at the time the bill was in progress, that it was intended, that the Minister for the time being should not interfere in the election of the new Court of Judicature in any way whatsoever. How could this be reconciled to the conduct adopted? A conduct at once so indecent and so degrading to them, that if the right honourable gentleman dared rise and avow, that the lists were prepared by his orders, and delivered by his authority, he would pledge himself to move the severest censure of that House upon the right honourable gentleman. And indeed, it was the duty of the House to institute an inquiry, in order to ascertain what he had stated as matter highly culpable on the part of the Treasury; and the House could take no means so effectual of doing that, as ordering their doorkeeper to the bar. He desired not to be misunderstood as meaning to cast any sort of slur on the characters whose names were in the written lists; more respectable characters he knew not, and so far was he from wishing it to be conceived that he intended to throw any imputation upon them, he was not without hopes, that they would feel that he was combating *their* cause, and would all vote with him. With these impressions, he trusted that he could *successfully* move, " That Mr. Joseph Pearson, doorkeeper, be " now called in and examined in relation to the said com-" plaint."

Mr. *Francis* seconding the motion, added, that he had not attended the ballot, as he had uniformly professed himself adverse to the constitution of a court of judicature, so un-

Mr Francis.

con-

conftitutional in its origin and principle, and fo inimical
to the natural rights of Britifh fubjeéts, in every particular
of its inftitution, powers, and proceedings. Upon the face
of the matter, it ftruck him that the eleétion had been partially conduéted, and that an inquiry was neceffary. This
ferved to confirm his former fufpicions of the extreme unjufti-
fiablenefs of the inftitution, and that the tribunal was meant
to be thruft forward as a rod of minifterial power, to fall
heavy on thofe whofe opinions led them to take an adverfe part
againft adminiftration; but to be lightly handled, with refpeét to others, who might conduét themfelves in a manner
more accommodating, and more pliant to the wifhes and
wills of the powers in being.

Sir Jofeph Mawbey. Sir *Jofeph Mawbey* remarked that the motion was needlefs,
and that all the arguments urged in fupport of it were rather
infulting to the Houfe, as they went upon the fuppofition,
that part of it was liable to undue influence, when proceeding to exercife its capacity of eleétors of the new Court of
Judicature. For his own part, he by no means wifhed to
inquire from whom the doorkeeper received the papers he
delivered; they had not influenced him, nor did he believe
they had influenced any gentleman who ballotted. They
might juft as well proceed to inquire by whom all the various papers, put into their hands from time to time in the
courfe of the feffion came, fuch as petitions for bills and other
things, an inveftigation which (to give it the gentleft term)
muft be a fhameful trefpafs upon the valuable moments of
the Houfe.

Mr. Chancellor Pitt. Mr. Chancellor *Pitt* expreffed his wifhes that a complaint
of fo frivolous and idle a nature would not occafion much
debate on a day, when agreeably to notice, other great and
important topics were to be taken under confideration. The
two heads of an affertion into which the honourable gentleman had divided his chaarge, firft, that the written lifts having been delivered, was a violation of the privileges of the
Houfe, and next that it ftood forward as an inftance of the
Minifter's having attempted to interfere in an eleétion vefted
in the members of that Houfe, by Treafury influence, were
each of them fo obvioufly ill founded and delufive, that they
fcarcely merited a ferious anfwer. In refpeét to the fuppofed
breach of privilege, there had been none. For what fpecific
privilege of the Houfe did the faét affumed in argument, but
without a fhadow of proof, trench upon? Suppofing even
that it were true, that the written lifts had been prepared
and delivered as the honourable gentleman had afferted, where
was the breach of privilege? And as to the idea, that the minds
of gentlemen were liable to be influenced, upon having a written lift of names put into their hands to do what they pleafed
with

with, unaccompanied by any requeft or any compulfion to vote for any one name in the lift, that fomething more than infinuation (for the honourable gentleman had that day invented a new fhade of affertion) was too infulting to the Houfe to be tolerated a moment.   But would any man imagine that the honourable gentleman or his friends had, in ferious truth, any concern for that impartiality in the conftitution of the Court of Judicature, for which they were now fo eager to profefs themfelves the advocates, when their conduct on the day of the bollot was confidered ?   It was in the power of forty of them by ftaying and doing their duty by balloting, to have put any name upon the lift and had it returned; for, with fuch attention to a fair and impartial election of the Court had the Act been framed, that it was fo worded, that no Minifter, were he fo inclined, or were he fo prefuming as to think fo meanly of the members of that Houfe, as the honourable gentleman had chofen to ftate them, had it in his power to prevent any name from being put upon the lift that forty members chofe to ballot for.   Inftead, however, of the honourable gentleman and his friends taking this fair and becoming mode of infuring a return of impartial characters, according to their ideas of impartial characters, they had deferted their duty and abondoned the ballot.   It was evident, therefore, that the attempt fo made to raife a clamour, was merely an attempt to throw impediments in the way of public bufinefs, and to create alarm in the minds of the people, by ill-founded and frivolous complaints.   Of the gentlemen who balloted he could obferve, without dread of contradiction, that their characers were too fpotlefs either to need praife or fhrink from cenfure.

Mr. *Fox* faid, that he could not without equal indignation and furprife obferve thofe very perfons who had, night after night, in nearly all their fpeeches, when he was in office, and conducting his India Bill through the Houfe, attacked him, and charged him with having given himfelf the nomination of the perfons who were to act under the bill, when he rofe up as Secretary of State, and fuggefted their names for the election of the Houfe, at this moment contending that to deliver Treafury lifts was no interference of the miniftry, and that the minds of gentlemen were left as free, as before they faw thofe lifts.   When he had the honour to ftand up in his place, and nominate Earl Fitzwilliam, Mr. Montague, and the other great and refpectable characters, who were to have been in the commiffion inftituted by his India Bill, was it not again and again faid to him, by the honourable gentleman, and all round him at that time, " You are nominating " your own *creatures*; you talk of the Houfe of Commons

Mr. Fox

" making

" their election; the majority of the House of Commons
" always vote with the Minister on great public points, and
" consequently the Minister who nominates within these
" walls, elects, and not the House of Commons!" This
language had been so often urged, that no man who heard it
at the time could have forgotten it, nor would any man, he
believed, be hardy enough to deny it. Where was the difference between his standing up publicly as a Secretary of State
and nominating, taking upon himself at the same time the
responsibility for so doing, and the Treasury's nominating,
by circulation of lists, except indeed the difference between
open and occult, between public and avowed, secret and concealed nomination? That the Treasury had *compelled* gentlemen to vote for any given list of names, Mr. Fox declared
he would not say; but he would say, they had *canvassed*, and
the event shewed that their canvass had been successful; for
though there had been *fifty-seven* names returned upon the
issue of the ballot, the whole *forty* that the canvassing lists
contained, were, he observed, in the number. Nor was it to
be wondered at that the Treasury canvass had proved successful; for, notwithstanding the ridiculous arguments and assertions urged and maintained by the honourable gentleman and
the honourable Baronet above him, that the House were not to
be influenced by a Minister, daily experience proved that they
were; and that they were, he should never be afraid to assert,
without meaning to cast a slur upon the House or any part
of it. The delivery of written lists was, indeed, the ordinary
mode of canvass adopted without doors, on various occasions;
but, however decent in those, it was highly indecent in the
recent instance of the preceding day. The accusation of
his having neglected his duty in not balloting, it was sufficient to answer, by professing himself an avowed enemy to almost every part of the bill; and therefore he would not (and
who, in reason could) expect it to meet with the least support.

Mr. Drake, junior.　Mr. *Drake*, junior, argued in favour of the supposed essential difference between publicly and officially nominating in
the manner the right honourable gentleman had done, when
Secretary of State, and the delivering out lists of names
anonymously in the manner complained of. He thought
there was no want of decorum in that, though he had seen
a want of decorum in those who had deserted their duty and
avoided the ballot. He said that he stood in a peculiar predicament, with regard to the subject of which he treated, but
he would nevertheless contend that those very respectable
gentlemen who balloted, had done themselves great honour.
The paper in question had not influenced him; he was the
spaniel of no Minister, the invariably attached adherent of no
party.

party. He would not fetch and carry for either, but might fay of himfelf in the language of a familiar motto, " *Nullius in verba.*" As to the India bill of the right honourable gentleman (Mr. Fox) although he met it as a *cordial opponent*, candour obliged him to allow that, in *fome* good effects, it *might* have furpaffed his.

Mr. *Martin* faid, that when the right honourable gentle- **Mr. Martin.** man canvaffed for Weftminfter, he believed, he thought it neceffary to do fomething more than barely write his name on a piece of paper, and leave it with the party canvaffed. He had expected fomething ludicrous when he faw the honourable gentleman rife to make his motion, but was more convinced he had been fporting with the Houfe, when he witneffed the folemn gravity with which the motion had been feconded. Mr. Martin declared that he had received one of the papers containing forty names; that it had not influenced his ballot in the leaft; and that he thought it would be an idle piece of bufinefs to have their old fervant brought from the door and placed at the bar of the Houfe.

Mr. *Francis* anfwered, that he was not aware of having **Mr. Francis.** difcovered more gravity than ufual when he feconded the motion—but be this as it might, the wit of the honourable gentleman would, doubtlefs, opperate upon him as an antidote to all ferioufnefs,

Mr. *Sheridan*, cenfuring the miftatements of his argument, **Mr. Sheridan.** complained of the right honourable gentleman's having pointed him out as as a perfon apt to treat that Houfe with infult and contempt. Nothing, he added, could be farther from his intentions, and as he had not the great abilities, the power, the influence of office, nor the other circumftances that right honourable gentleman poffeffed, to recommend him to the good opinion of the Houfe, the right honourable gentleman, he hoped, would not take from him his only poffeffion, a moft fincere refpect for the Houfe and all its members. Mr. Sheridan added, that he differed in one point from his right honourable friend near him; he meant to have balloted, though an enemy to the bill, but he had been prevented by accident.

The *Attorney General* begged leave to remind gentlemen of a **The Attorney General** fact which they feemed to have either forgotten or overlooked; and this was, that the Houfe of Commons did not, in reality, elect the Court of Judicature; they did not even elect fuch of their own members as were to make a part of it. The act directed them to return forty or more, of whom they chofe by ballot to return; and if they returned more than forty, another election by ballot vefted in the hands of the Judges, determine who the forty fhould be.

Mr.

Mr. Jolliffe.

Mr. *Jolliffe* contended, that the beſt way for the right honourable and learned gentlemen, and thoſe near them, to prove their own arguments, and to rivet conviction upon the Houſe, that the complaint was frivolous and ill founded, would be to call the doorkeeper to the bar, and proceed to his examination.

Mr. Vanſittart.

Mr. *Vanſittart* remarked, that he truſted the conduct of the Houſe, in reſpect to the ballot, as well as the very reſpectable names returned, would give pefect ſatisfaction in India, and convince the Britiſh ſubjects in that part of the world, as well as the natives, that an impartial Court of Judicature was inſtituted.

At length the queſtion was put, and the Houſe divided, when the numbers were,

Ayes	38
Noes	138

The Houſe being reſumed,

Mr. Sheridan.

Mr. *Sheridan* expreſſed his wiſhes, that the motion concerning the procedings, reſpecting the proposed plan of fortifying the dock-yards, would not occaſion much debate, or even meet with reſiſtance; but, previous to his making it, he ſhould imagine it would prove right to call gentlemen's attention back to the ſituation in which the Houſe ſtood at that moment, in reſpect to the ſubject. They would pleaſe to recollect that the Miniſter having given them to underſtand that, previous to their being called upon to vote, that the 50,000l. granted towards fortifications to be erected for the defence of the dock-yards in 1784, ſhould be ſo applied, the whole matter ſhould be referred to a Board of General Officers, naval as well as military, to inquire into the nature of the plan proposed, the poſſibility of doing without it, the neceſſity for having it, the wiſdom and policy of adopting it, and the expence which it would ultimately incur. He ſhould, alſo, beg leave to remind the Houſe of the turn of the argument of the right honourable gentleman, on the preceding Friday, when he formally announced his expectation, that when the Ordnance eſtimates were voted this ſeſſion, the application of the 50,000l. in hand would be deſired; at that time the right honourable gentleman had ſaid, that the Houſe would not now have the bare word of an individual, or of any Miniſter to rely on; but the report and unanimous opinion of a Board of the moſt reſpectable nature ever inſtituted, a Board compoſed of the firſt characters, in the naval and military line, now in being. What then (added Mr. Sheridan) was his aſtoniſhment, and what muſt have been the aſtoniſhiment of the Houſe, to find an honourable General, a member of that Board, riſe in his place and flatly contradict the right honourable gentleman, by denying that the reſult of the opinons

to

of that Board had been such as the right honourable gentleman had described, or that those opinions warranted any such declaration as he had advanced.

The right honourable gentleman had risen a second time and put the matter in issue between him and the honourable General; challenging the judgement of the House, and calling upon them to decide who was right and who wrong in his assertion? Where was the possibility for the House to judge, without either evidence or means of directing their determination? Assertion stood against assertion; and they, altogether uninformed as to the real merits of the fact in issue, and perfectly in the dark, were desired to decide? This was so obviously absurd, that he should have imagined, when the right honourable gentleman put the matter in issue, he would, of himself, have furnished those who were called upon to give judgement, with the means of forming their opinion: as he had not proceeded thus far, he meant to do it by his motion of that day, but concluding, that a great deal of matter improper to be laid before the House, might be contained in the detail of the Report of the Board of Naval and Military Officers, he had cautiously foreborne to make his motion too extensive; and had worded it so as to empower Ministers to lay such parts only of what papers the motion called for, before the House, as might be placed upon the table with the greatest safety to the State. If, however, his motion, in its present form, was to be found objectionable, and less objectionable words could be suggested, he would readily adopt them; and if the papers were furnished, and bore out the right honourable gentleman in his assertion, he would, for one, abandon all idea of opposing the proposal to suffer the money to be applied to fortifications. In conclusion, Mr. Sheridan moved for a copy of the appointment of the Board of Naval and Military Officers, of such parts of their instructions, and of their Report, as His Majesty's discretion might deem proper to be made public with perfect consistency to the safety of the State.

Mr. Windham seconded the motion.

Mr. Chancellor *Pitt* remarked, that he had listened to the observations of the honourable gentleman with more pleasure and congeniality of sentiment than he expected either to receive or feel; yet, though he joined with him in the main object of his argument, he must protest against some particular parts in which he could not think the honourable gentleman perfectly correct in his statement. Notwithstanding that he could not subscribe to the opinion of the honourable gentleman, that the whole of the instructions given by His Majesty to the Board of Officers might with safety be

M. Chancellor Pitt.

be made public; because, in many inftances, thofe inftructions went to very delicate points, and were of a nature likely to give information to thofe who might be our enemies in future, as would prove highly dangerous and detrimental; nay, as they were in fome cafes more delicate in their nature than even the Report itfelf, becaufe there were many fuggeftions in them which the Report did not anfwer, the Board of Officers having found a better method of coming at the Report: yet ftill, fuch parts of the Report as could with propriety be laid before the Houfe, it was highly neceffary it fhould be in poffeffion of, nor fhould he, by any means, endeavour to withhold them. He had certainly, as the honourable gentleman mentioned on a former day, objected to a motion which feemed calculated to give the Houfe information; but his reafon for doing fo was not to prevent information from being obtained, but becaufe the queftion propofed was in fact nugatory; as it required the commiffion appointing the Duke of Richmond, Prefident of the Board of Officers, to be produced, whereas no fuch commiffion had ever been made out; the inftrument by which his Grace had been appointed being the King's letter, and the fame method had alfo been ufed to conftitute the other members of the Board. He was furprifed to find, that the honourable gentleman had entertained an idea, that it was intended to have concealed the names of the gentlemen who comprifed the Board of Officers; for, if he remembered rightly, he had, on a former occafion, in fpeaking of the bufinefs, relied on the merit and refpectability of the members, as one of the fureft pledges of the juftnefs and accuracy of their Report, and of the advantage arifing from this confideration, the friends of the fortifications would be deprived, were the names of the gentlemen to be concealed. It did not appear requifite for him to fay any thing more on the Report of the Board, and the different points to which it went, than he had already troubled the Houfe with upon a former occafion, when he ftated, that it had been referred to the Board to report, whether a naval force fingly could give fuch effectual fecurity to our dock-yards as the nation might rely upon, with confidence in the event of a future war; whether fuch a fecurity could be obtained by the affiftance of an army alone, or by means of a naval and land force combined? To thofe queftions the Board had directly and fpecifically anfwered — That thofe invaluable parts of the kingdom could not be fufficiently fecured by either of the fuggefted modes of defence, not even by both conjoined, without the affiftance of fortifications.

He trufted that no arguments were now wanting to prove, that it was in the moft ftrict conftruction of the opinion of
the

the Board of Officers, that the measure was now brought forward, and that their opinion was explicitly and clearly in its favour. As to what the honourable gentleman thought proper to observe touching the sentiments of the honourable General behind him, he must beg leave to contend, that in this point, he had been extremely incorrect. The honourable General had by no means even hinted, that the opinion of the Board was averse from the system of fortification; but only declared, that their opinion was not, in his judgement, in favour of the measure to the extent in which he had stated it. On this part of the question, however, he and the honourable General were at issue, and the papers to be laid before the House would prove sufficient to determine which of them was in the right. Concerning the expence of those works that were proposed, he must appeal to the House, whether it had been the complection and character of his political and ministerial conduct, to regard with indifference the interests of the revenue, and the duties of public œconomy? Yet still anxious as he was to exert himself to the utmost in favour of those great objects (and he hoped that it would shortly appear, that his exertions had been attended with considerable success) he could, by no means consent, although for the very tempting prospect of diminishing the public debt, or relieving the burdens of the people, to abandon an object of greater moment, than even the diminution of the debt or the relief of the subject—the necessary defence of those naval magazines, our dock yards.—— He was glad to hear from the honourable gentleman a declaration that did him so much honour, as that he was ready to pledge himself, that if he should, on inspecting the papers now moved for, find, that the business stood upon the footing he had represented it, or sanctioned by the opinion of the Board of Officers fairly and clearly collected, he would then abandon his opposition—and for his part he was equally desirous of coming forward to meet the honourable gentleman with a similar pledge, which was — that if it should appear, that the Report of the Board of Officers did not fully and explicitly justify the measure, he would himself entirely relinquish it, nor should he in that case require a shilling from Parliament to carry it into execution. Upon the whole, he was so perfectly of the honourable gentleman's opinion, with regard to his motion, that he had prepared one of almost an exactly similar tendency, which he should propose to the honourable gentleman to adopt instead of his own, not because it was better adapted to the purpose, or any way properer in itself, but because in one instance it was more accurate in point of form, because it requested His Majesty to lay before the House the circular letters by which the Board had been constituted; whilst, on the other hand, the motion of the honourable gentleman, in consequence of his not possessing the fullest intelligence relating to the subject, required the commission, when, to speak truly, it was not in being.

General *Burgoyne* observed that he had listened with great pleasure to the generality of the arguments of the right honourable gentleman who spoke last. He was happy to find the matter in issue between them was likely to come fairly before the House. There was only one point in doubt with him. The whole of the instructions to the Board, in his opinion, might be laid on the table with perfect safety to the State. In the Report, he admitted, was much matter, of which the nature rendered it improper to be made public. With regard to the sentiments of the members of the Board upon the points submitted to their judgement, unless the whole was before the House, it was impossible for the House to determine justly, because cases, hypothetically put, admitted only of a direct answer, given under the admission of the hypothesis, whether probable or barely possible; instead of which, the House ought to have before them all the *data*, that they might judge whether the case, put hypothetically, was a case sufficiently within probability to deserve attention. He would by no means betray any state secret, or be guilty of a breach of the confidence under the seal of which he stood as a member of the Board in question, but, without incurring the imputation of speaking unguardedly or dangerously, he would say, that several of the cases submitted were mere *postulata*, and hypothetically as extravagant as if it were asked, Suppose, by some strange convulsion of nature, the straits between Dover and Calais should be no more, but that the coasts should meet and unite, would it not be politic, expedient, and absolutely necessary, to fortify the isthmus, or neck of land, between France and England? Absurd in the extreme as this hypothesis must be, several which were submitted to the Board appeared to him to have been equally extravagant and improbable: in short, so much beyond all bounds of reason, that it would be madness for that House to vote away the public money to a large amount, merely because to such hypothetical cases an unanimous opinion in the affirmative had been given. He had ever entertained an high opinion of the military skill of the noble Duke at the head of the Ordnance; but he had found him more expert and scientific in engineering than his partiality had suggested, insomuch, that he himself, though he had spent a great part of his life in the practice of tactics, and all the attendant circumstances, had returned from the Board with more lights upon the subject of engineering than he had carried with him to it. His opinion of the noble Duke,

therefore,

therefore, as a military character, was much heightened; and, in what he might in future find it neceſſary to ſay, he begged he might not be ſuppoſed to mean any thing perſonal. He ſhould, hereafter, probably take the liberty of troubling the Houſe much more at length with his opinion on the ſub-ject, and therefore it might not be amiſs to lay in his claim, when the inſtructions came before the Houſe, to treat them as freely as the King's ſpeech, generally conſidered there as the ſpeech of the Miniſter, was cuſtomarily treated in that Houſe. In ſupport of this claim, he muſt beg leave to remark that there was a mode of forming a ſyllogiſm by multiplying and branching out the main propoſition into numerous poſitions, and placing it in a variety of points of view by means of quſtions ſo put, that human reaſon could not withhold their affir-mative aſſent to any one of them, and yet every man's mind muſt deny the general reſult deduced.   And, upon this occa-ſion, he flattered himſelf that the Houſe would give him cre-dit for not conſidering the queſtion relative to fortificaticns with any party impreſſion or bias. The queſtion was beyond the reach of party, it was, in *his* mind, the moſt important and the moſt intereſting, whether conſidered as an official, a financial, or a conſtitutional queſtion, that ever came before Parliament. He, who made it a party queſtion, was unworthy to be he heard upon it.   In concluſion, General Burgoyne begged leave to know whether Adminiſtation deſigned to give the Houſe the whole of the inſtructions, or only a detached part.

Mr. *Chancellor Pitt* anſwered, that he muſt beg leave to contend that the argument of the honourable General was ſo far fetched as not to be capable of illuſtration, except by ſuppoſing a convulſion of nature, or ſo abſurd an event as the junction of Dover and Calais, by a new created iſthmus.— Could the Houſe poſſibly imagine that the moſt reſpectable Board of land and ſea officers that ever ſat were likely to be impoſed upon by ſuch frivolous and viſionary hypotheſes.— As for the honourable General himſelf, all, acquainted with his unrivalled ſkill in all the departments of literature, as well as of war, knew very well that no logical ſubtjlty could poſ-ſibly ſo far triumph over his reaſon, at to lead him on through a ſeries of inquiry and inveſtigation by means of ſuch data and hypotheſes as were in themſelves undeniable and ſelf evident, but which tended to a concluſion, which, though it could not be refuted by argument, the mind was yet *deter-mined* to deny.—And it was ſtill more inexplicable how ſuch an impoſition could be practiſed under the direction of a per-ſon who, high as he before ſtood in the opinion of the honou-rable General, was raiſed ſtill higher by his conduct at that Board; and from whom, enlightened as the honourable Gene-ral's ral's mind had already been, he had received fresh elucidation and improvement.—With respect to the honourable General's assertion that the report of the Board was founded upon imaginary cases, he felt himself justified in replying, that he was ready to meet him upon this ground; for, though there were many hypotheses submitted to them, yet, upon the grand question of the necessity and propriety of the fortifications, their opinions were unqualified and specific. Nay, the Report itself, (and that in a part of it where the Board were unanimous, and which of course must have had the consent of the honourable General) did arrange the subject matter of their inquiry in such a manner, as should extend it to such objects, and such objects alone, as were necessary for their discussion.

Mr. Fox.   Mr. *Fox* declared, that he had entertained the hope that the candid observations of his honourable friend (General Burgoyne) would have met with that liberal species of animadversion which he really thought they deserved. There was nothing which had fallen from him which seemed to justify either the expression or insinuation that he had been led, step by step, from deduction, to a result which he was determined not to admit. Nobody would suspect that he was inclined to speak disrespectfully of his relations, but he knew the manner of reasoning of the noble Duke who presided at the board, and that it was his method to lead the mind insensibly through the medium of certain propositions which it might not be disposed to controvert, unwarily to conclusions in which it could not acquiesce.

Captain Bowyer.   Captain *Bowyer* expressed his disapprobation of the production of the papers intended to be laid before the House. He was suspicious they would convey information to the natural enemies of this country.

Captain Macbride.   Captain *Macbride* was of opinion, that nothing was to be dreaded from this circumstance. He was firmly convinced, that the safety of this country depended so much on its naval force, and so little on its external fortification, that he did not care though all the papers which belonged to this Board of Inquiry were lodged for inspection in the Marine Office at Paris.

Mr. Sheridan's motion was then withdrawn, and the Chancellor of the Exchequer's substituted in its place, which was carried unanimously.

Mr. Fox.   Mr. *Fox* hoped the Ordnance estimates would not be brought forward in consequence of the production of the above papers on Monday, as originally intended.

Mr. Chancellor Pitt.   Mr. *Chancellor Pitt* did not wish to urge this point, but saw reason for postponing it to a more distant period than Wednesday.

Mr. Courtenay.   Mr. *Courtenay* moved for the production of the copy of the estimates of the engineers at Portsmouth, for building the forti-

tifications, together with the Report thereon of the engineers
of the Tower, which was agreed to *nem. con.*
Adjourned.

Friday, 17th February.

Mr. *Jenkinson* remarked, that, having on a preceding day Mr. Jen-
intimated his earneft wifhes to draw the attention of the kinfon.
Houfe to a fubject of much importance to the commerce of
this country, he muft now beg leave to afk if it was their
pleafure that he fhould open his motion, or defer it to another occafion. [Here fome gentlemen cried out " hear him,"
and he immediately proceeded.] He faid that the bufinefs to
which he alluded referred to two fubjects, both of which
were intimately connected. Firft, the intercourfe between
His Majefty's Weft-India iflands and the United States of
North America; and fecondly, the intercourfe between the
faid United States and His Majefty's European dominions.
Very heavy and violent complaints had been made, as well
by the people of Jamaica and the other iflands in the Weft
Indies as by their agents here, againft the reftrictions, confining the importation into thofe iflands by Britifh-built
veffels navigated according to law; nor could he adopt an
eafier mode of proving how groundlefsly the complaints were
urged, than by informing the Houfe what the operation of
thefe regulations was. The imports into Jamaica, during
the laft three years, were one third greater than in any of
the laft feven years previous to the war. Bread and flour fo
abounded in the ifland, notwithftanding the hurricane, that
the Governor was obliged to iffue an order prohibiting the exportation of provifions to any of the neighbouring foreign
iflands; a needlefs injunction, if they themfelves had not enjoyed plenty at the moment. In the exportation of rum
alfo, the ten laft years became by far the moft profperous.
Lumber, ftaves, and fuch other articles as fell under the defcription of allowed imports, were likewife as abundant as
ever, though fomewhat dearer, becaufe they came dearer now
to the Americans themfelves. Thefe were certainly very
agreeable effects of the regulations, but their political advantages to this country were equally great. Exclufive of
the fecurity and fatisfaction which the merchants of this
country muft experience from difcovering that when they
did not fupply the freight, they had at leaft the advantage of
ufing their own veffels; they had reafon to exult over the
employment of an additional body of no lefs than 4000 feamen, and upwards of 700 veffels, and to confider fuch a
circumftance as of the higheft public utility. There were,
however, two reafons which induced him, on the prefent occafion, rather to fuffer the power to remain with His Majefty

jefty to continue the regulations, than to bring them to a final conclusion by an act of Parliament. He understood (not from official information, but from report) that there was another petition, now signed by the inhabitants of Jamaica, against the continuance of this system, which he would not preclude from discussion by a previous determination; rather wishing that all those who affixed to it their signatures might enjoy more time to become reconciled to the measures by the extension of its benefits and the assurance of its advantages. With respect to the more important, or, at least, more intricate, confideration of the state of our commerce with the United States of North America, he should observe, that their vessels, notwithstanding their separation from this country, were not only on a footing with the vessels of the most favoured nation, but absolutely on equal terms with those of our own subjects. They resorted to our harbours precisely under the same advantages, except, perhaps, that, after foreign voyages, they underwent somewhat of a more strict examination. On the other hand, their return for these favours was of the most extraordinary kind, as there was no country against which their prohibitions were so severe, or their conduct so violent. He felt an ardent wish that these might meet with full leisure and ample time to confider how much their own interest depended on the encouragement of British commerce. With Portugal they had no trade, and still less with Spain. In the Mediterranean they could not venture from too well-grounded apprehensions of the corsairs; and, almost with the individual exception of tobacco, their principal articles were not, by the words of the treaty, to be imported either into Old France or any of its islands. But the circumstance of all others the most singular and striking was, that, although deprived of any other market for their salt fish, except through the British settlements, they refused to suffer British vessels to go for the purpose of buying of them this commodity. Having mentioned the instructions sent by various States to the general Congress, relative to an arrangement of commerce with Great Britain, the majority of which were extremely absurd; and, of all others, the most ridiculous was that of one State, which recommends articles to be signed whenever Congress were unanimous on the subject, Mr. Jenkinson expressed his earnest hopes that matters might remain in their present state, at least for another year, and therefore begged leave to move, " That an act, made in the twenty-third year of " the reign of His present Majesty, entitled, ' An Act for " preventing certain Instruments from being required from " Ships belonging to the United States of America; and to " give to His Majesty, for a limited Time, certain Powers

                                                        " for

" for the better carrying on 'Trade and Commerce between
" the Subjects of His Majesty's Dominions and the Inhabi-
" tants of the said United States,' might be read ;" and the
same was read accordingly.

Mr. Jenkinson next moved, " That an act, made in the
" twenty-fourth year of the reign of His present Majesty,
" entitled, ' An Act to extend the Powers of an Act, made
" in the twenty-third Year of His present Majesty, for
" giving His Majesty certain Powers for the better carrying
" on Trade and Commerce between the Subjects of His
" Majesty's Dominions and the Inhabitants of the United
" States of America, to the Trade and Commerce of this
" Kingdom with the British Colonies and Plantations in
" America, with respect to certain Articles therein men-
" tioned,' might be read ;" and the same being read accordingly, it was ordered, That leave be given to bring in a bill,
for farther continuing the said acts, for a time to be limited;
and that Mr. Jenkinson, Mr. Attorney General, and Mr.
Solicitor General, do prepare and bring in the same.

Mr. *Burke* now rose, and requested that the Journals of   Mr. Burke.
the year 1782 might be consulted for the forty-fourth and
forty-fifth resolutions of the 29th of May. These were
now read, and are as follow :

" That for the purpose of conveying entire conviction to
" the minds of the native princes, that to commence hosti-
" lities without just provocation against them, and to pursue
" schemes of conquest and extent of dominion, are measures
" repugnant to the wish, the honour, and the policy of this
" nation, the Parliament of Great Britain should give some
" signal mark of its displeasure against those, in whatever
" degree entrusted with the charge of the East-India Com-
" pany's affairs, who shall appear wilfully to have adopted
" or countenanced a system tending to inspire a reasonable
" distrust of the moderation, justice, and good faith of the
" British nation."

" That Warren Hastings, Esquire, Governor General of
" Bengal, and William Hornsby, Esquire, President of the
" Council at Bombay, having, in sundry instances, acted in
" a manner repugnant to the honour and policy of this na-
" tion, and thereby brought great calamities on India, and
" enormous expences on the East-India Company, it is the
" duty of the Directors of the said Company to pursue all
" legal and effectual means for the removal of the said Go-
" vernor General and President from their respective offices,
" and to recal them to Great Britain."

Mr. Burke now said, that it was not without considerable
uneasiness that he discovered that the task of introducing to
the attention of the House the solemn and important business
                                                          of

of the day was on the point of falling to his lot, when (as
all to whom he had the honour of addreffing himfelf would
certainly allow) it might have been brought forward, in the
plentitude of weight and efficacy, by the right honourable
member, (Mr. Dundas) whofe propofitions were the very
bafis of the refolution, the contents of which had only in
the preceding moment been recited. A party, of all others,
the moft interefted in the awful progrefs and ultimate refult
of any proceedings which might arife, had, with becoming
dignity of character, called firmly on him to advance his
charges; and fo pointed was the nature of his invocation,
that it rendered it impoffible for him to evade the execution
of his duty. Under thefe circumftances, moft feelingly did
he lament, that, as the unwelcome confequence of a devolution, caufed partly by the natural demife of fome, the political deceafe of others, and, in particular cafes, a death to
virtue and to principle, he fhould now remain alone engaged
in the attempt to keep the honour and the confiftency of the
Houfe in their unfullied luftre, to impart vigour to its intentions, and to facilitate and fix the efficacy of a fentence,
fubfequent to the paffing of which a period of four years had
actually elapfed. On the prefent occafion, he trufted that,
in common juftice, he fhould not be confidered in any other
character than as the mere agent of the Houfe, who, at the
very time to which he referred, had fixed upon Mr. Haftings as an object of their particularly marked and formal accufations. His province, therefore, was fubordinate, confining him within the neceffary endeavour to accelerate the
accomplifhment of a point aimed at moft indubitably by the
Houfe, and which ought, perhaps, much earlier to have
been fulfilled. Whofoever acted under the fanction of the
authority of the Houfe might certainly, without arrogance,
affert a claim to its protection, as far at leaft as the word
protection would bear to be interpreted as that candid and
honourable conftruction of a procedure to which all, determined upon the pureft and moft unaffailable adherences to
what they deemed a rectitude of conduct, were thoroughly
entitled. For the purpofe of rendering the whole Houfe
(but more efpecially its new-elected members) poffeffed of a
full idea concerning the nature of every preceding vote which
bore affinity to the tranfactions and affairs of India, he muft
beg the favour of carrying the recollection of thofe to whom
he had the honour of addreffing himfelf to matters of a re-
moter date; a review, during which, fenfible of the impropriety of trefpaffing too long upon their attention, he fhould
confult as much as poffible a brevity in his defcriptions.—
They might remember that, during the courfe of the year
1764, or, at leaft, near to that period, the Eaft-India Com-

pany difpatched Lord Clive to their fettlements in that quarter, for the purpofe of there becoming inftrumental to the introduction and eftablifhment of certain principles of Government, then regarded as indifpenfably requifite for preferving, in lefs precarious fecurity, and amidft the influence of a wifer policy, the territorial poffeffions of Great Britain. The fucceffes of this noble Lord furpaffed even the fanguine expectations of thofe who were inclined to give him credit for achievements of the firft importance; and with fuch aftonifhing rapidity did the moft extenfive and rich domains of this almoft completely vanquifhed region become appurtenances to our Eaft-India Company, that mankind were left at a lofs whether moft to wonder at the fudden inundations of profperity, or the at-once-accumulated riches which marked the brilliancy and vigour of its exiftence. From this æra did opulence bring forward one of its too cuftomary and baneful effects, by throwing open all the channels of ungovernable corruption. The moft enormous abufes were in a moment piled, each upon the other, till every fpot of Britifh territories in the Eaft Indies became a fhocking theatre of that variety of crimes, to which the luft of avarice and ambition fo frequently impels the worthlefs part of human kind. Difgrace became naturally interwoven with the commiffion of enormities; the honour of Englifhmen not only loft its luftre, but received an ignominious ftain; and, whilft the Princes of the Eaft confidered with deteftation the violent and unpardonable meafures of the fubjects of Great Britain, the States of Europe, with equal indications of abhorrence, adopted and difperfed their fentiments. When Lord Clive returned to England, it was deemed abfolutely requifite to inveft, with the prefidency of the Council at Calcutta, and the governorfhip of Bengal, fome perfon to whom the principles of Government in the Eaft Indies, as arranged and confolidated into a fyftem by the noble Peer, were not barely intimately known, but perfectly congenial; and, doubtlefs, it was for this reafon that Mr. Warren Haftings became removed from Madras to the government of Bengal. In this train, the tendency of which was obvious, affairs proceeded, until the Parliament, grown fenfible of the neceffity of fcrutinizing their merits by the moft ferious and ample inveftigations, threw open and continued their inquiries concerning the actual ftate, whether upon a general or a particular ground, of the Company in the Eaft Indies. From one period to another, feveral Committees were appointed; and various proceedings alfo took place, in confequence of their Reports. At laft, during a moment, which was the dreadful prelude to one of the bittereft and moft difgraceful to the national misfortunes, the war againft America burft forth;

yet, even through the continuation of hoftilities, upon our fide, at once frantic and ineffectual, the fituation of affairs in the Eaft Indies, far from having been forgotten, became a frequent object of the clofe attention of the Houfe of Commons, who, in the year 1781, thought fit to eftablifh, in two feparate and totally diftinct departments, a Secret and a Select Committee. A right honourable and learned gentleman (Mr. Dundas) was, upon this occafion, placed at the head of the Secret Committee; and particularly, from his inveftigations and propofitions, had refulted a well-known ftring of refolutions, from amongft which he (Mr. Burke) had juft felected one concerning Warren Haftings and William Hornby, Efquires; a refolution not couched in terms which could at all fuffer even the flighteft equivocal interpretation, but conveying againft them, as powerfully as it was poffible for words to point the meaning, the moft direct accufation of negligence of duty, and of improper proceedings throughout the courfe of their enjoyment of high official fituations. Surely it was a theme for univerfal aftonifhment, that when the right honourable and learned gentleman had difcovered, from an acute and indefatigable inveftigation of occurrences, that even every tittle of this ftriking refolution was grounded upon the ftrong foundations of the moft unanfwerable truths, he fhould, with a degree of coldnefs almoft approaching to indifference, have remained contented with the inactive fequel of his great and arduous tafk which, at its conclufion, (diffimilar, indeed, from its extraordinary and fpirited beginning and procedure!) funk into little more than a faint perfuafion to the Houfe to adopt and vote the refolution. An honourable gentleman (General Smith) at prefent not enjoying a feat among the Commons, moved, on a former occafion, for the Select Committee, when another honourable gentleman (Secretary to the Board of Control) feconded the motion : and, certainly, it would have appeared becoming in this honourable gentleman, if he had fubmitted the matter to the ferious attention, and not have left him (Mr. Burke) to engage in a matter which was more peculiarly and immediately his own province. Of the Select Committee (Mr. Burke added) that he was an unworthy member; but he could venture to affert, that although he, or even his affociates, might have been outftripped by others in thofe vigorous and deeply-fcrutinizing powers of the mind, fo greatly beneficial when it is neceffary to unravel a vaft and intricate combination of occurrences, at once important and alarming, yet no perfons whatfoever could have exceeded them in zeal and affiduity. From the moft unabated and ardent attention, manifefted by the Committees to every point fubmitted to their opinion, had arifen an immenfe and well-digefted body of

evidence,

evidence, forming, indeed, a moſt voluminous pile of Reports for the table of the Houſe, yet not leſs than highly intereſting throughout every part of its amazing bulk, although the labours of any ſeven preceding Committees had fallen conſiderably ſhort of ſo extended and comprehenſive an arrangement.   That ſuch abſolutely was the caſe could not, in fair argument, be diſproved, even by a noble and learned Lord, highly diſtinguiſhed on aecount of the pre-eminence of his office, yet more an object of celebrity as being in the full vigour of great influence, and extraordinary talents; nor leſs conſpicuous as *keeper of the royal conſcience*; in which ſingular and exalted character he thought proper to obſerve, in an auguſt aſſembly, that the Reports of this Houſe concerning the ſituation of affairs in the Eaſt Indies, were ſcarcely of more conſideration than *idle fables*; thus treating them like the fanciful adventures of Robinſon Cruſoe, or the wild chimeras of any writers of romance!   But neither wit nor ridicule, from howſoever brilliant or venerated a quarter they might proceed, could invalidate the nature and force of theſe Reports; and therefore, in defiance of either the keen ſeverity of raillery at once unmerited and groundleſs, or the impoſing plauſibility of an inſidious ſtile of argument, ſhould he reſt his own particular accuſation againſt Mr. Haſtings, as a delinquent of the firſt magnitude, upon the united authority of the very heavy charges to which he ſtands expoſed in theſe Reports, and of the ſtring of reſolutions remaining upon the journals of the twenty-eighth of May, in the year 1782; a matter which, coolly and impartially conſidered, muſt totally exempt him from the imputation of preſſing more upon the attention of the Houſe than they already had admitted and declared.   One ſtriking proof that the Commons of Great Britain had not, amidſt their inveſtigations of the affairs and occurrences in the Eaſt Indies, proceeded with either precipitation or wantonneſs, or without the moſt deliberate and ſound advice, and that their labours were deemed entitled to very high regard, might fairly be deduced (in fact, the premiſes would not admit a different concluſion) from the honourable manner in which, at the cloſe of the ſeſſion of 1782, the ſubject was recommended, in a ſpeech from the Throne, as calling for the ſtricteſt parliamentary inveſtigations.   Nor did this example ſtand long alone.   It was followed by a ſecond, not leſs pointed and convincing, when, from the ſame exalted quarter, expreſſions, particularly gracious, were dropped, in favour of the progreſs made by the Houſe, at the opening of the enſuing ſeſſion, with reſpect to an examination into the nature of meaſures and occurrences in the Eaſt Indies.   Having read to the Houſe the extracts from the ſpeeches in queſtion, Mr. Burke remarked, that they

ought

ought to operate as an irresistible incitement to their following up the point until they should have detected every various delinquency, and brought the most criminal offenders
to exemplary atonements.   In explanation of the process
whereon he meant to enter with respect to Mr. Hastings,
against whom, with a degree of warmth amounting to an appearance of defiance, he had been loudly called upon to advance his accusation, (and against whom he certainly should
advance it, were the papers for which he meant to move
thrown open to his inspection,) he must beg leave to remind
the House, that three several examples of the mode of proceeding against state delinquents were on record; and that,
according to the exigencies of particular cases, each had been,
at different periods, adopted.   The first was a direction to
the Attorney General to prosecute.   From this measure,
Mr. Burke said, he must acknowledge himself totally averse,
because he had reason to believe that the honourable and
learned gentleman, now vested in that high official situation,
to which his truly respectable character and professional abilities rendered him equal, in every sense of the expression, did
not discover any zealous inclination to support the point in
question, and bring it forward under the weight and sanction
of his powers, to impress the House with a due sense of the
measures which it behoved them to pursue, in order to bring
delinquents (should such be found) to signal punishments:
nor, indeed, did he conceive that a trial by jury was, of all
others, the most unexceptionable and best-devised for the
purpose of obtaining ample justice against an offender so great
and elevated (if opulence, talents and connections could ele-
vate) as the person whom he felt it as his duty, on this occasion, to pursue.   As little was he prepossessed in favour of
an application to the Court of King's Bench, from an idea,
that the magnitude of the trial (which he anxiously wished
to have brought forward in that shape, which would the most
certainly facilitate the progress and ultimate decisions of impartial justice) would overwhelm the varying multitude of
lesser causes of *meum* and *tuum*, assault and battery, conver-
sion and trover, trespass and burglary, together with an in-
numerable tribe of different misdemeanors.   Contending,
therefore, (as he described himself) against the mode of prosecuting through the Attorney General, against a trial by
jury, and against the institution of a suit in the Court of
King's Bench, it might naturally be asked, whether he would
wish to introduce a bill of pains and penalties, and to collect
the evidence which such a mode might render requisite?
To this question he should not hesitate to reply, that the procedure must press, with the severity of injustice, upon the
party prosecuted, and tarnish, in no slight degree, the cha-
                                                        racter

racter and honourable dignity of the Houfe; of which the. members would thus appear to prefent themfelves a motley fet, at one moment in the capacity of accufers, and at another moment in the deciding rank of judges: and, certainly, it appeared an act of violence to force a fuppofed criminal into an anticipation of his defence, and to order him to attend, together with his counfel, at the bar, for the purpofe of ftating (in the prefence of an affembly, the members of which prepofteroufly prefided in the two-fold capacity of ac- cufers and of judges) to what ground he meant to refort for proofs of his innocence, when required to enter upon his ex- culpation in another place; the forms and rules of which, exacting evidences on oath, were more within the fpirit of the cuftomary practice of judicial trials. His invincible ob- jection to a bill of pains and penalties would of courfe lead him to the propofition of another mode; and this, at once antient and conftitutional, was a procedure by a bill of im- peachment; yet, even in the adoption of this meafure, he would not endeavour to introduce the ufual practice of firft moving an immediate bill of impeachment, and next infti- tuting a Committee for the purpofe of difcovering and ar- ranging articles, in order that they might ferve as its foun- dation: a recourfe which, in his humble opinion, carried with it an appearance of warmth and prejudice exceedingly re- pugnant to the juftice, dignity, and honour of the Houfe. With their permiffion, he fhould move for papers, from the contents of which he would endeavour to collect the feveral articles into their neceffary points of view; and when thefe fhould, in the contemplation of the Houfe, feem (as, without rancour, and, in the cool fpirit of impartial juftice, he could venture to intimate his belief that they *would* feem) charges of an atrocious nature, he then defigned to move for an im- peachment at the bar of the Houfe of Lords. This grave and folemn meafure would not only prove congenial with the weight and high authority of the reprefentatives of the Peo- ple of Great Britain, but moft powerfully contribute to the attainment of all the aweful and decifive confequences which could arife from juftice. On this occafion it was fuperfluous to dwell upon the indifputable neceffity of acting with the moft guarded caution and the cooleft impartiality. In the very moment when an accufer brought his charges againft another, was he, in a confiderable degree, himfelf ftanding under a ftate of accufation! Confcious how religioufly he was obliged to act upon the fureft grounds, he chofe the line of conduct to which he now alluded, perfuaded that this, of all others, might be purfued, without the leaft danger of either plunging into error, encroaching upon the purity of law by violent oppreffion, or deviating, in any cafe, from that

invariably

invariably equitable point to which the courfe of real juftice perpetually ran. He lamented (but he felt it unavoidable) that the inquiry muft become perfonal; nor was he *now* to learn, that if, in the prefent inftance, the people of India could be permitted to make a choice, they would prefer procedure, of which the refult might difcover the exiftence of peculation, yet not reveal the peculator; might bring into the face of day the proofs of fcandalous corruption, yet hide equally, from all inquiring eyes, the corruptor and the corrupted; might make it manifeft with what invincible fatality the torrent of outrageous vice broke down and dafhed away each obftacle before it, yet kept the vicious individuals entirely concealed from human penetration; and, in a word, might imitate the verdict of a coroner; declare that murder had taken place; but add, that it was committed by perfons unknown. For the purpofe of tracing peculation to the peculator, corruption to the corruptor, and vice to the vicious, were the various Committees employed from time to time in obedience to the votes and orders of the Houfe; and the refult was, that the Committee, at which a fpirited and truly irreproachable individual (Mr. *Gregory)* prefided, during the courfe of three fucceffive years, *did* (as well as two fubfequent Committees) *declare,* that it was impoffible for the Government in the Eaft Indies to be foul, and the head of Government pure. Under all thefe circumftances, and keeping in his view the refolution of the Houfe accufatory of Mr. Haftings, Mr. Burke declared that he fhould confider himfelf juftified in all his fucceeding motions, of which the firft would be,

" That copies of all correfpondence, fince the month of
" January 1782, between Warren Haftings, Efquire, late
" Governor General of Bengal, and the Court of Directors,
" as well before, as fince the return of the faid Governor
" General, relative to the prefents, and other money, parti-
" cularly received by the faid Governor General, be laid be-
" fore this Houfe."

Mr. Windham feconded this motion.

Alderman *Le Mefurier* confidered it as reprehenfible that the honourable gentleman fhould not have ftated to the Houfe all the papers for which he meant to call; neither had he opened the points to which thofe papers were meant to be applied. This, doubtlefs, was always cuftomary; and indeed common fenfe required that fuch a mode fhould conftantly prevail, as the Houfe would, otherwife, become drawn on, ftep by ftep, till they could not know how to recede, in like manner as they had heard the preceding day of men being deluded by a feries of logical deductions, till they were drawn to a refult which their underftandings denied. The refolutions

Alderman Le Mefurier

tions (unlefs he greatly miftook) had paffed in a very thin Houfe; they ought not therefore to be made the ground of fo ferious a proceeding. Mr. Haftings had proved himfelf a meritorious fervant of the Company, and in giving him that character, he fpoke impartially, as he was a perfect ftranger to Mr. Haftings, and did not even know his perfon; but from all which he had feen of the records of the Company during the two laft years, throughout which period he had been in the direction, he faw no reafon whatever to fuppofe Mr. Haftings fuch a delinquent as the honourable gentleman had thought proper to defcribe him. The honourable gentleman had chofen to indulge himfelf in fome remarks relative to the trial by jury, and therefore, furely after fo public an avowal from that fide of the Houfe of an opinion againft trials by jury, whenever the new court of judicature, inftituted under authority of the Eaft-India bill, fhould fall again under difcuffion, they would not hear the gentlemen on the other fide, expreffing their difapprobation of it in fuch vehement terms, as was their ufual cuftom. In conclufion, the Alderman again expreffed his ardent wifh, that the honourable gentleman would, in common candour, ftate to the Houfe the whole of the papers for which he meant to move.

Mr. *Dundas* remarked, that, previous to their decifion on the prefent fubject, a variety of pointed ftrictures, manifeftly levelled at him during the courfe of the right honourable gentleman's obfervations, induced him, at one time, to imagine that he was himfelf the criminal whom the right honourable gentleman had determined to bring to juftice. He was glad, however, on that occafion, and he fhould always rejoice if gentlemen, when they meant to fay any thing which bore allufion to his conduct, would fay it in that Houfe, and in his prefence, when he might be fuppofed enabled by thefe means to anfwer it, and to make that fort of reply which the accufation might appear to merit. He never was afhamed, nor need he blufh to meet all who had any thing to fay againft him, face to face, and he rather wifhed that they would act in that manly way, and not attack him in anonymous libels, and delufive pamphlets, crammed with falfe and illiberal charges brought againft him behind his back, and circulated with induftry through every corner of the kingdom. From many parts of the right honourable gentleman's fpeech, it appeared, that the right honourable gentleman had been of opinion, (which he, indeed, had freely communicated to the Houfe,) that *he* ought to have been the perfon who fhould have taken upon him the office of the accufer of Mr. Haftings. Why the right honourable gentleman fhould have chofen, for one moment, to entertain fuch an opinion, or upon what ground it was that he had formed it, he was utterly

Mr. Dundas.

at a lofs to imagine, becaufe at no one period of his life-time
had he ever faid, or even dropped the moft diftant hint that he
meant to become the accufer of Mr. Haftings; but, on the
contrary, he had again and again declared, that he had no
fuch intention; and he appealed to thofe who fat with him
on the Secret Committee, two of whom he faw oppofite to
him, (Colonel North and Mr. Ellis,) whether he had even
glanced at fuch an idea? He had, undoubtedly, been the
perfon to fuggeft the ftring of refolutions which appeared
upon their journals; and he did not feel the fmalleft fcruple
to admit, that the fame fentiments which he had entertained
refpecting Mr. Haftings, at the time of propofing thofe refolutions, he harboured concerning him at that moment; but
were thefe fentiments, from which it was warrantable to in-
fer, that he fuppofed the conduct of Mr. Haftings fuch as
made him a fit object for a criminal profecution? Far from
it. To what did the refolution, upon which the right honourable gentleman had laid fo much ftrefs, proceed? To nothing
more than the recal of Mr. Haftings; a matter which he, at
the time, thought expedient, and had recommended to the
Houfe in this particular light; all which gentlemen who
were prefent muft well remember. For his own part, he
had not the fmalleft objection to go over all the matter which
had been difcuffed at the time, and to ftate to the Houfe upon
what ground it was that he thought it advifeable to recal
Mr. Haftings in 1782. With refpect to the conduct of Mr.
Haftings previous to 1782, the breach of the treaty of Poorunder, and the great and expenfive eftablifhments which Mr.
Haftings had made in India, he fhould briefly remark, that he,
on thefe two occafions, thought him highly culpable at the
time, and ftill he entertained the fame idea; but he did not
think that the procedure of Mr. Haftings amounted to criminality. He had examined his conduct minutely; and he always found, that when there was any improper conduct ob-
fervable in Mr. Haftings, every poffibility of annexing a criminal intention to it eluded his grafp, and there was always
fome letter of the Court of Directors, or fome ftrong reafon
to juftify Mr. Haftings at the bottom. In order to explain
the expenfive eftablifhments in India, he fhould beg leave to
read a letter written home by Mr. Haftings in 1782, in
which, upon that fubject, (Mr. Dundas now read a letter,)
Mr. Haftings complained of the fituation he was in, in confequence of fo many writers being fent out to him, declaring,
that he had at that time two hundred and fifty young men,
the younger fons of the firft families in Great Britain, all
gaping for lacks, and fcrambling for patronage, in the hopes
of getting fortunes foon enough to return in the prime of
life, and fpend the remainder of their days in their native
                                                        country.

country. This remonstrance (Mr. Dundas added) was received in England in the beginning of the year 1783,—and what was the attention paid to it? During that immaculate year, when Sir Henry Fletcher sat at the head of the Board of Directors, so far from a restraining hand being extended over the increase of the establishments of India, no less than thirty-six writers were actually sent out. Indeed he had not the list of the writers about him, but it was pretty obvious from what shop they came. The right honourable gentleman (Mr. Burke) had considered that part of the letter as essential, having marked a part of it by an alteration in the printing. Nor was the hand of the right honourable gentleman much less visible in some of the dispatches of the Court of Directors of that period, from the style in which they were written. To return to Mr. Hastings, Mr. Dundas added, that he had since 1782 done essential services to the Company, and had received the thanks of the Court of Directors; not that he meant to shelter himself under their minute; had he been a Director, most undoubtedly he should have signed the minute of thanks, being thoroughly convinced that they were merited by Mr. Hastings. And, upon this occasion, he felt it necessary to declare, that, although he thought it expedient to have recalled him in 1782, on account of the breach of the treaty of Poorunder, and on account of the extremely expensive establishments introduced by him in India, yet he much rejoiced that this resolution had not been carried into effect, because in such a case he should have proved the means of depriving the Company of a most valuable and useful servant, and the Public of a Governor General of India remarkable for uncommon ardour, abilities and capacity. Mr. Dundas observed that he should not advance the least objection to the motion, nor would he have troubled the House at all, had not so much been said personally to himself, that the House, he was persuaded, must have felt that it was due to them, that he should rise and give some explanation on the points to which the right honourable gentleman had directed his allusions.

Mr. *Fox* declared that he had not the smallest idea of speaking during the course of the debate, nor would he have interrupted the honourable gentleman (Mr. Rous) who was on his legs at the same time when he rose, had not some observations fallen from the right honourable and learned gentleman (Mr. Dundas), under which it was impossible for him to remain a moment silent. The only way in which he could meet the matter, was to oppose assertion to assertion; and to declare upon the word and honour of a gentleman, that if, in talking of the thirty-six writers sent out in 1783, when Sir Henry Fletcher sat at the head of the Board of East India

Mr. Fox.

India Directors, and when he had himself the honour to be in administration, the right honourable and learned gentleman meant to infinuate, that he had been concerned in sending out any, he was completely and perfectly mistaken. In the whole course of his life, he never had sent out, or rather procured to be sent out to India, but one single writer, and that was at the time when the Earl of Shelburne, now Marquis of Lansdown, presided over His Majesty's Councils. That, upon his word of honour, most solemnly pledged to the House, had been the only writer for whom he had ever procured a recommendation, and succeeded. Indeed, if the House would recollect a little, it was not very likely, that the administration in which he had the honour to be, should stand remarkably well with the Board of Directors, as it was well known what their intentions were at the time, with a view to effect a reform of the Company. Mr. Fox added, that he considered it right to say thus much in consequence of the infinuation of the right honourable and learned gentleman, and the manner in which it had been conveyed to the House. Previous to his sitting down, he should beg leave briefly to touch upon the consistency of the right honourable and learned gentleman, who, when hard driven to the point, and obliged, as it were, to defend his own conduct, had done that, which heaven knew the right honourable and learned gentleman could do at all times, with his opponents face to face, let the argument bear as much as it would against him; but what sort of a defence had the right honourable and learned gentleman made? He had been reduced to the necessity of admitting, that he at one time entertained an opinion that Mr. Hastings, with respect to certain points, proceeded in a manner highly culpable; nay, he had added, that he was still of the same opinion, although almost in the same breath, certainly in the same speech, he had declared that he entertained a high opinion of Mr. Hastings, and praised his conduct as warmly in the latter part of his observations, as he had abused it in the former part. And what points had the right honourable and learned gentleman chosen to select as the points in which he considered Mr. Hastings as having been highly culpable? Merely the two points of the Rohilla war, with the breach of the treaty of Poorunder, and in having introduced expensive establishments in India. Gracious heaven! did the whole idea which the right honourable and learned gentleman entertained of the culpability of Mr. Hastings amount only to this? Had the House heard nothing of Corah and Allahabad? Of Cheyt Sing? Of the Begums? And of all the long catalogue of crimes committed in India, to the infinite disturbance of the peace of the country, to the misery and even butchery of the natives, to the destruc-

.tion

tion of all confidence in Britifh faith, and to the everlafting difgrace of the Britifh name and character in Hindoftan? Mr. Fox now read the refolution immediately preceding that in which the Houfe refolved in 1782, that Mr. Haftings and Mr. Hornby fhould be recalled, and appealed to every man of common fenfe, whether that marked and ftrong cenfure did not go immediately to Mr. Haftings and Governor Hornby? It was not in language to exprefs difgrace more ftrongly than to declare that the delinquents ought to receive fome mark of parliamentary difpleafure. Certainly thefe two refolutions, and the obvious conftruction of both, with the vote of recall paffed at the India Houfe, in which Governor Haftings was permitted to refign in confequence of his long and meritorious fervices, was not a little ftrange.—How was this mode of recall to be reconciled to the refolution which ftigmatized Mr. Haftings, and declared it as the opinion of the Houfe that he deferved fome mark of parliamentary difpleafure? Was it not a contradiction infulting to that Houfe, and inconfiftent to a fhameful degree? The right honourable and learned gentleman thought proper to declare that he would not have fheltered himfelf under a minute of the Board of Directors, but that had he been a Director, he would have figned that minute likewife; and, therefore the right honourable and learned gentleman, who had himfelf prevailed upon the Houfe of Commons to refolve in a grave and phlegmatic form, but in ftrong and energetic phrafe, that Governor Haftings deferved parliamentary cenfure would have given that gentleman thanks for his long and meritorious fervices. What egregious inconfiftency! For the word *long* in the minute of recall, undoubtedly comprehended the whole of the fervices of Mr. Haftings, as well thofe before 1782, as thofe fubfequent to this period. During the commencement of the debate, a right honourable gentleman, (Mr. Burke) had been cenfured by a worthy Alderman, (Le Mefurier) for his fuppofed remark in refpect to trial by jury. The worthy Magiftrate had mifunderftood his right honourable friend, who had not exprefled any difapprobation of the general principle of trials by jury, but merely obferved that the caufe under confideration was of too much magnitude for the cognizance of the Court of King's Bench, and had propofed to appeal to a tribunal and a form of trial as ancient as the conftitution itfelf, of which it was a part. Thus had his right honourable friend evinced, that the higheft fpecies of offenders might be brought to trial, without reforting to any novel experiment on the conftitution, but in a manner conformable to ufage, and before an ancient, legal, and conftitutional tribunal. All this amounted to one powerful proof, that the new Court of Judicature,

which

which took away the birth-right of Britons, made *that* evidence that was not evidence before, and obliged criminals to accuse and to convict themselves, was not only a tribunal unconstitutional in its origin and its principle, and tyrannical and oppressive in its practice, but altogether needless.

The Chancellor of the Exchequer.

The *Chancellor of the Exchequer* remarked that he should have contented himself with giving a silent assent to the motion, had he not heard such extraordinary language used by the right honourable gentleman who spoke last. He should however have been ashamed of his own feelings, could he have tamely suffered such insinuations to be made, and that by a man so circumstanced as the right honourable gentleman, without expressing some part of that indignation with which his breast was filled, and in which he trusted that no person of generous and honourable principles could avoid taking a part. What had been the charge made against his right honourable and learned friend? A charge of inconsistency, in now bearing testimony to the merits of an individual whom, upon a former occasion, he was supposed to have considered as an object of censure. And by whom was this charge advanced? Let the House compare the charge and the party from whom it proceeded, and then judge whether he deserved censure for suffering his temper to be somewhat ruffled by so barefaced and so shameless a conduct.—Yet, indeed the right honourable gentleman had not deviated from his consistency of argument, when having first taken it for granted that his right honourable friend had, during a series of years continued to vent the most injurious and violent charges, to load with the grossest and most extravagant reproaches, and to threaten with the severest punishment a certain individual; he inferred that he was now become a convert in his supposed opinion, and had taken upon himself, from his own recent practice and experience, to dictate the form of words in which the recantation of his friend ought to have been made. [The members on the other side of the House cried out, hear him! hear him!] But his right honourable friend had no need of such a tutor as the right honourable gentleman, nor had he committed so egregious an absurdity as the right honourable gentleman thought proper to lay to his charge with a force of colouring which would have led the House, had they not too well known the person from whom it came, to believe that his heart was in truth capable of feeling and abhorring the meanness and unbecomingness of the conduct he had imputed to his right honourable friend. Eager to fix this imputation upon his right honourable friend, the right honourable gentleman had gone so far as to use the most unjustifiable language, no less than a direct charge of falsehood, for which, however, finding

ing

ing even the moſt violent members of the Houſe apparently
ſhocked, he had apologized by ſaying, that he did not mean
to apply the word in its generally offenſive ſenſe (an abuſe of
words into which the warmth of the right honourable gentleman's temper often betrayed him), yet he would ſtill contend that his right honourable friend's attempt to prove,
that thoſe reſolutions which had been read, were ſuch a pledge
of his diſapprobation of Mr. Haſtings's general conduct, as
muſt ſtamp with inconſiſtency any ſubſequent approbation
of any part. He ſhould regard his time as wretchedly loſt
were he to anſwer ſuch a miſerable attempt at wit, as the
right honourable gentleman had made, when he talked about
meeting him face to face, but he held himſelf in readineſs
fairly to meet any appearance of even plauſible argument.
The right honourable gentleman ſeemed determined to repreſent the acquieſcence which his right honourable friend
had acknowledged to the principle of the vote of thanks of
the Directors, as an unanſwerable proof of his having changed his opinion with reſpect to thoſe parts of Mr. Haſtings's
conduct which he had formerly cenſured : and yet, whoever
read with calm impartiality the vote alluded to, could not
remain one moment under difficulties to diſcover, that in
adopting the ſpirit and tenor of that vote, his right honourable friend could not have proceeded beyond the line of
mere thanks to Mr. Haſtings for ſome recent inſtances of
his conduct, cautiouſly guarding againſt the moſt diſtant
encomiums upon thoſe preceding parts which were the objects of his ſevereſt and moſt animated reprehenſion.

It did not, however, in the leaſt excite his aſtoniſhment to
find that one ſpecimen of the right honourable gentleman's
idea of conſiſtency was the poſition, that where one fault
could be found in any perſon, no merit ought, by any means,
to be admitted, but that uniform reproach and unremitting
cenſure ſhould always prove the conſequence of a ſingle difference of opinion. The right honourable gentleman could
not, ſurely, feel a neceſſity for coming to ſo full an explanation of his ſentiments on that head ; becauſe his conduct
had already made them ſufficiently public. For his own
part, he ſhould not meaſure his opinions by perſons, but by
principles : and, this was true conſiſtency ; for, always to
oppoſe, and always to agree with the individual, except upon
principle, was the worſt of all ſorts of inconſiſtency ; it
was, however, ſuch as the right honourable gentleman need
not have taken ſo much pains to hold up as that which he
thought the proper line of conduct ; for, his actions were,
in this caſe, the full teſt of his ſentiments. In purſuance of
that doctrine—to abide by principles, and not by perſons,
in forming an opinion of men's conduct, there could be
nothing

nothing more reconcileable than the propriety of condemning
the party on one set of principles, and of acquitting, nay,
of applauding him on another. This his right honourable
friend had done with respect to Mr. Haftings.—Considering
his procedure under certain parts of his administration, and
when embroiling the affairs of India by unnecessary and expensive wars; exciting the distrust and animosity of the
native princes against this country, by infraction of treaties,
and the extermination of a whole people, no doubt but he
must have highly resented and disapproved of such a conduct;
but again when he contemplated the exertions of his almost
unprecedented talents in the unexpectedly great business of
restoring peace and tranquillity, re-establishing a confidential intercourse with the neighbouring powers, and redeem-
ing the credit of the government, he would act highly inconsistent with those feelings and principles, which, upon a
former occasion, excited his indignation, if he were not at
once to acknowledge and to applaud the merit which had
produced such good effects. He held it absolutely necessary,
in point of justice and right, to examine the whole of the
public conduct of any servant of the people, to give him due
credit for such parts as were meritorious, as well as to censure him for such as were culpable; and, for his own part,
he should not hesitate one moment to declare that, however censurable some parts of Mr. Haftings's conduct might
be made to appear, he must, notwithstanding, consider such
as were praise-worthy as intitled to the warmest approbation;
nay, as a sufficient ground for reward and thanks, could they
be proved to predominate over whatsoever was exceptionable. The two right honourable gentlemen on the other
side, had contended that his right honourable friend, in moving the resolutions which were read, expressly pledged himself to institute a criminal inquiry, of which those resolutions
were to stand forth as the foundation. This position he
must positively deny, as the object of those resolutions was
manifestly of a very different tendency, and simply went
to establish the necessity of Mr. Haftings's recall, not on
account of mal-administration, but because having lost the
confidence of certain neighbouring Princes, he would (as
it was then conceived) lose the power of reducing the con-
fused and unsettled state of those countries to order and
regularity. Were it to be admitted, according to the apparent idea of the right honourable gentleman, that a vote for
the purpose of recalling a Governor, on motives of policy,
ought necessarily to be considered as a ground of a criminal
prosecution,—such a doctrine would draw after it the most
monstrous consequences; for it must either reduce Parliament to the necessity of hesitating concerning such a measure,

fure, however urgent the occasion might prove until after
a full examination of the conduct of the Governor, or it
must lead to the greatest oppression, by rendering a profecution indifpenfable, although no adequate inquiry might have
been inftituted to determine on its propriety. At all events,
it was unanfwerably demonftrable that, at the paffing of
thofe refolutions, they were not intended as a foundation for
any criminal proceedings, becaufe they contained in themfelves the whole of the object for which they were calculated; incontrovertibly eftablifhing the pofition that it appeared neceffary to introduce and maintain a confidence with
the princes of India. Certain Governors in India having
alfo loft that confidence, it was advifeable—What?—to punifh? No! but to recall thofe Governors.——Whether the
conduct by which the confidence of the native Princes was
loft, had been occafioned by the execution of orders from
home, or refulted from the imprudence of the Governors
themfelves, was a queftion by no means involved in either
the propriety or impropriety of the recall, becaufe to be the
agents in a fyftem of which the people of India difapproved,
would as effectually deftroy the confidence of thofe people as
to have become the original devifers of it. Therefore, however guilty Mr. Haftings might poffibly prove, the refolutions now referred to, were by no means a charge againft
him; becaufe whether innocent or guilty, his return from
India was apparently neceffary at the time, and thofe refolutions only went to point out and ftate how abfolutely fuch
a neceffity exifted.

The right honourable gentleman had dwelt on the extermination of the Rohillas with all the exaggerated and heightened colouring with which he was in general ufed to grace
his argument; there was no perfon who had heard him, but
would have imagined that this event had been, in fact, attended by the unexampled barbarity, even not lefs than the
maffacre of all the wretched inhabitants of the country,
without diftinction of age, fex, or condition; and he had
alfo reprefented it as a fubject, on which his right honourable friend thought fo highly as to make it a matter of fpeculation and inquiry, whether fuch a proceeding put in the
eftimate with a fum of forty lacks of rupees were juftifiable
or not. His right honourable friend had never entered upon
fuch an inquiry; neither did he fuggeft any fuch doubt;
having barely ftated in his refolution, that the defolation of
the country was not neceffary towards the recovery of the
money; nor had he at all gone into a confideration of the
meafure itfelf, with refpect either to its juftice or humanity,
but fimply with an eye to its efficacy towards the object
which it was intended to promote. But this was not the
only

only mark of difingenuoufnefs from the right honourable gentleman, becaufe he was by no means juftified for having reprefented in fuch melancholy language, the extirpation of that people, fince it was not as he had appeared to infinuate, a deftroying and cutting off the lives of the people, but merely the removal of them to a different place. He fhould not be furprifed to hear himfelf reprefented, in confequence of what he was now faying, as having attempted to defcribe the forcing a people from their poffeffions and removing them to a diftance, as in itfelf exceedingly infignificant, and, of courfe, not liable to the reproach of injuftice and inhumanity; but he had perfonally experienced fo much of that uncandid manner of arguing, that he could now coolly difregard and defpife it. He did indeed confider fuch an extermination (though far fhort of letting loofe all the horrors of fire and fword, as the right honourable gentleman had endeavoured to reprefent the affair of the Rohillas) in a moft horribly alarming point of view, and fo repugnant to every fentiment of human nature, that nothing could poffibly juftify it except the ftrongeft motives of political expediency, and that, throughout, irrefragably fupported by all the invincible principles of neceffary juftice.

The right honourable gentleman who introduced the debate had thought proper to fet off with an attack upon his right honourable friend for not having come forward in the prefent cafe as the profecutor of Mr. Haftings.—He had already fhewn why it was not his right honourable friend's duty to adopt the meafure on the idea of his having been pledged to it by the refolutions.—But, perhaps, the right honourable gentleman imagined that his right honourable friend would have proved the moft proper perfon to have conducted the bufinefs of the profecution, and, for that reafon, independently of the notion of his having been committed, wifhed him to have taken it upon himfelf. He muft confefs that if there were any real guilt to be inveftigated, and any punifhment to be inflicted, he joined in opinion with the right honourable gentleman, that his right honourable friend would indeed prove full as proper a perfon to take the lead, and full as likely to accomplifh all the purpofes of public juftice, as thofe gentlemen into whofe hands the profecution had fallen. But as another right honourable gentleman obferved that there were occafions, when the bounds and eftablifhed rules of juftice ought to be overleaped, and a profecution conducted rather by violence and refentment, than by the dull forms of ordinary proceeding; perhaps confidering the prefent bufinefs in that point of view, the gentlemen who had taken it up, were the fitteft perfons to carry it through all its branches from the beginning to the end.

With

With respect to the breach of the treaty of Poorunder, and the seizing on the provinces of Corah and Allahabad, he must beg leave particularly to remind the House that, subsequently to the transactions in those provinces, which took place during either the year 1772, or 1774, an act of Parliament had been passed altering the whole system of East-India Government, and instead of a President and Council of Bengal, appointing Mr. Hastings, by name, Governor General of the whole of the settlements. It would therefore prove at once highly inconsistent and absurd to consider him at the present period in the light of a culprit for any measures taken previous to his nomination to that distinguished post, which in itself was the highest certificate of the approbation of Parliament. All the papers required were certainly very proper to be laid before the House, let the mode in which the prosecution should be conducted by the right honourable gentleman be what it might. He should, for the present, avoid giving any opinion respecting the several proposed modes of trial; but, as the right honourable gentleman had appeared to determine upon impeachment, as the best calculated to answer the end proposed, he hoped that he would as early as possible make the House acquainted with the different steps which he proposed to take, and as explicitly as possible mark out the nature and extent of the charges intended to be made.—He was happy to feel that he should come to the business with the most perfect impartiality; and should the right honourable gentleman bring fully home to Mr. Hastings the violent imputations of atrocious crimes, he, for his own part, far from screening, would wish to bring down upon him the most exemplary punishment.

Mr. *Fox* begged leave to remind the right honourable gentleman that the minute upon which he had invariably argued was the vote of the General Court wherein it was expressed that Warren Hastings, Esq. should be permitted to return home, in consequence of his *long* and *meritorious* services. — Mr. Fox.

Mr. *Dundas* said that he could assure the right honourable gentleman (Mr. Fox) that he had alluded to the vote of thanks of the Court of Directors. — Mr. Dundas.

Mr. *C. W. Boughton Rous* observed that he felt it requisite to meet with a reply that part of the right honourable gentleman's (Mr. Burke) speech, in which he had insinuated, that as he (Mr. Rous) originally seconded the motion for the Select Committee, it would have proved more becoming had he brought forward the business of that day. On this occasion the right honourable gentleman would please to recollect that he not only seconded the motion for the Select Committee, but acted as one of its members; and when its first object was the investigation of the state and proceedings of — Mr. C. W. Boughton Rous.

the fupreme judicature of Bengal. On this Committee did he fit during the fecond feffion; but, at length, the great object was, to his great aftonifhment and concern, moft materially departed from, and points actually foreign to its nature received the preference in difcuffion. During the third feffion his name was put, without any previous intimation, and even without his knowledge, on the Committee, whilft he remained abfent in Shropfhire. Not, therefore, attending, with what propriety could the right honourable gentleman think of felecting him as the neceffary perfon to move an impeachment againft Mr. Haftings; againft Mr. Haftings whom he had not confidered as a criminal?

Mr. Francis.

Mr. *Francis* obferved that the ftrong impreffions made upon General Clavering's mind and his own, relative to the extremely barbarous mode of profecuting hoftilities againft the Rohillas, proceeded from informations given to them by a Britifh officer, then invefted with the command of the troops employed on the occafion.

Mr. Vanfittart.

Mr. *Vanfittart* contended, that in general the nature of the Rohilla war was little underftood; and that the *extirpation* of the Rohillas had *never* taken place. Mere chance, inattention, or error had introduced the word *extirpation*; and thus it ftood, falfely and abfurdly tranflated from a term (of a different meaning) in the Perfic language.

Ld. North.

Lord *North* remarked, that, on the prefent occafion he felt it neceffary to bring back to the recollection of the Houfe that, with their confent, he, during the year 1774, affifted in nominating Mr. Haftings Governor General of Bengal; that in 1776 the Directors (and this not improperly) removed him; but that a majority of the Court of Proprietors overpowered their act, and once more confirmed Mr. Haftings in his government. It was once conceived that a certain gentleman (Mr. Laughlin Macleane) would have proved able to bring Mr. Haftings to a refignation of his government; but, when the former reached Calcutta, the latter difowned him and kept his poft. During no inconfiderable period, affairs profpered under the adminiftration of Mr. Haftings. The circumftances of the Rohilla war were moft imperfectly underftood in England, previous to their inveftigation and fubfequently faithful and copious defcription by the Secret and Select Committees. Then, indeed, did cenfure alight upon the conduct of Mr. Haftings; and not only this gentleman, but even the Court of Directors, were deemed reprehenfible for the breach of the treaty of Poorunder. Lord North added, that, for his own part, he did not then think it prudent to recal Mr. Haftings, Great Britain being on the eve of a war with France, who was likely to turn her arms againft the Englifh territories in the Eaft Indies; but

not

not lefs likely to find their progrefs effectually checked by military meafures refulting from the plans of fuch a vigorous and able mind as that of Mr. Haftings.

When General Clavering, Colonel Monfon, and an honourable gentleman near him (Mr. Francis) arrived in India, and fecured a majority in Council, the Government became, of all others, the beft conducted, yet was not of very long duration, two of the gentlemen dying. With regard to the charge of inconfiftency, about which fo much had been faid, his right honourable and learned friend muft give him leave to contend, without meaning to impute inconfiftency either to him or to any other individual, that a manifeft want of confiftency appeared between the refolution which declared that Mr. Haftings had acted in a manner difgraceful to the national honour, and deferving of parliamentary difpleafure, and the vote of recal, which fpoke of his *long* and meritorious fervices; for the word *long* indifputably went to the extent of comprehending *all* his fervices; and furely no abfurdity could be more glaring, whilft this refolution remained upon the Journals in all its full and unrefcinded force.

Major *Scott* rofe next, and faid:

Mr. Speaker, as the right honourable gentleman who opened the bufinefs of this day, amidft all his declamations, has not thought proper to bring a fingle charge againft Mr. Haftings, I fhall not intrude myfelf long upon the indulgence of the Houfe. It is true he has promifed a great deal; but I have been accuftomed to the right honourable gentleman's pledges on former occafions. He has thought proper fometimes to defcend from the high and important ftation he fills in this country, to the rank of a common pamphleteer; and I now hold in my hand, Sir, a fpeech publifhed by Mr. Dodfley, as what the right honourable gentleman faid in this Houfe on the 1ft of December, 1783, before I had the honour to be a member of it. But when it appeared to the world in the fhape of a pamphlet, I had an opportunity of meeting the right honourable gentleman upon equal terms. I replied to it, and I appeal to the good fenfe of every man in the Houfe, and out of the Houfe, who is not tinctured by party prejudices, to declare whether I have not fatisfactorily refuted every charge of every kind that the right honourable gentleman brought againft Mr. Haftings. His fpeech and my anfwer are before the public, and they have pronounced in my favour. The charges are numerous; they are the effence of all his reports; and if they had been true, Mr. Haftings deferved to have loft twenty lives, if he had had them, for the magnitude of his crimes. I will go farther, Sir, as I have already refuted what the right honourable gentleman has afferted, I am not afraid of pledging myfelf to

Major Scott.

T 2 refute

refute all that he may hereafter produce in the courfe of this inquiry. The right honourable gentleman now propofes to procced againft Mr. Haftings; but how does he do it? He comes forward this day to move for papers, in order to found his charges upon. If the right honourable gentleman was a fair accufer, who acted from a regard to public juftice, and not for private vengeance, would this be the mode of his proceeding? Year after year the right honourable gentleman has pledged himfelf to God, this Houfe, and to his country, to prove Mr. Haftings a moft notorious delinquent. Laft year, feven weeks before the Houfe rofe, the right honourable gentleman declared his intention of profecuting Mr. Haftings; but 'it would have faved time, it would have enabled the Houfe to go on this bufinefs the fecond day of this feffion, if the right honourable gentleman had then moved for the papers he now intends to call for, and it would have been the conduct of a manly, fair, and honourable accufer, if the right honourable gentleman had given Mr. Haftings fome intimation of his mode of proceeding, by ftating to the Houfe what he has now ftated. Such conduct would indeed have been fair, honourable, and parliamentary, but it would not have been the conduct of a man who takes the Duke of Parma for his model, " *Dolus* " *an virtus quis in hofte requirit.*" This, Houfe, however, will not I truft adopt the fentiments and conduct of the right honourable gentleman. I have a confidence in the honour and juftice of this Houfe, and I am fure that they will protect a man who is univerfally allowed to have performed great and important fervices to his country, from unqualified abufe, and unmerited calumny. The right honourable gentleman has talked much of the labours of his Committee, and the accuracy of the reports—but, Sir, I affert that the Reports of the Select Committee are partial and unjuft; that the moft unwarrantable means were ufed to criminate Mr. Haftings in thofe Reports, and that whenever any evidence appeared that ferved to exculpate him, it was fuppreffed. I do not make this charge lightly. I pledge myfelf to prove it; and if I do not prove it, I will confent to be called a calumniator in the face of this Houfe. Nay, Sir, I will now ftate to you two curious facts. The Select Committee fummoned a gentleman of high rank in the Company's civil fervice before them. I was in the committee room, an open committee room, as a fpectator, and was turned out very civilly by the right honourable gentleman—who then afked various queftions of the perfon who had been fummoned, but finding that his anfwers were not tending to the purpofe the right honourable gentleman wanted, he told the Committee there was no neceffity to examine the gentleman they had summoned.

summoned. Will the House approve of this mode of proceeding? The Committee summoned an officer of high rank before them, Lieutenant Colonel Robert Stuart; the right honourable gentleman examined him, as to what he deems his strong hold, the state and condition of Oude. Colonel Stuart's answer to the right honourable gentleman's first question was perfectly satisfactory that Oude was in a ruinous state; but unfortunately the Colonel attributed, in his reply to the next question, the ruin of Oude to its true causes—to causes that followed from measures which were not the measures of Mr. Hastings. He then examined him as to the Begums and their eunuchs. Colonel Stuart stated instances of their disaffection and intrigues many years ago, so early as 1776. What was the consequence? The evidence is completely suppressed. I engage to prove to every man of common sense that that evidence was most material for the exculpation of Mr. Hastings, and that it contains more matter of fact than half the Reports, but it was wholly and completely suppressed. The most attentive reader of the Reports knows nothing of Colonel Stuart or his evidence. The House and the nation know the scandalous uses to which these unjust, and partial, and imperfect Reports were applied upon a great occasion, which fortunately failed. I do not mention the matter lightly; I accuse that Committee of the grossest partiality, and I am ready to prove it. Long before I had the honour of a seat in this House, I have often sat with surprize and astonishment in the gallery, while the right honourable gentleman has been describing in terms more glowing than I supposed the warmest imagination could have invented, the murders, robberies, oppressions, and cruelties practised by British subjects in India. Upon these occasions, Sir, I have been sometimes led to think that the greatest part of my life has not been passed in the fertile plains of Bengal, but in some distant quarter of the globe, so remote were the right honourable gentleman's descriptions from the real state of facts. Upon this subject I shall say more when the condition of Almas Ally Cawn, with his unfortunate wives and children, and the oppressed Princes and Begums, shall come regularly before us. The right honourable gentleman's character was once high and reputable in this country. Why it is not so now, is perhaps owing to his intemperate persecution of a man whose merits are universally acknowledged. And I repeat it, Sir, that the most unjustifiable means have been used to depreciate his character, means that however unworthy the dignity of a member of this House, taking up a great public subject, upon great public principles, are strictly consistent with the character of a man who takes the Duke of Parma for his model, and professes to attack Mr. Hastings

upon

upon the grounds that that General attacked Henry the Fourth—But the right honourable gentleman has now ſtated that he will produce ſpecific charges as ſoon as he gets the papers he means to move for.   I hope there will be no delay. I promiſe the right honourable gentleman, upon my honour, that I will aſſiſt him in the production of papers as far as I can ; but though I do not wiſh to narrow his ground, yet I hope the Houſe will underſtand that the right honourable gentleman's pledge was made previous to the exiſtence of any of the papers that he now may move for, and I confide in their juſtice and honour not to permit any unneceſſary delay —and here I hope I ſhall be in order, if I ſay I ſpeak the ſentiments of Mr. Haſtings on this ſubject : I had the honour to be long employed for that gentleman ; by his return to England, my agency has of courſe expired ; but I entertain for him the warmeſt ſentiments of affection and regard. My own reputation too is concerned in the iſſue of this buſineſs ; but that, Sir, is of very ſmall conſequence, compared to the importance of this inquiry — I ſpeak this for Mr. Haſtings, when I ſay, that he moſt anxiouſly wiſhes for an inquiry into his conduct, the moſt rigid that this Houſe can adopt, that he wiſhes it to be brought down to the very day of his departure from Bengal, and to riſe or fall in the opinion of this Houſe and this country by the reſult of this inquiry. But while he expreſſes his ſolicitude for an inquiry, he throws himſelf with confidence upon the honour and juſtice of this Houſe ; and he truſts they will not ſuffer his character to be the ſport of calumny for three years to come, as it has been for three years paſt.   He truſts the Houſe will protect him from that general unqualified abuſe to which he has been ſo long ſubject ; and as this Houſe is not actuated by the principles of the Duke of Parma, he hopes that the right honourable gentleman will be directed to bring ſpecific charges to which plain and direct refutations can be given.   I ſay for myſelf, Sir, that already there has been unneceſſary, intentional delay.   The right honourable gentleman, acting as a member of Parliament, can give no one reaſon why he did not ſtate to this Houſe laſt June what papers he wanted, and what mode he meant to purſue.   Acting as the Duke of Parma, he had good cauſe to proceed as he had done.

And now, Sir, before I ſit down, I beg to ſay a few words in reply to what fell from the noble Lord relative to the Rohilla war, the ſale of Corah and Allahabad, and the ſtoppage of the King's tribute.   The Rohilla war was not, I avow, the war of Mr. Haſtings.   It was founded on meaſures which were adopted before Mr. Haſtings arrived in Bengal, and on meaſures which he diſapproved.   I was a Lieutenant in Bengal, and upon the ſervice which produced the Rohilla war.

I ſhall

I shall state my facts from a record now upon your table; from the Fifth Report of the Secret Committee, presented to the House by the right honourable and learned gentleman below me.   It there appears, Sir, that in consequence of a threatened invasion of the Mahrattas, a treaty was entered into between Sujah Dowlah and the Rohillas, one condition of which was, that on the expulsion of the Mahrattas from Rohilcund, by the joint forces of Sujah Dowlah and the Company, the Rohillas were to pay forty lacks of rupees to Sujah Dowlah. To this treaty General Sir Robert Barker, on the part of the Company, was the guarantee.   This agreement was faithfully performed on the part of the English, and Sujah Dowlah.   We marched under the command of Sir Robert Barker into Rohilcund.   We pursued the Mahrattas across the Ganges, forded it after them, and continued encamped on the banks of the Ganges till the rains set in, when we returned to our own provinces.   The money was demanded by Sujah Dowlah, and refused.   In such a light did the conduct of the Rohilla chiefs appear to Sir Robert Barker, that in three several letters now on your table he pressed the Governor and Council to empower him to act against them, and states the faithless and treacherous conduct of the Rohillas to be proverbial and notorious throughout Indostan. The Rohilla war was afterwards undertaken by Mr. Hastings, in consequence of this breach of treaty.   The Directors at first, when they heard it, allowed that it was justly undertaken, though they lamented the necessity.   But afterwards this war was used as an instrument by the Government at home to effect the removal of Mr. Hastings.

There is another point I wish to set this House right in; for notwithstanding all that has been said on the subject of the Rohilla war, it is not yet understood either in or out of the house.   The Rohillas were not a nation, as the right honourable gentleman (Mr. Fox) stiles them.   The inhabitants of the country called Rohilcund are Hindoos; they may probably be two millions in number, and they have never been disturbed in their possessions.   The Rohillas invaded Rohilcund in 1742, when the Mogul empire was in its decline; and attempts were made to drive them again across the Ganges, but they succeeded in conquering and possessing the country.   I believe their number did not exceed fifty thousand.   Of these at least twenty-five thousand are now in Rohilcund with Fyzulla Cawn, and the remainder were forced across the Ganges, which the right honourable gentleman, in glowing terms, calls the extirpation of a whole nation.

With respect to the stoppage of the King's tribute, and the sale of Corah and Allahabad, these circumstances seem as little understood as the Rohilla war.   With regard to the first,
Mr.

Mr. Haftings found fome arrear exifting on his arrival in Bengal. This he withheld, and determined to pay no farther fum till he received the orders of the Company ; and why ? becaufe the King had gone with the Mahrattas to Wihly, and was actually a prifoner. What did the Company do ? They approved what Mr. Haftings had done, and they particularly ordered that not a rupee fhould be paid to the King without fpecial orders from England. Will you blame Mr. Haftings for this ? As to the fale of Corah and Allahabad, they were to remain by Lord Clive's treaty in the poffeffion of the King, for the fupport of his dignity. He ceded them to the Mahrattas. What was Mr. Haftings to do ? either to allow the Mahrattas to poffefs them, or to take them himfelf, or to yield them to Sujah Dowlah, to whom they had formerly belonged. He did the latter, and received fifty lacks of rupees for them. The Company very highly approved the tranfaction. And I defire to afk, whether, amidft the various changes that have happened, fometimes this government poffeffing more power, and fometimes lefs, in the management of the Company's affairs, any man or fet of men have ordered that the arrears of tribute fhould be paid to the King, or Corah and Allahabad reftored to him ? Certainly they have not ; and it is as ridiculous as unjuft to blame Mr. Haftings on thefe grounds.

Now, Sir, a very few words as to what fell from the noble Lord relative to the refignation of Mr. Haftings. He fays, that after the Company had fupported Mr. Haftings, his agent, or vakeel, Colonel Macleane, refigned the government of Bengal for him. Will the noble Lord detail to this Houfe the fecret management that brought about this refignation ? If he will, I can affure the noble Lord that Mr. Haftings will be much obliged to him ; for to this hour he is ignorant of it. But, Mr. Speaker, the proceeding is palpable. If Mr. Macleane did really poffefs authority to refign for Mr. Haftings, why not produce it to the Directors ? Was that done ? No. The powers were infpected by three Directors only, and one of the three declared they were no powers ; but the Court agreed to fanctify them, and the refignation was accepted. We know the confequences ; and I think now, as I always thought, that in that bufinefs Mr. Haftings and General Clavering were both ufed ill, and both kept in the dark. But the noble Lord fays, after General Clavering's death he continued Mr. Haftings ; and he affigns two unanfwerable reafons for fo doing ; firft, that it was the wifh of his conftituents ; and fecondly, that Mr. Haftings poffeffed vigour and abilities : but I really, Sir, am a good deal furprized at a diftinction the noble Lord makes. I have a great refpect for the noble Lord, and am not apt to treat lightly whatever falls from him ;

otherwife,

otherwife, Sir, I fhould be very much inclined not very fe-
riously to animadvert upon a curious diftinction that he attempts to draw between the original appointment of Mr.
Haftings by name in this Houfe in 1774, and the continuation of him three feveral times, when his firft commiffion
expired. It is true, the name of Mr. Haftings was not mentioned in 1779, or in 1780, when he was re-appointed each
time for one year, or in 1781, when he was re-appointed for
ten years : but this I fay, Sir, that the noble Lord appointed
him at thefe feveral periods, in point of fact, as much as he
originally appointed him in 1774, and he has affigned an anfwerable reafon for fo doing, that he poffeffed vigour and abilities, and was approved of by the Company. I only wifh
to obferve, that at thefe periods the Rohilla war, the fale of
Corah, the charges of peculation, and the Mahratta war, were
known, and had been canvaffed over again and again in England. And now, Sir, I fhall fit down with repeating, that
on the part of Mr. Haftings, I eagerly and anxioufly exprefs
my wifhes for an inquiry ; and I am confident that this Houfe
is too fenfible of what is due to its own dignity, its own honour, and its own virtue, to be influenced in the courfe of
that inquiry by the principles of the Duke of Parma.

Mr. *Burke* anfwered, that he never failed to preferve the utmoft calmnefs of temper, if attacked merely by perfonali- Mr. Burke.
ties, but he could not hear that the Rohillas were extirpated,
and a whole people deprived of their exiftence, without confiderable warmth and indignation. Doubtlefs, it was wrong ;
it was a weaknefs in him to give way to his feelings upon
fuch a trifling occafion, and he would endeavour to amend his
fault. The honourable gentleman had moft certainly explained the matter of the Rohillas very curioufly, and not lefs
fatisfactorily to the Houfe. The Rohillas were ftrangers,
and therefore they had no right to the country in which they
lived. Undoubtedly, the Englifh had a better right, and a
clearer title ; they were not ftrangers, but the aboriginal native inhabitants, men with fwarthy complections, children of
the fun, and, from their infancy, poffeffors of the foil ! This
being the cafe, to be fure they did wifely to extirpate the Rohilla race, and extinguifh a whole people. Mr. Burke obferved, that the honourable gentleman's declaration, that he
had refuted all his charges, and that if he made twice as many
he would refute them alfo, reminded him of the gallant Boba-
dil in the play, " Twenty more ! Kill 'em !—Twenty more !
" Kill them too !" The champion, doubtlefs, was invincible,
or he would not have talked fo valiantly. His threat was
equal to a reply once publifhed to a fermon on the 30th of
January, which was entitled, " A Reply to all the Sermons
" that ever have been, and to all that ever fhall be preached

" on the 30th of January.". As to his having omitted any of the evidence received by the Select Committee, the Report in question had not been drawn by him ; but if it had, the fact might have been the same, as every Committee in drawing up their Reports, enjoyed a right to exercise their own judgements, and insert just as much, or omit just as much, of the evidence as they might judge proper : but if there was cause for complaint,. an opportunity would offer for urging it. As to his acting upon feelings of private enmity, he felt no malice against any man ; if any lurked in his mind, it was unknown to him, and was a vice of disposition with which nature cursed him, and which he had neither yet discovered, nor, of course, subdued and eradicated. As to his having sent out writers to India, as a right honourable and learned gentleman asserted, what crime was there in that fact? or how did it disqualify him from calling the conduct of Mr. Hastings in question? The only misfortune was, that in truth, though he had lived so much in the world, and enjoyed so large a circle of acquaintance of all sorts and degrees, he never once had made a director, nor sent out, or procured to be sent out, a single writer to India ; no, not one ! The right honourable and learned gentleman was out in his conjecture. Again, the right honourable and learned gentleman knew him by his style, and had discovered him in the dispatches of the Board of Directors in 1783. What a miserable judge of style must the right honourable and learned gentleman be, when it so happened, that he never had written a line in any one dispatch of the Board of Directors in the whole course of his life ! The right honourable and learned gentleman held an office, the duty of which was extremely singular ; his duty was to think what another man should say ; for, as head of the Board of Control, the right honourable and learned gentleman dictated what others signed, and thus the dispatches sent to India contained the right honourable and learned gentleman's sentiments, with the Board of Directors' signatures. Now, had he been concerned in writing the dispatches of the Directors in 1783, he should have done little more than revise them, and perhaps have corrected their style ; in fact, he should have acted as the Directors' clerk ; and this, surely, was an office of low degree, and little worth his notice.

Mr. Dundas.

Mr. *Dundas* declared, when he mentioned the thirty-six writers sent out in 1783, he did not entertain the most distant idea of insinuating that the right honourable gentleman had any hand in the disposal of these employments but merely stated the fact. He did not know who had sent them out, and it was to him a matter of perfect indifference. In regard to what he had said of the right honourable gentleman's having a hand in the Directors' dispatches of 1783, if the fact were

were as the right honourable gentleman had ftated it, undoubtedly he had been miftaken : the reafon of ftating it was,
becaufe that in reading lately upon the fubject of the trade of
a particular part of India, where the queftion was, whether
it fhould be carried on by a monopoly, or be made an open
trade, an admirably well-timed letter had come into his hand,
and finding the ftile remarkably good, he had exclaimed to a
friend near him, " this is furely Mr. Burke's writing !" but
in that conjecture he meant the right honourable gentleman
no difhonour ; however, he now found that he had robbed the
Directors of a degree of credit which was due to them, and
placed it to the account of the right honourable gentleman.

Mr. *Fox* remarked, that if the obfervations of the learned Mr. Fox.
gentleman concerning the thirty-fix writers were his real fentiments, he fhould not have rafhly thrown out the fact in the
manner he did in his former fpeech, when from talking of the
fhop from whence they came, and the pure Board of Directors of 1783, moft undoubtedly the infinuation had all the
effect of an affertion; that thofe who were in power in 1783
abufed that which they had determined to reform, and thus
increafed the numerous and dreadful evils already prevalent.

Mr. *Dundas* anfwering, that the right honourable gentle- Mr. Dun-
man had miftaken his meaning, added, that he fhould, not- das.
withftanding, perfift in declaring, that he knew the fhop
from whence the writers came.

The queftion was now put and carried.

Mr. Burke then moved, " That there be laid before this
" Houfe, copies of all minutes of confultation and corref-
" pondence to and from Bengal, Bombay, and Madras, rela-
" tive to a contract or agency with Mr. Auriol, Secretary to
" the Board of Council General, for a fupply of rice to Ma-
" dras and Bombay.

" That there be laid before this Houfe, copies of all papers
" relative to the revenue and contracts of opium, fince the
" year 1782, fo far as the fame relates to any contract
" made during the government of the faid Warren Haftings,
" Efq.

" That there be laid before this Houfe, copies of all mi-
" nutes of confultation and correfpondence between the Go-
" vernor General and Council and the Refident at the Dur-
" bar of the Nabob of Bengal, fince the month of January,
" 1780, together with an account of the expenditure and
" diftribution of the ftipend allowed to the faid Nabob, toge-
" ther with the actual employments now held, and thofe for-
" merly held, by Mahomed Reza Khan, and the orders of
" the Court of Directors thereon.

" That there be laid before this Houfe, copies of all mi-
" nutes of confultation and other proceedings relative to a

" charge

" charge made by the Governor General, Warren Hasting,
" Esq. against John Bristow, Esq. late Resident at Oude,
" for disbursing large sums of money from the treasury of
" Oude without permission of the Nabob, or the permission
" and sanction of the Company's Govenment of Bengal, and
" without accounting for the same."

Mr. Chancellor Pitt. Mr. Chancellor *Pitt* observed, that could he suppose the existence of any intention, either to break new ground, or move for papers not mentioned in those Reports of the Committee to which, during the progress of the debate, allusions had been so often made, he should take the liberty to insist upon the right honourable gentleman's (Mr. Burke) explaining the nature of them to the House.

Mr. Dundas. Mr. *Dundas* remarked, that as, upon this occasion, his ideas thoroughly coincided with those of his right honourable friend, he felt himself justified in submitting them, even with earnestness, to the serious attention of the House.

Mr. Burke moved, " That there be laid before this House
" copies of all other correspondence during the residence of
" John Bristow, Esq. together with the documents therewith
" transmitted from the province of Oude, and also the an-
" swers thereto, and of all proceedings relative to his conduct
" during the said Residency, from the month of October,
" 1782."

Mr. Chancellor Pitt. Mr. Chancellor *Pitt* contending that this motion went to the production of new matter, and must, if carried, stretch out the subject unnecessarily into a wider field, declared himself determined to oppose it.

Mr. Dundas. Mr. *Dundas* remarked, that it behoved the right honourable gentleman (Mr. Burke) to expatiate concerning the nature of every new point, in order to illustrate which, he might esteem it proper to call for papers.

The Speaker now complained of illness ; in consequence of which, soon afterwards the House adjourned.

Monday, February 20.

Capt. Macbride. Captain *Macbride* begged leave to inform the House, that on the morrow he should move for copies of the reports of the estimates for fortifications, so far as the concurrence of the gentlemen in the naval department, who were upon that board, was concerned, to be laid before the House. This measure he could safely pursue, as the drift of it did not in the least tend to the proclaiming of what it was not proper to make known.

The order of the day being called for, to resume Mr. Burke's motion, relative to the production of such papers and documents as he esteemed necessary to ground his impeachment of Mr. Hastings upon, and the same being read,

Mr.

Mr. *Burke* defired to acquaint the Houfe, that, in order to obviate the imputation of prolixity, in the purfuit of a bufi-nefs in itfelf great, and therefore requiring a degree of delibe-ration equal to its confequence, he would withdraw his for-mer motion of the preceding Friday, that " there be laid be-" fore the Houfe copies of all other correfpondence during " the refidence of John Briftow, Efq. together with the do-" cuments therewith tranfmitted from the province of Oude, " and alfo the anfwers thereto, and of all proceedings rela-" tive to his conduct during the faid refidency, from the " month of October, 1782," and fubftitute, according to the advice of a worthy alderman who fat near him, a motion, " That there be laid before this Houfe, copies or duplicates of " all correfpondence, minutes of the Governor General and " Members of the Council, and inftructions relative to the " ftate and condition of the country of Oude and its depen-" dencies, and of the reigning family thereof, together with " all charges made by the late Governor General of Bengal " againft the Refident Middleton, and the Affiftant Refident " Johnfon, and the Refident Briftow, as well as all corref-" pondence, minutes of the Governor General and Members " of the Council, and inftructions which may not be com-" prehended in the foregoing, relative to Almas Ali Khan." Many circumftances were involved, from the relative fitua-tions of agents in the bufinefs. The fituation of Mr. Briftow and of Refident Johnfon, in allufion to the periods at which he aimed, were entirely brought to light ; and their different tranfactions in the affairs of that country, when thrown into their various points of view, would caft a farther elucidation on the fubject.

Mr. *Dundas* contended, that the Reports of the Select Com-mittee were not fufficiently decifive to warrant a determina-tion of the Houfe to profecute Mr. Haftings criminally; and therefore he wifhed to be convinced how far the right ho-nourable gentleman (for as yet he had received no argument to enable him to alter his opinion) would infift on calling for a number of papers, without giving any precife idea to the Houfe, how far thefe papers were either connected with, or related to, the fubject of criminality which he intended to bring forward. He had not, hitherto, by changing the mo-tion, obviated that objection in his mind ; and he wifhed to fee fome motive alledged, which would explain the right ho-nourable gentleman's determination how far his drift related to the fubject of impeachment.

Mr. *Burke* begged leave to remind the right honourable and learned gentleman, that, in all criminal inquiry, the accufer, who, by becoming fuch, took upon himfelf the *onus probandi*, had a right to affume two things ; of which the firft was, that

Mr. Dun-das.

Mr. Burke.

a fup-

a suppofition of guilt in a perfon who filled a ftation of confequence and honour, entitled the accufer to an hearing; and
the next, that fuch documents, proofs, or papers, as the perfon accufing faw or efteemed neceffary to fupport the charge
which he undertook to bring on, ought to be free and accef-
fible. A refufal muft be attended with a double injuftice.
If the accufer wanted collateral or explanatory aid, he ought
not to be denied it, for by its aid he could digeft, explain,
fimplify, or methodize thofe facts of which he was in prior
poffeffion; or if, on the other hand, the grounds of accufation could be extenuated, if the feverity of the charge could
be abated, nay, annihilated, a denial of that opportunity to
the accufer was an injuftice to the accufed. Were the hand
of power to deny him fuch documents as he called for, he
muft then reft himfelf upon the fole conviction of having
done his duty. He felt it a heavy and painful tafk, that the
burden fhould have fallen to his lot, who was connected only
with acquired power, the friends he had being fuch as thofe
upon whom Heaven had beftowed fome of the greateft talents which nature could poffefs; a concurrence of circumftances had rendered that tafk to him inevitable, and a collection of proof made it alfo upon him a duty. He had heard,
and he was convinced of it, that he had to encounter fome of
the firft weight, the firft importance and opulence of this
country; he forefaw all this, and relying upon the juftice of
his caufe, he would perfevere. The people would not, he
was informed, follow at his heels; this was a queftion which
he never afked himfelf, or, at leaft, never put in competition
with the awful fenfe which he entertained of that duty,
which he owed to the interefts of humanity:—he was not to
be popular; the people of England would reject him in fuch
a purfuit — in what purfuit? In the purfuit of the caufe of
humanity?—What! for having taken up the caufe of the in-
jured and oppreffed fellow fubjects of the people of England
in India! for attempting to procure an atonement to Indian
nations, who had been fcourged by their iniquitous fervants
—was he to be unpopular? O! miferable public! let him
then remain the object of perfecution, he entreated, and practice a leffon which he had learned in his earlier infancy, and
which he would remember to his lateft breath, " Bleffed are
" they who are perfecuted for juftice fake, for they fhall have
" their reward;" that reward which he fhould endeavour to
enjoy a confcious poffeffion of; and if thofe people who
raifed monuments to their benevolence, by forming afylums
and receptacles for human mifery, are juftly ranked for fuch
deeds amongft the benefactors to mankind, does not the man
who pulls down tyranny, eradicates cruelty, and avenges the
oppreffed,

oppreffed, deferve a title to the good opinion of his fellow creatures?

The downfal of the greateft empire which this world ever faw, has been univerfally agreed upon to have originated in the mal-adminiftration of its provinces. Rome never felt within herfelf the feeds of decline, till corruption from foreign mifconduct impaired her vitals, and as Midianus, an elegant commentator upon the orations of Cicero obferves, " *prevaricatione teftimonii*," by prevarication of teftimony, the inroads of corruption deftroyed the political frame and then were all things at ftake. But even then, a man of the firft families and connections, and rank in the ftate, was brought to punifhment. Verres, the governor of Sicily, was accufed by Cicero for the mal-adminiftration of the province committed to his care. The connections of the accufed were fome of the moft fplendid and opulent of Rome; among thefe were the Hortenfii, and even the Metellii. It was not a party for or againft Government, it was the Government itfelf which adopted the profecution, and no lefs than one hundred and fifty days were granted to the accufer to collect the materials for his accufation, and that from a province fo near as Sicily is to Italy; and the juftice of the Roman fenate allowed not only the time for digefting the matter of the accufation, but alfo opened, without referve, all the cabinets including the documents for which the accufer called. Can it now be faid that the caufe of juftice is in liberal hands, if documents which the accufer demands are to be retained? The bufinefs referred to a country in a remote fituation, from whence proofs have come in abundance; and the fuppreffion of them was no argument againft the veracity of the charge. The period was not long elapfed, fince a certain right honourable gentleman, the Cicero of the age (Mr. Dundas) obtained the moft ample intelligence of thofe miferies which prevailed in the Eaft Indies, a wretched facrifice to Englifh avarice and ambition. The right honourable gentleman brought forth a bill of pains and penalties againft one of thofe characters, whom the Houfe confiderd as an object within its reach. How far he purfued the point the world faw; and yet the difficulties he had to encounter in the purfuit of the matter in inveftigating his fubject, were totally removed by the general and concurrent difpofition of every party with whom documents were depofited neceffary to accomplifh his views. The right honourable and learned gentleman had a willing Adminiftration; a body of India Directors difpofed to his purpofe; and the conclufion of the bufinefs was in the remembrance of every one. Mr. Burke added, that for his own part, he only called for what the hand of power had no excufe for detaining. If the papers for which

he

he asked, were necessary to his purpose; the detaining them was unfair; and those who detained them must either plead design or ignorance of their purport; but whether to the purport or not, a refusal was unjustifiable; and if those who refused them were ignorant of their contents, they were guilty of neglect: yet, if, after all, the desolation of a province (and that no insignificant province) under a British government, a province which extended fifty-three thousand square miles, the internal wealth of which was, in every calculation, equal to eighteen millions sterling, at a period before it experienced those calamities which only rendered it an object fit to be abandoned; if the desolation and ruin of that province, the oppression and destruction of its nobility, were not sufficient inducements with the House to vote him the papers for which he moved, and if no other ground would be esteemed sufficient but that of specifying his charges, although he knew that he was acting inconsistently with the standing and established orders and practice of the House to comply with such a desire, yet for the sake of removing these objections, calculated to impede the business he undertook, he would wave all that attachment to regularity, because it was his inclination to adhere to, and comply with the wishes of those who opposed him, in order to substantiate the truth as soon as possible.

Scott   Major *Scott* answered, that the right honourable gentleman could not evince more readiness than himself to proceed upon that ground. As to the affair of Oude, the ruin of that country, which was painted in all the eloquent and forcible language of which the right honourable gentleman was so capable, had taken a very contrary turn to what was stated in the adduced instance; he would commit himself and join issue, when he could inform the House, that the nation of Oude, so far from being ultimately in that state of poverty and wretchedness as not to be able to repay the sum of near 800,000l. due by them to the East-India Company, had, at a later period, by the prudence of Mr. Hastings, been enabled to pay that sum which it owed, notwithstanding the positive assertion of an honourable gentleman opposite to him, that they never would be able to pay it: and such was the exertion of Mr. Hasting, in accomplishing this salutary purpose for the benefit of his employers, that he received the thanks of the Directors of the East-India Company for his meritorious services in establishing that solvency in the country of Oude.

Considering the debate in a resumed point of view he felt himself at liberty to refer to the affairs of Benares and Cheyt Sing. When a right honourable gentleman opposite to him, (Mr. Fox) framed his bill two years ago, he took up that
subject

subject on manly and liberal grounds, and made these fair allowances which the merits of the case required; an inquiry was set on foot, and as he himself had not then the honour of a seat in the House, he was therefore precluded giving such information as he now had it in his power to afford. On the news of the French war breaking out in 1778, the Supreme Council of Bengal, after deliberating on the measures most proper for their pursuit, resolved, that each zemindar, or dependant on the Government, should furnish his quota towards the general exigencies of the state. Five lacks of rupees were demanded of Cheyt Sing; to this demand a demur was made; and Mr. Hastings entered the Council irritated that a dependant of the Bengal sovereignty, who by stipulation was obliged to comply in furnishing his share towards the exigencies of the state, should resist the tenor of his agreement. An order was consequently issued, that two battalions of sepoys should be sent to enforce obedience; and that the additional expence of these troops should also be levied for their expences in addition to the five lacks of rupees which was his quota. It was premised to Cheyt Sing, that this money was only to be levied for the exigencies of the war, and that after its conclusion the expence would cease: this argument however had no effect; for the next year the same means were found requisite—and what person will, under these circumstances, coolly and impartially say, that if Mr. Hastings's life and fortune were aimed at, in compelling a refractory dependant to furnish his quota, the grounds could possibly admit of any justification?

Major Scott was now entering into a more detailed conversation on India business, when

Mr. *Wilberforce* begged leave to remind the honourable gentleman that he wandered far from the question, which was the production of papers, and not a recital of India transactions; he therefore wished that the Speaker would interfere, that the House might return to the consideration of the subject before them. **Mr. Wilberforce.**

The Speaker agreed that the question was departed from, to which Major Scott immediately acceded.

Mr. *Fox* requested the honourable gentleman to consider that he was making an appeal to him on a subject irrelevant to the question, and he would not wish to be regarded as giving an assent to what came before him extra judicially. **Mr. Fox.**

Mr. *Francis* contended, that the authority of the Supreme Council was not by any means a check upon Mr. Hastings; because, after the death of Colonel Monson, who with him and General Clavering were appointed to that Board, there was no control upon the Governor, who, in the executive **Mr. Francis.**

power acted as he judged proper; and whatever might be the design of those who thought differently from Mr. Hastings at the Council Board, his authority carried all before it. The affair of the zemindar Cheyt Sing, was, at least in his opinion, iniquitous; and in Council he opposed it on the grounds that the demand had been made without right; but he would not stray from the business before the House; let the papers moved for be produced, and as the honourable gentleman and he now understood each other, they ought to join issue, and leave the decision to the event.

Mr. Chancellor Pitt.

Mr. Chancellor *Pitt* expressed his earnest wishes to be considered as impartial in the business before the House, and when he gave an opinion, or happened to differ from the gentlemen opposite to him, it was not from any insurmountable partiality, for he should always strive to make his conduct a greater proof of his disposition than his words: yet he could not refrain from saying, that the more he informed his mind by recurring to precedents in similar cases, the more grounds he saw to insist for explicit reasons to intitle the House to concur in the production of papers which tended to the criminal accusation of any man; and as the right honourable gentleman had expressed his willingness to comply with the general wish of the House, by assigning what were his particular motives for calling for the papers [Here Mr. Burke said, it was not from a voluntary concession of his that he would, in this stage of the business, explain his motives; but if no other remedy was left, he would even go so far, though he knew it was irregular] Mr. Pitt thanked the right honourable gentleman for not suffering him to remain in an error, but was sorry they were not of opinion in so material a point. And whilst throughout a criminal prosecution he could find all authorities operating in his favour, when he required an explicit and an open charge to ground the production of papers on as collateral evidence, he hoped he would be considered as acting for, and pleading the cause of, every individual in the kingdom, either now or hereafter, who might be liable to prosecution, and whose innocence he would always presume to consider as existing, unless evident facts could be substantiated. He should contend that degrees of guilt are measured by circumstances, which either extenuate or aggravate; and in a charge where the House of Commons became accusers, he thought that the old mode which introduced the fact immediately before the House deserved a preference over that just now insinuated in the present business, where the mode of inquiry is only fishing for business.

Mr. Fox.

Mr. *Fox* observed, that the method suggested by his right honourable friend seemed more in favour of the accused person fon than that which was stated to be the customary process; for in the latter, the House assumes to itself the power of accusing at once; but in that now offered, he saw the House trying the merits of the case like a grand jury, before it would proceed to inquiry; and if there was any deviation from the established forms of the usual practice it was in favour of the supposed delinquent, who thus enjoyed a chance of acquittal thereby, which the other mode precluded.

Mr. *Burke* begged leave to assure the House, that should Mr. Burke. they call upon him to specify any of the charges he would comply; and he thought himself in possession of such a volume of evidence, as would enforce conviction before the tribunal to which he intended to refer it: such evidence as neither influence nor connection could withstand, nor corruption awe; nay, such as would cause the justice of this country to exert itself. Amidst a multitude of other enormities, it would appear, that the country of Oude had been desolated; the ladies of the royal family plundered; the nobility stripped of their property; armed soldiers quartered on the inhabitants to extort their property, and many other crimes too deeply marked by violent barbarity, under the command, and by the directions of, Warren Hastings, Esquire.

The motion was put by the Speaker, when

Alderman *Le Mesurier* took notice, that the book, since Alderman the year 1782, now moved for, amounted to six volumes in Le Mesurier folio, and from what appeared to him, six others prior to that date might perhaps be necessary for the right honourable gentleman's purpose; he thought therefore that a reasonable time should be allowed to the clerks.

Mr. *Burke* now moved,

" That there be laid before this House, a copy or Mr. Burke. " duplicate of the proceedings of the Governor General " and Council of the 23d of September, 1783, on the or- " ders of the Court of Directors relative to the women of " the Nabob of Oude's family.

" That there be laid before this House, copies or dupli- " cates of all correspondence relative to the conduct and " behaviour of the military forces in Oude, and of any " farming or managing, or proposal to farm or manage " any revenues, by any British officers in the Company's " service in that province, or the dependencies thereof.

" That there be laid before this House, copies of all " the correspondence of Major Palmer, a private agent to " Warren Hastings, Esquire, Governor General of Bengal, " at the Court of Oude; as also of Major Davy, another

" of the private agents of the said Warren Hastings, in Oude,
" together with their instructions.

" That there be laid before this House, an account of all
" allowances made from the revenues of Oude to the English
" Resident and assistants, agent or agents, or other English
" in a civil capacity, or to any other officers in the military
" service, over and above the pay and ordinary allowances,
" with copies or duplicates of all correspondence relative
" thereto, not comprehended under the other orders of this
" House.

" That there be laid before this House, copies or dupli-
" cates of all proceedings relative to the Rohilla and Bidgi-
" gur prize money, not contained in the Reports of the Com-
" mittees of this House.

" That there be laid before this House, copies or dupli-
" cates of all correspondence and other proceedings relative
" to the wife and the mother of Cheyt Sing, and the taking
" of the place of their residence.

" That there be laid before this House, a copy or dupli-
" cate of all correspondence relative to the state and altera-
" tions in the government, and concerning the landed reve-
" nues, or the appointment or removal of any naib, or de-
" puty, or deputies, in the province of Benares, and the
" appointment thereto or removal therefrom, of any Resi-
" dent since the settlement with Rajah Myhipnarain.

" That there be laid before this House, extracts of any
" letters shewing an account of the number of the persons
" which the Begums of Oude have at any time stated they
" were under the necessity of maintaining.

" That there be laid before this House, copies or dupli-
" cates of all minutes of consultation or other proceedings
" relative to the Governor General of Bengal's last deputa-
" tion to Lucknow, and the resolution not to send a Resident
" thither, together with the instructions and powers given to
" the said Governor General.

" That there be laid before this House a copy or dupli-
" cate of a letter from the Governor General and Council
" of Fort William, to the President and Select Committee
" of Bombay, dated 26th December 1781, and received by
" the Lively, 24th May 1783.

" That there be laid before this House, copies or dupli-
" cates of all correspondence and proceedings relative to the
" Nabob of Farruckabad, not reported in the Reports of the
" Carnatic or Judicature Committees.

" That there be laid before this House, copies or dupli-
" cates of all correspondence and other proceedings relative
" to a Mahometan seminary established at Calcutta.

" That

" That there be laid before this House, copies or dupli-
" cates of all correspondence, or other proceedings relative to
" the appointment of, or the attempt to appoint, Richard
" Joseph Sulivan, Esquire, late Secretary to the Select
" Committee at Madras, to be ambassador from the Nabob
" of Arcot to the Governor General and Council at Cal-
" cutta; and also to be ambassador from the Governor Ge-
" neral and Council of Calcutta to the Nabob of Arcot; and
" also to be ambassador from the Governor General and
" Council to the Nizam or Soubah of the Decan, from the
" date of the proceedings which have been reported by the
" Committee of Secrecy appointed to inquire into the causes
" of the Carnatic war.

" That there be laid before this House, a Letter from
" Warren Hastings, Esquire, to the Court of Directors, re-
" lative to their censure of his conduct at Benares, ordered
" by the said Warren Hastings to be printed, and also the
" answer of the Court of Directors thereto.

" That there be laid before this House, a copy of a pa-
" ragraph in the letter of the Court of Directors to the
" Governor General and Council of Fort William, dated
" 10th March 1785, permitting the Governor General,
" Warren Hastings, Esquire, to resign the government of
" Bengal."

The several motions passed, and the House adjourned.

Tuesday, 21st February.

No debate, on account of the small number of members
within the House.

Wednesday, 22d February.

Mr. Fox observed, that when he had the honour to present Mr. Fox.
the petition of the shopkeepers of Westminster, praying a
repeal of the act imposing a tax on retail shops, he had no
instructions to move, that the petitioners might be heard
either by themselves or counsel; but having understood since,
that such was their desire, he begged leave to move, " That
" the retail dealers, inhabitants of the city and liberty of
" Westminster, who have petitioned this House for a repeal
" of an act passed in the last session of Parliament, for
" granting to His Majesty certain duties on shops within
" Great Britain, be at liberty to be heard by themselves or
" counsel in support of the said petition, before the Com-
" mittee of the whole House, to whom the petition of
" the retail shopkeepers of the city of London is re-
" ferred."—The motion passed.

Mr.

Mr. *Baſtard* remarked, that before the Houſe proceeded to enter upon the diſcuſſion of the great queſtion of fortifying the dock yards, he conceived they ought to have the fulleſt information on the ſubject which could poſſibly be procured. He ſhould, therefore, as the time of the Houſe would become fully occupied by the debates likely to enſue upon that day, he would barely move that " an humble addreſs be " preſented to His Majeſty, that he will be gracioufly pleaſed " to give directions, that there be laid before this Houſe a " copy of the third datum referred to in the extracts from " the Report made to His Majeſty by the Board of Land " and Sea Officers appointed by His Majeſty to inveſtigate " and report on the proper ſyſtem of defence, and on the " expediency and efficacy of the propoſed plans for better ſe- " curing the dock yards at Portſmouth and Plymouth."

Mr. Chan-
cellor Pitt.

Mr. *Chancellor Pitt* replied, that when information was demanded by any honourable member, he always felt the ſtrongeſt inclination to have it granted, where it was poſſible to afford it conſiſtently with the intereſts and ſafety of the nation. That the information now required was not of that deſcription, he apprehended, needed no other proof than barely to read the title of the paper called for by the honourable gentleman's motion; he accordingly read it for the Houſe, and it appeared to be an account of the places and means by which an enemy could with the moſt facility effect an invaſion.

Mr. Baſ-
tard.

Mr. *Baſtard* anſwered that he could not conceive that any bad or dangerous conſequences could poſſibly reſult from laying upon the table the copy of a Report made at ſo remote a period; but as he held a copy of the Report in his hand, he would read it as a part of his ſpeech. Mr. Baſtard was proceeding to read the report, when

Mr. Chan-
cellor Pitt.

Mr. *Chancellor Pitt* begged leave to interrupt the honourable gentleman by aſſuring him that he could never acquieſce in any member's reading, as a part of his ſpeech, a paper, purporting to be an official document, without ſtating to the Houſe how he had obtained it, that ſo they might know it to be authentic. It was alſo, whether authentic or not, irregular, and highly improper for any paper of ſuch a nature to be exhibited without an order of the Houſe for producing it, for only the Houſe at large could judge of its neceſſity and uſefulneſs. Any information that could be derived from the Report now moved for, would in itſelf prove abſolutely nugatory; becauſe the reſult of the Report by a Board of military and naval officers, (whoſe competence no gentleman could poſſibly queſtion) comprehended and involved the reſult of the former Report; and from this former Report, and from the nature of the ſubject of that Report which he had
juſt

juſt read to the Houſe, it would appear that nothing but its general reſult could with ſafety be made public.

Mr. *Baſtard* replied that he wiſhed not by any means to infringe upon the orders or practice of proceeding in that Houſe, and if he had done ſo in any degree, he begged it might be imputed to his not being ſufficiently experienced in their mode of proceeding. With regard to the Report, as he found it to be irregular to read it, he would not proceed, but would content himſelf with ſaying, that the whole jut of the queſtions and anſwers in that Report went to eſtabliſh it as a poſition not to be diſputed, that an enemy might effect an invaſion if no attempt was made to oppoſe and repel their efforts, juſt as if a perſon were to aſk, if an enemy could make a landing behind the Speaker's chair? and the anſwer given was to be, " Undoubtedly ; if no endeavour is " exerted to prevent it."

Mr. Baſtard withdrew his motion.

Captain *Macbride* obſerved that he roſe to move for a paper, which, in his idea, could not poſſibly produce any inconvenience, or afford the leaſt information to the enemies of the country, which might affect the ſafety of the State. When the Board of Inquiry ſat at Plymouth, the naval officers entered a minute on their proceedings, inſiſting on having before them the Report of Lieutenant Hawkins, engineer, who had inſpected the coaſt of Whiteſand Bay ; that Report had been before them, and when that was ſeen, and the opinion of the naval officers upon it, it would be found that the naval officers' opinion was directly in the teeth of the fortifications. The Captain concluded with moving " That there be laid be- " fore this Houſe, a copy of the Report of the Board of " Naval Officers appointed in 1784, to inquire if an enemy " can land in Whiteſand Bay."

Mr. *Chancellor Pitt* again declared his uneaſineſs at being obliged to withhold from any honourable gentleman ſuch aids and materials as he might judge neceſſary either for his own information, or that of the Houſe, on a ſubject of ſuch importance as the preſent ; but his duty as a ſervant of the public, and as reſponſible for the ſecurity of the nation, moſt ſtrictly forbade him to give his aſſent to the motion that had been made. The Report of Lieutenant Hawkins was on a ſubject of a very delicate nature, and related to the practicability of an enemy's landing on Whiteſand Bay, and the coaſt adjacent from the Ramhead to Eaſt Looe, an extent of ſeveral miles, and it alſo gave a particular detail of the tides, the ſoundings, the ſmall harbours and inlets, the anchorage, and other material objects to be conſidered, with regard to the practicability of an enemy's landing, as well as of the various circumſtances of ſituation, of diſtance of ground,

and

Mr. Baſtard.

Captain Macbride.

Mr. Chancellor Pitt.

and of the time and difficulty which muſt attend the landing
of troops, horſes and artillery, and the probability there was,
in caſe of their landing, that they would be able to penetrate
the country in order to make an attack on the dock yards,
together with the time which it might be expected frigates
could remain upon the coaſt for the purpoſe of effecting and
covering the debarkation ; from which it muſt appear to the
Houſe how exceedingly incompatible with wiſdom and policy it would be to have it laid before the Public in the manner now demanded.

Captain
Macbride. Captain *Macbride* begged leave to aſſure the Houſe that he
diſclaimed any intention of moving for papers which might
convey information to the enemy, and obſerved that the landing muſt be effected before the enemy could proceed to penetrate the country, and that, conſequently, the naval part of
the queſtion was eſſential to the Houſe, as a primary conſideration to any conſequences which might take place, after
the enemy had once landed. He ridiculed the idea of our
having it in our power to communicate any intelligence reſpecting the Britiſh coaſts to the enemy, for they knew them
full as well as we did ourſelves, as every body might recollect, when it was conſidered that the French fiſhing boats
were perpetually over in our bays and harbours ; beſides, was
it to be imagined that they would attempt to land in corners,
and on ſuch parts of our coaſts which they muſt perceive our
cruizers carefully avoiding, as dangerous in the extreme?

Mr. *Chancellor Pitt*, diſclaiming any feelings of a perſonal
nature on the ſubject of the Report moved for, which, he
ſaid, it was impoſſible to impute to him with any ſhadow of
either propriety or juſtice, added, that it was impoſſible for
him, who knew the honourable gentleman's zeal for the ſervice of his country, and the great reputation which he had
acquired in the diſcharge of his profeſſional duty, to ſuſpect
for a moment, any but the pureſt intentions to have influenced him in making his motion. He argued againſt the attempting to go into the detail of the Report, in conformity
to the wiſhes of the honourable gentleman oppoſite, by obſerving, that as the ſubject matter of the Report was of ſuch
a nature as appeared to the Houſe to be improper for them to
inveſtigate, and as they had, as it had been well ſaid in that
Houſe, " ſent the queſtion to an arbitration," by directing
that a Board ſhould be appointed for the purpoſe, becauſe the
buſineſs could be done more effectually and more ſecretly in
that mode than by a parliamentary inquiry, it was departing
from the principle of the Houſe now to enter upon the minute parts of the ſubject, which it had already avowed itſelf
incapable of examining with propriety. He demanded an
explanation from the honourable gentleman, whether he had
                                                      intended

intended to ftate that the land officers diffented in their opinion from the report of Lieutenant Hawkins, or that the naval officers had difapproved of the fyftem of fortifications *in toto*, a pofition which, as the honourable gentleman had not abfolutely affirmed, he could, without any rudenefs, directly contradict, as the very firft article of the Report went to eftablifh the neceffity of fortifications by an unanimous vote of the whole Board.

Captain Macbride withdrew his motion.

General *Burgoyne* begged leave to point out two omiffions in the extracts from the Report of the Board of Naval and Military officers which appeared to him material. He did not mean to caft any imputation whatever, or to have it imagined that he thought the omiffion wilful; he did not believe they were; but he thought it right to mention them. Although he was as fully prepared upon the fubject as ever he fhould be, yet he had a motion to make for fome papers, to which he did not forefee the poffibility of an objection, but which, in his humble judgement, were fo important and fo highly neceffary to be before the Houfe, that the Houfe would not be ripe to proceed to difcufs the queftion of fortifications, till after the papers fhould have been put upon the table. The General then moved for " a return of the infan- " try in the kingdom, the number of effectives, and the de- " ficiencies to complete the eftablifhment in the year 1779."

This motion occafioning another converfation of fome length;

Mr. *Martin* profeffed himfelf an advocate for all the information which it was poffible to procure, but declared that not one of the papers moved for upon that day, went to the removal of the objection which he felt to the propofed fyftem of fortification, and that was, that the adoption of that fyftem would make an increafe of the ftanding army neceffary, a matter which he was too much of a Whig to give his confent to, notwithftanding the good opinion he entertained of the noble Duke at the head of the ordnance, and the great partiality of his mind to His Majefty's prefent Minifters, who he hoped would long remain in poffeffion of His Majefty's confidence, and the confidence of the People. Mr. Martin concluded by remarking that he did not confider the queftion of fortifications as perfonal, nor did he fpeak from private motives of any kind, but he thought it his duty to declare his genuine fentiments, and he hoped that every friend of the Minifter would alfo give his genuine fentiments refpecting the fubject.

Mr. *Chancellor Pitt* anfwered, that he entirely coincided in principle, (as in general he had the good fortune to do, with the honourable gentleman) that an increafe in the ftanding

General Burgoyne.

Mr. Martin.

Mr. Chancellor Pitt.

army would indeed occasion an almost insurmountable objection to the accomplishment of the plan under consideration; but he assured him and the House, that they need be under no apprehensions of any such necessity arising from the fortifications proposed being carried into execution. He would, he declared, undertake to prove to the satisfaction of every unprejudiced person, that so far from rendering it necessary to increase the standing army, they would operate in the direct contrary way, and afford the means of defending the kingdom, in case of an invasion, with a much smaller force than was at present necessary. As to the paper moved for he could see no sort of necessity for it, as it appeared to him to relate to one of those matters which formed the immediate duty of the executive government.

Mr. Fox.

Mr. *Fox* remarked that if, the right honourable gentleman really meant to resist such a motion as that of his honourable friend, it would be better to say at once, fortification was not a fit question for that House to discuss; for how was it possible for the House to form any opinion respecting the propriety of making fortifications, if they were not allowed the means of judging upon the subject? It was admitted, he conceived, on all hands, that fortifications must necessarily be considered in one of these two lights: they would either prove a strength to the kingdom, or they would add to its weakness, and in case of an invasion, strengthen the enemy. This must depend altogether on our capacity of manning them, and keeping them in our own hands; and how was that matter to be decided and ascertained? It could be known only by two means, and, for his own part, he should presume no good Minister would resort to the supposition, as to what might happen to be the internal force of the kingdom at any future period,—he surely would not, but would look back to what the internal force of the country had been during eras of danger. He would not take upon him to pronounce that the year 1779 was the best year to be selected for the objects of the motion, or whether it would not be proper to select a series of years, in order that the matter might be more fairly viewed and determined; but at any rate he saw not the utility of the House's proceeding to the debate upon the fortifications, without having some such papers before them as those for which his honourable friend had moved.

Mr. Chancellor Pitt.

Mr. *Chancellor Pitt* replied, that he should have looked upon it as a reasonable and fair opinion for gentlemen to entertain, that His Majesty's Ministers would not come to Parliament to require money for the erection of fortifications without having first duly considered the prospect of being able to garrison them properly; and that was what he meant when he gave it as his opinion that the object of the motion

seemed

feemed to him to relate to one branch of the peculiar functions of the executive government. If, however, the Houfe thought it a fubject neceffary for them to inquire into. he had no fort of objection to confent to the motion except that which naturally arofe in his mind at feeing the attendance of a full Houfe on a fubject of great importance, and having gentlemen difappointed and fent away without entering on the bufinefs which they expected to have finifhed. He could not, however, conceal his aftonifhment that the right honourable gentleman fhould not have before now made up his mind on that part of the fubject, as he believed he could fafely fay, that the fyftem of fortification had been at one time under the confideration of the right honourable gentleman himfelf, and by him as a Minifter received with approbation. He fhould, therefore expect, that when the bufinefs came regularly forward, the right honourable gentleman would have no objection to ftate and explain the reafons that had induced him to alter his opinion, if he had in fact changed it upon the fubject. He fhould by all means confent to the motion, notwithftanding his regret at having the bufinefs of the day poftponed; but he hoped that this was the laft intended delay of the kind, and begged that if any gentleman defired more information than had been already granted, he would now move for it, as he fhould by no means confent to any farther procraftination on any pretence whatfoever.

Mr. *Fox* replied that his honourable friend meant to have Mr. Fox. made the motion yefterday, but it was well known that he could not do it as there was no Houfe; and with refpect to himfelf, he really had never read the Report till it was printed; and therefore could not be a judge whether the papers now moved for would be neceffary or not, before the Report was delivered out to the members of that Houfe. As to what the right honourable gentleman had faid of his having at one time minifterially confidered and approved of the propofed fyftem of fortification, he would venture to advance one pofition, and the right honourable gentleman might wreft it to whatfoever conftruction he thought proper; and this was, that whatever opinion he might have lightly taken up at a former period upon any given fubject, which at a diftance of time came to be more immediately under his confideration, and he after a fecond and maturer deliberation found reafon to think differently, he fhould never be afhamed of acknowledging that he had changed his fentiments.

Mr. *Courtenay* remarked, that the paper might be refufed, Mr. Courtenay. for better reafons than any which he had heard advanced that night; as the producing it would give either the Public or the Houfe no very favourable impreffion of the accuracy, correctnefs, and principle on which the noble Duke had

profecuted

prosecuted this important investigation. It would perhaps appear, that the Board of Naval and Land Officers had previously determined, that 22,000 men were amply sufficient for the defence of Portsmouth and Plymouth, without their having any return of the military establishment before them; and consequently without knowing whether such a number of troops could be supplied. On the same principle they must have determined, by implication, on the strength of the military establishment of France, as they must have exactly ascertained the number of troops with which the supposed attack could possibly be made; and against which 22,000, in their opinion, would prove an adequate defence and security. It appeared therefore not a little astonishing, that these two most essential points were absolutely fixed by the noble Duke and the Board, though it was now admitted by the Chancellor of the Exchequer, that no return, even of the military force of this country, had been laid before them; still less could they have discovered the capability of France for the expected attack.

At length the motion amended passed thus:

" That an humble address be presented to His Majesty, " that he will be graciously pleased to give directions, that " there be laid before this House, a state of the British army, " as distributed in the different parts of the world, in the " months of June and December, in the years 1778, 1779, " 1780, 1781, and 1782; and likewise of the foreign troops " in the pay of Great Britain at those several periods.

" That an humble address be presented to His Majesty, " that he will be graciously pleased to give directions, that " there be laid before this House, a state of the distribution " of the land forces in South Britain, in the month of August, " in the years 1779, 1780, 1781, and 1782."

Ordered,

That the said addresses be presented to His Majesty by such members of this House as are of His Majesty's most honourable Privy Council.

The House adjourned.

Thursday, 23d February.

No material debate took place.

Friday, 24th February.

Major *Scott* remarked, that, during every minute subsequent to that in which a right honourable gentleman (Mr. Burke) had moved for papers, his eagerness and anxiety to see them all produced continually increased; and, therefore, had he

he gone twice to the East-India House, for the purpose of difcovering in what probable time they would become fubmitted to the inveftigation of the Houfe. He had been informed that morning, that the greateft part of the papers
were already prepared, and he would wifh to move, that fuch
as were ready, fhould be prefented, without any delay, that
the Houfe might have an early opportunity of perufing
them. He could affure the Houfe, that the only anxiety he
felt was, to bring forward the bufinefs as quick as poffible;
and that anxiety had been increafed by his obferving what
was doing out of doors, where the moft fcandalous mifreprefentations of what had been faid in that Houfe were zealoufly and infidioufly difperfed. He well knew that fuch
mifreprefentations could not affect the Houfe, on whofe juftice and impartiality he had the firmeft reliance; but when
falfe and injurious calumnies were afferted, and when thofe
calumnies were imputed to a member of that Houfe, with a
view of affecting the character of a man who had long enjoyed a very high office abroad, it became a matter of great
importance, that no ftudied or unneceffary delay fhould be
ufed, in bringing forward thofe charges, to fubftantiate which
the papers were moved for. Major Scott then read an extract from a newfpaper, that *" perfons living under the protec-
" tion of the Britifh Government had, in India, actually been
" put to the torture by the orders of* Mr. Haftings." This was
an affertion totally void of foundation. The honourable
member (he was informed) had faid no fuch thing. Of this
matter Mr. Haftings remained in total ignorance; and abfolutely certain it was, that no Englifhman had either au-
thorized or countenanced fuch an atrocious act of cruelty;
yet as the report was framed moft mifchievoufly to deceive
and to exafperate the Public, he fhould beg leave to move
that all papers whatfoever fhould, in the firft moment of being ready, become fubmitted to the infpection of the Houfe.

The Speaker told the Major his motion was informal and
unneceffary.

Mr. Pye moved, that the bill for reducing all the laws relating to the militia into one act of Parliament be committed
for Wednefday fe'nnight.

Mr. *Rolle* having obferved, that as any bill defigned to in- Mr. Rolle.
troduce a novel fyftem for the militia muft, by its nature,
become a point of deep importance, concerning which the
country fhould, if poffible, be previoufly confulted, expreffed
his wifhes that a longer time had been allowed. The affizes were coming on; it appeared therefore to be highly
proper that the bill fhould not be hurried through the
Houfe, but that it fhould at leaft wait till after the affizes,
and till the refpectable grand juries had been allowed to pafs
their

their judgement upon it. He added, that he was not afhamed of meeting his conftituents and confulting them as to their wifhes upon great public occafions: if the bill was not to be urged on farther at prefent, he fhould have an opportunity of feeing his conftituents and knowing their fentiments, an information which could not be acquired, were the defign of referring the bill at a very early moment to a Committee to be carried into execution.

Mr. Pye. Mr. *Pye* anfwered, that the bill was not to be confidered as a new bill, but merely as a bill reducing all the militia laws into one act. There were alfo parts in the bill which furely would meet the approbation of the Houfe as they went to favings; in particular, a claufe enacting, that the men fhould be balloted for five years inftead of three: he hoped therefore, that the bill, which certainly contained very novel matter, would be allowed to ftand committed for Wednefday fe'nnight.

Mr. Rolle. Mr. *Rolle* begged leave to remind the honourable gentleman, that he had himfelf mentioned a circumftance of confiderable importance, and fufficient in his mind to induce the Houfe to agree to poftpone the commitment of the bill; he fhould therefore move by way of amendment, that the bill be committed for the 3d of April.

[When it had been obferved that the circumftance of changing the period which the men were to ballot for from three years to five, was not a part of the printed bill, but was left blank for the Houfe in the Committee to decide as they thought proper,]

Mr. Rolle remarked that he had during the recefs, written to an honourable gentleman oppofite to him, to know what were to be the alterations in refpect to the militia that were to be introduced into the bill; and the honourable gentleman had written him in anfwer, that the bill was not fufficiently digefted for him to ftate what they were: as therefore the honourable gentlemen who had undertaken to prepare the bill, had fpent fo much time about the fubject, furely other country gentlemen ought to be permitted to have an opportunity of confidering the bill maturely, and confulting their conftituents refpecting it.

Mr. Marfham. Mr. *Marfham* acknowledging this circumftance, faid, that he had in return fent him word, that the whole of the bill was not at that time digefted, but he had at the fame time informed him of the propofal to change the period of balloting the men for five years inftead of three; the honourable gentleman therefore had been apprized of that occurrence upon which he now feemed to lay fo much ftrefs long enough to confult his conftituents refpecting its nature.

Mr.

Mr. *Jolliffe* remarked, that when he felt the magnitude and importance of a bill in which he could not avoid confidering all ranks within the kingdom as parties deeply interefted, his prepoffeffions became the ftronger in favour of the motion : the bill therefore ought not to be hurried in its progrefs, but time fhould be given to the grand juries who would be convened at the enfuing affizes, to fee the bill and form an opinion upon it ; fo that if the people thought proper they might inftruct their reprefentatives upon the fubject, and the Houfe in their decifion upon it might act agreeably to the known fenfe of the country. The propofals to ballot the men for five years inftead of three, and to call out the militia annually, were points upon which he was not perfectly decided, but he fhould declare his fentiments at the proper time. He begged not to be mifunderftood, nor to have it fuppofed that he was an enemy to the militia; no man in that Houfe was a more fincere friend to the inftitution, and he thought it unfair in the honourable gentlemen who had turned their attention more particularly to the fubject, and prepared the bill, to charge every member of that Houfe who was not willing to give his immediate confent to the putting the country to the expence of calling out the militia every year, with being an enemy to the inftitution; indeed he thought the right honourable gentleman (the Chancellor of the Exchequer) had been ufed rather hardly the other day in having it imputed to him that he was no friend to the militia, merely becaufe he was not willing to give a decided opinion upon that important point till he had heard it fully difcuffed and debated, and by that means had afcertained the fenfe of the Houfe in general refpecting it. With thefe ideas, he was perfuaded that the Houfe would confider him as fully juftified, when preffing earneftly upon their minds the neceffity of fetting apart a longer period for a deliberate inveftigation.

Lord *Mahon* faid, if the fact were, that the fenfe of the country ought to be taken, either by giving time for the grand juries to fee the bill and have an opportunity of confidering it previous to its being paffed, or by any other means, and it were true that a blank was left for words to be inferted enacting how long the men fhould be balloted for, that was a ftrong reafon for the bill's being fent to a Committee as foon as poffible, in order that the blanks might be filled up; becaufe, by that being done, the country would fee what the bill really was, and be capable of judging whether the alterations were for the better or the worfe. If the country ought to fee it, what could they learn from a blank bill? The idea of fending it into the country before the blanks were filled up would be abfurd and ridiculous in the

the extreme; and therefore would he advife, that the bill
fhould go to a Committee on Wednefday fe'nnight, and
after that, be printed with all the amendments made by the
Committee.

Mr. Rolle.

Mr. *Rolle* faid, that he had gone to the meeting of gentlemen who had undertaken to prepare a new militia bill,
and had been given to underftand, that no gentleman but
fuch as had ferved in the militia could be admitted: he
knew that his conftituents would oppofe feveral of the regulations, and he wifhed to give them time to confider them
fully.

Mr. Chan-
cellor Pitt.

Mr. Chancellor *Pitt* obferved, that he could fcarcely
have believed it poffible, that a converfation upon a fubject
which, in its prefent ftage at leaft, required but a fhort
difcuffion, could have become extended to a long debate—
An honourable member (Mr. Rolle) feemed defirous of
poftponing the commitment of the bill till after the affizes,
in order that the feveral grand juries might have an opportunity of judging of it, and fuggefting their fentiments to
their reprefentatives; but he did not fee how that very laudable inclination of the honourable gentleman to hear the
opinion of his conftituents fhould induce him to wifh to
poftpone the commitment, however it might be an argument for deferring to pafs the bill. He, for his part, fhould
be for the commitment on the earlier day; but he did not by
any means pledge himfelf as to his opinion, whether he
fhould vote for a delay in appointing a time for the third
reading of the bill or not; for, though he looked upon the
bufinefs as of the utmoft confequence, and thought it highly
proper on fuch occafions for the Houfe to give every opportunity to the nation at large to form their judgements and
opinions concerning them, yet he was inclined to think the
prefent a diftinct and feparate queftion, and not being on
the general policy of a militia, but on a mere matter of regulation, it was a fubject fitter for a parliamentary than a
more popular difcuffion, He apprehended, that the queftion
between a long or a fhort interval, from the commitment
to the third reading of the bill, would be entirely governed
by the ftate in which it fhould leave the Committee: if it
then appeared to contain any thing new, any thing doubtful, or any thing likely to create a great variety of opinion
in the Houfe, he fhould then fuppofe it would prove the
general fenfe of gentlemen to allow a long day for the third
reading; but otherwife, he could fee no reafon for deferring
it. Every man in the kingdom agreed in opinion on the
propriety and ufefulnefs of the militia, as a great refource
of national defence, and therefore on that head there could
be no variance of ideas; the only matter in difpute would be
how

how to render it moft efficacious toward the great end of its inftitution, the defence of the kingdom. If it fhould be found, that it was not abfolutely neceffary for the purpofe, that it fhould be called out every year, then no gentleman could oppofe the faving of fo much money as the embodying of it would neceffarily demand: but if, on the contrary, it appeared, that by not embodying of it annually, it would become lefs ferviceable, or in any degree inadequate to its end, then furely there could be no doubt of the neceffity of annually calling them out notwithftanding the expence, whatever it might be, that fhould be thereby incurred.

Mr. *Marfham* begged leave to animadvert upon one particular point which had been ftated by the honourable member who began the debate, and that was in refpect to the honourable gentleman's having been denied admiffion when he came while fome other gentlemen and himfelf were engaged upon the fubject. There was a general meeting advertifed, to which every gentleman who was a friend to the militia was invited to come, and every member of both Houfes of Parliament: that meeting chofe a Committee, and having done fo, it would have been exceedingly improper for the Committee to have been open to whoever chofe to attend it; becaufe in that cafe it would have been impoffible for the Committee to have executed any bufinefs, and the very end of its inftitution would have been loft. The honourable gentleman had to blame himfelf therefore for not having attended the general meeting. *(Mr. Marfham.)*

Mr. *Pye* declared, that he had never entertained the leaft idea of excluding the honourable gentleman (Mr. Rolle) from the meeting to which he had alluded; he had, on the contrary, in perfon, afked him to accompany him to the St. Alban's Tavern to the meeting. *(Mr. Pye.)*

The *Secretary at War* brought up the return of the military force of the kingdom in the years 1778, 1779, 1780, 1781 and 1782, with a fpecific account of the diftribution of it, as ordered on Wednefday laft. *(The Secretary at War.)*

General Burgoyne moved that it fhould be printed.

Mr. Chancellor *Pitt* obferved, that although a warm advocate for the neceffity of prefenting all proper information to the Houfe, he muft beg leave ftrenuoufly to contend againft the production of papers moved for by the honourable General, left danger fhould enfue from their becoming points of notoriety. He could not but think, that to let the papers lie on the table, would be fufficient for the information of fuch gentlemen as intended to make ufe of them in argument in the courfe of Monday's debate; nor could he think, without pain, of the confequences of the growing cuftom of intro- *(Mr. Chancellor Pitt.)*

introducing official papers almost as often as they were desired.

The House adjourned.

Monday, 27th February.

Mr. Chancellor Pitt.

Mr. Chancellor *Pitt* begged leave earnestly to submit to the most serious and deliberate attention of the House, a proposition which, in his humble opinion, it behoved them to adopt previous to their forming themselves into a Committee of Supply; in order that it might serve as a direction to that Committee in what manner to regulate that kind of vote which naturally might be expected from them at the close of the debate. Little, indeed, was his astonishment excited, when he reflected with how prejudiced a comment great numbers of the public had chosen to describe the question for discussion; because, as much within as beyond the walls of Paliament, its real nature had been concealed by an insidious colouring; to give a lasting force to which, all arts were put in practice.

The system of fortification had been dragged forth to public view as deserving the severest censures which could be thrown on any measure of Government; and there had been attempts to excite against it, the feelings, the passions, and even the most estimable prejudices of the nation. It was represented as novel in its principle, as unconstitutional in its tendency, by laying a foundation for the increase of the standing army, and as calculated to divert into either a useless or a dangerous channel those resources which ought rather to be applied to that great foundation of our strength, of our glory, and of our characteristic superiority over the rest of the nations of Europe—our Navy. Those were in themselves substantial objections, and such as, if they did really apply to the case, ought to carry with them an insuperable authority: but he was come down prepared with such arguments as he flattered himself would appear to the House sufficient to answer, and even overturn, them all; and in order that the whole scope and object of his reasoning might be the more readily and clearly understood, he would state, at the outset, the nature of his proposition, which he had so worded as to comprehend the whole of the several principles on which, in his mind, the question was to stand. He had, on a former day suggested, that the most regular mode for debating the subject would arise in the Committee of Supply, when the question would be, whether to vote the whole of the annual ordnance estimates, which would amount to about 300,000l. or to vote only 250,000l. and by such means prevent the application of the 50,000l. voted in a former session for the

purpose

purpose of fortifications, from the object for which it had been intended, by obliging the Board of Ordnance to apply it to the current service of the year; and, by so doing, to put an effectual stop to the whole system. From many things, however, which had fallen from gentlemen on the other side of the House, he was induced to wish, that a different method of arguing the question should be adopted; and he accordingly devised the present mode, as best calculated, in his opinion, to afford an opportunity of discussing, in their fullest extent, every principle which could possibly be involved in the proceeding, as well as those in opposition to it as those in its favour. It was also more consistent with the great importance of the subject to bring it immediately before the House, in the form of a specific resolution, recognizing a great and momentous principle, and founded on that principle, an instruction to the Committee, than to send it to the Committee at once, as it were incidentally and collaterally. The resolution which he proposed, before he sat down, to move to the House was,

" That it appears to this House, that to provide effectually for securing His Majesty's dock yards at Portsmouth " and Plymouth, by a permanent system of fortification, " founded on the most œconomical principles, and requiring " the smallest number of troops possible to answer the pur- " pose of such security, is an essential object for the safety of " the State, intimately connected with the general defence of " the kingdom, and necessary for enabling the fleet to act " with full vigour and effect, for the protection of com- " merce, the support of our distant possessions, and the pro- " secution of offensive operations in any war in which the " nation may hereafter be engaged."

He felt it impossible to contemplate this important question without regarding it as a portion of that momentary system which challenged, from its nature, the utmost care of all administrations whatsoever; a system upon which rested the security and the glory of the national defence. And, in order to judge of its necessity, towards that great object, he should attempt, but with much pain, to bring back the recollection of the House to the unfortunate and calamitous situation to which we were exposed in the late war, much in consequence of our want of those fortifications which it was the aim of the present question to provide. A considerable part of our fleet was confined to our ports, in order to protect our dock yards; and thus we were obliged to do what Great Britain had never done before—to carry on a mere defensive war; a war in which, as in every other war merely defensive, we were under the necessity of wasting our resources, and impairing our strength, without any prospect of

　　benefiting

benefiting ourfelves but at the lofs of a great and valuable part of our poffeffions, and which at laft was terminated by a *neceffary* peace. Shame and affliction were brought upon us by the American war. Was the Houfe ready to ftand refponfible to pofterity for a repetition of fuch difgraces and misfortunes? Were they willing to take upon themfelves the hazard of tranfmitting to the next generation thofe dangers and thofe confequent calamities which they had themfelves fo bitterly experienced? The fubject of fortifications was not now for the firft time to be difcuffed; it had been before the Houfe during the courfe of the laft feffion, and from what paffed then, together with what had been done in confequence of it, he thought there was very little room, compatible with confiftency of conduct, for that oppofition which he apprehended was intended to be given to the prefent meafure. The Houfe, in the laft feffion, had feemed well aware, that fuch an inquiry as was neceffary towards forming a proper judgment on the fubject, was by no means a proper one for it to go into. It had been, on all hands, agreed, that it was, in a great meafure, a queftion of confidence, and they had, therefore, acquiefced in his propofal of fending it to the arbitration of a Board of Land and Sea Officers, to be conftituted for that exprefs purpofe. That Board had, of courfe, been appointed, and confifted of every thing that was great and refpectable in the two profeffions; they had given the fubject an higher degree of confideration and refearch than had ever been known on fuch an occafion in any other age or country. The Report made by that Board was in itfelf fo direct, and fo conclufive, as to the neceffity of the meafure, that it ought in itfelf completely to determine the queftion, fhould it even appear that the reafons of a collateral nature advanced in oppofition to it were entitled to the authority which fome perfons feemed inclined to give them. Concerning the queftions, " whether the dock yards could properly and effectually be defended by a naval force alone; by a military force alone; or by a naval and military force combined? or whether it was neceffary that fortifications fhould be erected for their defence? and if fo, what fort of fortifications were likely to be moft effectual?" The Board had anfwered, that neither a naval nor a military force, nor even both united, could afford a fufficient fecurity for the nation to rely upon; but that the fortifications were abfolutely neceffary, and that, of all modes of fortification, the mode fuggefted by the Mafter General of the Ordnance was the moft eligible, as being the moft adequate to the defence propofed, capable of being manned by the fmalleft force, requiring the leaft expence to erect, and particularly as affording an increafing degree of fecurity, as they were erected; infomuch as,

that

that if any given portion of them were completed, and the remainder unfinished, yet even that part so completed would afford a great deal of strength. Such were the characters and abilities of the officers who composed that board, that it would naturally follow as the highest degree of inconsistency, were the House, after having referred the various branches of the detail of the inquiry to the Board of Officers, to reassume that duty which they had already declined as being out of their reach, and attempt to revise and correct the Report of the Board. All that the House ought to attend to was the general result of the Report of that Board; for, it was itself incapable of investigating the subject minutely, and by detail; much less was it capable of correcting or deciding on the Report of the Officers. In order to diminish the credit of the Report, (for the credit of the persons who framed it could not be impeached) attempts were made to prove, that the instructions given to the Board of General Officers were such as confined them to the necessity of coming to one certain result, by means of *data* proposed for their consideration, which were all merely hypothetical, and afforded no latitude to them for the exercise of their own judgement. But how was it possible this could have been the case, when to the two first *data* the whole Board were unanimous in giving their opinion, and their opinion on those *data* were entirely conclusive on the whole of the subject, for they went (and *that* unanimously) to establish the necessity of fortifications?—Was it credible that a Board, consisting of such men, could possibly be duped by chimerical and absurd hypotheses, so absurd and so extravagant, that he recollected the honourable General had stated them as tantamount to a *convulsion of nature?* Was it to be supposed that they could be so easily misled and drawn unanimously into an opinion on a subject of such magnitude, and contrary to their own conviction? But, in fact, it was impossible to impute any such delusion in the present instance, for the answer to the first *data* was absolutely unqualified, and positive, and recognized the necessity of fortifying the dock yards; the second enforced the same necessity, it was true, with a proviso:—but of what? the expence of their erection, and our ability to furnish a force to man them. It was not fair to argue that the whole result of the Report was founded upon *data* in themselves improbable and ill grounded, when, in truth, the principal *data* by which the several parts of the Report had weight, were not the original *data* referred to the Board, but such as they thought necessary to substitute and adopt, as a foundation for their ultimate opinions. This idea was in itself so absurd, that the very words in which it had been expressed (and which he had before repeated) appeared as if the gentlemen who

who had ufed them were in collufion with the Houfe, and endeavouring to put their own oppofition into the moft ridiculous point of view. He fhould think it an infult to the officers concerned in the Report, if he thought of faying any thing more in anfwer to a fuggeftion fo much to their difhonour, as that they had been fo egregioufly and fo palpably duped by an article fo fhallow, and of courfe fo eafily detected. Some reliance had been placed in former converfations upon the diffent of certain members of the Board, with refpect to their opinion, touching particular parts of the fubject. The inftances of diffent, however, were not many, and they were fuch as he flattered himfelf could not ftand as an infuperable objection to the general refult. He felt himfelf rather in a difagreeable fituation, at being obliged, in arguing the fubject before the Houfe, to attack the opinion and authority of any individual member of the Board; but with refpect to one of the two very refpectable land officers (General Burgoyne) who had in any inftance diffented from the reft, his uneafinefs was the lefs poignant, becaufe the honourable General was on the fpot to explain and fupport his own judgement; though even ftill he felt for the honourable General, who, he knew, would not think himfelf at liberty to enter fo deeply into feveral of the more delicate parts of the queftion, as, perhaps, were his own juftification alone concerned, he might wifh to do. But refpect to the other officer (Earl Percy) his feelings were more diftreffing, becaufe he was obliged to canvafs his opinion in his abfence. Thofe two officers had joined with the reft of the Board in their two firft unanimous opinions, with refpect to the neceffity of fortifications towards the defence of the dock yards; but they afterwards, by a fubfequent propofition, declared, that notwithftanding fuch neceffity, yet they were ufelefs, becaufe we were not mafters of a fufficient military force to man them. He begged the Houfe for a moment to confider the conclufion which would follow from fuch premifes; becaufe if nothing but certain fortifications could poffibly afford protection to our dock yards, and if we were unable to garrifon thofe fortifications when erected, what muft prove the confequence? Deplorable in the extreme. It muft be, that we were unable to protect them at all. The nation, however, need not defpond at the profpect thus unintentionally (he was convinced) prefented to them by the noble Earl, for whofe character he had the higheft veneration, and whofe noble difintereftednefs, together with the brilliant example which he held out to the nobility of the age, in the active fervice of his country, and the uniform tenor of his conduct, were fufficient to add luftre, even to the rank which the noble Earl already filled. They need not defpond at this uncomfortable

profpect;

prospect; for the papers laid upon the table, in consequence of the motions made by the enemies of the measure, clearly proved, that we should by no means stand in need of a greater force for the purpose of defending those fortifications, than we could easily afford to that service. It would appear from one of those papers, that in the year 1779, we had about fifty-three thousand men in South Britain, who were constantly and uniformly increasing, until the year 1782, to upwards of seventy-one thousand. There was also another paper on the table that had been demanded by the gentlemen on the other side, which gave an account of different cantonments in which those troops had been stationed during that period; a paper which he could not think in any way material for the government of the present question, unless the right honourable gentleman opposite was ready to undertake to prove, that, like all the other arrangements made during the course of the American war, the disposition of the army through England was the very best and wisest which human ingenuity could devise. It appeared, however, from this paper, that the number of troops stationed in such cantonments, as might be considered within reach of Portsmouth and Plymouth, was in 1779 above sixteen thousand men, and that it had in the year 1782 amounted, by a progressive increase, to twenty-one thousand five hundred in each case, including that most invaluable resource of national defence, the militia. Let gentlemen judge from this state of our military force, whether it would in case of an invasion prove difficult to furnish a sufficient garrison for the proposed works. But when it was to be considered, that our forces in Great Britain bore scarce any proportion to those which we were obliged to distribute through our then extensive dominions, and that from our present situation it was not likely that any such distraction of our military power would ever again take place, it might be looked upon as able to command a force fully adequate to the maintenance of the fortifications, without in any degree derogating from the respectable defence of all our other dominions. On this part of the subject, some gentlemen had thought proper to throw into derision and ridicule the whole inquiry of the Board of Officers, as if they had proceeded to investigate the question of fortifications, without having any state of the probable means of supplying those fortifications with troops for their defence laid before them. But he would only desire the House to turn over the names of the land officers who sat at the Board, and then to say, whether there was any foundation for such a reflection. —Was the Duke of Richmond —Was Sir Guy Carleton — Was Sir William Howe— Was Lord George Lenox, who commanded at one of those places —Was Earl Cornwallis (his respect for whom he should extenuate

tenuate were he to attempt to exprefs it) — Was Sir David
Lindfay, who commanded in another of thofe places—Was
Sir Charles Grey, who commanded in a third, and who befides, ferved in the courfe of the war with the greateft brilliancy, in the remoteft parts of the globe—Was General
Roy, who at the time was Quarter-mafter-general to the
whole — Were all thofe gentlemen to be fuppofed ignorant of
the general military ftrength of the kingdom? Or was it to
he contended that, to enable them to form an opinion on fo
broad and extended a queftion, it was neceffary that the re-
turns of every regiment fhould have been laid before them?
Surely gentlemen would not perfift in fuch weak and ground-
lefs arguments! There was, befides, in the Report, another inftance of difagreement in opinion; that however, he conceived,
ought not, and could not carry any very great weight; not
from the perfon from whom the diffent came being at all deficient in authority and confideration, but from a circumftance ftanding on the face of the Report itfelf. The name
of an honourable officer (Captain Macbride) appeared to a
diffent to the anfwer given by the Board to the third datum.
It was to be obferved that this datum, together with its anfwer, was omitted in the Report as containing matter not
fafe to be made public. This confideration rendered it impoffible for him, confiftent with his duty, to attempt to examine it in detail, and to combat the opinion of the honourable officer upon its own ground; but yet he had a ftronger
argument than any other he could be mafter of, and that was,
the opinion of the honourable officer himfelf, who had, fix
weeks before, as appeared from the minutes of the Board,
given, together with all the other members of the Board,
his opinion directly in favour of the principle which that
datum was calculated to eftablifh. If he was miftating the
honourable officer, he begged to be fet right; but he believed
it would be evident to any gentleman that would look at the
Report, that he was perfectly correct——

Captain
Macbride.   Captain *Macbride*, admitting that the ftatements of the
right honourable gentleman were perfectly exact, remarked,
that ftill he could not avoid embracing his former idea that
the opinion of the naval officers was fully in the teeth of the
fortifications propofed at Plymouth; and for this affertion he
had Admiral Barrington's authority, whom he had feen and
talked with upon the fubject during a part of the interme-
diately preceding days. The fact was that the naval officers
were not permitted to have an opinion of their own manifefted.

Mr. Chan-
cellor Pitt.   Mr. Chancellor *Pitt* again rifing, remarked that as he had
courted the corrections of others to fall upon the accidental
(certainly not voluntary) errors in his ftatements, fo it could
not

not follow that he experienced the least concern, but rather
pleasure, when he discovered the honourable gentleman cor-
roborating instead of refuting his representation. The honourable officer, then, had formerly united with the rest of
the Board in an unanimous vote upon the subject of the
third datum, and had afterwards, after an interval of six
weeks, retracted that vote, and entered another on the minutes of the Board diametrically opposite to it—thus each
opinion had the authority of the name of the honourable
officer; and if any dilemma arose in forming a judgement
between them both, it became easily solved by referring to
the Report itself, in which it would appear, that though each
opinion was equally supported by the honourable officer, yet
the casting voice between his first and second opinion was
given by the whole Board, by which he acted in favour of
his former opinion, and of course there could be no room
for the House to hesitate a moment which of the two they
ought to adopt. There was another circumstance which he
thought necessary to state under the head of the dissents from
the general purport of the Report, that he might answer it
in order; although it did not arise out of the Report itself,
but had been taken up in that House for the first time by the
honourable officer, when he stated that the fortifications proposed to be erected on the lands adjacent to Whitesand Bay,
were directly in the teeth of the opinion of all the sea officers.
He begged the House to attend particularly to the two distinct branches into which that part of the question was divided; one of a naval, the other of a military consideration.
That which more immediately demanded the judgement of
the naval service was the practicability of the enemy effecting a landing at all upon the coast, together with the various
circumstances of tides, winds, soundings, currents, and anchorage which might be necessary, and the probability there
was of all those concurring so as to enable an enemy to land
at all, and to remain long enough off the coast to cover and
complete their debarkation; the other subject was for the discussion of the land officers singly, and had for its object the
most effectual method of so fortifying the coast, as to prevent the enemy, should they effect a landing, from penetrat-
ing the country. The opinion of the sea officers was, that,
in certain circumstances it was possible for an enemy to land;
and he could only account for the objection of the honourable officer against fortifying a coast on which an enemy might
(as it was admitted) land, by that gallant spirit and bravery
which would at all times induce him to turn his thoughts
more to the animating and brilliant prospect of attacking his
enemy, than the less glorious, but still prudent, duty of providing for his own defence. But, in furnishing the part of

the country in queſtion with forts, they ought not to confine themſelves ſolely to the idea of an enemy's landing in White-ſand Bay. They ſhould conſider whether it would be prac-ticable for him to land in any place to the weſt of Plymouth; for if he could do ſo, then were theſe forts abſolutely neceſ-ſary for the defence of that town and its dock yards; they were the very poſts which an enemy would moſt eagerly en-deavour to occupy, becauſe from them they would be able to bombard the dock yards. All perſons who knew our coaſts; and ſuch as, to their own honour and the glory of their coun-try, were acquainted with the coaſts of our enemies, knew alſo that it was abſurd to think of fortifying every part of them which could afford a landing-place for the purpoſe of an invaſion. The conſideration was, where would an inva-ſion prove moſt detrimental; and, upon that ſpot to erect ſuch fortifications that not only an invaſion by ſea ſhould not become practicable, but that, if an enemy ſhould have been able to land in another place, he might not alſo be able ſuc-ceſsfully to attack them there. He hoped to hear no more of Whiteſand Bay; for it was not the defence of that Bay, it was the defence of the dock yards of Plymouth which was intended; it was not a landing there alone which was to be prevented; it was a landing on any part of the coaſt which was to be defeated, at leaſt as far as it had an attack on Ply-mouth for its object; and if Whiteſand Bay were ſurround-ed by a wall of adamant, ſtill Plymouth could not continue ſafe unleſs thoſe grounds were fortified. He hoped, and be-lieved that he had completely done away the whole force of the diſſents of the ſeveral officers to whom he had alluded; and now he ſhould attempt to anſwer objections of another nature—It had been thrown out (and the gentleman ſeemed much inclined to build upon the poſition) that the whole ſyſtem of fortification was new and unprecedented in this country; but, this idea he was prepared to combat in the moſt direct and poſitive manner. The ſyſtem of fortifica-tion did always make a part of the general defence of Eng-land, and he would prove it by the moſt inconteſtible re-cords of hiſtory. Even during the reign of King Henry the Eighth, there was a proviſion made, by ſtatute, for fortify-ing certain parts of the coaſts. The ſtatute he would not take upon himſelf to read, becauſe the terms in which it was couched were become obſolete, and almoſt unintelligible. The ſame policy was obſerved by Queen Elizabeth, and formed a conſiderable part of the defence provided by that great and glorious Princeſs againſt the expected attack of the Armada. In the leſs proſperous reigns of the Stuart Princes the ſame ſyſtem was occaſionally continued, and again adopt-ed by our illuſtrious deliverer, William the Third. During
the

the reign of Queen Anne, at the time when the victories of the British arms were forming an era in the history of Europe, at which England looked back with pride, and other nations with amazement, did our ancestors think it incompatible with their fame, with their liberty or their constitution, to fortify the most vulnerable parts of their coasts, as it was now proposed to do?——On the contrary, there was a resolution of the Commons, not even at the desire of the Crown, laying down the necessity of fortifying the dock yards against any possible invasion, and those resolutions were founded upon estimates of plans which had been made under the reign of King William. The estimates of those fortifications amounted to a sum which, considering the difference between those days and the expensive times in which it was our misfortune to live, gave no great room for a charge of prodigality against those who had digested the present plan. ——The money then voted was 300,000l. which, when compared with the value of money at this day, would not appear as a very trifling sum. To come down to a later period, a period to which it might be supposed he was somewhat partial ——the last war——the last war! would to heaven we could call it the last war—Not indeed the last war, but the last on which Britons could reflect without either a sigh or a blush—— the war of contrast with the last! the war in which the name of Briton was exalted above the highest and the proudest of nations; by successes as stupendous, and conquests as glorious as our late miscarriages and defeats had been calamitous and disgraceful. What was the policy of the Administration of that day? That it was exactly similar with what was now recommended he would prove by one or two short extracts from the Statute Book.——The first was from an act of 22d Geo. II. for providing fortifications for the dock yards; and the second was for a fortification for some more insignificant place (Milford as well as he could remember) in which the very grounds of the policy now inculcated were recognized; that by procuring adequate means for domestic defence, the nation would become more at liberty to send its fleets abroad either for the purpose of defending her foreign settlements, or carrying on the operations of offensive hostility into the center of the enemy's possessions. Thus it might be seen, that in the very best days of this country, the system of fortification was uniformly practised and encouraged; but even in a much later period, and during the administration of the right honourable gentleman (Mr. Fox) opposite to him, the very identical plan of fortification then under discussion had been considered, and an estimate for carrying them into execution was presented to the House. He supposed that the right honourable gentleman who contended for the propriety

of

of Minifters being always ready to make up their minds on every fubject which related to the force of the country, and who had himfelf, it appeared, made up his mind on the fubject, was now ready to give his reafons for that change of opinion which, it was to be feared, he intended on the prefent occafion to avow.   For his own part, notwithftanding the great abilities and uncommon verfatility of talents which the right honourable gentleman was well known to poffefs, he apprehended that he would not be able to reconcile to any princip'es of confiftency, his practice of making up his mind when in adminiftration, and unmaking it with fo much facility when out of office.   He fhould, however, expect to hear that particular circumftance fully explained, as far as fo extraordinary a change of opinion in fuch a peculiar variety of circumftances could admit of explanation.   As to the neceffity fuggefted as likely to enfue from this meafure of augmenting the ftanding army, nothing could prove more void of foundation.   It had been unanimoufly reported by the Board of Officers, that the plan of fortification propofed, was the beft calculated for the defence of the dock yards of any other which could be devifed, and that it was fuch as was capable of defence by the fmalleft number of troops.   Would any perfon then contend that a fmaller number of troops, independant of fortifications, were able to defend a place better than a large body affifted with the beft poffible fortifications? Such an idea was too abfurd to be argued againft; and yet, in fact, it was the only idea on which that topic of oppofition could poffibly be maintained.   Should we, in cafe of an invafion, truft folely to our ftanding army, then there would be a neceffity of augmenting to a moft enormous degree that army on which the whole fafety of the kingdom was to reft. Was this the way to vindicate and fecure our liberties? If we did not keep up fuch an army, then we fhould be reduced to the neceffity of recurring to foreign affiftance; perhaps to the protection of mercenaries, bribed by our money, and who, when we had no longer occafion for their fervice, would prove as ready to turn their arms againft ourfelves.   Was it lefs defirable for us to be defended by the walls of Portfmouth and Plymouth, garrifoned by our own militia, than to purchafe the protection of Heffian hirelings? The plan was objected to upon the ground of the expence which would attend it, and of the probability that we could not expect to be free from a war until it fhould be completed, and that we fhould derive no advantage from them at the time of the greateft neceffity.   As to the latter of thefe objections, he requefted the Houfe to recollect the words of the Report upon the table, from which they would learn that the plan of fortification propofed to be adopted was one calculated even in an

unfinished

unfinished and imperfect state, to afford great means of defence; and that every part of them, though wanting all other assistance, and standing singly by itself, would prove highly useful and of course desirable. Thus, every part would be answerable to the great object; and so far from rendering it necessary for the House to hold itself committed to a constant and periodical expence until the whole was completed, the fact would be, that every year the necessity of adding to the fortifications must diminish, because every year the dock yards would receive additional strength. As to the expence attending the building of the works, he flattered himself, that his sentiments and ideas on the subject of the finances of this country, was not a backward feature in his political character——He hoped that he had not shewn himself remiss in any endeavours which could possibly tend to raise the revenue from that deplorable state to which it was reduced by the melancholy process of the late war. It was too well known how much his feelings were engaged, not only by the duty of his station, and by his attachment to his country, but by considerations of his own personal reputation, which was deeply committed in the question, to exert every nerve, to arm all his vigilance, and to concenter all his efforts towards that great object, by which alone we should have a prospect, by relieving their burdens, of transmitting to our posterity that ease and comfort which ourselves felt the want of, an efficient sinking fund of the national debt, to accomplish which was the first wish of his heart; and this, as well by every means of prudent, well-regulated œconomy, as by a rigid collection of the revenue. But was he to be seduced, by the plausible and popular name of œconomy? He would not call it only plausible and popular, he would say the sacred name of œconomy, to forego the reality, and for the sake of adding a few hundred thousands more to the sinking fund, perhaps render for ever abortive the sinking fund itself. Every saving which could, consistent with the national safety, be made, he would pledge himself to make; but he would never consent to starve the public service, and to withhold those supplies without which the nation must be endangered.

The relieving by every such means as his duty would suffer him to adopt, the burdens of the people, and removing that load of debt by which she was oppressed, was the grand and ultimate end of his desire; it was the pedestal to which he would wish to raise a column which should support whatever pretensions he might have to reputation and popularity; but let it be well considered, how far the objects of necessary defence and of public œconomy could be reconciled, and let the bounds that divide them not be transgressed. Let it be well weighed, what a certain security for a lasting peace there

there was in a defencible and powerful situation, and how likely weakness and improvidence were to be the forerunners of war. But should a war happen, where was œconomy? What was become of the finking fund? The very expences of one year's loan would amount to more than the whole of those fortifications which might have secured us peace, because they would have diminished or effectually destroyed all temptation or hope of success in an attack. In this point of view, as the means of preventing a war, he should conceive, that the first million which would be applied as the foundation for the finking fund, might not be better applied than a million of money for the fortifications; not that a million would prove necessary, but he chose to state it as high as any other gentleman (let his talents of exaggeration be what they might) could possibly carry it. There was also another part of the subject which ought to have the greatest weight of all, and this was, that these fortifications being calculated to afford complete security to the dock yards, would enable our whole fleet to go on remote services, and carry on the operations of war at a distance without endangering the materials and seeds of future navies from being liable to destruction by the invasion of an enemy. It had been insinuated, that the second datum in His Majesty's instructions had been used to draw forth an acquiescence from the Board of Officers upon an unreasonable supposition of the fleet being absent for an improbable time. He believed there were few gentlemen could forget, that at no very distant period, even since he had the honour of a place in His Majesty's councils, the fleet had been absent for a time nearly equal to that supposed in the datum, upon a service which this country could not have dispensed with without sacrificing the most brilliant success which attended us in the late war; a success of such lustre as to spread an irradiation over the more gloomy scenes in which we had been involved. Had we been then in fear of an attack upon our coasts, which from reasons not proper to be mentioned, we happened not to be, Gibraltar, and the renown of defending it, must have been for ever lost. But it was not only by foreign expeditions that we might lose the aid of our fleet in case of an invasion; it might so happen, that our fleet, though in the very Channel, might be prevented by contrary winds, tides, or other contingencies, from arriving to the assistance and relief of the dock yards. What would then prove the situation of this country? The enemy might, in one day, in one hour, do an irreparable injury, and give a mortal stab to the very vital principle of our national vigour; might effectually destroy the seeds of that navy from which alone we had to hope for commerce, for safety, and for reputation. On the whole, he really thought

thought the present rather a question to be considered as connected with our 'naval establishment, than that of either our army 'or ordnance, as it was calculated to give liberty to the fleet which had hitherto been confined to our coasts, and as it were to the defence of those dock yards, without the security of which the very existence of the navy, or even of the nation, must be no more. Were it to be asked, why the sum required for these fortifications had not been demanded for strengthening the navy, he should answer fairly, that he thought the same sum laid out upon the fleet, would by no means afford a proportional strength to what would be derived from the fortifications. The money which would prove sufficient to accomplish those works, would not build as many ships as would answer for the defence of those invaluable harbours of Portsmouth and Plymouth. There was, besides, a certain degree beyond which the navy of this country could not go; there was a certain number of ships, beyond which she could neither build nor man any more: what that line was, he could not, nor would it be proper for him to point out; yet necessarily such a line must exist in the nature of things—but there never could be any line drawn to limit the security which we ought to provide for our dock yards. What could be the reason that gentlemen on the other side of the House seemed so anxious to impede this measure? Were they bold enough to stake themselves upon a question of such awful magnitude, and to stand forward with such decided vehemence as the opponents of a measure, which Parliament, thinking itself incompetent to scrutinize, had referred to the highest professional authority in the army, and in the navy, which had received the sanction of that authority, and which the Ministers of the Crown, who could have no personal feelings on the subject (except such as from considerations of their own ease and advantage were adverse from it) and who could have no temptations towards it, but a strong sense of its indispensable necessity, declared themselves so much interested about, as to be unable to rest upon their pillows so long as it remained in suspence. He called upon the House to beware how they suffered themselves to be lightly drawn into a line of conduct which might involve their posterity (nay themselves) for if they continued in their present weak state, they might accelerate the danger in the heaviest calamities.

He begged leave to know, if a few years ago, when the fleets of the enemy were hovering over Plymouth, they felt themselves inclined, with arms across, and that listless security in which they now seemed to indulge, to debate the question of fortifying the dock yards? He was happy in
reflect-

reflecting upon the great abilities, the high rank, and the reputation and virtue of the right honourable gentleman, because having so much at stake, he would become the less apt to infist upon an opposition pregnant with so much mischief as the present, and because the remorse which they must otherwise feel, if they should hereafter find, that they had involved their country in the most dreadful calamities on grounds less important and consequential than the sanction of the right honourable gentleman. He flattered himself that more arguments were scarcely necessary to prove, that the proposed system of fortifying the dock yards was absolutely necessary for the preservation and security of the sources of our marine in case of a future war, and that the system in question had received the unanimous sanction of a Board of Land and Sea Officers, consisting of the most respectable and experienced characters in the two services; and that they had in their Report pronounced the plan the best adapted to its purpose of any which could be devised, grounded on the most œconomical principles, and requiring the smallest number of troops to man. Viewing it properly, it was a naval question, and as such it ought to be considered, because while it gave security to the vital springs and sources of our marine, so far from rendering an increase of the military force of the kingdom necessary, as some gentlemen, from a laudable jealousy of the standing army, and from a natural and zealous regard for the Constitution, had been led to imagine, it would actually tend to enable Government to keep up a less military establishment than otherwise must be maintained. Thus circumstanced, he should rest all his hopes of support solely upon the power of his arguments to prove what he had asserted in that respect —— Having read the words of two preliminary resolutions, which he remarked would prove declaratory of the opinion of the House upon the subject (should they think fit to adopt them) and which, by being voted previous to their going into the Committee of Supply, would lay a foundation for their future proceedings, and rest their votes in the Committee upon a perspicuous and permanent footing. Mr. Pitt concluded with moving his first resolution as follows:

" That it appears to this House, that to provide effec-
" tually for securing His Majesty's dock yards at Portf-
" mouth and Plymouth, by a permanent system of fortifi-
" cation, founded on the most œconomical principles, and
" requiring the smallest number of troops possible to answer
" the purpose of such security, is an essential object for the
" safety of the state, ultimately connected with the general
" defence of the kingdom, and necessary for enabling the
" fleet

" fleet to act with full vigour and effect, for the protection
" of commerce, the support of our distant possessions, and
" the prosecution of offensive operations in any war in
" which the nation may hereafter be engaged."

Mr. *Bastard* observed, that feeling how exceedingly it be- Mr. Bastard.
hoved him to oppose as much as possible, the prosecution of
a system of which the accomplishment would menace the
probably irretrievable destruction of all the leading interests
of his country, he should beg leave to make his comments
upon the brilliant, but too groundless, arguments of the right
honourable gentleman who spoke last. Most cordially was
he inclined to give him all his share of credit for having,
during the course of the preceding session, consented that
the matter should be referred to a Board of Inquiry, constituted of naval and land officers of the first rank and character; yet he must reprobate the manner in which that
Board had been managed, and lament, that three of the
most skilful and experienced of its nominated members,
(Lord Townshend, General Conway, and Lord Amherst)
should have been excluded from taking their seats at it, in
consequence of a paltry manœuvre played off by the noble
Duke at the head of the Ordnance, who had procured himself to be appointed President of the Board. Where was
the boasted fairness and impartiality of the reference when
such a manœuvre was practised; as it is well known that
officers of long standing could not sit at the Board at which
a junior officer presided? He had never heard but of one
engineer who was fond of fortifications, and founded them
upon the same principles as those to which the noble Duke
discovered the most glaring partiality, the data which met
his eye so frequently in the printed extracts from the Report;
the engineer to whom he alluded was no less than the re-
nowned Don Quixote de la Mancha. Don Quixote always
called for datas, and proceeded to build his fortifications
upon those grounds; the noble Duke's fortifications appeared
totally as Quixotich. He desired to remind the House, that
the nation had always been jealous of every thing which
looked like an increase of the standing army, and asked
whether one great argument in defence of the militia, and
what greatly recommended the institution to Englishmen,
had not been the circumstance of their mixing so much with
the people in their Houses, and whether that did not tend
to preserve to them their character of citizens rather than
to hold them out as soldiers? The militia had been called
the school of the army; if that description was true, would
it not be more justified by shutting them up in fortresses,
and keeping them separate from their fellow subjects?

Might not these strong holds be termed seminaries for soldiers, and universities for Prætorian bands? And was it not likely that the militia would come out of garrison with minds rather prepared for joining the regular army than inclined to return to mix with their countrymen employed in civil avocations? How unconstitutional was the tendency of the proposed system: it was so much the object of odium and detestation in the county which he had the honour to represent, that if the fortifications which were intended to be raised there should be erected, the people on whom it appeared that a reliance was placed for assistance in manning them, in case of necessity, would refuse to lend the least assistance whatever. He felt but little difficulty in discovering, that the great object was to relinquish that method of defence which, from the very prudent choice and sanction of our ancestors, had risen into weight and full celebrity. He, for one, could not repress his indignation at the idea of tearing the ensign of the British glory from the mast head, and fixing it to a standard on the ramparts of a military garrison: and he must assure the right honourable gentleman, that the sense of the country was clearly and decidedly against the system, as he would see from the description of gentlemen who would take a share in the opposition of the day. Neither those to whom he alluded, nor himself, acted either from party motives, or with a view to factious purposes. They stood up the advocates of their country in a moment which seemed to threaten it with serious danger, from the adoption of a system as absurd as impolitic; but they stood up like independent men, unconnected with any party, and as ready to support the Minister when he appeared in the right, as determined firmly to oppose him when they were satisfied that he was in the wrong. In conclusion, he moved to leave out from the word " House," to the end of the question, in order to insert, " That fortifi-
" cations on so extensive a plan as proposed by the Board are
" inexpedient."

Mr William Lemon.   Sir *William Lemon* said that he could not avoid admiring in his honourable friend (Mr. Bastard) the public spirit evinced in his having manfully stood up from the first mention of it, the uniform opposer of a system, which, as it tended to introduce a departure from the old mode of defending the island by a naval force, could not but give alarm to every well-wisher to his country. How ill-timed was it to recommend a plan of fortifications to the House, when it had not been ascertained whether that constitutional force, the militia, was to be called out annually or not! This, added to the appearance of a design of abandoning the cultivation of our marine, and relying rather on the army and military erections for security, must create much jealousy in that

House

House as well as without doors, in consequence of the unconstitutional tendency of such a conduct. Were the proposed system of fortification adopted, it should be considered
as the fatal era from whence the decline and ruin of our navy might be dated. He, indeed, meant not to impute any
bad design to the present Administration in recommending
the plan proposed, nor to hint a suspicion of the friendly inclination of the Prince on the throne to the liberties of his
People; but long experience had proved, that when every
thing wore the appearance of security, and the country had
a thorough confidence in the King and his servants, more
than ordinary caution ought to be exercised by the People,
whom it then became less than ever to be ready to allow a
system to be adopted, that in the hands of a weak Prince
and wicked Ministers might grow into a formidable engine
of prerogative, and be turned against their freedom and the
constitution. Admonishing the Minister against pursuing
steps which would lead him astray from the favour, and strip
him of the confidence of the People, Sir William concluded with giving his hearty assent to the amendment.

Mr. *Wallwyn* begged leave to recommend it to the right
honourable gentleman to drop the idea of persisting in a plan
against which the Public in general were extremely averse.
He declared that Report confidently said that the right ho-
hourable gentleman's mind was not with the system, and
that he was by no means a sincere friend to it. [The Chancellor of the Exchequer here complaining of the injustice of
such an imputation, declared that the Report was most grossly
false and wholly groundless.] Mr. Wallwyn said that he
spoke of it merely as a Report, and he had hoped that the
Report was true. " To be or not to be," a powerful maritime state appeared to him " the question." Till the right
honourable gentleman could urge some argument which
amounted to a solution of the problem which he had started,
viz. that the proposed system of fortification, which must
necessarily require a number of men to garrison, would nevertheless be a means of diminishing the quantum of the standing
army requisite for the defence of the kingdom, he should
think it his duty to oppose the system, as directly militating
against the ancient mode of insular defence, as prejudicial to
the increase of our navy, and as dangerous to the constitution.
He concluded by giving his support to the amendment.

General *Burgoyne* declared that he felt himself extremely
embarrassed between what he ought to divulge, and what he
knew; between the data which were in the extracts from
the Report, and those that were not there; but he would endeavour to explain his sentiments on the subject. At the
Board of Inquiry when the members of it assembled, the

Mr. Wall-
wyn.

General
Burgoyne.

B b 2   noble

noble Duke gave them his plan with the data to confider, and called for their plans in return. What individual even if he had prepared a plan, would have chofen to commit himfelf with it in that manner, againft a plan produced by the Prefident of the Board, after its having been under his confideration and improvement for two years? They were therefore reduced to the neceffity of giving their replies to the data fuch as they were, leaving the probability of them to reft on their propofer. Many of thefe data held out fuppofitions moft extravagant, but they were put fo artfully, that it was impoffible not to anfwer them in the affirmative. However deniable the general conclufions might be, he deemed the whole a lift of improbable poffibilities, and therefore confidered the idea of defending the kingdom by fortifications as inconfonant to the genius of our conftitution, and irreconcileable with the fecurity of the liberties of the People. He fhould have fuggefted various other modes of defence of the kingdom, had he been called upon, but all of them maritime. The kingdom might have been defended by fending a fleet off Breft, by fending a fleet to the mouth of the Mediterranean to prevent a junction between the fleets of France and Spain, and by other deftinations of our fleets, as the relative fituation of other powers might make it proper. He now ftated from the papers for which he had moved laft Wednefday, the number of troops, including cavalry, which had been in Plymouth, and Scilly, and in Portfmouth, during the refpective years of the late war, contending that there had never been above eight thoufand men, including three or four regiments of cavalry in Plymouth, any one of thofe years. He compared it with the twenty-two thoufand men which would be wanted to man the new fortifications (twelve-thoufand at Plymouth, and ten thoufand at Portfmouth) and afked why had the inquiry of the Board of Officers been confined to thofe two dock yards? Were we vulnerable no where elfe, or in no other dock yards? Was not Chatham dock yard worth looking at? That dock yard, and the pafs there, were, he maintained, of as much confequence as either, if not both the two others. The General concluded with declaring, he fhould give his vote for the amendment.

Lord Hood.   Lord *Hood* profeffed himfelf a friend to the plan of fortifying the dock yards. No argument could be derived from what this country had done formerly with her navy. The navy of France was very formidable, and fo was that of other powers; regard therefore muft be had to the prefent relative fituation of the marine of other countries compared with our own marine, and it was from their powerfulnefs at fea, that it became a wife and prudent meafure to fortify our dock yards.

yards, by which means the whole of our navy would be free to be sent out upon any one or more services in case of war. In the case of our having a large convoy of merchant ships coming home from the East or West Indies, and knowing of the enemy's having sent out a fleet to meet and intercept them, in order to save the commerce of the country from a fatal blow, our business would be, instantly to send as large a fleet as we could spare to seek the enemy. This we could not do, while our dock yards rested solely for defence on our navy; because, if we sent the whole of our fleet, France might have a sufficient body of men on her coasts, all ready for embarcation, and those she might send across the water in frigates, and such other vessels as were unemployed by her, and fit for the purpose. They might come here, effect the business, do us an irreparable mischief, and get away before our fleet returned; or even they might do the mischief, and instantly surrender prisoners of war. For his part he was decidedly of opinion that it was proper to adopt the proposed system, and that France and other maritime powers of Europe had of late much increased their naval force; and that Great Britain could not be too cautious in securing the source of our marine from surprise and distress.

Captain *Macbride* said that much absurdity marked the conduct of the noble Duke, respecting the manner of endeavouring to enforce conviction to his own liking on the Board of Naval Officers at Plymouth. The noble Duke had played off a piece of mummery there, which disgraced him in the eyes of the whole country. He sent a parcel of boys in a boat who were to try to effect a landing, whilst others on shore were to endeavour to repel them. They had fastened a capstern on shore, and by that means, and the help of a rope, drew themselves up the cliff. Thus he declared that he would teach a milliner's apprentice to draw a large gun, by the help of a coach and horses, up to the cross of St. Paul's. The noble Duke had used great art with the naval officers to persuade them to be of his opinion. All the places which they had examined were perfectly secure from any danger of an enemy landing at any of them. He knew a place, however, where an enemy might land. The right honourable gentleman (Mr. Pitt) need not be alarmed, for he was not going to tell where the place was. He begged leave to urge the expediency of taking care of the navy, and not cheating the Public of their money, as was the case at the end of the war before last, when ships of a smaller size than usual were built, which were good for nothing. He must beg leave to express his surprise at the illiberal imputation which had been thrown upon the spirit of the inhabitants of the country at large, and of his constituents in particular. His honourable
friend,

Capt.
Macbride.

friend, (Mr. Baſtard) on the appearance of the enemy, had marched in at the head of two thouſand men from the country, when there were only at the time five hundred ſtand of arms in ſtore, with thoſe they took charge of the priſoners and conducted them to Exeter. And the gentlemen whom he had the honour of repreſenting, had; with a laudable zeal and ſpirit, formed themſelves into two companies, clothed and arrayed themſelves at their own expence, and continued to do duty during the remainder of the laſt war. To that ſame independent ſpirit, when Government preſumed to dictate to them in the choice of repreſentation, he was indebted for the honour of a ſeat in that Houſe.

He ſhould now proceed upon the vindication of the conduct of himſelf and of the other ſea officers of the Board, not without complaining that the grounds of his diſſent were not laid before the Houſe; eſpecially as he had declared, that no part of the objections which he had made againſt the fortifications, or of the papers for which he had moved, tended to ſhew the weakneſs, but, on the contrary, the ſtrength of the coaſt and country, he craved permiſſion to read extracts from his minutes of the papers he had moved for, which were to the following purport:

LIEUTENANT HOCKINGS' CONCLUSION.

I beg leave to obſerve in this extent of coaſt (from Ramhead to Loo) above ſeventeen miles, the fifteen paſſes in Whiteſand Bay are in a manner ſo difficult of acceſs to an enemy, not only from the great rockineſs of the ſhore, but alſo from the openings of the ſmall bays or receſſes in the coaſt leading to theſe paſſes being ſo narrow, that ſhould the wind and tide not be favourable at the time of landing, the enemy will run great riſk of being carried on the rocks. It is, however, certain, ſhould the enemy effect a landing at any of theſe ſand paſſes, they are undoubtedly acceſſible, and by which he may gain the ſummit of the coaſt.

But when the great irregularity of thoſe paſſes is conſidered in their numerous windings and turnings up ſteep cliffs, it appears an enemy will not find it ſo eaſy an operation to force them, particularly if defended by ſmall breaſt-works and a few choſen troops at the head of each paſs. However, to render the acceſs ſtill more difficult, and throw every obſtruction poſſible in the way, ſo as to retard an enemy's attempts, it would be proper to break up thoſe footings, either by filling the paths with ſtones and earth, or ſcarping the ground, which would take off the favourable aſpect of thoſe paſſes, and render them inacceſſible.

It is remarkable, that the high ſtone and earth fences of the different fields along the coaſt, at a ſmall diſtance from

the

the fummit of the cliffs, and paffes between Ramhead and Loo, form a ftrong line of entrenchment to line the coaft if properly defended.

LAND OFFICERS' PROVISO.

Horfe Guards, June 18, 1785.

We have confented to the Report of Lieutenant Hockings being entered on the Minutes, as it has been propofed by fome of the members, but we defire not to be underftood as acceding to it in all its parts: with refpect to the number of places where an enemy can land, and the proper words for this purpofe, we rather chufe to reft our opinions on the Report which the Naval Officers of this Board may have made on this fubject than on the Report of Lieutenant Hockings.

We the under-written Sea Officers defire the following note may be inferted in the Minutes after the provifo of the Land officers.

. The Report of Lieutenant Hockings, engineer, refpecting Whitefand Bay and coaft adjacent, with the plan accompanying, correfpond with the fentiments we entertain of the difficulty of effecting a landing there if properly oppofed, it being no road-ftead, and fo much avoided by our own fhips, we can hardly fuppofe the fleet of an enemy will hazard an anchorage there.

S. BARRINGTON,
M. MILBANK,
T. GRAVES,
W. HOTHAM,
J. MACBRIDE,
A. S. HAMMOND.

Captain Macbride now obferved, that he had corrected grofs miftakes in the Report of the fhape of the country, part of which was his own eftate. Having likewife read the Duke of Richmond's order to Lieutenant Hockings, engineer, which was given without the knowledge of the Sea Officers, he remarked, that it appeared to the Board, that Lieutenant Hockings was clandeftinely employed by the Duke to invalidate the opinion of the Sea Officers; when it was found to produce the contrary effect, Lieutenant Hockings, who before was thought well qualified for fuch an employment, became treated as ignorant and prefumptuous, and as a perfon unknown until a refpectable member of the Board, in the engineer department, faid, that he had been bred up under him at Gibraltar, and gave an honourable teftimony of his character and abilities. Thus, how ridiculous was the conduct of of the noble Duke, who, by every art and fineſſe in his power, had endeavoured to warp the naval opinions in favour of his ſyſtem — failing in that, he had recourſe to a piece of mummery, which expoſed him to the ridicule of the whole country. Captain Macbride obſerved, that he had Admiral Barrington's authority to ſay he agreed in opinion with him, and was even ready to come and declare it at the bar of the Houſe of Commons. Indeed the whole conduct of the noble Duke, who more properly guided than preſided, was without precedent, and it was the firſt Board of Officers in Council, where queſtion and anſwer came from the Preſident and the ſenior members. In every other caſe the junior officer gave his opinion firſt—in this caſe it was reverſed for very obvious reaſons. In concluſion, the Captain profeſſed himſelf averſe to all unneceſſary fortifications whatſoever.

The hon. G. Berkeley   The honourable *G. Berkeley* obſerved that ſo much had been ſpoken upon the ſubject, and ſo many abler perſons had delivered their opinions, that he ſhould only trouble the Houſe with recapitulating what he had aſſerted in a former debate, long previous to the appointment of the Board of Officers; but he could not help taking notice of what had fallen from a right honourable gentleman (Mr. Fox) on a former day, which had been now re-echoed, viz. that the plan aſcribed to a noble Duke was unconſtitutional. He wiſhed that when he choſe to make a panegyric upon himſelf and his noble relation, that he had ſtated to the Houſe, in that maſterly language which made him the admiration of mankind, what he knew and felt; that the noble Duke would be the laſt man in England to patronize, and would die ſooner than propoſe any plan which could militate againſt the conſtitution of this country. Making theſe remarks, he muſt beg leave to be underſtood, that, like the right honourable gentleman, no ties of blood, nor any other conſideration, could induce him to give his vote for any thing which he did not think perfectly right. As to his own idea, of their being unconſtitutional, he could not conceive they were more ſo than any others which were already begun or finiſhed in England; and to render them ſuch, recourſe muſt be had to the honourable General's (Burgoyne) catalogue of improbable poſſibilities. Concerning the neceſſity of ſome fortifications, eſpecially at Plymouth, to which he meant to confine himſelf, he was enabled to ſpeak with as much, and it would not be arrogance to ſay, more, certainty than any man in that Houſe; and if they did not chuſe to give him credit for what he aſſerted, they might call the general officers commanding there, and aſk them their opinion of fortifications at the critical and important moment when the French fleet were off Plymouth,

mouth, of which he was a spectator; and he hoped not an idle one; and would be bound to say, that not a soul there but wished for fortifications. He must beg leave to assert, that the enemy could have landed, and he would not go into suppositions like his honourable friend (Macbride) as to winds and weather, but declare, that it could have been effected at any hour of the day or night of the time which the enemy remained there, and at the very spot which these forts were meant to defend. For his own part he thought, that the most strenuous opposers of the plan would not ensure us a permanent peace, nor would they ensure us, in case of a war, the same honour and abilities at the head of the Admiralty which the noble Lord now there, or his predecessors possessed; he did not know, but if a war happened, we might be cursed with the same mismanagement in that department which we experienced during the war, when our fleets were sent sculking away, and our coasts, our convoys, and our docks, left totally unprotected. Indeed when the honourable General had moved for papers, he thought it was for the purpose of investigating and probing into the errors of the last war, and to make the noble Lord (North) that vigilant Minister, account for the losses which we had sustained in America, and those which we were near suffering at home. This circumstance must operate as a reason for his supporting the plan; but another and a stronger was, that as a sailor and a well-wisher to the service, in which he would give way to no man, he felt an anxiety to see the fleet properly employed in war in annoying the enemy; for he only agreed with the best writers upon the subject when he said, that England in a war with France ought always to act on the offensive; as, in acting otherwise, she gave up all her natural advantages and inspirited the foe. Granting this position, it followed that the proposed fortifications would be of essential use, as instead of cramping the operations of the fleet, it must assist them, because the Commander in Chief would act with more vigour against the enemy when he knew our coasts and our dock yards to be safe and protected. In such a plan of war as this, he thought that his honourable friend (Captain Macbride) would join him, as he would have an opportunity to display that spirit of enterprize in *la petite guerre*, for which he was so distinguished; yet he found, that instead of assisting, he had opened his lower tier against it: but he knew that he depended upon his constituents for defending that part of the coast; yet doubtless he would have acted more for the safety of them, if he had voted a breastwork for them to fire over, as he was sure that they would have felt more comfortable behind that, and taken better aim, than if opposed face to face with a French grenadier.

With refpect to the language of the honourable Member (Mr. Baftard) for that county (Devon) he was aftonifhed, he was confounded, to hear him affert, as the language of his conftituents, that they would not defend the country, or give their affiftance in cafe of an attack, if this queftion was carried. Surely the bleffings of peace and a few years cannot have altered their ideas fo much; for during the laft war, he remembered that very gentleman heading fome hundreds at Plymouth; and fo far from thinking the fortifications wrong, they were employed in repairing and ftrengthening the wretched ones then upon the fpot. He would now intreat the Houfe to take notice, that fo much had been faid of our weaknefs, and our true fituation had been laid fo open, that if thefe, or fome works were not erected, and a war to enfue, he trembled for the confequences; but thofe gentlemen who had oppofed them muft anfwer for the event. He wifhed that they might not find an old, but homely, proverb verified, " That they had been " penny wife and pound foolifh."

Captain Bowyer. Captain *Bowyer* pronouncing himfelf a friend to the original motion faid, that juftice, and a fenfe of his duty to his country, obliged him at the fame time to declare, that a greater degree of attention ought to be paid to the navy, when the fortifications were going on than ever, and that both ought to go hand in hand together. The neglect of the navy during the laft peace was highly reprehenfible; and he therefore recommended it to Minifters, to take particular care that a number of young men were properly trained up and educated for the fervice, fo that in cafe of a rupture there might be a fufficient number of them qualified for pettty officers. The want of this was feverely felt at the commencement of the laft war.

Sir Charles Middleton. Sir *Charles Middleton* remarked that when the matter had been firft agitated a feffion or two fince, he had great fcruples upon the fubject; but he was now perfuaded, that the propofed meafure was wife, prudent, and neceffary. The fecuring the dock yards was certainly a great object, but a ftill ftronger reafon operated upon his mind in its favour, and that was, it would enable us to have the full ufe of our navy in cafe of a war. This was likely to be a moft effential advantage; and had we poffeffed it laft war, he was firmly of opinion we fhould not have failed fo often as we had done, becaufe, although we might not be equal to our enemy upon the whole in point of naval force, yet there occurred feveral fituations at fea, in which we might make ourfelves equal.

Col. Barré. Colonel *Barré* faid, that he fhould put his decifive negative upon the pofition, that it was either right, or wife, or
expe-

expedient, to fortify the dock yards; and if the abstract question were to depend on his answer, he declared that he would say no to it in the most direct and unreserved manner. With regard to the argument of his right honourable friend, who had opened the business with so much eloquence, he must deny it, and every part of it. When the House had done him the honour to adopt his advice last session, was it to be imagined, that by his recommending a Board of Naval and Land Officers, men of high rank, known experience, and admitted abilities, to inquire into, and report the most proper and fit mode of defence of the kingdom, he meant a paltry, narrow, circumscribed plan of fortifying two dock yards? He had not the smallest idea of any such scheme. He had been struck with the grand conduct of the wisest Princess that ever reigned, who, at a period of extreme peril, had taken advantage of the collective wisdom of both services, the navy and army. He had read a pamphlet published under the auspices of the noble Duke, on the subject of fortifications, during the last year, and meeting with a passage which provoked his indignation, it occasioned his coming down to the House in the preceding session, on the day when the ordnance estimates were to be voted, and while sitting in his place and hearing the arguments which were then urged, he rose and delivered his opinion, in the course of which, warmed, and glowing with the importance of the matter in discussion, he had asked with some emphasis, " Who was the " man that dared limit the extent of the navy of England, " or circumscribe the exertions of this country in the increase " of her marine!" That question he must put again, because the attempt was again made to commit so presumptuous an act; an act little short of treason to the state! It gave him infinite pain to differ in opinion from his right honourable friend before him; but his duty to his country demanded that he should speak out, and let no personal attachments, however strongly they clung about his heart, stand between him and the exercise of his honour, in doing his utmost in endeavouring to avert the disgrace (perhaps the ruin) which awaited the remaining parts of the British empire, if so rash, so mischievous a plan as that in contemplation was permitted to be carried into effect. The Colonel recapitulated all which had passed upon the subject during the last session, and said, that the sort of Board of General Officers, and the objects to which they were to direct their attention, as well as the manner of directing it, were far, far different indeed from the constitution of the Board which had been instituted; the mode of their proceedings, the result of their inquiry, and the Report they had made, the whole of which was so curious, that it was worth the while of the House to trace it re-

gularly,

gularly, and view it collectively. Having recapitulated all the steps taken from the period of his advising the institution of a General Board of Naval and Military Officers, to the day of the Extracts from the Report coming before the House, he marked every part of the proceeding, and held it up as a series of instances of artful management, misapplication of time and talents, and useless inquiry. The Board which he meant, was a Board of great respectable, and independent characters; men who had no vote to give, no favours to look for, no frowns to fear; men who would have done their duty without a consideration whom the result would please, or whom it would displease. Their object was to have been to inquire into and report the best mode of defence of the kingdom, and in pursuit of such an object they would not have confined themselves to two petty spots, but would have acted on a large scale, and cast their eyes round the kingdom. They would not have compressed their business into ten ten days at Portsmouth, and ten days at Plymouth, but have employed a due proportion of time in a deliberate discharge of their duty. If Portsmouth and Plymouth ought to be fortified, Chatham, and Sheerness, and Dover, and Harwich, and Yarmouth ought to be secured likewise; nor should the North pass unregarded

The noble Duke had great abilities and great assiduity; he was astute, logical, and a perfect master of argument in debate — No wonder that he was too much for a set of brave officers, used chiefly to out with their lower-deck tier and make ready for action. The noble Duke was fond of engineering,

"*Diruit, ædificat, mutat quadrata rotundis;*"

and (to do him justice) he was no bad engineer. Let him employ himself in engineering, but not at the expence of the Public! The Colonel next compared the Duke's qualifications for contriving and carrying into execution this or any other plan of fortification, with those of General Conway, Lord Amherst, or Lord Townshend, all of whom (he said) by procuring himself to be appointed President of the Board, he had excluded from their seats at that Board. Having dilated on their respective services and characters, he then remarked, that the office of Master General of the Ordnance was a civil employment, and frequently holden by a person not a military officer. He instanced the case of the Duke of Montagu. He mentioned, as in his idea, another characteristic of the noble Duke, at this time Master General, that he was never known to give up a point in his life; and that, he said, added to his being so astute, rendered it impossible for the respectable Naval and Land Officers who sat at the

Board

Board to cope with him on a logical contest. He defired not to be underftood as meaning to caft any imputation on the gentlemen who had conftituted that Board; he revered their characters, and bowed to their authority; it was the mode of inftitution reforted to, and not the men whom he condemned. In fpeaking of the ufeleffnefs of fortifications, he ftated the erecting untenable lines of circumvallation, as giving ftrength to the enemy; and inftanced in proof his affertion, the fact of Lord Amherft's having poffeffed himfelf of the lines of Ticonderoga, which the enemy, out of weakness in point of numbers, had abandoned, and which ferved Lord Amherft as an ufeful fhelter for his men from the enemy's fire. He could only account for a right honourable gentleman (Mr. Pitt) having taken fo active a part in recommending fo wild and ufelefs a project, by fuppofing that his confcience had been furprized, or he would not have affifted at all. He fhould now beg leave to refer the Houfe to a lift of papers, copies of which had formerly been laid on the table, whence it would appear, that we had, during the laft war, 120 fail of the line at fea, and 95,000 feamen on board, when the Houfe had only voted 80,000, notwithftanding the number of Britifh feamen on board privateers, and notwithftanding alfo the great drain occafioned by fo many of the profligate of England, Scotland, and Ireland, having flown to America, entered on board their fhips and other foreign veffels and fought againft their country. The peace had been marked by the epithet of a neceffary peace; but it was a great and glorious peace; and notwithftanding what had been uttered in that Houfe and without doors about it, the author of this happy event daily received the gratulations of the whole kingdom for having wrought fo happy a work. The noble Marquis when he made it was aware of his danger; he had honoured him with his confidence, and had faid, " I know that if I do not make a peace immediately " I can keep my place; if I do make it, I fhall effentially " ferve my country, at this time finking under the weight " of almoft exhaufted refources, and utterly incapable of " continuing war; but I fhall lofe my fituation: I difdain " however all confiderations of a perfonal and felf-interefted " nature, I will make a peace, be my rifque what it may." This was the magnanimity with which he acted, but the confidence which the Court of Verfailles had in him made the arduous tafk fomewhat lefs difficult, and the country was now experiencing the bleffings, the wealth, and the vigour that had flowed from the tranquillity which had been effected. In conclufion Colonel Barré defired not to be underftood as meaning to hold himfelf out as a fkilful engineer; he was none, nor could he pretend to any great military fkill: he

had

had been long invalided, moft honourably indeed, more fo than he deferved.

The hon. James Lut-trell

The honourable *James Luttrell* (in reply to Colonel Barré) obferved, that the fortifications were the only queftion fince the peace which had drawn forth the attention of that refpectable Minifter to the important bufinefs of Parliament; and retorted on the Colonel his profufe compliments to our invincible and unlimited navy, as ill fuited to grace the terms of that peace which could not be thought glorious by comparifon with the former peace; and he hoped no hiftorian would ever be able to praife it by comparifon with any future peace, which an enemy fhould dictate upon the afhes of our dock yards.

He lamented that it was not proper to lay before Parliament the whole proceedings of the Military Board. He wifhed the nation knew their danger, if that would induce them to apply a remedy—He alfo wifhed to do juftice to the impartial and judicious proceedings of the Military Board. He read the queftions referred to them by His Majefty's inftructions, which he faid were plain and diftinct; he alluded alfo to the firft unanimous refolution of Land and Sea Officers contained in the Report, which ftated, that they had availed themfelves of His Majefty's permiffion to alter the data, and the very firft datum fo altered declared unanimoufly that fortifications were neceffary for the fecurity of the docks in the cafes of abfence of the whole fleet, or fuch other caufes as might prevent the fleet from affording its protection to the docks.

To this datum the Sea Officers were unanimous— It was enough for them to fay, the docks ought to be fortified; they were not called upon to give any opinion on the conftruction of forts; that belonged to the Engineers and General Officers. If the Sea Officers had thought fhips fufficient for the protection of the docks, they could eafily have anfwered the firft queftion, whether a naval defence could be relied on for the defence of the docks?

The Sea Officers had pointed out where an enemy could land, and fully anfwered all maritime queftions; but except fuch parts of the conftruction of a fort as was meant to operate againft fhips, and to guard the entrance of a harbour, they had not at Portfmouth given any opinion, neither did he think them authorifed by His Majefty's inftructions in the Report to give any opinion refpecting the beft fyftem of fortification for land defence at Plymouth. The Sea Officers had alfo expreffly declared, after recommending gun boats, water, and fignal houfes, for Plymouth, that they had no other improvement or other fyftem of defence to fuggeft.

He

He conceived his gallant friend (Captain Macbride) saw difficulties for an enemy to surmount in Whitesand Bay that he would not call difficulties if opposed to him in any operation on the enemy's coast — That to say a landing might be effected if unopposed, mixed a land question with a sea question. Unopposed might mean to oppose with ten guns or a thousand guns; and an enemy is not unopposed, if, instead of risking the fate of the dock upon the possible event of landing, the object for landing was removed by giving perfect security to the dock. He compared Whitesand Bay with Gabruse Bay in America, to shew that greater natural difficulties, added to the opposition of fortifications, had not been sufficient to prevent the British troops from landing in the teeth of the enemy's batteries of troops, for the important object of taking Louisbourg; and argued, that great difficulties will always be undertaken for a great object.

He went over the so-often-repeated grounds of the instances of our fleet in the last war abandoning the defence of the docks, and the difference between the policy of a general system of fortification to guard against an enemy whose numbers and preparations should be equal to an invasion of this kingdom against the collective force, and the policy of guarding our docks, the vital parts of the kingdom, from an enterprize of 20 or 30,000 men, in the temporary absence, or in case of the inferiority of our fleet, against our dock yards.

He went into some detail to shew, that the French, without additional expence in war, only by keeping 15 or 20,000 men upon the opposite coast, and when occasion required, by laying embargo on their coasting vessels, would be at all times prepared in war to push across the Channel under protection of their fleet, an expedition against our dock yards. If forty sail of the line were to be kept in check by French troops, it allowed a French army virtually to operate as an increase of their navy, because a superior French fleet could force a landing; if our fleet should be inferior and forty sail of the line at Brest would oblige us to keep forty sail of the line to oppose it, except in the case of French troops so situated as to force a landing near our docks if we suffered our home fleet to be inferior to the enemy. Under this check of preparation for invasion, we could not send abroad reinforcements; and for the miserable œconomy of saving 500,000l., Jamaica, Barbadoes, Quebec, or our most valuable possessions in the East, might fall a sacrifice, and commerce and convoys be abandoned, owing to the inferiority of our fleet in those seas compared with those of the enemy, and our home fleet being confined to Channel service.

He

He reminded Mr. Fox of his argument at the opening of the feffion, threatening us with alliances between the Dutch, the French, the Spaniards, and the Emperor, and a combination of naval force againft us unparalleled in any former period of our hiftory. If it was true, that money could be found to build as many fhips as all thofe powers combined, it was no increafe of naval ftrength to build more fhips than we can poffibly man, and in the laft war we never manned an equal number of fhips to France and Spain alone, and an enormous increafe of our feamen was by no means probable. We were told the French did not like to attack us, and that they would not keep 15 or 20,000 men in the towns and ports of the oppofite coaft; but by what magic, as extraordinary as any convulfion of nature, could any member of that Houfe fet bounds to the ambition of France, or limit the number of her troops, where great objects in view muft juftify great expence, great rifk, and great efforts? We were told a future war may be a war of alliance—the object of thefe fortifications is to fet the navy at liberty for offenfive war, as well as for the defence of our foreign dependencies: and of all wars, a war of alliance ought to be an offenfive war; becaufe, if each ally only acts on the defenfive, there would be no conquefts made by either to balance, in the terms of peace, the loffes which one of the allies, or more than one might fuftain: and the peace which could not partially be made for the benefit of the one, muft end in difgraceful and inglorious terms of peace for the whole.

To relieve our navy from local ftationary fervice thefe forts were meant to be erected — If we are weak, it is the more neceffary: but even if we could launch half our forefts, and cover the wide ocean with our numerous fleets, he wifhed them to go forth for offenfive war, for extenfion of empire, protection of commerce, and for the glory of the Britifh arms; but ftrongly reprobated their being obliged to lie idle, ftationary, and fheltered in our ports, a mere defenfive, inglorious, unprofitable force.

Speaking of the bad confequences and imbecility of the American war, he concluded by obferving, that although it had been faid, the fun of Britain's glory is funk in our weftern hemifphere, we had the confolation to fee a glorious fun rife in our own horizon, which though accufed of not being yet in its meridian, had already fhed its happy influence on this ifland, fo as to reftore vigour to the Conftitution, and fuch ftrength to the roots of our refources as promifes the faireft profpect of growing profperity, and of the future happinefs and welfare of the Britifh empire. He inferred that there were no grounds for defpondency, nor for profufion, but that to grant the neceffary fupplies for fo

impor-

important a service, was state œconomy, as well as sound policy.

He entered into some detail to justify the estimates for the fortifications. He remarked on several parts of the Report, and insisted there were but two negatives to some additional fortifications being necessary. That all admitted the noble Duke's system would completely defend the docks in case of the absence or inferiority of our fleets—but if we reject that security, and keep an equal home fleet with the enemy, for our defence, he feared such a measure must, in its consequences, eventually reduce our Sovereign from being monarch of an empire, to be King of the single island of Great Britain.

Mr. *J. Hawkins Browne* expressed the highest satisfaction at discovering that a zeal for the navy was universal on all sides of the House; and he trusted that this would always be the darling service of this country; but he was astonished to hear the importance of the navy urged as an argument against those fortifications when it was the only argument in their favour, for these fortifications were not intended to substitute a new species of defence for the kingdom in lieu of our navy, but to protect our dock yards, and our dock yards only, which were our vital and vulnerable parts, because they were the gem and support of our navy. A right honourable member (Colonel Barré) had observed that magnanimity was the best public virtue in times of vigorous enterprize, or in those moments of imminent danger which we experienced in 1779, and in 1782. Granted, yet prudence was a rational virtue as well as magnanimity, and the most fit to be exercised when we had a prospect of long continuance of peace, as he hoped we now had, and when we might contemplate to advantage our former dangers, and pursue the wisest means to prevent the return of them. Fortifications, he observed, were not new in this country; large sums had been lavished upon them during every former war; but this was the first time that a regular plan had been laid before that House not dictated by the pressure of immediate necessity, not dependent upon the opinion of any Minister, nor the caprice of any Master General of the Ordnance, but approved by the first military and naval characters in this country. This was to him, and must be to most members of that House, in a great measure, a question of confidence. But, in whom were we to place confidence, if not in the executive Government, calling upon us for the public defence, and supported by the names which appeared in the Report, a Report to him perfectly satisfactory, and in the most essential parts unanimous. He concluded by pressing strongly upon the House if, in consequence of their rejection of this plan, and their refusing

Mr. J. Hawkins Browne.

refusing this confidence, they should live to see our dock yards destroyed, and the seeds and sources of our future navies annihilated, how they could ever forgive themselves, or make atonement to their constituents and the Public?

Mr. Courtenay.

Mr. *Courtenay* said, he hoped for the attention of the House on this very important, comprehensive question, as he would endeavour to compress what he had to say in as few words as possible, and would not trespass on their patience either by prolixity or repetition. At the same time he begged leave to declare, to prevent all possibility of misconstruction, that in opposing the present system of fortification, he acted from no personal spleen to the noble Duke at the head of the Ordnance department. He had always been treated with great civility and flattering attention by the noble Duke, and should always esteem the approbation he (Mr. Courtenay) had received of his official conduct from so accurate and discriminating a judge, as a singular honour. Mr. Courtenay then adverted to the very peculiar circumstances under which the Board of Land and Naval Officers was constituted. It certainly never was understood, when the House of Commons reposed that unbounded confidence in the Chancellor of the Exchequer—he would appeal to gentlemen on both sides of the House, whether they entertained the most distant ideas at the time—of any intention to make the noble Duke President of such a Board, whose sole object and express purpose it was to investigate and report on the merits of a plan of fortification projected by the noble Duke himself. If there was nothing reprehensible but the indecorum of such an appointment, he should take but little notice of it; but when, by this management, the country was deprived of the abilities and assistance of some very able and experienced officers, it deserved the severest animadversion. He did not profess to give any invidious preference to one military man over another, not being a judge of the competent merits of military officers; but this he begged leave to say, that in a general view, age, experience, and long service, gave a decisive superiority in the military profession. Still he acknowledged there were sometimes, but rarely, illustrious exceptions to be met with; there were extraordinary characters who mastered every science, rather by intuition than study. But surely the most partial of the noble Duke's friends would scarcely venture to rank him among beings of this very uncommon and superior class. He would therefore submit it to the House, as he was sure it would incite indignant feelings in their breasts, when they were told, that General Conway, Lord Amherst, and Lord Viscount Townshend, found themselves at once degraded and excluded, by receiving a circular letter from the Secretary

tary of State, to place themfelves under the control and command of the noble Duke. The Public were infulted by having their names oftentatioufly difplayed in the Gazette, at the very moment they found themfelves obliged to decline the fervice. For how could General Conway, Lord Amherft, and Lord Townfhend, confiftent with their own dignity, and with military honour, ferve as members of a Board of Land and Naval Officers under the Duke of Richmond? The only alternative left them was to decline the fervice, regretting, at the fame time, that the very difagreeable and embarraffing fituation in which they were placed, obliged them to take fuch a ftep. The next thing the Public had a right to ex-pect was this—that able and experienced officers fhould be fubftituted in the room of thofe who were thus ftudioufly, and, perhaps he might add, affiduoufly excluded.—Was this the cafe?—No.—Why was not Sir Henry Clinton's name placed on the lift? Early diftinguifhed for his military fkill and fpirit; the friend and favourite of the Hereditary Prince. Would it be fufpected that he had adopted the fentiments of the Prince of Brunfwick, on the expediency and utility of fortifying Portfmouth? Did the Houfe know the opinion the Hereditary Prince gave on that fubject? What he did fay probably did not apply to the noble Duke; for he only faid (after viewing the works and pofts with a military eye) that no officer who knew how to manœuvre and ftation a corps of troops properly, would dream of defending Portf-mouth by fortifications. Let us now contemplate the noble Duke, Prefident of the Board, declaring *ex cathedra*, laying down his hypothetical fyllogifms, proving his own data by the *modus ponens*, and confuting all objections by the *modus tollens*, amidft the applaufe of his own Engineers, amidft the roar of his own artillery.

The noble Duke judicioufly attacked them with the only fpecies of weapons with which they were unacquainted, and obtained an eafy, decifive, and glorious victory. Suppofe we now revert to the probable expence of thofe projected fortifications, and obferve their progreffive increafe, even on the noble Duke's own eftimate. In the year 1783, four or five hundred thoufand pounds were ftated as fufficient to com-plete the intended works at Portfmouth and Plymouth for the fecurity of the dock yards.—In 1785, 692,562l. were ftated as the probable amount, in the Military Memoir pre-fented to the Houfe, and figned by the Mafter General, and the other members of the Board of Ordnance. In the year 1786 the eftimate of the charge for completing the works, amounts to 760,097l. almoft double the original fum, not-withftanding this laft eftimate had been reduced by the œconomical labours of the Committee of Engineers at the

Tower, who had cut off near 50,000l. from Colonel Dixon's calculation. This able and experienced Engineer had added a third, aud affigned this reafon for doing fo, to provide for extraordinaries which he could not forefee.—However, he was called upon to fpecify what he had already faid, he could not forefee, and on his not complying, 50,000l. was ftruck off his eftimate by the Committee of Engineers, which at leaft was a fhort and compendious mode of deciding the queftion. Now, if we add a third more on the whole of the eftimate for 1786, it will amount to very nigh a million. The Chancellor of the Exchequer ftated it fo. Now fuppofing the fortifications compleated, and a million expended, the bare intereft of the fum is 50,000l. If we add to this, three or four per cent. for repairs, (no unreafonable computation) befides the intereft on that capital which ftill remains to be laid out in artillery, ftores, &c. the whole annual charge perpetually entailed on this exhaufted and impoverifhed country will be 100,000l. at leaft. To fome gentlemen this might appear but a trifle ; but let it be confidered that every burden is of a mixed and blended nature, not folely to be eftimated from the fum raifed, but connected with the capacity of the people to bear it. Before the late unfortunate war, before the glorious prodigality of the German war, the people of the country were perhaps better able to bear an annual charge of 500,000l. than 50,000l. at prefent. Mr. Courtenay then alluded to what fell from an honourable gentleman (Mr. Walwyn) that the profufenefs of the Chancellor of the Exchequer in this inftance might induce the Public to impute his conduct rather to private political motives than enlarged patriotic principles. For his own part, he reprobated fuch an idea ; ftill he could not anfwer for the invidious conftruction of others, who might conceive it poffible for the Chancellor of the Exchequer to facrifice a million to gratify the whim, conciliate the obftinacy, and infure the precarious attachment of one capricious, projecting individual. However, if a political, he would not fay, cordial, friendfhip could be promoted by fuch means, he had little objection. If the hands of Government could be ftrengthened by fortifying the dock yards, a million was but a' trifle to effect fuch a falutary purpofe. If the principle was fairly avowed by the Chancellor of the Exchequer, or any of his vouching friends, he would vote for the noble Duke's fortification ; confident as he was, that it would promote peace, unanimity and concord in the Cabinet, where it was fometimes fo much wanted, and always fo effentially requifite. Befides, the beneficial effects would not ftop there—faction would be depreffed and confounded ; the petitions on the table would be withdrawn ; the murmurs and complaints of the

People

People would ceafe, if it was once avowed that the Houfe of commons had generoufly voted away a million of their conftituents' money, for the fole and exprefs purpofe of cementing an alliance between two fuch great perfonages as the Mafter General of the Ordnance and the Chancellor of the Exchequer. To eftablifh an adequate fund for the payment of the intereft, and other incidental expences, he hoped the fhop tax would be made perpetual, and the produce of it unalienably applied to the building of fortifications.

Mr. Courtenay then begged leave to obferve, left the panegyric paffed on the noble Duke in an eulogium, by an honourable gentleman (General Burgoyne) fhould make too ftrong an impreffion on the Houfe, that the noble Duke's fkill was rather problematical, and indeed holden in very flight eftimation, by profeffional officers with whom he had converfed on the fubject. He had been told that there was a battery erected at South-Sea Caftle by the noble Duke himfelf; nobody difputed the honour of it with him; it was his own unclaimed dividend: many of the guns were fo injudicioufly placed, that they would not bear on the defigned object; the buoy on the fpit; on firing, their recoil endangered the battery; and the narrow enclofed cafements were fo well contrived, to prevent the efcape of the fmoke, that, on quick firing, the gunners muft perifh like bees fuffocated in a hive. What fhould we think of the noble Duke's line of defence, from Stokes Bay to Frater Lake, above three miles in extent? He would appeal to any military man, whether an enemy's column might not, with the utmoft facility, and with very little danger, penetrate between his two projected Forts? and his boafted works muft then fall at once. Was it ever difcuffed, or was it ever moved as a propofition by the noble Duke, and fubmitted to the Board, whether Magazines (bomb proof) might not be built in the center of Portfea Ifland, at a very inconfiderable expence, and whether an immenfe fum might not be faved by confining our military works to that ifland alone? A bomb-proof magazine (he fpoke from the unqueftionable authority of an excellent engineer) of about four hundred rods of brick wok, would hold almoft double the quantity of combuftible ftores contained in the dock yard at Portfmouth.

This at 10l. per rod	-	-	4000	0	0
Filling up the infide	-	-	1000	0	0
			5000	0	0
Another a Plymouth	-	-	5000	0	0
			10,000	0	0

In

In fhort, the very refpectable Board of Naval and Land Officers were attacked by furprife, and furrounded and befieged by the noble Duke's new-raifed corps of data, axioms, poftulata, lommas, corollaries, and hypothetical fyllogifms, and foon found themfelves reduced to furrender at difcretion. Serioufly, they found themfelves abfolutely precluded from confidering the general defence of the kingdom, combined in all its circumftances, on a large and comprehenfive view; and only fpecially appointed to examine the noble Duke's plans for Portfmouth and Plymouth, and report accordingly. Mr. Courtenay begged leave to remark, that the Chancellor of the Exchequer had always, and indeed, rather triumphantly, laid it down as an incontrovertible datum, that the very exiftence of our fleet depended on the ftores in our two dock yards. Was the fact fo? Thank heaven it was not; the right honourable gentleman had again that day, with his ufual eloquence, in all the fafcinating pomp of declamation, enobled and dignified — hemp, tar, pitch and oakum, turpentine and fail-cloth, by the name, ftile and title of the feeds and ftamina of the future navies of England. Was this the language of a Britifh ftatefman? Was this the language of a well-informed, enlightened Britifh Minifter? For his part, he had always formed a very different idea on the fubject; he had always thought that the feeds and ftamina of our fleets confifted in an unbounded commerce, in the fuperior fkill and gallantry of our naval officers, in the hardinefs and intrepidity of the Britifh failors; in the freedom of the Britifh conftitution, which diffufed a fpirit of independence to the loweft individual of the community. Such were the true ftamina of our navy; of that navy to which Britain was indebted for her empire and her glory, and which had extended her fame to the extremities of the globe.

" In vain the nation has confpired her fall,
" Her trench the fea, and fleets her floating wall."

But could the right honourable gentleman be ignorant, that there are ten times the quantity of naval ftores in the merchants warehoufes in the river, than were ever at one time in the king's ftores at Portfmouth or Plymouth? How many fhips of the line were launched laft war from flips in the river? Where did the Eaft-India Company build the Afia, Ganges, and the Bombay? Did not a noble Earl (of Lonfdale) contract with a private builder for the fhip which he defigned as a prefent to the King; but to his great regret, was moft unluckily prevented from accomplifhing his patriotic defign, by that neceffary peace which a noble Earl made, and the Chancellor of the Exchequer figned. Mr.

Courtenay

Courtenay then expatiated on the fpirit and generous exertions of the country gentlemen of England, who had laft year compelled the Minifter, however reluctant, to fufpend the noble Duke's plans, and even put his office in commiffion, and now by their perfeverance and patriotifm, would probaby put an end to a fcheme pregnant with every mifchief. If this military projector was not checked in his career, none could know what confequence might enfue. A Mafter General, with his Committee of engineers, like the Leputan Philofophers, in their flying ifland, might hover over the kingdom in an Ordnance balloon, defcend in a moment, and feize on any man's houfe and domain—(Mr. Cary would not be the only fufferer) draw out their fcales and compaffes, or fketch out their works. The country gentlemen would find their terraces converted into baftions, their flopes into glacis, their pleafure grounds and fhrubberies into horn works and crown works, to which they have hitherto borne an irreconcileable averfion. But where was this fyftem to end? Who could fet bounds to it? If Portfmouth and Plymouth were to be covered with military works to preferve the naval ftores, London fhould be fortified on the fame principle. Ridiculous as this project might now appear, there was once a ferious defign entertained of carrying it into execution. For the truth of the fact, he would appeal to the venerable records of the Court of Aldermen, to the authentic minutes of the Board of Ordnance.

When the Pretender, in the year 1745, or, to fpeak more courtly language, the Grandfon of James II., had flipped the Royal army and advanced as far as Stone, the Court of Aldermen took no falfe alarm:—The Lord Mayor fent a circular letter to every member, commanding his attendance, conftituted himfelf prefident, drew up a fet of inftructions to direct their proceedings; and after a long debate, it was at laft unanimoufly agreed to apply to the Duke of Newcaftle to fend them an engineer; as, on fuch an arduous occafion, they did not choofe to entruft the defence of the metropolis to the city furveyor—his office, therefore, like the noble Duke's, was put in commiffion, Colonel Lafcelles was actually appointed for this duty, and was directed to wait on the Lord Mayor and Aldermen with a plan and eftimate, but an exprefs critically arriving, with an account of the Highlanders retreat to Scotland, put a ftop to this wife project.— If we were refolved to provide againft all poffible dangers by fortification, why fhould not Newcaftle, Sunderland, and many other important places be fecured in this way? The noble Duke, from a principle of gratitude, would not leave our collieries expofed to an attack; and they would equally affect the partial attention of the Chancellor of the Exchequer;

quer; as he had early, with infinite fagacity, perceived in them the stamina of future taxation. Mr. Courtenay then alluded to what a right honourable gentleman (Colonel Barré) had rather, he thought, invidiously introduced, a fort of comparifon between the commiffion iffued to Sir Walter Raleigh and others, the firft military characters of the age, in the reign of Queen Elizabeth, and the late circular letter and inftructions to the noble Duke. This was tender and delicate ground; otherwife, he had a ftrong inclination to fay—*Rex facit Elizabeth olim; nunc eft Regina Jacobus.* Mr. Courtenay faid, he now clearly perceived why the right honourable gentleman had, with his ufual point and energy, objected to the Mafter General's having a feat in the Cabinet, as our navy was to be increafed, our army diminifhed, by the fingular expedient of building fortifications. If we were to credit the Chancellor of the Exchequer (though all this appeared an Ordnance conundrum to him) why might not the want of allies be fupplied in the fame manner? It was only one ftep farther; on this fuppofition the right honourable gentleman (Colonel Barré) might juftly apprehend, that the Mafter General would act confiftently with his own principles, and oppofe any alliance in the cabinet, left it fhould make his fortifications lefs expedient and neceffary. Indeed, this was the moft fingular, and at the fame time the moft verfatile project that ever was devifed. In other ages, and in other countries, the increafe of the military eftablifhment was always deemed effential when the fortifying fyftem took place, otherwife it became relative weaknefs.

But the noble Duke had fo contrived it (and the Chancellor of the Exchequer became his voucher) that it would reduce our ftanding army, increafe our fleet, and furnifh us with firm and fteady confederates in the day of peril. By a fort of fecond fight, we were to difcover allies in pentagonal forts, and a fquadron of the line in a chain of redoubts. Mr. Courtenay obferved, that feveral gentlemen had juftly ftigmatized the fortifying fyftem as dangerous and inimical to freedom and the conftitution. He fhould take the liberty of offering to the Houfe the fentiments of a great and political writer on the fubject: Baron Montefquieu expreffly applauds the watchful jealoufy of the Englifh, in not permitting the executive government to erect military works and fortifications, as by fuch means defpotifm may be eftablifhed under the fpecious pretext of protecting the kingdom againft a foreign enemy. Hiftorical facts confirmed the principle.—In the reign of Charles the Firft, the glorious efforts of our anceftors would not have proved fuccefsful, if Portfmouth had then been furrounded with the prefent projected works; and Lord Clarendon juftly remarks, that the poffeffion of this

place

place was almoſt reckoned deciſive in the conteſts between the King and Parliament. However, he did not mean to draw any invidious parallel betwen thoſe inglorious and the preſent auſpicious times; but we might not always be bleſſed with a gracious Prince; we might not always have a mild, unaſſuming virtuous Miniſter.

" A King might ariſe who knew not Joſeph."

Still it was the duty of the repreſentatives of the People to guard poſterity againſt thoſe evils which they were not apprehenſive of ſuffering themſelves. Mr. Courtenay concluded, by calling forcibly and with energy on every man, who felt for the rights and liberties of his country, who venerated the glorious Conſtitution of England; as it behoved every man to reflect ſeriouſly, before he gave his voice on a propoſition of ſuch dangerous tendency. The propoſition moved by the Chancellor of the Exchequer on the ſuggeſtion of the noble Duke, went directly to depreciate the Britiſh navy, and to ſubſtitute a new and fallacious mode of defence in its room. A new and degrading ſpecies of diſcipline was to be introduced. The Britiſh ſoldier was to be left

" To lurk in the trench, and ſkulk behind the line."

On his conſcience and honour he believed the vote of that night would be deciſive; fatally deciſive indeed, if the amendment propoſed by the honourable gentleman (Mr. Baſtard) was not carried.

Lord *George Lenox* begged leave to aſſure the honourable gentleman who ſpoke laſt, that he was not thoroughly grounded upon the facts to which he had adverted. In one inſtance he erred extremely; for it was a truth, that at the fortification of South-Sea Caſtle, built by the Maſter General of the Ordnance, neither the defect of letting its guns run back at the time of firing, nor of ſmothering the men with their ſmoke, had ever taken place. The honourable gentleman had a manner of delivering his ſentiments which might divert himſelf, but he muſt appeal to the honourable General near the honourable gentleman, if the fact did not differ moſt materially from ſuch ſtatements.

General *Burgoyne* declared, that thus called upon, he could not as a man of honour refuſe to ſay, that he had ſeen the fortreſs, and that he had not obſerved the inconvenience in queſtion.

Mr. *Courtenay* anſwered, that he had not aſſerted the fact as falling within his own knowledge, but had merely ſtated, that ſuch a circumſtance had been related to him by an engineer.

Lord Geo. Lenox.

General Burgoyne.

Mr. Courtenay.

The House doubtless would hear the sentiments of others on this particular point.

The honourable *Charles Marsham* remarked, that his objection to the proposed system of fortifications must chiefly rest on the difference of opinion which prevailed between the Naval and Land Officers who formed the Board of Inquiry. In all points of so peculiar a nature, the authority of the Land and Sea Officers would have great weight with him; and had he reason to think that the Board had been fairly and impartially constituted, and that their opinions were unanimous in favour of the proposed system, he should, in that case, have given his vote in its support; but in consequence of what he had heard from the honourable and gallant officer near him (Captain Macbride) he was led to imagine that the reverse was the fact. An honourable gentleman (Sir Charles Middleton) had argued in favour of the proposed system of fortification, and he also should beg leave, in order to shew what had been the prevailing opinion of the best and wisest statesmen on the subject of insular defence, when the danger of invasion was most dreaded, to trouble the House with an extract of a letter written by Sir Nicholas Throgmorton to Secretary Burleigh in the reign of Queen Elizabeth; it ran thus :—" In any wise, Mr. Secretary, tend your force, cre-
" dit, and devise, to maintain and increase your navy by all
" the means you can possible; for in this time, considering
" all circumstances, it is the flower of England's garland;
" animate and cherish as many as you can to serve by sea—
" Let them neither want good deeds, nor good words. It is
" your best and most cheap defence, and most redoubted of
" your enemies and doubtful friends, there is not so many
" perils in it, as there is to depend upon fortresses; neither
" the charges be like."

Viscount *Mahon* declared, that in his opinion, the increasing the army was not the best way to increase the navy; but he always conceived, that a standing army ought to be an object of constitutional jealousy in this country. No consideration whatever should have induced him to support this plan of the noble Duke (Richmond) if it had not been proved to the House, that this plan would tend to decrease instead of increasing the number of troops necessary to be employed to defend the dock yards.

He then read the following extracts from the Report of the Board of Land and Sea Officers, who had been appointed to examine the Duke of Richmond's plan of fortifications :

" Your Majesty's Land Officers (at Portsmouth) are una-
" nimously of opinion, that the proposed finishing of works
" already begun, the improvements to old ones, and the
                              " plan

" plan for rebuilding South-Sea Castle, will, together with
" the new works proposed, give a reasonable degree of secu-
" rity to Your Majesty's dock yard at Portsmouth, for the
" time and under the circumstances of the data, with a gar-
" rison of the numbers before specified (regulars and militia)
" which the Land Officers are of opinion is sufficient for its
" defence; whereas the present works, even when repaired,
" finished, and improved, would require a larger force for
" their defence, with which they would still be ineffectual
" for the purpose of securing this dock yard."

" Your Majesty's Land Officers (at Plymouth) are una-
" nimously of opinion, that a garrison (of the numbers be-
" fore specified, regulars and militia) appears sufficient, if
" the proposed new works and repair of old ones are executed,
" and that for the present works, even when repaired, a
" much larger garrison would be ineffectual for the pur-
" pose of securing the dock yard."

And at the end of this Report, a still stronger fact is
proved, viz.

" The works we recommend, appear to us to be calculated
" upon the most œconomical principles, and to require the
" smallest number of troops possible to answer the purpose of
" effectually securing Your Majesty's dock yards at Portf-
" mouth and Plymouth."

(Signed)

Richmond,	James Pattifon,
Guy Carleton,	Sam. Cleaveland,
Will. Howe,	James Bramham,
Geo. H. Lenox,	William Green,
Cornwallis,	William Roy,
David Lindfay,	George Garth.
Charles Grey,	

Viscount Mahon concluded by observing, that the question
was not whether there should be fortifications or no fortifications to defend the dock yards; but whether the present existing fortifications, which require a very large body of troops
to man them, and which are not adequate to the defence of
the dock yards; or whether the plan proposed by the Duke of
Richmond, which will require a much smaller number of
troops to man them, and which will give security to the dock
yards, ought to be preferred.

Mr. *Sheridan* declared, that he gave the noble Viscount
full credit for the principles he had professed, with respect to
the Constitution; and that he did sincerely believe that the
noble Viscount would not vote for the measure then under
discussion, but upon a supposition, that its tendency was rather to diminish than augment the military power of the

E e 2 Crown;

Crown; upon this ground therefore he would meet him, and he was sanguine enough to believe, that the noble Viscount might be induced to alter the opinion which he had declared, unless indeed, he was restrained from exercising his free judgement upon the subject; an apprehension which a late speech of his had suggested, a speech in which the noble Viscount had expressed himself so full of dread and horror, at the means by which a Tory foe, in another place, had, both by sap and storm, assailed those constitutional bulwarks which the noble Viscount had so zealously endeavoured to erect for the protection of our decayed election rights, that it was almost reasonable to presume that the noble Viscount might have entered into a serious compact with a noble Duke, his former ally, on this subject, for reciprocal assistance on their two favourite objects, by which the noble Viscount was peremptorily to support the plan of fortifying the dock yards in that House, or the noble Duke would no longer engage to assist him in fortifying the Constitution in the other. But what was the noble Viscount's argument? He had rested the matter entirely upon the ground taken by his right honourable friend (Mr. Pitt) that the pursuing this system of fortification, would actually diminish the standing army in this country, and that the number of troops being so diminished, there would be proportionally less cause for that constitutional jealousy, with which all parties agreed it was our duty to regard the increasing military power of the Crown. That this system of defence by fortifications, could, under any circumstances, have the effect of reducing the standing army, he must beg leave utterly to deny. Some plausible arguments indeed had been adduced in support of this notion, which, however, when sifted, would be found fallacious and contradictory; for the present, however, he would wave that point, and admit implicitly, that the standing army of the country would be reduced by the measure proposed precisely in the proportion stated by the noble Viscount; it then, however, remained to be proved, that, giving the noble Viscount his premises, he was right in his conclusion. When we talked of a constitutional jealousy of the military power of the Crown, what was the real object to which we pointed our suspicion? What was the datum, as the fashionable phrase was, upon which they proceeded? What!—but that it was in the nature of Kings to love power, and in the constitution of armies to obey Kings. This, doubtless, was most delicate ground to touch upon; but the circumstances of the present question called for plain dealing; and for his part, he could not be suspected, even in the smallest degree, of alluding either to the present Monarch on the throne, or to the army under his command. He agreed most sincerely, to the dis-

tinctions

tinĉtions taken with refpeĉt to both, by a worthy baronet who
had fpoken before him; but, at the fame time it muft be
admitted, that whenever we fpoke of a conftitutional jealoufy
of the army, it was upon a fuppofition that the unhappy
time might come, when a Prince, mifled by evil counfellors, and againft the fuggeftions of his own gracious temper,
of courfe might cherifh the difaftrous notion, that he could
become greater by making his fubjeĉts lefs, and that an army
might be found fo forgetful of their duty as citizens, fo
warped by feelings of falfe honour, or fo degraded by habits
of implicit obedience, as to fupport their military head in
an attempt upon the rights and liberties of their country !
The poffible exiftence of this cafe, and the probable coin-
cidence of thefe circumftances, was that to which every gentleman's mind muft point, when he admitted an argument
upon the fubjeĉt; otherwife we burlefqued and derided the
wifdom of our anceftors, with the provifions of the Bill of
Rights, and made a mere mockery of the falutary and facred referve with which, for a fhort and limited period, we
annually intrufted the executive magiftrate with the neceffary defence of the country. This plain ftatement being
really the cafe, to what, in fuch a crifis, were we to look ?
Were our apprehenfions only to be direĉted to the length of
the mufter roll of men in the King's pay ? Were we to
calculate only the number of foldiers whom he could encamp at Hounflow, or the force of the detachment which
he might fpare to furround the lobby of the Houfe of Commons ? No ; the jet and fubftance of the queftion lay briefly
here : In which of the two fituations now argued upon,
would the King and his evil advifers find themfelves in a
ftate of the greateft military force and preparation, and moft
likely to command and to receive a military fupport ? In
this point of view would it be argued, that thefe fortreffes
which were to become capable of refifting the fiege of a foreign enemy landed in force, would ferve as a fufficient
ftrength in the hands of the Crown, when the enemy was
his People ? Would no ftrefs be given to the great and important diftinĉtion, already ably urged, between troops
eleĉted and feparated from their fellow citizens in garrifons
and forts, and men living fcattered and entangled in all the
common duties and conneĉtions of their countrymen ? Was
this an argument of no weight when applied to the militia,
who were to form a part of thefe garrifons ; or would it,
even for a moment, be pretended that men under fuch circumftances, and in fuch difciplined habits, were not a
thoufand times more likely to defpife the breath of Parliament, and to lend themfelves to the aĉtive purpofes of tyranny and ambition, than the loofe and unconneĉted bodies
which exift even with jealoufy under the prefent fyftem ?

It

It was unneceffary to prefs the diftinction; the fact was, that thefe ftrong military holds, if maintained as they muft be in peace, by full and difciplined garrifons; if well pro-vided, and calculated to ftand regular fieges, as the prefent plan profeffed, and if extended to all the objects to which the fyftem muft inevitably lead, whether they were to be confidered as inducements to tempt a weak Prince to evil views, or as engines of power in cafe of an actual rupture, would in truth, promife tenfold the means of curbing and fubduing the country, than could be ftated to arife even from doubling the prefent military eftablifhment; with this extraordinary aggravation attending the folly of confenting to fuch a fyftem, that thofe very naval ftores and magazines, the feed and fources of our future navies, the effectual pre-fervation of which was the pretence for thefe unaffailable fortreffes, would in that cafe become a pledge and hoftage in the hands of the Crown, which in a country circum-ftanced as this was, muft infure an unconditional fubmif-fion to the moft extravagant claims which defpotifm could dictate.

What could poffibly prove more fallacious than holding out expectations that a fyftem of defence by fortifications could, in fact, end in a retrenchment of the ftanding army! The firft fallacy in this argument ftood forward in the fup-pofition that the fyftem of defence by fortifications was ne-ceffarily to ftop, when Portfmouth and Plymouth fhould become fecured, and that the reafoning upon which the ex-tenfive works for thofe places were juftified, would not apply to any other parts of the kingdom, however their importance called for defence, or their fituation expofed them to attack. The fhorteft method of refuting this idea, was fimply to fuppofe the fame Board of Officers, acting under the fame inftructions, and deliberating under the fame data, going a circuit round the coaft of the kingdom, and directed to report upon the various places in their progrefs, and let any perfon fairly confider the fuppofitions under which they make their prefent Report, and then hefitate to confefs that they muft, of neceffity, recommend a fimilar plan of de-fence proportioned to the importance of every place to which their attention was directed. It was fuperfluous to dwell upon the circumftances which no longer permitted us to confider Holland in future otherwife than as a province of France, or which rendered it equally reafonable to look with an eye of apprehenfion to the neighbouring coaft belonging to the Emperor; becaufe, the fact was evident that, in the cafe of this country being engaged in a war againft a power-ful confederacy, (upon the fuppofition of which alone the prefent fcheme was recommended and juftified) every motive

of

of prudence muſt compel us to direct an attention, as vigorous and vigilant to the eaſtern as to the ſouthern coaſt of this country. It was not poſſible for the Houſe to remain at a loſs to diſcover various places which, with Chatham and Sheerneſs (where moſt extenſive lines had actually been begun under the auſpices of the noble Duke) muſt neceſſarily be provided for in the new ſyſtem of protection ; and for his own part, indeed, he could wiſh that any perſon would compute the ſtationary defence neceſſary for ſuch places, in addition to the twenty-two thouſand men demanded for Portſmouth and Plymouth, and allow likewiſe for any moving force in the country, and then decide what chance there was that this prolific ſyſtem would terminate in a reduction of the ſtanding army !

Concerning the probability of our being able to furniſh men for the conſtant maintenance of theſe garriſons, he felt it requiſite to obſerve that the argument had been, not a reference to our preſent peace eſtabliſhment, but to the extent of the ſervice during the moſt extravagant periods of the laſt war ; which, in other words, was to hold out a notion that we might ſpeedily again look to a time when we ſhould become able to expend for the purpoſe of war fifteen millions of money in the courſe of a ſingle year ! At the very moment when the right honourable gentleman was holding out the reduction of our debt by a few hundred thouſand pounds, as the triumph of his adminiſtration, and the corner ſtone of that pillar upon which his fame was to become emblazoned ! But, even ſuppoſing this to be poſſible, and conſidering the reference to our eſtabliſhment in the laſt war as juſt, the right honourable gentleman had taken an unfair advantage of the argument ; for when he ſtated the numerous armies which we had upon the continent of America, as reſources from which we were in future to garriſon theſe forts, and increaſe our home defence, he ought alſo to have taken into his account the enormous floating eſtabliſhment which attended upon thoſe armies, and which being converted into an efficient naval defence at home, would make both his fortifications and his garriſons unneceſſary.

To the attack which the right honourable gentleman (Mr. Pitt) had choſen to make upon the late Adminiſtration, he ſhould beg leave to anſwer that, in whatever point of view he was, that day, to regard the right honourable gentleman, whether as that glorious orb which an honourable gentleman (Mr. Luttrell) had deſcribed him to be, whoſe influence and power was more than to compenſate to the nation for the loſs of an hemiſphere ; or whether his luſtre was calculated rather to dazzle and ſurpriſe, than to cheriſh and invigorate ; whether he merited the leſs complimentary language

guage of his right honourable friend (Colonel Barré) who obferved, that his confcience had been furprifed in this bufinefs; or whether he had capitulated upon regular approaches; whether he had been fuccefsful in repelling the infinuation of another gentleman, that he was not in earneft in this caufe, by the vehemence of his manner, or had confirmed it by the weaknefs of his argument; whether the right honourable gentleman moft deferved the praifes or the reproach which he had received, he would not embarrafs himfelf by pretending to determine; but only obferve, that one part of his conduct had moft aftonifhingly efcaped the panegyric of his friends—he meant the fpirit and enterprize with which, taking his hint probably from the fubject in debate, he had endeavoured to carry the war into the enemy's country, and purfue meafures of offence and attack, while every pafs at home was left unfortified and defencelefs.

For what was the ground of this ftrenuous charge? The late Adminiftration (as the right honourable gentleman afferted) had fubmitted part of this very plan to the judgement of Parliament, but at the defire of the Houfe withdrew that part for reconfideration; and now, if, upon reconfideration, they had in any refpect altered their opinion, it was the groffeft inconfiftency of conduct and dereliction of principle!—an extraordinary charge, and particularly fo from the gentleman by whom it was urged! He had reconfidered many fubjects, without afpiring to the merit of an obftinate adherence to his firft opinion. He had reconfidered his American intercourfe bill, and had publicly avowed that he had parted with every idea which he once entertained upon that fubject. — He had reconfidered his India bill, and before it was engroffed, had fcarcely fuffered one word to remain which belonged to it when it was brought in.—He had reconfidered his Irifh refolutions, in every part, provifion, and principle; and, having firft offered them as a bounty to Ireland, he had reconfidered the boon, and annexed a price to it, and then reconfidered his own reconfideration, and abandoned his own indifpenfable condition! And yet this Minifter, whofe whole government had been one continued feries of rafh propofition, and ungraceful conceffion, held it out as a palpable enormity in others, that reconfideration fhould have produced alteration of fentiment, and that too upon a fubject where the firft opinion muft have been taken upon credit, and the fecond was called for upon minute information and authentic inquiry. In the fame excellent fpirit of reconfideration, many honourable gentlemen round the Minifter, who had formerly given a decided opinion againft the fortifications, were now folicitous to argue in their favour. As an effectual defence of the conduct of the late Adminiftration, he could prove, by referring to the eftimates and journals of 1783, that they had not the leaft occafion to refort to the juftification of having changed their minds in confequence of better information; for the fact was, that they never had, even in the flighteft degree, committed themfelves in either any opinion or approbation whatever of the prefent plan.

Concerning the hiftory of the rife and progrefs of fortifications in this ifland, upon which the right honourable gentleman had laid fo much ftrefs, as if he had proved, that what was not new, muft be conftitutional, and that the point which had been often tried, muft be fit to be carried into execution; he fhould maintain, that every word urged on this fubject made againft the caufe which it was brought to fupport; for experience, even by their own ftatement, convinced us of nothing but that the nation had invariably been deluded and defrauded upon this unprincipled plea of fortifications; that much had been done and undone, many fchemes and many projectors tried; many millions fpent, and the object avowedly as diftant as ever! So that repeated proofs of paft deception were all which they urged as arguments for prefent confidence; and it was modeftly expected, that they would believe, that becaufe a point had been always unfuccefsfully attempted, it was now at laft certain of being wifely accomplifhed.

The right honourable gentleman (Mr. Pitt) had chofen eagerly to dwell upon a pretended charge of inconfiftency which he advanced againft au honourable naval officer (Captain Macbride) and which, although the latter had omitted to reply to it, had no other foundation than the right honourable gentleman having thought proper to confound the opinion of the land officers with that of the fea officers. With refpect to the Report itfelf, he was ready to admit, that thofe who had entrenched themfelves in conftitutional objections only, refufing to be bound by the advice and authority of any Board of General Officers or Engineers whatfoever upon fuch a fubject, had taken ftrong and refpectable ground; and that thofe alfo, who had argued the fubject more with a reference to the ftate of the revenue of the country, and had feemed to confider the meafure as advifeable, or otherwife, according as it fhould prove confiftent with the neceffary principles of œconomy, were undoubtedly intitled to every attention. For his own part, however, he did not go to the extreme of the reafoning ufed on either of thefe topics—every hour produced inftances where practices highly dangerous by their precedent, and evidently infringing on the eftablifhed rights of the fubject, were reforted to, unavoidably perhaps, for the purpofe of retrieving and maintaining that public credit, without which the affairs of this country were completely defperate.

The right honourable gentleman had pledged himfelf not to prefs this bufinefs, unlefs he could make it appear to be a meafure not lefs effential to national fafety than even the prefervation of national credit. Upon this line of argument, the dangers to be apprehended to the Conftitution, which were ftated as eventual and remote, muft, of courfe, give way, and the point of œconomy was wholly out of the queftion.

The right honourable gentleman had alfo contended, that the decifion of a Board fpecially appointed for this inquiry, and confifting of perfons eminently qualified for the judgement expected from them, was the beft anthority which the country could obtain on the fubject, and afforded a furer guide for the opinion and conduct of that Houfe, than either the arguments or the information of its individual members could fupply. To this he had already affented, and now repeated his affent; nor did he hefitate to renew the pledge to which the right honourable gentleman had appeared fo anxious to fix him, that he, for his own part, mindful of the terms upon which the queftion was fufpended at the clofe of the laft feffion; he would reft contented to abide by the decifion of a Board fo defcribed, and to withdraw his objections to the plan, if it could be fairly made appear that thefe gentlemen, (whofe names and characters he freely admitted did intitle them to the confidence which was claimed for them) upon a full inveftigation of the whole of the fubject propofed laft year in Parliament to be fubmitted to their inquiry, and being left to their own free and unfettered judgement in forming their decifion—had reported, as their decided and unqualified opinion, that the plan propofed by the noble Duke, and then under difcuffion, was a meafure which it became the wifdom and prudence of Parliament to adopt. Upon this point they were at iffue, and the Report in his hand was the only authority to which he fhould appeal, and the fole ground upon which he fhould argue.

Yet, previous to the leaft difcuffion of the matter of the Report, he could not omit to take notice of many circumftances attending the manner of its formation. Far from meaning to reflect upon the Officers who compofed the Board, he muft beg leave to fupport the complaint which had been urged by the right honourable gentleman (Colonel Barré) who firft fuggefted this reference, that, in violation of the confidence repofed in Minifters, they had not referred the queftion of a fyftem for the general defence of the country to the Board, giving them due time and materials for forming their opinion upon the great and extenfive fubject, but had merely required from them a fhort anfwer relative to two points of attack under certain data of their own impofing.

Many

Many powerful, perhaps unanfwerable, objections had been made againſt the appointment of the noble Duke to be Preſident of the Board. Some honourable gentlemen had alluded to peculiar circumſtances of the noble Duke's perſonal character; he had been deſcribed as a man who was never known to give up a point; but whether this was the caſe or not, or whether there was ſome principles of public profeſſion, to which the noble Duke had not very rigorouſly adhered, he would not pretend to decide, as he might be ſuſpected of ſpeaking from party prejudices. There was one characteriſtic, however, of the noble Duke's mind, which he thought might be fairly mentioned, as it was a peculiarity which had been publicly brought forward in argument by high authority in that Honſe; and if now referring to it, he were to repreſent that noble perſonage as of a temper eager to extravagance, and vehement in the extreme, if he were to deſcribe him as a perſon who, having taken up a juſt principle, was capable of defeating all ſalutary proceeding upon it, by driving on with a heated imagination to the moſt flighty and prepoſterous concluſions, the right honourable gentleman oppoſite to him (the Chancellor of the Exchequer) would become his authority. He was the perſon who had led him and the Houſe into that opinion, as muſt be in the recollection of every honourable gentleman, who, during a former ſeſſion, heard that right honourable gentleman diſcuſs the noble Duke's principles of parliamentary reform, and recollected the terms of indignant ridicule with which he had cautioned them againſt the ſchemes of ſo viſionary a projector. If, therefore, he was arraigned for following any plan of the noble Duke's with a peculiar degree of jealouſy, he ſhould leave his juſtification in the abler hands of the right honourable gentleman.

Yet the noble Duke deſerved the warmeſt panegyrics for the ſtriking proofs which he had given of his genius as an engineer, which appeared even in the planning and conſtructing of the paper in his hand! The profeſſional ability of the Maſter General ſhone as conſpicuouſly there, as it could upon our coaſts. He had made it an argument of poſts, and conducted his reaſoning upon principles of trigonometry, as well as logic. There were certain detached data, like advanced works, to keep the enemy at a diſtance from the main object in debate. Strong proviſions covered the flanks of his aſſertions. His very queries were in caſements. No impreſſions, therefore, was to be made on this fortreſs of ſophiſtry, by deſultory obſervations, and it was neceſſary to ſit down before it, and aſſail it by regular approaches. It was fortunate, however, to obſerve, that

notwithftanding all the fkill employed by the noble and
literary Engineer, his mode of defence on paper was open
to the fame objection which had been urged againft his
other fortifications; that if his adverfary got poffeffion of
one of his pofts, it became ftrength againft him, and the
means of fubduing the whole line of his argument.

The points which (Mr. Sheridan faid) he fhould conceive
that he had diftinctly eftablifhed from the authentic document before the Houfe, notwithftanding the mutilated
ftate in which it appeared, were—firft, that not one word,
hint, or fuggeftion on the part of the naval officers tending
to give any approbation, either directly or by implication,
to the fcheme of fortification then in debate, was to be
found in that paper, but that, on the contrary, from the
manner in which a reference was made to the minutes of
the naval officers, of which the refult was withholden, a
ftrong prefumption might be grounded, wholly independent
of the information which the Houfe had received from members of that Board, that thofe minutes did contain a condemnation of the plan. He did not expect to hear it argued
that the refult of thofe minutes could not be communicated,
becaufe they were mixed with dangerous matters of intelligence; they had fhewn a fufficient degree of ingenuity in
the manner of having extracted them from the Report; and
it would prove extraordinary indeed if wherever the judgement was unfavourable, it fhould have been fo blended and
complicated with matter of detail and dangerous difcuffion,
that no chemical procefs in the ordnance laboratory could
poffibly feparate them; while, on the contrary, every approving opinion, like a light fubtile oily fluid, floated at the
top at once, and the clumfieft clerk was capable of prefenting it to the Houfe, pure and untinged by a fingle
particle of the argument or information upon which it was
produced.

In the fecond place, he fhould contend that the opinion
given by the land officers in favour of the plan, was hypothetical and conditional: and that they had unanimoufly
and invariably, throughout the whole bufinefs, refufed to
lend their authority to, or to make themfelves refponfible
for, the data or fuppofitions upon which that opinion was
to be maintained. This circumftance deferved the more
particular attention of the Houfe, becaufe the Report had
been fo artfully managed, as in many points to appear to
fupport a right honourable gentleman (the Chancellor of
the Exchequer) in a contrary affertion.

Next, he regarded himfelf as unanfwerably juftified in
concluding that the data themfelves were founded upon a
fuppofition of events fo improbable and defperate, that the
exiftence

exiftence of the cafe contained in them, carried with it not the imminent danger of Portfmouth and Plymouth only, but the actual conqueft of the ifland.   Upon this occafion, he did not think much detail of argument was neceffary, after he had, at leaft in his opinion, irrefragably eftablifhed, that the cafe alluded to, in the words often recurred to — " under the circumftance of the data,"—was literally this, " The abfence of the whole Britifh fleet for the fpace of " three months, while an army of thirty or forty thou- " fand men was ready on the enemy's coaft to invade this " country, that enemy to chufe their point of landing, to " land and encamp with heavy artillery, and every necef- " fary for a fiege, while no force in Great Britain could be " collected in lefs than two months to oppofe them."   By no means could he admit as a fact that, even taking it for granted that the enemy fhould decide to affault no part but Portfmouth and Plymouth, he fhould, with moft polite hoftility, fcorn to ftrike a blow at the heart of the empire, but in the courtly fpirit of a French duellift, fhould aim only to wound in the fword-arm; yet even under this idea, muft he deny that thefe only objects provided for, could be faid to be effectually fecured.   For, firft, it was not made out that the enemy might not either land or march to the eaftward of Plymouth, where no defence was pretend- ed; and, fecondly, the whole queftion turning upon a fup- pofition of our being inferior at fea, in that cafe a pre- fumption of the fafe return of the inferior fleet and its beating the fuperior fleet, was the fole refource for the re- lief of the befieged dock yards, the defence of which was exprefsly ftated in the Report, to be calculated only as againft the force, and for the time expreffed in the data; fo that the enemy having it obvioufly in his power, while mafter of the fea, to recruit his own army, as well as to keep the other expofed parts of this kingdom in check and alarm, and thereby to prevent the poffibility of our affem- bling and uniting a force fufficient to raife the fiege, it fol- lowed that if either the enemy's army exceeded the number fuppofed, or that the time was prolonged beyond the period calculated, the whole of this effectual fecurity vanifhed un- der their own reafoning, and we fhould merely have pre- pared a ftrong hold in the country for our foe, a hold which the circumftances under which he was fuppofed to make the attack, would enable him for ever to retain.

Mr. Sheridan now proceeding to his remarks concerning the diftinction which had during the debate been taken rela- tive to the different perfons who were fuppofed to form the oppofition to the prefent plan, faid that he had heard the old infinuations of party views reforted to by thofe who

defended

defended the original motion; and fome honourable gentlemen who moft ftrenuoufly oppofed it, had, however, in a
kind of language which he could not avoid taking notice of,
difavowed any party feeling or connection with the party
in queftion. With refpect to himfelf, he was happy that
the bufinefs had worn fo little the appearance of party as it
had; and although he had moved for and obtained the Report, which had been fo much difcuffed, and upon which
fo much had turned, he had proved himfelf ready and anxious
(as the perfons alluded to well knew) to refign the bufinefs
into the hands of the refpectable gentleman who had upon
that day fo ably brought it forward. He could never, for
one, fubmit to the imputation, that the party with whom he
had the honour to act were fupporting or oppofing any
meafure upon motives lefs juft, lefs fair, or lefs honourable than thofe which influenced any other defcription of
gentlemen in that Houfe. The prefent queftion could not
even be pretended to be purfued with party policy, as there
was not a perfon in the Houfe who could avoid confeffing
that party purpofes would be better gratified by entangling
the right honourable gentleman in the purfuit of this obnoxious and unpopular fcheme; but the gentleman who had
upon that day led the oppofition to it, had been fo wifhed to
take fuch a lead, becaufe it appeared among the moft effectual means of warding off an injury from the country;
otherwife to be enlifting under leaders for the day, or
courting the temporary affiftance of any defcription of gentlemen, would, in his opinion, prove a conduct as impolitic as undignified. On the other hand, to recede from
any important conteft, becaufe gentlemen unconnected with
them were likely to have the credit of the event, would de-
fervedly caft on them the reproach of being a faction and
nor a party. But this was not their conduct; they could
defend their fituation upon fyftem and principle; however
reduced their ranks, they were more defirous to prove they
were in the right than to increafe their numbers. He was
confident, however, that the gentlemen to whom he might
be fuppofed to allude, were too liberal to fet a lefs value
upon their fupport that day becaufe it was unaccompanied
by adulation, or any endeavour to canvafs for their future
connection. Let us (added Mr. Sheridan) upon this night
be firmly embodied in a caufe we equally approve. Let us
do this great fervice to the country; then feparate, and feek
oppofing camps. Let them return with the double triumph,
if they will, of having conferred an important benefit on
their conftituents and the nation, and a real obligation on
the Government. Let them have the credit with the country of having defeated the Minifter's meafure, and the merit
with

with his friends, of having refcued him from a perilous dilemma. Leave us only the filent fatisfaction that, without envying the reputation of thofe whom we were content to follow, without being piqued by infinuations againft our motives, and without debating whether the Minifter might not be ferved by our fuccefs, we gave an earneft and zealous affiftance in defeating a meafure, which, under the fpecious pretence of fecuring our coafts, ftrikes at the root of our great national defence, and at the heart of the conftitution itfelf.

Mr. *Fox* remarked, his honourable friend had gone fo fully into the whole of his fubject, and had argued it fo clofely, that it was unneceffary for him to take up much of the time of the Houfe. He would therefore fpeak only to a few points, fo perfonal to himfelf, that the Houfe, as he conceived, would think it highly neceffary for him to take fome notice of them. The right honourable gentleman (Mr. Pitt) had pretty ftrongly infinuated that the fyftem of fortification, now in contemplation, was a part of that identical fyftem which he (Mr. Fox) had, when in office, propofed to the Houfe. This was not by any means a correct reprefentation of the fact; for, in truth, he never had propofed any plan of fortification whatfoever; but in the ordnance eftimates of the year 1783, a fpecific fum was afked for the purpofe of going on with Fort Monkton, and another fmall fort which had been begun; yet, a demur arifing upon the fubject, he had agreed in the Committee to take the two charges out of the eftimate, and referve them for future confideration; and the remaining part of the eftimate was voted without them. In his opinion, a right honourable gentleman (Colonel Barré) had well faid, that it was not by fortifying Portfmouth and Plymouth merely, that we were to look for a defence of the kingdom from either invafion or dangerous attacks; becaufe, undoubtedly, there were other vulnerable parts of our coaft which required attention as well as thofe propofed to be fortified. As to the late peace, fome obfervations concerning which had given fuch offence to a right honourable gentleman (Colonel Barré) he fhould ftill deny that it had been either a *neceffary*, or a *great and glorious* peace; and contend, that in the relative ftate of this kingdom, at the time, compared with the ftate of other powers, we had a right to expect a much more advantageous treaty. If, however, we had been great and glorious, thofe who remained in office, and enjoyed a fhare in making it, had divided the rewards of it in a manner fingularly ftriking. For themfelves they had taken places and emoluments, and left the perfon, who was fuppofed to have been the principal negotiator of it in full poffeffion of all the encomiums which
the

the warmeft of his panegyrifts could beftow. But eafe and praife were the true objects of genuine ambition. Thefe they liberally beftowed upon the noble Marquis (Lanfdown) thefe fubftantial recompences, thefe folid honours, have they nobly fecured to him, in his favourite retirement, in his fequeftered happinefs, in ruftic peace, and undifturbed repofe. For themfelves, on the contrary, have they not referved all the cares, the anxieties, the fatigues, the folicitations, and the emoluments of office? Generous partition!—fubftantial fame for their patron; mere official reward for themfelves! 'Tis the extreme of abfurdity to imagine, on party confiderations, that the carrying the propofed amendment can prove an object of the flighteft eftimation. Who can conceive that either I or my friends fhall be one ftep nearer the acquifition of office or of power, whether the Duke of Richmond's fortification plan fucceeds or fails? If defeating the Minifter, even in points which he has unequivocally fupported to the utmoft of his power, could have ferved us in a party light, how came it that, notwithftanding the numerous defeats which he has endured, he continues unfhaken, and even more firm than ever? Has the whole failure of the Irifh propofitions in the leaft affected him as a Minifter? Did his fhameful defeat in the queftion of the Weftminfter fcrutiny either prejudice *him*, or ferve *me*, in a minifterial light? Did his abandonment of the Manchefter tax take an atom from his confequence? But, in fact, he is a Minifter who thrives by defeat, and flourifhes by difappointment. The country gentlemen oppofe him upon one occafion, only to give him more ftrength upon another; he is beaten by them upon one fubject, only to be affifted by them in a fucceeding one; if he falls by the landed intereft to-day, he is fure to rife by them to-morrow with added energy and recruited vigour." In conclufion, he muft beg leave (Mr. Fox faid) to remind the Houfe, that the right honourable gentleman had, as ufual, availed himfelf of his machinery in his opening fpeech. He had drawn into his argument the American war, and the coalition. He was a little furprifed that the poor India bill had efcaped. Thofe topics, however, the right honourable gentleman might bring forward as often as he thought proper. No part of his conduct was he afhamed of; and although clamour, artfully raifed, and induftrioufly kept alive, might for a while put a falfe and injurious conftruction upon it, time would diffipate the cloud of prejudice, and convince all men how egregioufly they had been duped and deluded. And here he fhould avow that he retained all his great party principles upon conftitutional queftions; and that it was this circumftance which formed the line between him and the right honourable gentleman. " I ftand (faid he) upon this
great

great principle. I fay that the people of England have a right to control the executive power, by the interference of their reprefentatives in this Houfe of Parliament. The right honourable gentleman maintains the contrary. He is the caufe of our political enmity; to this I adhere; to this I pledge myfelf, and upon this ground I mean to vote for the amendment."

Lord *North* contended that the propofed fyftem was repre- LordNorth. henfible on the grounds of policy and œconomy; and that if every Mafter General of the Ordnance were to be indulged in conftructing fuch plans of fortification as his caprice approved, there would be no end to the expence. What was began by one Board of Ordnance would be pulled down by another, and new works would become erected, which would again be pulled down by the next. It was therefore highly neceffary to take up fome determination with refpect to the fubject, and not continue to proceed upon fo unfettled, fo various, and fo expenfive a fyftem. An honourable gentleman (Captain Berkeley) alluding to a noble Earl (of Sandwich) who, during a former adminiftration, prefided at the Board of Admiralty, had lately talked of the curfed management of the Navy during the late war; and to this honourable gentleman he fhould beg leave to anfwer, that although the American war was not by any means a fubject which came within the purview of the original motion, or of the amendment, he fhould not have the fmalleft objection to meet the honourable gentleman upon that topic, whenfoever he might think proper to bring it forward; when he did, howfoever he might differ from the opinion of many gentlemen on the other fide of the Houfe, (from fome whom he faw oppofite to him, he believed that he fhould not differ widely,) and howfoever he might even differ from his right honourable friend, and many honourable gentlemen who fat near him, he fhould contend and maintain that no lofs had been imputable to any mifconduct or mifmanagement of his noble friend, who at that time fat at the head of the Admiralty Board, but that every ill fuccefs had arifen from the nature of the war, from the neceffary divifion of our marine force, and from the powerful combination of marine ftrength with which Great Britain had to contend. In conclufion, Lord North declared that he fhould vote for the amendment.

Mr. *Dundas* anfwered, that it was with a view to meet the Mr. Dundobjections ftarted by the noble Lord, that the fyftem of forti- das. fications then under confideration had been propofed. It was by the Houfe's laying down a regular and permanent fyftem that an end would be put to the expenfive practice which had prevailed of indulging one Mafter General of the Ordnance with this plan, and another General with that, and fo on, pulling down and abandoning as faft as fortifications were erected. Mr. Dundas contended, that a mode of defence which would give fecurity to our dock yards, and preferve the vital fources of our Navy from the danger of being deftroyed during any future war, was an object, in his mind, of fo much value and importance, that 700,000l. or even a million of money, (as fome honourable gentlemen had ftated it) would prove a cheap price to pay for the purchafe. The queftion was, would the Houfe go to that expence for the attainment of an object fo immediately connected with the future exiftence of our Navy, or would they avoid it? To fuch a queftion he fhould not imagine that any man in his fenfes, who was not mifled by prejudice, could hefitate a moment to reply in the affirmative. He relied a good deal on the opinion of the Board of Officers, who, he muft contend, had delivered it as their unanimous opinion, not only that fuch a fyftem of fortification was abfolutely neceffary, but that it was the particular plan which could be erected at the fmalleft expence, and would require the feweft foldiers to man.

Mr. Wyndham.

Mr. *Wyndham* remarked, that, in his opinion, the right honourable gentleman (Mr. Dundas) who fpoke laft had argued the queftion fairly, and was the only advocate in favour of the propofed fyftem, who had put it upon its right ground. The queftion fhortly came to this point: A plan of fortification was propofed, and it muft coft 700,000l. Would the Houfe, or would they not agree to pay that price for it? Mr. Wyndham having fo ftated the matter in iffue between the two fides of the Houfe, added, that they would act unwifely and imprudently, were they to accept the bargain upon the terms propofed. Fortifications in general were infecure and dangerous means of defence, and of all others the moft unfit for us to adopt. *Spem pro pretio emere, ridiculum eft*, was an eftablifhed maxim, but *detrimentum et periculum pro pretio emere, ridiculum eft*, was ftill more undeniable, and therefore he fhould vote for the amendment, on the ground, that to pay 700,000l. for fortifications, would be to lavifh fo much of the public money, for the purchafe of alarm and danger.

Mr. Chancellor Pitt.

Mr. Chancellor *Pitt* remarked, that, notwithftanding his having trefpaffed, during fuch a length of time, upon the patience of the Houfe, he flattered himfelf that, even at a very advanced hour, they would not refufe their wonted indulgence, efpecially after they had heard fo much, to render a reply from him indifpenfably neceffary. Upon this occafion, he muft beg leave to contend, that the queftion was clearly a naval queftion, and that it had been made appear, in his mind, unanfwerably, that if the plan were adopted, a fmaller army eftablifhment

eftablifhment would become neceffary than had hitherto been kept up. An honourable gentleman (Mr. Walwyn) as a new member, and evidently not much ufed to public fpeaking, was indeed excufable for having mentioned the report which he had heard; but that report was ill founded: he was, however, greatly hurt at finding fuch a report hazarded within thofe walls; and he had been ftill more aftonifhed, when he heard fomething fall from a right honourable gentleman (Colonel Barré) whofe infirmity he was extremely concerned to underftand had forced him to, withdraw, which looked like an infinuation darkly wrapped up under the words, *that his confcience had been furprized,* and which feemed to have been directly aimed at the fame end. He had only to fay, that he confidered both the one and the other (if the meaning which he had affumed really belonged to them) as founded in the blackeft malignity, and as highly injurious to his character. The Chancellor ended with repeating his affurances, that the propofed plan was intimately connected with the future welfare and propriety of the Navy; and that unlefs fome fuch plan were foon adopted, the country and that Houfe would have to lament, and to blame themfelves for rejecting a meafure fo much to the national advantage, and on which the prefervation of their liberties, and of the conftitution itfelf depended!

The gallery was now cleared, and the Houfe immediately divided on the motion, " that the words propofed to be left out ftand as part of the queftion."

Tellers — For the Ayes, Mr. Steel, and Mr. M. A. Taylor; for the Noes, Lord Maitland, and Captain Macbride.

Ayes - - - - 169   Noes - - - - 169

The numbers being equal, the Speaker having remarked, that, under his inability to fay any thing new upon a fubject which had been already fo thoroughly debated, and being too much exhaufted by fatigue to enter largely into it then, even if he poffeffed talents enow to do it in a manner which would tend to throw any new light upon it, he would content himfelf with merely giving his vote againft the original motion, and declaring that the Noes had carried the queftion.

Mr. Fox faid, that the motions which his right honourable friend (Mr. Burke) was to have made on the preceding day, for papers relative to Mr. Haftings, could not be made before Wednefday; on which day they probably would be made by his right honourable friend, who was then prevented by illnefs from attending his duty in that Houfe; a fortunate circumftance for the right honourable member (the Speaker) as it had given him an opportunity, which he otherwife would not have had, of gaining immortal honour to himself, by his casting voice upon the subject of fortifications.

The following Members voted for the Duke of Richmond's Plan of Defending the Forts and Dock Yards of this Kingdom by Military Fortifications.

A.
Lord Apsley
R. P. Arden
James Amyatt
John Aldridge
H. Addington
T. Aubrey
J. Aubrey
J. W. Adeane
B.
R. W. Bootle
F. Baring
J. Baring
John Buller
G. Berkeley
G. Bowyer
J. Blackburne
H. Beaufoy
Ch. Boone
C. Brandling
G. B. Brudenell
P. Bathurst
J. H. Brown
W. Bellingham
E. Bearcroft
N. Bayley
A. Brodie
C.
Sir R. Cotton
Sir G. Collier
W. Chaytor
Hon. W. Cornwallis
R. Colt
John Calvert
J. F. Cawthorne
H. Cruger
F. C. Cust
J. Calvert
C. A. Crickitt
J. Crutchley
Earl of Courtown

Lord F. Campbell
J. Campbell
Ilay Campbell
D.
H. Duncombe
Wm. Devaynes
L. Darell
Lord Delaval
H. Drummond
Sir E. Dering
J. Dawes
H. Dalrymple
A. Douglas
G. Douglas
E.
Earl of Euston
E. J. Eliot
J. Eliot
J. T. Ellis
J. W. Egerton
S. Estwick
Sir A. Edmonstone
G. N. Edwards
F.
Sir Adam Ferguson
G.
Marquis of Graham
Hon. W. W. Grenville
J. Grenville
B. Gascoyne
James Gordon
R. Gamon
Philip Goldsworthy
H.
J. J. Hamilton
Sir S. Hannay
Lord Hinchinbrook
Sir H. Hoghton
Lord Hood
Sir R. Hill

B. Hammett
A. Hood
G. Hardinge
J. Hunter
J. W. Heneage
Sir J. Henderson
P. Home
J.
C. Jenkinson
T. Johnes
P. Johnstone
K.
Sir L. Kenyon
T. Kempe
John Kynaston
Sir C. Kent
L.
E. Loveden
Sir W. Lewes
Sir James Langham
Sir E. Littleton
Lord G. Lenox
James Luttrell
C. Lefevre
M.
Lord Mahon
James Macpherson
W. Macarmick
R. Mackreth
H. W. Mortimer
R. S. Milnes
Thomas Masters
Tho. Masters
Sir C. Middleton
W. Mainwaring
Lord Mulgrave
Lord Muncaster
W. Middleton
P. Le Mesurier
J. Macnamara
P. Metcalf

G. Med

G. Medley
R. Manners
Sir W. Mansell
D. Murray
J. Moore
William Macdowal
J. Murray
Earl of Mornington
Sir J. Mawbey
N.
Edward Norton
Ed. Nugent
R. Neville
O.
G. Osbaldiston
P.
P. P. Powney
W. Pitt
H. Phipps
W. M. Pitt
H. Pierse
Sir J. Pennyman
William Pulteney

E. Phelipps
J. J. Pratt
C. Phipps
D. Pulteney
R. Penn
R. Preston
R.
C. W. B. Rouse
Sir T. Rich
George Rose
D. Ryder
E. Rushworth
Sir C. F. Ratcliffe
S.
W. Selwyn
Sir Jam. Stuart Dent
J. Scott
Sir R. Smith
J. Smith
Sir C. Sykes
J. Sutton
G. Selwyn
S. Smith

T.
Earl of Tyrconnel
S. Thornton
R. Thornton
H. Thornton
V.
J. C. Villiers
W.
W. Waller
W. Wilberforce
D. Watherstone
B. Watson
J. Wilmot
W. Williams
W. Wemyss
S. Whitbread
N. W. Wraxall
J. Wilkes
Y.
P. Yorke
W. Young
Sir G. Yonge.

Thomas Steele }
M. A. Taylor } Tellers.

And the following voted against the Plan:

C. W. CORNWALL, Speaker.

A.
F. Annesley
Sir J. St. Aubyn
James Adams
W. Amcotts
W. P. Acourt
W. Adam
J. Anstruther
B.
R. Burton
Sir F. Bassett
W. A. Boscawen
J. P. Bastard
Sir C. Bampfylde
F. J. Browne
H. Bankes
J. Bond, jun.
J. Bullock
J. Burgoyne

H. Bridgeman
R. Benyon
L. E. Bentinck
Sir H. Bridgeman
Visc. Beauchamp
W. H. Bouverie
C.
W. Colhoun
J. Crewe
J. Call
Edward Coke
J. Cleaveland
Sir G. Cooper
Sir W. Coddrington
P. A. Curzon
J. Cotts
H. Cecil
D. P. Coke
J. Courtenay

P. Crespigny
E. Cotsford
H. S. Conway
W. Conway
F. Charteris
Sir W. Cunynghame
D.
W. Drake, jun.
J. Dawkins
Hon. G. Damer
Visc. Duncannon
P. Delme
W. Dickinson
C. Dempster
Sir Tho. Dundas
E.
Hon. Rd. Edgecumbe
Sir J. Eden
W. Ewer

W. Ellis

W. Ellis
Sir J. Erfkine
W. Evelyn

F.
R. Fitzpatrick
T. Fane
H. Fane
H. Fenton
P. Francis
Sir J. Frederick
Chas. James Fox
J. Fitzherbert
T. F. Freeman
E. Foley

G.
W. Grinfton
J. Grigby
J. B. Garforth
C. Greville
J. L. Gower
A. Goddard

H.
J. Hunt
D. Howell
A. Holdfworth
J. Hare
F. Honywood
W. Huffey

I.
Lord Inchiquin
J. C. Jervoife
Sir J. Jervis
G. Jennings

K.
R. Kinfmill
K. P. Knight

L.
Sir W. Lemon
J. Lambton
W. Lawrence
B. Leithieulier
L. Ladlow
J. Lifter
D. Long
E. Leeds

M. Loyde
R. Lafbrooke
J. Lowther
Lord Lifburne

M.
Sir W. Molefworth
J. Mortlock
— Mitford
Sir J. Morfhead
E. Mundy
James Martin
Sir J. Miller
Lord Middleton
E. Morant
C. Marfham
F. Montague
C. Meadows
A. Moyfey
E. Monckton
Sir H. Mackworth

N.
N. Newnham
D. North
W. Norton
J. Nichols
C. Norton
G. A. North
J. Nefbit
R. Nicholas

O.
J. Ord
W. M. Owen

P.
Sir P. Parker
W. Praed
Sir R. Palk
J. Purling
W. Plomer
Lord Penrhyn
F. Page
J. Pelham
H. Pelham
C. Penruddock
J. G. Phillips

R.
P. Rafhley
J. Rolle
Sir W. Rawlinfon
C. Robinfon
J. Rooke
Sir M. W. Ridley
Sir J. Roufe

S.
Earl of Surry
C. Stewart
T. Scott
W. C. Sloper
J. Stanley
J. Sawbridge
Lord Chas. Spencer
Lord R. Spencer
R. B. Sheridan
S. Salt
J. Stewart
R. Skene

T.
J. Tempeft
R. Thiftlethwayte
C. Taylor
Sir J. Thorold
G. W. Thomas
J. Townfhend

V.
G. Vanfittart
R. Vyner
General Vaughan
Sir G. W. Vanneck

W.
W. Wrightfon
W. Weddell
J. Webb
J. Walwyn
H. Walpole
W. Wyndham
J. Whitmore
Lord Weftcote
Sir W. W. Wynne

Lord Maitland } Tellers.
Captain Macbride }

The following papers are so indispensably requisite for the elucidation of various parts of the preceding debate, that we flatter ourselves our readers will favourably accept a respectful mark of attention, which will save them the trouble of references in any other quarter.

My Lord,   *Whitehall, 8th April,* 1785.

I HAVE the honour to transmit to your Grace a copy of a circular letter written to the several officers named *, who, together with naval officers, have been appointed, by the King's command, to compose a Board for investigating, and reporting to His Majesty on the proper system of defence, and the expediency and efficacy of the plans which have been proposed for better securing His Majesty's dock yards at Portsmouth and Plymouth; and His Majesty having thought proper to appoint your Grace to be President of the said Board, I am to signify to you his royal commands, that you do hold yourself in readiness for this service; and am to acquaint your Grace, that His Majesty's instructions will be transmitted to you as soon as possible.

I have the honour to be, my Lord,
Your Grace's most obedient, humble servant,
SYDNEY.

His Grace the Duke of Richmond,
&c. &c. &c.

C I R C U L A R   L E T T E R.
(C O P Y.)

My Lord, or Sir,   *Whitehall, 8th April,* 1785.

HIS Majesty having judged it of the utmost importance, that the most effectual means should be provided in time of peace, for rendering His Majesty's principal dock yards as secure as possible against any attempt upon them that may be expected in a future war, plans of permanent works for this purpose, for Portsmouth and Plymouth, have, by the King's commands, been laid before His Majesty by the Master Ge-

---

* General Duke of Richmond, General Conway, Gen. Lord Amherst, Gen. Lord Townshend, Lt. Gen. Sir G. Carleton, Lt. Gen. Sir W. Draper, Lt. Gen. Sir W. Howe, Lt. Gen. L. G. Lenox, Lt. Gen. Sir R. Boyd, Lt. Gen. Burgoyne, Lt. Gen. Earl Percy, Lt. Gen. Earl Cornwallis, Lt. Gen. Sir D. Lindsay, Lt. Gen. Sir C. Grey, M. Gen. Pattison, M. Gen. Cleaveland, M. Gen. Bramham, M. Gen. Green, M. Gen. Roy, M. Gen. Garth, M. Gen. A. Campbell.

neral

neral of the Ordnance. But in a work of such magnitude and expence, so necessarily connected with the general system of defence for the kingdom, His Majesty, desirous of having the opinion of a Board composed of land and sea officers of experience and abilities, who should fully investigate the subject on the spot, has been pleased to appoint the officers before mentioned, with naval officers, who will receive their instructions from the Admiralty, to be members of this Board, for investigating and reporting to His Majesty on the proper system of defence, and the expediency and efficacy of the proposed plans for the better securing His Majesty's dock yards at Portsmouth and Plymouth.

And as the object of the inquiry peculiarly belongs to the office of the Master General of the Ordnance, His Majesty has been pleased to direct, that the Duke of Richmond shall be President of this Board.

His Grace is to give notice to the members of the time and place where they are to assemble, and is to appoint some intelligent officer to act as Secretary.

His Majesty, confiding in your zeal and talents for this service, has been pleased to appoint you a member of this Board; I am therefore commanded by His Majesty to direct you to hold yourself in readiness for this service.

His Majesty's instructions for your proceedings will be transmitted to the President. His Majesty has been pleased to direct, that an allowance of 40s. per day shall be made to you, and to each of the land officers, members of this Board, during the time you shall be employed on this service, and 20s. per day to the Secretary; as likewise an allowance of 2s. per mile to each member, and 1s. 6d. per mile to the Secretary, for such journeys as they may actually take in consequence of this order.

I have the honour to be, Sir,

Your most obedient, humble servant,

SYDNEY.

SIR, *Admiralty Office, 14th April, 1785.*

THE King having been pleased to direct, that a Board of sea and land officers should be forthwith appointed (whereat the Duke of Richmond, Master General of the Ordnance, is to preside) for investigating the proper system of defence, and reporting upon the expediency and efficacy of the plans which have been prepared for the better security of His Majesty's dock yards at Portsmouth and Plymouth, for His Majesty's information: and the Lords Commissioners of the Admiralty having in consequence judged fit that you, together with the several flag officers and captains of the fleet,

fleet *, who have been duly apprized of their Lordships' intentions herein, should be selected for the sea officers, whereof that part of the Board to be assembled at Portsmouth, for such special purpose, is to be composed : I am therefore directed to signify their Lordships' desire, that you will hold yourself in readiness to attend the Duke of Richmond, and other members of the Board, at Portsmouth, when so required by his Grace, for the discussion of any maritime propositions incidental to this appointment; and to communicate your opinions, how far the same may appear more or less eligible to be adopted for the benefit of His Majesty's service; and otherwise to proceed in the premises as required by the King's instructions given to the Duke of Richmond, for His Majesty's information, accordingly.

But whereas some previous and more particular inspection of the coast and shores, to which the inquiries addressed to you and the other naval officers of the Board relate, may be necessary in the progress of your deliberations, you are permitted to take to your assistance therein such Captains of the guard ships, naval officers, pilots, or other resident persons having knowledge of the navigation of the ports and parts of the adjacent coasts and shores to be examined, as you shall think proper.

After the necessary inquiries have been terminated at Portsmouth, where your stay will be requisite for carrying on the service of the port, Admiral Pigot will be to proceed with the Board, as senior officer in the naval branch, on the similar investigation of the system of defence proposed for the dock yard at Plymouth.

And I am farther to inform you, that you and the other naval officers of the Board will be paid, for your travelling charges and subsistence, while you are employed on this service, such allowance, out of the contingencies of the Ordnance, as is to be made, by His Majesty's commands, to the respective officers of his land forces, nominated for the same occasion.

I am, Sir,
Your most obedient, humble servant,
PH P. STEPHENS.

N. B. Admirals Montagu and Pigot being excused from the above service, on account of their indisposition, Vice Admiral Barrington was directed to proceed upon it in their stead, as senior officer in the naval branch.

* Admiral Pigot, V. Ad. Barrington, R. Ad. Lord Hood, Captains Hotham, Sir J. Jarvis, Bowyer, Macbride, Sir A. Hammond, James Luttrell.

INSTRUCTIONS.
GEORGE R.

Inſtructions for our right truſty and right entirely beloved
couſin and counſellor Charles Duke of Richmond, Lenox,
and Aubigny, Maſter General of our Ordnance, whom
we have thought fit ſhall be Preſident of a Board of
Land and Sea Officers, appointed under our royal authority, to inveſtigate, and report to us on the proper ſyſtem
of defence, and on the expediency and efficacy of the
propoſed plans for better ſecuring our dock yards at Portſmouth and Plymouth.   Given at our Court at St.
James's, the thirteenth day of April 1785, in the twenty-
fifth year of our reign.

UPON the receipt of theſe inſtructions, you are to
give notice to the members named in the incloſed liſt, of the
day on which they are to aſſemble at Portſmouth, and fix
the hour and place where they are to meet.

As ſoon as ſeven of our ſaid land officers, and five of our
ſaid ſea officers are aſſembled, they are to proceed to buſineſs,
and to adjourn from time to time as they ſhall ſee occaſion.

You are to appoint ſome intelligent officer to act as ſe-
cretary, who is regularly to enter in a book the proceedings
of the Board.

In caſe of difference of opinion, the reaſons for ſuch difference are to be ſtated, either jointly or ſeparately, and are
to be ſigned by each member preſent.

The matters treated of, and the opinion of the members, are not to be divulged without our royal permiſſion.

As the inquiries neceſſary to be made, to enable the
Board to give a well-informed opinion on this important
ſubject, muſt branch out into a variety of matter, we have
directed that they ſhould be arranged under ſeparate heads;
which have been accordingly prepared for this purpoſe, and
are hereunto annexed.   On theſe the Board are to report
their opinion to us.

Under each head is added a ſet of more minute and detailed queſtions and obſervations.   The anſwers which the
Board will give to them, will form the baſis of their more
general concluſions.   Theſe queſtions, with the anſwers, as
well as theſe inſtructions, the ſeparate heads, and the Report, are to be entered in a book, containing the proceedings of the Board; which are alſo to be laid before us, that
we may be able at any time to refer to the grounds on
which their opinions have been formed.

If any other matter not contained under thoſe heads or
queſtions, ſhould occur, and appear to the Board, to throw

more

more light on this subject, they will add it to their Report, with any farther observations they may think proper to submit to our consideration.

The first part of the subject referred to the investigation of the Board is, in general terms, the proper system of defence for Portsmouth and Plymouth; which will naturally lead them to consider, whether a system of naval defence alone; a system of land defence, from troops alone; or a system of naval and land defence combined, can be relied on for the protection of the dock yards of Portsmouth and Plymouth; or whether fortifications are necessary: if they are, the second part of the subject referred to this Board, viz. the expediency and efficacy of the proposed plans, will next require their attention.

But before they can agree on any system of defence, it will be necessary for them to agree on the nature and extent of the attack against which it is to be calculated, and on the circumstances to which the kingdom may be reduced by the events of war, when called upon to defend its dock yards.

Note.—(Then follow six data, stating circumstances that may prevent the fleet from affording effectual protection to the dock yards, the force of the enemy against which it may be prudent to guard, the number and sort of troops that may be had for the defence of these places, and the time it may require to collect the strength of the country from other parts of the kingdom. These six data are omitted, because the matter they contain is not proper to be divulged; and because the Board established two new data in place of the two first, and considerably varied two of the others.)

The Board will vary or add to these data as they shall see occasion.

The heads and questions under them will best explain the manner in which the Board is to proceed in applying these data.

We have ordered that such naval assistance as may be wanted at the Ports shall be given; and that such engineers and artillery officers as the Board may wish to examine, shall attend them; they will also have the proper plans and surveys laid before them.

It will be necessary for the naval officers to examine the shores, as well as for the land officers to study the country, which must undoubtedly take up time; but we hope that the Board will be able to make their Report by the first week in June.

With

With refpect to calculations of expence, or making out plans upon any ideas that may be propofed, the Board will give their directions for this purpofe, either to the engineer on the fpot, or to the Committee of Engineers at the Tower, as they fhall fee occafion; and their Reports are to be entered in the proceedings of the Board.

As accurate eftimates can only be made on works which in every particular are fettled, and upon detailed drawings and fections of them, fuch computations as may give a general idea of the probable amount of the expence will be fufficient.   G. R.

Extracts from the Report made to His Majefty by the Board of Land and Sea Officers, appointed by His Majefty to inveftigate and report on the proper fyftem of defence, and on the expediency and efficacy of the propofed plans for better fecuring the dock yards at Portfmouth and Plymouth, bearing date the 24th day of June 1785.

MEMBERS Prefent.

At PORTSMOUTH.	At PLYMOUTH.
G. D. of Richmond, Pref.	G. D. of Richmond, Pref.
V. Ad. Barrington,	V. A. Barrington,
Lt. G. Sir Guy Carleton,	Lt. Gen. Sir Guy Carleton,
Lt. G. Sir Will. Howe,	Lt. Gen. Sir Will. Howe,
Lt. G. L. Geo. Lenox,	Lt. G. Earl Cornwallis,
Lt. G. Burgoyne,	Lt. G. Sir David Lindfay,
Lt. G. Earl Percy,	Vice Ad. Millbanke,
Lt. G. Earl Cornwallis,	Lt. Gen. Sir Charles Grey,
Lt. G. Sir David Lindfay,	Major G. Pattifon,
Lt. G. Sir Charles Grey,	Major G. Cleaveland,
Major G. Pattifon,	Rear Ad. Graves,
Major G. Cleaveland,	Major G. Bramham,
Rear Ad. Lord Hood,	Major G. Green.
Major G. Bramham,	Major G. Roy,
Major G. Green,	Major G. Garth,
Major G. Roy,	Capt. Hotham,
Major G. Garth,	Capt. Macbride,
Capt. Hotham,	Capt. Sir A. Hammond.
Capt. Sir John Jarvis,	
Capt. Bowyer,	
Capt. Sir A. Hammond,	
Capt. James Luttrell.	

Report of the Board of Land and Sea Officers appointed by Your Majefty to inveftigate and report on the proper fyftem of defence, and on the expediency and efficacy of the propofed plans for better fecuring the dock yards at Portfmouth and Plymouth.

Having

Having fully taken into our confideration Your Majefty's inftructions, under Your Majefty's fignet and fign manual, dated the thirteenth day of April 1785, and obferving that Your Majefty has been gracioufly pleafed to allow us to vary or add to the data contained therein, as we fhould fee occafion, we have availed ourfelves of Your Majefty's permiffion fo to do; and as, in confequence of fuch alterations, fome heads and queftions under them appeared to us to have been already anfwered in fome of the data, we conceived any difcuffion of them became unneceffary, as will more fully be feen in the minutes of our proceedings herewith laid before Your Majefty.

We, therefore, in obedience to Your Majefty's comm nds, beg leave humbly to report to Your Majefty, that we have agreed on the following data, as the grounds on which our fubfequent opinions have been formed.

Firft datum, agreed to unanimoufly by both Land and Sea Officers at Portfmouth and Plymouth.

That it is perfectly right, neceffary, and wife, effectually to provide in time of peace for the fecurity of Your Majefty's dock yards at Portfmouth and Plymouth, by fortifications capable of refifting fuch an attack as an enemy may be able to make upon them during the abfence of the fleet, or whilft, from other caufes, the fleet may be prevented from affording its protection to the dock yards.

Second datum, agreed to unanimoufly by both land and fea officers at Portfmouth and Plymouth.

That, as far as is confiftent with due confiderations of expence, and the probable ftrength of the land forces, it will be advifeable to provide a defence by fortifications for the dock yards at Portfmouth and Plymouth, againft the chances of the fleet, or fuch part thereof as might give them protection, being abfent for—(a certain time named, which is omitted, as not being proper to be difclofed).

Note,—The third datum, ftating the force of the enemy, againft which it may be prudent to guard, the number of embarkations, and the detailed account of fhips proper for this purpofe, and agreed to unanimoufly by both land and fea officers, is omitted, as it cannot be proper that fuch particulars fhould be difclofed.

The fourth datum, afcertaining the precife number and fort of troops which may reafonably be expected to be had for the defence of Portfmouth and Plymouth, as eftablifhed by the Land Officers, and an obfervation thereupon, is of a nature not to be difclofed. The diffent of Lieutenant-general

neral Burgoyne and Earl Percy, is in substance contained in their proviso, under another head herein-after stated at full length; but the particular reasons contained in the dissent of Lieutenant-generals Burgoyne and Earl Percy, are for the same reason omitted.

The fifth datum, agreed to unanimously by the land officers, ascertaining the time that it may require before the strength of the country can be collected from other parts of the kingdom in such force as to defeat such an attempt as is supposed, is for the same reason omitted.

Your Majesty's Land Officers at Portsmouth and Plymouth are unanimously of opinion, that such is the situation of the present works, that no finishing, repairs, or improvements, without additional works, can, under the circumstances of the data, afford that degree of security to the dock yards,—(for the time mentioned in the preceding datum) as may enable Your Majesty to employ your whole fleet, if necessary, on foreign service.

Note.—All the details relative to the insufficiency of the present fortifications, unanimously agreed to by the Land Officers, are omitted.

Your Majesty's Land Officers, both at Portsmouth and Plymouth, are unanimously of opinion, that a system of detached forts is the most proper for the purpose of protecting the dock yards.

Your Majesty's Land Officers, both at Portsmouth and Plymouth, are unanimously of opinion, that the system of detached works, as proposed, has, in the extensive situations of Portsmouth and Plymouth, this advantage, that the security to be derived therefrom will not be wholly delayed till the whole of the proposed plan is executed, but an additional degree of strength will be acquired as the detached works are progressively finished.

Your Majesty's Land Officers, both at Portsmouth and Plymouth, are unanimously of opinion, that the situations of the several places therein specified, are well chosen for detached works.

Your Majesty's Land Officers at Portsmouth and Plymouth, are unanimously of opinion, that the new works proposed are well adapted to those situations.

Note, — The detail of the peculiar advantages of these works, unanimously agreed to by the Land Officers, is omitted.

Your Majesty's Land Officers at Plymouth are unanimously of opinion, that the distance of the situation proposed, in lieu of Merrifield, from the dock, appears too

great

great for the circumstances of the data; and would, if fortified, require a greater garrison and greater expence, and would not afford the same security to the dock yard as Merrifield, and therefore the land officers must give the preference to Merrifield.

Your Majesty's Land Officers at Portsmouth are unanimously of opinion, that the proposed finishing for works already begun, the improvements to old ones, and the plan for re-building South-Sea Castle, will, together with the new works proposed, give a reasonable degree of security for Your Majesty's dock yard at Portsmouth, for the time and under the circumstances of the data, with a garrison of the numbers before specified (regulars and militia) which the land officers are of opinion is sufficient for its defence; whereas the present works, even when repaired, finished, and improved, would require a larger force for their defence, with which they would still be ineffectual for the purpose of securing this dock yard.

Your Majesty's Land Officers at Plymouth are unanimously of opinion, that a garrison—(of the numbers before specified, regulars and militia) appears sufficient if the proposed new works and repair of old ones are executed; and that for the present works even when repaired, a much larger garrison would be ineffectual for the purpose of securing this dock yard.

Your Majesty's Land Officers having taken into consideration the whole situation of Plymouth, are unanimously of opinion, that the proposed new works, in addition to the old ones, when properly repaired, as suggested in our proceedings, (with a garrison of the numbers before specified, regulars and militia) will give a reasonable degree of security for Your Majesty's dock yard at Plymouth for the time and under the circumstances of the data.

Your Majesty's Land Officers, as far as they were respectively concerned at Portsmouth or Plymouth, do report to the Committee of Engineers at the Tower, which they have unanimously agreed to adopt, it appears, that the expence of the works proposed for securing Your Majesty's dock yards at Portsmouth and Plymouth, will be as follows:

Note. — This paper has been already delivered to the House.

Your Majesty's instructions under the 23d head, having required, what improvements or alterations, or what other system of defence the Board would suggest, the unanimous

mous opinion of Your Majesty's Sea Officers is, that—(a certain number therein specified) of gun boats at Portsmouth and Plymouth, will form a great arm of defence against an invading enemy.

And Your Majesty's Land Officers entirely concur in this opinion with the Sea Officers, considering these gun boats as a great improvement in the defence of those places.

Your Majesty's Land and Sea Officers beg leave to recommend a set of signals to be established on the projecting head lands—(of certain parts of the coasts therein specified) with intelligent mariners to make them, as of essential advantage in conveying early intelligence of the approach of an enemy, and for the protection of commerce.

Your Majesty's Land and Sea Officers unanimously recommend—(an improvement in the supply of fresh water at Plymouth, if to be had at a reasonable expence).

The Board has no other improvement, or other system of defence, to suggest to Your Majesty.

Lastly, Your Majesty's Land and Sea Officers humbly beg leave to observe, that they make this Report to Your Majesty, in full confidence, that the providing an additional security to the dock yards at Portsmouth and Plymouth is in no respect inconsistent with the necessary exertions for the support of the navy; which they consider as the first object of attention for the safety and prosperity of the kingdom.

(Signed)
Richmond, Lenox, and Aubigny,

Sam. Barrington,	Tho. Graves,
Guy Carleton,	Hood,
Will. Howe,	James Bramham,
Geo. H. Lenox,	William Green,
John Burgoyne,	William Roy,
Percy,	Geo. Garth,
Cornwallis,	William Hotham,
David Lindsay,	John Macbride,
Mark Millbanke,	John Jarvis,
Charles Grey,	Geo. Bowyer,
James Pattison,	A. Snape Hammond,
Sam. Cleaveland,	James Luttrell.

Captain Macbride entered the following objection to the third datum, on the subject of the enemy's force against which the Board thought it necessary to provide.

I object to this datum, because it is founded upon a calculation of a large imaginary force. My idea of a descent goes only to the probability of an armament that may possibly
bly

bly confift of—(a certain force which he fpecifies) which I think fufficient to provide againft.

To the queftion, What improvements or alterations, or what other fyftem of defence the Board would fuggeft?

Lieutenant-general Burgoyne, and Earl Percy, Vice-admiral Millbanke, and Major-general Green, ftated, that they had none to fuggeft under the circumftances of the data.

Rear-admiral Graves ftated, that he had none to fuggeft under the excefs of the data.

Vice-admiral Barrington, Rear-admiral Lord Hood, Captains Hotham, Bowyer, Sir Andrew Snape Hammond, and the honourable James Luttrell, ftated, that they thought it more properly belonged to the Land Officers of this Board, than to them, as the minutes of their proceedings will fhew, to enter into any fyftem of defence or fortifications, except fuch parts as are intended for a defence againft fhips of war, and the propofals they have offered for gun boats.

Captain Macbride ftated, that he had no farther improvements to fuggeft; but entered his objections to the propofed fyftem of defence.

> Note—Captain Macbride's objections are omitted, becaufe they contain detailed defcriptions of the coaft-roadfteads, currents, tides, and bottoms, and anchorage, by no means proper to be divulged. Captain Macbride concludes his objections with thefe words:

I am therefore of opinion that no new works are at prefent neceffary to be erected at Plymouth.

(Signed)   John Macbride.

On the Board having declared it to be their unanimous opinion, that no member is precluded, by the data agreed to by the Board, from fuggefting any other fyftem of defence, on thofe or any other data, for the confideration of the Board, in anfwer to the queftion contained in the 23d head under His Majefty's inftructions;

The following provifo was added:

But we do not think ourfelves required, as individuals, by His Majefty's inftructions, or any queftions under them, to produce any other fyftem, or other data.

(Signed)

S. Barrington,	Will. Green,
J. Burgoyne,	Will. Hotham,
Percy,	John Jarvis,
M. Millbanke,	Geo. Bowyer.
Tho. Graves,	

Rear-admiral Graves, in affenting to the article of the Report expreffing the full confidence of the Board, that the providing an additional fecurity to the dock yard at Plymouth, is in no refpect inconfiftent with the neceffary fupport of the navy; to avoid being mifunderftood, defired to explain himfelf by the following provifo:

I perfectly agree with the reft of the Board, as to the importance of the Royal Navy towards the fafety and profperity of this maritime and infular kingdom; but would not have it implied, that I think any new fyftem of additional land fortifications for the fecurity of Plymouth neceffary.

(Signed)   T. Graves.

Lieutenant-generals Burgoyne and Earl Percy, Vice-admiral Millbanke, Rear-admiral Graves, and Captain Sir John Jarvis, on figning the Report, beg leave to reprefent to Your Majefty as follows:

That our proceedings have been founded upon the fuppofition of the whole fleet being abfent (for a certain time) as mentioned in the fecond datum, and therefore that the enemy may bring over an army (of the force mentioned in the third datum) with an artillery proportionate to an attack on Portfmouth and Plymouth, having (a certain time) to act in, uninterrupted by the Britifh fleet, as mentioned in the third datum: the bare poffibility of fuch an event we do not pretend to deny; but how far it is probable that the whole Britifh fleet may be fent on any fervice requiring fo long an abfence, at a time when the enemy is prepared to invade this country with (a force as that mentioned in the third datum) we muft humbly leave to your Majefty's fuperior wifdom; and therefore, whether it is neceffary, in confequence of fuch a fuppofition, to erect works of fo expenfive a nature as thofe propofed, and which require fuch garrifons to defend them.

(Signed)

J. Burgoyne,   T. Graves,
Percy,   J. Jarvis.
M. Millbanke,

Lieutenant-generals Burgoyne and Earl Percy, on agreeing to the erecting of new works, and to the fyftem of detached forts being the moft proper for the prefervation of the dock yard at Portfmouth, entered the following provifo:

We approve of the fyftem of detached works, and we agree to the above, under the circumftances fettled in the data, provided the expence to be incurred fhall not exceed fuch fums as the State can afford to grant for thefe purpofes, and that the number of troops fuppofed to be allotted by the

fourth

fourth datum, can be spared for the defence of Portsmouth, consistently with the general defence of the kingdom.
(Signed)

> J. Burgoyne,
> Percy.

To which proviso the rest of the Land Officers, members of this Board, think it their duty to add:

That we the under written humbly desire that it may be understood by Your Majesty, that we never entertained an idea that any expence to be incurred should exceed such sums as the State could afford for these purposes, as we apprehend was fully stated in our second datum; or that we meant to recommend works requiring a greater number of troops to defend than could be spared for the defence of Portsmouth, consistently with the general defence of the kingdom.

On the contrary, the works we recommend appear to us to be calculated upon the most œconomical principles, and to require the smallest number of troops possible to answer the purpose of effectually securing Your Majesty's dock yards at Portsmouth and Plymouth. We conceive that such numbers can be spared for this purpose; we consider such protection to be an essential object for the safety of the State, and intimately connected with the general defence of the kingdom; but we do not consider it to be our province minutely to enter into a consideration of the abilities of the State to provide the necessary supplies for this purpose.

(Signed)

Richmond, Lenox, and Aubigny,	
Guy Carleton,	James Pattison,
William Howe,	Sam. Cleaveland,
Geo. H. Lenox,	James Bramham,
Cornwallis,	William Green,
David Lindsay,	William Roy,
Charles Grey,	George Garth.

R I C H M O N D, &c.
President of the Board of
Land and Sea Officers, &c.

COPY of an Estimate of the expence of fortifying His Majesty's Dock Yards at Portsmouth and Plymouth, by the Committee of Engineers at the Tower; annexed to the Report made to His Majesty by the Board of Land and Sea Officers, appointed, under His Majesty's Royal authority, to investigate and report to His Majesty on the proper system of defence, and on the expediency and efficacy of the proposed plans for better securing His Majesty's dock yards at Portsmouth and Plymouth.

For erecting new works on Portsea Island.
For six brick towers on the beach, between Cumberland Fort, and South-Sea Castle, 3300l.
For a pentagonal fort at Hilsea lines, 95,381l. 10s.
For two redoubts at Hilsea lines, 2640l.
Total for new works on Portsea islands, 101,321l. 10s.

For the purchase of land on Portsea island.
For the supposed value of land to be purchased for the fort at Hilsea lines, 2600l.
Total for new works, including the purchase of land on Portsea island, 103,921l. 10s.

For erecting new works on the Gosport side.
For a pentagonal fort proposed at Stokes bay, 135,970l. 13s. 11d.
For a pentagonal fort proposed near Frater lake, 111,278l. 11s. 8d.
Total for the new works on the Gosport side, 247,249l. 5s. 7d.

For the purchase of land on the Gosport side.
For the value of the land at Stokes bay and Fort Monckton, as set by the jury, 11,747l. 16s. 7¼d.
For the supposed value of land to be purchased for the fort near Frater lake, 10,000l.
For the purchase of land at Gosport, 21,747l. 16s. 7¼d.
Total for new works including the purchase of land at Portsmouth, 372,918l. 12s. 2¼d.

For erecting new works on the Plymouth division.
For the proposed pentagonal fort on the heights of Maker, including advanced works, 119,588l. 5s. 5d.
For the proposed pentagonal fort on the heights of Merryfield, 101,964l.
Total for new works in the Plymouth division, 221,552l. 5s. 5d.

For the purchase of land in the Plymouth division.
For the value of land for the fort on the heights of Maker, as set by the jury, 13,945l. 7s. 6d.

For

For the fuppofed value of the land for the fort on the heights of Merryfield, 14,000l.

Total for the purchafe of land in the Plymouth divifion, 27,945l. 7s. 6d.

Total for new works including the purchafe of land for Plymouth, 239,497l. 12s. 11d.

For the repair and improvement of the old works on Portfea ifland.

For Cumberland fort, with the additional alterations now propofed, 3444l. 17s.

For the repair and improvement of Lumps battery, 1971l. 19s. 7d.

For ditto—of Eaftney battery, 3232l. 0s. 7d.

For the repair of the old works round the town of Portfmouth, 10,715l. 13s. 9d.

For completing the works round Portfmouth Common on the reduced plan, 26,929l. 17s. 0¼d.

For taking down South-Sea Caftle and building a fquare redoubt in lieu thereof, 10,080l. 8s.

Total for old works on Portfea ifland, 87,379l. 15s. 6¾d.

For the repair and improvement of the old works on the Gofport fide.

For repairs and additions to Block-houfe fort, 1054l. 19s.

For completing Fort Monckton, 32,457l. 12s. 3½d.

For completing the lines at Wevill and Priddy's Hard, 8248l. 3s.

Total for old works on the Gofport fide, 41,760l. 14s. 3½d.

Total for old works at Portfmouth, 129,140l. 9s. 10¼d.

For the repair and improvement of the old works at Plymouth.

For reveting the North Glofter and Second Devon redoubts, 5748l. 12s.

For repairing the citadel, 1955l. 3s. 11¼d.

For repairing the battery on the Haut, 3l. 9s. 10d,

For ditto Eaftern King, 4l. 8s. 4d.

For ditto Weftern King, 4l. 3s,

For ditto Paffage Point, 2l. 8s.

For repairing the works on St. Nicholas ifland, 110l. 0s. 7d.

For repairing the lines round Plymouth-dock town, 694l. 1s. 9d.

Total for old works at Plymouth, 8522l. 7s. 5¼d.

RICHMOND, &c.

GENERAL

GENERAL ABSTRACT of the whole Expence for Fortifying the Dock Yards at Portsmouth and Plymouth.

	For repairing and improving the Old Works.	For the New Works proposed.	For the Purchase of Lands.	Total.
On Portsea Island, - -	87379 15 6¾	101321 10 0	2600 0 0	191301 5 6¾
On the Gosport Side, - -	41760 14 3½	247249 5 7	21747 16 7½	310757 16 5¾
Total expence to fortify the dock yard at Portsmouth, -	129140 9 10¼	348570 15 7	24347 16 7½	502059 2 0½
Total expence to fortify the dock yard at Plymouth, -	8522 7 5½	221552 5 5	27945 7 6	258020 0 4¾
General Total of Expence, - - £.	137662 17 4	570123 1 0	52293 4 1½	760079 2 5¼

N. B. Provided no new works are erected, and the works round Portsmouth Common are completed, as proposed in 1783, the expence of old works will be increased as expressed in the eleventh article of this Report, relative to Portsmouth, - - - - - - 70630 0 0

Consequently the total amount of old works will then be - - - - - - 208292 17 4

RICHMOND, &c.

Tuefday, 28th *February.*

No material debate.

Wednefday, 1ft *March.*

The Houfe having refolved itfelf into a Committe of Supply, the eftimates of the Navy (which had been previoufly referred to the Committee) were taken into confideration, when Mr. Brett rofe and moved,

1. " That it is the opinion of this Committee, that a fum " not exceeding fix hundred and ninety-two thoufand, three " hundred and twenty-fix pounds, eighteen fhillings and " eight pence, be granted to His Majefty for the Ordinary of " the Navy, including half pay to fea and marine officers for " the year 1786."

2. " That it is the opinion of this Committee, that a fum " not exceeding eight hundred thoufand pounds be granted " to His Majefty towards buildings, re-buildings and repairs " of fhips of war in His Majefty's yards, and other extra " work, over and above what are propofed to be done under " the heads of wear and tear, and ordinary for the year " 1786."

The queftion was put, and the refolutions carried.

The faid refolutions were ordered to be reported on the morrow.

Captain *Macbride* begged leave to trefpafs, during a fhort time, upon the patience of the Houfe, whilft he endeavoured to draw their attention upon a point of great moment to the welfare of the ftate.   From the papers upon the table he had difcovered, that amongft the fhips intended for repair were feveral frigates, and fome fhips of 60 and 64 guns.   This appeared to him a very impolitic plan of proceeding, as every profeffional man knew that a 60 or 64 gun fhip was no match for a French 74; and our having fo many of the former accounted for our frequent defeats when fingle Britifh fhips met and encountered fingle French fhips in the courfe of the laft war.   The French had now not above three or four 64 gun fhips; for we had taken the major part of the reft of that fize from them, and they built chiefly 74 gun fhips.   Policy therefore dictated, that we fhould keep pace with them, and imitate their example.   If we had done fo before, and kept more 74 gun fhips afloat during the laft war, he was perfuaded that the country would at this time have been in a very different fituation from that in which it ftood.   He rofe to complain, that the fyftem of repairing fmall fhips at an enormous expence was purfued; it was, he could affure the Houfe, a pernicious fyftem, and burdened the Public with a

heavy

heavy expence to no manner of purpofe.   He faw in his lift a great number of frigates and fmall fhips fet down to be repaired.   The repairs of one were eftimated at eleven thoufand pounds, and of another at fifteen thoufand.   It would be much better to let them fall to pieces, put a few more thoufands to each fum, and build good 74 gun fhips in their place.   How much fuperior was the merit of 74 gun fhips over fmaller fized veffels.   He verily believed, that if the number of our fhips were reduced one third, the navy of England would prove one third the ftronger.   But for the fake of increafing the patronage of the Minifter, or of the Admiralty, the lift of fhips, and confequently of captains, was unneceffarily fwelled to an enormous amount.   He had heard that an officer (Commodore Johnftone) who had rapidly rifen to high command, declared in that Houfe, (before he had the honour to have a feat there) that a 60 gun fhip and a frigate, or two or three frigates together, were an equal match for a French 74, or an 80 gun fhip.   He was aftonifhed that no feaman, a member of that Houfe, had given him an anfwer at the time.   If that honourable gentleman, who might now more properly be ftiled an honourable Director than a Commodore, fhould ever again advance fuch a doctrine, and he fhould be prefent, he would affure the Houfe that the honourable gentleman fhould not go without an anfwer.   According to that honourable gentleman's doctrine, by the paper in his hand, he could make our matches for a fmall fleet of French 74 gun fhips, by oppofing fmall fhips and frigates to them; but, agreeably to his own opinion, and he believed that moft of his brother officers, who had feen much fervice, a very few French 74 gun fhips would blow the whole lift out of the water.   He wifhed that the honourable Director had been prefent to hear what he thought and faid upon the fubject.   That honourable gentleman had, however, been fince favoured with an opportunity of reducing his theory to practice in Port Praya Bay, and therefore he would fay no more upon the fubject.   The Captain then returned to his argument, to prove the folly of putting the nation to a heavy charge for repairing fuch fhips as the lift in his hand contained.   There were among them feveral fhips, known as bad fhips, and not worth repairing.   He inftanced the Afia and Solitaire, and faid, that if a war fhould take place, thofe fhips and feveral others would be found to be of very little fervice.   To what purpofe was it then to repair fuch fhips as would endanger the lives of the officers and feamen, many hundreds of whom had been facrificed during the courfe of the laft war, by being fent to fea in bad fhips?   Another thing againft our navy was, that the French

74 gun

74 gun fhips were 2000 tons burden, while our 74s had been reduced to 1600 tons. If the Admiralty would build 74 gun fhips equal to thofe of the French, he was perfuaded that the officers and men would do their duty, and the country would be well ferved.   In a 64 gun fhip the Commander who met a 74 was well off if he efcaped capture.   He particularly inftanced the benefit of failing with the lower tier out, and faid, he faw an honourable friend of his whom he had often paffed and envied laft war, in confequence of obferving him proudly carrying his lower tier out at the time that he dared not fhew a fingle gun of that tier.   In conclufion, he expreffed his earneft wifhes, that if conformably to his natural expectations he fhould not, during the continuance of the debate, become an ear-witnefs of unanfwerable arguments in favour of a vote for the prefent eftimate, and the habitude (in his idea, impolitic and dangerous) of repairing fmall-fized fhips at an enormous expence, he fhould difcover a firm intention amongft thofe entrufted with the management of the naval departments totally to give up the practice.

Mr. *Drake*, junior, defired to know whether the money received for the fale of the materials of old and condemned fhips, and old ftores, after the fhips were broken up, had been brought to any account in favour of the Public? By the prefent eftimates it appeared that the public were debtor to their amount, and therefore he wifhed to know how the credit fide of the account ftood, and he put the queftion then, as it was an acknowledged fact a vaft number of fhips had been broken up fince the war ended. *Mr. Drake.*

Mr. *Brett* affured the honourable gentleman, that the fums received for old materials and old ftores were regularly paid over to the treafurer of the navy, and put by him to the account of the Public, and applied to naval fervices, in like manner as any other money which came into the hands of the treafurer of the navy was applied. Accounts of the monies received for old ftores up to given periods have frequently been called for and laid upon the table; nor ever, upon this fubject, had the moft diftant refervation been fuffered to take place. *Mr. Brett.*

Captain *James Luttrell* defired his honourable friend (Captain Macbride) to recollect, that frigates and fmall fhips were of effential ufe to this country, being principally employed for the purpofes of commerce. Indeed it was fcarcely poffible to carry on commerce without them, not to mention the extreme difficulty of keeping a large convoy of merchantmen tolerably together at any rate; for indeed, without frigates it would be abfolutely impoffible to do it. There were other fervices for which frigates and fmall fhips were peculiarly *Captain James Luttrell.*

adapted, and therefore while we had occasion for such ships, and we had a number of them, it would be madness not to keep them in repair and fit for service. He submitted it to his honourable friend's candour, whether it was not rather the province of the first Lord of the Admiralty than of that House to direct what classes of ships should be repaired and kept in order for service. The noble Lord now at the head of the Board was as correct a judge of the subject as any naval officer, and, in an equal degree, the statesman and the seaman. The country therefore might trust the management of the navy safely in his hands; and his honourable friend might rest assured that proper and useful ships only would be repaired and employed.

Captain Macbride.

Captain *Macbride* answered, that, in his humble opinion, no arguments which had fallen from his honourable friend who spoke last were sufficiently cogent to induce him to relinquish his position, that 74 gun ships were the sized ships we ought to build, and that it would be sounder policy to let most of those which were in the estimates this year, rot and tumble to pieces, than to lay out eleven thousand pounds on the repair of one, and fifteen thousand on that of another. He saw an honourable Baronet (Sir Charles Middleton) in his place, to whom he wished to address a few words; and these upon a different topic, though a topic relative to the navy. What he meant was, to learn if it was intended to persevere in the absurd system of suffering the ships to remain in their coppered bottoms during the whole of the peace? If that matter was intended, there would be no occasion to argue whether one sized ship or another should be built, for we should soon have no navy to send to sea. Mischievous were the effects of suffering the ships to remain coppered in still water. The copper corroded, and ate more into their bottoms than either worms or time. The consequence would be, that the instant ships which had long lain by were sent to sea, their bottoms would drop out, and thousands of brave seamen would perish in the ocean. It was a mistaken notion, that copper-bottomed ships did not get foul; they were as foul after laying by a time, as ships not sheathed with copper. The old custom was to take the ships into dock annually and triennially, and let them have their trimmings. When that practice was followed, our ships were kept in good order and condition; and if the coppered ships were not looked to, they would all be ruined. Admiral Barrington and he had together examined a coppered ship under repair, and that they found the bolts corroded and eaten away, notwithstanding the prevailing idea that they would not corrode. The evil to be dreaded from the neglect appeared to him of so serious a nature, that he thought, if something were not done immediately to prevent it, it, an inquiry ought to be commenced in that House, and the facts which he had stated ascertained. The nation would then see its danger. The French had discovered the folly of the practice, and for some time left off sheathing their ships with copper. We ought to do the same, or at least to take off the copper when the ships were to lay long in still water, and put it down when the ships were wanted to be sent to sea. A ship might be sheathed with copper in a tide, and therefore no time would be lost. His remarks (whatever gentlemen who were not professional men might think) were of infinite importance. He hoped therefore that he should have an answer from the honourable gentleman opposite to him, and find that contractors had not entirely seized upon the understandings of official men, and filled them with such a whimsical and dangerous fondness for such idle and new-fangled schemes, as to occasion them to shut their eyes against the natural and alarming consequences of such proceedings.

Captain *Leveson Gower* said, that he must call to the recollection of his honourable friend that sheathing ships with copper was a new matter; that it had not been introduced above ten years; and that it was therefore as yet in experiment: but he did assure his honourable friend, that it was watched with the utmost caution, and its effects observed and guarded against with all possible attention.

Captain Leveson Gower.

Sir *Charles Middleton* trusted that the honourable gentleman (Captain Macbride) would give him full credit when he declared, that he had no interest whatever in the sheathing ships with copper; that it was customary when any proposal was offered, for it to come before the Navy Board, and with their approbation it was referred to the yards to know if it were practicable in the opinion of the workmen. It then came back to the Navy Board with the report of the proper officer, and it was afterwards sent to the Admiralty for their consideration, and if meeting with their approbation was acceded to, and put in execution. Had his honourable friend been so obliging as either to have called at the office, or to have favoured him with a private application, he should have felt the highest pleasure in communicating to him the general nature of such matters as fell under his immediate cognizance; but little did he expect that motives of delicacy and caution would not have prevented the agitation of the subject in the House; and he was sure that, under cooler recollection, his honourable friend would join issue with him in the opinion that discussions of this kind could not be publicly brought forward without manifest impropriety and danger,

Sir Charles Middleton.

Captain *Luttrell* remarked, that although the sentiments of his honourable friend were at variance with his ideas respect-

Captain James Luttrell.

ing

ing either fortifications or the size of ships to be repaired, their thoughts were congenial upon the subject of copper-bottomed ships. That matter was of most serious consequence; a question infinitely more important than the question of fortifications! The proposed fortification plan would have cost the nation 700,000l., or at most a million; but should the mischiefs which his honourable friend had stated as likely to ensue, in consequence of suffering our navy to remain in their copper kettles, come down upon us, the expence would be many millions, and the whole navy of England stand exposed to ruin. It was therefore of the first importance that it should be inquired into, because what was the result? either the whole navy was safe and sound, or the complete reverse was the case. Let gentlemen weigh the matter a moment in their minds, and they would, he doubted not, be of opinion, that it ought to be a serious and immediate investigation in the proper quarter. He therefore coincided with his honourable friend; but thinking with him as he did, and willing as he should be to institute an inquiry, he would not agree to institute one in that House directly. He should advise that the matter be left to the executive government, and to that department to which it properly belonged, and he had not the smallest doubt of its receiving the most ample and zealous notice; but should the contrary happen, and the baneful absurdity of suffering the ships to continue in their copper kettles still prevail, he for his own part was determined either to introduce or second any motion which might ultimately bring the matter under the effectually-reforming consideration of the House.

Captain Macbride.   Captain *Macbride* contended, that in his legislative capacity, and as one of the representatives of the People, he possessed the most indubitable right to say in his place what he had before thrown out; nor would he by any means admit that it was a fair answer to him, or to any other gentleman who agitated a matter so essentially interesting to the nation, as the future well-being and even the future existence of the navy, for any person in office, to refer them to office, or to say, " why did not you ask me in private?" The properest spot for the discussion of subjects of this nature was the House of Commons, in which he should not cease to examine them as frequently as opportunities might arise.

Mr. Drake.   Mr. *Drake* said, that he meant no disrespect to the honourable Baronet, for whom there was not a gentleman present who entertained a higher respect; but he must declare, that if such answers were to be given upon matters, so interesting in their nature, to gentlemen of that House, which was the tutelar guardian of the public purse, the true interpretation of the

the honourable Baronet's language was, "I, office, demand, "you, the Public, pay."

Captain *Leviſon Gower* obſerved, that the coppering ſhips was as yet an experiment, and that its effects were duly watched. To what his honourable friend (Captain Macbridge) had ſaid in preference of 74 gun ſhips to 64s, he muſt beg leave to declare, that the argument came rather oddly from his honourable friend, who laſt war commanded a 64 gun ſhip, and had been offered a 74, which he declined accepting.

Captain *Macbride* anſwered, that in vindication of the conduct which the honourable Captain had with truth imputed to him, he ſhould beg leave to remind him, that his crew in the 64 were all men which he had recruited, as brave a ſet of hands as ever ſailed; they liked him, and he liked them, becauſe he knew he could depend upon them. If he could have been permitted to have taken them with him into the 74 gun ſhip offered to him, he would gladly have accepted the ſhip; but not being favoured with this indulgence, he choſe to remain in the 64 gun ſhip, on board of which were his old and gallant ſailors.

Captain *Berkeley* remarked, that the quickſilver in his honourable friend's barometer was apt to riſe rather too high when he got up to ſpeak in that Houſe, and generally reached extreme heat. He thought that it had got to that point then, in regard to what he ſaid of copper-bottomed ſhips; and he dared take upon him to aſſert, that his honourable friend had not previouſly applied to office upon the ſubject, for if he had, he was perſuaded that he would have met with an handſome reception, would have been heard with attention, and obtained every poſſible ſatisfaction afforded him. There was a matter in his mind exceedingly well worth attention, beſides what his honourable friend had ſuggeſted, and this was the building of ſhips. We were not only in point of policy to build ſhips of the ſame ſize as thoſe which conſtituted the navy of France, but we neceſſarily muſt build them ſo as to adapt them to the depth of water of our own harbours. For his part he wiſhed extremely that the Navy Board, inſtead of truſting merely to the ſurveyors of the navy, would imitate the example of France, and grant premiums for the beſt drafts of men of war. He meant the beſt plans in point of ſize, tonnage, &c. &c. &c.; this would give the Board the advantage of all the ingenuity of the kingdom, as well as the judgement of the navy ſurveyors; and he heartily deſired that ſome able contriver could ſhew how a 74 gun ſhip drawing no more water than a 64 could be built. If ſuch a plan could be found, it would prove an eſſential national advantage. Indeed the conſtruction of our ſhips in general ought

ought to be more particularly attended to. He owed it to the valour of the same honourable gentleman, then in his eye, to whom he was indebted for his naval education, that he commanded at this time one of the finest ships in the British navy. That ship was a proof how much better the enemies ships were built than ours were; and also how much better the materials were. Nothing could give him more joy than to perceive that all the ships belonging to the fleet were at length brought into a state of equal excellence.

Mr. Hopkins. Mr. *Hopkins* said that, among a great number of new ships, only two of the whole were 64 gun ships.

Mr. Sloper. Mr. *Sloper* observed that, as it was on all hands agreed, that coppering the bottoms of ships was an experiment, he thought the experiment ought to be tried on a few ships only, and not on the whole navy at once.

The question was put and carried.

Mr. M. A. Taylor. Mr. *M. A. Taylor* gave notice that he should on Tuesday next move for leave to bring in a bill, to extend an act of the last session, respecting Courts of Conscience, in order to make it general throughout England.

The House adjourned.

Thursday, 2d *March.*

Sir John Jarvis. Sir *John Jarvis,* intreating the earnest attention of the House to what he described as a subject of the greatest importance, added, that it had been observed by an honourable gentleman, (Captain Macbride) during the debate of the preceding Wednesday, that 18,000l. 15,000l. and 11,000l. were expended upon ships, which after all, proved unserviceable. In this assertion, an honourable baronet (Sir C. Middleton) had attempted to correct him, but he believed that there was too much truth in it to admit of refutation. He did not mean to charge the Navy Board with any wilful neglect; but, perhaps, there were abuses which they could not correct, and this, of the repair of old ships, most likely was one of them. With the leave of the House, he would state the method according to which the business had proceeded.—When the Navy Board wish to have a ship repaired, an order is sent to taste her and found her bottom. She is then bored in several places, and if the augur brings out sound wood, she is marked S; if rotten, she is marked R. But, the masters, whose duty it is to perform this office, do not always attend their duty, and ships of great burden and force are tasted by the apprentices. Therefore, for want of due care in this respect, very great abuses are committed.

As one instance of fallacy, in the year 1775, or 1776, a ship which he had a natural regard for, (the Prince) was
tasted

asted in this way, and ordered to be broken up. When the workmen came to strip her planks, she was discovered in a sound condition, and reported to be in a state capable of being refitted. Yet, notwithstanding, the Board ordered her to be broken up immediately; and a part of her hulk now lies at Plymouth.

Another instance, but of a direct contrary nature, and which corresponded exactly with Captain Macbride's assertion on the preceding Wednesday, happened within his knowledge. A ship was taken into dock to repair; but upon stripping her, she was found so rotten, that the master builder could not, as an honest man, proceed; he therefore reported her rotten state to the Board; he, nevertheless, was peremptorily ordered to go on: and the builder afterwards told him, that she cost more in repairs than would have built a new ship of the same force. These were objects of great importance, which ought to be carefully looked into, and corrected. Another subject of equal consequence impressed itself upon his mind, and that was the suffering the copper sheathing to remain on the ships, during their continuance in ordinary. He could assure the House, that if it was an idea that the copper preserved them in a state fit for immediate service, it was not only a most egregious mistake, but a very dangerous error; for the contrary was the fact, as the copper corroded the bolts in spite of every precaution. Of this truth, the French were so thoroughly convinced that immediately upon laying up their ships, they stripped off the copper sheathing. In submitting these weighty considerations to the House, he had barely fulfilled his duty; nor could he avoid adding how happy he should esteem himself could he have the honour of finding the majority of the House in a disposition congenial with his own, to root up and totally prevent the growth of evils so enormous and alarming.

Captain *Macbride* said that he considered the case of the Asia as not less deserving the attention of the House. Upon her return from India, she underwent a heavy and expensive repair, the amount of which might easily be found in the books: afterwards she made only one trip to Gibraltar, and now so large a sum as 18,000l. is again to be bestowed upon her;—surely this was bad policy, to call it no worse. His objection went only to ships of an avowedly bad character, to expend money upon the fruitless repairs of which were criminally to dissipate a portion of the public treasure.

Mr. *Brett* observed it was usual after a ship had been tasted or bored in several places, that when she came to be stripped, she should be found worse. As to the particular instances alluded to by the last honourable Speaker but one, he was

utterly

utterly unacquainted with them, and therefore could give no account refpecting their nature. But he could by no means join the honourable Captain (Macbride) in his idea of throwing away all the 60 and 64 gun fhips. There was another circumftance included in the idea of building our line of battle fhips upon a large fcale—Would the honourable gentlemen pleafe to recollect the depth of water in our harbours? That was one reafon why we could not turn our attention entirely to large fhips. Concerning the affertion, that we were not a match for the enemy laft war, he believed the fact was, that we had taken feveral of the enemy's fhips before they had taken a fingle one from us; and furely this did not manifeft fuch an inferiority as was fuggefted.

Capt. Macbride.

Captain *Macbride* anfwered, that he never had a defire to throw away all the fmaller line of battle fhips, but only thofe of bad character. With regard to the depth of water in our ports, the objection was futile and frivolous to an eminent degree. Did we not dock the largeft of the enemy's fhips in our docks, and bring them into our ports? there could then remain no reafon for repairing old and unferviceable fhips inftead of building new ones which might add to the extent and vigour of our navy.

Mr. Huffey

Mr. *Huffey* obferved, that at the moment when the Houfe was going to vote away 14 or 16,000l. of the People's property, they had ftrong inftances of flagrant abufes pointed out by two gallant officers, who were an honour to their country; and yet it had, during a former debate been urged, that the Admiralty would grow jealous of inveftigating fuch matters in that Houfe. This was a doctrine which he by no means admitted; and he hoped, that the gallant officer would perfevere in his inquiry. The Houfe, on a very late occafion had fhewn that there was ftill fome fpirit and virtue left in the nation—a great many gentlemen had the welfare of their country at heart; and all thofe would certainly join and fupport him. In his opinion the Houfe was the proper place to canvafs thefe abufes; and he trufted that no gentleman would be frightened from his duty—Let the Houfe lay out what fums they chofe upon the navy, but let it not be wafted away upon idle projects when prudence required it for ufeful fervices.

Captain Macbride.

Captain *Macbride* faid, that he did not underftand there was at prefent any inquiry; and he hoped, from what had been dropped, that no neceffity for it would arife; if there fhould, he pledged himfelf that he would not fhrink from his duty.

Captain Bowyer.

Captain *Bowyer* obferved, that none of the inftances of abufe defcribed had come within his knowledge.—The refolution was then put by the Speaker and carried.

The

The House having next refolved itfelf into a Committee of the whole Houfe, Mr. M. A. Taylor in the chair,

Mr. *Beaufoy* rofe and faid,

Mr. Taylor,

As I had the honour of prefenting to the Houfe the Report for the confideration of which they have now refolved them- felves into a Committee, I muft intreat their indulgence for a few moments, while I briefly defcribe the plan which the Refolutions contained in the Report are meant to recom- mend.

Mr. Beau- foy.

In bringing forward this bufinefs, I have pleafure in con- templating the intimate connection it has with thofe impor- tant interefts that have this day fo ftrongly and fo juftly en- gaged the attention of the Houfe, I mean the naval interefts of this kingdom : and I have alfo pleafure in recollecting, that it is a bufinefs to which the members of the Houfe have re- peatedly fhewn themfelves favourably difpofed; for in the two laft feffions of Parliament, as well as in the prefent, they ap- pointed a Committee expreffly for the purpofe of afcertaining the moft effectual means of extending the fifheries of Great Britain.

It was in confequence of the inquiries of the Committee of the laft year, that I was enabled to propofe to the Houfe a bill, which they did me the honour to approve, for remov- ing the reftraints which unwife and improvident laws had im- pofed on the progrefs of the fifheries on the northern and weftern coafts of the ifland.

It is in confequence of the inquiries of the Committee of the prefent year, that I am now enabled to propofe what may be confidered as the fecond part of the fyftem — a plan for improving the fifheries in the eaftern feas of the kingdom.— This defirable object the Report before you propofes to ob- tain, by transferring from foreigners to our own country- men, from Dutchmen to Englishmen, the valuable fifhery for turbot. It is in our *own feas* that all thefe fifh are taken— it is to our *own markets* that almoft all of them are brought : yet they are taken by Dutchmen ; they are brought to mar- ket by Dutchmen ; all the profits arifing from the fale of the fifh, all the advantages refulting from the encouragement of feamen and the maintenance of naval ftrength, all the benefits both public and private which the fifhery affords, are at this time monopolized by the *Dutch.* Thofe advantages the Re- port upon your table propofes to transfer to the people of this kingdom.

The principle of the fyftem is, that our *countrymen* fhould be preferred to *foreigners* ; that *Englifh fifhermen* are intitled to fome advantage in our *Englifh market* ; and that it is more to the intereft of Britain to encourage her *own fifheries,* reward the industry of *her own* people, to increase the number of her *own* seamen, and to add to her *own* naval strength, than it can be to encourage the fisheries, or reward the industry, or promote the naval strength of *Holland*, a country which is always a rival, and sometimes an enemy.

Before I proceed to move the different resolutions which I shall have the honour of submitting to the judgement of the Committee, perhaps, Sir, it may not be unnecessary, nor altogether uninteresting, briefly to describe the nature of the fishery to which these resolutions relate.

The turbot fishery begins about the latter end of the month of March, at which time the Dutch fishermen assemble on that part of the Dutch coast which lies a few leagues to the south of Scheveling; from thence as the warm weather approaches, the fish, in order to avoid the heats, retire farther and farther north. During the months of April and May they continue on the bank which is generally called the Broad Fourteens, and which runs nearly parallel to the coast of Holland from the latitude of Scheveling to a latitude considerably to the north of the Texel. Early in the month of June, the fish remove from the Broad Fourteens, to the banks that surround the small island of Hylingland which lies westward of Hamburgh, off the river Elbe, but at a considerable distance at sea: there the fishery continues to the middle of the month of August, at which time it is over for the year.

Having thus described the times when, and the places where the turbot are caught, the next object of inquiry is the mode of taking them. At the beginning of the season the fish are caught with a sort of drag net, which is drawn along the banks, and which sweeps from the sand, the various species of flat fish which lie there, such as soles, plaice, thornback, and, among the rest, turbot: But when the season for the removal of the fish is arrived, and the turbots retire from the banks on the coasts of Holland to those in the neighbourhood of Hylingland, the depth of the water, and the unevenness of the ground render the use of the drag net wholly impracticable. The fishermen are then obliged to have recourse to the hook and line. The line that is employed for this purpose is not of the sort that is held by the hand, and that is furnished with a single hook; for the line employed in the turbot fishery is generally more than two miles in length, and is furnished with six or seven hundred hooks, which are placed at the distance of several yards from each other; so that when the line, as the vessel drives, is thrown into the water, and sinking by means of its leads, a considerable length of ground is occupied by the successive hooks. Besides the leads that are employed to sink the line, several anchors are fastened to it at different distances, in order to prevent its drawing with the

tide,

tide. The hooks, during one part of the feafon, are baited with the common fmelt, and during the other with a fifh that refembles the eel, except that its colour is different, and that its head is drawn out to a kind of bill; which, in fhape, is like that of a bird, and from which it takes its name of gore-bill. Fortunately this fifh is found in great abundance on the weftern coaft of the ifland.

Thus it appears, that, at the firft of the feafon, the tur-bots are taken only with nets, and at the latter end of it only with hooks; but during the middle part of the feafon, before the removal of the fifh from the coaft of Holland, both me-thods are in ufe.

Such, Sir, is the nature of a fifhery which levies on this kingdom a large annual contribution for the maintenance of the naval ftrength of the Dutch.

To the *Dutch* that money is given that would fupport eight hundred feamen for the fervice of the Britifh Govern-ment. — The *Dutch* are allowed to poffefs themfelves of an employment that affords them a perfect knowledge of the na-vigation of our feas; and that in a future war would enable them to pilot the fhips of their new ally to the very Thames itfelf.

To effect a transfer of this fifhery from the Hollanders to our own countrymen, two expedients are propofed in the Report.

The one is a tax upon the tonnage of foreign veffels import-ing turbots into this kingdom:

The other is a fmall bounty, as an additional encourage-ment to our own people.

That either a tax or a prohibition on foreigners fhould be laid, cannot, I fuppofe, be doubted; but fome doubts may poffibly arife on the comparative advantage of the two modes of proceeding. For my own part, I fhould think the tax the preferable meafure; becaufe, while it equally infures to the Britifh fifhermen the poffeffion of the trade, whenever they are prepared to take the whole upon themfelves, it does not in the intermediate time exclude all other channels of fupply.

The other expedient fuggefted by the Report is, as I ob-ferved, a bounty in favour of our fifhermen.

In recommending a bounty, I am fenfible that I advife a meafure which ought on very few occafions to be adopted, fince there are very few on which it can be juftified. For this reafon I am anxious that the prefent bounty, if approved by the Committee, fhall be founded on fuch principles, and be circumfcribed by fuch rules, as fhall render its operation lefs expenfive to the Public, yet more effectual to its end, than bounties have generally proved.

That

'That an attempt to afcertain the rules by which, on thefe occafions, the liberty of the Legiflature ought to be governed, will not, I am perfuaded, be confidered as trivial and uninterefting, when the Committee recollect, that, in the courfe of the laft year, no lefs a fum than 94,000l. was paid to one fingle fifhery.

The firft principle, generally fpeaking, which ought to be obferved in the grant of a bounty, is, that the term of a grant fhould be limited. For, as the intention of the Legiflature in giving the bounty is the encouragement of a trade, which, if once eftablifhed, would afford a reafonable return on the capital employed, but in which the inexperience of the fubject renders him unwilling to engage, the bounty, it is evident, like the caufe from which it takes its rife, fhould be of temporary continuance.

Conformably to this maxim, I would beg leave to propofe that the bounty on turbots fhould be limited to the term of five years. — A fecond principle of a judicious bounty is, that the fum granted by the Legiflature fhould diminifh gradually, rather than be all at once and fuddenly withdrawn: for if the external fupports on which a trade has been accuftomed to lean fhould be abruptly removed, much violence to the interefts of the trade muft unavoidably enfue: whereas if the aid which is given by the Legiflature is diminifhed by degrees, the trade will be brought naturally and eafily to reft on its own bearings. I would, therefore, fuggeft the expedience of declaring, that, after the term of three years, the bounty on turbot fhall begin to diminifh, fo that, in the courfe of the fourth year, not more than two thirds of the former annual fum fhall be diftributed; and that in the fifth year only one third fhall be given; by which means the trade will be preferved from the danger of a fatal fhock, when, at the end of the fifth year, the aid of Parliament fhall wholly be withdrawn.

A third principle of a judicious bounty is, that the extent of the expence which it brings on the Public fhould, from the firft, be clearly afcertained. The Public have a right to the means of comparing the value of the object to be obtained with the amount of the fum that muft be given for obtaining it; for, otherwife, how can they be fure that they are not making an injudicious and improvident bargain. In purfuance of this maxim, I will take the liberty of propofing, that, during the three firft years of the term, the bounty fhall not exceed four thoufand pounds per annum: that during the fourth year it fhall not exceed three thoufand pounds; and that during the fifth year it fhall not exceed two thoufand pounds.

The

The last principle, with the mention of which I shall trouble the Committee, is, that the bounty should be given on the commodity produced, rather than on the instrument of its produce. I would say, for example, that a bounty for the encouragement of agriculture should be given on the corn, rather than on the plough; that a bounty for the establishment of a wearing manufacture should be granted on the cloth, rather than on the loom; and that a bounty for encouraging a new fishery should be given on the fish, rather than on the vessel; for, on this plan, the public expence cannot out-run the benefit received, and the bounty will operate as a reward to industry, not as a means of insuring idleness from loss.

Such are the principles on which, as far as I can judge, bounties in general should be granted; and, trusting to the hope that they will meet the approbation of the Committee, I should now move the several resolutions, were I not aware that the whole plan is open to one very obvious objection, which, before I proceed, it becomes me to obviate. The objection is, that, as during a part of the season the turbots are caught upon banks that are contiguous to Holland, the Dutch may perhaps exclude our fishermen from the trade by excluding them from the coast.

That the Dutch have this power cannot be disputed; but that they will think the exercise of it politic or safe I never can believe; for let them once establish, as a practical maxim, the opinion, that every nation has a right to exclude from its coasts all fishermen but its own, and what will become of the fishery which they themselves carry on for herrings not only upon our coasts, but almost in our very harbours? What will become of their pretensions, to consider Braffa Sound as the first, and Peterhead as the second, of their fishing stations? or on what ground will they claim the indulgence of following the fish upon our shores, from the north of Aberdeenshire to the southernmost parts of Suffolk? Will they hazard the loss of the fishery which first made them a people? Will they hazard this ancient source of their independence, this best support of their wealth and of their naval power? I cannot imagine that what they emphatically call their great fishery will thus be sacrificed to the preservation of a fishery of subordinate importance. Should this, however, be the case, their decision will be fortunate for Britain; for we shall then, in conjunction with the Irish, be possessed of little less than a monopoly of the herring trade; the Swedes, our only other rivals, not being likely, for reasons easily assigned, to maintain their competition long.

Upon these grounds I feel no hesitation in submitting to the Committee the different resolutions that are intended to
form

form the basis of the bill, which I hope I shall be permitted to offer to the House, confident that from such a bill one or other of two important advantages must certainly ensue — the acquisition of the valuable fishery for turbots, or the still greater acquisition of the Dutch fishery for herrings.

Mr. Hussey. Mr. *Hussey* having observed that no member of the House could possibly incline with a sincerer ardour than himself to the support of any plan devised for the improvement, vigour, and extension of our fisheries, added, that as the point in question was probably new to many honourable gentlemen, and certainly at present beyond the line of his experience, he could wish to know whether it would not answer better for the Chairman to report a progress, and request permission to sit again, in order that, during the space of two or three days, the resolutions might lie upon the table for the inspection of the members, who thus might prove enabled to give their votes upon the clearest and most decisive grounds? Unless this should prove the case, he must beg leave to intimate to the honourable gentleman his wishes that he would favour the House with a more ample and open explanation of his meaning and intentions. Could he ascertain that, as a natural consequence of bearing away a material portion of the fishing trade from the Dutch, London would become supplied in proper quantities with turbot? The allusion of the honourable gentleman to the 94,000l. bounties granted to the Greenland fisheries (pursuits of the first moment to this country!) was just and well timed. Would the honourable gentleman please to inform him through what means the London market would receive a sufficient supply of fish?

Mr. Beaufoy. Mr. *Beaufoy* answered: — The honourable gentleman complains of the novelty of the business submitted to your consideration, and insinuates a suspicion of an attempt, on my part, to take the Committee by surprise. Is then the honourable gentleman so little attentive to the proceedings of the House, as not to know that more than a fortnight has elapsed since they appointed a Committee to take into consideration the state of the British fisheries? or if he did know that such a Committee was appointed, why did he not attend their meetings, which were open to every member, and at which the most satisfactory evidence was given? or if this would have required more time than he chose to bestow upon the subject, why has he not read the two Reports which the Committee has made, and which are printed by the order of the House? With such opportunities of knowledge, the honourable gentleman's want of information is chargeable only on himself, and ought not to be pleaded as a bar to the progress of a business for which all but himself are perfectly prepared.

The

The honourable gentleman expreffes his zeal for the Greenland fifhery, and thinks that 94,000l. of the public money was laft year wifely expended for its fupport. Far be it from me to fuggeft an idea in any degree adverfe to a fifhery that employs, in enterprizes of unufual hardihood, more than fix thoufand of our feamen; but allow me to obferve, that, on the loweft computation, every feaman fo employed brings on the Public, in confequence of the bounty, an expence of no lefs than 13l. 10s. per annum; whereas the feamen that fhall be employed in the fifhery which is now propofed will not occafion to the Public a greater annual expence per man than 4l. 10s. at the moft, and that only for the fhort period of five years.

Now if the former expence is not thought extravagant, the latter, which is comparatively fmall, cannot reafonably be cenfured.

I am afked by what means the Legiflature will prevent a fraud fo eafily practifed by the fifhermen, as that of purchafing from the Dutch the turbots they have taken, and importing them as Britifh caught? This queftion certainly merits an anfwer. Every fifhery is obvioufly attended with two feparate advantages; that of taking the fifh, and that of bringing them to market. Now, certain it is, that, if Britain cannot fecure both thefe advantages, the acquifition of one of the two will always be an object of importance.

Upon this occafion, however, I am perfuaded that both will be found of very eafy attainment. Among the different meafures recommended in the Report which is now under your confideration, is that of beftowing premiums on the three veffels whofe refpective crews fhall have caught, in the courfe of the feafon, the three greateft quantities of turbot; the confequence of which expedient will be, that the crew of each veffel will have an obvious intereft in preventing the crew of any other veffel from purchafing turbots from the Dutch, as fuch purchafers would fwell, by unfair means, the quantity of turbots apparently caught by the purchafers, and, if not difcouraged, would deprive of their premium the veffels to which it would otherwife be paid.

Thus the crew of each veffel will have the ftrongeft incitement to watch over the conduct of the crew of every other veffel; and as the fifhery veffels carry on their bufinefs on the fame banks, and in view of each other, there is reafon to believe that this check will be effectual.

A fecond means of preventing the fuggefted fraud will be the requifition of an oath, before the receipt either of the premium or of the bounty, that the fifh were Britifh caught. Now, though an oath, generally fpeaking, is of little avail when the party taking it has an intereft in fwearing to a falfehood, falſehood, and no other perſon has an intereſt in detecting the perjury, yet where there is an intereſt that prompts to vigilance, and urges to detection, the ſecurity which the Public derives from an oath is far from being weak.

I muſt own, however, that it is chiefly to a third conſideration of much greater force than either of thoſe I have mentioned, that I am led to believe that the fraud of purchaſing fiſh taken by the Dutch, and importing them as Britiſh caught, will not often be committed. The conſideration is, that in all caſes of fair competition between the Engliſh and the Dutch, the former have conſtantly obtained a clear and acknowledged ſuperiority. Not many years have elapſed ſince the Dutch had no leſs than one hundred and ſixty veſſels in the fiſhery to the Greenland ſeas; but now, and the recital of the fact fills me with exultation, we have brought them down to ſixty, while, in the very laſt year, Britain ſent to that fiſhery no leſs than one hundred and fifty ſail.

In the whale fiſhery to the ſouthern ſeas Britain has obtained a ſtill more decided aſcendency: from the coaſts of Brazil, and the ſhores of Falkland's Iſlands, eaſtward to the Cape of Good Hope, a Dutch fiſhing veſſel is ſcarcely to be found. The Americans themſelves fail in the competition, and Britain poſſeſſes the fiſhery unrivalled, and almoſt alone. Even the Dutch fiſhery for herrings, the favourite object of their moſt vigorous purſuit, no longer maintains its rivalſhip with the Engliſh; for, in the laſt year, the Dutch employed but one hundred and thirty-three ſail, while Scotland and Yarmouth, independently of the reſt of the iſland, ſent out two hundred and fifty veſſels. With theſe facts in my view, I can never believe, that, in the fiſhery to which our preſent conſultations relate, the ſlow and torpid induſtry of the Dutch will be more ſucceſsful than the ardent ſpirit of enterpriſe and vigour of exertion which mark the proceedings of the Engliſh. I never can believe that they who, in every other purſuit, have given proof of unrivalled ſkill, will, in this, have any permanent temptation to employ ſuch clumſy inſtruments as the Dutch. Unleſs, therefore, the honourable gentleman has better arguments to urge than thoſe he has drawn from his own inattention to the buſineſs, and from the partial eſtimate he has formed of the activity of the Hollanders, I am not, I hope, preſumptuous in thinking that the propriety of the motion before you, as tending to increaſe the wealth and promote the naval ſtrength of the kingdom, is ſtill unimpeached.

Mr. Ald.
Watſon.

Mr. Alderman *Watſon* remarked, that it greatly excited his ſurpriſe when he heard the honourable gentleman compare the turbot fiſhery to that of Greenland. It was like an attempt to trace affinity between the herring and the whale; and in

either

either cafe the fimile would prove equally warrantable! At once extenfive and important were the benefits and refources which the nation acquired from the Greenland fifhery! A fifhery which had preferved invincibly fecure (what was within that Houfe denominated) the wooden walls of England! Yet doubtlefs the propofed plan for taking the turbot fifhery into our own poffeffion was full of merit, and promifed much to benefit the nation. Under this idea, he hoped that the bounties would be rendered general, and not impoliticly narrowed.

Mr. *Beaufoy* again replied: — As far as I am able to judge from what has paffed in the debate, the objections of thofe who are the moft hoftile to the meafures propofed are now reducible to a fort of apprehenfion that the people of this kingdom will not be willing to engage in the fifhery for turbot; upon which apprehenfion is founded an argument, that, till the Legiflature is fatisfied as to this fact, it would be very impolitic to impofe a reftraint on the fupply that is brought by foreigners.

In anfwer to this doubt, I am happy to have an opportunity of faying that the feveral owners of twelve different veffels belonging to Gravefend have fent me a written affurance that if the plan recommended in the Report fhall be adopted by the Legiflature, thofe veffels will immediately be fent on the fifhery for turbots. Another affurance was alfo given me by a deputation from the fifhermen of Harwich, that, from their town alone, fix and twenty veffels would be fent on the turbot fifhery. Now, if eight and thirty veffels are already preparing from thofe two places alone, exclufive of what may be expected from other parts of the kingdom, I cannot be much deceived in flating to the Committee that there is reafonable ground for believing that our own fifhermen will be able to furnifh the market with an abundant fupply.

All, therefore, that is requefted from the honourable gentleman who moft objects to the plan, (if, on behalf of our poor fifhermen, he will permit me to flate the requeft) is, not that he will facrifice a fingle dinner, or deprive himfelf of a fingle article of luxurious fare, but merely that, in laying out his money, he would have the goodnefs to prefer his countrymen to foreigners.

Since, then, there is no reafon to doubt the abundance of the fupply, the argument for delay falls wholly to the ground. On the other hand, the near approach of the turbot feafon ftrongly urges to difpatch; for, to thofe who are willing to engage in this fifhery, the lofs of a few days may prove the lofs of the whole year: and allow me to add, that, at a time when more than a thoufand fmugglers on the eaftern and fouthern coafts of the ifland are unemployed, who muft, however,

Mr. Beaufoy.

ever, foon have recourfe to fome means of obtaining a liveli-
hood, either confiftent with, or deftructive of, the interefts
of the revenue, it is material to furnifh thofe men as fpeedily
as poffible with an occupation which, having in it fomething
of chance and enterprife, correfponds, in a certain degree,
with their ancient habits of life, and, at the fame time, by
enabling them to extend the naval ftrength of the country,
entirely coincides with the beft interefts of Great Britain.

Mr. Rolle.

Mr. *Rolle* faid, that, anxious to preferve from every material injury the fifhery eftablifhed upon the coaft of Devon,
and facilitating the great fupply for the London markets by
land carriage, he could not avoid expreffing his hearty wifhes
that fome little time at leaft might elapfe previous to the execution of the plan propofed in favour of the turbot fifhery by
the honourable gentleman.

The Mar-
quis of Gra-
ham.

The Marquis of *Graham* contended, that as the fifhery
would open during the courfe of this month, the fcheme, unlefs directly adopted, would become loft for a year.

Mr. Ald.
Sawbridge.

Mr. Alderman *Sawbridge* obferved, that the plan was too
unexceptionable not to refift the general imbecility of the
arguments which were advanced to overthrow it. The dread
of lofing a fupply for the London markets had not the leaft
foundation; becaufe, were our people to fail, the Dutch
would find it anfwer to pay the ten fhillings a ton duty on
the fifh which they might bring, and raife the prices accordingly: nor need gentlemen, in either cafe, defpair of fitting
down to dine upon a turbot.

Sir John
Jarvis.

Sir *John Jarvis* declared, that, in his opinion, the fcheme
merited adoption for a variety of reafons. As much did he
wifh it full fuccefs as he difliked to obferve Dutchmen, without either the aid or need of pilots, running up and down the
Channel, into the Thames, and all our rivers. This was an
habitude, of which the political circumftances of the country
would juftify a wifh for its fuppreffion.

The three feveral refolutions now paffed.

The order of the day for the adjourned Committee, to
which the petitions, praying a repeal of the act of the laft
feffion, granting to His Majefty certain duties on retail fhops,
had been referred for confideration, to fit again, having been
read, Mr. Taylor took the chair; immediately after which,

Sir Watkin
Lewes.

Sir *Watkin Lewes* rofe, and obferved, that, having upon a
former occafion intimated to the Houfe his defign of moving
for a repeal of the fhop tax, he fhould now take the liberty
of intruding himfelf ftill farther upon their patience with a
brief defcription of the motives inducing him to profecute a
tafk, which, however zealoufly he had the caufe at heart, he
could, with pleafure, confign to any of thofe numerous
members whofe influence and abilities were far fuperior to his
own;

own; yet, having the honour to be one of the reprefenta- tives of the metropolis which was principally affected by this partial and oppreffive tax, he fhould ill difcharge his duty, or deferve the confidence of his conftituents, were he not to exert the utmoft of his abilities to relieve them from fo heavy a burden. He conceived that the fubject might be comprifed in a very narrow compafs; nor would he enter into any ex- traneous matter, but endeavour to comprefs his fentiments in as few words as poffible. When he confidered the arguments upon which the tax was fupported during the laft feffion of Parliament, that it would fall upon the confumer, the opera- tion of which they had not then experienced, and when he recollected the teftimony of the refpectable perfons who ap- peared at the bar, and proved to a demonftration that it ope- rated as a perfonal tax, and that it could not be impofed upon the confumer, he entertained hopes that the gentlemen who were fupporters of the tax before would become converts to his opinion. The right honourable gentleman (Mr. Pitt, the Chancellor of the Exchequer) had ftated the tax as amounting to 140,000l.; but he did not think it right to take it at the higheft calculation: he would, therefore, take it at 120,000l. That compared with the affeffment on the table for three quarters of a year, amounted only to 55,000l.; adding ano- ther quarter, it would amount to 73,000l., very little above half the fum which it was propofed to raife, taking the deduc- tion of thofe perfons paying rent from 15l. to 25l. per an- num, who could not pay the parifh rates, and were exempted. He fhould appeal to the right honourable gentleman, whether it was a tax which he ought to perfevere in; for a more ex- ceptionable tax he could not propofe. Befides, when they confidered that moft of the great cities and towns throughout the kingdom petitioned againft this tax, all declaring and bearing an uniform teftimony, that it would operate as a perfonal tax, and would not be impofed on the confumer, what members who heard him could deny that it was a partial and oppreffive tax upon a defcription of men, who, with the utmoft induftry, could hardly maintain their fami- lies, and who were entitled to their protection, particularly as not one of the reprefentatives in that Houfe took a fhare of the burden. The tax ought to be repealed *in toto*, with- out any modification, and therefore he fhould move, "That " the Chairman be directed to move the Houfe, that leave be " given to bring in a bill to repeal an act paffed during the " laft feffion of Parliament, entitled, An Act for granting " certain Duties on Shops within Great Britain."

Mr. Alderman Sawbridge moved, as a preliminary pro- ceeding, "That the evidence fhould be read over," defiring that Sir Watkin would withdraw his motion, to give way for

its

it. This being complied with, the chief part of the evidence was read over at the table; after which

Mr. Alderman *Sawbridge* rose, and said, that the right honourable gentleman, when he introduced the tax, had declared, that it would fall upon the consumer, and that the consumer would ultimately pay it. The reverse of this had been stated at the bar to have been the operation of the tax, which stood proved a personal tax, and a tax which the shopkeeper must pay out of his own pocket, without a chance of recovering any part of it. The inability of many of the shopkeepers of this metropolis, on whom the tax principally pressed, to pay it, had been established by the clearest testimony; and therefore he hoped the House would not persist in so partial, so unjust, and so diabolical a tax, but that the right honourable gentleman would meet the wishes of the People, and comply with the prayer of the petitions, by consenting to repeal it. The question was not a party question: it ought to be treated on its own merits, independently of any other consideration. His political principles were well known; and whenever a party contest was the matter in hand, he was never ashamed to avow his reasons for supporting the side of the question taken by those with whom he generally acted. If any thing of party had mixed with the question, it would have been his object that the Minister should not repeal the bill; because if any one step could weaken his credit without doors, and shake his popularity more than another, he was satisfied it would be for him to persist in keeping a bill in force which had deservedly drawn down upon it such general odium and detestation throughout the cities of London and Westminster, the borough of Southwark, and almost every capital city and town in the kingdom; but the fact was, that exclusive of the desire which he had to get the act repealed, in gratification of the anxious wishes of his constituents, who would readily contribute their share towards the public exigencies of the state in common with the rest of their fellow subjects, it was his sincere opinion that the act ought to be repealed; that the tax was a bad one, and would not produce any thing like the money for which it was given. He begged leave to remind the right honourable gentleman, that one quarter of the year remained to be collected; and that if the right honourable gentleman would consent to repeal the act, he was persuaded that he would render the collection of the quarter due a very easy business; for, in that case, the shopkeepers, knowing it was to be the last for which they were to be called upon, would pay it with great chearfulness.

Mr. Alderman *Newnham* declared that he could not avoid considering the tax as replete with partiality, injustice, and
oppression;

Mr. Ald.
Sawbridge.

Mr. Ald.
Newnham.

oppreffion; particularly becaufe almoft the whole weight of it fell upon the fhopkeepers of the city of London. They had a more than fufficient fhare of difadvantage to cope with before. Well known was their readinefs at all times to contribute to affift the public neceffities, provided that they were called upon to contribute equally with the reft of the People; but it was unfair to feleft them out to pay a very heavy tax, which was not felt by others infinitely more capable to pay it than they were. As the Minifter had been faved the expence of the fortifications, which, in his mind, (Mr. Newnham faid) appeared rather calculated to deftroy the conftitution than to defend the kingdom, he might well afford to give up the paltry fum which the fhop tax was likely to produce. Under thefe circumftances, he flattered himfelf either that the right honourable gentleman would, upon cool conviction, refolve to meet the motion with his deferved report, or that the debate might take fo powerful and juft a turn as to draw him, even againft his inclinations, into a majority of the Houfe.

Mr. Alderman *Hammett* remarked, that he confidered the tax as one of the moft critical and important points that ever fell under the inveftigation of Parliament. If not repealed, a principle of taxation of the moft dangerous nature, a principle ftriking at the very foundation of the Conftitution, would become eftablifhed; a principle that Parliament might take the money, by a tax, out of the pocket of any particular individual, or any particular defcription of individuals: a principle to which he, for one, never would give his confent; nor to any tax, no part of which the members of that Houfe were to pay themfelves. What right had they to tax one fet of men more than another? If fuch an abominable principle obtained, any man worth two hundred thoufand pounds might be felected, and one hundred thoufand taken away from the man whether he chofe it or not. Let every man make the cafe his own. If one man could be fo unjuftly taxed, it might be a man's own cafe, if he were equally rich, the next time. He detefted all perfonal taxes; for all taxes ought to operate equally on every man according to his property and affluence. The fhop tax did not. He had a large property in houfes, and yet neither he nor any of his tenants paid towards it. The tax on attornies he always thought an unjuft one; becaufe a poor fellow, who came and afked permiffion to draw a few leafes, and the attorney who kept many clerks, and was in full and profitable practice, each paid five pounds a year licenfe. Was that fair, was it equitable? The Houfe would pleafe to recollect, that he happened to be the firft man who objected to the tax in his place, and all which he had predicted of it had been fulfilled, and the witneffes had proved it

Mr. Ald. Hammett.

it at the bar. Exclusive of this, he had endeavoured to probe the truth : he had asked if the bookseller could increase the price of his books, or the printseller of his prints, and he found neither of them could do it. On this occasion he had referred himself to an irreproachable and enlightened individual, (Mr. Alderman Boydell) and found, as he expected, that the sentiments which he entertained concerning the tax were such as strongly militated against its flagrant and oppressive partiality.

Sir Joseph Mawbey. Sir *Joseph Mawbey* observed, that his constituents, to whose opinion he, in this case, implicitly assented, detested the personality of the tax, and most severely reprobated it as an intolerable grievance : nor should he have absented himself during the investigation of its demerits, but that extreme indisposition confined him to his house.

Sir Edward Astley. Sir *Edward Astley* professed himself a friend to the tax when it was originally proposed. He had expressed his satisfaction, because (as he then declared) he thought the shopkeepers deserved it, for having for some time entered into a combination to defeat the operation of the receipt tax. He had last year strongly urged the right honourable gentleman to make the receipt tax effectual by some proper regulations : if that were done, it would produce a large sum.

Mr. Amyatt Mr. *Amyatt* (an advocate for either the repeal of the bill, or some modification) said, that if shopkeepers were permitted to charge five per cent. on their book debts, he believed they would be contented.

Mr. Loveden. Mr. *Loveden* declared that his constituents, satisfied with the tax, only wished for the abolition of hawkers and pedlars.

Mr. Thornton. Mr. *Thornton* remarked, that he felt it necessary to explain his reasons why, having, during the course of the preceding session, given a vote in favour of the bill, he now resolved to meet it with his opposition. The manner in which he had then conducted himself had been misrepresented to his constituents, and had drawn down upon him a degree of unpopularity, greater perhaps than had ever fallen upon a representative of any place before. As open and ingenuous conduct was always to be preferred, he thought it incumbent on him to declare the fact, and he would have the courage to say, that though he might possibly repent the vote he had last year given, he did not repent the motive that impelled him to give that vote, which was a consideration of the great exigency of public affairs ; a conviction that taxes, at once irksome and severe, must be imposed on the subject, and an idea that, in a choice of difficulties, the tax on shops was as fair a tax as any other that had then been suggested. He had since that time received the instructions, and indeed the repeated intreaties of his constituents, to support a motion for the repeal

peal of the tax, and he fhould vote accordingly. He would advife the right honourable the Chancellor of the Exchequer to relinquifh a tax fo extremely odious and unpopular to fo large a body as the fhop tax was. Unlefs he thought proper to purfue this meafure, at the divifion of the Houfe he doubt-lefs would perceive moft of the reprefentatives of counties and populous cities and towns giving their voice in oppofition to his own. The moft refpectable part of the Houfe would fhrink from his fide, and the chief (if not the whole) of his diminifhed political phalanx confift of the members for de-cayed and rotten boroughs.

Mr. *Drake* obferved, that, amidft the drudgery of atten- Mr. Drake. tion to parliamentary bufinefs in a Committee room, it was not to be fuppofed that he had enjoyed time to prepare him-felf with any powerfully-digefted force of argument in favour of the motion, and therefore he fhould reft fatisfied with en-deavouring to make fuch irregular attacks as feemed requifite for the defence of the ground which he defigned to chufe. When the tax was firft propofed, the Houfe were neceffarily obliged to confider it fpeculatively, and to act upon what it was thought it would produce. Since that time affertion had become evidence, and experience was oppofed to theory. It had been proved to be a partial and oppreffive tax, and the fooner it was repealed the better. He conceived it to be a perfonal tax, and not a tax on confumption; but if it were the latter, it was impoffible but that a great deal more money would be levied on the Public than would go into the Exche-quer. He reminded the Houfe what had been the cafe when a duty on wines, amounting to the rate of one penny the bot-tle, was impofed; at that time the retailers charged two pence, and, in fome cafes, five pence advance on that penny. An honourable gentleman had fuggefted, that if fhopkeepers were allowed to charge five per cent. intereft on their book debts, it would make them willing to acquiefce under the fhop tax. For his part, he did not admire that fcheme; be-caufe he feared the fhopkeeper would, if that were adopted, often lofe both principal and intereft. It would be an eafy way of fettling accounts to men who owed more than they really could or would pay. When the claim was made, fuch men would fay to the fhopkeeper, " Oh! charge me five per " cent. intereft; let the account go on, and make a great ca-" pital of it!" and thus the whole would be loft. A repeal was the beft way of quieting all fcruples, and fettling all dif-gufts. He expreffed an ardent wifh to fee two right honour-able gentlemen (Mr. Fox and Mr. Pitt) united in their coun-try's fervice. Were that the cafe, what might he not expect of benefit to Great Britain! He profeffed the moft enthufiaf-tic admiration of the latter's (Mr. Pitt) virtues and talents.

He

He declared it was not a defire of having his right honourable friend facrifice to popularity, that prompted him to advife a repeal of the bill.   He was not fo ignorant of the world as to remain, at the prefent hour of his life, a ftranger to the tranfient nature of popularity; nor, although perfectly convinced how pleafing to a liberal mind the confcioufnefs of enjoying the approbation of the multitude muft always prove, could he fet fo exorbitant a value upon public praife as to become miferable in the extreme when he did not enjoy it.

Mr. Powys.   Mr. *Powys* remarked, that as he had not hitherto been favoured with inftructions from thofe whom he had the honour of reprefenting, it was not to be fuppofed that he could addrefs the Houfe with that degree of authority which accompanied the remarks of either the worthy magiftrate (Sir Watkin Lewes) who opened the debate, or an honourable gentleman (Mr. Thornton) who fpoke laft but one.   He had neither received any inftructions nor intimations, and therefore he fhould look to the petitions on the table, being of opinion that the petitions of the People, let them come from whom they would, always deferved the refpect and attention of every member of that Houfe.   To the fort of evidence given at the bar he had liftened very clofely.   He gave the witneffes the credit of being extremely well informed; but there were fome pofitions of theirs to which he could not reconcile his mind; in particular, their declaration that the competition between the capital fhopkeeper and the petty fhopkeeper would prevent their enabling themfelves to reimburfe the charge of the tax by a diftribution of it on the articles they deal in, was a pofition to which his own opinions would never fuffer him to affent.   He alfo revolted at the idea of the capital fhopkeepers abforbing the fmaller fhopkeeper.   Why would that be more probable in future than it had been hitherto?   There always had been both defcriptions; and the one had the fame degree of power over the other, and yet the petty fhopkeepers were not abforbed.   He was inclined to confider it as a tax on confumption, which would in time find its level.   He did not like, at any rate, to repeal it merely becaufe it was unpopular. He recollected that the receipt tax was, at one time, equally unpopular, and fo would every tax be which raifed a good deal of money.   If the prefent could be proved to be perfonal, it muft be repealed; but it had not yet been fo proved.   A tribute of confiderable applaufe was certainly due to the right honourable gentleman (Mr. Pitt) for every ftep in his political procedures, as far as they refpected the finances of the nation, from the firft moment to the prefent of his prefiding over the government of affairs; nor did any act entitle him to a greater fhare of panegyric than the rapidity with which he had funded the unfunded debt.   In conclufion, Mr. Powys obferved, that

he

he meant to render himself at leaft one exception to the remark which an honourable gentleman had thought proper to
make during the courfe of the debate, that the minifterial
phalanx muft, on the prefent occafion, confift of the members for decayed and rotten boroughs. In this defcription he
did not clafs; and yet his vote would go in oppofition to the
motion of the worthy magiftrate.

Mr. *William Stanhope* obferved, that although he enjoyed
the honour of being a reprefentative for (Kingfton upon Hull)
one of the moft extenfive and opulent commercial towns within
the kingdom, his conftituents had not hitherto directed him
to meet the fhop tax with an oppofing voice; nor indeed
could he, for his own part, conceive why fuch an impoft was
improper. The fhopkeepers would contrive that the confu-
mers fhould pay it, and that it might be fo laid as to be a fair
tax. With regard to the prefent tax, it certainly ought to be
altered. The criterion by which it was laid was moft abfurd.
The colour of a man's door was juft as certain a rule to judge
what his fhop was worth. There were a great many people
who paid very high rents for their houfes, and yet who did
very little bufinefs; and again, there were others in directly
the reverfe fituation. He ftated the cafe of Mr. Gray, the
buckle maker, or feller, in New Bond Street, and oppofed it
to an artificial-flower maker's fhop in the upper part of the
ftreet. The former did a great deal of bufinefs, and kept his
country houfe, and the latter did very little, and yet the latter
paid a much higher rent than the former. This was certainly
hard upon the flower maker. A variety of fimilar inftances
might be cited. Might not a better end be anfwered, were a
fhop to become affeffed feparately, valued at a third of the
rent, and that third taxed in proportion?

Mr. *Francis* declared he had no intention to embarrafs the
right honourable gentleman in the bufinefs of taxation and
finance; he difclaimed any fuch idea. He rofe merely to
fpeak in behalf of that lower order of fhopkeepers whofe
voice was not very likely to reach that Houfe: he meant the
petty fhopkeepers who dwelt in houfes from 5l. to 15l. a year.
The fhopkeepers of that defcription muft be extremely dif-
treffed by the tax, and theirs was a cafe which rather appealed
to the compaffion of the Houfe, than came forward with any
other ground of appeal.

Mr. Chancellor *Pitt* faid, that it gave him no inconfiderable pleafure to embrace an opportunity of rifing fo foon after
an honourable gentleman (Mr. Francis) who had uttered obfervations which reflected the higheft credit upon the benevolence of his heart; and he trufted that, previous to the conclufion of thofe remarks with which he muft beg leave to
trefpafs upon the attention of the Houfe, he fhould convince

Mr. Wm. Stanhope.

Mr. Francis.

Mr. Chancellor Pitt.

the honourable gentleman that, upon the prefent occafion, his breaft was not deftitute of proper feeling. He entirely concurred in opinion with an honourable gentleman who began the debate, that the queftion before the Houfe was one of the utmoft confequence, but that it alfo lay within a very narrow compafs. The whole of the objections to the tax might be claffed under two feparate heads; the one applying to the juftice of the Houfe, the other fimply to its compaffion and humanity. The firft of thofe objections was, that the tax was perfonal; that it was impoffible to lay it on the confumer; and that it was of courfe highly partial and oppreffive. The other objection was, that, in certain cafes, it fell with a heavy weight on perfons who were abfolutely incompetent to pay it at all. As to the firft, he declared himfelf to labour under very difagreeable feelings, in being obliged to avow, that, notwithftanding the very intelligent manner in which the witneffes at the bar had given their teftimony, yet they had by no means brought home a conviction to his mind of the truth of the grievance of which they complained. He was not furprifed at the great refiftance which appeared to be given to the meafure, when he confidered how unwilling people were in general to pay any tax at all, and how ftrongly their prejudices were excited againft the prefent tax in particular, by perfons who had firft found it their intereft to give it the moft violent degree of oppofition in Parliament, and had afterwards endeavoured with all their induftry to impart and communicate that violence to the people abroad. It had originally been argued in favour of the tax, that it would be made to operate as a general impoft upon confumption, and it was now attempted to be proved that it could not be made fo to operate, but muft remain a burden on the fhopkeeper. The averfion of the fhopkeepers themfelves was adduced as an argument in favour of this conftruction; for it was taken for granted, that if the fhopkeeper could at all indemnify himfelf, he could do it to an extent out of all proportion greater than he was entitled to do, and therefore that his diffatisfaction muft neceffarily arife from the impoffibility of indemnifying himfelf at all. In his opinion, the oppofition could be as eafily accounted for from the natural prejudices of mankind, by which the perfons paying the tax were inclined to overlook the additional profits they might make by an advanced price on their commodities, becaufe thofe were fcattered and minute in their parts, and to lay a greater emphafis on the tax they had to pay, though not greater in amount, becaufe it was to go out of their pockets in a lumping fum. The particular part of the queftion, which related to the practicability of laying the amount of the tax on the articles of the trade, appeared to him to have met with great mifre-
prefentation,

prefentation, and a very unfair inquiry. He had endeavoured to elucidate that inquiry by a queftion which he afked one of the witneffes, whofe anfwer had been alluded to by an honourable gentleman oppofite to him. The queftion was, By what criterion were the charges of the retailers of any commodity to be regulated? The anfwer was one to which he could not fubfcribe, By the prime coft. If this were the cafe, what regulated the diff. rence of prices charged by the wholefale dealer or manufacturer and the retailer? There were, he apprehended, a variety of confiderations which ought to weigh with a trader in fixing a price on his commodity : befides the prime coft, he was to eftimate the other expences as well as the trouble which might attend it ; the bringing it to market, and, if it was a commodity unfit for immediate confumption, the manufacturing it to a ftate of perfeclion, were attended with a degree of labour and attention for which he was to indemnify himfelf by his price. It was not merely by the prime coft that the retail price was to be governed, but by every other incidental expence attending the bufinefs ; fo that the retail fhopkeepers might as eafily advance their prices, in order to indemnify themfelves from the tax, as they could for the purpofe of anfwering any other charge they might incur. The principal topics which could be adduced to prove the poffibility of the fhopkeepers to lay on their commodities, without giving an unfair opportunity of competition to the more confiderable traders, had been already anticipated, which was, that if thofe could meet the inferior dealers in a competition favourable to themfelves with the tax, they alfo do it equally without the tax, and therefore would long fince have entirely overborne and abforbed the whole trade to themfelves. The nature of the competition in trade was not a competition to underfel others, fo much as to fell at a rate which would procure the dealer a proper living profit. What this profit was, depended upon the circumftances of the trader, and was that general profit which would enable him to live in a ftile fuitable to his rank among people of that clafs ; from whence it muft appear, that a confiderable trader could not eftimate his profits by thofe of another, an inferior one, but muft make them keep pace with the proportion between their feveral capitals. Thus the inferior trader kept pace in his proportional profits with the fuperior ; and if the fuperior ventured to underfel the inferior, his proportional profit, which was in fact his living profit, muft become diminifhed, which would effectually prevent his attempting to do fo. — It was fomething extraordinary that it fhould be contended, either that no advance at all could be made in the prices of the articles of the retail trade, or that if any advance fhould be made, it muft be to fuch a degree as would burden the Public

N n 2　　　　　with

with a tax infinitely greater than that impofed upon the fhopkeeper. Thus the principle of competition was powerful enough to enable the trader to practife a heavy impofition againft the Public, but not fufficiently to protect and indemnify himfelf from a fmall burden. But neither of thofe extremes were to be expected; for, in the firft place, on the principle that every trader expected a general proportional profit upon the whole of his capital, adequate to that capital, and therefore would not attempt to underfel the inferior trader, as by fo doing he would diminifh that proportional profit; fo the danger of lofing all their bufinefs would prevent any of them from going fo far in increafing their prices as to impofe upon the Public in the degree which had been fuggefted. In trades of any peculiar myftery or fkill, perfons might endeavour to ftretch their profits to an unreafonable length, becaufe no fuch danger of rivalfhip exifted there as in other cafes; but, in that particular inftance, to extend the profit too far would leffen the confumption: in the ordinary courfe of bufinefs, however, any attempt to raife a too exorbitant compenfation on the Public would raife up competitors, and defeat the object. The abfurdity of fuppofing that the addition of a fmall burden on the fhopkeepers would in any degree deftroy the general level of trade, muft appear to thofe who fhould reflect upon the difference between the rents of houfes at the prefent time from what they were thirty years ago, and from what they poffibly might be thirty years hence; and this increafe fhould be confidered in the fame point of view as the prefent tax, with this difference, that the proportion of the tax was in favour of the lower orders of fhopkeepers; whereas the increafe of rents had no fuch proportion. Did this increafe then give any unfair advantage to the fuperior fhopkeeper? If fo, how had the inferior ones kept their ground? And if they could keep their ground againft a general rife in rents, why not equally in the circumftance of an additional tax, not general and equal, but calculated to maintain a proportion favourable to the poorer claffes? Hence it muft follow, that the general principle of a proportionate profit to the capitals of the different traders would prevent a competition dangerous and deftructive to the inferior fhopkeepers; and that the natural difpofition of all traders to endeavour at a competition, where it could be done confiftent with that principle, would prevent a too exorbitant compenfation from being raifed upon the Public. It had been argued, that the rent of the houfe was not a fair criterion to judge of the degree of trade carried on by each individual; but it was the faireft method by which it could be afcertained; for if one fhopkeeper paid thirty pounds a year for a houfe of equal dimenfions to that for which another, in a lefs-advantageous

tageous fituation, paid only twenty, they acted fo certainly either with a view of felling more articles, or of getting a higher price for thofe they did fell : if the trader fold more, then certainly his fhop, independent of the houfe, was, in fact, more valuable, and of courfe more an object of taxation ; but if he fold at a higher rate, then certainly it could not be contended but that there was a poffibility for a tradefman to indemnify himfelf for any extraordinary expence he might be at by an advance of his prices ; and he would not fuppofe that any gentleman would attempt to argue that a tradefman could apportion the fum of ten pounds, to be made up by an advance of price on his trade, and yet be at a lofs to indemnify himfelf for a tax infinitely lefs, and which bore a proportion decidedly in favour of the inferior dealer. It was worthy of obfervation, how the native force of reafon, in fome inftances, without felf-confcioufnefs, got the better of prejudice. An honourable gentleman (Alderman and member for the city of London) had ftated it as impoffible for any trader to indemnify himfelf for a tax, by raifing the price of his commodities ; but ftill the honourable Alderman, on a fubject in which his particular paffion and interefts were not engaged, had fhewn, in the courfe of the evening, that he was not in reality fo ignorant of the operations of taxation as he had pretended ; for when, in a former debate, it had been fuggefted, that, by impofing a tax of ten fhillings per ton on Dutch fifhing veffels, the city of London might be deprived of her fupply of a certain favourite article, the honourable Alderman had anfwered the objection by obferving, that there was no danger of the market being deferted ; for if our own fifhermen did not fupply it fufficiently, the Dutch would, notwithftanding the duty, bring in their turbot, and indemnify themfelves for the additional ten fhillings per ton impoft by adding it to the price of the fifh. Such an argument was the more fingular, as it was made on the very eve of a debate in which the honourable member, no doubt, was prepared to hold one of a directly contradictory nature. An honourable gentleman, for whofe opinion he had the higheft refpect, obferved, that we had now experience inftead of theory, and evidence inftead of affertion, to convince us of the injuftice of the tax ; but as to experience, we had as yet had none, for the tax had been paid but in a very few inftances ; and befides, we could not expect to find the event of fuch a fubject completely fulfilled until time fhould have fuffered the trade affected by the tax to have fubfided to its level. As to the evidence produced, it was in fact nothing but affertion, and the affertion of men labouring under ftrong prejudices ; fo that, upon the whole, he could fee no reafon for agreeing to the motion for a total repeal, however it might

become

become proper to mitigate the tax in some instances. This
brought him to a second class of objection, which was the
heavy burden it imposed upon persons absolutely incapable,
and on others not very well qualified to bear it. From motives of compassion to persons whom he should wish to protect and cherish as a very deserving, and though not an opulent, a respectable part of the community, he was extremely
willing entirely to remit the tax to such as were so poor as to
be excused the payment of parish rates; and those who came
next to them in their title to pity, and though not quite so
indigent, were nearly unable to pay it: such should, with
his consent, be considerably eased. Those persons must be
ascertained by their rents being under twenty or twenty-five
pounds. Thus the very poorest class would become wholly
exonerated, and that immediately above it materially relieved. But in consenting to this, he was directed solely by
motives of humanity, and not by any considerations of the
impropriety of the principle of the bill, which he continued
to approve, notwithstanding all the efforts which had been
made to depreciate and condemn it. If he could be convinced
that the tax were really objectionable, he would most chearfully acquiesce in its repeal; and he supposed there was no
gentleman in the House that would for a moment hesitate to
comply with the wishes of the inhabitants of the city in
which they all lived. For his own part, he declared that he
would by no means resist their desires merely because the measure was originally of his own framing; and he was happy
to say, that if gentlemen should really think the tax either
oppressive or unjust, that the situation of the public finances
were not such as could afford them any excuse for persisting
in it; but he flattered himself that he was not so far mistaken
in his opinion of the generosity and spirit of his countrymen
as that the relief which he was ready to grant to the more indigent part of them would not give ample satisfaction to the
more opulent, and make them chearfully acquiesce in the
burden which (if the House thought proper) they were still to
bear. But he begged leave to warn the House against a too-
ready compliance with a requisition for the repeal of a tax,
as it might form a precedent to endanger every branch of the
revenue; for it was difficult to find any tax whatsoever,
against which very plausible exceptions might not be made,
and from which many people would not be found averse. On
the subject of the proposed modifications he should say little,
because if the House agreed to the total repeal, it would
prove useless; and if they did not, the modifications and ex-
emptions would become sufficient. It had been proposed to
value the shops at one third of the rent of the house; but
this would answer no end towards regulating the tax; because
the

the proportional value, according to that eftimate, would ftill be uniform, and therefore the tax on each muft bear the fame *ratio*; but if they were otherwife, an honourable friend of his (Mr. Stanhope) had fhewn an exception in the inftance of two houfes; the fhop belonging to one of which did not amount to above one-tenth part of the value of the whole, whereas in the other the fhop was worth one half. As to the allowing fhopkeepers intereft for their book debts, (which, however it might be a compenfation, was certainly no modification of the tax) he thought, in fome points of view, it would prove defirable, and he would willingly comply with it; but he apprehended it was what the traders themfelves did not wifh for. A worthy Alderman (Mr. Hammett) felt warmly under the impreffion of the prejudice which obvioufly poffeffed his mind; but if the pofitions which he had laid down were admitted, as to what was not a fair principle of taxation, nine tenths of our revenue muft be given up as built upon an erroneous principle. Perhaps a perfeverance in the attempt to give ftability to the fhop tax would either prevent the flighteft acquifition of popularity, or leffen, if not annihilate, whatever fhare of it might, at any preceding period, have been acquired; yet, although no circumftance could prove more flattering to his heart than the enjoyment of the approbation of his fellow fubjects, nor any endeavour become a ftronger object of his mind than that which tended to earning from their generous partiality a tribute of honourable praife, the welcome, the dear reward of having confulted their actual welfare, he fhould prefer (what, in his humble opinion, he might deem) their interefts to their gratifications, and their real fervice to their imaginary caufes for contentment. The important duties of his ftation fhould never, even for a moment, lofe their firft afcendency in his recollection; and, amidft the principles which a becoming idea of the weight of thefe muft naturally infpire, he would regard all marks of popular applaufe as merely perfonal confiderations, and therefore not worthy to weigh a fingle feather in the fcale againft his efforts to procure, on grounds of unexceptionable juftice, advantages for the revenue.

Mr. *Fox* faid, that the right honourable gentleman who fpoke laft might reft affured that he admitted, without even the flighteft exception, the juftice of his arguments in favour of the neceffity of perpetually endeavouring to introduce, and to promote advantages for the national revenue, and of refufing (unlefs the moft powerfully-unanfwerable reafons could juftify a contrary procedure) to relinquifh a tax, from the produce of which he might have reafon to expect a fum of great amount. So fully was he perfuaded that his fentiment became not only every minifter, but every member of

Mr. Fox.

that

that Houfe; and fo deeply was he, at the fame time, convinced, that, in matters of finance, and of taxation, the unpopularity of any particular impoft ought not to be the reafon for its being abandoned : that much as he profeffed of refpect for his conftituents of Weftminfter, and ftill more, as
he felt of regard and reverence for thofe whom he confidered
as his firft conftituents, the people at large, whofe interefts he
held himfelf bound to watch over, and, as far as in him lay,
to guard, protect, and defend within thofe walls; yet, notwithftanding the numerous petitions on the table, and notwithftanding the inftructions which he had received from
thofe whom he immediately reprefented, and their known
wifhes, he made no fcruple to declare, that he would have
fupported the right honourable gentleman in refifting a motion for the repeal of the fhop tax, had he not been fully convinced that the tax was radically bad ; that it was founded in
the groffeft partiality and injuftice ; and that no modification
whatfoever, much lefs the fort of modification propofed by
the right honourable gentleman, could cure its defects, or
render it fit to be endured. The motion for its repeal fhould,
therefore, have his firm fupport, and in giving his vote for a
repeal of the act *in toto*, he hoped he fhould not be confidered
as an enemy to the revenue. When the tax had been originally propofed, he objected to it, and then declared, that,
though the right honourable gentleman chofe to call it a fhop
tax, it was in fact an additional houfe tax, partially applied to
houfes, of which fhops made a part. That was undoubtedly
the ftate of the cafe, and confequently it was not the firft,
but the fecond fhop tax ; for the tax on houfes had operated
partially, and to the difadvantage of fhopkeepers ; inafmuch
as fhopkeepers, compared to all other defcriptions of houfeholders, paid by far the higheft rents of any perfons in the
kindom. To lay a new burden on the fhoulders of that defcription of people, who were too heavily burdened before,
was oppreffive and unjuft ; that, therefore, were there no
other, was a ftrong reafon, and indeed it ought to operate
as an unanfwerable one with the Committee for agreeing to
the motion for a repeal of the act. The right honourable
gentleman had put the cafe, that if houfes were to rife in rent
confiderably all over the kingdom fome years hence, what
would then be the fituation of fhopkeepers, and would they
have any reafon to complain that they paid higher rents than
they did at prefent? If the right honourable gentleman meant
merely that if money grew cheaper, and all forts of property fetched a larger proportion of money in price proportionably, in that cafe, things would juft remain in the fituation in which they ftood at prefent ; but if the right honourable gentleman meant (and fo indeed he muft mean, if he

meant

meant any thing) that the houses of shopkeepers only were at any given period to be raised in their rents all over the kingdom, he had then very fairly described the additional tax in question, the shop tax, because that tax operating upon shopkeepers only, did what the right honourable gentleman had stated: it raised the rents and swelled the capitals of shopkeepers' houses all over the kingdom, at the same time that it raised the rents of no other houses.   How extreme was the injustice of selecting that useful body of people, the shopkeepers, as objects of not only separate and distinct, but oppressive and unjust taxation.   With regard to the right honourable gentleman's two points, (which he had laboured so much to establish) that the tax was not personal, and that it might be laid on the consumer by the shopkeeper who paid it in the first instance, both those positions must he deny in the most unequivocal manner, and declare that the tax was a direct personal tax on the shopkeeper, and that it was utterly impossible for him to repay himself by laying it on the consumer, without putting the Public not merely to five times the charge of it, as an honourable member near him had stated to have been the case in regard to the duty imposed on wine some years since, but to forty, or perhaps one hundred times the charge.   On this occasion, he must beg leave to remind the Committee, that nothing could be more easy than to ascertain exactly to what the sum of additional duty per hogshead upon wine came, and what would prove the amount of that duty when divided into gallons, and from gallons into bottles.   If, then, in a case so easy, obvious, and intelligible, the retail dealer had barefacedly charged the Public five times as much for every bottle as he paid to the Exchequer, what an advantage must not be unavoidably made where the distribution of the tax was privately laid on a variety of small articles?   In fact, the consumer, if he paid the tax at all, must imperceptibly and insensibly, even to the shopkeeper, pay it over, and over, and over again ; but he defied the right honourable gentleman to prove that any shopkeeper either had, or could charge it to the consumer.   Being, therefore, undoubtedly a personal tax, he should advise the right honourable gentleman, in this instance at least, to give way, and offer some tax, less exceptionable, in its stead.   He had himself, when the subject was under discussion last session, mentioned a tax which he had thought preferable, though he was very ready to admit, that the tax to which he alluded was extremely open to exception.   He meant a new general house tax.   That he thought, exceptionable as it was, was less exceptionable than the shop tax.   In point of exceptionableness, it was chiefly so, as that it would bear harder on shopkeepers than on any other perfons, becaufe they paid higher rents (as he had obferved before) than any other defcription of houfeholders. In fhort, the tax was fo radically bad, that no modification could cure its defects. The right honourable gentleman, in the greater part of his argument, had gone to prove that the tax was not perfonal, and that it muft find its level and fall on the confumer. If this were true, what was there to recommend his modifications? The right honourable gentleman had ftated that he would take off and modify the portion of the tax to be paid by all fhopkeepers who lived in houfes at lefs rents than twenty and twenty-five pounds, which would confiderably lighten the load, and exonerate the fhopkeeper. Would it? Of what would it exonerate him? Of the money paid by the confumer! For if the confumer was to pay the whole of the tax, the confumer would be exonerated by the modification propofed, and not the fhopkeeper. In like manner, the generous and compaffionate bounty of the right honourable gentleman, in fact, amounted to nothing; becaufe if the confumer really paid the tax, the poor fhopkeeper, who was not to pay towards the tax, if he was excufed the payment of parochial taxes, was excufed from paying that which, according to the right honourable gentleman's argument, was to come out of the pocket of another. The right honourable gentleman had thought proper to hazard the remark, that the tax would, no doubt, find its level; but that the fhopkeepers had not yet found out how to make its diftribution. This was an extraordinary thing to fay of men, the daily bufinefs of whofe lives was to lay out large fums to purchafe articles in the grofs, and to draw back and collect the fums fo expended by a multitude of minute profits. How ftrange and idle to impute the fort of ignorance in queftion to thofe men, who, of all others, were moft in the habits of making fuch a diftribution as that which it had been faid they had not difcovered how to make! In fact, the laying the tax on the confumer at all was impoffible. Upon this occafion he fhould inftance his own receipt tax, which every body knew was to this day paid by the perfon who received the money, although he had a legal right to oblige the perfon paying it to pay for the receipt. Mr. Fox declared, that though he did not pretend to be above popularity, but, on the contrary, was fhocked and affected when it fell to his-lot to become unpopular, yet he would, at all times, in fpite of unpopularity, ftand up an advocate for a tax after it was once propofed, unlefs, as in the prefent inftance, he thought the tax radically bad, and unfit to remain unrepealed. The prefent tax was a perfonal tax, and at the fame time partook of the nature of a tax on the confumer in the worft manner, becaufe it left the power of diftribution folely to the difcretion of the fhopkeeper,

keeper, and what was more exceptionable, to be by him fecretly exercifed. The requifite to make a perfonal tax pala-
table was, to lay it fo that its operation fhould be general, if
not univerfal. The fervants' tax was an unexceptionable perfonal tax, but (he feared) ill collected. The argument of a
worthy Alderman (Mr. Hammett) was certainly well grounded in regard to the principle of taxation, though it went a
great way farther than he was ready to go upon the fubject;
but the right honourable gentleman (he thought) went much
farther himfelf, when he had afferted that nine tenths of the
revenue depended upon taxes raifed upon the principle which
the honourable Alderman had reprobated: the principle of
impofing mere perfonal taxes, and thofe fuch as did not affect
themfelves. Whenever taxes were under confideration, one
material defect in the conftruction of that Houfe manifefted
itfelf, and that was, that the city of London, which paid, in
general, fo large a fhare of all the taxes, had not a greater
proportion of reprefentatives to fecure it its due weight in determining of what taxes fhould confift. The right honourable gentleman, notwithftanding, deferved a tribute of applaufe for fuch modifications as he intended to introduce;
and, for his own part, under a total averfion from the whole
of the bill, he fhould be glad to difcover that, with the aid of
the right honourable gentleman, fome portion of it might become repealed, if it were vain to hope to fee it actually
thrown out of Parliament. An event of this laft defirable
and happy nature would refcue the fhopkeepers of London
and Weftminfter from the burden of an almoft intolerable
grievance. Anxious to emancipate them from fuch unmerited oppreffion, he felt it a duty which, upon the prefent occafion, he fhould moft chearfully fulfil, to vote in favour of
the motion for an abfolute repeal of the act paffed during the
courfe of the preceding feffion.

Sir *Gregory-Page Turner* declared that he had laft year voted
for the tax confcientioufly, but that he fhould now vote for its
repeal, as the act was partial, in not including wholefale
dealers.

Mr. Alderman *Watfon* declared that he rofe not to call upon
the compaffionate feelings of the Houfe, but upon its juftice,
to which the fhopkeepers of London and Weftminfter had
fubmiffively appealed. An honourable Baronet (Sir Edward
Aftley) had obferved, that he was againft the tax being repealed, as the fhopkeepers had entered into a combination to
defeat the receipt tax. This he was glad to hear, becaufe it
put the matter on its true ground. It feemed, then, that
the Houfe had voted the tax on a principle of vindictivenefs,
and in order to punifh the fhopkeepers of London for having
dared to difapprove of a former tax.

Sir G. P.
Turner.

Mr. Ald.
Watfon.

Q o 2   Mr.

Mr. Ald.
Townshend

Mr. Alderman *Townshend* now rose, and declared, that he could not avoid calling the honourable member who spoke last to order, and reminding him, that a declaration that the House ever imposed taxes on the subjects from a principle of punishment and vindictiveness, discovered that kind of freedom which must be deemed insufferable within the walls of Parliament.

This point having been adjusted,

Mr. Ald.
Townshend

Mr. Alderman *Townshend* rose a second time, and remarked, that the tax had from the first been called an unjust and oppressive tax; assertion was now evidence; the right honourable gentleman had originally opened it as a tax of a personal nature, and had, at the same time, talked of abolishing hawkers and pedlars, as a compensation to the shopkeepers; but it was clear that the abolishing hawkers and pedlars would have been no compensation to the shopkeepers of London and Westminster. This idea, in that form, was consequently unjust, because the tax operated oppressively chiefly in the metropolis, and there no compensation existed at all. The idea, however, was afterwards changed, and, instead of hawkers and pedlars being abolished, the doctrine that the shop tax would be paid by the consumer was taken up and maintained. The tax, therefore, had been introduced upon a fallacious principle, and on that ground of objection, were there no other, it ought to be repealed. In order to prove how ill founded the doctrine was, that the shop tax was a tax on consumption, he must remind the House of the increase of the land tax, and ask if any gentleman could give an instance that a load of hay, of corn, or of straw, had fetched more on account of the increase of the land tax? In like manner, if a gentleman raised the rent of his farm, and the farmer brought a load of the produce to market, would he not be laughed at if he were to demand an inordinate price, and to alledge as a reason for so doing that he paid a high rent? Every person knew that the farmer must, in that case, be governed in his demand by the fair average and ordinary market price of the day. With respect to wool and cloth, could a dealer in either get more for his wool per tod, or his cloth per yard, on the plea of his paying an increased rent? He would give the right honourable gentleman warning in time of his danger: if the tax were not repealed, he could have no conception of the extreme odium which he would incur throughout the kingdom. Its partiality was intolerable. What must the petty cheesemonger in Bishopsgate Street, who lived next door to Mr. Long's, and could scarcely afford to live on his own cheese parings, think, when he daily saw Mr. Long drive out, lolling in his coach at his ease, and knew that he did not pay a penny

penny towards the shop tax, though he was forced to contribute to it himself?

Mr. *Grigsby* said, that, old fashioned as the custom appeared, he was determined to obey the instructions of his constituents : he rose, therefore, to declare, that he had consulted them, and that, upon meeting the shopkeepers of the two largest towns in the county [Suffolk] he had the honour to represent, they were generally satisfied with the tax, and declared, that if it were extended to other descriptions of traders, such as warehousemen and bankers, they should become still more satisfied.   Another matter that was foreign to the subject then under discussion, Mr. Grigsby said, he wished to speak to.   When the question of reform had been in debate last session, he was out of the house, and was absent about twenty minutes.   During this absence, he understood, that a noble Lord, not then in his place, had risen and noticed to the House, that he had seen some advertisements signed by a member of that House, inviting his constituents to furnish him with instructions on the question of reform ; but as that member had not said a word, nor was there any petition on the table from Suffolk, he presumed that county was content with the existing state of the representation. The fact (Mr. Grigsby added) was, that he had, in consequence of his advertisements, seen his constituents at the time ; that they had assigned their reasons for declining to convene a meeting of the county, and had left it to him to act as he thought proper.

Mr. Alderman *Newnham* observed, that it appeared to him to be a very extraordinary case for the freeholders of the county of Suffolk to have instructed their representative to recommend it to the House, instead of repealing the shop tax, to extend it to warehousemen and bankers.   There was not, he believed, any warehousemen in the county, and not above two bankers.   It was extraordinary that any member for a county should have pursued so wild a measure

Mr. *Grigsby* declared that he had said the *shopkeepers*, not the *freeholders*, of Suffolk had told him that they should be glad if the tax were extended to warehousemen and bankers.

Sir *Richard Hill* said, that he presented a petition, praying for a repeal of the shop-tax act, from the county of Salop, and that he had come down determined to vote for the repeal ; but the modifications the right honourable gentleman had proposed would (he had no sort of doubt) reconcile the shopkeepers of Shrewsbury, and indeed of every town in the county, to the tax.   He, therefore, should vote against the repeal.

Mr. *Macnamara* observed, that he had, in like manner, received instructions from his constituents to vote for the repeal ;

Mr. Grigsby.

Mr. Ald. Newnham.

Mr. Grigsby.

Sir Richard Hill.

Mr. Macnamara.

peal; but he believed, that had they been aware of the proposed modifications, they would have gladly accepted of the tax upon thofe terms. He, therefore, fhould vote againft the entire repeal of the act.

The Committee now divided —

Ayes - - - - - - - - - - 93
Noes - - - - - - - - - - 176

Majority - - 83

The Chairman was directed to report; and, as foon as the Houfe was refumed, the report was ordered to be brought up on the morrow.

The Houfe adjourned.

Friday, 3d March.

Mr. Burke.

Mr. *Burke* begged leave to fubmit to the moft ferious attention of the Houfe, the fubjects of motions which had been made for papers relative to particular tranfactions in the Eaft Indies. Upon this occafion, he confidered it as his duty earneftly to repeat, that thefe motions were unavoidably requifite for the acquifition of papers which belonged to the whole body of charges, and without which it would prove impoffible to go fully and fairly into the inveftigation of this important matter; he trufted, therefore, that no objection would arife againft their being granted. He fhould make three motions, all, in a great meafure, connected with each other. They went to the treaty of peace with the Mahrattas, and were for the purpofe of bringing into evidence proofs requifite to eftablifh the charges againft Mr. Haftings in that particular tranfaction. His firft motion, to which he hoped to receive the concurrence of a majority, was, " That there be laid before this Houfe, " copies or duplicates of all papers relative to the laft peace " with the Mahrattas, or any demand made by the Mahrattas " concerning the ceffion or reftoration of any territories now " in the poffeffion of the Company, or its allies, or of the " payment of any chout, (or fourth part of the revenues) or " of any fum in lieu thereof, or concerning any payment of " money, or loan, to any of the faid Mahrattas, made or paid " fince the 1ft of January, 1779."

Mr. Dundas.

Mr. *Dundas* remarked, that as the contents of the papers for which the right honourable gentleman thought fit to move muft, if rendered public, occafion that matter to tranfpire which ought, from motives of the foundeft policy, to remain an actual fecret to all the powers of the Eaft Indies, he, for his own part, was determined fteadily to oppofe fo dangerous a propofition. All this refiftance was due from him, in confequence of his attachments to the interefts of his country;

for

for the fake of which he could not fubmit to fee carried into the world a full (or even a contracted) relation of circum- ftances refpecting any of thofe fteps which led to the conclu- fion of the peace with the Mahrattas. Firft, he fhould take the liberty to aver, that the late peace in India had never be- come the object of complaint, but merited, and it received, every man's applaufe. The benefits arifing from it were great; they were, in fact, the falvation of the Britifh empire in Afia. That peace broke one of the moft powerful confe- deracies ever formed againft our poffeffions there; and had it not been concluded in the manner in which Mr. Haftings fo happily effected it, our power in that part of the world muft certainly have experienced its total diffolution. The plans under which this happy event was effected were extremely improper to be made public, becaufe they led to difcoveries of the means by which the different confederate powers were ren- dered jealous of each other; to the intrigues by which the Rajahs were induced to diffolve their league againft the Bri- tifh empire; and they would bring out fecrets of infidelity which muft tend to do the moft material injuries to our inte- refts. It was impoffible to feparate the motion fo as to effect the purpofe which it fought, without incurring the evils which he forefaw, and therefore he fhould not comply with its terms. The Houfe might fay to Mr. Haftings, You fhall not ftate this: you fhall not ftate that in your defence, be- caufe it muft deeply affect our interefts in India; but when Mr. Haftings comes upon his trial, who is it can prevent him from going into the fubject of the Mahratta peace at large, and broadly ftating whatever he knew? The difcuffion of the Mahratta peace would lead to a difcovery of what alliances we had formed in India, and to a full inveftigation of the po- litics of that country; matters very improper to become re- vealed to foreign powers. From motives of fuch uncommon cogency muft he contend againft the requifitions of the right honourable gentleman; nor did he doubt but that the Houfe, fenfible of the propriety, and even the neceffity, of fuch a refiftance, would, upon this occafion, honour him with their fupport.

Mr. *Frederic Montagu* obferved, that, under his ufual ideas that whatfoever arguments might be delivered by the right honourable and learned gentleman who fpoke laft, they muft command attention, it was not without fatisfaction that he difcovered his refiftance to the motion placed folely upon a public ground, where the decifion with refpect to its pro- priety might prove entirely unexceptionable. The right ho- nourable gentleman (Mr. Burke) had come forward as a de- termined accufer, and the charges which he made contained neither light nor novel matter. The fubject had been dif-

Mr. Fred. Montagu.

cuffed

cuffed for a number of years, and before many Committees. The right honourable gentleman's abilities fhone with more than common fplendour in the bufinefs; his diligence and attention were unwearied. But, notwithftanding this perfeverance, and thefe virtues, he much feared, that, like many other great perfons, he muft truft to pofterity for the benefit of his labours; for there feemed little probability of bringing this point to iffue in his lifetime. As to the danger arifing from the difclofure of the circumftances of the Mahratta peace, he really faw it not in the light in which it was attempted to be placed by the right honourable and learned gentleman. He hardly could perceive how the mixed government of the Indian princes fhould enter into the detail of the parliamentary proceedings in England. If the minute papers were moved for, there was a negative put on the motion; there was an end to all inquiry. What was to become of juftice, if the ftrong hand of the Minifter was raifed on fuch occafions againft the attainment of equity? If, on the prefent occafion, he took the liberty to ufe the word Minifter, it was not without a tolerably well-grounded fuppofition, that, not merely upon this, but upon feveral other political occafions, the right honourable and learned gentleman came forward as effectively the Minifter. In conclufion, Mr. Montagu faid, that, for the reafons which he had already ftated, he was determined to give the motion of his right honourable friend an affenting vote.

Mr. Burke.   Mr. *Burke* contended that the objections of the right honourable and learned gentleman went not only to the firft motion, but ftrongly and directly to the other two; and he was the more furprifed at this oppofition, when he contrafted his conduct in the year 1782 with his proceedings in the year 1786. The amafing change of opinion on the fame fubject carried to the mind a kind of aftonifhment, that, in fo fhort a time, fo great a difference of fentiment could become effected. As to the arguments ufed by the right honourable and learned gentleman in fupport of the refufal of the motions, they had, when confidered, a moft ftrange appearance. They went to this—that the papers could not be granted, becaufe they would prove how and in what manner the different powers in India had been facrificed to each other. Thefe were not indeed the exact words, but they conftituted the meaning to the full extent. Thus extraordinary was the caufe affigned for endeavouring to prevent the papers from an appearance upon the table of the Houfe; but if the reafoning of the right honourable and learned gentleman had any force at all, it ftruck down his ftrange pofition, that the papers ought not to be produced at all.

Mr.

Mr. *Dundas* called Mr. Burke to order. He infifted that he never entertained an idea of the powers in India being in-duced to betray each other by the circumftances under which the Mahratta peace was effected.

Mr. *Burke* anfwered, that nothing was fo far diftant from his intentions as to engage in merely verbal altercations. Of little confequence was it whether we had prevailed upon the powers in the Eaft Indies reciprocally to betray one another, or whether we had betrayed to them every ally we had in that part of the world. If the right honourable gentleman meant to do Mr. Haftings a fervice in refufing to let thofe papers be laid upon the table, he fhould have begun with eftablifhing that there was no guilt in the tranfactions; that our allies were not betrayed; and that our engagements and promifes had all been fulfilled with the princes who had fo ftrongly charged us with breaking them. It happened rather unfor-tunate for the right honourable and learned gentleman, that his own words were the ftrongeft teftimony againft his argu-ments, and this he hoped to prove. It had been argued on a former day, that if the prefent inquiry was to feek after crimes, the papers could not be granted; but that if a direct charge was made, there fhould not be any objection. That fpecific charge was not brought forward: it was committed in detail to writing; and if the right honourable and learned gentleman wifhed to hear it, it fhould be read to him. In-deed great part of it muft be in the right honourable and learned gentleman's recollection, if he turned to the Report of that Committee in which he once was fo active a member; but little notice fhould be taken of what thofe people fay who fo eafily forget. The matter, however, was of too fe-rious a nature to be dropped, becaufe he had ftopped the right honourable and learned member's memory. It muft, he faid, and it fhould be brought forward, if there was a poffibility of obtaining juftice in Parliament. Indeed the prefent objec-tion to the motion for neceffary papers carried with it an ill omen, and portended, that, in all matters of ftate, it would be impoffible to bring high delinquents to an impartial trial, when Minifters put a negative upon the evidence that was neceffary to that purpofe. As to the excufe which the right honourable and learned gentleman made of the Mahratta peace being fo falutary, and fo honourable, he denied the juf-tice of the affertion, and took upon himfelf to declare, that it was the direct contrary, and that our national honour and reputation were facrificed in that very peace. It was to prove this, and to bring the charge directly home to Mr. Haftings, that the prefent motion was made. The charge was of a po-litical nature: the crimes were political; and therefore the politics of both countries were involved in the event. The objection of betraying politics was, therefore, frivolous, because the whole being of a political nature, it was impossible to come to the matter of fact without a knowledge of those very politics which it seemed to be the intention of Ministers to conceal. As to the defence of, or rather the panegyric on, the conduct of Mr. Haftings, he should refer the right honourable and learned gentleman who made it to the forty-four resolutions which he moved against that very Mr. Haftings; which resolutions stood on the Journals of the House. They stood by themselves as a monument, to record the unanimous sentiments of the Committee, as approved by Parliament. Six of these resolutions were now violated by the opposition of the very gentleman who proposed them, and without any other argument to support the change of opinion than the very curious one, that Mr. Haftings had made a good peace. What had the peace to do with the antecedent crimes? The right honourable gentleman stood pledged on the Journals of the House to do that which he now declares to be unsafe. What did all this amount to? What must the world think of the business? That we were a nation of thieves and robbers, afraid of inquiries into facts, and therefore stopping the progress of investigation, lest we might impeach each other, and the truth come out. It was, in a narrower point of view, laying the crimes of the individual upon the shoulders of Parliament, and making the House of Commons answerable for that which alone belonged to Mr. Haftings. If the right honourable and learned gentleman meant really to be serious, it was his duty to step forward, and not only to assign indubitable reasons why the disclosure of the particulars respecting the Mahratta peace would give umbrage to the foreign powers, but unanswerably to prove that the resolutions were in the least likely to force the Government into the disgraceful act of betraying secrets which ought for ever to remain inviolable.

Mr. Dundas.

Mr. *Dundas* here again called the right honourable gentleman to order, who, he said, was arguing on the principles of motions not yet offered to the House. There had been but one read, and to that he wished he should confine himself.

Mr. Burke.

Mr. *Burke* infifted that he had not infringed upon any of the regulations of the House, or wandered beyond the subject in general with which the first motion stood connected, and with which the other two were collaterally related. The infidelity which the conclusion of the Mahratta war exemplified to our allies, the breach of treaties, and the forfeiture of solemn promises, were a part of the great charge against Mr. Haftings; but it would be impossible to substantiate that part, if Government withheld the evidence. He specifically charged Mr. Haftings with having betrayed the allies of this country,

and

and with having given them up. The Mahratta peace contained perfidy, and was fraught with ingratitude and cruelty to those who ought to have been sheltered and protected by us. The difference between him and the right honourable and learned gentleman was this:—He (Mr. Burke) brought accusation—he (Mr. Dundas) pronounced a panegyric: the one advanced his charge upon proof—the other fled from it. There were three parties in this business. The House stood as the accuser, Mr. Hastings as the accused, and a party was neuter. This latter was the Minister. The prosecutor is in possession of the facts; but then there is a necessary evidence to testify to the truth of these facts, and that evidence is in possession of the neuter party, which neuter party being determined to keep it back, the consequence must be the acquittal of the culprit. In respect to the danger mentioned by the right honourable and learned gentleman, which was to arise from making public these papers, if a negative proof to the contrary was allowed, he could fairly bring it home to the understanding of any gentleman in the house, that no danger could possibly arise more than had already happened. This is not a manœuvre respecting the Mahratta peace, of which the powers in India are not already in complete possession; and the consequence is, that they have already combined against this country for the purpose of extirpating the British power in Asia. The sovereigns there are as well informed as any sovereigns in Europe: they have their intelligence regularly; they have their newspapers and their newswriters, and the best and most authentic intelligence of all the powers both in Europe and in India. The circumstance of the treachery used to the Rajah of Gohud, of the breach of treaty with that unhappy prince, now driven from his territories, and a wanderer in the East, are well known—too well known to be concealed: that poor fugitive now holds up his hands, and implores the British Parliament; he abjures them by their own consistency, by the faith of treaties, by the honour of their nation, to do him justice, to fulfil their promises, and to punish the man who caused that honour to be sacrificed, that faith of nations to be broken. There was one thing which he wished the House to consider; that the disaffections in India, by our breach of promise, and by other unpardonable crimes committed under the authority of the late Governor General, might, and no doubt would, induce France to take an advantage of the most pernicious consequences to our eastern possessions. As to the concealment of transactions respecting the Mahratta peace, he should take the liberty to observe, that if they were to be a secret, they were only to be a secret to the House of Commons. The world was already in full possession of every matter which the right

ho ourable

honourable and learned gentleman with such caution wished to conceal ; and if the House did not agree with the producing the papers now asked, they shut the door against the truth, and against a principal truth, which led to the most material evidence.   The confistency of the right honourable and learned gentleman throughout the whole of the transaction was admirable.   He first, in the strongest terms which words could convey, reprobates the whole government of Mr. Haftings : then, on a change of politics, comes with a set-off against that which he reprobated.   The set-off was a panegyric on the Mahratta peace.   He must beg, therefore, to turn to the Journals of the House to bring to the right honourable and learned gentleman's memory that to which he had then agreed to : it was in No. 20, in the Appendix to the Tenth Report.   As to the Ranna of Gohud, it was clear that in the treaty it was meant to desert him, although the promise of support was held out.   The words were, " as " long as he behaves with propriety ;" and out of that prolific root constructions shooted forth, which were his ruin : constructions which were a complete defeazance of treaty —— a defeazance which proved that he was facrificed — that he was given up — that he was betrayed under the security of a British promise.   This conduct, he infifted, was such as difgraced us with the whole world ; the eyes of Europe were upon us in the present proceedings.   The conduct of Mr. Haftings was well known, and justice, exemplary justice, was expected.   What, then, would prove the remarks of all mankind, when they heard that the evidence, in the posseffion of Government, to bring that state criminal to justice, was withholden, because, forsooth, it would publish that which was already public ; because it would make known that which was already no fecret ; because it would difcover to the powers in India that fystem of politics with which they are already well acquainted.   If, on the present occafion, the members of Adminiftration and their adherents should prevent the fuccefs of the motion, all the world would, with reafon, confider the name and character of a British Parliament as buried under indelible difgrace.   In fhort, if the prefent motions were not granted, he faid, the refufal would difgrace the British Parliament with the whole world.

The gallery was then ordered to be cleared, that the queftion fhould be put, when

Mr. Fox.   Mr. *Fox* rofe, and defired to be favoured with a ferious anfwer to his neceffary queftion, Whether the profeffions of a determination to perfift in a refufal of the papers were actually fincere? Surely there was nothing in the rule of conduct which the gentlemen of the other fide laid down for themfelves that did not argue moft powerfully and convincingly

cingly for their production. If a specific purpose was neceffary to be mentioned, and the object of the motion requisite to be explained, there was a pointed and specific charge in the treatment of the Ranna of Gohud, who was allowed, and indeed mentioned in former treaties, as the ally and friend of Great Britain, and neglected in the general peace which terminated the Mahratta war. This was the fact, as it appeared uncontradicted, and the House ought surely to inquire whether such desertion of the friends of this country was justifiable in the Governor General. To withhold any information on this subject would be not only unjust to Mr. Hastings, who was accused, but indecent to the House, whose honour was so much concerned in the full and rigorous examination of such a conduct. There was no behaviour whatsoever which would operate more injuriously to the British interest, either in this or any other quarter, than to find that its friendship was no protection to its allies. An unwarranted defertion, if such it could be proved, must certainly be considered as a great misdemeanor; and nothing was more necessary either to the character or vindication of the person accused than to explain the grounds on which he was justified. There might possibly exist a plea of necessity for this proceeding, and, for the present moment, he would admit that it did exist. But when there was a certain assurance the allies and defendants of Great Britain had been abandoned by her in a negociation, there was a crime *prima facie* evident, and the proceedings in that negociation should certainly be laid before the House, in order to convince them of that necessity. It would be very unfair, and indeed very improper, if gentlemen should have these feelings barely when their own honour or their own characters were at stake, and seem wholly unconscious of them, when the question was against the character of others. Thus the Ministers of the time, when the late peace was concluded, knew the defection from the Loyalists to be a conduct so much in need of justification, that they very decently came down to the House, in order to excuse themselves on the ground of necessity. Whether such necessity existed, this was not for him to discuss; but the means of inquiry on the subject were undoubtedly open. Why not then pursue the same line of conduct on the present occasion, when positive and direct charges were brought against the measure? If motives of necessity recommended the treachery, why was that necessity not explained? And if principles of policy dictated the conduct, why was not that policy made known? It was indeed alledged, that the interests of the country might be endangered by the disclosure which the papers would make: but in our Constitution there were both advantages and defects, and the same must also be true of

every

every other conſtitution and ſpecies of government. We, however, were of opinion, that the advantages which we conſtitutionally poſſeſſed by far outbalanced the diſadvantages; and it was one of the leading principles, to prefer the reſponſibility which belonged to our officers and miniſters before the ſecrecy which was deemed ſo neceſſary in other countries. Then ſuppoſing (for he was far from admitting it) that ſome injury might be apprehended from the production of theſe papers, it was only the neceſſary conſequence to which every inveſtigation was liable; and there could be no inquiry of a public nature, in which circumſtances did not come out which might better have remained a ſecret. The Houſe, then, would do well to reflect what a precedent they were laying down, for all future public officers to take advantage of. For if this excuſe ſhould once be admitted, there was no circumſtance, and no ſituation, to which it would not be found to apply. A right honourable and learned gentleman (Mr. Dundas) had, on this, as well as a former night, endeavoured to play off the conduct of Mr. Haſtings, poſterior to the Reports of the Committee, againſt the delinquency of his former meaſure, to which the right honourable gentleman had borne ſuch full and ample teſtimonies in the courſe of theſe Reports. But what was the meaning of this language, or what other ſentiment did it expreſs but this? " I " think his conduct ſince that period laudable and good, and " I wiſh you to think ſo with me; but, in the mean time, " I am reſolved that you ſhall have no reaſon to think ſo " beyond my aſſertion, and I will deny you the information " which is neceſſary to convince you of it." Sufficient had been the remarks of his right honourable friend to prove, that not even the moſt trivial cauſe exiſted for thoſe apprehenſions of danger which gentlemen on the other ſide of the Houſe, for reaſons beſt known to themſelves, thought proper to expreſs; and therefore he truſted that the Houſe would call for arguments leſs frivolous, before they gave their ſanction to the withholding of the neceſſary papers.

Mr. Chancellor *Pitt* remarked, that he could not avoid expreſſing his aſtoniſhment at the unmerited rigour experienced on this occaſion by his right honourable and learned friend, only becauſe he had laid down a principle (apparently indiſpenſable on ſimilar occaſions) that no vote ſhould paſs for the production of papers, unleſs their neceſſary application to a ſpecific object were demonſtrable beyond the power of diſpute. The right honourable gentleman who took the lead in this proſecution had expreſſed and acquitted himſelf with a degree of candour and openneſs which redounded much to his credit: but he certainly did not offer arguments of ſufficent force to evince the neceſſity of producing

Mr. Chancellor Pitt.

theſe

thefe papers.   Difpofed as he was to act through the whole
of the bufinefs with the utmoft impartiality, he could fee nothing in the conduct of Mr. Haftings refpecting the Mahratta
peace which did not deferve the higheft commendation.   He
had indeed effected it by diffolving a league of the moft
powerful Indian princes which could poffibly become confederates for our deftruction ; and he was aftonifhed that any
man, who ever was a minifter, who ever looked forward to
be a minifter, could think of cenfuring fo fuccefsful and glorious an achievement.   When this country fhould, at any
time, be threatened with, or engaged in a war with its natural enemies, was there any Minifter who, in oppofing the
houfe of Bourbon, would not think it the moft meritorious
of all fervices to be able to diffolve the family compact ? and
precifely in the fame fituation was Mr. Haftings refpecting
the Mahratta peace.   He made it at a time when the continuance of war would have proved abfolute and inevitable
ruin, and he completed it with an addrefs and ingenuity
which did him immortal honour.   He was not fo converfant
in Indian politics as the right honourable gentleman who preceded in the debate ; but he certainly confidered this part of
Mr. Haftings's conduct in that light which he juft now mentioned.   How far other charges might be fubftantiated againft
him, remained yet to be determined.   It was certainly a point
of juftice that delinquents fhould be punifhed ; but this fhould
be done with the niceft regard to public fafety.   When fufficient ground of guilt was laid down, there was certainly a
reafon for laying afide thofe prudential maxims which, on
flight and curfory accufations, fhould be moft ftrictly adhered to.   If the papers now called for were granted, there
would of courfe enfue various difcoveries which might have
ruinous confequences to our officers in India.   There were
certainly means ufed to detach the different princes one from
the other ; but to difcover the mediums through which this
policy operated would deftroy the future confidence in Britifh
politics, and the field of negociation which it was fo effential
to the profperity of this county to enjoy ; and it might not
only be a bar to our future operations, but effect the fituations
of perfons now in India, who were inftrumental and ferviceable
able in bringing about that great object.   A right honourable
gentleman had attempted to prove that thofe proceedings
could be no fecret in India, becaufe all intelligence of that
kind was fully communicated in the Indian Gazette.   In order to fhow the weaknefs of that argument, he would only
remind him of that period when his right honourable friend
(Mr. Fox) went into office, when his country was labouring
under the preffure of a war againft combined and powerful
...es.   His policy at that time was to detach a part of that
                                                confederacy

confederacy by offering feparate terms to the Dutch, and, at the fame time, propofing exclufive terms to the Americans. The attempt was certainly laudable, and, though unfuccefsful, the right honourable gentleman had undoubtedly the merit of deferving well of his country. But would it, therefore, be juft to affert that any country in Europe knew the detail and particulars of thefe negociations, becaufe there were Gazettes in England and Holland? Certainly not. The right honourable gentleman had, however, ftrengthened his arguments by reafoning not only on the motion immediately before the Houfe, but alfo on others which he intended to put. He fhould applaud fuch a conduct in general, as it would fave much time, and be equally proper where the connection between them was fo intimate. But he would not admit him the full extent of his obfervations in accufing a right honourable gentleman of oppofing all his motions, while he argued only on one particular fubject. There was one of his motions which he certainly would not oppofe, becaufe there was laid a fufficient ground of inquiry : he meant that refpecting the Ranna of Gohud. However he might differ with him refpecting the propriety of the Ranna of Gohud being excluded from the peace, he certainly thought it a fair fubject of interrogation. This man, he underftood, previous to the Mahratta peace, had entered into a feparate negociation with Moodhajee Scindia for himfelf, without the knowledge or concurrence of the Governor General of Bengal. After being detected in this act of infidelity, it was not ftrange that he fhould not be admitted to the benefit of a peace which was meant to ferve the friends, and not the foes, of Great Britain. It was not againft fuch a motion that his objections fhould ever be brought forward ; and even with thefe ideas did he hold himfelf fully juftified in pofitively refifting that motion, of which one confequence muft be a difclofure of fecrets which found policy required us to preferve inviolable.

Mr. *Fox* faid, that he felt it neceffary to bring into clearer points of view fome allufions ftarted during the courfe of the debate, and even touched upon beyond the walls of Parliament. Thefe went to the fubject of his negociation for a feparate peace with Holland. He was well aware that the right honourable gentleman did not mention it by way of blame, nor did he wifh to impute to him any fuch intention ; but as it had fo often been glanced at, he was glad to have the opportunity of fpeaking two or three words to it in this public manner. He was forry that the Houfe was fo thin of members, but he was pleafed to fee fo full a gallery. When this meafure, of detaching Holland and America from the confederation which was formed againft us, was firft propofed,

was

was only three days in office, and consequently was obliged to meet those people in the Cabinet from whom he was accustomed to differ upon political subjects; and yet, what was a circumstance that did not often happen, he had the honour to propose that measure with the unanimous concurrence of all His Majesty's Cabinet Ministers. This he thought himself at liberty to mention, because, though it might be improper to state the dissensions or disagreements in the Cabinet, there would certainly be no impropriety in mentioning their unanimity. He would farther observe, that this policy was by no means ineffectual as to some of its objects, though, in others, it certainly had not the wished-for success: for these gentlemen who were then in office might well recollect, that the disposition of some courts in Europe was not then extremely favourable to the country, and that the measure how alluded to had at least the effect of averting these consequences which might otherwise have been apprehended.. Having said this much for the allusion, he would next return to the propriety of admitting the present papers. He observed, that it was expressed in the treaty subsisting between the Company and the Ranna of Gohud, that he was to be protected by the powers of Great Britain against their mutual foes. In consequence of which, he had lent his services during the war, and was to have been of course included in the peace. There were also (according to Mr. Hastings's own letters) several other Rajahs and Princes who had the same, or similar, claims upon the protection of Great Britain; and yet it appeared from the Mahratta peace, that none of them were included in the provision of it. This was not the time to argue from what motives, or upon what policy it was done. But the omission was *prima facie* evidence of either treachery or guilt, to obviate, or to substantiate which, was the object of the present motion, and was, in his judgement, a debt claimed as well by the justice due to the sufferers in India, as to the dignity of Parliament and the acquittal or condemnation of Mr. Hastings. He agreed with the right honourable gentleman, that it was not sufficient ground for the production of all papers, to say one gentleman is the prosecutor, and would pledge himself to prove their application to the object in view. But, in the present case, the production of the papers could not be followed by any political peril whatsoever, and the strongest reasons existed in favour of the disclosure of their contents.

Mr. *Burke* remarked, that the right honourable gentleman, (the Chancellor of the Exchequer) like a cautious warrior, instead of attacking the main body of the forces of his enemy, had remained satisfied with mere skirmishes and the pillaging of the stragglers in the rear. He by no means asserted the

Mr. Burke.

Gazette informations to be that on which the princes of India moſt relied for information; but he contended, that ſo complete was their knowledge of every circumſtance relative to that peace, that what was made ſecrets of in the Houſe of Commons of England, were matters of notoriety in India, and had been publiſhed in moſt of their papers. But the ſource of their intelligence was ſuch as could not fail them; for the moſt enormous ſums were expended in procuring ſpies, even in official ſituations in our ſettlements; and, by comparing notes, they had fully and ſubſtantially diſcovered that treachery which our officers employed againſt them individually; the conſequence of which was, that they had now formed a league of an offenſive import againſt our ſettlements, which would be beſt and moſt effectually oppoſed, by taking ſuch meaſures here as would ſhew them that theſe offences, at leaſt, were not to have the ſanction of the Parliament of Great Britain. Having read ſeveral extracts, as well from the Reports of the Committee of Secrecy, as from the treaties which lay upon the table, Mr. Burke expreſſed his hopes, that, as he undertook the arduous and diſagreeable duty of moving certain reſolutions which could lead the Commons of Great Britain into an effectual proſecution of the man whom they had before condemned, he ſhould be allowed thoſe papers which he deemed neceſſary for the purpoſe, as well as for the juſtice which we owed the miſerable inhabitants of a deſolated country, whoſe injuries he had never loſt ſight of, and was determined to perſevere ſince the firſt moment he became acquainted with them, and in whoſe cauſe he would not relax his exertions. If, on the contrary, a majority ſhould, by their diſſenting voices, deprive him of the opportunity to gather up materials indiſpenſably requiſite for the moſt complete ſubſtantiation of his charges, he muſt avail himſelf of ſcattered pieces, and try from theſe to ſtamp validity upon his accuſations.

[The Houſe was again proceeding to divide, and the ſtrangers ordered to withdraw; but the debate continuing for ſome time longer, the gallery was again opened. In the interval between excluſion and admiſſion, Mr. Pitt and Mr. Wyndham ſpoke.]

Mr. Wilberforce.

Mr. *Wilberforce* profeſſed himſelf much unacquainted with Indian politics, and would therefore confine himſelf to a recommendation to the Miniſter to be extremely cautious how he ſhould ſuffer any papers to be produced which were likely to do injury to the ſtate. The danger of producing thoſe papers at a time ſo near the tranſaction of the peace, might have the moſt ſerious conſequences to thoſe who were concerned in the buſineſs, and who might perhaps be in confidential ſituations with thoſe very princes whoſe ſecrets they
might

might have revealed. He cautioned the House not to be led into any warmth from the circumstances which were liable to be mentioned on these occasions, requesting, at the same time, that the gentlemen on the other side would not persist in harrassing Ministers with a demand of papers which they knew could not be complied with.

Mr. *Burke*, in reply, said, the honourable gentleman had acted the part of a wise man in offering his advice, when he was certain it would be taken; but at the same time might have spared his reproachful admonition to him, who had certainly no design of embarrassing Ministers by his conduct. But he thought it no good omen to the cause, if papers of so simple and fair a nature were subjects of embarrassment to those now in power.   Mr. Burke.

Major *Scott* contended that the Rajah of Gohud was not entitled to any provision in the peace then made. He also vindicated Mr. Hastings with regard to the omission of another Rajah in the Mahratta peace, which was done at his own request. He then observed, that the difference now subsisting between the right honourable gentleman (Mr. Fox) and Mr. Hastings was not greater than that which prevailed between him and his noble friend in the blue ribband; nor were his charges more severe against the one than against the other. In all the proceedings against Mr. Hastings, and amidst all the abuse poured out against him, he (Major Scott) had never entertained the smallest apprehensions, nor ever made any overtures of accommodation. On the other hand, when the right honourable gentleman brought in his India bill, an intimation was given, in a private conversation, which he had with a person of authority, that matters might be accommodated; and he made no doubt, had Mr. Hastings then come home, he would have heard nothing of all this calumny, and all these serious accusations.   Maj. Scott.

Mr. *Fox* immediately rose, and said, that, on a subject which concerned his honour and character, he would not hesitate a moment to offer himself again to the House. He would first premise, that at no period could he declare that offers were made to him, either by Mr. Hastings or his agents, in order to bring about an accommodation; for if there had, he would instantly have treated them with the most absolute and marked refusal. At the same time he would assert, upon his honour, that no proposal whatever was made to Mr. Hastings or his friends, with either his knowledge or his concurrence; and he was also certain that no such proposal ever came from any of his colleagues. So that whoever made, or even hinted at such an offer as coming from him, did it without the smallest shadow of authority. Indeed it frequently happened, that, during consultations which he had with his   Mr. Fox.

friends on the subject of his India bill, it had often been intimated to him, that it would be better to drop all proceedings against Mr. Hastings, as being a powerful enemy; but he would never listen to any advances of this nature: nay, so far was this from being understood an authoritative offer by the honourable gentleman (Major Scott) himself, if any offer had been made, that he objected to him in that House, that he made the complaints against Mr. Hastings the principal ground and excuse for the provisions of his bill. If so, then how absurd would it be to require, or even to accept, his support of it.

Maj. Scott.

Major *Scott* still insisted that the proposal had been made to him; but as the gentleman from whom it came was not now present, he would wave all farther explanations until he saw him in his place.

After this the House divided on Mr. Burke's motion, when the numbers were,

Ayes - - - - - - - - - - 44
Noes - - - - - - - - - - 87

Majority - - 43

Mr. Burke now moved the following motions:

" That No. 20 of the Appendix to the Tenth Report,
" which was made from the Select Committee, appointed to
" take into consideration the state of the administration of
" justice in the provinces of Bengal, Bahar, and Orissa, con-
" taining copy of a letter from Mr. Hastings to Colonel
" Muir, dated Chunargur, 10th September, 1781, and also
" translate of an agreement between Colonel Muir, on the
" part of the English Company, and Mahajee Scindia for
" himself, dated 15th October, 1781, might be read;" and
the same was read accordingly.

" That the articles of agreement, made and concluded at
" Fort William, in Bengal, between the Governor General
" and Council, for the affairs of the East-India Company,
" on behalf of the said Company, on the one part, and
" Maha Raja Luckindar Bahadur, Ranna of Gohud, for
" himself and his successors, on the other part, inserted in
" No. 239 of the Appendix to the Sixth Report, which was
" made from the Committee of Secrecy, appointed to inquire
" into the causes of the war in the Carnatic, and of the
" condition of the British possessions in those parts, might be
" read;" and the same was read accordingly.

Then the question being put, " That there be laid before
" this House, copies or duplicates of all papers relative to the
" last peace with the Mahrattas, or any demand made by the
" Mahrattas concerning the cession or restoration of any ter-
" ritories now in the possession of the Company, or its allies,

" or

" or of the payment of any chout, (or fourth part of the
" revenues) or of any sum in lieu thereof, or concerning any
" payment of money, or loan, to any of the said Mahrattas,
" made or paid since the 1st of January, 1779," it passed in
the negative.

Mr. Burke then moved,

" That there be laid before this House, copies or duplicates
" of all letters concerning the delivering up of Ragonaut
" Row, the Rajah of Bopal, or the Ranna of Gohud, or
" concerning the terms by which Futty Sing Guicawar, as
" also all letters of Lieutenant-colonel Camack, or Colonel
" Muir, pointing out the nature and extent of our connec-
" tions with each of the Rajahs engaged with the Company
" in any act of hostility, and the claims which their past ser-
" vices may have given them to our protection."

" That an act, made in the 13th year of the reign of His
" present Majesty, intituled, ' An Act for establishing cer-
" tain Regulations for the better Management of the Affairs
" of the East-India Company, as well in India as in Europe,'
" might be read;" and the same was read accordingly.

" That there be laid before this House, copies or duplicates
" of all letters concerning the delivering up of Ragonaut
" Row, the Rajah of Bopal, or the Ranna of Gohud, or
" concerning the terms by which Futty Sing Guicawar, as
" also all letters of Lieutenant-colonel Camack, or Colonel
" Muir, pointing out the nature and extent of our connec-
" tions with each of the Rajahs engaged with the Company
" in any act of hostility, and the claims which their past ser-
" vices may have given them to our protection." It passed
in the negative.

Ordered, " That there be laid before this House, copies or
" duplicates of all correspondence relative to the Ranna of
" Gohud, not included in the Reports of the Committee of
" Secrecy, and to any application from him concerning the
" proceedings against the said Ranna by Scindia, the Mah-
" ratta General, together with all the minutes, or other pro-
" ceedings thereon, since the year 1781."

The House adjourned.

Monday, 6th March.

Mr. *Lewis* brought in the bill for building a bridge across   Mr. Lewis.
Menai Strait, from Carnarvonshire to the Isle of Anglesea,
which was read a first time, and ordered to be read a second
time. On the motion being put, " That this bill be read a
" second time upon that day fortnight,"

Mr. *Parry* observed, that he had been instructed by his   Mr. Parry.
constituents (who meant to oppose the bill) to desire that sufficient

cient time might be allowed them to fend up witneffes, which they wifhed to have examined againft the bill; and therefore he fhould move, by way of amendment, to leave out the words, " this day fortnight," and infert the words, " this day " month."

Drake,   Mr. *Drake*, jun. defired the Houfe to underftand, that they were called upon to vote for deferring the prefervation of human lives; for fuch, in fact, was poftponing the paffing of fuch a bill as the prefent. Not longer fince than the 5th of December, fixty or feventy people were loft in croffing the Menai. The account of that fatal accident muft have harrowed up the feelings of every gentleman prefent; and he hoped that it would ftimulate their humanity to difplay itfelf in giving all poffible efficacy and expedition to the paffing of a bill which had fo laudable an object for its purpofe.

Mr. Burton and one or two other gentlemen fpoke on the fubject, when the Houfe proceeded to divide; but, after the gallery was cleared, it was given up; and the Houfe determined that the bill fhould be read a fecond time upon the twenty-firft.

The order of the day, for going into a Committee of Supply, having been read, Mr. M. A. Taylor took the chair, when

Mr. Chancellor Pitt rofe, and moved, as modifications of the act impofing certain duties upon retail fhops,

" That all the duties charged by an act, made in the laft " feffion of Parliament, intituled, ' An Act for granting to " His Majefty certain Duties on Retail Shops,' (except the " duties charged upon any houfe, the annual rent whereof " fhall be thirty pounds or upwards) do ceafe, determine, " and be no longer paid or payable."

" That in lieu, and inftead of the duties charged upon " fuch houfes, there fhall be raifed the following rates: that " is to fay, for and upon every houfe or other building, any " part of which fhall be ufed as a fhop, for the purpofe of " felling by retail any goods, wares, or merchandizes, of " the yearly rent or value of five pounds, and under ten " pounds, there fhall be paid the annual fum of four pence " in the pound of fuch rent: for and upon every fuch " houfe, &c. of the yearly rent or value of ten pounds, and " under fifteen pounds, there fhall be paid the annual fum " of eight pence in the pound of fuch rent: for and upon " every fuch houfe, &c. of the yearly rent or value of fif- " teen pounds, and under twenty pounds, there fhall be paid " the annual fum of one fhilling in the pound of fuch rent: " for and upon every fuch houfe, &c. of the yearly rent or " value of twenty pounds, and under twenty-five pounds, " there fhall be paid the annual fum of one fhilling and

" three

" three pence in the pound of such rent: and for and upon
" every such house, &c. of the yearly rent or value of
" twenty-five pounds, and under thirty pounds, there shall
" be paid the annual sum of one shilling and nine pence in
" the pound of such rent."

Mr. Alderman *Le Mesurier* expressed his hopes, that, as Mr. Ald. Le-
the two resolutions were perfectly new to the Public, the Mesurier.
right honourable gentleman would not call upon the Committee to vote them immediately, but let them lie upon the
table during the space of two or three days, in order that the
metropolis might have time to know what they were, and
how, in consequence of their nature, the tax would become
lightened. He feared that the two resolutions would afford
but little satisfaction to the shopkeepers of London, upon
whom the weight of the tax chiefly rested. The alteration
of the quantum of tax to be paid for all houses rented at 20l.,
25l., and 30l., could not prove any alleviation to the majority of the shopkeepers of London, Westminster, and Southwark, because in very few of the streets of the metropolis,
and so more especially in that part of it called Southwark
did the shopkeepers reside in houses so low rented as from 20l.
to 30l. He was not one of those to grudge another his good
fortune, merely because he had not the happiness to be equally
fortunate; and therefore he rejoiced that the country shopkeepers were to obtain material alleviation, as they must necessarily be in consequence of the modification which the
right honourable gentleman had just proposed; but he might
be permitted to remark, that the modifications in question
were an additional proof of the partiality of the tax with respect to the town shopkeepers.

The motions passed.

The estimates of the Ordnance having been referred to the
Committtee of Supply,

Captain *James Luttrell* stated, that, during the course of the Captain J.
present year, no debt had been incurred; neither did any un- Luttrell.
provided services exist: a circumstance unparallelled, he believed, at any prior period. Such was the œconomy of the
Board, that they had so far enforced their plan of proceeding
as to avoid calling upon the House for any thing, except
what appeared in the estimates; and these stood as follows in
their relation to the charge of the Office of Ordnance for the
year 1786:

L A N D

LAND SERVICE.

ORDINARY.

	£.	s.	d.	£.	s.	d.
Salaries and rents to the Master General, principal officers, clerks, and attendants, employed at the Tower — — —	15266	8	—			

And at the following places, viz.

	£.	s.	d.
Greenwich, Windsor, Hampton Court, and St. James's — — —	226	—	—
Woolwich — — —	1334	10	—
Purfleet — — —	541	5	—
Gravesend and Tilbury — —	255	—	—
Chatham — — —	600	—	—
Upnor Castle — — —	80	—	—
Sheerness — — —	380	—	—
Feversham — — —	290	—	—
Dover — — —	120	—	—
Portsmouth — — —	814	15	—
Priddys-hard — — —	170	—	—
Plymouth — — —	644	15	—
Keyham Point — — —	170	—	—
Storekeepers at Pendennis, Scilly Island, Chester Castle and Liverpool, Berwick, Carlisle, Tinmouth Castle and Clifford's Fort, Hull, Yarmouth, and Landguard Fort —	430	—	—
Guernsey — — —	448	2	6
Jersey — — —	448	2	6
Isle of Man — — —	166	—	—
Rent for use of land and houses —	554	17	—
Establishment of the laboratory at Woolwich, and for proving powder — —	1876	5	—
Establishment of the office of Inspector of Artillery, and for proving guns — —	923	7	6
Establishment of the office of Superintendant of Military Machines — —	282	17	6
	£. 26022	5	—

	£.	s.	d.
One half of which is charged to the Sea Service —	13011	2	6

Pay of Civil Officers and Artificers at

	£.	s.	d.
North Britain — — — —	554	10	—
Gibraltar — — — — —	1411	7	6
Jamaica — — — — —	292	—	—
St. Christopher — — — —	584	—	—
Antigua — — — — —	584	—	—
Dominica — — — —	584	—	—
Carried over —	£. 17921	—	—

					£.		
	Brought over				17021	—	—
St. Vincent	—	—	—	—	584	—	—
Barbadoes	—	—	—	—	584	—	—
Grenada	—	—	—	—	584	—	—
Bahama Islands	—	—	—	—	474	10	—
Quebec	—	—	—	—	861	15	—
Halifax	—	—	—	—	662	5	—
New Brunswick	—	—	—	—	629	12	6
St. John's and Placentia, Newfoundland	—	—	—	1277	10	—

Pay of mafter gunners at the feveral garrifons and batteries in Great Britain, and of the gunners at St. James's Park and the Tower of London, with their allowance for coals and candles   3416 17 6

Charges incident to the Tower and the feveral other forts and garrifons in Great Britain, Guernfey, and Jerfey, in taking remains of ftores, pay of labourers, books, paper, coals, candles, cartage, meffages, and poftage of letters   —   18000 — —

Ordinary repairs of fortifications, bridges, gates, platforms, barracks, ftorehoufes, pallifadoes, making new and repairing old carriages in the feveral forts and caftles in Great Britain, Guernfey, and Jerfey —   —   —   15000 — —

Furnifhing beds, bedfteads, fheets, &c. and repairing the fame, at the feveral forts, caftles, and garrifons in Great Britain, Guernfey, and Jerfey   —   —   —   4379 4 7

Expence of ftores and ammunition for garrifons, and fmall ftores for the common duty of regiments, in Great Britain, Guernfey, and Jerfey   —   —   —   6000 — —

Cleaning and repairing fmall arms in the Tower   —   2000 — —

Pay of the corps of Engineers   —   —   10402 10 —

Pay of the royal regiment of artillery, confifting of 3282 men, officers included   —   —   106465 11 2

Eftablifhment of the civil officers, profeffors, and mafters of the Royal Military Academy at Woolwich   —   1798 12 6

Eftablifhment of draughtfmen in the Tower of London, for fervice in Great Britain and foreign garrifons   —   2025 15 —

Pay of fuperannuated and difabled men, half pay of reduced officers, widows' penfions, and allowances to officers for good fervices, purfuant to His Majefty's warrants   —   20569 21 6

Sums to be paid at the Treafury, and at the Exchequer, for fees on the fum of 300,096l. 17s. 1d. being the amount of this eftimate   —   —   —   646 — —

Ordinary   —   £. 213382 14 9

E X T R A O R D I N A R I E S.

NEWFOUNDLAND.

	£.	s.	d.	£.	s.	d.
For repairs of fortifications, barracks, and quarters for officers, staff, contingencies, and current service	3000	—	—			
For fuel for the troops	1500	—	—			
				4500	—	—

QUEBEC.

For staff, contingencies, and current service	1500	—	—

JAMAICA.

For staff, contingencies, and current service	1500	—	—

BAHAMA ISLANDS.

For contingencies and current service	1000	—	—

WEST-INDIA ISLANDS.

For staff, contingencies, and current service	6000	—	—

GIBRALTAR.

	£.	s.	d.	£.	s.	d.
Pay of the company of artificers	4492	10	10			
For staff, contingencies, and current service	3840	—	—			
For excavation of the Souterrain works	1181	11	6			
For re-establishing quarters, and repairs of barracks	3900	—	—			
For ordinary repairs of fortifications, storehouses, magazines, &c.	3300	—	—			
For providing and burning lime	1350	—	—			
For supply of bricks and other materials, to carry on the foregoing works	1200	—	—			
For repairing roads, drains, communications, &c.	450	—	—			
For extraordinary repairs of works	10000	—	—			
				29714	2	4

SCOTLAND.

For repair of the several forts, castles, and barracks in Scotland, staff, contingencies, and current service	5000	—	—

TINMOUTH CASTLE, &c.

For repair of the batteries and works at Tinmouth Castle, Clifford's Fort, and Tinmouth barracks	1000	—	—

CINQUE-PORTS DIVISION.

For staff, contingencies, and current service	1000	—	—

FEVERSHAM.

For buildings, necessary works, and implements for carrying on the manufacture of gunpowder	2000	—	—

Carried over	£. 53214	2	4

| | Brought over | — | £. 53214 | 2 | 4 |

CHATHAM.

	£.	s.	d.

For repair of the barracks at Chatham, and for repairs of Gillingham, Cockhamwood, and Howness Forts, staff, contingencies, and current service . — — 1500 — —

For repairs of the powder magazines, &c. at Upnor Castle — — 1000 — —

2500 — —

SHEERNESS.

For repair of the breakwaters, staff, contingencies, and current service — — 1000 — —

WOOLWICH.

Towards the extraordinary expences of the laboratory — — — 2000 — —

For staff, contingencies, and charges, attending the barracks — — — 1000 — —

3000 — —

PORTSMOUTH.

For staff, contingencies, repairs of old works, and other buildings, at Portsmouth, and various places in the division, and for current service 6000 — —

For the works near the dock yard — 3000 — —

9000 — —

GOSPORT.

Towards carrying on the works at Fort Monckton 10000 — —

For staff, contingencies, and repair of barracks and the lines — — — 1000 — —

11000 — —

PLYMOUTH.

For staff, contingencies, and repairs of the citadel, and various places in the division, and for current service — — 2000 — —

REGIMENT OF ARTILLERY.

For contingencies — — 5000 — —

Extraordinaries	—	—	86714	2	4
Ordinary	—	—	213382	14	9
Ordinary and Extraordinaries	-	£. 300096	17	1

RICHMOND, &c.
Master General of His Majesty's Ordnance.

W. HOWE, JAMES LUTTRELL, G. CRAWFURD,
J. ALDRIDGE, THO. BAILLIE.

In conclusion, Captain Luttrell moved, "That a sum,
"not exceeding twenty-five thousand pounds, be voted for
"the expence of Ordnance for land service for the year
"1786," meaning to apply the 50,000l. in hand to the same
use.

Mr. Herbert.

Mr. *Herbert* stated, that, as the intended system of fortifications, for the defence of the dock yards, was set aside,
something ought to be done towards quieting the claims of
those persons whose lands and houses had been taken from
them to make room for the fortifications, and who had not as
yet been able to receive the value, the rent, or any sort of
return.

Mr. Holdf-
worth.

Mr. *Holdsworth* observed, that, in having given his vote
against the system proposed, he did not mean that it should
be imagined that his opinion was that no fortifications were
necessary. He only designed to vote against the proposed system, or any other which went upon the idea, that the whole
of our navy might be out of port at one time: an idea
which he could subscribe to as very likely to happen. He
had taken the trouble to examine the present estimate, and
compare it with the Ordnance estimate at the commencement
of the last peace: he wished, therefore, to ask the honourable gentleman opposite to him two or three questions, and he
really should ask them with no other view than a desire to obtain information. The amount of the Ordnance estimates altogether was much larger this year than in the year to which
he had referred. He wished to know the reason? The corps
of engineers, and the royal regiment of artillery, were also
considerably increased in numbers, and consequently in expence. He should be glad to know why this was so? Another question he wanted information upon was, Whether the
expence of invalids was included in the charges for engineer
corps and artillery?

Mr. Lut-
trell.

Mr. *Luttrell* answered, that the Ordnance estimate for the
present year, when examined, would be found to be, on the
average of a number of years, about the same with the estimates of the last peace: that, in fact, the expences of the
department of Ordnance were more increased under several
heads than usual, and that next year there would be greater
charges still under the head of extraordinaries. This increase
was unavoidable. With regard to the corps of engineers,
great complaint had been made at the commencement of the
last war that there were so few engineers; and therefore the
corps had been augmented in number, and consequently the
expence incurred on that account was larger. The regiment
of artillery was also increased. Mr. Luttrell professed himself ready to give honourable gentlemen any explanation on
any part of the subject which they might wish to receive.

Sir

Sir *Grey Cooper* said, that he rose not to speak to the question, but merely to the form and order of their proceedings.
The motion appeared to him irregular. The amount of the
Ordnance estimate was 300,000l.; therefore, in point of form,
the resolution should state that sum, and afterwards, in the
Committee of Ways and Means, provision might be made
for the 50,000l. in hand, in consequence of the system of
fortification round the dock yards, for which it had been
voted, having been advanced.

Mr. Chancellor *Pitt* remarked, that he perfectly coincided
with the opinion of the honourable Baronet, that the motion
was inaccurate, and that the whole amount of this estimate
ought to be voted in the Committee of Supply, and the
50,000l. lying in the Exchequer be brought to account in the
Committee of Ways and Means, and there disposed of for
the service of the year. Although the House had come to no
specific resolution on a former night, when the subject of the
fortifications was before them, declaratory of its sense of that
measure, the words of his motion having been negatived,
and those proposed to be substituted in their stead having been
withdrawn, yet, as their general opinion was easily collected
from what had passed in that debate, it should be a law to him,
however he might regret the failure of a plan which he did
most sincerely think extremely beneficial to the Public. He
joined in opinion with an honourable friend, that the whole
system of fortifications had not been condemned, but that
the sense of the House was only to be understood as being adverse to fortifications to the extent in which they had been
proposed; and he was perfectly convinced that the principles
on which gentlemen had argued and voted against the fortifications were extremely meritorious and well meant; nor did
he by any means pretend to hold that those who opposed them
were bound to suggest any plan of fortification or security for
our dock yards in room of that which they had rejected. It
was the duty of His Majesty's Ministers alone to devise the
means of public defence, and of Parliament to approve or
condemn; and if those means which appeared to Administration to be the best were rejected, they were bound to produce
such as they thought next best. In the present estimate it
would be found that there were two sums stated for the purpose of fortifications; however, part of the general plan
which had already been disapproved by Parliament (he apprehended) would come within the description of such parts of
it as seemed to be excepted against by such gentlemen as were
in opposition to the whole. There was a sum of 10,000l. for
Fort Monckton, and of 3000l. for completing the lines at
present subsisting for the defence of the dock yards, which,
from being unfinished, was nearly in the same state as if a

successful

Sir Grey Cooper.

*Mr. Chan-
cellor Pitt.*

succefsful attack had been made, and a breach accomplished. If, therefore, it were not to be completed, it would be abfolutely ufelefs, and it would confequently prove more advifeable to level the whole, and convert the materials to fome other purpofe. Thefe lines were calculated to protect the dock yards from immediate deftruction, in cafe an enemy fhould debark at the moft obvious and practicable places of landing at South-Sea Caftle, or the place where Fort Monckton ftood; and therefore, together with that laft-mentioned place, he apprehended the fenfe of every gentleman was, that if any part of the plan ought to be adopted, it was that which related to the completing thofe two works.

Mr. Fox.

Mr. *Fox* faid, that it gave him much pleafure to reflect, that, when the right honourable gentleman expatiated upon the nature of minifterial refponfibility, his remarks were unexceptionable. He had very properly declared that he had no right to demand from any gentleman, who voted againft the fortifications, a plan to fupply the place of that which had been rejected. It was, however, a different language from that which he held upon the late debate concerning this fubject; but he fuppofed the conduct of the right honourable gentleman on that occafion proceeded from the effects of difappointment. It was undoubtedly the duty of Minifters to furnifh plans for the public defence and fervice, and to fubmit them to the judgement of that Houfe, who had nothing to do but fimply to approve or reject; and, in cafe of the latter, Minifters were to fupply the place of fuch plans as were rejected with others lefs exceptionable. The very meaning of the word refponfible was a fufficient proof that it could not apply to the whole Houfe of Commons; for how could they anfwer to a charge which alone implied refponfibility? Indeed, from the fingular manner in which the queftion alluded to had been determined, it would prove more eafy to fix the refponfibility on one individual perfon; but he fhould be very forry to hear it contended, that the Speaker of the Houfe, or the Chairman of a Committee, fhould be regarded as anfwerable for the votes of that Houfe. For his own part, he could not entertain the moft diftant idea of oppofing fo flight a charge as 3000l. for the completion of the unfinifhed works at Portfmouth; yet he muft beg leave to fignify his earneft wifhes that Adminiftration would not venture to folicit this grant from the Houfe without a previous declaration that the unfupported ftate of the dock yards rendered it indifpenfably requifite.

Mr. Chancellor Pitt.

Mr. Chancellor *Pitt* anfwered, that the right honourable gentleman had ventured to throw out an infinuation which called for an immediate reply. He chofe to fignify that his approbation of the fentiments which he (the Chancellor of

the

the Exchequer) had uttered during the course of the present debate was much greater than any which he could confer upon those opinions which he delivered during a preceding day, concerning the subject of fortifications: opinions which he acknowledged himself ready to consider as the effects of disappointment. Mr. Pitt professed himself willing,to grant that he was most severely disappointed; yet was it, he asked, a disappointment of a personal object? Of such a disappointment only he should be asked to shew the effects; but he was always ready to avow the sense which he should feel of a disappointment in his hopes of promoting the public welfare. On such occasions he experienced, and constantly should experience, concern for the sake of the Public only; and he flattered himself that his disappointment at the rejection of any plan of his would, at all times, proceed from the same causes which might induce him to propose his plans — his anxiety for the welfare of his country. On such occasions, therefore, he should give the right honourable gentleman leave to make use of the language which he had uttered, but which he was also fond of proceeding to, when he was less entitled to this freedom, and when he must not expect to meet with so ready an acquiescence on his part. It was, however, rather singular that the right honourable gentleman should now approve of his language on this day, and have disapproved of it before; for it happened that on both days his language had been exactly the same—that it was the duty of His Majesty's Ministers, and of no other, to contrive and produce proper plans for the public service; and if that House disapproved of such plans, then to suggest others in their stead; and although they were not answerable for such misfortunes as might arise from the rejection of their plans, yet they were highly accountable if they should omit the means, whatever they might be, of remedying the evils resulting from the rejection of the original plan; but he imagined that so soon after the event of the last debate on the subject of fortifications, it would not be expected that Ministers should come forward at that time with a new system. He went over the general grounds of the former debate, and pointed out the different objects to which the consideration, first of the Ministers, and afterwards of the House, ought to be directed, when any new system was to be adopted, as first, whether to fortify the landing places most adjacent to the dock yards, whether to fortify the dock yards themselves only, or whether to fortify both; for as to the fortifying the country surrounding the dock yards, that seemed to him to be the part of the plan of which chiefly the House had expressed its disapprobation. In conclusion, Mr. Pitt remarked,

that,

that, in his idea, the services to which the right honourable gentleman alluded were positively necessary.

Mr. Fox.   Mr. *Fox* replied, that none of the observations which had just fallen from the right honourable gentleman were sufficiently cogent to gain over his retraction from the remark, that all responsibility rested with Ministers, and not with that House; but he was ready to admit that the right honourable gentleman had put it very fairly in his last speech, notwithstanding he had chosen to persist in calling his language of that day, and on the 28th instant, one and the same language. For his own part, he would vote for the present estimate, without exception, as the sum asked for fortifications was so small, and, in confidence, the right honourable gentleman having declared, that he considered the repair of Fort Monckton, and other works, as unavoidably requisite.

Colonel Norton.   Colonel *Norton* declared, that, in voting against the extensive plan of fortifications on the 28th of February, he meant no more than to signify his objection to that particular plan.

Ld. Hood.   Lord *Hood* observed, that he rose to correct some misapprehensions of the opinions with which he troubled the House on a preceding night. His argument had not gone to the idea, that the whole of our navy would be out at sea at the same time, but merely to prove that any thing which tended to give internal security at home, so as to enable our home fleet to be free to act as the occasions of war might require, was extremely eligible, and fit to be adopted. He would elucidate what he meant, by putting a case which, doubtless, would render his meaning obvious to his right honourable colleague, and to every man present. If the enemy's fleet should come to the mouth of the Channel, with a view to intercept and capture our merchantmen as they either sailed home from the East and West Indies, or on their way to both, would it not be admitted that we ought to send our home fleet to fight there? It would, he imagined, be granted on all hands, that we should. Suppose, then, the enemy had previously stationed a large body of troops on their coast, with a view to seize a fit opportunity of landing them on our island, in order to strike some effectual blow; and when our home fleet came up to the enemy, they should sail into the ocean, ought we in that case to follow them? He believed no body would deny that we ought; because if we did not, we immediately manifested to all mankind that this country could only maintain a defensive war, and every body knew that a defensive war was what this country could never support. Then the case being so circumstanced, if our dock yards were fortified, the enemy would be checked upon their invasion, and our home fleet might nevertheless be away. Under this consideration it was that he had voted for the
proposed

propofed 'fyftem' of fortification ; nor did he doubt but that the unanimity with which the land and naval officers approved of the plan for erecting fortifications was, in part, grounded upon motives fimilar to his own.

Captain *Macbride* contended that the naval officers did not unanimoufly approve of that plan. They had been tricked into an appearance of granting their approbation of what, in fact, they did not approve. The Report was artfully drawn, and the provifoes and objections fo tranfpofed as to make the naval officers feem to have changed their opinions. When he came to the Horfe Guards, and was called on to fign, he objected, and faid, " Surely his name ought not to appear as " approving the plan ;" when he was told, if he did not fign, it would not appear that he had been of the Board. He indeed approved highly of introducing a fluice of frefh water into Plymouth dock yards, which would, he fuppofed, incur an expence of about 20,000l., and prove exceedingly advantageous.

Mr. *Baflard* declared his opinion to be ftrongly in favour of fortifications of fome fort ; and faid, that whenever a proper plan fhould be propofed, and fairly fubmitted to a board of naval and military officers, and it fhould be afterwards fanctioned by their approbation, he would vote for fuch a plan as fatisfactorily as he had voted againft that of the noble Duke at the head of the Ordnance.

Mr. Alderman *Hammett* fpoke in juftification of the plan for which (he faid) he had voted. The noble Duke, he declared, was as firm and zealous a friend to the Conftitution as any man living. He had great and fhining talents, and reflected luftre on every Cabinet of which he was a member.

Captain *Luttrell* begged leave to advife his honourable friend (Captain Macbride) who, he faid, had lately turned orator, not to imitate the example of chimney fweepers, and the loweft of the rable, in calling names, and dealing out perfonal abufe, when debating in that Houfe. Talking of the naval officers having been tricked out of their opinions by a noble Duke, was an infult to their underftandings.

Captain *Macbride* replied, that the honourable gentleman might reft affured he would not take him for his pattern.

Mr. *Dempfter* lamented exceedingly that he fhould fee an Ordnance eftimate amount to fo large a fum in time of peace. He declared that he had taken the trouble to examine the Ordnance eftimates voted for many years paft; that from the peace of Utrecht to the next war, the amount had been no more than 91,000l. a year, and from the peace of Aix-la-Chapelle to the American war, (diftinguifhed by Mr. Pitt's glorious conduct of it) the eftimate had never arifen above 110,000l., or thereabouts. He ftated alfo what it had

Captain Macbride.

Mr. Baftard.

Mr. Ald. Hammett.

Captain Luttrell.

Captain Macbride.

Mr. Dempfter.

amounted to from the peace of Paris till the laft moft unfortunate American war, and then ftated the amount of the
Ordnance during the Duke of Marlborough's wars in the
reign of Queen Anne, contending that the eftimate at this
day (a day of profound peace) was higher in amount than it
had been during the Duke of Marlborough's wars. He condemned the voting 2000 additional feamen this year, and
faid, that we ought to be rigidly œconomical now that we
had no enemy to cope with but the three per cents. the four
per cents. the long annuities, and other funds. He advifed
the Minifter to wage a warm and vigorous war againft thofe
enemies.

Captain *Berkeley* adverted to what had fallen in the debate
on the fortifications from an honourable General, (Burgoyne)
who had faid that he would defend this country by having an
Auftrian army on the banks of the Rhine. Whatever alliances we made, of courfe they would contain ftipulations
obligatory upon us in return for the matters ftipulated on their
part to perform in our behalf. He adverted to the barrier
treaty, in which the Dutch had engaged to build forts for
the Emperor, and afked whether we would build forts in
Holland, if we were told it was unconftitutional? The tendency of his argument went to prove that it was more eafy
to talk of alliances than to form them, and that fortifying
our dock yards would have infured us fecurity without
pledging us to perform fervices for allies which might prove
extremely inconvenient.

Mr. Alderman *Sawbridge* protefted that no man had entertained a higher opinion of the œconomy of the noble Duke,
and of his zeal to preferve the freedom of election; he was
forry, therefore, to be under the neceffity of accufing him of
grofs wafting of the public money, and a direct attempt to
fubvert the freedom of election. Thefe charges, however,
he would undertake to prove. Mr. Sawbridge then ftated,
that certain veffels belonging to Queenborough were employed
by the Ordnance in carrying ftores. Thefe veffels coft Government a great deal annually, full 1500l. a year; and when
a noble Vifcount (Townfhend) prefided at the Board of Ordnance, a fcheme was projected to employ three hoys inftead
of thefe veffels, by which an amafing faving would have been
effected: in fact, the whole expence muft, by this excellent
reform, have funk fo low as 600l. The plan was ordered to
be adopted when the late Miniftry were difmiffed; but the
noble Duke had continued the veffels ever fince. This gave
the Board of Ordnance an election influence at Queenborough, infomuch that during the laft election one candidate
declared that he had been fent down by the Navy Board,
while another faid, that he came from the Board of Ordnance.
Mr.

Captain
Berkeley.

Mr. Ald.
Sawbridge.

Mr. Sawbridge now afked leave, and was permitted, to read, as part of his fpeech, the enfuing letter, written, he faid, and fent to the papers by one of his friends:

" To the Duke of RICHMOND.

" MY LORD,

" I T is not my intention to enter into an examination of your political conduct. Apoftacy from principle, and defertion of connections, have been fo common in the prefent unfortunate reign, that it would be a wafte of time and labour to expatiate on the perfidy of an individual. I mean to confider you only in your official character. Your conduct in the military department of the Ordnance is now very generally underftood, and univerfally reprobated. The firft profeffional men in the country have fully expofed the hardfhip of thofe oppreffive regulations in the corps of engineers, by which, under the fpecious name of reform, you have aimed only at an extenfion of your power, and the futility of thofe vifionary projects of defence, which are as inconfiftent with your repeated declarations as with every military principle; I fhall, therefore, confine my obfervations to the civil branch of your office, and, comparing your conduct with your profeffions, refpecting the fpecific abufes of which you have moft loudly complained, leave the Public to judge of the juftice of your pretenfions to the character of a reformer.

" When you entered into office, you thought proper, in the courfe of a very long fpeech in the Houfe of Lords, to enter much at large into the abufes of the department you was called upon to fill, and to arraign, in very fevere terms, the conduct of your predeceffors. You particularly complained, that, for the purpofe of parliamentary influence, the Board of Ordnance had been entirely compofed of members of the Houfe of Commons. ' Great and extenfive,' you obferved, ' is the power and weight of the Board; moft ' of the fhipping employed in their fervice is taken up from ' Queenborough, with a view to influence the election for ' that place.' You pledged yourfelf, in the ftrongeft manner, to put an end to the corrupt prodigality which you had reprobated, and to deftroy that undue influence which, upon your avowed principles, was incompatible with the fafety of the Conftitution.

" There is no difficulty in ftating what your conduct ought to have been after thofe voluntary profeffions, after this laboured detail of projected reforms. The People had a right to expect that the members of the Board would be appointed without any view to parliamentary arrangements.

ftill

still less to the little politics of a county. That you would observe a strict neutrality in the elections for the borough which you had particularly described as under the influence of the Ordnance; neither exerting that influence yourself, nor permitting it to be exerted by others. That you would inquire whether the Public had been served on the cheapest terms by those freemen of that borough, whose transactions with the Board you deemed of so suspicious a nature; and would discharge every useless vessel, retrench every needless expence, and introduce the most rigid œconomy, especially in those articles of expenditure where œconomy and reduction of influence might go hand in hand.

" In no respect have you justified the confident expectations of the Public. I shall not dwell on the indecency of bestowing on Sussex gentlemen almost every appointment of value and consequence. In some instances, perhaps, the ties of private friendship, and a sense of gratitude for past services, may have operated even on your mind; in others, no motive can be suggested for your conduct, but that of extending your influence. It is true that most of the gentlemen, who were the object of your favour, were not at that time possessed of seats in the House of Commons. It would not have been prudent to have began your official career with a gross and public violation of recent professions. You, therefore, adopted the happy and honourable expedient of first introducing your friends into office, and then endeavouring to bring them into Parliament.

" The borough of Queenborough, to which, in your speech in the House of Lords, you called the public attention in so particular a manner, appears to have engrossed no inconsiderable share of your own   That attention has, however, been directed not to the reduction, but to the support of the extensive influence in the elections for that place, to which you succeeded on your accession to power; which you derived solely from your official situation; which, in other hands, had called forth your bitterest invectives; and which you have kept up at the public expence, and exerted without decency or moderation. In a very few weeks after you had delivered the speech to which I have referred, you took measures to bring in one of your friends on an expected vacancy for Queenborough, which I have great reason to believe you engaged in a negociation with Sir Charles Frederick to procure. While Lord Rockingham was pursuing his system for reducing the influence of the Crown, you was preparing to exert that influence; while Mr. Crewe's bill, to prevent revenue officers from voting at elections, was passing through the two Houses, under the auspices of the Administration of which you was a member, you was endeavouring to defeat

the

the good effects of that falutary meafure, which you did not dare openly to oppofe.

" When you refumed your office on the removal of the Portland Adminiftration, and one Parliament having been diffolved by prerogative, another was to be packed by corruption, you refumed your attempt, and united your intereft with that of the Admiralty, for the purpofe of forcing two members on the town of Queenborough, in oppofition to the known wifhes of a great majority of the independent freemen. The open and fhameful exertions of the influence of Government, to which I was a witnefs during the conteft, have been equalled perhaps, but I am fure never exceeded, under the moft profligate Adminiftration which this country has ever experienced. Commodore Bowyer, who was one of the Court candidates, declared from the huftings, at a public meeting of the electors, that he came there at the exprefs requeft, and that he ftood in the intereft and recommendation of Lord Howe; and Mr. Aldridge, who was your candidate, avowedly canvaffed in his official capacity of principal Storekeeper of the Ordnance.

" The influence of which you have thus unwarrantably availed yourfelf, is principally derived from the employment of an unneceffary and (in time of peace) unprecedented number of Ordnance veffels at Sheernefs, in the rivers Thames and Medway, for the purpofe of conveying ftores on board the King's fhips; moft of thefe veffels, inftead of being taken up by contract, as is the practice at Portfmouth and Plymouth, have been put on the eftablifhment, at an enormous expence to the Public, for the emolument of freemen of Queenborough, of whom the mafters and mates are entirely compofed. In proof of what I have advanced, I will ftate the annual expence of thefe veffels from the beft eftimate I have been able to procure.

" The mafter of the Marlborough gun hoy, at Sheernefs, of about ninety tons, is allowed 160l. per annum to provide three men, and a houfe, which lets for 16l. more; and the repairs of this veffel may be fairly eftimated at 70l. more — total expence to Government 246l. per annum. The Frederic powder boat, at Sheernefs, of about thirty-five tons, is at prefent on what is called the old eftablifhment, which confifts of a mafter and mate, whofe falaries (the mafter being allowed 2s. 6d. per day, and the mate 2s.) amount to 82l. per annum; and the men, when a veffel on this eftablifhment is on fervice, are hired from the gun wharf at 1s. 6d. per day each. Although this veffel is in fuch bad repair as to be totally unferviceable, and the pofts of mafter and mate are therefore become mere finecures, you thought proper, on the death of the mafter, fome time fince, to reward the fervices
of

of a freeman of Queenborough, who had been active in your interest, by appointing him to succeed. The Ligonier powder boat, at Chatham, of about forty-five tons, is on the new establishment, which consists of a master and mate, whose salaries (the master being allowed 60l. per annum, and 72l. to provide two men, and 30l. per annum for a boy, and the mate 48l.) amount to 210l., and the repairs cost 70l. more — total 280l. per annum. The Lord Townshend, of forty-five tons, at Woolwich, is on the same establishment, and costs 250l. per annum; the salaries of master and mate amounting to 210l., and the repairs to 40l. The Amherst, of forty tons, at Purfleet, costs 232l. per annum; the salary of the master amounting to 162l., and the repairs to 70l. There are also two contract vessels on the same station, which cost 409l. That at Chatham, of about ninety tons, is hired at 12s. per day; and that at Sheerness, of about seventy tons, at 10s. 6d.

" On the whole, the gun hoy and powder boats on this station, in constant pay, cost Government the annual sum of 1499l. Of this expence 1090l. is incurred by the establishment, which consists of five vessels, and two hundred fifty-five tons of shipping, and provides for eight freemen of Queenborough; and 409l. only by two vessels of one hundred and sixty tons of shipping, hired by contract.

" From this statement it is evident that the employment of established, in preference to contract vessels, is perfectly inconsistent with every principle of œconomy. Those on the new establishment, on an average, cost each 75l. per cent. more than a contract vessel of the same burden. The Amherst, of forty-five tons, at Portsmouth, was hired at 8s. per day, (145l. per annum) while Lord Townshend was Master General.. I have been informed by persons of much judgement and experience, that three vessels, which might be taken up by contract for 600l. per annum, would be fully sufficient, in time of peace, for the ordinary service of the Ordnance at Sheerness, and in the Thames and Medway, which now cost 1499l. If that is the case, there is an unnecessary expenditure in that article of 150l. per cent. But whatever may be the specific amount, I am justified in affirming, that very great profusion is practised; and that that profusion, in its effect and operation, has a corrupt influence in the elections for Queenborough.

" These abuses, which duty and consistency called on you to put an end to, seem to be not only connived at, but openly protected and encouraged. While Lord Townshend presided at the Ordnance, a plan of retrenchment was adopted, and the Queenborough vessels were ordered to be discharged, on the report of Captain Dickinson, one of the superintendants of
the

the fhipping, to which the confideration of that bufinefs had been referred by a minute of the Board. On your return to office, not contented with inftantly rejecting that plan, and reftoring that very expenfive eftablifhment which your predeceffor had abolifhed, you thought proper to relieve your Queenborough friends from the troublefome control of Captain Dickinfon, and to transfer the fuperintendance of their veffels to Mr. Webb, who is a freeman of that place. One uniform principle pervades every department of the Ordnance; while the Mafter General fits as Prefident of the Board of Inquiry into the efficacy of his own plan, the manager of a borough intereft is employed to watch the expenditure, and to check the prodigality from whence that intereft is derived.

"A FREEMAN of QUEENBOROUGH."

" Feb. 18, 1786."

Captain *Luttrell* replied, that he fhould admit that Captain Dickinfon had reported to the noble Vifcount (Townfhend) that the Public would reap advantage from carrying ftores by three hoys, inftead of by the four veffels, called the Townfhend, the Conway, the Ligonier, and the Frederic; yet no mention had been made concerning what thefe would fell for, and what the three hoys would coft. On fubfequent examination, however, it appeared, that the four old veffels might be worth 35ol. a piece, but the hoys would coft 115ol. each. For this reafon the project had been abandoned. With regard to the election influence, that ftood exactly the fame, whether the hoys or the veffels had been adopted, as the men were to have been the fame as thofe already employed.

Mr. *Courtenay* said, he confidered the amount of the Ordnance eftimate as fo trifling a confideration, weighed againft the late greater queftion of the fortifications, that he meant not at firft to have fpoken in the debate; but he now felt it neceffary to explain the whole bufinefs of the Queenborough veffels, and to ftate, that Captain Dickinfon was a naval engineer, bred up under a noble Vifcount, (Howe) at prefent fitting at the head of the Board of Admiralty, and perfectly competent to decide refpecting the hoys. That had the laft Mafter General of the Ordnance (Vifcount Townfhend) continued in office, the hoys would certainly have been adopted to the faving of 3000l. yearly; yet what could be more ridiculous than the œconomy of the noble Duke! (of Richmond.) When he firft entered that Houfe, he came in loaded with farthing fandbags, and could fcarcely totter under their weight to the table, though fupported by a pair of the beft beech crutches which all Suffex could produce! His œconomy that year was wonderful; for, after retrenching in
every

every minute particular, the noble Duke had faved the nation full 14l. 9s. 5¼d. Mr. Courtenay mentioned the new addition to the Ordnance Office, in Old Palace Yard, as an inftance of one work of public expence not put into the eftimates, and as a proof that the honourable member's (Captain Luttrell) boaft, that the eftimates contained the whole of the expenditure, was unfounded.

Captain Luttrell.   Captain *Luttrell* anfwered, that the erection of the new building in queftion came under the head of repairs, ftated by the Tower department, and that all buildings were mentioned under the fame head during the time of the laft Mafter General of the Ordnance.

Mr. Steele.   Mr. *Steele* faid, that he recollected that a charge of having written a letter to a noble Duke, at that time at the head of the Adminiftration, complaining of his Grace's not having turned out two Cuftom-houfe officers, who had voted againft the honourable magiftrate on fome election, had been, fome few years fince, handed about; and it was not, therefore, ftrange that an attempt fhould have been made to impeach the noble Duke's known regard for the freedom of election, when even the honourable Alderman's zeal for the fame fpecies of freedom had not efcaped calumny.

Mr. Ald. Sawbridge.   Mr. Alderman *Sawbridge* begged leave to remind the Houfe, that he offered to prove the facts which he had ftated; would the honourable gentleman do the fame? One thing, however, he muft fay in reply, that, throughout the whole courfe of his life, he had not enjoyed the honour of writing a letter to any noble Duke whatever.

Mr. Sloper.   Mr. *Sloper* obferved, that the Committee were going to a vote, without knowing the reafon for its taking place. The 10,000l. for repairing Fort Monckton, and the 3000l. for the works at Portfmouth, were both of them portions of the fyftem, the greater part of which the Houfe had decided fhould not be carried into execution. The noble Duke had affumed credit for œconomy in the office over which he prefided. But did the prefent eftimate by any means difcover that he was entitled fo much to plume himfelf upon his frugality?

Mr. Powys.   Mr. *Powys* remarked, that he was nearly on the point of embracing an opinion, that no gentleman fhould fpeak on the fubject who was unprepared, either with a charge againft the noble Duke, or a panegyric upon his official virtues. He meant to deal in neither, but merely to afk a queftion—what fortifications were meant to be carried on? The old upon the large fcale, the new ones according to part of the noble Duke's plan, or were the old ones to be finifhed on a reduced plan?

Mr.

Mr. Chancellor Pitt faid the latter; but Mr. Powys and fome other gentlemen objeted to voting the 10,000l. for Fort Monckton, and 3000l. for the works at Portfmouth, as they were parts of 32,000l. and 20,000l, till the queftion of fortification was finally fettled.

Mr. Chancellor *Pitt* rofe again, and contended that the Mr. Chancellor Pitt. plan rejeted by the Houfe confifted of three different plans combined; and fince the Adminiftration would not be permitted to have the whole of the plan, they fhould try to have as much of it as the Houfe, by whofe opinion they were glad to be guided, were willing to adopt; but as it certainly would make the prefent vote ftand more diftint and clear if the two articles of Fort Monckton and the works at Portfmouth were taken out of the eftimate, he would confent to withdraw them, and fo reduce the fum to be then voted, by taking off 13,000l.

This was confented to, and, at length, the eftimate reduced, was voted.

Mr. Burke now moved that queftion for papers, relative to Delhi, which the order of the day had been moved upon during the courfe of the preceding Friday.

Mr. *Dundas* faid, that he would not mifpend the time of Mr. Dundas. the Houfe fo much as to go again over thofe reafons which he had on Friday fo amply ftated in detail; reafons inducing him to refufe his confent to thofe motions, which, if carried, would reveal fecrets that policy required fhould be concealed. The motion was one of that defcription, and therefore he muft objet againft it.

Mr. *Sheridan* complained of that manner of refufing mate- Mr. Sheridan. rial papers, without ftating any particular fpecific reafon for fuch refufal; but what he principally rofe for, he faid, had been in order to give the Houfe an explanation of that charge, or rather infinuation, refpeting him, which an honourable gentleman oppofite to him had advanced. The Committee would recollet, that when he heard of the matter on Friday evening, he had ated in the manner which he hoped they would think moft proper for him to adopt under the circumftances of the cafe as they then ftood. He had fince that had an interview with the perfon, with whom he had talked upon the fubjet, and who indeed he had commiffioned to go to the honourable gentleman oppofite to him, who he did not doubt would do him the juftice fully to explain to the Houfe when he fat down, that he had been miftaken in his fact, having been fatisfied by the gentleman in queftion that he was miftaken. In order to make the Houfe more clearly underftand what he meant, it would be neceffary for him to ftate a little of fome opinions, which he had ever referved in his own mind, and did not intend to have ftated, had not this bufinefs made it neceffary. With regard to India affairs, he had thought there were but two lines of conduct to be purfued after thofe emphatic refolutions of the 28th of May, 1782, had been voted. The one was to recal Mr. Haftings immediately by the ftrong arm of Parliament, and punifh him exemplarily; the other, to bring in an India bill, in which, on grounds of expediency, on account of the times not bearing fo ftrong a meafure, and the difference of opinion refpecting it, no retrofpect fhould be had, but all the claufes fhould look to the future. So thinking, when the India bill of his right honourable friend was preparing, the latter meafure appeared to him moft expedient to be followed, more efpecially as the time for calling home Mr. Haftings, by act of Parliament, was, in his mind, gone by, and therefore he had fent a friend to the honourable gentleman oppofite to him to know whether Mr. Haftings would come home, if recalled. In the courfe of the converfation which he had with his friend, the intended India bill was certainly mentioned, but merely as matter of converfation, and not as a propofition to the honourable gentleman. This he had the happinefs to fay was the true ftate of the cafe, as the gentleman in queftion had affured both him and the honourable gentleman oppofite to him, and that there had not been the moft diftant idea of bartering with Mr. Haftings for his fupport of the India bill.

Maj. Scott.   Major *Scott* perfectly admitted that the gentleman whom he had feen originally on the bufinefs had confirmed, fince Friday laft, every fyllable which the honourable gentleman had uttered; and he begged leave to thank him for fo fair a ftatement of the tranfaction. He only differed from him in one particular: he had always conceived that the converfation about Mr. Fox's India bill had been the principal, and the queftion as to whether Mr. Haftings would come home, or would erect the ftandard of rebellion in India? the acceffary point and caufe of the meffage to him. Moft certainly the gentleman with whom he converfed had affured him it was not, and he was bound to think fo now. But he would ftate to the Houfe why it was natural for him to have thought fo at the time, and the matters had very ftrongly impreffed his mind in that way ever fince. In the firft place, he had no powers from Mr. Haftings to treat of his refignation, and he had ftated as much at the India Houfe three years ago, by reading a part of Mr. Haftings's inftructions to him; and, as a farther proof that fuch had been the impreffion which he had received, he muft beg leave to read from the Morning Chronicle the following paragraphs, and anfwers, which had appeared in it on the fubject in 1783:

Morning Chronicle, Nov. 22, 1783.   " Mr. Fox, in his fpeech on Tuefday, declares, in refpect to Mr. Haftings, that

that his bill was not meant to have *any retrospect*; that it depended entirely on the *friends* of the Governor General, whether what was past should be buried in *oblivion*, or the *whole* of Mr. Haftings's conduct should be exposed to the severest parliamentary animadversion. Should the *friends* of Mr. Haftings throw obstructions in the way of a parliamentary reform, this, in addition to their unparalleled enormities, would unquestionably justify a *bill of attainder* in the evidence already in the possession of the House. Let not Mr. Haftings's friends deceive themselves, by expecting that those men, who, from *factious views*, were *predetermined* to oppose every plan for reforming the abuses of the Company, will support them afterwards in procuring *impunity* to Mr. Haftings; they ought to recollect, that the *late Lord Advocate* is the person who not only moved the severest censure against Mr. Haftings, but also carried through a vote for his recal. The temper, the connections, the influence of Mr. Dundas over his friend, (Mr. Pitt) and the rest of the leading characters of opposition, are too notorious to escape the observations of the most inattentive."

Morning Chronicle, Nov. 24, 1783. " A paragraph of a very extraordinary nature having appeared in this paper on Saturday, with a view of intimidating the agent of Mr. Haftings, and his friends, Major Scott conceives himself called upon, by the duty he owes to his principal, and to his country, (in which he has an hereditary stake, and is therefore as much entitled as any Englishman can be) to give his sentiments upon the most pernicious scheme that was ever brought forward to the public view. Mr. Haftings and his friends equally despise *threats* and promises. Will the Public suppose, or can Mr. Haftings's friends be so weak, that men, who have pursued Mr. Haftings with a degree of inveteracy and malice which is unparalleled in the annals of this country, now wish to stop short, out of tenderness to that gentleman? Mr. Fox knows perfectly well that neither Mr. Haftings nor his friends are actuated by factious views. He knows also, that they *fear no retrospect*, and *wish for no oblivion*. And he not only knows, but feels, that the purity of Mr. Haftings's character, and the integrity of his conduct, have placed him beyond the reach of malice. Mr. Haftings has said boldly and openly, ' If I am a violator of public ' faith, do not censure me; punish me with death.' His friends in England say the same; and they assure Mr. Fox, or *his friend*, who has thrown out the *threat of a bill of attainder*, that they will meet it with the same readiness, and oppose it with the same firmness, as they have done the *threat of delinquency*, and the fallacious Reports of the Select Committee. Major Scott must be the most infamous man indeed, if he could be induced, by any confideration upon earth, to facrifice the caufe of the Eaft-India Company, after that Company have fo honourably fupported the Governor General againft every attempt to remove him. With refpect to Mr. Dundas, the Public will-be pleafed to recollect, that he difavowed every idea of delinquency in Mr. Haftings: he never was pledged to God, the Houfe of Commons, and the nation, to remove Mr. Haftings on any other ground than that of *expediency*; and he argued for that expediency thus:—— The Mahrattas will not make peace with Mr. Haftings, becaufe he has forfeited their confidence. The refult has proved that Mr. Dundas was miftaken."

Morning Chronicle, Nov. 26, 1783. " The correfpondent who fent the paragraph relative to Mr. Haftings to the Morning Chronicle of Saturday, cannot but exprefs the utmoft aftonifhment at the defperate effrontery of that gentleman's agents. After Mr. Haftings has been convicted, in the only way it was poffible to convict him, of the moft *flagitious delinquency*; when it is on the records of Parliament, and admitted by himfelf and his agents, that he received a bribe of 100,000l., without deigning to affign a motive for his acceptance of it; to have extirpated a whole people, who had never given him any caufe of offence, for a fum of money; when his ruinous contracts, extortions, and monopolies, are confeffed by his warmeft friends — is the *ambaffador* of *fuch* a man to be fuffered to brave the public juftice, and to tell the nation that *Mr. Haftings laughs at the impotent vengeance of the Britifh Parliament!*"

Morning Chronicle, Nov. 27, 1783. " Major Scott is exceedingly unwilling to draw the attention of the Public from the great fubject now before them, by intruding upon their notice any matters which could only affect Mr. Haftings perfonally, becaufe that gentleman's hour of trial *muft come*, and then the nation will be able to judge how far he has deferved the treatment he has met with fince the 22d of March, 1782. The writer of a paragraph in yefterday's paper has, however, jumbled together fo many charges, that a fhort reply is abfolutely neceffary.

" Mr. Haftings has never been convicted of *flagitious delinquency*. It is *not* admitted by Mr. Haftings, or his agents, that he received a bribe of 100,000l., without affigning his reafons. His letters to the Court of Directors are full proof of the contrary. Mr. Haftings did not extirpate a nation. The Rohilla war, here alluded to, had been fully explained. Mr. Haftings has not given away ruinous contracts, or eftablifhed monopolies; nor has he been guilty of extortion. Major Scott's letters to Mr. Burke have fully detected the falfe ftatements contained in the Ninth Report of the Select Committee.

Committee. Major Scott neither wished to brave, nor to fly from public justice, *though he rejected the offer of an act of oblivion for his principal, provided he would remain silent during the present attack upon the East-India Company.* If it were necessary to go now into the subject, one short sentence from the Ninth Report of the Select Committee would prove that Mr. Hastings, so far from being convicted, is not yet charged with delinquency; for the sublime Reporter says, page 53, ' The ' Reports of your Committee are *no charges,* though they ' may possibly furnish *matter for charge.*"

Doubtless neither the House nor the Public were warranted to suppose that these paragraphs came from the honourable gentleman, (Mr. Sheridan*;) but they certainly came from some where: they did not fall down from heaven on the compositor's letter case; and as they ran in the same stile with a right honourable gentleman's (Mr. Fox) speech on opening his India bill, they certainly came from some friend of that gentleman.

Mr. *Sheridan* rose once or twice to correct Major Scott, and to beg that he would let the House know that it had been their mutual friend, and not he, (Major Scott) who set him right as to the real purport and end of the message. Mr. Sheridan.

Mr. *Fox* expressed great satisfaction that the matter had been so well cleared up, and repeated what he had thrown out on Friday, the instant he heard the insinuation made, assuring the House that he never had entertained a thought of compromising with Mr. Hastings, as the speech which he made on opening his India bill had sufficiently proved. It was likewise clear that he had been concerned in no treaty of the kind in question, or it would have been natural for him to have waited to have learnt how the treaty went on before he opened his bill. Mr. Fox.

Mr. Chancellor *Pitt* refused to comply with the motion, as tending to affect the policy of India, by opening the secrets of negociations in that country, which the peace and tranquillity of Hindostan rendered absolutely necessary should remain undivulged. Major Brown's letter he treated as the unauthenticated effusion of a chimerical projector, that might neither deserve the credit of the House, nor affect the character of Mr. Hastings. Mr. Chancellor Pitt.

Mr. *Burke* read part of Major Brown's letter from Delhi, and of Mr. Hastings's letter from Lucknow, as a portion of his speech, and declared that if the insinuation of an honourable gentleman had been true, and he had been deserted by Mr. Burke.

* On this occasion the Printer declared, upon his honour, that the paragraphs in question did not come to him from Mr. Sheridan, or from any member of Parliament.

his

his honourable friend, and by all mankind, the great cause he was engaged in should not have been abandoned, but, even standing alone, he would have proceeded.

The House divided on the question —

Ayes - - - - - - - - - - 34
Noes - - - - - - - - - - 88
                                        _____
                        Majority - - 54

A motion having been immediately afterwards made for copies of three letters — two from Major Brown at Delhi, and one from Mr. Haftings at Lucknow,

Mr. *Fox* remarked, that if the papers stated in the question were refufed, there was an end of afking for papers, however material to the profecution those papers might be, and however free from any imputation of being dangerous or likely to affect the policy of India. He could not believe, however, that His Majefty's Minifter would go the length of refufing the three letters in queftion; if he did, what a fhameful fact would it not eftablifh? Would it not then appear in broad and ftriking colours, that a right honourable gentleman had perfuaded that Houfe to vote a number of ftrong refolutions, to not one of which he meant that they fhould ever give force and efficacy? Of the papers now called for, the Houfe could already perceive the tendency, fince, in the preceding debate, they had heard the moft material paffages read and argued on. They muft, therefore, be aware, that no harm whatever could arife from producing them and making them public; he and his friends had duplicates of them already in their poffeffion, and were perfectly mafters of their contents. In refufing to let them formally be laid upon the table, the other fide of the Houfe would ftand without excufe. Mr. Fox contended that it was, in his mind, impoffible that they fhould do fo; if they did, and pleaded that their granting the papers would affect the policy of India, he muft declare, that ever fince he fat in Parliament, he never had witneffed fo difgraceful a conduct; his comfort, however, would be, that, however the Minifter might withftand every individual motion for papers, and prevent any thing like evidence from being obtained, however he might rely on the power of his majorities in that Houfe, there was another tribunal to which he muft go for trial, the tribunal of the Public, who would judge for themfelves; and however the right honourable gentleman might reft fatisfied, in affigning as a reafon for rejecting his right honourable friend's motions, that, if granted, they would affect the policy of India, a reafon too general to be combated, and which, if admitted as a fufficient juftification for refufal in every cafe, would amount to a direct vefting of Minifters with the power of protecting every delinquent, however criminal,

minal, and of quashing every inquiry and every accusation, however founded, at a single stroke. The right honourable gentleman might stand assured, that, though that House would rest content, the honour of the nation would not be satisfied, nor would the People be pleased at seeing their representatives act in a manner so disgraceful to themselves, and so foreign to the purposes of substantial justice. Mr. Fox now exclaimed, "What a precious farce is daily acting " within these walls!" We see the friends of Mr. Hastings affecting to be eager that every paper called for should be granted; we see the King's Ministers rising to declare that every thing that can properly be granted shall not be refused; we hear other gentlemen, who call themselves independent men, saying, By all means let the House know the whole, and be put into possession of every necessary species of information; and yet we see the same men all of them dividing together to enforce a negative to a motion for such information, and we see them helping each other out with hints and whispers during the debate, and pointing to matters apposite to the argument on their side the question, in like manner as my right honourable friend and I would assist each other when we are maintaining the same point and arguing for the same purpose.

Mr. Chancellor *Pitt* expressed his hopes that he should not be thought less grounded in presuming to withstand the present motion, if he did not follow the right honourable gentleman's example, and make a speech full of angry words, delivered with all the vehemence of passionate expression. Notwithstanding what the right honourable gentleman had thrown out by way of threat, no menaces should intimidate him, or induce him to quit that line of conduct which he felt it to be his duty to pursue. The present motion he should reject, and he trusted the majority of the House would support him in that rejection, when he informed them that it was neither more nor less than the same motion which the House had just decided against admitting, only put into another shape. The right honourable gentleman had misrepresented his arguments: he had not nakedly stated that the reason of his refusing his consent to the motion just negatived was because the papers then moved for would, if agreed to, affect the general policy of India, but because they would materially affect the policy of India, by leading to discover and make public certain secrets in the different negociations which had been carried on, the discovery of which would tend to disturb the tranquillity of that country, and lead to consequences highly injurious to the British interests in India. For the same reason, he must refuse his assent to the present motion, and for the same reason he should continue to refuse

his

Mr. Chancellor Pitt.

his affent to any other that fhould appear to him liable to produce a fimilar effect : nor would the right honourable gentleman's ufing expreffions infulting to any individual near
him, or, what was ftill lefs defenfible, infulting to the majority of that Houfe, operate upon his mind in the leaft. He
fuppofed the glow of eloquence which they had juft heard
was to be accounted for by the right honourable gentleman's
having warmed himfelf with the conception of it in the lobby,
and being determined that a few happy thoughts and ardent
expreffions fhould not be loft upon the Houfe; if fo, the
right honourable gentleman had fulfilled his defign ; whether
to the fatisfaction of thofe who heard him, much lefs to their
conviction, the Houfe would decide by their vote, which he
trufted would go in fupport of the vote they had juft given,
and that the motion before them would, like the preceding
one, of which, in point of tendency and effect, it was the
exact counterpart, receive an exprefs negative. Mr. Pitt faid
that he had before been, together with the right honourable
gentleman, to the tribunal of which he talked, and he was
ready to meet him there again. He complained of gentlemen's reading papers as a part of their fpeeches, which were
papers produced before a Secret Committee, obtained from
thofe who had betrayed their truft : fuch a practice cut up all
the principles of political fecrecy by the roots.

The Houfe adjourned.

Tuefday, 7th March.

Mr. M. A. Taylor. Mr. *Michael-Angelo Taylor*, having moved for leave to
bring in a bill to regulate the courts of confcience throughout the kingdom, obferved, that he had, during the courfe
of the preceding feffion, brought in a bill, which paffed into
a law, to regulate thofe courts in London, Weftminfter, and
Southwark ; that the bill was merely experimental; but he
had been informed from all quarters that it produced beneficial
effects. This made him turn his attention to the prefent bill;
and he had received the approbation of many refpectable gentlemen in Briftol, and other cities and confiderable towns,
who declared that the eftablifhment of fimilar regulations
amongft them would prove a fource of great convenience.
Amidft a variety of abufes and evils, one was, that a man
might be imprifoned for life for fo fmall a fum as 15s. or 20s.;
and even could the miferable wretch raife the money to pay
the debt, ftill he was detained for his fees. This was fhocking to humanity, and called loudly for redrefs. The bill went
likewife to another point. He had obferved, that perfons in
a comparatively low condition fat as judges in thefe courts,
and were totally unqualified in every refpect. One claufe of
it,

it, therefore, went to eſtabliſh a qualification of 20l. per annum freehold, or 500l. perſonal property. The time limited by the bill for imprisonment by theſe courts he intended to be twenty days for any ſum not exceeding 20s., and forty days for any ſum not exceeding 40s.

Mr. *Francis* expreſſed a wiſh that ſome method could be deviſed to oblige thoſe perſons, ſo qualified, to attend the duty, as he verily believed that the diſagreeableneſs of the taſk threw the execution of it into the hands of thoſe inferior perſons deſcribed by the honourable gentleman. *Mr. Francis.*

Mr. *Taylor* replied, that, when his bill was paſſed into a law, it would be eaſy to compel ſuch perſons by *mandamus*.—— Leave was given accordingly. *Mr. Taylor.*

Mr. Taylor, the Chairman of Ways and Means, brought up the reſolution of the Committee ; immediately after which

Sir *John Miller* offered a propoſition to the Houſe, that the 50,000l., now unappropriated, in the Exchequer, might be applied to the purpoſes of bringing freſh water to Plymouth dock, to the building of gun boats, and ſuch other beneficent uſes as might appear neceſſary. *Sir John Miller.*

The Speaker informed him that it was utterly out of order for the Houſe to receive ſuch a propoſition, and that it muſt be ſubmitted to the Committee of Supply.

The reſolutions were reported, and agreed to by the Houſe.

The Honourable Mr. *Marſham* gave notice, that he ſhould, on the firſt open day, move the Houſe for leave to bring in a bill to extend the proviſions contained in Mr. Crewe's bill, which prevents perſons enjoying certain places under Government for voting at elections for members of Parliament, to the Navy and Ordnance ſervice. *The hon. Mr. Marſham.*

The Speaker named the enſuing Thurſday.

Mr. M. A. Taylor reported the ſeveral reſolutions of the Committee on the ſhop tax. The ſame were received by the Houſe, and agreed to without oppoſition.

Mr. Baſtard moved, " That there be laid before this Houſe, " an account of the perſons convicted of any offences, and " who have been, in conſequence thereof, ſent on board the " hulks in the river Thames, or on board any other hulk, or " priſon ſhip, in any other place, or confined in any priſon " within this kingdom, ſince the 1ſt of January, 1775, ſpe- " cifying the offence and time for which ſuch perſons were " ſentenced to be tranſported or impriſoned reſpectively, and " which of them have been diſcharged, and at what time, " and on what account, and whether ſuch perſons ſo diſ- " charged have, at any time, and when, been convicted of " any, and what, ſubſequent offence, or offences." Ordered.

Mr. Baſtard then moved " for the expences of ſuch as had " been confined on board the hulks, ſpecifying the time,

" and when difcharged, and whether they have been fince
" convicted."

The Attorney General contended that the order could not
be complied with.

Mr. Chan-
cellor Pitt.

Mr. Chancellor *Pitt* obferved, that he forefaw that it was
the intention of the honourable gentleman to move fome propofition relative to tranfporting felons. This was a fubject
of great intricacy. Several new modes of difpofing of the
convicts had been pointed out, every one of which was attended with fuch difficulty and expence, that Government
was not a little embarraffed what method to take confiftently
with the public fafety. He begged leave to remind the gentleman, that it is much eafier to point out a grievance (and
fuch this certainly was) than to apply a remedy.

Mr. Man-
waring.

Mr. *Manwaring* expreffed his concern that no efficacious
meafure had hitherto been devifed. Between three and four
hundred convicts were now under fentence in the metropolis,
fome condemned for three, four years, and upwards, and their
time was now going on ; fo that in a few years numbers would
be let loofe upon the Public to commit depredations, unlefs
otherwife difpofed of. If Government did not act with vigour, it would damp the adminiftration of juftice. Even the
Judges themfelves were at a lofs what to do, becaufe there is
no proper mode exifting for difpofing of them.

Mr. Ald.
Watfon.

Mr. Alderman *Watfon* doubted whether the motion could be
complied with, becaufe the books were burnt in 1780. He
obferved, that if fome fpeedy method were not taken to fend
them out of the kingdom, the magiftrates ought to efcape
cenfure if they could not afford protection to the inhabitants.

The Earl of
Surrey.

The Earl of *Surrey* faid that it was better to bear the expence than fubmit to the danger.

Mr. Baftard's motion was then put, and carried.

Mr. Chan-
cellor Pitt.

Mr. Chancellor *Pitt* begged leave to introduce a fubject of
the utmoft importance ; but he fhould at prefent only mention
certain preliminaries ; and thofe were the feveral accounts
which would draw the ftate of the finances into one point of
view. His intention was to take every poffible ftep to give
full and complete fatisfaction to the nation in a matter of
great and national concern. For this purpofe the accounts
fhould be reduced into eftimates by a Committee. It was,
therefore, his intention to defer any particular ftatement ;
and for the fame reafon he had no idea of entering into the
minutes, or into any fpecifical reafoning on the various and
complicated branches of the public revenue, the actual expenditure, and the probable methods of laying the ground
work of a permanent plan to reduce the heavy burdens of the
nation. He fhould firft afk leave to move for a Select Committee of nine, to be chofen by ballot by the whole Houfe,

on

on the morrow, to whom all the accounts are to be submitted, and by them reduced into estimates. These being printed for the use of the House, he should then submit his propositions to their judgement and candour.

Mr. *Pitt* then made his motions, which were as follow :

" That the several accounts and other papers, presented to
" the House in this session of Parliament, relating to the pub-
" lic income and expenditure, be referred to the considera-
" tion of a Select Committee, and that the said Committee
" be directed to examine and state the same, and also to report
" to the House what may be expected to be the annual
" amount of the said income and expenditure in future."

" That the number of the said Committee be nine."

" That the said Committee be chosen by way of balloting."

" That the members of this House do, to-morrow at two
" of the clock, prepare lists, to be put into glasses, of nine
" persons' names, to be the said Committee."

" That the said glasses be placed upon the table, and the
" said lists, held up between the finger and thumb, be put
" into the glasses at the table by the members called over for
" that purpose, according to the counties and places they
" serve for, as the said counties and places are entered in the
" return book."

Mr. *Fox* agreed with the right honourable member, that *Mr. Fox.* when papers, complicated and various as those of necessity must be, required investigation, it was always a good measure to refer them to a Select Committee; but he thought that nine was rather too confined a number. However, he should make no objection ; but, on the contrary, be happy to give every assistance in his power.

Sir *Grey Cooper* expressed his wishes that an instrument or *Sir Grey* schedule of all the papers might be made. He did not consi- *Cooper.* der the accounts of two years revenue expenditure as a suffi- cient space of time for the Select Committee to make a fair estimation, whereby to ground a permanent plan. He rather thought it should be extended to three years.

Mr. Chancellor *Pitt* answered, that he rejoiced to discover *Mr. Chan-* so few objections to the mode which he had the honour of *cellor Pitt.* proposing ; and, therefore, when the Committee should have made their report, and the House have taken time to consider and digest it, he would proceed to what was commonly called opening the budget. He could assure the House that we were fortunately now in a situation to begin a plan to rescue the nation from her difficulties.

Mr. *Francis* now rose, and said,

Mr. SPEAKER,

I rise to move for leave to bring in a bill to explain and *Mr. Fran-* amend an act passed in the year 1784, for the better regula- *cis.*

U u 2   tion

tion of the East-India Company's affairs. I am deeply fensible, Sir, of the difficulty of the task I have undertaken. To move for the essential alteration of an act of the Legislature, against the sense of a majority of this House, and to encounter the abilities which were employed in framing it, and which are likely to be exerted in defending it, is not an attempt, to me at least, of inconsiderable magnitude. I can very truly assure you, Sir, that if I were not thoroughly convinced that what I propose to do is necessary to be done; if I did not think myself bound by a special duty to make the attempt, and if I were not conscious that my motives for making it were honest and upright, I should neither have the confidence to undertake such a labour, nor a degree of resolution sufficient to go through with it. The considerations which have called me to this duty will, I trust, support me in performing it. When I say that I have the sense of a majority of the House to encounter, I mean to pay the greatest tribute to their honour and to their justice; since I presume and expect that they will nevertheless hear me with indulgence; that they will listen to arguments opposed to their present impressions, and be led perhaps by the reflections which such arguments may suggest, to condemn and undo an act of their own.

There is one preliminary word, including a solicitation, which I shall offer to the House, and particularly to the right honourable gentleman (Mr. Pitt) who brought in the bill: it is, that they would separate and distinguish the substance of what I have to submit to their consideration from my manner of delivering it. That the right honourable gentleman himself, if, through the disorder and embarrassment with which I may speak, he can discover and collect the force and meaning of what I would express, and if that meaning should appear to him to deserve consideration, he will, in the first place, allow it due weight in his own mind; and then, if he should think fit to answer me, that he will give my arguments the advantage of his own expression, and encounter them in the armour with which he himself shall have invested them. However he may disregard personal invectives or personal attacks, he ought not to undervalue any efforts that are seriously employed in the discharge of a public duty. It is the condition, perhaps the burden, of his station, to listen to all men with patience and attention, and to collect information wherever it can be found. Between the right honourable gentleman and me there is no competition; and if there were, it ought not to be decided by inequality of arms. In desiring the right honourable gentleman's assistance against himself, I certainly invite him to a conduct that will do him honour. There is but one thing more honourable to the human character;

racter; and that, I am not without hopes, may be the result of this day's debate. If, fortunately, from the reflections which I mean to submit to the House, the right honourable gentleman's own measure should stand condemned, or considerably impeached, in his own mind, I persuade myself that he will frankly acknowledge his conviction, and act upon it.

Before I enter upon the essential part of my task, there is an explanation to be stated to the House, external to the merits of the motion which I mean to make, yet materially connected with it. This explanation regards the time and circumstances in which I act. It is matter of public notoriety, though not regularly before the House, that the India bill was received in India a year ago with great discontent, and that petitions against it were preparing to be sent over to be laid before Parliament. On one side, then, I may be suspected of a base intention to avail myself of the present temper of the discontented parties for some mischievous purpose; and, on the other, I may be charged with acting precipitately and unfairly to the petitioners themselves, in not waiting for their petition. To the first imputation I say, that my opposition to almost every part of the bill, but particularly to the inquisition and judicature, was known and declared from the moment when it was introduced, and that I have invariably held the same language, and expressed the same sentiments concerning it. My objections to the measure were no way connected with my opinion of the reception it might meet with in India. Some gentlemen, who ought to have been better informed than it appears they were, took upon them to assure the House, that they had no doubt of its being perfectly well received there; they assured us it would be received with open arms. I will not deny, that, on my own principles, perhaps I might have been strictly bound to have moved for an alteration of this law in the course of last session; but I had reasons for not doing so, which I hope will be thought valid. The attention of the House was wholly engaged in the commercial arrangement with Ireland. The most exceptionable parts of the India bill were not to begin to operate till a year or two afterwards; but, principally, I wished to give time for the sense of the House to cool upon its own act, and for the general judgement of the nation to be collected on the merits of the measure. With respect to any impression which the bill may have made in India, or any measures taken there to obtain a repeal of it, I beg it may be understood that the business I am engaged in, and the part I take in it, stands wholly independent and unconnected with any thing said or done in India: that if the law, instead of being received as it has been, had been accepted by the parties immediately concerned in it as a benefit, I should not indeed

deed

deed have been fo forward and officious as to wifh to protect them againft an inquifition and a trial which they were willing to fubmit to, or to reftore them to rights which they were willing to relinquifh; neverthelefs I fhould have taken the fame courfe I now take. I fhould equally have moved for an alteration of this law, that a precedent might not be eftablifhed, either with or without their confent, dangerous to the Conftitution of this ifland, and to the rights and fecurity of the community at large.

To the fecond objection I anfwer, that although I act independently of the petitioners, I am as much in earneft as they can be to promote the object of their petition. What I am going to do cannot injure, and may affift them. In the matter, I take for granted, we are agreed. In the matter I feel myfelf bound by confiderations of duty here, which they are not equally concerned in. Next to the object itfelf, it is my wifh, and fhall be my endeavour, to accomplifh it in a way moft honourable to Parliament, and moft confiftent with its dignity — I mean by an appeal to the juftice of Parliament, and to nothing but its juftice. The object of the petitioners may be obtained, and the dignity of Parliament may be preferved together. For this latter purpofe it is material, nay it is effential, that Parliament, in the revifion of its own act, fhould proceed on its own motion without the influence of any external impulfe whatfoever. On this fubject I need not enlarge. The reflections that belong to it are obvious.

There is one plea, however, which I muft beg leave to enter in this place againft all infinuations that have been, or may be, hazarded againft my integrity in the part I take in thefe tranfactions; namely, that nothing faid or done now in England, concerning this law, can affect the minds or influence the conduct of our fellow fubjects in India. The law made its impreffion a twelvemonth ago. Whatever the confequences of that impreffion may be, they do not depend on any thing which can be ftated now, or foretold concerning them, and which cannot reach India till many months hence. It is a common artifice for the real author of a misfortune to endeavour to fhift the refponfibility of his own meafures from himfelf to the perfons by whom thofe very meafures were moft ftrenuoufly refifted. By this fort of ftratagem the forefight of an evil is converted into the caufe of it, and the prophet is made anfwerable for the mifchief he foretold. Former predictions on the prefent fubject have already been fulfilled by events, which are themfelves prophetic.

Having thus far cleared the ground and opened the way to my object, the firft thing I fhall attempt fhall be to fubmit to the Houfe a fhort diftinct view of the law as it ftands, comprehending the fundamental governing principles that confti-

tute

tute its effence, and the prominent features that form, if I may ufe fuch an expreffion, the countenance, the *vultus*, or general volition of the law. An explanation of this kind is the more neceffary, becaufe I know in fome inftances, and have reafon to fufpect it may be true in many, that this law has not been attentively read, nor hitherto very carefully confidered; and I confefs that I am not forry to think fo. If I thought the reverfe were true, my hopes of fuccefs to-night would be confiderably abated. As it is, I derive fome encouragement from your neglect. Befides this, Sir, by beginning with a view of the principles, a minute examination into the detail of the bill will, in a great degree, become unneceffary to my purpofe. If thefe leading principles are fuch as the Houfe, on a fair review of them, fhall think it right to adhere to and confirm, it would anfwer no purpofe of mine to fhew that there were miftakes or inconfiftencies in the detail. Defects of that kind belong to all human inftitutions, and are eafily corrected. On the other hand, if the principles of the law fhould, on a fair review of them, be reprobated by the Houfe as falfe, abfurd, and unconftitutional, the great and effential part of my tafk is accomplifhed, I fhall have ftruck a decifive blow at the root of the tree. The body of it muft fall and bring the branches to the ground.

This law, Sir, obvioufly divides itfelf into three great departments, and is therefore to be confidered generally under three points of view: firft, the arrangement made for the diftribution and eftablifhment of power at home; fecondly, the arrangement made for the government of the Company's affairs abroad; and finally, the inftitution of a fpecial inquifition and of a new judicature in England, for the difcovery and trial of offences committed in India. The firft, I affirm, ftands in direct contradiction to every rational principle of good government; the fecond ftands in the fame contradiction, not only to principles, but to experience; and the third introduces a capital and dangerous innovation into the criminal jurifprudence of this country, for no purpofe of juftice whatfoever, that might not have been equally, if not better, obtained by the judicatures that exift already. I ftate my propofitions in terms of great referve and moderation, compared with my opinion, and hope that I fhall be able to prove much more than I affirm.

In the firft place, Sir, I ftate it as a matter of fact, that, with refpect to the governing power of the India Company in England, the conftant and notorious complaint was, that the power of the Court of Directors was defective and infufficient to enforce obedience among their fervants abroad, or to punifh their difobedience. To remove this caufe of complaint, and to fupply this defect, recourfe has been had at various times to the authority of the Legiſlature; and the profeſſed object of every bill that has been offered to Parliament, for the better regulation of the Company's affairs, has been to ſtrengthen the executive power of the Company; that is, of the Court of Directors, either by giving them additional powers, or by removing the impediments thrown in their way by the interpoſition of the Court of Proprietors; who did, in reality, diveſt the Directors of all their power. Now, Sir, I admit that the general object of creating a power at home, ſufficient to enforce and ſecure obedience abroad, was proper, wiſe, and neceſſary. Let us ſee what courſe the preſent law has taken to arrive at this juſt and neceſſary object. It leaves the oſtenſible power of the Company with the Court of Directors. By them all orders and inſtructions for the governments in India are to be prepared, and by them they are to be ſigned; by them alſo all appointments to the ſervice are apparently to be made : thus far the fact, or the appearance of the fact, is conſiſtent with the principle. I cannot admit a ſuppoſition that the Legiſlature entertained the leaſt diſtruſt of the integrity, or even of the wiſdom, of the Court of Directors. I cannot ſuppoſe it poſſible that the Legiſlature, profeſſing to interpoſe its power for the improvement of inſtitutions, or the correction of abuſes, ſhould have continued the moſt delicate of all truſts, and the moſt important of all powers, namely, that of the executive government, in the very hand that was believed to have betrayed or abuſed it, or in any hand whatever that was deemed to be unequal to the performance of the duty. The law declares its confidence in the Directors, ſince it continues, profeſſedly at leaſt, to veſt in the direction an equal power to that they had before. The law clearly ſuppoſes them to have hitherto made a proper uſe of ſuch power as far as they were able to exert it, and therefore profeſſes to confirm and enlarge it ; but, the moment you turn over the leaf, you will find that all the ideas and proviſions are reverſed : that the law aſſumes a new principle utterly incompatible with that on which any new power could properly be given to the Directors, or any of their former power could properly be left in their hands. It abandons all idea of ſtrength and vigour in the executive power. Inſtead of uniting that power in ſome one Board, which could alone make it efficient, the law divides it between two Boards, whoſe operations, from the particular nature of that diviſion, can not act vigorouſly, even when they act together; and when they counteract each other, muſt not only be feeble, but ridiculous. Power, in whatever manner it may be divided between different political perſons, is generally impaired by a diviſion ; but the ſpecial diviſion of it made by this bill is more extraordinary than even the idea of dividing it at all.

It

It places all the nominal power of the Company in one set of men, and all the real power in another. The power that appears to command, is itself commanded, and obedience is expected to the authority of men, whom the law itself declares to have no authority at all. If the Company's servants were disobedient in former times, when they knew that the orders they received were really the act of the persons who signed them, what are we to expect at present, when they know, because the law itself tells them so, that the Directors are nothing but formal instruments in the hands of another Board, and that they are obliged to put their signatures, not only to letters and instructions which they have not drawn up, but to letters and instructions drawn up in notorious contradiction to their declared sentiments? A more effectual contrivance to excite and irritate a spirit of disobedience could hardly have been thought of. What language will the servants hold now to their employers, but this in effect?—— " We were ready to have obeyed you ; but we know that the " orders we have received are not yours : we know that they " are directly opposite to your sentiments." A more plausible pretence for disobedience cannot easily be imagined. Sir, I am not reasoning upon imaginary cases. The law has established two jurisdictions over the same object. We know that they have already clashed in one very important instance, and I have reason to believe that they continue to do so in many others. The very moment the Directors began to act, the Board of Control began to counteract ; and the Directors, in the end, were forced to sign orders, against which they had previously protested.

The bad consequences of such a system are obvious in theory, and visible in fact. What good effects it has produced, and how it can possibly produce any, must be explained by those who approve of it. The burden of that explanation makes no part of my undertaking. They who are of opinion that a double government, in which every apparent act of power of one hand is the real act of power of the other ; in which the power that controls is itself controlled ; in which the power that commands is itself commanded ; in which the power that acts is known to act against its own sentiments ; that such a government can be wise in theory, or efficient in practice, will support the present law as it stands, for I have stated nothing which the law itself does not most explicitly enact. They, on the contrary, who may think that a single ostensible government is better than a double one ; that it provides better for the uses of power, and better fixes and secures a determinate responsibility to answer for the abuse of it, will join with me in affirming, that the executive power of the Company ought to be vested in one Board, or in one set of men; and whether they prefer a Court of Directors, or any other form of government, they must equally concur in my conclusion, that this part of the present law defeats its purpose, if that purpose was to create a government, vigorous on one side, and responsible on the other; and that, as long as the present law is in force, the Company's affairs are under a government directly the reverse of what all governments ought to be, and the particular situation of their affairs most urgently demands.

I have stated that the defect, or grievance, at home was, want of power over the service abroad. If that proposition be true, it includes the supposition that the servants abroad abused the power with which they were entrusted, and were disobedient and refractory to that which the law had placed over them. There would have been no occasion to increase or strengthen the power at home, if it had not met with a resistance which it could not overcome; but I need not have recourse to any implication, however clear and obvious. Every bill that has been brought into Parliament on this subject takes the affirmative for granted, considers disobedience as a fact as well as a crime, and denounces various penalties against it. The present law declares, that the wilful disobeying, or the wilfully omitting to execute, the orders of the Directors, shall be deemed, or be taken, as a misdemeanor at law, and punishable as such. Now, Sir, I would ask the right honourable gentleman, if such disobedience has existed, who are the persons most likely to have been guilty of it? In what persons was such disobedience most important in the instance, and most dangerous in the example? Undoubtedly, he will answer me, the persons in the highest trust and authority in India; they alone could disobey; they alone could execute and enforce the orders of the Directors; they alone are answerable, not only for their own offences, but for every offence which they promoted by their participation, which they permitted by their negligence, or encouraged by their example. The conclusion from this reasoning unavoidably fixes the charge of disobedience upon the highest power; and the charge of breach of duty upon the highest trust established in India. It necessarily fixes both upon the Governor General and Council of Bengal. No man, who knows any thing of India, will affirm, that if that Council had been determined to do their duty themselves, they could not have compelled all the subordinate ranks of the service to follow their example. Sir, this very law fixes its eye upon the Governor General and Council, and does, in effect, charge upon them, or the majority of them, all the capital offences which it reprobates and prohibits. What is the power in India that can pursue schemes of conquest and extension of dominion but

the

the Governor General and Council of Bengal? What power can declare war, or commence hostilities, or enter into any treaty for making war, but the Governor General and Council? The subordinate Presidencies could have adopted no hostile measure of any kind which the superior Council might not have instantly countermanded, if it was proposed; and arrested, if it was begun. There was no possibility that Madras or Bombay could carry on war, without the concurrence and assistance of Bengal. Besides that, they have no resources of their own; any member of each of those Presidencies might have been removed by the Governor General and Council, if he attempted it. In all the late wars, therefore, the Governor General and Council must be considered as principals; but it is well known that, in all those questions, the Council was not unanimous. The measures which this act so expressly condemns were the acts of a majority; but even that majority was fictitious, since it consisted of the Governor General, and one member of the Council, against the remaining two. In truth, the Governor General's casting voice decided every thing; for, although the Council ought to have been composed of five persons, the unfortunate death of General Clavering threw the whole power of government into the hands of two persons, of whom one, by an unreserved concurrence of opinion, united his vote and authority in that of the other. Such was the gradual devolution of power in Bengal, until it ended in a point, until it vested in the Governor General alone, until it centered in effect in the person of Mr. Hastings. His colleague is to answer for the surrender of the power; but Mr. Hastings is especially answerable for the use that has been made of it. The fact is, that, under the government of a single person, armed with a really undivided power, which the constitution of the Council never meant to give him, all those principles, which the present law condemns and prohibits were brought into action, and produced all those effects which the present law professes to look back to with indignation, which it threatens hereafter to punish, or promises immediately to correct. From these premises it might naturally be expected, that the law, when it condemned certain acts, and reprobated certain principles, would have limited and restrained the power of those persons who had done such acts, and avowed such principles. For what reason the law should act on a conclusion opposite to its own premises, as in fact it has done, has never been accounted for. From the acknowledged abuse of power, the inference of this law is, that such power ought to be strengthened and increased. It states the experience of former abuses, and refuses to be guided by it. In the first place, it reduces the Council from five persons to four; that is, it professes to strengthen by

X x 2   contracting

contracting it into fewer hands; and then, in order to unite the power of the whole Council in the hand of one perfon, it entrufts the Governor General with the perpetual exercife of a cafting voice as long as the Council confifts of an even number, and is equally divided; that is, it unites the power and divides the refponfibility. One would think that they who had feen to what purpofes the power of the cafting voice had been applied, when it accidentally fell into the hands of a Governor General, would never have propofed to annex it in perpetuity to that office. But, taking the bill on its own principles, and admitting that it might be right to give a con-ftant predominant power to the Governor General, I affirm that this is the very worft way of giving it. That it does not give it with certainty, and that the framers of the law were afraid or afhamed to look their own principle in the face. If a Governor General ought to have fuch power, it ought to have been avowedly ftated, and directly given; otherwife it may happen, that the power, which you fay is neceffary, may, in fact, never veft in the Governor General; at all events, his tenure of it is precarious; of courfe the meafures of the government muft fluctuate with every acci-dent that gives or takes away the operation of the cafting voice. By thefe obfervations, I am far from meaning to ad-mit that the object is in any degree wifer than the mode. In my mind, the means are abfurd, and the end is dangerous. I fpeak from long obfervation and experience, and with all the deliberation and conviction of which my underftanding is ca-pable, when I affirm, that, to unite all the powers of go-vernment in India in one perfon, would be a dangerous mea-fure in one view of it, and a ufelefs meafure in every other. That it may be the caufe of irretrievable mifchief, and can anfwer no good purpofe, which may not be more effectually accomplifhed by another courfe. I well know, Sir, that, at fight of any great diftrefs, or mifmanagement, or abufe in public affairs, the firft idea that is apt to prefent itfelf to the mind is that of creating a dictator. When I fay that this is the firft idea that prefents itfelf, I mean that it is not the re-fult of experience and reflection. I will not argue upon the wifdom of fuch an inftitution in a political fyftem, very dif-ferent from ours. An arbitrary monarch, or a republic, may perhaps delegate all their power, for a limited time, to one perfon, with fafety and effect. The dictator had power of life and death; and I will not undertake to deny, though I am far from meaning to admit, that a remedy of fuch vio-lence, if it did not kill, might poffibly cure. But remedies of this dangerous vigour are incompatible with our Conftitu-tion. You cannot give the power; and, if you could, it would anfwer no good purpofe. My propofition is, that, for

every

every good purpose attainable under our Constitution, a Governor and Council is a much stronger power than any that can be exercised by a single person.

As to any man who may have demanded such power for personal purposes of his own, I treat him, as I suppose this House would instantly do—I lay him entirely out of the question. But let me suppose the case of a man of unquestionable honour and integrity, who should insist on being vested with exclusive powers, with an undoubted intention of making the best use of them. To him I would say, " Sir, the confidence which you seem to repose in your judge- " ment does not entitle you to mine. I know, from expe- " rience, that cases occur in the government of India, in " which the advice and control of a Council are not only " useful, but necessary, and in which the most prudent Go- " vernor will be the readiest to take advice. A wise Gover- " nor will not only take advice, but he will be glad to have " the constant check and inspection of a Council over his ac- " tions. No man, whose intentions are upright, will feel " himself fettered, or distressed by such advice and inspec- " tion."

But it will be said that the plans and views of a Governor General, however proper and judicious, may be thwarted and defeated by factious opposition, and by divisions in the Coun- cil. To this I say, that, *prima facie*, a Governor is just as, likely to be a factious man, and to have bad intentions, as any given member of the Council: nay, the presumption is against him in proportion to the superiority of his rank and influence. The elevation of power is apt to make men giddy; and the exercise of it, I fear, has no direct tendency to improve their morality. In all the divisions under Mr. Hastings's government, the Court of Directors fixed the blame upon him. The two Committees of the House of Commons, who have inquired into our conduct, have done the same. Let it be admitted, nevertheless, that a majority of the Council is most likely to be in fault, and that they thwart the Governor General on factious principles, and for interested purposes of their own. If that should really hap- pen, take care that you fix the blame where you ought to fix it. If you do not, you are unjust in the first instance, and that injustice will mislead you in the subsequent choice of your measures. Before you apply a remedy against faction, take care that you distinguish between the merit of the insti- tution itself, and that of the persons who are appointed to fill it up. The wisest institution that human wisdom has been able to contrive, may be defeated by an improper choice of persons. On the contrary, a poor and feeble system, honestly, wisely, and vigorously executed, may be attended with all the
effects

effects of a virtuous government, and many of the advantages of a strong one. If, when you have instituted a Council on the wisest principles, you fill it up with men of no ability or experience; with men of a questionable character; with men whose general principles are not previously known to one another; or, in short, with men whose rank and reputation in life give you no pledge or security for their good behaviour; and if then you find your Council distracted by factions; if then you find the wise measures of your Governor General resisted and defeated, do not condemn the institution, but blame yourself for the weak or shameful choice you have made of the persons, to whose hands you have committed the execution. On this point I desire to be understood to speak generally, and not to allude to any fact or individual whatever. Now, Sir, let me suppose, that, under the same institution, the choice of persons were to be directly the reverse of that which I have described: that none but men of proper rank, acknowledged ability, and unquestionable integrity, and whose general principles were known to, and approved of, by each other, were appointed to this Council; will any man say that a Council, so composed, is likely to thwart and embarrass a good Governor by a factious opposition to his measures? No, Sir; they will not weaken his authority by opposition, but they will make him powerful indeed by their support. A Governor General understands nothing of his situation, if he thinks that any power, directly vested in his hands, will carry half the sway with it, that will always accompany the united acts of a Governor and Council. If he trusts to his own exclusive judgement, I tell him, he will find himself surrounded by some of the most artful men that exist: on one side, by natives, who, without our general knowledge, are infinitely sagacious, who observe us attentively, and understand us perfectly; and on the other by some Europeans, who, in every thing but their habit and complection, are perfect Asiatics. No single unassisted English judgement is a match for such men, and for such peculiar faculties, as will collect about him from the moment of his arrival. If again he relies on his exclusive power, I tell him, that, for want of clear and accurate knowledge, he will rarely venture to exert it. Every man who approaches him will tell him a different story, or give him a different opinion. He will often doubt, and, when he doubts, he will not act at all. No vigorous determination can exist in a good mind, that is not produced by knowledge or conviction; but even his power, when he exerts it, will be feeble and ineffectual against the universal combination and clamour of all ranks, and of all interests, which will be formed to counteract him in every measure that tends to reduce exorbi-

tant

tant emoluments, or to correct any abuse, from which individuals derive an advantage. In this respect, however, our
fellow subjects in Bengal have full as much morality as we
have. In parallel circumstances, the same thing would happen in England; but, in a great community, the reformer
has the voice and approbation of a majority to encourage him.
In a very narrow circle he will have no part of the society in
which he lives to support him against the rest. They will
all make common cause against him, and, sooner or later,
overcome his resolution, or break his heart. Upon the whole,
I am of opinion, that, in a plan of general reform, an united
Governor and Council may do much—a single person can do
nothing. For the truth of this proposition I would readily
appeal to Mr. Haftings himself; and I would state the argument to him with an admission of all the personal preferences
and objections which that gentleman could wish to establish.
Let it be imagined, then, that the Legislature, instead of
forcing him to act with men of unequal rank in life, of opposite views, of a suspected or doubtful character, and of an
impracticable temper, such as General Clavering, Colonel
Monson, and myself, had united him with men of his own
cast and disposition, with men whose general views and principles determined them to give him the same cordial and vigorous support which he constantly and uniformly received from
Mr. Barwell; then would he say, that a Council, so constituted, and so acting firmly together, would not have possessed
in itself, and given the Governor a stronger power than any
that could have been vested singly in his person, or any that
he alone could have ventured to exert. I am much mistaken,
indeed, if, on a case so stated, Mr. Haftings's opinion would
differ from mine. This, at least, I may affirm with certainty, for my late honourable colleagues as well as for myself, that if the personal character, political views, and public principles of Mr. Haftings and Mr. Barwell had been such
as, concurring with our own, had engaged us to unite cordially with Mr. Haftings, and to give him a steady and vigorous support, we should have thought his government not
only more wisely calculated for all the purposes of council
and deliberation, but even stronger in the execution, than any
power that could have been vested in him alone; and that it
would have carried an opinion, a dignity, an authority, and
a sway, along with it, which no faction could have resisted,
no combination could have withstood.

From all these premises, I come to my conclusion on the
second general division of the bill, that the reduction of the
Council from five to four was an unwise measure; that every
idea of vesting great exclusive power in any single person, is,
at once, useless and dangerous; that, for all good purposes,

an

an united Council is infinitely more powerful than a single person can be; and that even if the principle, on which the present law proceeds, were ever so just and necessary, I mean that of giving special powers to a Governor General, this law does not act up to its own principle, or provide for its own object. The power it gives is meanly and indirectly given, and it provides no security for its continuance, for a single day, in the Governor General's hands. On the whole, therefore, if you disapprove of the principle of giving exclusive power to a single person, you must condemn this law for having given too much; but, if you approve of the principle, you must then condemn the law still more strongly for having given too little.

We are now to consider the third great division of the bill; and, on this subject, I confess I expect not only a general attention, but a general concurrence and support. However indifferent and uninteresting the good or bad government of the East-India Company's affairs, or the welfare of the people subject to their power in India, may have been to the nation at large, or to a majority of this House, or to any individual member of it, there is not a man in the kingdom to whom the subject, that now calls upon you for your attention, ought to be indifferent. At first sight, it may perhaps appear to affect only a part of our fellow subjects who are at a distance from us. If that were true, I still should think it my duty to appeal to you in their behalf. This law declares that they are not so distant as to be out of the reach of its power. To whatever extent we carry that power, let us take care to shew that our justice goes along with it. Let no man in India have reason to say, that he is included in the power, and excluded from the justice, of the Legislature. But, Sir, it is not for them alone that I have undertaken this heavy task. The instant suffering is theirs: the consequence and the danger is yours. *Res agitur vestra.* A capital innovation is made in the criminal jurisprudence of England. New principles are introduced, not only in the system of our laws, but into the manners of the people. A new tribunal is erected for the trial of misdemeanors committed in India, and armed or accompanied with powers unheard of in this country. The ancient established mode of trial by a jury, and by the country, is renounced as imperfect and inadequate; a new and arbitrary system of inquiry and trial is established in the room of it; and all this is done for reasons and pretences equally applicable to any other sort of crime, and any other species of offender. This system, considered as a fact, I deem to be unjust and arbitrary. Considering it as a precedent, it holds out a general menace to the whole kingdom: it acts directly upon a few, but it threatens us all.

If,

If, by the immediate acquiescence of the parties—if, by their voluntary surrender of their rights, the instant injustice of the fact could be palliated or removed, the danger of the precedent would be increased; for who would regard a distant menace, if he who was actually wounded were to suppress his resentment, or to admit, by his silence, that he had no reason to complain.

In agitating this part of my subject, the principle I set out with, and the main ground I take, is not only supported by the obvious dictates of policy and reason, but by the highest authority by which Parliament can be instructed. The authority I speak of is at all times entitled to submission and respect; but to the respect and submission of this House of Commons in particular, and of the present Administration, its claim is special, and not to be resisted. At the first meeting of the present Parliament, we received an admonition from the Throne, which, I am sorry to say, was very little regarded in our subsequent proceedings. The words His Majesty made use of ought for ever to be remembered —

" The affairs of the East-India Company form an object " of deliberation deeply connected with the general interests " of the country. While you feel a just anxiety to provide " for the good government of our possessions in that part of " the world, you will, I trust, never lose sight of the effect " which any measure, to be adopted for that purpose, may " have on our own Constitution, and our dearest interests at " home."

To insure the success of the present motion, I desire no better pledge or security than that the House should keep this wise admonition in their view, and be governed by it. The principle contained in it has already been successfully exerted, though, in my judgement, very erroneously directed, against a law proposed by a right honourable gentleman (Mr. Fox) near him — against a law, which, in no shape, invaded the Constitution, or affected any domestic interest that ought to be dear to us. The part which the nation in general took in that transaction has only proved the facility, in some cases, of substituting words for meaning, and of totally overturning the sense by the sound. The charter of a monopoly was confounded with the great charter of our freedom, and that single word *charter* decided the question. When the principle I have alluded to had done all the duty demanded from it, it was still indeed adhered to in terms, and delivered with great and awful solemnity, as an instruction to this House; but it was at that very moment completely abandoned in fact, and another, directly opposite to it, assumed, and acted upon. In little more than a month after the King had cautioned us, from the throne, " never to lose sight of the effect which any

" meafure, to be adopted for the good government of India,
" might have on our own Conftitution, and our deareft inte-
" refts at home," a bill was brought into Parliament, which
I affirm, and I have no doubt of being able to prove, attacks
the Conftitution of England in its foundation, and not only
threatens, but invades, the fecurity of every intereft that
ought to be deareft to us at home; which not only fhakes the
defences of our domeftic eftablifhment, but acts upon principles which ought not to be admitted under any government
or conftitution, or in any human fociety whatever. I defire
it to be underftood, Sir, that, in every thing I am going to
fay, I keep the King's fpeech in view as a beacon or land-
mark, by which my courfe fhall be directed. In the firft
place, allow me to ftate, in a fhort, general view, what it is
that this part of the law enacts. It begins with compelling a
fet of men whom the law itfelf, in fome fort, prejudges to
be criminal, whom it ftrongly fufpects, at leaft, if it does
not accufe, of having acquired fortune by corrupt practices,
if not by violence and extortion, to deliver an exact inventory of their property, on oath, as foon as they arrive in
England. Now, Sir, with refpect to men perfectly innocent and unfufpected, the beft that can be faid of the law is,
that it is harmlefs. If that were all, it would then be equally
ufelefs. From thofe who are innocent you can extort no
confeffion: but I deny that it is in no cafe a hardfhip and injuftice to an honeft man, to oblige him to declare publicly the
exact amount of his fortune. Numberlefs cafes might be
ftated, in which it might be, to a very honeft man, a very
arbitrary act of oppreffion. It might even happen, that the
act might be oppreffive in proportion to the innocence of the
party; for, though his poverty might prove his innocence,
it might eafily happen that many a man would wifh to have
his innocence proved by any other kind of evidence. We do
not live in times in which poverty is refpectable. I fear the
contrary is true, and that the law which compels an honeft
man to difcover the narrownefs of his circumftances, whatever it may intend, will, in effect, only ferve or affift to fling
difgrace upon ill fortune, and to make the moft honourable
poverty ridiculous. Men of this defcription ought certainly
to be fpared.

Now, Sir, admitting it to be an equitable fuppofition, that
guilt and fortune go together; admitting it to be a found
principle of juftice, that men fhould be tried rather by their
wealth than by their actions, let us fee how the law operates
on thofe whom it may have reafon to fufpect — on men who
may really have acquired an immoderate fortune by very unwarrantable, perhaps very criminal, means. See whether the
option, which the law holds out to fuch perfons, be likely to
produce

produce any good effect whatever. It obliges the parties to chufe between a condemnation of themfelves by a difcovery of their guilt, and a concealment of their guilt by perjury. If this be the option, what is like to be the choice? That a man, accuftomed to criminal practices of one kind, will be extremely fcrupulous about committing another crime to protect the firft; or that, being already guilty, he will make himfelf ftill more guilty in order to efcape punifhment. In my mind, Sir, all the effect of the law will be, to invite him to add one crime to another, and if he be already guilty of extortion, of oppreffion, of cruelty, to endeavour to cover it by perjury. In general, it is neither prudent nor equitable to place any man between a great danger, or a great temptation, on one fide, and a moral or religious obligation on the other. The law fhould be tender of creating fuch dilemmas. To impofe fuch a teft on men whofe integrity you already fufpect, is worfe than imprudent. It is an invitation to falfehood; becaufe it annexes the expectation of impunity for one offence to the commiffion of another.

The law then, Sir, in the cafe of any complaint made to the Court of Exchequer, of wilful concealment of property, or defect, or evafion in the difcovery, proceeds to fubject the party to anfwer interrogatories, on oath, at the difcretion of the Court. In both inftances it revives a mode of inquifition and conviction which the Conftitution of this country holds in abhorrence, and which our anceftors vainly imagined they had extirpated for ever, when they abolifhed the Star Chamber. With refpect to the interrogatories, it might be fufficient to fay, that they are liable to the fame fundamental objection with the method propofed for extorting a difcovery in the firft inftance; namely, that they place a perfon, who, by the fuppofition, is criminal, between the neceffity of condemning himfelf by his veracity, or acquitting himfelf by his falfehood. But thefe interrogatories carry the fame abfurd and wicked principle a great deal farther. They fuppofe the party to have been guilty of perjury in the firft inftance; and they call upon him either to convict himfelf of that crime, or to cover it by a feries of new perjuries in his anfwers to the interrogatories. I have ftated the principles of the new inquifition as I find them avowed and eftablifhed, and fhall leave them, without argument, to the fenfations and to the judgement of the Houfe. To make it felt that they are arbitrary and abfurd, requires no argument. The moment they are ftated, they are condemned.

The law, having now exerted the utmoft of its power to extort a difcovery of guilt by the confeffion of the guilty, proceeds to fupply the defects of that mode by another courfe, which indeed feems to promife a greater probability of fuccefs, but, in my judgement, is ftill more deteftable than the other, becaufe it holds out rewards to treachery and bafenefs, and tends to corrupt and deftroy all the little morality we have left in private life. This law formally introduces into the inmoft receffes of perfonal confidence and friendfhip the worft of all the inftruments that ever have been employed by power without right. It acknowledges the office of fpy and informer to be ufeful in the general intercourfe of fociety, and rewards him with a fhare in the fuccefs of his information. Sir, the man who difcovers a crime, and brings a criminal to punifhment, performs an honou ple duty to the Public; but he who fearches into the circumftances of another, who inquires in order to accufe, and who accufes in order to profit by the amount of his difcovery, can be nothing but a traitor in private life; he never can be a ufeful fervant to the Public. But the temptation held out by this law is not confined to common fpies and informers; it goes to perfons much better able to difcover the amount of a concealed fortune, to perfons whom you have particularly trufted—your agent, your fecretary, your banker, or your friend. Who knows but that the invitation of the law may feduce a fon to betray his father, a brother to betray his brother, and, what is worft of all, perhaps fome perfon, whom you have effentially ferved, to betray his benefactor. The very money you have lent him, if, whether wilfully or not, you fhould have omitted it in your account, will enable him to accufe you of concealment, and entitle him to fhare in the forfeiture that follows. I appeal to every thing that is honourable and virtuous in this Houfe — Is there an object of penal juftice, againft any particular fet of men, adequate to the price you muft pay for it, if you fuffer fuch principles as thefe to be introduced not only into the laws of the kingdom, but into the manners of the People?

This appeal to the general fenfe and judgement of the Houfe, I truft, will not be ineffectual: but the juftice of my caufe entitles me to look every where for affiftance. There is a particular body of men, powerful in this Houfe, and in this kingdom, who, I think, are bound by many fpecial confiderations to take part with me in the prefent queftion — I mean the gentlemen who have unaccountably been mifled to give their confent to a law which bears hard upon their former companions, and upon all the connections they have left in India. I appeal to them as to men of honour, and put the queftion ftrongly upon their character, whether they will deliberately inflict upon others fuch reftraints and penalties as, I imagine, they would have thought unjuft againft themfelves? whether they will look back with fympathy and concern to the fituations in which they were lately placed? or whether, having quitted their fituations, they will content
themfelves

themselves with holding to all their deserted friends and companions the base exclusive language of personal escape and security — *Occupet extremum scabies.* — Sir, I am aware of the turn that may be given to an argument of this nature. It is directed *ad homines,* and with them it ought to have weight. But, in order to give point and direction to this appeal, and to make it intelligible by application, I desire leave to suppose that all the gentlemen alluded to were for a moment represented by one person, and that that person were my honourable colleague in the government of Bengal, now a member of this House, (Richard Barwell, Esq.) To him at least I have some right to address myself. I would request him to consider whether, if, before he left India, before he had remitted home and invested in England the honourable reward of his labours, (and certainly the labours were considerable, if we are to measure them by the amount of the reward) it had been proposed to him to give or refuse his concurrence to a law which should oblige him, the moment he arrived in England, to make a public declaration on oath of the amount and particulars of his fortune, which should compel him to submit to interrogatories on oath concerning the truth of every particular of that declaration, and which should hold out temptation and seduction to his agents, to his friends, and to every man in his confidence, (by the promise of sharing in his fortune) to find out some error in his account; whether, if such a proposition had been made to him, he would have thought it a just and reasonable law against himself; whether he would have assented to it with chearfulness, or rejected it with indignation. I certainly meant to call upon him, if he had been present, to answer explicitly for himself; yet I think I know my honourable colleague's ideas and principles on this subject sufficiently to venture to answer for him. I will venture to affirm for him, that he would not have entirely approved of these inquiries into the state of his fortune, much less of the encouragement held out to his particular friends to accuse him. If I form a just judgement of my honourable colleague's principles, he will assist me in protecting others from an inquisition which he would have thought oppressive to himself. I cannot believe that he would apply any other measure to the actions of others, but that which he would willingly abide by for his own.

I come now, Sir, to the consideration of the tribunal and mode of trial which this bill creates, and substitutes in the place of the ancient trial, which every man in this land is entitled to, even the felon, the murderer, and the parricide, when he throws himself upon his country; that is, to be tried by twelve indifferent persons, as nearly as possible of his own level, and by the law of the land. Let us see what
this

this tribunal is, how it is conftituted, and how it is to act. In the firft place, Sir, it profeffes to confift of thirteen perfons, whom I will fuppofe for a moment to be chofen with all the indifference which the law affects. If they be really fo chofen, it will not follow that, with refpect to ten of them, namely, the four Lords and fix Commoners, any advantage is gained over a jury in point of knowledge, or any other judicial qualification ; for I believe it will not be denied that a fpecial jury of Englifh gentlemen is juft as likely to be qualified for this or any other judicial office, as any ten members of the Lords and Commons taken at a venture. But the pofitive difadvantages of the new tribunal are many and obvious. The Lords and the Judges are not peers of the criminal. An inftitution, that calls on fuch perfons for a verdict, renounces every ufe and advantage which the laws of this country annex to the trial of facts by our Peers. In favour of what ? In favour of a tribunal, in which every one of the component parts is placed in a fituation in which they were never placed before. This tribunal abandons the wife and ancient feparation of the verdict from the judgement, and unites in the fame perfons the verdict, the explanation of the law, and the fentence. Lords and Judges are called upon to find the facts, and the Commoners, if they will, may determine the law, and pronounce the judgement. The vote of the Commoners, on a point of law, is juft as valid as that of the Judge.

With refpect to the method of chufing the pannel, I fhall avoid faying any thing that may appear invidious or perfonal. My caufe is too powerful to want the affiftance of perfonal reflections. I ftand on public ground, and fhall take no other. I ftate it, therefore, only as a matter of fact, not only not denied, but defended, that, in the very firft inftance of chufing the pannel, out of which the new tribunal is to be finally felected, the choice was made by Treafury lifts diftributed among the members of this Houfe, and that the perfons named in thofe lifts have been appointed. I ftate the fact without obfervation, and fhall leave it fo to the reflections of the Houfe.

The law proceeds to prefcribe a courfe, by which the whole pannel of three Judges, twenty-fix Lords, and forty Commoners, fhall be finally reduced to thirteen perfons, whofe names are to be inferted in a fpecial commiffion, in order to form the new tribunal. On this part of the proceeding I obferve, that, admitting the neceffity of changing the form of adminiftering criminal juftice, it does not follow that there is any neceffity for renouncing the fundamental principles on which that juftice has been hitherto adminiftered in England. Your profeffed object is to create an impartial tribunal.

unal. The formation of a jury is so contrived, that it is scarcely possible it should not be impartial; then why abandon the forms established for the choice of a jury? The present law does so without reason or necessity. It allows the party a right of peremptory challenge only against thirteen of the Peers and twenty of the Commoners. Now, supposing it proper to admit of none but peremptory challenges, why should the exercise of that right be stopped as long as a number of Lords and Commoners remain sufficient to form the tribunal: if, on the contrary, it be proper to limit the number of peremptory challenges, why should you restrain the party from challenging the remainder of the pannel for cause assigned? This, I affirm, is not only an unnecessary departure from the ancient constitution of juries, but a denial of right, completely unjust and absurd. It is unjust to force the party to include his challenges for a cause assigned within the number which you allow him to make peremptory. The result may be, that you will allow no peremptory challenge at all, since it may very easily happen that all his peremptory challenges may lie against persons against whom he might be ready and desirous to object for specific reasons. But can any thing be conceived more absurd than that the law should yield perhaps to his malignity, perhaps to his caprice, and refuse to listen to his reason?

Against the three judges there is to be no challenge allowed, for reasons, I presume, deduced from the sanctity of their character and the respect due to their station. To the former I shall only say, that judges may be better men than we are, but they are men; and that cases occur in which an exception to a judge, even in the discharge of his proper office, would be deemed valid, and would force him to retire. To the latter I say, that a judge has no right to carry along with him the respect due to his proper station, when he descends to any other. I will not challenge him as long as he maintains the post at which the Constitution placed him; but if he accepts of another office, if he takes upon him to find the facts, if he condescends to be a juryman, he must accept of that office with all its conditions. He has no claim to the privilege of a judge, while he does that which no judge in this kingdom ever did before. But is it impossible that one of the three judges may be an enemy of the party accused? Would you really appoint such a judge to try such a party? and, if the objection were so stated, would you affirm that it deserved no attention? If, even without supposing a direct enmity, two men were known to have stood on terms unfriendly to each other, would you appoint one of them to judge the other? Let me appeal to the honour of the learned gentleman opposite to me, who knows what has passed in India. If I were the

the person accused, would he chuse Sir Elijah Impey to be my judge? That gentleman, I presume, would decline the office. But for myself I can affirm, that if he should be accused, I would never sit in judgement upon him. I may be prosecutor—I may be evidence against him—but I will never give a judicial vote in any cause in which Sir Elijah Impey may be party, unless I can safely give it for him.

The tribunal, at last obtained, professedly consists of thirteen persons. For what reason this small number should afterwards be reduced to seven is not explained. The whole power of the thirteen is finally committed to a *quorum* of seven, provided one of this number be a judge. In so very small a number it might be thought, that an unanimous judgement might safely be demanded. In finding the facts, at least, it might be expected that their verdict should be unanimous; but in this tribunal a new and dangerous principle of decision is assumed. The sense of the court is to be bound and determined by a majority of votes; that is, the facts may be found, the law determined, and the punishment awarded by four persons out of seven; and the court may be so composed and divided, that possibly one Lord and three Judges may find all the facts against the finding of three Commoners, or *vice versa*, that four Commoners may determine the law against the three Judges. What they will do I know not; but this is what they may do under the present institution.

We are now to consider the course and conduct of the trial. With respect to the trial of crimes in general, I presume it will not be denied that two conditions are essential to the due administration of justice, at least that they have been hitherto thought so in England. The first is peculiar to our Constitution, that the jury shall not separate before they have agreed upon their verdict. The law is cautious of exposing the virtue of jurymen to the temptations which might be thrown in their way, if they were suffered to go out of court, and disperse before they had found their verdict. The law will not even confide in their judgement so far as to suffer them to listen to any extrajudicial evidence whatever. When once they are shut up, all access to them is forbidden. Let the House compare the wisdom of these precautions with the latitude allowed to the present tribunal. The commissioners may adjourn from day to day *ad libitum*. They may mix in society, and listen to all manner of discourses upon the subject matter of the charge depending before them. If the party accused be a very guilty man, he must be wealthy in the same proportion; and if the evidence should appear to go against him, what security have you that he will not attempt to corrupt the integrity of one or other of the commissioners, fioners, whom he or his agents may meet out of court and converfe with every day? Since a majority is to decide, it may happen that, by corrupting one out of feven, the judgement may be in his favour. In all thefe obfervations, Sir, I earneftly defire it to be underftood that I fpeak of inftitutions, and not of perfons. The Lords and Commoners, who compofe the prefent pannel, are honourable men; fo we are all: but let it be remembered that laws are made to guard againft what men may do, not to truft to what they will do. Admitting corruption to be impracticable, there are other forts of influence, againft which the virtue of men fhould equally be defended. The language of perfonal enmity, or public odium, on one fide, or of intereft, folicitation, or compaffion, on the other, may engage the paffions, or bias the judgement of the judge. But if any of thefe Lords and Commoners fhould be connected with the Adminiftration, and if the party accufed fhould be a perfon whom the Minifter fhould think it neceffary to feduce or intimidate; whofe fortune, for example, might entitle him to a feat in the Houfe of Commons, then look to the confequence. Who will venture to affirm that it is impoffible for a commiffioner, fo connected, to found the inclinations of the Minifter; to apprife him what turn the trial is likely to take, and to receive his inftructions from time to time for his own fubfequent conduct. Of the prefent Minifter I am ready to admit, that fo bafe a practice is not to be fufpected. Concerning his perfonal honour, I am ready to take every thing for granted that his warmeft friends can fay of him. My argument is applied generally to things, not to men, and ftands abftracted from all perfonal confiderations whatfoever.

The fecond great confideration, which I deem to be effential to the adminiftration of juftice, and which is admitted to be fo not only in this country, but in every other where juftice is really adminiftered, is, that the trial fhould be in open court. The law of England does not allow that juftice can be done in fecret; therefore will not fuffer the doors of a court of juftice to be fhut. The wifdom of our anceftors has deemed the infpection of the public eye upon the proceedings of the court to be a powerful guard over the virtue of the judge; and the beft and wifeft of our judges have thought it no impeachment of their integrity. An open trial obliges the judge, in every queftion that comes before him, to chufe between his duty and the lofs of his reputation. On the face of the prefent law, I fee nothing that provides for and fecures a public trial: for any thing that appears to the contrary, the commiffioners may fit, in clofe recefs, in one of the chambers of the Treafury. If I am miftaken on this point, I wifh to be corrected, for I should be sorry to load the law with an ill-founded imputation.

Sir, it requires but little ability to shew the dangerous nature and effect of these invasions in the plan and system of the laws of England. He who is able to state the fact, demonstrates the consequence. But we have been told already, and I expect we shall be told again, that necessity supersedes all principles; that there is no alternative; that offences committed in India are of such a nature, that it is impossible to bring them within the cognizance, and of course to subject them to the verdict of a jury. It may be so: but I own it is a proposition that passes my understanding. When, by virtue of the powers already vested in the courts below, the necessary evidence, from depositions taken in writing, shall be obtained from India, why the whole of it may not be reduced to distinct issues of fact, on which a jury may pronounce as well as any other tribunal, is a question to which I am not able to conceive a satisfactory answer. We are not speaking of political offences, of crimes against the state, which, in many cases, perhaps can only be established by a minute examination of letters, instructions, and correspondence, and by a careful deduction and inference from intricate proceedings to certain motives. The declared and only object of the present law is to prosecute and bring to speedy and condign punishment persons guilty of the crime of extortion and other misdemeanors. These offences, if committed, are matters of fact, on which it remains to be proved that a jury of English Commoners cannot find a verdict, but on which a court, consisting of Judges, Lords, and Commoners, can very well find a verdict, declare the law, and pronounce a judgement. I distrust my own knowledge too much, and see too much legal learning opposed to me, to undertake to prove a negative to that proposition. Yet even that task would have been undertaken, and I doubt not with success, by a learned gentleman, (Mr. John Lee) whose heart, as well as his learning, goes with me on this subject, if a severe illness, unfortunately for me and for the Public, had not prevented his attendance this day. I lament his absence, though I know I shall not be left without some powerful legal support. Strictly and properly, the burden of the proof lies on the affirmative. They who innovate are bound to shew a sufficient positive reason for the innovation. They are bound to the direct proof of this clear, distinct proposition; namely, that a jury is absolutely incapable, and cannot by any means be made capable of trying an act of extortion, or other misdemeanor, committed in India. No doctrine, that does not clearly and distinctly go to the full extent and meaning of this proposition, will support the present law. The innovation

tion is avowedly founded on a suppofed neceffity, and no alternative. But if a jury either is, or can by any means be made capable of the fervice, you have an alternative; the neceffity does not exift, and you have no pretence to innovate. Sir, this will be a ferious undertaking for men of rank and character in the profeffion. It is not a trial of fkill between cunning knowledge and unlearned reafon: it is not a victory of legal argument over an unlearned individual, contending for his birthright, which, on fuch a queftion, will fatisfy the fenfe and judgement of this nation. The learned perfon, who ventures to affirm that the propofition is true in the terms in which I have ftated it, fhould remember that his character is at ftake, that he acts under the infpection of the public eye, and that he is going to chufe between his duty and the lofs of his reputation for ever. I will tell him too, that I have good reafon to believe, though I do not directly affert, that the firft law authorities in this kingdom are againft him. I truft he will find it fo when the queftion comes to be agitated, as ere long it muft be, in another place.

Before I conclude this part of my fubject I flatter myfelf the Houfe will allow me to remind them of the little triumph that prevailed when a right honourable friend of mine (Mr. Burke) declared very lately, that, after long and ferious deliberation, he preferred the trial by impeachment to that of profecution in the courts below, for the purpofe of bringing a capital Indian delinquent to juftice; as if my right honourable friend had thereby abandoned the trial by jury, and furnifhed the advocates of the prefent tribunal with reafon to conclude that his opinion on this fubject coincided with theirs. I hope to be able to convince the Houfe that the conclufion was precipitate, and the triumph premature. I fhould indeed have thought myfelf unfortunate if the fentiments of my right honourable friend had differed from mine on this important queftion. I fhould have diftrufted my own moft deliberate judgement, and fhould have acted with hefitation and reluctance even upon the moft deliberate conviction. The relation in which I ftand to my right honourable friend, gives him every claim over me that belongs to authority, and juftifies fubmiffion: it is that of a being that is inftructed, to the being that inftructs him. Sir, I am not here to pronounce my right honourable friend's panegyric; nor, if I were equal to the tafk, would I now venture to undertake it: it would lead me to reflections that would utterly difcompofe me—to the recollection of virtues unrewarded, and of veteran fervices growing gray under the neglect, if not ingratitude, of his country. If fame be a reward, he poffeffes it already: but I know he looks forward to a higher recompenpe. He confiders and believes, as I do, that, in fome

other

other exiſtence, the virtues of men will meet with retribution; where they who have faithfully and gratuitouſly ſerved mankind, " ſhall find the generous labour was not loſt."

On the point in queſtion there is no difference between us. His opinion comes in aid to mine : our minds are united, and our principles act together. If it be a contradiction to ſay, that, for the puniſhment of crimes of a ſpecial quality and magnitude, the trial by impeachment is the ſafeſt, the moſt effectual, and the beſt; but that, for offences of a lower order, the eſtabliſhed trial by jury ſhould ſtill be adhered to. He who maintains the affirmative, charges that very contradiction upon the laws, the inſtitutions, the practice, and the wiſdom of England, ever ſince Parliaments had a being. I am not afraid of erring with ſuch powerful and venerable authority. The trial by impeachment is founded on a popular right, coeval with the Houſe of Commons: it is as well known and as well eſtabliſhed in our Conſtitution as the trial by jury, though it cannot occur ſo often. There are caſes of crimes and of criminals, to which no other form of proceeding is adequate, to which no other mode of trial is commenſurate. In ſuch caſes, the trial by impeachment does that which no other trial can accompliſh. It not only forces the crime to an inquiry; it not only demands juſtice againſt the criminal, and inſures his puniſhment; but it provides for another object, which, in ſome inſtances, is not leſs intereſting and neceſſary than even juſtice and puniſhment. It clears the honour of the nation in which ſuch crimes are committed, and to which ſuch criminals belong: it vindicates the character of this country from reproach in the judgement of mankind. Theſe are the occaſions in which the pre-eminence of the wiſdom and juſtice of England diſplays itſelf over all other nations. Other nations may rival us in our crimes — but there the competition ends. In England alone the dignity of the trial riſes to a level with the eminence of the crime. When the Houſe of Commons impeaches, it is a ſolemn appeal to the judgement of the world. When crimes are charged, by which the happineſs, if not the exiſtence, of whole nations has been affected; by which ſtates and princes, and all the higheſt orders of men as well as the loweſt have been reduced, by the baſe and iron hand of upſtart power, to miſery and ruin, the trial by impeachment makes proclamation to the kingdoms and princes of the world to attend and look on, while the democracy of England advances in perſon to the charge, aſſumes the noble office of accuſer, and forces the crime to trial before every thing that is great, and noble, and wiſe, and learned, and venerable, in our country. The crime, the criminal, the proſecutor, the judges, the audience, and the trial, produce and conſtitute a ſcene

which

which no other country can exhibit to the world. Let us hope that the necessity of so solemn a proceeding will not often exist hereafter. The Constitution has wisely reserved it for crimes of special magnitude, and rare in proportion to their greatness. The same Constitution has provided, with equal wisdom, for the punishment of offences of an inferior rank by another course, equally appropriated to its object. Let my right honourable friend proceed, therefore, to the discharge of that elevated duty, to which his eminent abilities call him. There are still other duties to be performed by inferior abilities. While he travels on in the high road of impeachment, I shall endeavour to attend his course in a narrower track, but in a parallel path. The lines we act in neither cross nor diverge: they are equally directed to the same general object of justice, and they run together.

Now, Sir, the principal part of my task is completed; for, generally speaking, my present purpose is not so much to institute, as to correct. I mean to take away a great deal, but not to enact much in the place of it. In other circumstances, I should have thought myself bound to attempt a great deal more. If I had been united in views and sentiments with the acting Administration of the country, and might therefore have hoped for their support in the plan, and their hearty concurrence in the execution of a new law on this subject, I certainly should have extended my thoughts to a comprehensive positive institution for the better government of India; but, since I do not stand in that predicament, I must adopt another conduct, conformable to my situation. I must take care that whatever I propose, *rebus sic stantibus*, whether to correct or to enact, the thing I propose may execute itself, and not depend for its success on the temper of Administration. I must take care not to aim at any thing but what may really be attainable under the present circumstances; and finally, that while I am endeavouring to do good, I may be sure of doing no mischief. Acting on these limited principles, I shall proceed to state to you briefly and generally what I propose to do. If the motion should be carried, my purpose is to extirpate out of this bill the principal evil that belongs to it; to revert to that which was good before, or which, if not perfect in itself, has not been improved by innovation; to strengthen that good, if it be feeble, and not to enact much by positive institution. I would rebuild the house I live in from the foundation, if I could; but since that is not in my power, I will endeavour to repair it.

Protesting, as I continue to do, against the form in which the executive powers of the India Company in England are actually distributed, and declaring, as I do, that, in my opinion, a more absurd system of government could not have been

been imagined, I shall leave it as it stands. I perfectly know that an attempt to alter it would have no chance of succeeding; nor would I trust the execution of a better system in the hands of men who were adverse to it.

With respect to the government of Bengal, the alteration I shall propose is no more than to revert to the former constitution, which this law has very unwisely altered. I would replace that government in a Governor General and four counsellors, with nearly the same powers with which they were invested by the acts of 1773 and 1781. This alteration is easy, and will execute itself. It has an accidental advantage too, which may recommend it to the favour of those who possess the patronage of the Company. It revives a fifth office of counsellor, with ten thousand pounds a year.

With respect to all that part of the law which creates an inquisition, which compels the subjects of Great Britain to answer interrogatories on oath, which endeavours to corrupt the virtues of private life by promising to make men rich, if they turn traitors and informers, and which deprives the subjects of this kingdom of their great chartered right, of their common-law right, and of their unalienable birthright, a trial by their peers, my intention is to tear it out of the statute book — I would erase it, if I could, from the memory of mankind—I would replace the criminal law of England in the state in which it stood. If the powers already given to the Court of King's Bench, for the purpose of obtaining evidence from India, be insufficient, I have no objection to enlarging them. If the formality of pleading, or the present rules of evidence, or any other formality, stands in the way of justice, let the law be altered; but when the evidence is once collected and prepared, let it be submitted to a jury. With respect to written evidence, though I allow it must be accepted, since, in some cases, it may be impossible to obtain any other, yet I think the present law abuses that concession, and carries the admission of written evidence to a most dangerous excess. It is enacted, " That all writings which shall have " been transmitted from the East Indies to the Court of Di- " rectors, by their officers and servants resident in the East " Indies, in the usual course of their correspondence with the " said Court, and which in any manner relate to the subject " matter of the charge, may be admitted to be offered in evi- " dence." The correspondence, so described, I dare say amounts to above a hundred large folio volumes every year: it comprehends not only the proceedings of the superior councils in India, but those of their subordinate councils, and all the correspondence of all of them with every individual with

whom

whom they have any transaction or intercourse whatever. The law declares that every thing contained in this enormous heap of writing may be admitted to be offered in evidence, and then the Court is to sift and examine it. The task would be a heavy one, even if a clear, certain rule could be established for distinguishing the credible parts of such evidence from the rest. The effect of this clause will be to make the Company's correspondence an indirect channel of accusation between man and man, and to fill it with every thing that interest, jealousy, or malignity can invent, or that ignorance and folly can believe, on any subject. I will not now attempt to state any precise limits for this dangerous admission of written evidence. In general, I shall only say, that authentic copies of the orders of the Court of Directors may be admitted as evidence, when the charge is for disobedience; and that every man's writing, or an undoubted copy of it, may be evidence against himself. On this point I hope to be assisted with legal advice, and to be able to state my opinion with greater precision, if I am permitted to bring in the bill; and here I shall conclude.——They who may differ from me in opinion cannot reasonably impute the part I have taken in this business to any personal apprehension or interest of my own. As to myself, I stand as clear of the law as if I had never been in India; and as to particular friends or connections, I have now but very few in that country: those few, I fear, have not prospered. If any of them are rich, they have no occasion to stay there. If any of them are conscious of having used improper means to acquire a fortune, they will naturally shelter themselves under the present law, by returning to England before January, 1787. I attack this law, because, in fact, it holds out protection to the guilty, and tends to corrupt the innocent; because it introduces false principles into the administration of justice; because it is unjust in its immediate application, while it establishes a precedent dangerous to this kingdom; because it takes away the trial by jury; because it invades and alters the Constitution; and because it shakes the security, and threatens the liberty of every subject of Great Britain.

I therefore move, " That leave be given to bring in a bill " to explain and amend an act made in the twenty-fourth " year of the reign of His present Majesty, entitled, ' An " Act for the better Regulation and Management of the Af- " fairs of the the East-India Company, and of the British " Possessions in India; and for establishing a Court of Judi- " cature for the more speedy and effectual Trial of Persons " accused of Offences committed in the East Indies."

Mr. Wyndham seconded the motion.

Mr.

Mr. *Dundas* remarked, that when the honourable gentleman (Mr. Francis) who fpoke laft, adverted to a new judicature for the trial of perfons accufed of extortions and other mifdemeanors in the Eaft-India fettlements, he certainly included in that divifion of his ftrictures upon a bill which he propofed to amend and mollify, what did not immediately belong to it; and this was, the obligation impofed upon the fervants of the Company at their return to Europe, to account on oath for the property which they might have acquired during their refidence in India. He fhould not, for the prefent, enter into the full extent of the queftion, but fay fomething concerning each part of it, referving the remainder for a future occafion, not far diftant, when the fubject would again be brought by him before the Houfe. The honourable gentleman complained, that in the alteration which had been made in the government of the Company's affairs at home, the refponfibility was fo divided between the Board of Control and the Court of Directors, that it became impoffible to afcertain, in cafe of mifcarriage, where the fault exifted. To this he would anfwer, that at prefent the refponfibility was infinitely more direct and complete than it had been before; for, when the Board of Control, and the Court of Directors coincided in their orders, then each body was anfwerable, but when they differed then the Board of Control was liable to account; by which means the refponfibility was rendered more tangible, as it was in fome inftances transferred from a fluctuating and uncertain body, as the Court of Directors were, to one of a permanent conftitution, the Board of Control, and in other inftances extended to them both. It might happen in the former fyftem for the whole body of Directors to be changed between the time of adopting a particular meafure and the difcovery of the bad confequence refulting from it; who then was to be called to account? The criminality would appear, but the authors of it could not be found. As to the honourable gentleman's complaint, that the executive authority of the Company had been feparated from the patronage, that, he muft contend, was the moft valuable and beneficial part of the whole fyftem; becaufe, when the executive power was in the Directors, the patronage which they enjoyed tended very much to fetter and embarrafs the exercife of that power; for every order of theirs being calculated to affect their fervants in India, and thofe fervants being appointed by themfelves, and of courfe out of their own families and connections, it followed that they had private feelings with regard to them; which private feelings and affections, from the natural prejudices and weaknefs of humanity, materially inter-

fered

fered with their conduct respecting the Public. Now the separation of those two powers of executive government and patronage would effectually remedy that inconvenience; and the Board of Control having no such ties of friendship and affection to the servants of the Company, would have no other object in the execution of their office but the benefit of the Public. As to the alteration in the governments in India, he was decidedly of an opinion contrary to that given by the honourable gentleman; and though he should feel great uneasiness in being obliged to enforce his own theory in opposition to the experience of the honourable gentleman, yet that uneasiness would undergo a diminution in consequence of the authorities with which he could meet the honourable gentleman's personal knowledge of the subject; for there was not a person whom he had conversed with who had not condemned the former state of the government of that country, and among the rest he could bring as an instance, a noble Lord (Macartney) who had declared, that none but a madman would consent to accept the government while it remained upon its former footing. He must also beg leave to insist, that the honourable gentleman's proposal for remedying the disease of a casting voice [Here the House and Speaker laughed] was by no means adequate to the object; for the appointing five persons to the council would not prove sufficient, unless it could be contrived that those five persons should all live, for otherwise, the determination of many questions must depend upon the casting voice, and it was extremely probable, that during a long series of years, no question would be decided except by a casting voice. On one part of the subject the honourable gentleman seemed to ground his principal objection to the present system, it was that which established a new judicature for the trial of delinquents returned from India. On this head he could not but differ most widely from the honourable gentleman. This judicature, he should admit, was represented by some persons at home, and he believed was looked upon by many others in India, as a most dangerous and exceptionable measure; but he had reason to think that in general it was considered in a very different point of view. He could venture to affirm, that the present mode of trial had all the advantages attending the trial by special jury, and none of its disadvantages; that although the defendant had no right of challenge, yet there could be no objection to that defect, because the court was appointed in such a manner, as to leave no room for the necessity of admitting challenges, which existed in trials by jury: all persons who might be supposed to entertain any bias or prejudice, either from their having been too intimately acquainted with the circumstances, and therefore being liable to a fufpicion of having been predetermined; all who had ever been in India, all who were connected with the India Company, or who could be fuppofed under the influence of government by means of employments, were excluded.

The court confifted of perfons of high rank and character, and fuch as could not afford the fmalleft reafon to apprehend any injuftice or partiality from them, unlefs under the ftrange idea, that juftice and impartiality were things not to be found amongft mankind in any clafs, and if fo, then no judicature could be thought upright. In anfwer to the doubts which the honourable gentleman had expreffed arifing from the danger of the judges being corrupted, he thought himfelf juftified in contending, that if there were any foundation for fuch an apprehenfion, there was alfo as much danger in every other trial, for even before a jury the judge had great weight and authority; he could pofitively determine on the competence and admiffibility of evidence; he had great influence in eftablifhing its credibility; and befides, it was part of his duty to fum up the whole and put upon it that conftruction which feemed to him moft proper; he had, in fhort, in many inftances extenfive power, and in others great influence, until that ftage of the trial in which the jury were clofeted for their final determination: and as the three judges were to be appointed, one by each court, there was no doubt but fuch of them would be appointed by their brethren on the bench, as appeared to them moft proper from being leaft liable to any unfair impreffion or prejudice. A right honourable gentleman (Mr. Burke) when opening proceedings againft the Eaft-India governor, Mr. Haftings, and expatiating upon the different modes of bringing a delinquent from that country to juftice, had difclaimed the trial by jury as not calculated for the cognizance of fuch accufation; and in fo doing he was certainly extremely prudent; he himfelf knew too well how difficult it was to proceed by a bill of pains and penalties; becaufe, when on a former occafion he adopted that method, he found numbers of gentlemen who, though willing to profecute the accufed, and to inflict an adequate punifhment where guilt was proved, yet declared, that they would then, and on all occafions, fet their faces againft a bill of pains and penalties: the only remaining method therefore of proceeding was by impeachment, which the right honourable gentleman to whom he laft alluded had adopted in the profecution at that moment depending, as the only way by which juftice could be expected. Of the two modes of trial, that by the prefent judicature, and that by impeachment, he thought the former as unexceptionable as the latter; as well from the

purity

purity of its appointment, as from the numbers of which it confisted; for the court of the Lord High Steward might confift of as few members as the Eaft-India judicature; and the House of Lords, when they fat in the high court of Parliament, were not fubject to any challenges, to which this court, though not actually, yet, from the mode of its conftitution, might be faid virtually to have become liable. The honourable gentleman exprefled his uneafinefs, that no provifion had been made to prevent the Court from proceeding to trial with fhut doors; but he apprehended that the omitting to mention any fuch matter in the bill was by no means a fanction for adopting a cuftom fo diametrically oppofite to the common law, which directs, that all courts of judicature fhall be open, and which of courfe, the prefent one muft be in compliance with the rules of the common law, which are always to continue in force unlefs particularly avoided by the exprefs words of a ftatute, which not being done in this act, there could be no pretence for the doors of this court being fhut. On this occafion he fhould beg leave to inftance the election bill, framed by a late member of the House (Mr. Grenville) in which there was no particular injunction preferve fecrecy in the proceedings of the Committee to be appointed under it; and yet, in purfuance of the principles of the common law, their doors were always kept open. The complaint made of the power which the Court had to adjourn from time to time, was one which, like fome of the others, proceeded from the principle, that human nature was fo depraved that no fecurity could be expected againft wickednefs and temptation. He fhould therefore attempt to give no anfwer to it upon that principle; but only inftance the laft-mentioned judicature under the election bill, and alfo in the cafe of trials before the House of Peers, where it was the conftant practice to adjourn *de die in diem*, and yet in either cafe was it ever pretended that there was any danger of undue influence being ufed by His Majefty's Minifters, as was now attempted to be fuggefted. — Another confideration which tended to prove the abfolute impracticibility of reforting to trial by jury was, the great fcope of evidence that in general it would be neceffary to produce on fuch occafions: as, for example, in the cafe of Sir Thomas Rumbold, and alfo in that of Mr. Haftings; the evidence was fo various and voluminous, that it was phyfically impoffible that any jury could have ftrength fufficient to go through it without retiring to reft, and without other refrefhment.

As to the objection which he had heard made againft the admitting the writings and correfpondences from the Eaft Indies to be admitted in evidence, he apprehended that gentlemen were not fufficiently acquainted with this part of the

fub-

subject: they seemed to think, that all writings whatsoever coming from that country were intended by the act of Parliament to have full validity given to them as evidence in the newly-established court; but this was by no means the case; for every paper was liable to be scrutinized according to the common rules as well of admissibility as of credibility, which were used with respect to other witnesses; and if any should appear to come from a person prejudiced or interested in the event of the trial, it would be considered as wholly inadmissible; or if it should prove inconsistent, contradictory, and improbable, it would then be considered as incredible. It was no new thing to bring the correspondence of the Company's servants as evidence into a court of justice; because the act of 1773 had made a provision for the purpose, declaring such papers to be competent evidence; and indeed, in most instances, it would prove impossible to investigate a complaint from that country without recurring to such sources of information; and besides the other arguments tending to vindicate the departure from the trial by jury in this instance, the necessity of admitting such evidence was a very strong one; for, however expedient it might be in some cases to adopt new rules of evidence, it would prove extremely dangerous and improper to habituate the minds of the common juries of the country to such a change: because, being in certain cases used to look upon that as evidence which the peculiarity of the matter alone rendered so, they might, in cases where no such peculiarity existed, be inclined to receive similar impressions from similar documents, and by those means the rules of evidence might become fluctuating and liable to change, a circumstance to the full as dangerous and as necessary to guard against, as any change in the other forms of judicature could possibly be. As to the novelty imputed to this departure from the established practice of trial by jury, no such did exist, for it had long since been adopted both in the army and navy, and no person ever pretended, that any precedent was likely to flow from the institution of naval and military courts martial, dangerous to the constitution and laws of the country.

Respecting that part of the subject which related to the oath required from persons returning from India, to ascertain the amount of their acquisitions in those parts, he had not completely made up his mind; but having intended to bring the subject before the House in a short time, he had been in the habit of considering it attentively, and should, in a few days, come to a settled opinion concerning it. The reason of his doubt was the variety of sentiments he had met with in letters from India, some of which contained an approbation of the restriction, while others severely condemned it. It would how-

however anfwer part of the objections ftated by the honourable gentleman, to fhew, that all of them at leaft were not perfectly well founded, and that the inftitution was not liable to the whole of the obloquy thrown upon it. The honourable gentleman had cited an example, drawn from the cafe of his own colleague in the adminiftration of Bengal, and had faid, that if the queftion had been put to that gentleman, whether he fhould be fatisfied on his return to England to be called upon to take an oath of the nature prefcribed by the prefent fyftem, he thought it highly probable that he would anfwer in the negative. The honourable gentleman had ftated, that if the fervices of his faid colleague, were equal to his rewards, they muft have been great indeed; which words could have no other implication than that his rewards were greater than his fervices merited: was not this then a ftrong argument in favour of the oath; for, was it not as much as to fay, that if the oath had at that time been neceffary, the gentleman alluded to having it before his eyes, and having alfo objections to taking it as his circumftances then ftood, would have acted in fuch a manner as to have enabled himfelf to take it with a fafe confcience? By this means the evil would have been prevented, and this prevention was the chief object of inftituting the oath; for many perfons, though they might be inclined to fubmit to thofe temptations which that country was fuppofed to hold out, and which by fome were reprefented as being almoft too ftrong for flefh and blood to refift; yet, knowing that the confequence of doing fo muft neceffarily be either avowing their guilt, or adding to it the crime of perjury, they would be reftrained and prevented; and thus the oath would operate to ftrengthen and confirm their confciences.

The honourable gentleman had farther complained of the interrogatories which people were to be compelled to anfwer, after they had made a direct oath, and had reprefented it as a new thing thus to call upon men to acknowledge, that they had been guilty in the firft inftance of perjury. But furely if the honourable gentleman had confidered what were the ufual modes of examining upon oath in this country (for the principal method of fifting a witnefs, in order to afcertain the truth or falfehood of his teftimony, was to crofs examine and put fuch queftions to him, as in fpite of all his artifice and cunning fhould force him to fpeak the truth) he would find no ground of complaint, either as to the novelty or hardfhip of the regulation. Such was the cafe of bankrupts, who, though in matters that might affect their lives, were bound by law to anfwer fuch interrogatories touching their effects, as might be put to them by thofe intrufted with their affairs. On the whole, he fhould not give a negative to the prefent motion, becaufe because he had intended to bring forward one of an exactly similar nature, which he did not imagine he could do consistently with the forms of the house, if it were now rejected; he should therefore be satisfied with moving the previous question.

Mr. *Anstruther* complained of the attempt of the right honourable gentleman to take the merit of reforming the errors and mischiefs of the India bill out of the hands of his honourable friend. This, however, he must consider as a plain proof of the obstinacy of the gentlemen on the other side of the House, in passing a bill which now, at scarcely an interval of more than a year, appeared even to themselves, to call so loudly for alteration and amendment. He was of opinion, that it was by all means more desirable, that the alteration should proceed from the immediate motion of that House, than from the clamours raised against it in India; and therefore, which ever of the two honourable gentlemen was to have the honour of introducing it, he hoped that no time would be lost in bringing it to a speedy conclusion. He combated the doctrine of the right honourable gentleman, that the oath would operate so as to fortify and strengthen the consciences of the people in the East Indies, and prevent them from acting in such a manner as must reduce them to the alternative on their return to England, either of adding perjury to their guilt, or of furnishing a suspicion against themselves by declaring the truth. He combated this doctrine, on the grounds of its being a restraint only on the virtuous, on whom no such restraint was necessary, and as having no power whatsoever to restrain the abandoned, who alone ought to be the objects of coercion. It was also unfair and cruel, inasmuch as its operation being postponed for a long time, it would enable those who had, by rapacity and extortion, or other illegal means, already acquired a sufficient fortune to return home before it should take effect; whereas, those who, by a different line of conduct, had continued in indigence, were obliged to remain till after it was in force, and to become subject to it. He begged leave to ask a learned and right honourable gentleman (Mr. Dundas) and he should submit the matter to the candour of the House, whether it was decent or fair to treat British subjects, laudably serving their country in India, as common bankrupts; and to talk of them as men whose misconduct or misfortunes had subjected them to the bankrupt laws before the House had even the shadow of a proof that they deserved to be considered in so humiliating a point of view. He was surprised that the right honourable gentleman, from the facility with which he recurred to the examples of the army and navy, had not been led to reflect how the doctrine of setting aside the trial

by

by jury might hereafter be strengthened by the precedent now established. It might, on some future occasion, be thought advisable to extend this system to the West Indies, perhaps to other of our possessions; nay, to some part even of this island. If any opposition were then to be offered, how easily might it be answered—what objection to abolish the trial by jury in this place, when there are so many precedents in favour of the measure? Is not trial by jury at an end in the West Indies? Is it not suppressed in the East Indies? Is it not given up in the army and the navy? How then can you complain of its novelty? The right honourable gentleman had by no means established his argument to shew that the present institution was equally just and favourable to the subject as that of trial by jury; for in this the party might be condemned by a majority of the new Court of Judicature, which might consist of so small a quorum as seven, whereas a jury must be unanimous; and surely no person would attempt to argue, that it was as eligible to be tried by a tribunal, where the condemnation was in the power of four persons, as where it was necessary that twelve should give it their concurrence.

Mr. *Vansittart* remarked, that as the honourable gentleman who made the motion had particularly called on those members of the House who served in India, he rose to take some notice of one part of his speech, which alluded to the clause of the act of 1784, respecting the obligation on gentlemen to make oath of the amount of their property on their arrival in England from the East Indies. As that was deemed a hardship by gentlemen serving in India, he had no objection to give his consent to the repeal of it. With regard to the new court of judicature, he could not agree with the honourable gentleman, because he thought it a fair, impartial, and safe tribunal for any man to appeal to, and such a tribunal as no honest man would fear to face. *Mr. Vansittart.*

Major *Scott* said, that he should not have risen if the honourable gentleman who opened the debate had not pointedly called upon all the gentlemen who had served in India to deliver their sentiments. He had voted for every part of the bill as it now stood; but he was perfectly ready to declare that there was one part of it which he earnestly wished to see repealed — he meant that which compelled a declaration of fortunes. He could not agree with the right honourable and learned gentleman on the floor, (Mr. Dundas) as far as his information went, that there was a difference of opinion in India upon it. From all the letters which he had seen or received from Oude, or military gentlemen, he was led to conclude that it was deemed a peculiar grievance, and therefore he earnestly wished the repeal of it. But he trusted that gentlemen *Maj. Scott.*

tleman would recollect, that though he did vote for this obnoxious clause, yet he had invariably opposed both in and out of the house all the ill-founded clamour raised respecting the enormities committed by British subjects in India; that he could affirm, and always had affirmed, that there was in no part of the world, if they were taken collectively, a more respectable set of men than the gentlemen serving in India, or men who had deserved more of their country; but the clamour having been raised, he conceived such a clause, which would have proved the justice of the outcry, might have shewn how much the People of England had been misled; and he had no personal objection to it. It had, however, occasioned general dissatisfaction; and he hoped it would be repealed. With respect to the judicature, upon the fullest and most deliberate consideration, he did avow his complete approbation of it, and he thought if crimes were committed in India, which afterwards came to a trial here, it was impossible to find a purer court before which any man could so soon wish to be tried; for offences committed in India could not, he thought, be tried by a jury in the common modes of trial. There was one thing mentioned by the right honourable and learned gentleman (Mr. Dundas) which had given him very great pleasure indeed. From what he had thrown out, he trusted that such a firm and efficient government was to be established in India as would render the proposed judicature totally useless; for he was convinced that a steady and strong government abroad would prove fully competent to correct every abuse which might exist in that quarter. The honourable gentleman who opened the bill had dealt in panegyric and invective. He had mentioned Sir Elijah Impey, who was not present to defend himself; but if the honourable gentleman had been displeased with Sir Elijah Impey's decision, an appeal lay open to him.

Mr. Francis spoke to order, contending that the honourable gentleman had totally mistaken his meaning.

Major Scott replied, that he submitted with pleasure to correction, and would embrace a future opportunity of replying to the panegyric of the honourable gentleman.

Mr. Jolliffe observed, that it seemed agreed on all sides that the bill brought in by the right honourable gentleman, for the regulation of the government of India, was defective, and of course required amendment; that some thought the government at home improper; that others objected to the government abroad; but that all seemed to agree that it was capable of considerable reformation. The honourable gentleman near him (Mr. Francis) had moved for leave to bring in a bill for this purpose; it was therefore exceedingly ungenerous in the right honourable and learned gentleman to resist

- that

Mr. Francis.

Mr. Jolliffe.

that motion by a previous queſtion, when he declared at the
ſame time that he propoſed to make the very ſame motion
himſelf. This was taking all the merit from his honourable
friend; this was ſaying, " I agree with you entirely; but be-
" cauſe you have brought forward that which every body ap-
" proves, you ſhall not have the merit: I have the ſtrength
" in my hand; I will wreſt the honour and reputation from
" you of ſerving your country." With reſpect to the government at home, he was of opinion that the bill of the
right honourable gentleman (Mr. Fox) was the moſt calculated to produce good; for it gave to the State the government of the territory, which every body admitted was the
property of the State, and which that Houſe had voted to bo
ſo, and it left to the India Company the management of their
trade; this was all which they could claim. Concerning the
government in India, he differed from his honourable friend,
(Mr. Francis) becauſe he thought the government abroad, in
the hands of one, was more conſiſtent with an operative, executive government than divided among a number, who, in
all probability, would diſagree upon the manner in which the
various operations of government ſhould be conducted. By
being in one perſon, the country knew where to look for reſponſibility, and it was much eaſier to remove one perſon,
and appoint a ſucceſſor, than either to diſplace a body of men,
or to ſelect out of a number one or more at ſuch a diſtance,
whoſe conduct might be variouſly repreſented, and with reſpect to whom there might be much difficulty in judging.
The chief cauſe of his riſing was to enter his proteſt againſt
the new-adopted mode of trial; for he conſidered the trial
by jury as the great paladium of the Conſtitution of this
country; as the only ſecurity which Engliſhmen had for their
lives, their liberty, or their property; as the great barrier
for the People againſt the power of the Crown, or the influence of the ariſtocratic part of the country; every innovation on this right, every, the ſmalleſt, alteration of it ſhould
be watched and attended to with the minuteſt care. How
much, therefore, ſhould the alarm be taken at (not the deviation from this mode of trial, not an alteration in point of
form, or in matter of evidence, but) an abſolute ſubverſion
of it, by appointing a new, unheard of, unconſtitutional
ſyſtem, which, if admitted to be proper in the trial of the
delinquents from India, would equally hold applicable to any
other part of the dominions of Great Britain; and it might
be argued as fitting to extend to offences committed in the
Weſt Indies, in Ireland, or even in Scotland. No man could
ſay, if the principle were once admitted, to what it might
not be argued as proper to be carried. The right honourable
and learned gentleman was ſo ſenſible of this, that he had en-

deavoured to shew (but on the falsest grounds) that this mode of trial was in fact a trial by jury. He desired to ask in what respect it resembled it? A jury consisted of twelve persons; but this was an indefinite number, from thirteen to seven: a jury must be unanimous — a majority here determined; yet a jury must decide before they could separate; but this court might adjourn *de die in diem* as long as they pleased: a jury could have no intercourse whatever with the parties; yet these might have any communication they pleased with any or all of the parties: a jury were to determine the fact, and not the law; but these were to determine both fact and law. There was, in truth, no one thing in which they resembled a jury, except that they were sworn; but the greatest absurdity was, that as a majority of seven might determine, those who heard the trial might not be the same as those who gave the verdict; out of thirteen, seven might hear part of the trial, three might be absent, and three others hear another part, and, at last, six fresh attend and decide upon the whole, without having heard one word of the merits. The judges could not declare the law; for they might be overruled by ten, or by seven, or by four of the other members: so that what was not law might be determined to be law against the declared opinion of those who are appointed to declare the law in every court in the kingdom; the rules of evidence, one great security to justice, might, in every instance, be departed from, and the judges sit by spectators, unable to prevent such a violation of first principles of the law. In a court of law, the judge is answerable for the law which he lays down, that it shall be law of the land; but in this judicature no man was answerable for his conduct. This, he was sure, need only to be known to be reprobated: it required only to be divulged and understood, to call the universal voice of the country for its repeal.

Mr. Henni-ker.   Mr. *Henniker*, immediately before the previous question was put, rose (upon an idea suggested, that those who voted for it were pledged to support the intended amendment proposed by Mr. Dundas) to say that the grounds on which he supported the previous question were, that, on a competition between two honourable gentlemen (Mr. Francis and Mr. Dundas) to propose that amendment, he was thoroughly satisfied that the person who had a great share in the formation of the bill was the most proper to move for its amendment, and that when the whole was brought forward he should be then more competent to determine on the intrinsic merit of the mode of Indian government: yet he must beg leave to assure the House how much he spurned at the bare thought of irrevocably pledging himself to vote for the amendment suggested by the right honourable and learned gentleman, (Mr. Dun-

das)

das) unlefs it were to come home, in all refpects whatever, to his unbiaffed feelings and his fincere opinions.

The previous queftion, moved by Mr. Dundas, was carried.

Upon bringing up the Ordnance Report,

Sir *John Miller* obferved, that he fhould move for it's re- Sir John commitment, with the intent, that after he fhould have ftated Miller. his reafons for voting againft the late extenfive fyftem of Ordnance fortifications on the preceding Monday, he might fatisfy the Houfe that his objections to that fyftem did not, in any degree, go to the more immediate and neceffary accommodations and fecurities of the dock yards of Portfmouth and Plymouth, which he confidered as of the higheft importance to this country; and in order that the Houfe might be unapprifed of the object of his motion as well as to œconomife their time, their trouble, and their attention, he fhould now ftate to them the motion with which he intended to clofe his obfervations and opinions upon the fubject of our fortifications. He then read his propofed motion, to the following effect: " That the fum of 50,000l., granted in a former fef-
" fion to be employed in fortifying our dock yards, be now
" applied in the following manner, viz. in bringing frefh
" water to the dock yard of Plymouth; in building and fur-
" nifhing gun boats, agreeable to the unanimous approbation
" of them by the fea and land officers in their Report now
" on the table of this Houfe, as expedient for the defence of
" our dock yards; and for the erecting fuch bomb proofs and
" cafements within the faid dock yards as fhall be judged moft
" immediately neceffary, as well as moft effectual for prefer-
" ving ammunition, provifions, and ftores, from the fudden
" irruption of an enemy; and alfo for the erecting certain
" ports and eftablifhing certain ftations for fignals, as recom-
" mended in the fame Report."

Mr. *Rofe* anfwered, this was not a proper time to move Mr. Rofe. fuch recommitment, unlefs for the purpofe of diminifhing the amount of the fum now reported.

Mr. Sloper and Lord Maitland infifted that the honourable Baronet was founded in his motion to recommit the Report.

The *Speaker* alledged, that the Houfe was afked from the The Speaker Crown for the value of the Ordnance eftimates; that it was ker. the right of Parliament either to reject *in toto*, or to diminifh the fum applied for by Government. But that upon a Report of money granted, as in the prefent cafe, nothing but an intention of refufing or diminifhing the fum already granted (which he did not apprehend, and which indeed he faw by the motion which had been ftated to be no part of the honourable Baronet's intention) could juftify the prefent recommitment of the Report.

The Houfe adjourned.

Wednesday, 8th *March.*

No exceedingly material business took place, unless we except the choice, by ballot, of a Committee, to whom the several accounts and papers, relative to the public income and expenditure, are referred, who are to examine and state the same, and to report to the House what may be expected to be the annual amount of the said income and expenditure in future.

The following are the names of the gentlemen chosen:

Marquis of Graham,
Right Hon. W. W. Grenville,
Hon. E. J. Eliot,
H. Addington,
H. Beaufoy,
J. Call,
G. Rose,
J. Smyth,
W. Wilberforce,
} Esquires.

The House adjourned.

Thursday, 9th *March.*

In compliance with the request of Mr. Burke, who was on this day absent,

Mr. Francis.

Mr. *Francis* moved, "That a certain selection of the papers which had been laid upon the table, in consequence of the motion of his right honourable friend, for the purpose of grounding a charge against Mr. Hastings," might be printed. He begged leave to inform the House, that his right honourable friend considered these papers as more particularly necessary to the support of the projection; yet at the same time he felt it proper to remind them, that it did not follow that because these were so earnestly desired, no intention was entertained of making use of any of the rest: on the contrary, that it was his right honourable friend's intention to avail himself of the whole of the evidence to be derived from all the papers, as well of those which were not as of those which were to be printed.

Mr. Chancellor Pitt.

Mr. Chancellor *Pitt* argued in favour of the propriety of printing all the papers, persuaded that it would take up more time for the House to make the selection than the printing of the whole; yet upon reflection he must allow that the motion made by the honourable gentleman might be suffered to pass without farther inquiry; but, at the same time, he would beg leave to advise some friend of Mr. Hastings to move for the printing of such part of the papers as he might deem immediately requisite for his exculpation.

Major

Major *Scott* obferved that the honourable gentleman who **Maj. Scott.** made the motion, had himfelf been fo candid as to fuggeft to him the very fame advice as that juft given by the Chancellor of the Exchequer; which he fhould certainly follow, and for that purpofe look over the papers, in order that he might make his motion; as he wifhed that the papers which he meant to have printed might follow thofe moved by the honourable gentleman, as immediately as poffible, left the Public, reading fome papers which might appear to have a tendency to criminate him, and not enjoying the opportunity of perufing thofe which were expreffly calculated for his vindication, might receive impreffions deftructive of thofe favourable ideas which (he would venture to affert) ought to be entertained of his adminiftration in the Eaft Indies.

The motion of Mr. Francis paffed.

Mr. *Marfham* now moved for leave to bring in a bill for **Mr. Mar-** extending the provifions of an act introduced into that Houfe **fham.** by his honourable friend (Mr. Crew) for fecuring the freedom of elections, by depriving perfons employed in certain offices, as the cuftoms, excife, poft and ftamp office, of the right of voting, to the civil branches of the navy and ordnance offices. He underftood that fome people imagined he had intended to include the officers of the army and navy in his bill, but no fuch idea had ever entered his mind, nor, he fuppofed, that of any other member of the Houfe. So much benefit had refulted from the former bill, and that which he propofed to bring in, was fo exactly fimilar to it in principle, that he thought there was no fort of neceffity for him to fay any thing in fupport of his motion.

He then moved, " For leave to bring in a bill for fecuring " the freedom of election, by excluding perfons holding " places in the navy and ordnance offices from voting as " electors."

Mr. *Honeywood* obferved that many of his conftituents, fee- **Mr. Honey-** ing and feeling the good confequences of Mr. Crew's act, **wood.** which were particularly confpicuous in his part of the country, had expreffed a wifh for its extenfion in the manner propofed by his honourable friend, for which reafon, as well as from his own conviction of its propriety, he would fecond the motion.

The motion was put and carried.

Friday, 10th *March*.

Mr. Chancellor *Pitt* obferved, that, as at leaft an inaccu- **Mr. Chan-** racy of expreffion had crept into one of the claufes of the **cellor Pitt.** militia bill, he fhould firft correct it, and then beg leave to trouble the Houfe with his fentiments upon the fubject.

Endeavours

Endeavours had been used, (but, upon what justifiable grounds he believed it would prove more than difficult to discover) to represent him as hostile to the institution of the militia, because, when an honourable gentleman had applied to him for his opinion relative to one part of its regulation, he had declined at the moment to give an answer, wishing to suspend his judgement, until he could enjoy the advantage of hearing the arguments of those gentlemen who, from their being personally interested in the service, were most competent to the decision. The injustice of such a misrepresentation of his principles was so glaring, as scarcely to require an answer; for he had not given the smallest opportunity to any gentleman to say that he had expressed a doubt of the benefits and valuable tendency of the militia itself; he had only hesitated to consider whether, by a material saving to the public, the militia could be made equally beneficial to what it had been on its former establishment, with a view as much as possible to reconcile that great constitutional defence of the kingdom, which no man could value higher than he did, though he was certain every man in that House must prize it most highly) to the principles and practice of œconomy. He had made every inquiry in his power upon the subject from gentlemen much better qualified than himself, how to accomplish so desirable an object, and he found that it was the general opinion that the militia ought to be called out every year. Still, notwithstanding their being annually embodied, a considerable saving might be effected without any danger (as he apprehended and had been advised) to the service. Yet, if it appeared to gentlemen, many of whom were more capable of considering it in a military point of view than he was, that the mode which he should suggest would prove a means of rendering the militia less effective as a national defence, he would cheerfully give up his opinion; for, however anxious he was on all occasions to spare the public purse, yet he could never consent to starve so valuable and so necessary a part of the public service. It was always usual to keep the several regular regiments considerably under their establishment, in time of peace, because by so doing the army might become increased, in time of war, without adding to the number of the regiments, by filling them up to their full complement of men, which was certainly the most œconomical management that could be adopted, consistent with prudence and good policy, as it was more easy to make soldiers than commissioned, and more especially non-commissioned officers. And, in consequence of this mode being adopted, the regular regiments in time of peace never had above two thirds of their esta-

blishment

blifhment complete. He propofed that the fame principle fhould be applied to the militia; that the whole number of men fhould be balloted for and enrolled, but that only two-thirds of them fhould be employed. Thofe that were to be fo, being appointed for the actual duty, and to continue fo during the whole period of their fervice, by which means, one-third of the expence of their pay would be faved, deducting only fo much as would neceffarily go to defray the expence of the annual mufter, which would not amount, however, to above one thoufand pounds. There would, befides, be a farther faving of one-third in the article of clothing, which two favings would amount to about forty thoufand pounds; a fum of too great confequence to be thought lightly of. Still he was liable to alter his opinion, fhould he find againft him the general fenfe of the gentlemen, who had made the bufinefs their particular ftudy. And if the exempting one-third of the privates from the annual exercife, fhould be thonght by them likely to render the militia lefs ferviceable than it otherwife would be, he fhould moft willingly refign his opinion, and regret, that for the prefent he could only accomplifh one of thofe two moft defirable objects, the faving of the public treafure, and the promoting the beft conftitutional defence of the kingdom, —the militia.

Mr. *Rolle* thought the annual embodying of them was a prejudice to the morals of the people, as it gave them habits of debauchery and idlenefs, and they were diffatisfied when they returned to their wives and families, and confequently became much worfe members of fociety.

Colonel *Orchard* contended that the militia did not injure the morals of the people, and faid, that it appeared the more extraordinary, as his honourable friend had once confented to take a command in the fervice himfelf.

Mr. *Rolle* begged leave to correct the error into which his honourable friend had fallen. He had indeed offered, when the enemy was expected on the coaft of Devonfhire, to go down and raife five hundred men, but upon his honour, he had never offered to go into the militia.

Colonel *Orchard* replied, that, upon his honour, he thought he had made fuch an offer.

Mr. *Young* fpoke in favour of annually embodying the militia, that gentlemen might know their neighbours, and be able to inform themfelves of their characters, as to who were poachers, drunkards or quarrelfome, and alfo for the purpofe of rendering the corps more ferviceable.

Sir *Edward Aftley* obferved that the inftitution, confidered in a general point of view, merited not merely the approbation, but the warm encouragement of the ftate; yet he feared that,

Mr. Rolle.

Colonel Orchard.

Mr. Rolle.

Colonel Orchard.

Mr. Young.

Sir Edward Aftley.

that, in some respects, the present regulations of the militia were far from unexceptionable; and he was well convinced that it should be rendered as welcome as possible to the People. He thought twenty-eight days too short a period of time for the militia to be trained and exercised with any effect, He would, therefore, mention a proposal which appeared to him more likely to prove generally useful, and that was: that instead of five, the militia should be ballotted for four years only, and that they should be trained and exercised for two months together in every second year. Sir Edward observed, that when he rose to speak as a member of Parliament upon the subject of the militia, or any other topic, he considered himself as entitled to deliver his free sentiments, and that he was dealt unfairly by, if, because he disagreed from any proposition suggested as a regulation of the militia, he was deemed an enemy to the institution. At all periods, had he been ready sincerely to espouse the cause of the militia; nor did he think it the least honourable part of his life when he enjoyed the happiness of serving under an establishment so well adapted to the internal defence of the kingdom.

Captain Berkeley.

Captain *Berkeley* apologized for troubling the House on a question so remote from the line of his service; but he only rose to say, that a relation of his (his brother, earl Berkeley) whom no person could pretend to think the worst officer in the service, had been consulted on the subject, and had entirely coincided in opinion with the Chancellor of the Exchequer.

Mr. Drake.

Mr. *Drake* having acknowledged himself most zealously anxious for the prosperity of the militia, as the natural and constitutional defence of the country, added, that he considered the gentlemen who had dedicated their time without doors to modifying and digesting the bill, as delegates from the meeting which so laudably turned their attention to an object of great national importance, and therefore he should bow to their authority. The gentlemen of that description had signified their approbation of the proposal of the right honourable gentleman who so excellently managed the finances of the kingdom, and their sanction was a sufficient reason for him to vote for it. As to the objection started by an honourable gentleman, that calling out the militia was injurious to the morals of the men, he must beg leave to answer, that he had not studied the distinction between civil and military morals; if he had, the consideration would, probably, have given birth to some florid ideas; but perhaps it was as well that he had not. To reconcile public service with public œconomy was the great end of every good government; and, with this idea, he gave the right honourable gentleman at the head of the Exchequer full credit for the middie line of conduct which he had pointed out between expence and utility.

Sir *John Miller* remarked, that he felt it impossible to mention the institution of the militia, without the fullest expressions of applause. He admired it: he acknowledged its utility, and hoped the country would never be deprived of so constitutional a defence. With regard to the present bill, he relied chiefly on the abilities and experience of those who had prepared it, and from confidence in their judgement and zeal he would give it his support. The sword, he added, to which alone all human ordinances must submit, should in a free country be placed only in the hands of those, who had property as well as liberty to preserve and defend. With regard to Great Britain, the root of her power, offensive and defensive, lay almost exclusively in her navy and her militia; they were both therefore great national objects, and ought to be cherished and encouraged by that House. He traced the origin of the militia from the reign of Alfred, to the present period. That great and wise prince, by the aid of his militia, defeated a powerful invasion headed by Hastings, a warlike Dane. Henry the Second, to guard against external insult, and to provide for internal security, fixed an assize of arms, in conformity to which every subject was to be armed and disciplined. The militia of England in the time of queen Elizabeth, amounted to 140,000 fighting men, besides what Wales could supply, all of the inhabitants in which quarter were ready to receive and properly to entertain the contents of the Spanish Armada. In the reign of James the First, the militia of England consisted of 160,000 fighting men, all well armed and well disciplined. The civil war between Charles the First and the Parliament, diffused the ancient military spirit through the whole body of the People; and it was notorious, that the British name and British glory were never more revered than under Cromwell. Charles the Second imported, at the restoration, vice, profligacy, and debauchery. The military spirit of the nation was then lost. He distrusted the militia. Brought up in arbitrary principles, he suffered the institution gradually to decay, and substituted guards and garrisons, consisting at first of 5000, and afterwards of 8000 men, in their room. James the Second disarmed the militia, and substituted an army of 30,000 men, declaring to his Parliament that he had found the militia useless and unserviceable by experience, and insisting upon supplies to support his increased military establishment. The subsequent reigns of William and Anne were distinguished only by wars abroad and factions at home. Many attempts were afterwards made to revive a national militia, but in vain, till that great and ever to be revered Minister laid the fo long-wifhed-for foundation, upon which we were, he trufted, with the aid of his fucceffor in name, virtues, talents, and fituation, to raife a proper fuperftructure. He felt fhame and mortification at our being occafionally obliged to import foreign mercenaries to defend our commerce and conftitution, our liberties, our properties, and our capital! When the fit opportunity fhould offer, for his ftating his fentiments refpecting the lately-exploded fyftem of fortification, he would explain himfelf fully on that fubject. With regard to the prefent bill, he hoped the Houfe would go literally into the completion of it, and give thofe who had brought it forward full praife and ample aid, fo as to render the militia an honourable, an ufeful, and (as far as might be confiftent with their efficiency) an œconomical fafeguard to the country. The propofition of the right honourable gentleman (Mr. Pitt) for annually calling out two thirds of the militia, deferved, and fhould receive his beft encouragement, and every fupport in his power.

The Chancellor of the Exchequer's propofition was received, and the Houfe adjourned.

Monday, 13th March.

Mr. Francis Mr. *Francis* ftated to the Houfe, that, as certain meafures of very great public importance were now in agitation, he thought that fuch meafures ought not to be decided, until they had endeavoured to collect, in a conftitutional way, the general fenfe of the nation concerning them; namely, by calling the reprefentatives of the People together: that the impeachment of Mr. Haftings was an object of great public intereft and concern. That the meafure which it was faid the Chancellor of the Exchequer had in view, for applying the exifting furpluffes of revenue to the difcharge of debt, was a fubject of equal novelty and importance, and particularly called for the attention of a full Houfe of Commons: but above all, he thought, that, as Mr. Dundas had given notice of his intention to revife and correct the India bill of 1784, there ought to be a call of the Houfe for the fpecial purpofe of re-confidering that bill. That it had not been fufficiently attended to in the firft inftance, having been generally debated and carried in very thin houfes; that if the principles of this law, upon a more deliberate review of it, fhould be confirmed, they would take root in the Conftitution and might never be eradicated. The queftion concerned the public liberty, and ought not to be decided without a full reprefentation of the People.

He therefore moved, " That the Houfe might be called " over on Monday the 27th of March."

Mr. Fox feconded the motion.

Mr.

Mr. Chancellor *Pitt* remarked, that he could not avoid taking the liberty to obferve, that the honourable gentleman who made the motion, feemed to have deviated in fome meafure from his confiftency. When he moved himfelf for a repeal of the India bill, he had not confidered a call of the Houfe neceffary; but now, when this act was only agreeable to the ratification given to be explained and amended, he conceived a call of the Houfe to be moft indifpenfably requifite. He could not eafily account for this verfatility in the conduct of the honourable gentleman: the matter to which a right honourable gentleman (Mr. Burke) had directed the attention of the Houfe, feemed to him to be of great importance, and to, juftify, in fome refpects, the motion under contemplation. If he fhould have matters in fuch forwardnefs as to be able to fubmit them to the difcuffion of the Houfe about the time intended for the call, he would not oppofe the motion; and he would referve the right to himfelf, of bringing forward in the interim, any matter of finance, as a public concern, notwithftanding his concurrence in the motion for the call. *(Mr. Chancellor Pitt.)*

Major *Scott* declared, that he had only four papers to afk for relative to Mr. Haftings, which he was convinced would occafion no delay. He hoped that fome affurance would be given him by the right honourable gentleman (Mr. Burke) of his bringing forward his impeachment near the time of the propofed call of the Houfe. *(Major Scott)*

Mr. *Burke* declared, that the going through a period of thirteen years, collecting the facts relative to the fubject during that time, and arranging them in the form of a charge, was no matter of eafy accomplifhment. He had therefore undoubtedly a right to do this with caution, and agreeable to his own convenience. *(Mr. Burke)*

Mr. Chancellor *Pitt* wifhed that he fhould fix a period for his bringing forward this bufinefs as nearly as poffible. *(Mr. Chancellor Pitt.)*

Mr. *Burke* faid, that the period he would fix for this bufinefs was that day three weeks: then he would move the Houfe to refolve itfelf into a Committee on the charges againft Mr. Haftings, and fubmit what he had collected from verbal teftimony on the fubject. The names of the witneffes to be adduced on the trial, he would ftate in the Houfe upon the morrow. *(Mr. Burke)*

Mr. Chancellor *Pitt* conceiving this a fufficient reafon for delaying a call of the Houfe, propofed an amendment, that inftead of " this day fortnight," the words " to-morrow three " weeks" be inferted. *(Mr. Chancellor Pitt.)*

Mr. *Fox* contended, that this afforded no argument for fetting afide the original motion, as it was pufhed for other reafons than the impeachment of Mr. Haftings. *(Mr. Fox.)*

Mr.

Mr. Francis perſiſted in his former opinion.

The queſtion was put and carried.

Mr. Fox.

Mr. *Fox* declaring himſelf diſſatisfied with the deciſion on the preceding Monday relative to the production of papers, containing the correſpondence between Mr. Haſtings and Major Brown, then at Delhi, gave notice, that he would bring forward this buſineſs again on the enſuing Friday.

A motion having been made, that the Speaker do leave the chair, for the purpoſe of reſolving the Houſe into a Committee on the militia bill:

Mr. Rolle.

Mr. *Rolle* having expreſſed his wiſhes, that time might be given, added, that he had been informed by his conſtituents, that there were clauſes in it objectionable: he hoped therefore for the preſent, the blanks only would be filled up in the Committee, and that the report would not be made, as adopted by the Houſe, with precipitation.

The motion was then put, and the Speaker left the chair: the blanks were filled up, and the Houſe adjourned.

Tueſday and Wedneſday, 14th *and* 15th *March*.

On account of the want of attending members no buſineſs took place.

Thurſday, 16th *March*.

At bringing up the report of the Committee on the mutiny bill, reſpecting the new clauſe for ſubjecting the officers by brevet, receiving no pay, who ſhould be in command, to be tried by a court martial:

Col. Fitzpatrick.

Colonel *Fitzpatrick* deſired to know upon what principle of neceſſity or propriety ſo very extraordinary a clauſe was founded?

The Secretary at War.

The *Secretary at War* explained, that it was poſſible for an officer by brevet, who had no pay, to be in command, and that it had been thought right, that officers ſo circumſtanced ſhould be liable to be tried by a court martial for their conduct while in command.

Col. Fitzpatrick.

Colonel *Fitzpatrick* declared, that unleſs ſome caſe could be ſtated to the Houſe of the kind in queſtion, he ſhould think it ſcarcely poſſible for ſuch a caſe to happen, and therefore he ſaw no uſe in introducing ſuch a novelty into the mutiny bill.

The Secretary at War.

The *Secretary at War* begged leave to remind the Houſe, that he had given notice that there would be ſome new clauſes introduced into the bill, and had particularly called the attention of the Committee to the clauſes when he had propoſed them. With regard to the poſſibility of ſuch a caſe occurring, as that of a brevet officer happening to be in command, he

he hinted that fuch a cafe had occurred, and it had been
held, that the officer was not amenable to, nor could be tried
by, a court martial.

General *Burgoyne* fupported the objection, on the ground General
that it was introducing a new and dangerous principle into Burgoyne.
the mutiny act; that of fubjecting perfons who were not
paid by the Legiflature, and confequently were not under the
control of that Houfe, to martial law. He contended, that
the idea of making any man liable to martial law was founded
altogether on the circumftance of his receiving pay, voted
by the Houfe of Commons; and that the new claufe led to
confequences extremely alarming, as it would countenance
the keeping up an armed force in the country, that was
neither paid by the Legiflature, nor fubject to legiflative
control.

Mr. Chancellor *Pitt* defended the claufe as highly ne- Mr. Chan-
ceffary to clear up a matter of a doubtful nature. He ftated cellor Pitt.
the recent cafe of General Rofs, and mentioned, that upon
the laft reference to three of the judges, whether any officer
by brevet, and in command, was liable to a court martial;
one judge gave it as his opinion that he was; another gave
it as his opinion that he was not; and a third declared himfelf doubtful whether he was or not.

Ayes - - - - - - - - - 79
Noes - - - - - - - - - 17
—————
Majority - - 62

Mr. *Dundas* remarked, that as his new bill had lately Mr. Dundas
received, in a confiderable degree, the inveftigating notice
of the whole Houfe, he fhould not prefume to trefpafs too
much upon their patience by arguing diffufely concerning
its nature and its principles. He fhould imagine, that either
at the time of the fecond reading of the bill, or of its coming to the Committee, gentlemen might, with the greater
propriety, make their objections; objections to which he
fhould endeavour, as fatisfactorily as poffible to anfwer. At
prefent, he would juft ftate the heads of the principal alterations which he propofed to make in the prefent bill.——
Thefe were, firft, in regard to election of perfons to ferve
in council. As the bill of 1784 ftood, it confined it to the
fervants of the Company in India; but he meant that it
fhould comprehend alfo the fervants at home as well as thofe
in India. Another alteration was, an addition to the principle of the bill; for, inftead of leaving every thing to be
decided by the voice of the majority of the council at Calcutta, he meant to give the Governor General more power
than he at prefent poffeffed, and to let him decide upon every
meafure whether his council agreed with him or not. A
third

third alteration would be that of empowering the Governor General to nominate a succeſſor to ſit in council on the death of any one member, inſtead of the oldeſt in ſervice ſucceeding as a matter of courſe. He intended to entruſt the Directors with the power to decide as they thought it moſt for the benefit of their ſervice, whether the Commander in Chief ſhould have a ſeat at the council or not. At preſent the Commander in Chief enjoyed of courſe a ſeat at the council. A fourth alteration would be with reſpect to promotions in India: according to the bill of 1784, the Company's ſervants were all to riſe by regular gradation; but gentlemen would ſee in a moment, that, as there were different heads of ſervice, ſo a regular riſe muſt in ſome caſes prove inconvenient, and therefore he meant to divide the ſervants into their reſpective claſſes, and enact, that each claſs ſhould riſe regularly. In regard to the part of the bill, which obliged the ſervants of the Company on their coming home, to deliver in the amount of their fortunes, and alſo an account how they had diſpoſed of any part of their fortunes in India, upon oath; he had taken conſiderable pains to aſcertain what it was of which the gentlemen ſerving in India chiefly complained reſpecting that part of the bill of 1784; and he found that what chiefly diſtreſſed them aroſe from two operations of the diſcovering clauſes; the one was, the being obliged to give an account on oath, of the preciſe manner in which they had diſpoſed of any part of their fortunes in India, and the other the publicity of ſuch an account, by its being put upon record after it was made. He admitted that various ways might ariſe to occaſion gentlemen to diſpoſe of conſiderable ſums in India which no man would wiſh to have known. Particular ſums might be given to particular perſons; connections both male and female might abſorb a large portion of a gentleman's fortune; and it would undoubtedly be vexatious to have an authentic account of ſuch money made a matter of public record. He meant therefore to leave out of his bill the clauſe which reſpected the diſpoſal of every ſervant of the Company's money in India, and alſo to let the account of the fortune they brought home be made ſecretly, and kept ſecret unleſs in particular caſes where it would not prove right that it ſhould remain ſecret. Theſe alterations would, he truſted, relieve the minds of gentlemen in India in a great meaſure from the uneaſineſs which that part of the bill might have occaſioned, and at the ſame time the great end and object of obtaining an account of the fortunes which thoſe who returned home had made would be anſwered. Another alteration (and that the laſt) was, in reſpect to the mode of balloting for the petty jury to try perſons charged with

having

having committed crimes and misdemeanors in India, after their arrival in England. As the bill of 1784 stood, two hundred members were obliged to be present before the House could proceed to ballot. This was extremely inconvenient; and therefore he meant to omit that part of the bill which respected the two hundred members, and then the ballot might more easily be conducted, and in a way equally impartial, by having balloting lists prepared a sufficient time previous to the day of ballot; by which means a greater number of names would be before the House for election. Under all these circumstances, he felt it necessary to move "for leave to bring "in a bill to explain and amend the India bill."

Mr. Chancellor Pitt seconded the motion.

Mr. *Francis* remarked, that he did not entertain the most distant intention of opposing the motion, for that the bill of 1784 stood in need of great alteration and amendment was a fact universally admitted. He rose merely to give notice, that as soon as the motion should become disposed of, (which he presumed it would be immediately) he should move a proposition, which related to the bill just moved for. *Mr. Francis.*

Mr. Chancellor *Pitt* begged leave to call to the recollection of the honourable gentleman, that his right honourable and learned friend had given three days notice of his intention to move for leave to bring in a bill to amend and explain the India bill, whereas the honourable gentleman had not given any notice of his intention; he hoped, therefore, that as the report on the bill to modify the shop tax was designed to fall under the immediate consideration of the House, and as a right honourable gentleman opposite to him had signified his wish to enter, in some degree, upon the subject, the honourable gentleman would wave his motion for the present, and resume it at a more convenient season. *Mr. Chancellor Pitt.*

Mr. *Francis* answered, that his motion was so immediately connected with the motion then before the House, that he could not think of making it at any other time; but he did not conceive that it could be objected to, or that it would occasion the House a quarter of an hour's delay. *Mr. Francis.*

Mr. *Sheridan* remarked, that the excessive condescension and boundless good nature with which a right honourable gentleman (the Chancellor of the Exchequer) had risen to support his right honourable and learned friend's motion, was unparallelled! What an astonishing instance of true liberality of mind, in the very moment of having heard him declare that the purport and principle of his new bill went to cutting up by the roots the right honourable gentleman's own India bill, which the learned gentleman had proved by his speech to have been a very foolish piece of business. On this occasion, Mr. Sheridan added, that he should presume to warn *Mr. Sheridan.*

warn the right honourable and learned gentleman in time, that he ought to bring all the parts of his bill forward together, and not to imitate the conduct of his right honourable friend, (the Chancellor of the Exchequer) whose India bill, when first introduced, proved so imperfect and so improper, that it was obliged to be completely altered in all its parts in the Committee, and four and twenty new clauses were inserted. What the right honourable and learned gentleman called " an addition to the principle of Mr. Pitt's bill of 1784," was, on the contrary, a direct reversal of its principle, and the substitution of a new principle as to the particular point in question; for, by the bill of 1784, every thing in Council in India was to be carried by the majority of voices, whereas in the new bill every thing was to depend solely on the single opinion of the Governor General. And here he must desire to bring back to the remembrance of the House, that, on the first day of the session, they had been told by a right honourable gentleman, (the Chancellor of the Exchequer) that the reason why no notice of India had been taken in the speech from the Throne was, because the government of India had been established on a solid and permanent footing. Surely the information just given to the House, and the motion now under their discussion, appeared to operate like absolute contradictions against the existence of establishments of solidity and permanency!

The question was put and carried.

Mr. Fran-
cis.

Mr. *Francis* contended that his motion was of such a nature, that he scarcely thought it possible for any gentleman to object to it, since the doctrine which it tended to establish had been, at different times, professed by all of them, and recommended to their care and attention by the first authority in the kingdom — by His Majesty in his speech from the throne. It was an instruction to the gentlemen appointed to prepare the bill just moved for and ordered, highly necessary to be attended to, and would serve as a test of the principles of every gentleman in that House, and prove whether he was a friend to the Constitution or not. Mr. Francis now moved, " That it be an instruction to the gentlemen appointed to " prepare and bring in a bill to explain and amend an act " passed in the twenty-fourth year of His Majesty's reign, " entitled, ' An Act for the better Regulation and Manage- " ment of the Affairs of the East-India Company, and of " the British Possessions in India; and for establishing a " Court of Judicature for the more speedy and effectual " Trial of Persons accused of Offences committed in the " East Indies,' that, in preparing the same, they do never " lose sight of the effect which any measure to be adopted " for the good government of our possessions in India may
" have

" have on our own Conſtitution, and our deareſt intereſts at
" home; and particularly, that, in amending the ſaid act,
" they do take care that no part thereof ſhall be confirmed
" or re-enacted, by which the unalienable birthright of every
" Britiſh ſubject to a trial by jury, as declared in Magna
" Charta *, ſhall be taken away or impaired."

Mr. Sheridan ſeconded the motion.

The Houſe immediately divided —

Ayes - - - - - - - - - 16
Noes - - - - - - - - - 85
    ——
Majority - - 69

When the order of the day, for bringing up the Shop-tax
Committee report, was read,

Mr. *Fox* obſerved, that he ſhould give the Houſe leſs trou- Mr. Fox
ble upon the ſubject than he expected to have done when he
gave notice on the preceding Monday of his intentions to
offer his thoughts to them in regard to the modifications of
the ſhop tax propoſed by the right honourable gentleman
(the Chancellor of the Exchequer.) Since Monday a large
meeting of the moſt reſpectable ſhopkeepers in London,
Weſtminſter, and Southwark, had taken place, at which ſeveral reſolutions were agreed to ; and he had ſince been in-

* The trial by jury, or the country, *per patriam*, is alſo that trial
by the Peers of every Engliſhman, which, as the grand bulwark of
his liberties, is ſecured to him by the great charter, " *nullus liber
homo capiatur, vel impriſonetur, aut exulet, aut aliquo alio modo
deſtruatur, niſi per legale judicium parium ſuorum, vel per legem
terræ*."

The founders of the Engliſh laws have, with excellent forecaſt,
contrived, that the truth of every accuſation, whether preferred in
the ſhape of indictment, information, or appeal, ſhould afterwards
be confirmed by the unanimous ſuffrage of twelve of his equals, and
neighbours, indifferently choſen, and ſuperior to all ſuſpicion; ſo
that the liberties of England cannot but ſubſiſt ſo long as this PALLA-
DIUM remains ſacred and inviolate, not only from all open attacks,
(which none will be ſo hardy as to make) but alſo from all ſecret ma-
chinations which may ſap and undermine it, by introducing new and
arbitrary methods of trial by juſtices of the peace, commiſſioners of
the revenue, and courts of conſcience : and however convenient theſe
may appear, (as doubtleſs all arbitrary powers, well executed, are the
moſt *convenient*) yet let it be again remembered, that delays and little
inconveniencies in the forms of juſtice are the price that all free nations
muſt pay for their liberty in more ſubſtantial matters; that theſe inroads upon THIS SACRED BULWARK OF THE NATION are funda-
mentally oppoſite to the ſpirit of our Conſtitution; and that, though
begun in trifles, the precedent may gradually increaſe and ſpread, to
the utter diſuſe of juries in queſtions of the moſt momentous concern.

BLACKISTONE.

formed from that meeting, that it was their wish that he should state that they were by no means satisfied with the intended modifications, but that, so far from considering them as an alleviation of the tax with regard to them, they deemed them frivolous, delusive, and partial, since they left the whole burden of the tax upon their shoulders. " Such was the rooted disgust against the tax, that the shopkeepers, persuaded that no modification of it could palliate its personal and oppressive tendency, would rather wait until the ensuing session in the hope that the House would, in candour and in justice, consent to repeal it. altogether, than attempt to try now for any farther modification of it; and although they were perfectly conscious that it did not lie with them to suggest taxes, but that it was the immediate province of the Chancellor of the Exchequer and the House; yet had they authorised him to declare, that, objectionable as a general house tax was on many accounts, and partial and severe as its operation would prove upon them, they would gladly consent to pay a new general house tax, on condition of the repeal of the shop tax."

Mr. Ald. Newnham.

Mr. Alderman *Newnham* declared, that though he agreed in much of what had fallen from the right honourable gentleman, yet there was one point from which he must beg leave to dissent — the proposition of a new house tax in lieu of a shop tax. The shop tax was doubtless a bad tax, extremely partial and every way unwarrantable, and therefore he should be glad to see it repealed; and though the right honourable gentleman might (and he dared to say that he had) have stated the sentiments of the retail shopkeepers very fairly, yet he could not for a moment sit silent, while it was possible for the House to conceive that he would consent to take a thorn out of the side of the retail shopkeepers, and lodge it in the sides of his constituents in general. He thought it his duty in the most public manner to make this declaration in the House, and to add, that he would oppose a new house tax most strenuously, if ever it should be brought forward as a substitution for the shop tax.

The report was after this brought up, and the amendments made in the Committee agreed to.

Mr. Burke moved, " That the House should, on the ensuing Monday fortnight, resolve itself into a Committee of " the whole House on the East-India papers." As he was proceeding through a second motion for the attendance of several witnesses, at the same time,

Mr. Chancellor Pitt.

Mr. Chancellor *Pitt* rose, and expressed his hopes, that, in consenting to the motion, it would not be understood that he was bound not to oppose the examination of these witnesses

neſſes as to any points concerning which papers had been refuſed by the Houſe.

Mr. *Burke* anſwered, that, although he felt extreme con- Mr. Burke,
cern at the refuſal of the Houſe to grant him papers neceſſary
for ſubſtantiating ſeveral of what he deemed moſt material
charges, and ſhould rather ſuffer in his reputation in conſequence of this refuſal, he did not mean to examine witneſſes
as to thoſe points; for he not only ſaw that it would anſwer
no purpoſe, but knew that he ſhould be ſtrictly watched.

The perſons for whoſe attendance he moved were,

Sir Robert Barker,	Major Marſac,
Colonel Champion,	Captain Edwards,
William Alderſey, Eſq.	Colonel Muir,
Nathaniel Middleton, Eſq.	Colonel Popham,
J. Peter Auriol, Eſq.	David Anderſon, Eſq.
Sir John Doyley,	Major Williams,
Major Gilpin,	Balfour,
James Fraſer, Eſq.	Webber,
Captain Leonard Jaques,	—— Grady, Eſq.
John Hill, Eſq.	John Chandler, Eſq.

The Houſe adjourned.

Friday, 17th *March.*

The ſhop-tax modification bill having been read a third
time,

Sir *Watkin Lewes* moved a clauſe by way of rider, and was Sir Watkin
ſeconded by Mr. Thornton. Sir Watkin remarked, that Lewes,
from the title of the bill, impoſing a duty upon perſons keeping retail ſhops, he apprehended that victuallers were exempted from the tax; but as there were doubts reſpecting the perſons exempted, and the opinion of the judges was deſired on
the queſtion, he thought it right to explain the preſent and
the former act by a clauſe, that no perſon acting as a victual-
ler, and who had or ſhould take out a licenſe and act as ſuch,
ſhould become ſubject to the ſaid tax. This being made a
matter of converſation, and the Attorney General contending that victuallers were not ſubject to the tax, his opinion
anſwered the intention of Sir Watkin in moving the clauſe,
and therefore he withdrew it.

When the orders and buſineſs of the day, which were of
various kinds, had been gone through, the Speaker called to
Mr. *Fox:* that gentleman roſe immediately, and deſired that, Mr. Fox,
previouſly to his troubling the Houſe on the ſubject which he
wiſhed to bring under their conſideration, certain of the reſolutions of the 28th of May, 1782, might be read. He then
moved, " That the entries in the Journal of the Houſe, of
" the 28th day of May, 1782, of the ſix reſolutions reported

" from

" from the Committee of the whole Houfe, to whom it
" was referred to confider farther of the feveral Reports
" which had been made from the Committee of Secrecy, re-
" lating to the affairs of the Eaft-India Company, and which
" were then agreed to by the Houfe, might be read."

All thefe then were, as agreed to by the Houfe, read accordingly, as follows :

Refolved, " That the orders of the Court of Directors of
" the Eaft-India Company, which have conveyed to their
" fervants abroad a prohibitory condemnation of all fchemes
" of conqueft and enlargement of dominion, by prefcribing
" certain rules and boundaries for the operation of their mi-
" litary force, and enjoining a ftrict adherence to a fyftem of
" defence upon the principle of the treaty of Illahabad, were
" founded no lefs in wifdom and policy than in juftice and
" moderation."

Refolved, " That every tranfgreffion of thofe orders, with-
" out evident neceffity, by any of the feveral Britifh govern-
" ments in India, has been highly reprehenfible, and has tend-
" ed, in a chief degree, to weaken the force and influence, and
" to diminifh the refources, of the Company in thofe parts."

Refolved, " That every interference, as a party, in the do-
" meftic or national quarrels of the country powers, and all
" new engagements with them in offenfive alliance, have been
" wifely and providently forbidden by the Company in their
" commands to their adminiftrations in India."

Refolved, " That every unneceffary or avoidable deviation
" from thofe well-advifed rules fhould be followed with very
" fevere reprehenfion and punifhment for it, as an inftance
" of wilful difobedience of orders, and as tending to difturb
" and deftroy that ftate of tranquillity and peace with all
" their neighbours, the prefervation of which has been re-
" commended as the firft principle of policy to the Britifh
" government in India."

Refolved, " That the maintenance of an inviolable charac-
" ter for moderation, good faith, and fcrupulous regard to
" treaty, ought to have been the fimple grounds on which
" the Britifh Government fhould have endeavoured to efta-
" blifh an influence fuperior to that of other Europeans over
" the minds of the native powers in India; and that the dan-
" ger and difcredit arifing from the forfeiture of this pre-emi-
" nence, could not be compenfated by the temporary fuccefs
" of any plan of violence or injuftice."

Refolved, " That as an effential failure in the executive
" conduct of the Supreme Council, or Prefidencies, would
" make them juftly liable to the moft ferious animadverfions
" of their fuperiors, fo fhould any relaxation, without fuffi-
" cient caufe, in thefe principles of good government, on the
" part

" part of the Directors themfelves, bring upon them, in a
" heavier degree, the refentment of the legiflative power of
" their country, which alone can interpofe an effectual cor-
" rection to the general mifrule."
Refolved, " That it appears, that the Government Gene-
" ral had been previoufly in poffeffion of a letter from the
" Duan of the Rajah of Berar, containing overtures for me-
" diation for peace and alliance with the Pefhwa ; and that
" this material information was wholly fuppreffed by them in
" their difpatches to the Court of Directors; but a copy of
" it was fent, by the fame conveyance, to the private agent
" of Mr. Haftings ; and that, in thus neglecting to make
" immediate communication to the Court of Directors of
" fuch important intelligence, the Government General ap-
" pear to have failed in an effential part of their duty."
Thefe having been read,
Mr. *Fox* rofe, and obferved, that he was perfectly con- Mr.
vinced, that, previoufly to all endeavours for the fuccefsful
introduction of a motion for papers, effectually and fubftan-
tially, although perhaps not formally fimilar to that which,
during the courfe of a preceding debate, received the inveftigation, and (with concern he fpoke it) fuffered under the diffent of the Houfe, an apology was due to them upon the
principle that it muft always prove indecent frivoloufly to
trefpafs upon their attention. But if he ever had reafon to be
diffatisfied with the decifion of that Houfe ; if he ever thought
a motion of the firft importance to the honour and dignity of
the Houfe required a re-confideration, it was the motion for
the Dehli papers ; and that, becaufe the decifion the Houfe
had come to when they negatived it, had proved a decifion in
the teeth of the refolutions juft read, and in defiance of every
found and folid argument advanced in fupport of thofe refolutions ; in contradiction and controverfy of which arguments
no one rational idea or pofition had been ftated. It was,
therefore, for no light or trivial purpofe that he again begged
the Houfe, for the fake of its own dignity, for the fake of its
own honour, for the fake of national juftice and national character, to re-confider what they had decided upon, and, before they confirmed a denial of the Dehli papers, (which he
regarded as exceedingly material to the folemn and ferious accufations brought in that Houfe againft Warren Haftings,
Efq. ;) which denial, it appeared to him, they could not confirm, without loading themfelves with difgrace, and impeach-
ing their own honour and dignity, to weigh well what they
were about, to reflect a little on the frivolous point of view
in which fuch an ill-judged confirmation would place their
own refolutions, and the effect which it muft neceffarily have
upon the conduct of the Company's fervants in India. He
begged

begged them alſo to recollect, that in paſſing the reſolutions of May 28, 1782, they had holden out to the country powers of India a code of wiſe, wholeſome, and ſalutary laws, as the baſis of the conduct of the Britiſh government in India in future; and that the Houſe had, in fact, pledged itſelf to adhere to the letter and ſpirit of their own reſolutions. Theſe were ſurely great and important conſiderations, and conſiderations which ought to have a deep effect on the minds of gentlemen before they gave a vote, which muſt involve in it ſo many and ſuch intereſting conſequences. Some perſons had ſuppoſed that our Government and Conſtitution were attended by certain diſadvantages with reſpect to their intercourſe with foreign ſtates, ariſing from the public manner in which many important parts of our adminiſtration muſt neceſſarily be conducted; but from this evil (if an evil it was), a moſt important good would be found to reſult, when it was conſidered how far this publicity tended to create a confidence in all other nations, and how ſtrongly it contributed to bind us to certain defined and ſpecific modes of political conduct. From hence it aroſe that we could lay down (as we had done in the preſent inſtance) a particular ſyſtem of proceeding, for the due obſervation of which all thoſe ſtates might reaſonably look to us; an advantage not in the power of any arbitrary government whatſoever; for if a king were to iſſue an edict, ſetting forth the principles by which he intended to conduct himſelf with reſpect to foreign nations, it would be received only as a notification of the will of the Miniſter of the day, who, by death or diſgrace, might loſe his ſituation, and leave room for a ſucceſſor of different ſentiments, who, of courſe, would purſue a different line of conduct; whereas, with us, when the Britiſh Houſe of Commons publiſhed a ſyſtem of foreign adminiſtration, they not only committed the whole nation in the perſons of their repreſentatives, but abſolutely bound individually, as well all thoſe who had already been Miniſters, and enjoyed a proſpect of being ſo for many years to come, as thoſe who were ſo for the preſent. That he might, if poſſible, ſtill more impreſs the Houſe with a proper idea of the magnitude of the duty which they had engaged to perform, when they voted the reſolutions of 1782, he ſhould not heſitate to deſcribe them as meaſures of a ſtrong nature, and affording, he believed, the firſt inſtance of that Houſe's thinking that it became them to depart ſo far out of their immediate province as to interfere with any part of the exerciſe of the executive government; a circumſtance which they certainly would not have conſented to, but from the extraordinary complection of the caſe, which ſeemed to call for peculiar notice and peculiar proceeding. The Houſe never called for papers lightly, and he, for his own part, conſcious

that

that they ought not to do it lightly, never had nor would attempt to move any, which he was not convinced were absolutely neceſſary for ſome great and uſeful public purpoſe. The Houſe, he was aware, ought not to grant any other; and it was true, he willingly admitted, that papers neceſſary for ſome great and uſeful public purpoſe might be called for, the production of which would nevertheleſs be attended with miſchief to the ſtate, of ſuch a dangerous caſt as would more than overbalance the good which might ariſe from the purpoſe being anſwered for which they were moved, and which, therefore, afforded His Majeſty's Miniſters ſound and cogent reaſons for refuſing them; and, under ſuch circumſtances, it was undoubtedly their duty to refuſe them. But though he was ready to grant this, yet he held that in all ſuch caſes the refuſal ought not to reſt ſolely on the bare *ipſe dixit* of a miniſter; that many queſtions of confidence might, it was true, be agitated, on which a miniſter's word ought to be taken, but then ſomething at leaſt ſhould be ſtated in order to convince the Houſe that miſchief might ariſe if the motion were complied with. In regard to the motion in queſtion, the motion with which he ſhould conclude what he had to ſay, for the Dehli papers, it had been, on a former day, ſtated by his right honourable friend, (Mr. Dundas) the avowed accuſer of Mr. Haſtings, that thoſe papers were material to the matter in charge, and therefore they had been called for; but, material as they were, if they were not granted, his right honourable friend had declared, he already was in poſſeſſion of ſufficient materials to prove and make good every thing which he had ſaid at various times reſpecting the delinquency of the late Governor General of India; his character, therefore, was ſafe and on ſhore. This, which he was ſatisfied was perfectly true in reſpect to his right honourable friend, he wiſhed to be equally true in reſpect to that Houſe. He wiſhed that Houſe to be on ſhore and its character ſafe; and therefore it was that he ſhould again call for the papers. But, previous to this ſtep, he truſted that the Houſe would pleaſe to recollect upon what ground the papers had been once refuſed. It had been ſtated by the right honourable gentleman oppoſite to him, that the papers were not eſſential to the charge againſt Mr. Haſtings; that they proved nothing; Mr. Haſtings not having authoriſed Major Brown to enter into a treaty with the Shah; and thirdly, that they involved in them ſecrets reſpecting the negociations which, during the war, had been carried on in India, the divulging of which would tend to diſturb the tranquillity of the reſpective powers concerned in thoſe treaties, and to induce conſequences which might be attended with danger to the general intereſts of the Britiſh ſtate. For his own part, he was confident that he ſhould not

experience

experience much difficulty in proving that these grounds of
denial either did not apply, or were not sufficiently material
to justify withholding the papers; and to establish his position he might venture to rest much of his reasoning on the
letters of Major Brown to Mr. Hastings. It was manifest
that a treaty of offensive alliance had been negociated with the
Mogul, which was directly contrary to the express resolution
of that House. It was manifest, from Major Brown's letter,
that Mr. Hastings had authorised that negociation, and that,
in Major Brown's opinion, good faith, morality, and justice,
required that assistance should be afforded the Mogul, in compliance with the terms of that treaty. The emphatic words
of Major Brown's letter were, " we have offered to treat ; he
" has accepted : we have annexed conditions, he has approved
" of them." These words proved incontestably that the
treaty commenced by voluntary offer on our part; and the
subsequent words in which Major Brown in his letter proceeds to urge Mr. Hastings, for the sake of the good faith,
morality, and justice of the British nation, to send troops to
the assistance of the Mogul, to lay siege to certain districts of
country, in order to drive out the inhabitants, and to give the
lands to the troops for their subsistence, proved equally forcibly that the treaty was a treaty of offensive alliance. It was
evident that the resolution of the House had been trampled on
and contemned by Mr. Hastings in this instance; and it was
more than matter of suspicion that the treaty was never intended to have been concluded when it was begun. When,
during the former debate on the same subject, he was complaining that the resolution had been infringed by Mr. Hastings, who began to negociate a treaty of offensive alliance,
a right honourable gentleman (the Chancellor of the Exchequer) had thought proper to say across the house, " a treaty
" never completed;" and therefore he (Mr. Fox) must beg
leave to know whether he was to understand from those words
that it was taken as a merit that the Company's servants in
India got into this dilemma; they had violated the resolutions
of the House by commencing a treaty, which local or temporary policy might appear to make it expedient to commence,
and then they had violated the national faith by deceiving the
Mogul, and refusing to conclude the treaty so commenced;
thus proving to the princes of Hindostan how little security
was, on the one hand, afforded them by the code of laws held
out to them in the resolutions of the British House of Commons, and how little safety was, on the other hand, to be acquired by entering into treaties of alliance with the British
government in India He felt himself thoroughly justified in
contending that, in spite of any narrow principle which temporary distress or local circumstances might seem to call for,
such

such as keeping the Mogul out of the hands of the French, or of Tippoo Sultan, it ill became a nation of great weight and character, like Great Britain, to depart from general syftems, founded in wifdom and in juftice, on any fuch petty confiderations; that if fuch narrow policy were to juftify a departure from a great parliamentary fyftem, there was an end of the utility of laying down a code of laws, to be made the foundation of a government, of fimplicity, of publicity, and of good faith.   In fact, the whole of the negociation had been fecretly carried on by Mr. Browne, as the agent of Mr. Haftings.   With refpect to the ground of refufal of the papers, on the plea that their production would betray fome fecrets of negociation, the divulging of which muft difturb the tranquillity of the powers of Hindoftan, and prove dangerous to the fafety of the State, he muft candidly confefs that it was moft difficult to meet it with any argument, the other fide of the Houfe having given him fo little to lay hold of, and not having faid enough to enable him to guefs even at what the danger could poffibly be which would arife, were the ftate fecrets, which they fo much dreaded to lay open, to become divulged.   Situated, however, as he was in thefe refpects, he could, without hefitation, declare, that no government fecret of any kind could juftify the withholding papers which were to enable the Houfe to fupport and fubftantiate the refolutions to which they ftood folemnly pledged.   For what was it but to fay to the princes in India, " we know our fervants have " committed delinquencies, and we are convinced that they " have broken faith with you; but we muft not inquire into " their conduct, becaufe that would betray ftate fecrets, " that would develope State myfteries, which muft be kept " facred!"   Would not every man in India laugh at fo abfurd a reafon for refufing to do juftice? Would it not plainly appear that the Board of Control, and that Houfe, were following the exact fteps of the old Boards of Directors? That they were laying down complete fyftems of ethics in their orders and refolutions, but refufing to take the only means poffible to enforce their performance? The effect of fuch conduct was too manifeft to need an illuftration.   Inftead of reformation in India, it would encourage abufe, and increafe delinquency; the Board of Control and the Houfe of Commons would be anfwerable for having fuffered the Company's fervants, employed in the government of India, to believe themfelves fecure from inquiry, and fafe from punifhment. What was it but to put it in the power of a minifter to interfere in every inveftigation, and, by his fingle *veto*, put a ftop to the procefs, and defeat the aim of that Houfe in the exercife of its firft great conftitutional character — that of the grand inqueft of the nation? Armed with fuch a power, to what lengths might not a minister proceed? Every criminal, however notorious his delinquency, however numerous his crimes, however injurious to the national honour, would only have to secure the Minister's protection to be able to laugh at accusation, and set conviction at defiance! Much had been said by the ministerialists concerning secrets; but there could be no secret in question; nor could the papers called for possibly make any thing public which was not already well known in India. If it were asked why he, who was so strenuous for the publishing of every matter relative to India, and so urgent in contending that nothing respecting that country ought to remain a secret, did not hold the same argument with respect to the European powers, and in like manner maintain that nothing which regarded treaties and negociations between the Court of Great Britain and any Court of Europe ought to be made a state secret in that House, by any of His Majesty's Ministers, he would answer that question by proposing another. Had that House ever expressly laid down rules of administration for the executive government with regard to European powers? Most certainly it had not; and that for very clear and obvious reasons. Why had it done otherwise with respect to the administration of the executive government of the British possessions in India? Because from the series of abuses, mismanagement, and delusion, which had crept into the conduct of the executive government in India, the British honour was tarnished, and the native princes no longer had confidence in British faith. Nothing, therefore, but the interference of Parliament could redeem the national credit, and restore it in the eyes of the country powers in Hindostan. Having so interfered, and having laid down the code of laws which could alone support a system of government adapted to the nature of the case, and likely to regain the confidence of the native princes—a system of government founded on simplicity, publicity, and good faith, would that House, on the mere pretence of a state secret, without the smallest information to prove that there was a real state secret in the way, with nothing more than a Minister's *ipse dixit* for it, shut their eyes to what every man who was not wilfully blind must see the necessity of — to their proceeding to substantiate their resolutions and fulfil their promises, to which they all stood so particularly pledged? Even yet, however, he should not relinquish his hopes that his right honourable and learned friend (Mr. Dundas) would rescue the House from the disgrace of having been persuaded by him to vote resolutions, which, if the papers were refused, it would be fair to say he never meant should be acted upon. Let the right honourable and learned gentleman recollect what had been done last year by the Board of Control respecting the debts of the Nabob

of

of Arcot. If he did not know the circumſtance, he would poſſeſs him of it; but moſt probably he knew of it more correctly than he did; if he did not, however, he would inform him of the fact. It was this:—that ſo far from the management then made being attended to, new loans were at this time going on, and new debts contracting. Having moved for the Dehli papers, Mr. Fox concluded his remarks.

Mr. Chancellor *Pitt* obſerved, that could he entertain a wiſh to have the queſtion totally thrown aſide, his wiſh might, with facility, be completed; becauſe as no incontrovertible parliamentary reaſon could be aſſigned why a motion ſhould be made twice in the courſe of the ſame ſeſſion for the production of papers, more than for any other purpoſe, he might object againſt and abſolutely prevent its introduction; yet, in the preſent caſe, he would not avail himſelf of the ſtanding rule of parliamentary proceeding, as he felt an inclination to anſwer ſome parts of the right honourable gentleman's argument, and he ſincerely hoped that his motion was ſufficiently diverſified to allow of its being argued a ſecond time. He ſhould, in that hope, reply to the right honourable gentleman, and endeavour to compreſs his neceſſary remarks into as few words as poſſible. He agreed with almoſt every one of the right honourable gentleman's principles, as well with reſpect to the policy of the Eaſt-India government, as with reſpect to the right and duty of that Houſe to inquire into all the abuſes which might ariſe in it; but in the concluſions which the right honourable gentleman had drawn from thoſe principles, he widely and completely differed from him. He had formerly, in debate on a motion made by a friend of the right honourable gentleman, given his ſentiments concerning the ſubject of granting official papers for the purpoſe of facilitating a criminal inquiry, and he would again briefly repeat them. He was of opinion, that, on a motion for papers with ſuch a view, it was neceſſary firſt to ſhew a probable ground of guilt; next, that the papers required were neceſſary and relevant to ſubſtantiate that guilt; and laſtly, that the papers might be made public without any dangerous conſequence to the State. He ſhould argue the preſent queſtion on thoſe principles; and if the Houſe ſhould not be perfectly ſatisfied that on each of them the motion ought to be rejected, he ſhould acquieſce in their opinion. The right honourable gentleman had charged Mr. Haſtings with a number of offences, to which, as he contended, the papers now required had a reference. The firſt charge was, that he had entered into an offenſive alliance with the Great Mogul, and, by ſo doing, had acted in defiance, not only of the order of the Court of Directors, but of the reſolution of that Houſe, in approving of thoſe orders by which they had prohibited the

Govern

Government of Bengal from entering into any offensive alliance with the powers of the East. In the first place, those resolutions which, he admitted with the right honourable gentleman, were singular in themselves, and only to be accounted for and justified by the peculiar situation of the affairs of India, did not prohibit, in strict and implicit construction, every particular alliance of the nature alluded to, but only restrained a wanton habit of making such engagements; for it would prove highly impolitic and absurd, in all cases whatsoever, to forbid the making of offensive alliances, as situations might occur in which they would be indispensably necessary; but in the present case, it was needless to inquire into the latitude which was left to the servants of the Company in India, to exercise a discretion in the forming offensive alliances, as he could shew that, in this at least, there was no such alliance either formed or authorised by Mr. Hastings. The right honourable gentleman had entertained a presumption from the letter of Major Browne, that he had been commissioned by Mr. Hastings to negociate a treaty of offensive alliance with the Mogul, and this was the only ground of such a suspicion: The most satisfactory method of course, in which that question could be ascertained, was, to read parts of Major Browne's correspondence, and to try whether it contained any thing either to contradict or to confirm that presumption; this he had accordingly done, and should again read a part of it to the House, by which they would become enabled to judge how far the right honourable gentleman was justified in presuming, that Mr. Hastings had employed Major Browne to conclude the alliance in question.

It was necessary for gentlemen to look back upon the situation of India at the period when the transactions took place, by which it would be found, that then a most dangerous attack was made on the Company's possessions by the European enemy of this country, in conjunction with the most formidable of all the princes of India, Tippoo Saib: that the last-mentioned prince, well knowing the influence which the name of the Mogul had upon the feelings and the prejudices of his countrymen, was exercising all his endeavours to bring him over to his interests; that he was making him offers of assistance in re-instating him in the power and consequence which he had lost, and even of great sums of money to bribe him into his party; and that if he had succeeded, an insurmountable addition would have been made to the difficulties under which the English Government had to struggle: That in order to counteract this, it became necessary for the servants of the Company to exert themselves to the utmost to ingratiate themselves with the Court of Dehli, and by such

means fecure to their employers that great body of strength
and influence which would naturally refult from the countenance of the Shah; and this more efpecially, as the Mogul
had recently loft his Minifter, a perfon highly ferviceable to
the Britifh adminiftration, being clofely connected by ties of
friendfhip with the Vizier, who was a decided favourer of
this country; and that it was determined by the unanimous
voice of the Council to fend an ambaffador to Dehli, in order
to fecure as much as poffible an amicable difpofition in that
Court. That Mr. Haftings appointed Major Browne to the
embaffy, and that his inftructions were, firft, to fulfil the
formalities of refpect and compliment to the perfon from
whom the Company acknowledged to hold all their poffeffions; next, to condole with him on the death of his minifter; and laftly, to confult with him on the means of reftoring
him to that power and confequence which his predeceffors
enjoyed, but which he had been deprived of. He was alfo
to encourage with as much addrefs and delicacy as poffible,
overtures of an alliance and applications for affiftance from
the Bengal Government, but was expreffly directed to avoid
any pofitive engagements until he fhould have referred to
the Council the propofals made by the Mogul; and particularly, an account of the manner in which any force the Prefidency might afford him were to be employed, and the refources by which it was to be paid. Thefe were the objects
of Major Browne's miffion: the confequences was, that the
Mogul, unwilling to efpoufe the party of Tippoo Saib and
France, expreffed a willingnefs to enter into a treaty of an offenfive nature with the Government of Bengal, of which
Major Browne gave notice to the Council, who refufed to
enter into it. This circumftance of the attempts of the
French and Tippoo Saib, to unite to their joint powers the
authority of the Mogul, reminded him of what had dropped
from the noble Lord in the blue ribband during the courfe
of a former debate. The noble Lord had paufed for fome
time, to confider what connection there could poffibly be
between any European power and the Court of Dehli, and
had particularly alluded to France—" What," faid the noble
Lord " has France to do with Dehli?" and the noble Lord
attempted to turn into ridicule the idea of fuppofing that it
was neceffary to fecure that Court, to prevent its falling in
with the views of our enemies; but from the facts which appeared upon the face of Major Browne's letter, on which, for
other purpofes, fo much reliance had been placed, the noble
Lord might inform himfelf better refpecting the fubject, and
fee that France had very material objects in view in an intercourfe and connection with the court of Dehli. [The
Chancellor now read that part of Major Browne's inftructions

tions to which he had referred before, whence it appeared
from that gentleman's own words, that he was expressly
restrained from concluding or even proposing any treaty, until he had laid the whole progress of his negociation before the Council, and had their approbation to proceed
upon it.]

The Chancellor was now asked from the other side of the
House, what was the date of the letter?

He informed them; and added, that the date led him to
another circumstance entitled to particular observation, and
this was, that the letter bore a date subsequent to one of the
periods in which the right honourable gentleman supposed
Mr. Hastings to have given the instructions against which
he complained. If, therefore, any such instructions were
given, it must according to the right honourable gentleman,
have been at the time when Mr. Hastings met Major Browne
at Lucknow; but the right honourable gentleman had marked
that as the time when it was determined to depart from and
violate the treaty, so that it was impossible that he could then
have given any such instructions: thus, he apprehended, he
had sufficiently proved, that no such treaty was ever undertaken by Mr. Hastings, and so it became impossible that the
other charge, of having departed from and violated his treaty
could have any place or authority whatsoever. The right
honourable gentleman had also accused Mr. Hastings of prosecuting his negociations with the Mogul without the pri-
vacy of the Council, contrary to the duty of his station; but
here again were the records of the Council to contradict him;
for, as the letters of Major Browne proved, that he had not
begun a negociation for an offensive treaty at all, so it was
proved by those that he had never intended to do so without
applying to the Council for their encouragement. He should
now trouble the House with some brief remarks concerning
the charge of having suffered the Mogul to unite with the
Marattah powers, which a right honourable gentleman (Mr.
Burke) had said it was his duty, by force of arms to have
prevented; but before he went farther on that subject, he
begged gentlemen to advert to the inconsistency of one gentleman's complaining of a governor for entering into an offensive treaty, and another as bitterly inveighing against him
for not actually taking up arms, and this from persons who
appeared to go hand in hand in the whole proceeding! With
respect to this union of the Mogul with the Marattahs, he
should only observe, that if that had not taken place, one of
the other of these two circumstances must have occurred;
either he must have fallen into the hands of the French and
Tippoo Saib, or become connected with the East-India Company by such an alliance as was now so severely reprobated.
But

But in fact, if he were inclined to do what his duty reſtrained him from doing—to lay open ſecrets, of which the intereſts of the country required a concealment, he could eaſily prove, that the junction of the Mogul with theſe potentates was of the higheſt advantage to the Company.   The right honour-ble gentleman had objected to the mode in which the Court of Directors had inquired into the negociation with the Court of Dehli, making Major Browne the object of their inquiry inſtead of his employer, Mr. Haſtings, whom they entirely paſſed by; but ſurely it was a ſeverer method againſt the principal to apply to the agents in ſuch caſes, for it was putting him on his guard, and pointing out to him the ne-ceſſity of proving againſt his employer all ſuch facts as, if brought home to him, muſt, in the end, come upon himſelf, and was of courſe adding one perſon more (and him the moſt deeply intereſted) to the liſt of the accuſers; ſo that in truth, the calling upon Major Browne in the firſt inſtance, was the moſt likely way of bringing forth all the circumſtances againſt Mr. Haſtings, ſuppoſing the tranſactions to have been crimi-nal, whilſt it by no means tended to produce any thing in his favour.

From all this it muſt appear, that there was no preſump-tive grounds for a charge of criminality ſufficient to war-rant the diſcloſure of papers alledged to be of a dangerous ten-dency; but, as the right honourable gentleman had ſaid ſo much on that head, he ſhould take up as little of the time of the Houſe as poſſible to give him an anſwer.   He believed, if he were determined to prove to the Houſe, that the papers were really dangerous and improper to be made public, he could do it in a very ſhort and compendious way, to which he con-feſſed he ſhould prove extremely averſe.   This method, in ſhort, was, by producing them; for he would undertake to ſay, that were they to be read by the members, there could be but one opinion upon them, that of cenſure againſt him for conſent-ing to grant papers of a nature ſo extremely delicate, and ſo likely to injure our intereſts in India, by expoſing to each other the views and conſiderations under which each of the princes of that country had been governed in their arrange-ments with us.   He had (Mr. Pitt added) been called upon to point out how the production of the papers would prove dangerous; but ſurely by making the attempt he ſhould lite-rally incur the danger; for how could he explain the danger of communicating ſecrets, without in a great meaſure making the ſecrets themſelves known?   He had already ſaid as much, and perhaps more, than he could with ſafety ſay upon the ſub-ject; and doubtleſs it could not be ſuppoſed, but that if he conſulted his own caſe rather than his duty, he muſt wiſh at once to conſent to granting of the papers; and indeed, when

he

he confidered, that as yet, all the papers granted, were of a nature calculated to fupport the charges againft Mr. Haftings, and that thofe now moved for were fuch, as would place in a moft confpicuous point of view, the moft meritorious and brilliant part of his adminiftration, he could not help, from motives of compaffion and juftice, lamenting, that in compliance with his duty, he muft object to their production. The right honourable gentleman had attempted to fhew, that on the fame principles as thofe on which the prefent motion was objected to, any delinquent fervant of the Public might be fcreened from punifhment and the cenfure of that Houfe by the bare *ipfe dixit* of the Minifter, "That the documents "neceffary to the proof of his guilt could not be produced "with fafety;" but when circumftances fuch as he had mentioned, as well of the innocence, nay the merit, of the tranf-action imputed as criminal, as of the extreme delicacy of the papers demanded were urged, could it poffibly be faid, that the queftion refted upon the *ipfe dixit* of the Minifter? Or could a precedent be eftablifhed under fuch circumftances as the prefent which could ever apply to cafes wherein thofe or fimilar circumftances did not exift? Where, on the contrary, they occurred, he trufted that all precedents would prove unneceffary, and that the Houfe, guided by the plain rules of common fenfe and political expedience, would never meet fuch applications with their unmerited concurrence.

Mr. Sheridan.

Mr. *Sheridan* remarked, that in fpite of the extenfive talents and brilliant eloquence of the right honourable gentleman who fpoke laft, his obfervations were much too barren of folid argument to conftitute a refutation of the reafoning of his right honourable friend (Mr. Fox) who had unanfwerably contended for the production of the papers, upon the proof, which he as irrefragably eftablifhed, that they contained the cleareft and moft incontrovertible evidence, of a negociation for an offenfive alliance entered into by Mr. Haftings with the country powers; nor had his right honourable friend maintained by lefs unqueftionale allegations, that were thefe wonderfully fecret papers divulged, no danger whatfoever could accrue to the State from their publicity. For his own part he muft confefs, that were he to place an approving confidence in the meafures of an Adminiftration, and any honourable member fhould move a queftion for papers affecting the executive government of the country, and His Majefty's Minifters who were to be refponfible, fhould ftand up and declare, that the granting the papers would prove dangerous to the State, he would defift from preffing fuch a motion. But was this the cafe now? No; the right honourable gentleman, as His Majefty's Minifter, was not refponfible for the adminiftration of the executive government

of

of India; that government was not the government of His Majesty, whose name and authority had no connection with it; it was merely the government of a trading Company, conducted by their servants, and therefore all ideas of confidence in the King's Ministers were out of the question. What was the Board of Control? Nothing more than another Board of Directors, of a superior order indeed, and nominated by His Majesty in the first instance. But it was rather curious, that the right honourable and learned gentleman should be one of the persons (and perhaps the principal, in talking of India secrets, and refusing necessary papers on that ground) when he himself had formed his own motions for papers in 1781 and 1782, in the broadest and most general words; calling for all the papers relating to the revenue, all the papers relating to the civil government, and so on: at that time, and it was a time of war, nobody dreamt of a secret respecting India. How happened it then, that when the conduct of Lord Clive was under inquiry, when every other India inquiry was going on, that from the earliest periods it had never been discovered, that there might be a state secret in India till the year 1786. It was downright nonsense to talk with a grave face about secrecy and the dangerous tendency of letting the papers moved for be seen, when it was well known not only what were their contents, but every transaction to which they alluded.

In order more fully to convince the House that the papers would establish a most extraordinary series of duplicity in the conduct of Mr. Hastings, respecting the negociation with the Mogul, Mr. Sheridan went into a detailed investigation of every minute circumstance of the transactions of Major Browne, from the time of his leaving Calcutta, in October, 1783, to the arrival of Mr. Hastings at Lucknow, with all the relative facts of the flight of the son of the Mogul; of that Prince's reception by Mr. Hastings and the Nabob of Oude; the seizure of the old Minister of the Mogul by the Vizier Aphrafead Cawn, and the putting the Mogul into the hands of Madagee Scindia; reasoning upon each particular as he proceeded, and deducing such inferences as he conceived the premises clearly warranted: all these he contended, concurred in proving, that Mr. Hastings had acted in a manner so intricate and extraordinary, that though he by no means wished it to be understood as suggesting it either as a charge or an insinuation, that Mr. Hastings was conscious of being guilty, yet with the purest innocence on the part of that gentleman, the suspicion to which it gave rise (at least in his mind) was, that Mr. Hastings, from an idea, that the party he considered as his political enemies, were in power at home, might entertain a wish to provide himself a refuge at the

Court of Dehli.   On this occasion he must take the liberty to observe that much inconsistency had, to appearance, marked the conduct of a learned and right honourable gentleman, (Mr. Dundas) who discovered an aversion from either manfully standing forward himself as the first accuser of Mr. Hastings, or being at least a warm supporter of the accusation.   What could be the reason of the backwardness of the learned and right honourable gentleman, who had built his fame on his conduct as a conductor of Indian inquiries? Was it because he thought to secure that situation he had acquired by prosecuting one supposed delinquent, that he took pains to protect another?   Or was it from a kind of gratitude for East-India delinquency to which he had been so much obliged, that he chose to be his friend, and would not, as it were, kick down the ladder on which he had risen?   From whatsoever motives a conduct so singular had arisen, it was fair to point at the political versatility of the right honourable and learned gentleman, who could, in 1786, oppose the substantiation of resolutions, for which, in 1782, he had particularly moved.

Scott.   Major *Scott* rose next, and said: The right honourable gentleman (Mr. Sheridan) who spoke last, has treated the subject in debate in so extraordinary a manner, that I am absolutely lost in astonishment, and find it impossible for me to follow him; yet I will endeavour, Sir, by a plain and faithful relation of facts, to render the subject intelligible to the good sense of this House; but if I were to attempt to answer the honourable gentleman's ingenious arguments in any other way, I should assuredly fail in the attempt.   I shall never presume to dispute the abilities, the wit, or the ingenuity of the honourable gentleman, but I must lay claim to some knowledge of the subject before you; and in a debate on an India question, a residence of near sixteen years in that country may give me some advantage over the honourable gentleman, which it would be presumption in me to aspire to upon any other.   But before I proceed to detail the circumstances of Major Browne's negociations, permit me to remark upon a most extraordinary supposition in the conclusion of the honourable gentleman's speech; and I am glad he mentioned it, because it has been already mentioned in a former debate by a right honourable gentleman (Mr. Fox).   One way of accounting for Major Browne's proposal for the British government of Bengal to assist the King with troops, is, that it was entirely agreeable to Mr. Hastings; and what renders it so suspicious is, that these troops were not to have British officers.   The conclusion meant to be impressed upon the House was, and indeed it was stated too plainly to be misunderstood, that about the time this proposal came from Major Browne, Mr. Hastings had intelligence of certain events in England, namely,

namely, the right honourable gentleman's India bill, and that he was providing a secure retreat at Dehli, where he might resist the power of this country. An attention to dates over-sets this suspicion in an instant. The proposal for troops was originally made in October 1783, and the right honourable gentleman did not bring in his bill till the following month. No one can believe that I had the most distant idea of the heads of that bill; even the then chairman of the Court of Directors, Sir Henry Fletcher, professed his utter ignorance of it, till it was opened in this House: so that at once there is an end to this suspicion. At a subsequent period, in May 1784, Mr. Hastings had heard from me that the bill had been twice read, and committed. In his reply to that letter, he had prophesied the fate of the bill; he said it never would pass: and many gentlemen in this House have seen the letter. But, he added, that to him it was not of the smallest consequence, since not all the powers upon earth should detain him another season in India, unless upon one condition—that of having complete power from England; and of that he had not the smallest expectations. He kept his word, for he quitted in February 1775, seventeen days previous to the appointment of his successor in England. But admitting for a moment, that Mr. Hastings, feeling strong resentment for the unmerited reproaches cast upon him in England, in return for preserving an empire to Great Britain, had determined within himself to resist that bill: is there a gentleman in this House, who supposes that any thing so absurd, so preposterous, or so ridiculous, as what the two honourable gentlemen have insinuated, could have entered into his head? What, Sir, to trust himself with six miserable battalions of seapoys, without British officers, in a country where there have been, for the last ten years, almost as many assassinations and revolutions as months? No man who knows any thing of India, can, for a moment, entertain such a thought. There was one, and but one way by which such a plan could have succeeded, acting heart and hand with our countrymen in India: but Mr. Hastings at Dehli would have been more inconsiderable than Mr. Hastings in London. As the honourable gentleman has mentioned that India bill, I will tell him what were the feelings of Gentlemen in India upon it, as far as I have been able to learn them, from letters, and the information of those who were at the time it was heard of on the spot. Our countrymen there conceived they had rendered great and important services during the war, and that they were as successful there, as unhappily we were unfortunate every where else: they therefore read with indignation and resentment the virulent abuse which was universally bestowed upon them while that bill was in its progress

through

through this House; added to this, the general opinion was, that daily supercessions were to be expected, since removals and appointments in India were vested in the Commissioners. Mr. Haftings was generally, almost univerfally efteemed, or more than efteemed, and the caufe was a common one: if, therefore, he had entertained fuch ideas as the honourable gentleman would impute to him, Calcutta, and not Dehli, would have been his feat of government; but in truth, he was anxious to conclude his bufinefs with the Vizier, and to embark for his native country. Having ftated this, Sir, I fhall now beg leave to reply to all the ingenious arguments of the honourable gentleman by a ftrict relation of facts.

On the 20th of Auguft, 1782, Major Browne, was by the Governor General and Council, not by Mr. Haftings, appointed Minifter from the Britifh government to the Mogul: the inftructions were given by Mr. Haftings, with the knowledge and concurrence of the Board, and the material parts have been read by the right honourable gentleman below me. The policy of the embaffy has not been difputed. In March, 1783, thefe inftructions were refcinded. In October, 1783, before Major Browne had had an interview with the King, a propofition came from His Majefty and his Minifter, to the Governor General and Council for troops to affift him. The Marattah peace, which had not been ratified when Major Browne was deputed, was at this time fully fettled: Mr. Haftings recommended a compliance with the King's requeft, but his Council rejected the propofition, and there it ended. It is neceffary to obferve that at this time, and for fome months before, very violent difputes fubfifted in the Council, and Mr. Haftings was in a minority. Thefe difputes continued, till in the latter end of December the Board agreed to leave the province of Oude to the management of Mr. Haftings, he relieving them from the refponfibility, and he confenting to it. On the 20th of January, 1784, Major Browne's letter of the 30th of December, 1783, was received and fent in circulation to the other members. The bufinefs of Oude was at this time the great fubject of attention, and the Board had two months before declared to affift the King. In ten days after this, Mr. Haftings, ftill in a minority, quitted Calcutta, and expreffly confined by his credentials to the execution of that bufinefs for which he was deputed, namely, to affift the Vizier in fettling his country, and to recover the debts due from him to the Company. The power of removing Major Browne lay with the Board in Calcutta, who were not at that time, nor were till juft before his departure for Europe, very well inclined towards Mr. Haftings: they did not remove him; but there was no farther application from him or the King for military affiftance at that time. In

the

he month of May, while Mr. Haftings was deeply engaged
n arranging the affairs of the Nabob Vizier, the Prince ar-
ived in the vicinity of Lucknow; and I can affert it for a
act, upon the folemn affurances of Mr. Haftings, and every
gentleman then with him, that he was utterly ignorant of
his flight, and that he took every ftep in his power to prevent
his coming to Lucknow; but when it was not to be avoided,
he thought it proper to receive him in a manner fuited to the
dignity of the Prince's ftation in Indoftan. His anfwer to
he Prince was furely wife and true. The King and his Minifter afterwards fent a formal embaffy to require the Prince's
return, and Major Browne was charged with feparate commands from the King: whether Mr. Haftings was right or
wrong in his judgement, it is certain that he thought this a
favourable moment to affift the King. He earneftly preffed
his Council to grant him authority, but they peremptorily refufed it; and here this fecond negociation ended. Mr. Haftings never buoyed the King or the Prince up with an idea
that he had any power to affift them, without firft receiving
the fanction of his Council—One point is curious:

The right honourable gentleman has quoted two refolutions to prove, that to interfere unneceffarily in the difputes of
the country powers, is contrary to the wifh of this Houfe.
Mr. Haftings quoted a third to his Council, to prove that
it was the wifh of this Houfe that the firft favourable opportunity fhould be feized of doing him a fervice; for if the refolution does not mean thus much, it means nothing. I defire it may be read:

Refolved, " That it is the opinion of this Committee, that
" the conduct of the Company and their fervants in India to
" the King, and Nudjiff Cawn, with refpect to the tribute
" payable to the one, and the ftipend to the other, and with
" refpect to the transfer of the provinces of Corah and Illa-
" habad to the Vizier, was contrary to policy and good
" faith; and that fuch wife and practicable meafures fhould
" be adopted in future, as may tend to redeem the national
" honour, and recover the confidence and attachment of the
" Princes of India."

Now, Sir, this refolution is an ample juftification for Mr.
Haftings, if he could affift the King without an unneceffary
interference in the differences of the country powers; but as
his Council would not agree with him, he formally declared
that he could not affift the Mogul, though all parties agreed
in granting an afylum to the Prince, and the Nabob Vizier
cheerfully afforded him the means of fubfiftence.

I muft defire to obferve, that Mr. Haftings's deputation to
Lucknow had no connection of any fort with Major Browne's
negociations. There had been very violent difputes at
Lucknow

Lucknow between the Vizier and Hyder Beg Cawn on the one part, and Mr. Briftow on the other. Thefe were referred to Calcutta, and Mr. Haftings differed with his Council effentially upon the fuhjects in difpute. From May to December, 1783, thefe differences continued; and then the Council agreed to yield to Mr. Haftings, provided he would enfure the payment of the Company's debt. He acceded to the terms; he prepared, on the Vizier's invitation, to go to Lucknow: his offer was accepted by the Board, and his credentials confined him to the two points of affifting the Vizier, and recovering the balances due from his Excellency to the Company. Thefe were in fact the only two points on which Mr. Haftings was deputed, and therefore his credentials, which this Houfe has ordered to day to be printed, were in every refpect proper and ample. It is furely a ftrange conclufion to draw, that Mr. Haftings wanted to involve the nation in another war, becaufe he declared his opinion to his Council, that if powers were granted to him he would effectually affift the King, and make his fituation much more comfortable than it had been for years. If we are to judge from another event, we muft think that Mr. Haftings could have performed what he promifed. There was hardly a man in India who conceived a poffibility of his doing what he did to extricate the Vizier at Lucknow, or to recover the Company's debt. The honourable gentleman has faid that Mr. Haftings's letter of the 30th of April, and the poftfcript of the 13th of May, were printed by me, and publicly read in a Court of Proprietors, and that therefore it is abfurd to withhold the other papers. He is very near correct in this ftatement, but I will relate it exactly as it happened. I declare upon my honour that I did not receive a copy of that letter from Mr. Haftings, but merely a fmall letter upon a quarter of a fheet of paper, which came in the Company's over-land packet, and was delivered to me at the India Houfe. This letter, which many gentlemen have feen, contained the prophecy of Mr. Haftings, that the right honourable gentleman's bill would never pafs, and his mere declaration to return the following feafon to Europe; but I confefs I was very defirous to get at the letter to the Directors; and I will tell the honourable gentleman why. When the right honourable gentleman brought in his India bill, the Houfe and this country were told that the balance due from the Vizier to the Company was above 750,000l. and never could be paid, and it was ftruck out of the Directors' ftatement. Mr. Haftings's public letter contained authentic accounts that the greateft part was actually paid in April, 1784, and an ample fund provided for liquidating the remainder, as well as for the current fubfidy; and thefe funds have been fully fuffi-

cient,

cient, as later advices prove. Now, Sir, I do confefs, that the triumph of party, by which we are all apt at times to be actuated, did induce me to wifh that by fome means or other the public fhould be informed how erroneous the right honourable gentleman's ftatement in a very material inftance had been proved to be. The only way to get at the letter was to propofe its being read at a General Court. This we did: the Chairman (Mr. Devaynes) objected to it, but we were too anxious to get at the main point, to attend to his objections, and the letter was read. I had then a right to a copy of it, which I fent to Mr. Debrett to publifh; but being defired by feveral gentlemen not to publifh it, I prevented its coming out, even after it was printed. But when Mr. Debrett had actually procured a copy from another channel, I then thought he might as well fend mine forth; and this is the ftate of the tranfaction. It was a mere party triumph, and not a very unreafonable one, when it was confidered how deeply the right honourable gentleman had committed himfelf on the moft material point of the letter in queftion.

The honourable gentleman has afferted that the Vizier had no army except our forces, commanded by Britifh officers. Good God! Sir, where can he pick up his intelligence? The Vizier's army, I believe, confifts of 50,000 men, 15,000 of which are cavalry. Our force in his country confifted of one brigade at Cawnpore, fix battalions at Futtyghear, and a fmall corps at Lucknow; but his own army is very confiderable. I will affure the right honourable gentleman that I never faw Mr. Haftings's fecret letter of the 16th June, 1784, to the Secret Committee of the Court of Directors, till I read it in his letter book, fince this fubject was agitated. By that letter it appears that he gave the Court of Directors the earlieft intelligence of his views in favour of the King, and of their being counteracted by the refufal of his counfel to grant him powers. This following extract the honourable gentleman has not favoured us with, though the words are contained in the letter he has in part read: " My " object is, with the poffeffion of authority, to exhibit it as a " means of negociations, not to exercife it; and I am mo- " rally certain that had I poffeffed fuch a power at the time " in which the event I have defcribed took place, and while " the minds of the principal actors were enfeebled with the " recent agitation of it, I could have eafily dictated the " terms both of the King's deliverance from his prefent thral- " dom, and his fon's return." Mr. Haftings did not poffefs the powers the council continued to refufe the powers, and he did nothing; but was it criminal in him to afk for them, in order, as he thought, to perform a fervice acceptable to the Mogul, this nation, and the Eaft-India Company? I am fenfible,

fible, Sir, that I have not preferved a proper connection in the detail I have attempted to give you; I will therefore recapitulate in a few words what I meant to ftate to the Houfe, declaring at the fame time, that I have my information from Mr. Haftings; and that Major Browne himfelf will, in all probability, be in England in twenty days: Major Browne was appointed the 20th of Auguft, 1782, Minifter from the Government of Bengal to Dehli. His inftructions were read and approved by the Board, then confifting of Mr. Whelet and Mr. Macpherfon, and confequently were the Board's inftructions. From this time he had no farther communication with Mr. Haftings, nor any inftructions at any time from him but thofe which I have mentioned. Mr. Haftings did not once write to Major Browne, or fee him in Auguft, 1782, till after he left Calcutta himfelf in February, 1784. Various obftructions prevented Major Browne's arrival at Dehli, till a year and a half after his appointment; in March, 1783, the inftructions were refcinded. Mr. Stubbs then being added to the Board, and Sir Eyre Coote having returned from the Court for a fhort period, from May, 1783, to the 20th of January, 1784, Mr. Haftings was in a minority. In October, 1783, the propofal for affifting the King with troops was debated. Mr. Haftings was for affifting him; the other members were againft it; and there it dropped. The fame propofal was again repeated, though perhaps in different words, by Major Browne, on the 30th of December, 1783. This was received the 20th of January, 1784, and fubmitted to the Board, Mr. Haftings all the time in a minority. It does not apperr that the Board did any thing upon this matter, or that they ever took it up after; but Mr. Haftings is not to be cenfured for that; he left Calcutta a very few days after, and was much indifpofed at the time. The Council had the power of recalling Major Browne, if they thought he had exceeded his inftructions, which were, to encourage rather than to difcourage a propofition for troops. They did not recall him; nor did they reply to his letters as I know of: but with this Mr. Haftings had nothing to do. At a diftance of five months after the Prince's flight from Dehli, Major Browne came to Lucknow in June, 1784, earneftly intreated by the Mogul to explain the particulars of his fituation, and to folicit affiftance againft Affrafiab Cawn; but the propofal of the 30th of December, 1783, was to co-operate with Affrafiab Cawn and the King. Mr. Haftings deemed the moment a favourable one to affift His Majefty; he applied to his Council for powers; he wrote to the Directors over land that he had done fo: the powers were refufed and the bufinefs ended. Mr. Haftings left Lucknow in Auguft, and India the February following.

Lord

Lord *North* said, that, rising at so late an hour, he did not mean, by tedious remarks, to press upon the nearly worn-out patience of the House, but should sit down immediately after having made some short and necessary observations. The honourable gentleman (Major Scott) who spoke last, had declared that the Supreme Council at Calcutta refused to assist the Mogul with any troops: yet, strange to tell! in the letter from Major Browne were these words: "We offered to "treat; he accepted: We annexed conditions; he approved "of them." This, surely, was dealing in plurals!—We! not I! Might it not, therefore, without absurdity, be concluded, that the Council at Calcutta had said "no" to Major Browne, meaning that Major Browne should say "yes" at Delhi? But, doubtless, the ingenuity of the honourable gentleman could either explain away or bring into full consistency the singular disagreements in the accounts of the transaction. Having remarked that he felt it necessary to repeat his declaration, during the course of a preceding debate, that the French had nothing to do at Dehli, Lord North concluded by desiring his right honourable and learned friend (Mr. Dundas) to accept of his congratulations upon the vast renown which he had acquired by formerly moving the resolutions, and at the same time to give him credit for the assertion that had he now maintained them his political reputation would have received a most considerable increase.

(margin: Ld. North.)

The House divided—

Ayes - - - - - - - - - - 73
Noes - - - - - - - - - - 140
                                  ———
                    Majority - - 67

The House adjourned.

Monday, 20th *March.*

Mr. *Dundas* moved, "That the bill be committed for the ensuing Wednesday.

(margin: Mr. Dundas.)

Mr. *Francis* objected to so early a day, and observed, that not only on account of the great importance of the bill, and the material alterations which it made in the principles of the constitution, it ought to be suffered to go through all the usual delays of parliamentary proceedings, but because the unusual circumstance attended it, of its being brought in on the same day in which leave had been granted for it. He hoped, therefore, that the right honourable and learned gentleman would allow a longer interval for the commitment.

(margin: Mr. Francis.)

Mr. *Dundas* contended for the necessity of an early day, in order that the bill might go out to India with the ships shortly intended to sail. The circumstance of its being

(margin: Mr. Dundas.)

brought in on the day in which leave had been obtained, was
no reafon for delay, becaufe it did not proceed from any
haftinefs in the mover, but from the accident of the motion
for leave being made for two days by the difappointment of a
ballot for an election committee, which rendered it neceffary
to make every amends poffible in point of time.

Mr. Jolliffe.   Mr. *Jolliffe* expreffed his earneft wifhes that a delay of
fome days might be had on a queftion of fuch infinite importance, by which the conftitution of this country was to be fo
very materially altered. He forefaw that by this bill, the
trial by jury was to be laid afide; for the foundation was
hereby laid to fubvert and deftroy that deareft and moft valuable privilege of Englifhmen. Our lives, our liberty, our
property, and our characters were all dependent on this inftitution; and the eftablifhing a new mode of trial, was admitting the principle that trials might be had without juries,
which, if once eftablifhed, might be carried to any length.
It therefore was but right that the country fhould know
what an attempt was making. There was another great objection to this bill: it eftablifhed the moft enormous power
in the hands of Government that ever was heard of; it was,
in fact, the moft monftrous ftride to increafe the power of
the Crown that had been made at any period; and although
the prefent miniftry, or the next, might not mifufe it, the
confequences might prove dreadful. It was no lefs than
giving abfolute dominion into the hands of the government
over every man who came from India. He was to give an
account of his acquifitions to the Board of Control only,
and they might either proceed againft him for perjury, in delivering in a falfe account, or for peculation, or any crime
which they might charge againft him to have been committed
in India, or they might withhold the proceeding as they
pleafed. This put all the wealth of the Eaft entirely at their
difpofal. For thefe reafons, but moft efpecially on account
of the alteration of the trial by jury, he moved, " That
" the bill fhould be committed for Friday inftead of Wed-
" nefday."

The Houfe divided on the amendment—

Ayes - - - - - - - - - 19
Noes - - - - - - - - - 53
                               Majority - - 34

The original queftion for Wednefday was then put and
carried.

Sir Adam   Sir *Adam Fergufon* moved the petition of Mr. Ferguson,
Ferguson.   complaining of an undue election for Aberdeen; and moved,
" That it might be taken into confideration on Tuefday the
" 2d of May.

                                       The

The Earl of *Fife* rose, and informed the House, that Mr. The Earl of Fife.
kene, the member for the county of Aberdeen, was not in
own. He intended to be in town in two weeks. He had
o idea that there was any design of presenting a petition
gainst his election. Lord Fife added, that he had written
o Mr. Skene to hurry him up, and he was certain he would
be here about the end of this week. He desired to be understood, as not to insinuate the smallest wish for any delay in
hearing the merits of this petition; on the contrary, he did
pledge himself to the House for his honourable friend in his
absence, that the earliest day which they could name, con-
istent with their forms, and other business, would be the
most agreeable to Mr. Skene. Lord Fife therefore moved
an amendment to Sir Adam's motion, " That in place of the
" 2d of May, Thursday the 27th of April might be the
" day;" which, after some conversation, and the question
being put, was agreed to without a division.

The House adjourned.

Tuesday, 21st March.

Mr. Chancellor *Pitt* having observed that the subject to Mr. Chan-cellor Pitt.
which he must intreat the attention of the House required a
much speedier dispatch than was unexceptionably consistent
with the forms of Parliament, added, that the Voorberg, a
Dutch outward-bound East Indiaman, had been forced into
Dartmouth bay by stress of weather, with the crew in very
bad health; that numbers of the persons on board had died
since their arrival; that it was the opinion of physicians, that
if they continued longer on board, this fever would become
more dangerous, and that if they were brought on shore they
might be much more easily recovered; that such an alarm
had gone abroad among the people as rendered it impossible
to provide accommodation for them; that a petition had
been sent to His Majesty to relieve those unfortunate persons
in such a manner as he was enabled to have carried into execution; but that it was not in His Majesty's power to do any
thing without the assistance of Parliament. The House had
a precedent to go by in the quarantine laws, which he would
beg leave to recommend for their adoption in the present case,
and he hoped that where policy and humanity were so
strongly in favour of dispatch, the bill which he should move
for would be allowed to be brought in and passed during the
course of the day. The object of his bill was, to invest three
commissioners with powers to take a sufficient portion of
ground for the purpose of erecting temporary buildings, for
the accommodation of the crew at a proper distance (to be
expressed in the bill) from any dwelling houses; and were the

land-

landowners to perfift in a refufal to confent that they fhould be applied to thofe ufes, commiffioners fhould be impowered to enter upon them, allowing a reafonable compenfation to the proprietors. He therefore moved, " That leave be given " to bring in a bill to enable the perfons therein to be named " to provide proper places on fhore for the reception of the " crew of the Voorberg Dutch Eaft Indiaman, forced by " ftrefs of weather into the port of Dartmouth."

Mr. Min-chin. Mr. *Minchin* expreffed his wifhes that the utmoft circum-fpection might take place, in order to prevent a fatally infec-tious communication between the country people and the fick mariners.

Mr. Drake. Mr. *Drake* fignified his earneft hopes to the fame pur-pofe.

Mr. Chan-cellor Pitt. Mr. Chancellor *Pitt* contended, that the precaution was needlefs, inafmuch as the alarm among the people, which had made the prefent motion requifite, would totally fhut out all kind of dangerous intercourfe.

The bill was accordingly read a firft and fecond time, committed, reported, paffed, read a third time, and carried to the Lords.

The Houfe adjourned.

Wednefday, 22d March.

The order of the day having been moved for the Houfe to refolve itfelf into a Committee of the whole Houfe, upon the bill to explain and amend an act of the 24th year of the reign of His prefent Majefty, entitled, " An Act for the better " Regulation and Management of the Affairs of the Eaft-" India Company, and of the Britifh Poffeffions in India, and " for eftablifhing a Court of Judicature, for the more fpeedy " and effectual Trial of Perfons accufed of Offences com-" mitted in the Eaft Indies," the Speaker left the chair, and Mr. C. W. Boughton Roufe took his feat at the table.

Mr. Fran-cis. Mr. *Francis* remarked, that he fhould trefpafs but little upon the attention of the Houfe with ftrictures concerning the new powers given to the Governor General by the bill in queftion, becaufe as he had already entered into a wide and ample difcuffion of the fubject, it would prove not lefs tire-fome than unneceffary to travel a fecond time along a path fo beaten; but he trufted that he fhould not appear to prefs too much upon their patience whilft he followed up the amend-ments (according to the order in which they ftood) with fome natural obfervations. It appeared that the law of 1784, which (were credit given to the minifterial eulogiums on its merits) was fo perfect and fo completely provided for the good government of India, that not the fmalleft occafion
arofe

arofe to mention the fubject in the King's fpeech, had already
produced doubts, difficulties, embarraffments, and inexpedi-
ents; and he muft beg leave to afk whether that claufe, refpecting the nomination and appointment of the covenanted
fervants of the Company by the Court of Directors to fupply the vacant offices of Counfellors, was meant to extend to
perfons who were no longer on the lift of covenanted fervants? There was a bye law, or refolution of the Directors,
by which any perfon on their Indian eftablifhments, who
fhould have been a certain time in England, became difmiffed
from their fervice. Did the caufe therefore abolifh that bye
law entirely, or did it only remove the prohibition from the
office of Counfellor? Was long refidence in England to be
a bar to a man returning to a low office, but not to his being
appointed to an high one. That would prove a ftrange fituation; and yet it appeared to be the effect of the claufe. With
regard to the next claufe, which ftated its having been
enacted, that as often as the number of members of any of
the Councils of the three fettlements of Fort William, Fort
St. George, and Bombay, fhould, by death, or abfence, or
ficknefs, be reduced to two, had been productive of difficulty
and embarraffment, was that the fact? If it was, he fhould
be glad to know what difficulty and embarraffment it had
produced? The next claufe gave the Governors of the refpective prefidencies power to fill up any vacancy in Council, by appointing at their choice any perfon on the fpot; and
this power gave each Governor the command of the vote of
the perfon fo nominated. It alfo gave them a power of putting a junior fervant over a fenior, a matter which, in his idea,
appeared irreconcileable to the eftablifhed rules of the fervice; and as to the idea of fuch perfon's holding his feat till
the vacancy was duly fupplied, and then returning to the
office he before held, it was a moft abfurd idea to place and
difplace a man in a great office. How could he go back to
his fubordinate ftation? With regard to the next claufe, that
feparating the office of Commander in Chief from the office
of a Counfellor, he muft beg leave to remind the Committee
that the faith of Government had been pledged to General
Sloper when he went out Commander in Chief, that he fhould
hold his feat at the Council Board, and now that faith was
about to be broken on an *ex poft facto* law. The next claufe
by which the offices of Commander in Chief and Governor
General were united in the fame perfon, created a moft dangerous union of power in the fame hands. Was it meant
that Earl Cornwallis fhould take the field? What! take
the civil government of India, which refted on him alone!
That was a monftrou- idea; but even if that were proper,
the change was unneceffary, as Earl Cornwallis would command

mand General Sloper of courfe, as his fenior in the King's
fervice, whenever they were in the field together, provided
that a fingle company of the King's troops were joined to
thofe of the company. Another claufe empowered the Governor General, and the Governors of Fort St. George and
Bombay, to act without the concurrence of their refpective
Councils. Then why have a Council at all? By the fame
claufe the Council were to fign againft their opinions, and it
was provided that the Governor General muft take an oath.
Earl Cornwallis was a Peer. Would not the Houfe believe
him on his honour? Was his former oath ftronger than his
word of honour folemnly pledged? This was an odd obligation to impofe on a Peer, whofe word of honour decided
on the life and death of his brethren of the Peerage; and it
was not a little extraordinary that, by the words of the oath,
the Governor General was to fwear he was convinced. An
oath was furely no argument. It reminded him of Lord
Peter in Swift's Tale of a Tub. Was it to be imagined that
a cafe could exift, in which three perfons of character fhould
fay no, and one fhould fay yes, and that the one ought to
carry it. He declared folemnly that he could not conceive
fuch a cafe, and he defied any man to ftate one. It was to be
obferved too, that it muft be fome great emergency, yet that
emergency was fo doubtful and fo obfcure, that three honeft
men fhould affirm one way, and one the other, and then the
minority carried it. This law inverted the rule of evidence;
that was, the more witneffes they had to the truth of any
propofition, the lefs they were to believe. Why fhould not
the three Counfellors fwear as well as the Governor General?
It was furely better to have no Council; for by that courfe
they weakened the Governor's meafure, fince at laft the meafure was promulgated with a proteft againft it of the whole
Council. With refpect to vefting the Governor General
with exclufive powers, a right honourable and learned gentleman (Mr. Dundas), in the debate of the 7th inftant, faid,
that all the authorities which he had confulted, every man
from India to whom he had fpoken, were againft him (Mr.
Francis) in their opinion. He defired therefore to know
who thofe authorities were? Were they the body of the
Indians? He afferted that they were not competent judges
of fuch a queftion, and they (Mr. Dundas and Mr. Pitt)
declared they were a parcel of felons; at leaft they treated
them fo, and even worfe than the worft of felons were treated
by the laws of the land, and the adminiftration of criminal
juftice. Would they then go to fuch men for advice on a
matter of ftate and legiflation? There were in England but
three competent witneffes to that point, viz. Mr. Francis,
who, though appointed by Parliament, and conftantly approved

proved for fix years together by Minifters and Directors, nay encouraged from time to time with promifes and honours of rewards, had never once been confulted.　Mr. Haftings and Lord Macartney were the two others.　He mentioned himfelf firft, becaufe he would firft difpofe of the moft infignificant; and next he would fpeak of Mr. Haftings, who, though competent, was not a credible witnefs on the fubject of power, fince every law from every quarter implicitly accufed him of having abufed the power with which he was intrufted.　As to Lord Macartney, he was perfectly competent and credible.　But what had Lord Macartney faid ? That Houfe did not know.　He had not declared his reafons for declining the government.　They might be very different from an objection to the want of power in the Governor General; perhaps he thought the ftate of affairs defperate; perhaps he objected to the exifting Council as men with whom he could not fit.　But it could not be for want of power, for if it had, the Minifters who applauded him fo highly would not have refufed to have granted to Lord Macartney what they fo liberally granted to Earl Cornwallis.　The public judgement on the propriety of Lord Macartney's refufing the government of Bengal muft remain in fufpence until he fhould think it right to affign his reafons.　He doubted not but that they were valid; yet until they knew what they were, they could not acquit him entirely of what was *prima facie* a charge.　As to the inventories being to be depofited and filed among the fecret papers of the Board of Control, how was any perfon to inform againft the inventory in the manner prefcribed by the fixty-firft claufe ? Who could inform but the Secret Committee of the Directors, and the Commiffioners of Control and their chief Secretary ?　Did not that put all the Indians who came home completely in the power of Miniftry ?　Befides, how could they fwear who had not feen the inventory ? and who was to profecute, except the perfons to whofe fecret cuftody the inventory was committed ?　There was an end therefore to profecution. and the door was fhut againft all popular actions.　Under thefe ideas he felt himfelf warranted in declaring, that he thought the new bill far more exceptionable than the old bill, and therefore fhould move that the Chairman do leave the chair.

Sir *James Erfkine* having expreffed his aftonifhment that the members on the other fide of the Houfe fhould not have liftened with more attention to the well-directed arguments of his honourable friend, added, that he, for his own part, regarded as highly objectionable the idea of fending out a Governor General armed with the powers which the bill gave him.　It was erecting the ftandard of defpotifm in Bengal,

Sir James Erfkine.

gal, without any probability of the person so fortified being rendered responsible to the House for his conduct, because after the answer Ministers had given a few nights since, when papers, material to the inquiry about to be instituted into the conduct of Mr. Hastings, it was idle to talk of responsibility; for how could the conduct of any person, entrusted with an high official situation, become investigated if the papers tending to elucidate that conduct, and prove what it had been, were withholden and denied by Ministers?

Sir James asked for what reason, among other powers conferred on the Governor General, he was to be made Commander in Chief? He wished to know the policy, the expediency, and the necessity of such a measure. The army in India was of great importance. The attention which it required was sufficient to any capacity with whom its command should be intrusted. In cases of emergency, which might be expected to occur frequently in such a country as India, how was the Commander in Chief to divide himself among the several demands which the civil, the political, and the military departments had upon him? Was it practicable for any individual to do all of them justice, or possible for him on many occasions not to sacrifice one to another?

He blamed the judicature established by the bill of 1784, and lately ballotted for in the House. He asked what our countrymen, who served the Company and their country in India, had done, that so many of them were thus involved in one fatal proscription. One solid or convincing argument had never yet reached his ears upon the subject. He took it for granted that there was some reason, which however the author of the measure was ashamed, afraid, or, probably, too prudent to state. When that principle was once fairly and honestly avowed, he trusted it would be met by the House with that thorough and marked disapprobation which ought always to stigmatize such measures as are broached and brought forth in the teeth of the constitution.

He attached much of his remarks to the words *energy* and *dispatch* (which were mentioned in the printed paper which he held in his hand) as the grounds on which the powers specified were assigned to the first office in the new India Government; and he contended that the powers thus delegated, notwithstanding their unqualified extent, would not produce that effect; would not discover such characters in their operation. Thus the extension of authority which the Governor General, whoever he might be, was to enjoy by the act thus amended, would rather retard than facilitate the operations of Government.

He

He was loath to encroach on the patience and the time of the Committee, otherwife it would have been the eafieft thing in the world to have fhewn how almoft all the feveral provifions in the bill would produce the very reverfe of the effect which the propofer of them intended. He wifhed the Houfe to be apprized of this circumftance, and to view thofe regulations as fertile of confequences which every man in the Houfe undoubtedly wifhed to avoid.

The Chairman was putting the queftion, when

Mr. *Burke* declared, that the anxiety and indignation which Mr. filled his breaft, whilft he reflected upon the prefent meafure, was paft defcription; nor could he avoid bitterly complaining againft the indecency of fuffering a queftion of that kind to be put without the honourable gentlemen on the other fide deigning to fay one word in reply to fo much ferious and folid reafoning. But well did it become the learned and right honourable gentleman (Mr. Dundas) to remain filent! And much did he appear fatisfied, that if the majority of arguments was on one fide, the majority of nofes was on the other. The principle of the bill was to introduce an arbitrary and defpotic Government in India, on the falfe pretence of its tending greatly to the ftrength and fecurity of the Britifh poffeffions there, and giving energy, vigour, and difpatch to the meafures and proceedings of the executive government. He reprobated the whole of the idea, contending that an arbitrary and defpotic government was always fure to produce the reverfe of energy, vigour, and difpatch, its conftant features being weaknefs, debility, and delay. He referred to the Turkifh government, and every arbitrary government that ever exifted, in proof of his affertion. It was, he obferved, ufual to prefume the preamble to every Bill founded in truth; but as the prefent bill was only in a ftate of probation, he made no fcruple to affert, that the preamble of the claufe which laid it down as a principle that arbitrary power was neceffary to give vigour and difpatch, was a libel on the liberties of the people of England, and a libel on the Britifh conftitution; it gave the lie to all common fenfe, to all reafon, and to the uniform experience of ages. He denied that there ever had been a people abject enough to fubmit willingly to an arbitrary government; that however a prince, amiable in his private character, great, glorious, and fuccefsful in his victories abroad, wife and juft in his adminiftration at home, might prevail on his people to fubmit to his will, to which they were ready to refign themfelves, from the pride which they might too naturally feel at feeing fuch a character exalted, yet, in fo fubmitting, it was not from any fenfe of conviction, or an acquiefence in the principles of an arbitrary government. In the Turkifh government there were

principles of freedom, nor was there ever a government in the world in which there were not balances that diftinguifhed it from an arbitrary government. This had been lately experienced at Smyrna, where there were three different powers to check and control each other, and yet the Turkifh government had been blazoned forth by the advocates of arbitrary power as a true model of that fort of government. But, in fact, the whole of the bufinefs of India reform was a moft contemptible refult to fo much time and trouble as it had coft him and other members of that Houfe in inquiries into the abufes of the Eaft, and in preparing numerous and voluminous reports upon the fubject. He told Mr. Roufe that he little expected the whole was to end in his being feated in that chair, the Chairman of a Committee on fuch a bill as that upon the table. He thanked the honourable gentleman for his powerful affiftance in drawing up the firft Report of the Select Committee, and lamented that fuch a laudable defign fhould end in the learned and right honourable gentleman oppofite to him having endeavoured to erect a whifpering gallery for the Board of Control, which demanded auricular confeffion, and armed with the new powers the new bill was to give it, would prove a direct copy of the ear of Dionyfius. The bill was a Rawhead and Bloodybones, which had affumed various fhapes; and to prove that difpatch was a thing which defeated many projects, he fhould put the cafe — had the learned and right honourable gentleman come down to that Houfe at once, and faid out boldly, " my plan is defpotifm and an arbitrary government;" in that cafe the Houfe would have revolted at once, but now they had been taken by fap; they were tamely furrendering to principles that would have fhaken every fibre in the frame of their anceftors but to have heard mentioned in any other terms than terms of execration. He defcribed the progrefs of the India bills of the gentlemen on the other fide allegorically, and faid, profligacy had firft cried out, " Give me defpotifm;" but hypocrify, more artful and wilely, had faid, " No, let us come upon them by degrees, and then they'll fubmit to what would have frightened them at firft;" and fo an abortion of tyranny, like an imperfect foetus in a bottle, was produced and handed about as a fhew; at length the child's navel ftrings broke, and a full-grown monfter of tyranny, the bill upon the table, was brought forth. To adminifter arbitrary power as a cure for the ills of India, was like that man who faid he could apply one fhort and immediate remedy for the various difeafes of the human body — poifon. He declared that he confidered the prefent bill as pregnant with unconftitutional doctrines; Magna Charta and the Bill of Rights gave every man a trial *per judicium*
.trium,

prium, aut per legem terræ. This bill confirmed a new Court of Star Chamber, and prevented a poſſibility of a trial *per pares,* as would be the caſe if Earl Cornwallis ſhould be tried. What he, from the experience derived from many years attention, would recommend as a means of recovering India, and reforming all its abuſes, was a combination of theſe three things — a government by law, trial by jury, and publicity in every executive and judicial concern. Various were the arts played off by profligacy and hypocriſy ; and when hypocriſy might think proper to conclude her game, and let profligacy play her part,

> " Then ſhould the warlike Harry, like himſelf,
> " Aſſume the port of Mars ; and, at his heels,
> " Leaſh'd in like hounds, ſhould famine, ſword, and fire,
> " Crouch for employment."

Meaſures of this complection would indeed account for miniſterial taciturnity. It was the only ſpecies of conduct which could ſuit the queſtion which occupied the Committee. He deplored the fate of the country and the conſtitution from the ſpectacle which attracted their attention at this moment. What did theſe amendments recommend ? It was a ſyſtem of arbitrary government. Where were the feelings of Engliſhmen, who could hear what ſtruck him as the groſſeſt inſult which could be offered to a Britiſh Parliament ? And were they then reduced to that degraded and abject ſituation which forced them, inſtead of delivering the captives from thraldom, to forge for them new chains, to be the inſtruments of increaſing even the heavy misfortunes of ſlaves ? Was this the character of our forefathers ? No ; it had happened to us in theſe dregs of times, when public ſpirit, the liberties of mankind, the generoſity, the juſtice, the dignity of the nation, were all extinguiſhed. But nothing could aſtoniſh him more than to find that dignity, energy, and diſpatch, were expected to reſult from abſolute power. Was not even this abſurdity, groſs and monſtrous as it was, too palpable to be ſwallowed implicitly by a Britiſh Houſe of Commons ? He deſired to know where that arbitrary government exiſted, of which dignity, energy, and diſpatch, were the characteriſtics. To what had democracy, in all ages and all countries, owed moſt of its triumphs, but to the openneſs, the publicity, and the ſtrength of its operation. The imbecilities, inſeparable from the exertions of the beſt mind on earth, would always render the meaſures of an arbitrary government weak and imperfect. It was in direct oppoſition to all our theories and knowledge of human nature, to expect from one more than from many ; or that the opinion of an individual, in all caſes reſpecting the government

ment

ment and regulation of fociety, fhould be more folid than thofe which refult from the joint experience and wifdom of multitudes combined and matured for that purpofe. Yet, if he reafoned wrong, why had not the fame fyftem prevailed in the Britifh Government? The learned and honourable gentleman, in the completion of this wonderful fyftem, had roundly impeached the fagacity and integrity of our anceftors. They had confecrated, for the ufe of pofterity, a fyftem of government extremely different. How long it might retain the venerable garb which it had hitherto worn he knew not, but he fhrewly apprehended a defign was on foot, hoftile to that ancient and ftately fabric, which had been the wonder and admiration of all the wifeft, the beft, and the greateft of men, for many generations. This government, therefore, devifed by a Britifh Houfe of Commons, for one of our dependences, was the firft of the kind; it had no example among the nations the moft polifhed, or the moft barbarous; it was repugnant to every feeling of the human heart, and ftamped throughout with cruelty and outrage. He for his part fhould not have remarked on the fyftem at all, but merely to enter his proteft againft it; for he conceived it to be one of thofe grofs and extravagant abfurdities which was not fufceptible of reafon, on which men of fenfibility could not reafon, which it were a proftitution of reafon to be applied either for or againft. He defired to be fhewn what *data* human nature afforded as the foundation of fo outrageous a fyftem. Where were thofe facred principles of freedom in which the Britifh laws formerly originated? Gone, and fomething elfe was now fubftituted in their room. This perhaps was our deftiny, and, for ought he knew, it might be our duty to fubmit; but it was hard on thofe who regarded the Britifh liberties with affection. The period was however arrived, when the feelings of Englifhmen were put to the teft. He was forry they did not feem more alive, and that fuch a meafure as that before the Committee could be fuffered to make its appearance in the Britifh Senate. While he had a voice, however, it fhould be exerted in protefting againft an innovation thus fhocking and monftrous. Were the prefent an original meafure, it might have been proper to attack it in another manner, but it was no more than the completion of one. The gradation was obvious, and menaced the liberties of the country through every ftage of the bufinefs in the fame formidable manner. The right honourable and learned gentleman's bill began with reprobating five in Council. This was one preliminary ftep for augmenting the power of the Governor General. His learned and right honourable friend next, with all the fury of his eloquence, attacked a cafting voice. All this was hitherto
aiming

aiming at that arbitrary power which was the principal intention of the meafure, only obliquely. But having thus paved the way, a bold and unequivocal ftep is taken at laft to outrage this country and this Houfe with a propofition for the eftablifhment of a fyftem which our anceftors ftruggled and died to exterminate, which is incongruous to the habits and peculiarities of the national character, and which we cannot admit without facrificing at once all our prepoffeffions for the privileges of Britons, and the rights of humanity. He wifhed the Committee to recollect how this meafure had throughout facrificed the many for the few. He adverted to that claufe in the original bill of 1784, which rendered every individual who had been in India accountable for his fortune. It had been often enough obferved, and juftly, that this claufe was fufficient, in an honeft and independent Houfe of Commons, to have ruined the entire meafure. It afforded every fubterfuge which villainy could defire, and expofed honefty alone to ridicule and contempt. Did a principle like this become the Britifh Legiflature? It certainly did not; but it was adopted, and operated at this moment, to the difgrace of the country. In what manner were delinquencies now to be detected? It was taken for granted that no man could have a large fortune by honeft means, becaufe fo many had been known to bring home one by means that were not honeft. This principle was wrong, becaufe it, fuppofed that which was not true. Induftry would undoubtedly obtain its object by perfeverance there as well as here. Money might to a certainty be even more eafily obtained, as it was ten per cent. cheaper. A man of this kind might not like to give an accurate account of all his acquifitions, as it would in a great meafure prove impracticable. He ftated the cafe of a perfon high in office, who, by every fpecies of the groffeft peculation which his fituation might enable him to practice, fhould accumulate enormous wealth, but who, at the fame time, fhould wafte that ill-gotten revenue for the moft flagitious purpofes; although guilty of almoft every crime which human nature can perpetrate while in India, having thus diffipated his fubftance, he might be a poor man by the time he came home. It would not then be an object to profecute his delinquencies. For the meaning of this claufe was to lay hold on a man's fortune firft, and condemn him afterwards; to begin with the effects of his crimes, in order the more eafily and unanfwerably to prove his criminality. What was that but a literal tranfcript of what had been done in India during the adminiftration of Mr Haftings? It was the practice to examine the country, and wherever he found money to affix guilt. There was not a more dreadful fault that could be alledged
againft

against a native than that he was rich. The moment this
fact was fubftantiated guilt was prefumed ; and it was no
very difficult matter, with the powers he poffeffed, to realize
whatever charges he chofe to feign.   All this did he perpetually cenfure, becaufe he conftantly knew it to be a leading feature of that government for which Mr. Haftings was refponfible; it was one of the charges which he fhould endeavour
to fubftantiate.   But what encouragement did the meafure he
now condemned afford him for proceeding in the profecution
of a delinquency, which the Houfe would virtually approve,
by an adoption of what originated in the fame principle, and
might be directed to the fame object.   All which had yet
been faid of the judicature, which was now eftablifhed for
the purpofe of punifhing the delinquencies committed in India, fell fhort of its turpitude; it had no authority, example,
fimilitude, or precedent, in the hiftory of this country, except, perhaps, the Star Chamber of deteftable memory. This
inftitution, which had made the hearts of the whole nation
to quake and tremble, was compofed of Peers, Privy Counfellors, and Judges.   Lord Bacon, not much to his credit,
exclaimed, Where would any man wifh to be tried with
greater fafety ? He owned there was at leaft as much probability that a Court, conftituted of fuch refpectable members, was as likely to pronounce an independent and impartial fentence, as any felection which a Minifter could make
from his friends in that Houfe.   But was this to be compared to an Englifh Jury ? It certainly was not. The fafety,
the fatisfaction, and the confidence connected with this mode
of trial, arofe from the character of the jurymen.   They
were citizens, and not politicians; and each of them might
to-morrow return to the very fituation in which had been the
man whom they condemned.   This he confidered as the
great bulwark of our liberties, and the deprivation of it was
a punifhment hanging over the heads of thofe who probably
deferved it the leaft.   It was at the fame time, he readily allowed, fuch a judicature as became the crimes which were
likely enough to be fubjected to their cognizance. Whoever
brought home money fufficient to tempt his relations, or
friends, or others in the fecret, to betray him, would fall
under the lafh of fuch an inftitution. He remembered that
it had been faid of one King James, of Scotland, on viewing
the beautiful and rich gardens, and other fertile and delight-
ful parts of a great man's property, which lay on the banks
of the Tay, that he exclaimed, " What a *bonny traitor* would
" this *man mack !*"—meaning that his poffeffions were fufficient to tempt the grafp of rapacity thus armed with power.
Mr. Burke ftated, that the fituation of the Company's fubordinate fervants is often fuch as obliges them to have recourfe

o unfair practices, in order to support their dignity. The
Residents, for example, in Oude and Benares, the one had
not an allowance of above twenty-four hundred pounds, and
he other received about twelve: these salaries were by no
means adequate to the indispensable expenditure of these
gentlemen in their official situations or capacities. But
suppose either or both the Residents to have realized enormous fortunes, it was in the power of any of their depen-
dents, or others in their confidence, to present a statement
of the fact, and from that circumstance tempt them to a
collusion, in order to avoid the punishment of their crime.

Mr. *Fox* observed, that he thoroughly coincided in all Mr. Fox.
the sentiments of his right honourable friend who spoke
last, and felt equal indignation, sorrow, and surprise, that
a bill so directly the reverse in principle, and so objectionable in many of its parts, however proper in others, should
be delivered to the Committee in a manner so extraordinary,
without the author of it having thought it worth his while
to say a word in explanation of it. When the learned and
right honourable gentleman had first introduced it, he had
himself assigned a few reasons, if reasons they may be called,
for the several heads of alteration which he meant it should
contain, and he had himself said at the time, that he supposed at the second reading, or in the Committee, would be
the proper time to go into it more fully. Having given
them to expect by this that the learned and right honourable gentleman would have opened the contents of the bill
a little more at large, and stated the particular facts which
constituted the necessity upon which he presumed the essential difference had been made in the bill, compared to the
bill of 1784, he owned he was in some degree surprised at
the learned and right honourable gentleman's silence; but,
however, the right honourable gentleman might affect to
disregard what had fallen from his honourable friend behind
him, with an impression and a weight that he should imagine
no man could resist, and which was not more remarkable
for the splendour of eloquence with which it had been delivered, than for the truth of the arguments and the force of
the conclusions; what his right honourable friend had said
must be answered, and he felt himself extremely anxious to
hear in what manner the learned and right honourable gentleman would ward off the force of what the House had just heard.

Mr. *Dundas* answered, that he had not been silent out of
any disrespect to either of the honourable gentlemen, but
had barely reserved himself till they came to fill up the blanks
of the respective clauses, which he concieved to be the proper time for stating to the Committee upon what principle
it was that he proposed each particular alteration. Nothing
that

that he had yet heard, had induced him to change his mind in that respect, and therefore he must beg to be excused saying any thing farther till the fit opportunity came, which surely the honourable gentleman took an odd way of getting at, by moving that the Chairman should quit the chair as soon almost as he had got into it.

Mr. Powys.   Mr. *Powys* remarked, that although he should vote against the motion for the Chairman's leaving the chair, yet he begged not to be understood as standing pledged to support the whole of the clauses of the bill. Several of them he thought exceedingly proper, and some highly otherwise.

Mr. Fox.   Mr. *Fox* rose again and said he should not take the sense of the House upon the motion, but that extraordinary as such a motion might appear, yet it was by no means irregular or unusual to move that a Chairman leave a chair as soon as he came into it, by way of instituting a debate, and he should have imagined the honourable gentleman would have been glad of the opportunity the motion would have afforded him, of going into a general explanation of the clauses of the bill.

Mr. Drake   Mr. *Drake* censured (what he denominated) the unsteady, shuttlecock mode of proceeding in bringing bill after bill to amend and explain a subject of so much importance. He had heard a high character of Earl Cornwallis, and believed him to have been every way deserving of it; but if Government did not proceed in a more easy and settled manner, how did the House know, but before his Lordship reached Bengal, another bill might be proposed, his power detruncated and his authority lost?

Mr. Chancellor Pitt.   Mr. Chancellor *Pitt* inveighed against the ridiculous inconsistency of moving the Speaker out of the chair, merely for the purpose of moving him into it again, without doing any thing in consequence of his leaving it. But, gentlemen complained that they had not certain clauses prepared which they thought necessary to be added to the bill. In his opinion, sufficient time had been given to prepare every such clause; but had it been otherwise, an objection of that nature came with an aukward grace from gentlemen, who had themselves so recently prepared an entire new bill for the purpose of amending and altering the old one, and who of course must be provided with every thing they thought necessary for the purpose. The right honourable gentleman had boasted that he and his friends were desirous of putting off the necessity of answering the strong arguments of the right honourable gentleman; but he believed it would appear that they who endeavoured to move the Chairman out of the chair, were more desirous to postpone the discussion, than those who wished to continue him in it, until that stage of

bufinefs, in which alone fuch a difcuffion would be at all applicable. As for the arguments themfelves to which he alluded, though he could not pretend to fay he had not heard
them, the tone and voice in which they were delivered having rendered that impoffible, yet he muft declare that he
did not fufficiently underftand how they affected the queftion, then before the Committee, fo as to be able to attempt
any anfwer to them with a view to arguing the impropriety
of the Chairman's leaving the chair.

At length the queftion was put and loft. The Committee
then proceeded, Mr. Dundas propofing to fill up the blanks,
and to ftate his reafon for each particular claufe, as each
came under confideration.

Mr. *Sloper* reprobated the claufe which enacted, that the Mr. Sloper.
Commander in Chief fhould not in future be of neceffity one
of the Council. This was, he thought, extremely harfh and
unfair in refpect to the prefent Commander in Chief, and
therefore he fhould move as an amendment to confine the
claufe to future Commanders in Chief: and the rather, becaufe he thought it hard, that a Commander in Chief fhould
be recalled, without fome ground of complaint or reafon
being alledged.

Mr. *Fox* contended againft the idea, that military men Mr. Fox
were not liable to be recalled by their employers without fome
reafon being affigned. He faid that he ever would maintain, that
military men were liable to be recalled at the pleafure of thofe
in whofe fervice they were employed without any reafon whatever being affigned: but he neverthelefs thought the cafe of
General Sloper exceedingly fevere, as the taking from him
a right of fitting at the Council Board, which he already
enjoyed, *ex officio,* was an humiliating degradation of his
character.

Mr. Chancellor *Pitt* lamented over that unfortunate ftate Mr. Chan-
of public fpirit within the kingdom which would not permit cellor Pitt.
any queftion of political expediency to efcape refifting arguments upon perfonal and private confiderations. However,
fince fuch had become the practice he muft fubmit to it,
and would therefore anfwer the gentlemen upon their own
grounds. He could eafily account for the warmth which one
of the honourable gentlemen had appeared to feel on the fubject, where fo near a relation was fuppofed to be concerned;
it was natural, it was in fome degree laudable; but for the
right honourable gentleman who had taken up the fame
grounds there was no room for any fuch excufe. He would
undertake to prove, that the bill might not in reality affect
General Sloper, as had been urged; and he would alfo put
a queftion to the honourable relation of the General, whe-

ther, confidering fome circumftances which he fhould mention, any complaint could poffibly be made by his friends, fhould it even operate againft him in the manner it was apprehended. The General might probably ftill retain his fituation in the Council, nor was it fair in the honourable gentleman (Mr. Sloper) to glance at the fuppofed injuftice of recalling a General from his command without affigning any caufe. The right honourable gentleman himfelf had at firft joined in reprobating this doctrine, though towards the end of his fpeech he had inadvertently feemed to fall into it; and though he difclaimed the principle in general, he had adopted it in the particular cafe. He joined in opinion with his right honourable and learned friend, that a perfon might be perfectly eligible to the command of an army, without poffeffing thofe qualifications which were neceffary in a ftatefman; and that more efpecially, in the Bengal government, where certain talents which were, by no means requifite in the foldier, were certainly indifpenfable in a counfellor, and that more efpecially, as the new powers to be vefted in the Governor General, would lay the other members of the Council under the neceffity, whenever thofe powers fhould be exercifed, of entering in detail the whole of their arguments, on their journals, and taking a comprehenfive political view of every queftion which fhould fall under fuch a circumftance; befides, the greater the political abilities of the counfellors might be, the greater reftraint would be impofed on the Governor. He did not mean to argue upon the merits or abilities of General Sloper, as in reality they were no way concerned in the queftion, which only related to the eftablifhment of a general political regulation without any reference whatever to the particular individual; but he believed he could remind the Houfe, and the right honourable gentleman, of an inftance, that fhould General Sloper of deprived of his feat in the council in confequence of that claufe, it would appear to apply exactly in point. When on a former occafion, he had the misfortune to lofe a feat in the Cabinet, the perfon who was commander in chief, had the good fortune to retain his office, but no longer continued a member of the Cabinet, though he had been one before. The right honourable gentleman had a confiderable fhare in the arrangements which were made at that time, and he hoped he would explain to the Houfe, how fuch an alteration could take place in the fituation of a right honourable officer (General Conway) without involving him in the fame difgrace that it was now ftated would fall on General Sloper, by barely making it poffible for that to happen to the latter which had actually happened to the former. He could by no means agree to take into confideration the circumftances of General Sloper's

for-

fortune as an argument which either could or ought to weigh
one way or the other on the prefent queftion, for it would be
a dangerous and abfurd doctrine to eftablifh, that the Houfe,
in debating a queftion of a public nature, fhould be at all
influenced by motives arifing either from the wealth or the
poverty of any perfon whom that queftion might affect. But
the honour of General Sloper was by no means affected by
the clause; and one circumftance muft immediately filence
all arguments drawn from that gentleman's fituation:—
" When General Sloper accepted of the command in India,
" it was with a particular condition, that if this country
" fhould be fo fortunate as to acquire the affiftance of the
" abilities of Earl Cornwallis as Governor General, that then
" the office of Commander in Chief fhould be united with
" that of Governor, and to this condition General Sloper
" confented." He fhould therefore beg leave to afk the honourable gentleman fo affectionately zealous in the caufe of
his relation, whether the latter could with reafon either complain or repine?

Mr. *Sloper* anfwered, that Earl Cornwallis told him perfo- Mr. Sloper.
nally, that when he went out his going would not at all affect
General Sloper's fituation.

Mr. *Fox* remarked, that as the right honourable gentleman Mr. Fox.
(Mr. Pitt) had chofen fo particularly to advert to the cafe
of the Commander in Chief (General Conway) he, for his
part, fhould think it fufficient to anfwer, that when this gallant and enlightened officer fat in the Cabinet, it was in a
time of war, and when he no longer belonged to the Cabinet,
we were at peace. But to deprive General Sloper of the
right of a feat in Council proved every way injurious, as a
degradation of his character in the eyes of all India, and a
moft oppreffive reduction of his appointments from fixteen
thoufand to only fix thoufand pounds a year.

Mr. *Sloper* declared, that General Sloper had much rather Mr. Sloper.
be recalled, than fubmit to fo irkfome and ignominious an
alteration.

At length the Committee divided on Mr. Sloper's amendment, when the numbers were,

For the original words of the claufe,   151
For the propofed amendment,   -   -   65
                                          ————
Majority,   -   -   -   -   -   86

Mr. *Dundas* contended, that the claufe, empowering the Mr. Dundas
Court of Directors to unite the offices of Governor General
and Commander in Chief in one and the fame perfon, was
equally neceffary and politic, becaufe it introduced an opportunity of employing Earl Cornwallis in the two different
capacities.

Mr.

Mr. Fox.   Mr. *Fox* anſwered, that far from coinciding in the ſentiments of the learned and right honourable gentleman who ſpoke laſt, he regarded the clauſe as impolitic, inconvenient, and even dangerous.

Mr. Dundas   Mr. *Dundas* ſaid, that although a multitude of obſervations had fallen from a right honourable gentleman (Mr. Burke) whether in terms of brilliant eloquence or not, it was equally the ſame with regard to the real queſtion, about deſpotiſm, arbitrary government, and ſuch like topics, he ſhould conſider it as mere declamation, and the flights of a fanciful imagination, bearing no relation whatever to the true ſtate of the queſtion, and conſequently not invalidating the merits and ſtrict propriety of the clauſe, enabling the Governor to act in caſes of great emergency without the concurrence of his Council. Before gentlemen took upon them to charge the empowering the Governor General to act in caſes of emergency without the concurrence of his Council, as the introduction of arbitrary government, it behoved them to prove, that arbitrary government depended more upon one perſon governing than two; a poſition which he believed it would not be eaſy to make out. He had ever conſidered the governing by known laws the preſervation of all the rights and franchiſes of ſubjects; and trial in all caſes of property, by the eſtabliſhed judicature of the country, and the free exerciſe of public and private opinion, moral, political, and religious, as the invariable and undoubted proofs of freedom. While theſe remained, the liberties of the people would ſurely be as perfectly enjoyed as ever they had been, or were likely to be; this was the real ſituation of the caſe of India. The perſon intruſted with the adminiſtration of the country, was indeed inveſted with more power, but he had therefore the greater reſponſibility. Though in caſes of great emergency, he was allowed to act without the concurrence of his Council, yet he had ſtill his Council to adviſe with, and they were always about him as checks and controls upon his conduct. In fact, the Governor could do no more under the preſent clauſe than he could have done with the concurrence of his Council before; and in proportion as he had more perſonal power, ſo had the bill provided more ſecurity and more reſponſibility. On this occaſion he ſhould beg leave to remind the Committee, of the eſſential difference between a cabinet council and a popular legiſlative aſſembly of debate; in the latter, party difference produced variety of opinion and variety of diſcuſſion, all of which tended to elucidate what was obſcure, to aſcertain what was doubtful, and to digeſt and mature what was crude and unformed. Hence, in proportion as that Houſe debated a queſtion, it became more thoroughly underſ underftood ; and they all, let them be of what party they might, were better prepared to decide upon it ultimately.— The cafe was widely otherwife in refpect to a council of executive government ; in fuch an affembly, the fewer the voices, the lefs the party feeling ; and the greater the unanimity, the better the decifion ; the more vigorous the execution of the meafure decided upon, and the more probable its fuccefs. All the mifchiefs and all the misfortunes, which had for years taken place in India, he was fatisfied in his own mind, after long and attentive inquiry into the affairs of that country, arofe entirely from the party principles of the members of the different councils in exiftence there, and the factious fcenes which thofe councils had almoft uniformly prefented. When he faid this, he cared not who he offended, perfuaded as he was, that the fact was ftrictly what he had defcribed it to be : not that he meant to fuggeft, that the members of thefe councils had all acted from bad motives ; he neither intended to infinuate, nor did he himfelf believe any fuch thing : on the contrary, he believed, that had any one member of the Council, of which the honourable gentleman oppofite to him had been a member, had the power of governing India, unharraffed by divifion in Council, India would have been governed better, and our affairs there would, at this moment, have been in a more profperous fituation. For years the ftate of the government in India had been this : the Governor had carried every thing by one vote, and it had always been two to three if there were four prefent, and one to two if only three. The claufe was juftified on the grounds of policy and neceffity, and he trufted the Committee would lay out of their minds all prejudice and falfe colouring, and look at the real queftion. This being examined with cool impartiality, it might follow as an almoft invariable confequence, that the Houfe, or at leaft the majority, would not harbour the leaft idea of what had been fo ingenioufly defcribed as a minifterial defign to eftablifh a defpotic government in the Eaft Indies.

Mr. *Fox* obferved, that the right honourable and learned **Mr. Fox.** gentleman had totally fulfilled his expectations, by not advancing even one fingle pofition in fupport of the pretended neceffity of the propofed alteration, or in proof, that a government in the hands of a Governor General, was likely to turn out a better government than a government by Governor and Council. Where did the right honourable and learned gentleman learn the doctrine? Did he collect it from the papers laid before him when Chairman of the Secret Committee? Did he think that Mr. Haftings, who acted fo repeatedly in defiance of the orders of the Directors, and contrary to the advice of the Council at Calcutta, has afforded

forded a proof of it? Would the Rohilla war never have happened had Mr. Haftings poffeffed the power with which he defigned to inveft Earl Cornwallis? Would the treaty of Poorunder not have been broken? Would the affair of Cheyt Sing, and all the various mifchiefs which it drew down on our affairs, never have happened? Which of all the numerous facts ftated by the right honourable gentleman, in his own Reports, and in the excellent code of laws contained in his own ever-memorable refolutions, had afforded him proof of what he wifhed to imprefs upon the Houfe? The right honourable and learned gentleman, had chofen to compare the Council at Calcutta to a Cabinet Council. No one thing could be fo unlike unto another: In what did they refemble? He knew not the fingle particular alike in either. In a Cabinet Council the debates were fecret: no perfon knew (or at leaft ought to know) except themfelves, what was done. If any Minifter, for inftance, a Secretary of State, fhould, from morning till night, debate againft any particular meafure in his own department, fuch as the negociating or breaking of a treaty, and neverthelefs, being over-ruled by the majority, fhould carry that meafure into execution, he alone was refponfible, and this was the only way by which that Houfe or the Public could have any conftitutional knowledge of what paffed in His Majefty's councils. A government by a Council, was every way preferable to a government in the hands of a Governor General. Little did it excite his aftonifhment, that a right honourable gentleman (Mr. Pitt) fhould have fcattered fuch unbounded panegyric upon the powers of arguing and ftating opinions with which the new, but inactive, Council were to be vefted. It was natural for him, whofe great talent it was to ftate a thing well in words, and by dint of fuperior eloquence give it a beautiful and ftriking appearance, to commend that in which he excelled, and to confider the fphere of action as the inglorious fphere. It was no wonder that the right honourable genleman was always fuccefsful in what he faid; feldom in what he did! Look to his fpeeches; they were mafterly, they were convincing! Look to his actions, failure after failure! The one all powerful; the others miferable, impolitic, and abfurd! The Council, who were to argue and not to act, therefore very naturally became the objects of his eulogiums, while the actual exercife of the executive government was regarded as of much lefs eftimation. Let others act, the right honourable gentleman defired only to argue! The operation of the India bill framed by the right honourable gentleman, was ridiculoufly futile; and of courfe, the Board of Control became the moft inefficacious Board ever inftituted. What had that Board proved itfelf fit for but to perplex the

Direc-

Directors, to fend out orders, unfit to be executed, to India, and to fcreen public delinquents from an inveftigation into their conduct in the Houfe! Thefe were the fruits of a bill not two years old; a bill now neceffary to be altered, and perhaps a farther alteration and as great a change of it would come under confideration in the courfe of the next feffion!

Mr. Chancellor *Pitt* expreffed the pleafure which he felt that his reply to the right honourable gentleman could be confined within fuch narrow limits as to preclude from the neceffity of long trefpaffing upon the time and patience of the Houfe. And left after this remark, he fhould inconfif- tently trifle with either, he meant totally to throw afide thofe parts of the right honourable gentleman's fpeech which ap- peared folely calculated to exhibit the powers of inflammatory declamation. He attempted, for inftance, to infinuate that the Houfe had fcreened the late Governor General of India from punifhment, by withholding the papers moved for by one of his friends on a former day; but the abfurdity of fuch an infinuation would be manifeft to fuch gentlemen as would recollect that the very perfon who had moved for thofe pa- pers, avowed and boafted, that independent of them, they had fufficient ground for a full proof of the guilt of Mr. Haftings; and though they had fuch proofs, yet did they en- deavour by every inflammatory topic, to provoke the Houfe to demand documents not relevant to any charge whatfoever, and which, from their nature and defcription, could not be produced without manifeft detriment to the State. Thus they had firft rendered it neceffary for the Houfe, in com- pliance with its duty, to reject the motion, and afterwards in purfuance of the fyftem which uniformly appeared to govern them, had endeavoured to impute that neceffary refufal to the worft and moft corrupt motives; the defire of fcreening a criminal from juftice. With this fort of language from the right honourable gentleman the Houfe were long fince fa- miliar: and as he had already frequently found occafion to anfwer it, he fhould for the prefent be contented to pafs it by in filence rather than mifpend the time of the Houfe. The right honourable gentleman had faid, that he was fick of hearing the idea of refponfibility applied to an Indian admini- ftration. For his part he looked upon it that not only the fervants of the Public in India were refponfible, but that even the Minifters here were deeply fo, for the conduct of the af- fairs of thofe fettlements: they were refponfible not only for the good behaviour of the perfons whom they fent out, but for their continuance there, and for the fanction which they might give to the fyftem they fhould purfue, or the mea- fures they fhould adopt. This refponfibility, as had been argued by his right honourable and learned friend, was made

more

more broad and comprehenfive on the part of the new Governor General, by the frefh powers to be given him in the
bill. And in fact the very inftitution of thofe powers created
the additional degree of refponfibility, and made it more
ftrongly attach upon his conduct; for it was not an arbitrary
power put into his hands fubject to no check or control,
which was the true meaning of the term, arbitrary power:
it was only a difcretionary power to he exercifed in cafes of
great and urgent importance, and that under the moft forcible
reftraints, and the ftrongeft guards which could he imagined.
In the firft place, the whole of the confultations on the fubject, whatever it was, on which the Governor was to exercife his new authority, were to be recorded; alfo his reafons
for differing in opinion with his Council, were to be entered
on the minutes, together with an account of the circumftance which made him think it neceffary to take fuch a ftep,
and with thofe was to be contrafted the arguments of each
of the diffenting members of the council, which they were
required to enter by way of proteft for their own juftification, and the whole was to be fent home and laid before the
Court of Directors. With refpect to the doctrines laid
down on the fubject of arbitrary power, he felt himfelf fully
juftified in contending that it did not arife from the numbers
of the perfons in whom it was vefted, but from the want of
a proper check and control to which thofe perfons fhould be
liable in the exercife of it. To illuftrate this, he inftanced
the Britifh conftitution, in which the number of five hundred
gentlemen in that Houfe, and a confiderable number of peers
in the other, would not be a fufficient fecurity for the liberties of the People, were it not that the individuals who compofed thofe affemblies were a part of that People, and the
moment they paffed any law, became themfelves bound by
it, in common with the reft of their fellow fubjects. That
Houfe in particular was reftrained from the exercife of fuch
a power by the nature of its conftitution, being in a great
meafure, though not fo much as he and every other friend to
the liberties of the country muft wifh, elected by the People.
But take away thofe circumftances of reprefentation, however imperfect, in one Houfe, and of community of intereft
with the reft of the nation in both, and their numbers would
afford no fecurity whatfoever againft the exercife of defpotic
and arbitrary government. Nay, as had been already remarked by his right honourable and learned friend, in large
bodies, there was great danger to be apprehended of fuch
ftrides of defpotifm, becaufe in them the refponfibility would
prove lefs binding, by being divided among fo many perfons,
whereas, in the prefent cafe, being confined to one, it would
become an infurmountable barrier and reftraint. The right
honourable

honourable gentleman had, in his ufual ftile, made reflections upon him for having altered his fentiments upon the fubject of the powers neceffary to be vefted in the Governor General. It was his fingular misfortune, as the views of his
opponents made it moft inftrumental to their purpofes, to labour alternately under oppofite and contradictory charges;
at one time he was accufed of a prefumptuous and obftinate
adherence to his own opinions and propofals, and at others of
a too ready departure from them; of the two crimes the latter
was that of which he fhould moft willingly acknowledge
himfelf to be guilty; for, to facrifice the interefts of his
country to the pride of perfevering in his own opinions, he
thought would, indeed, be a moft flagrant breach of his duty
to the Public; but to change them where experience, or argument, or a more clofe inveftigation had fhewn them to be
wrong, was, he fhould humbly conceive, rather a fource of
commendation than invective. In this inftance, however, he
had not departed from any of his principles, but had, on the
contrary, given them a greater force and efficacy in the bill
then before the Committee. He had always entertained an
opinion that the authority of the Governor General ought
to be put on a different footing from what it had been, as
many evils refulted from the parity of power between him
and the reft of the council. In the former bill, therefore,
his powers had been enlarged by diminifhing the number of
the council, that fo the concurrence of one of the number
would prove fufficient to give him a majority, and his cafting
voice would more frequently be exercifed with effect; and
in the prefent bill the fame principle was ftill adhered to
and farther followed up, by giving him a power in extraordinary emergencies, and, with the numberlefs checks added to
prevent a wanton or corrupt exercife of that power, of fu-
perfeding, by his fingle authority, the votes of the reft of the
Board. Gentlemen had pretended to treat with ridicule the
idea of impofing an oath on the Governor General whenever
he fhould think proper to avail himfelf of this new created
power. But did fuch gentlemen really pretend to think, or
did they feel that an oath was no reftraint; or did they, when
they were complaining of the power itfelf, ferioufly object
to circumfcribing it with reftraints and limits? The right
honourable gentleman had gone back to the hiftory of Indian politics to prove, that had this power hitherto exifted,
it would have been attended with the moft mifchievous confequences during the adminiftration of Mr. Haftings, becaufe
that on all occafions when that gentleman had been over-
ruled by his council, he was prevented from putting into execution dangerous and deftructive meafures. Whatever might
be the opinion of Mr. Haftings, furely he had no right to

affume that every Governor General was to be as bad as he thought proper to reprefent him; and, for his own part, he was reftrained from entering into a difcuffion of that particular topic, becaufe it was fo intimately connected with the inquiry then depending on Mr. Haftings's conduct, that he fhould not be able to follow the right honourable gentleman without violating that delicacy which fo naturally belonged to a criminal profecution. Whatever might have been Mr. Haftings's demerits, the prefent claufe had nothing to fay to him, it was intended to remedy a defect in the conftitution of the Eaftern Government, from which bad confequences muft neceffarily refult in times of danger and difficulty; and to fay that fuch bad confequences would be overbalanced by preventing the Governor General from exercifing a power, in a manner as deftructive as a former Governor General had attempted to exercife it, was to fay, that having been unfortunate in one Governor General, it muft neceffarily follow that we fhould always be not lefs unlucky. This argument was founded in an idea that all public men were to be diftrufted. Such an idea as this ought by no means to be adopted. It was good policy to guard as much as poffible againft the mifconduct of Minifters, to provide as many reftraints as the nature of the fervice would admit, and to render it as difficult as poffible to efcape punifhment by concealment or otherwife; but it would prove a monftrous abfurdity to fet out upon the principle that they were all neceffarily corrupt; and, befides, fuch a principle would apply to the Members of the Council, as well as to the Governor General. The right honourable gentleman by a recourfe to experience, had attempted to prove that his honourable friend near him, (Mr. Francis) had for a confiderable time engroffed the whole powers of the council by his influence over the majority of the members; and that, during that time the affairs of the Company were better adminiftered than at any other period. If this were the cafe, it only ferved to prove that a more fit perfon might be found than Mr. Haftings, and that, therefore, it was abfurd to argue, from the fuppofed delinquency of that gentleman, the impoffibility of finding an able and upright governor. This the honourable gentleman himfelf feemed to have in view when he took upon him to enumerate the perfons that were competent to judge on the affairs of India. In the firft place having, at one word, ftricken off all thofe who had not been concerned in the executive government, he reduced the lift to three names only, that of himfelf, of Mr. Haftings, and of Lord Macartney. Of the two laft he had contrived to get rid in a very fhort and fummary way, and of courfe left himfelf as the only perfon fit to be confulted on the bufinefs. The right honourable gentleman,

tleman, (Mr. Fox) when arguing the impropriety of the clause upon the topic of experience, had affirmed that from the time that his honourable friend (Mr. Francis) had lost his influence in the council, by the death of one of the members, and that Mr. Hastings's power began to predominate, every thing went wrong. This argument, could it establish any thing, must prove that it was warranted by experience that the power should be lodged in the minority instead of the majority. What an idea! that because the consultations of the Council of Bengal were recorded, that circumstance rendered it the less expedient and safe to place an independent authority in the hands of the Governor! He admitted that, in that particular the constitution of the cabinet council at home was different from that of Bengal; but this difference, he contended, was one of the things which might be offered in favour of the new regulation, because the consultations being minuted and transmitted to the Court of Directors, would form one of the strongest restraints on the exercise of the discretionary power. The right honourable gentleman had endeavoured to triumph over his right honourable and learned friend for his appealing to futurity for the success of the system then under review; but in a measure so recent as the present, where there was no time for experience of its effects, and in which the framers of it had no other grounds to go upon but the consciousness of their own good inclinations and industry, what other test could they appeal to but that of futurity? As to the predictions of the right honourable gentlemen, he should only answer them by recalling the attention of the House to some of his former predictions on a part of the same subject. He had upon an occasion, not yet, he believed, erased from the minds of gentlemen, when he had a hope of carrying into effect a measure of the most destructive tendency to the prosperity of India and to the constitution of Great Britain, endeavouring to bring over people to his views, and to conceal, as much as possible, his true and real purposes—predicted "that " the East-India Company would shortly be bankrupt," and on this pretence, at that time unfounded upon any probable grounds of conjecture, he had been able to impose upon many members of that House, and had by means of that delusive prediction nearly accomplished his ruinous and most alarming project. This prediction had since sustained the ordeal of time, and it appeared to be egregiously false and contrary to fact; for so far was the East-India Company from a state of bankruptcy, that their affairs were in a most flourishing way; their resources increasing, their credit rising, and their expenditure retrenched; and there was every hope that the revenues of India would not only prove able in a

short time to pay off all its own incumbrances, but to contribute also to the relief of this country. With all these
particulars in their view, the Committee would, doubtless,
wisely exercise their own judgements, and decide how far
the right honourable gentleman, when exploring the womb
of futurity, and describing the colour, the nature, and the
consequences of East-India occurrences to come, was inspi-
red with the sacred powers of unerring prophecy!

Mr. Fox.   Mr. *Fox* answered, that could it have been possible, by the
artifices of misrepresentation, so to have tortured the meaning of his words, as to have impressed upon the House an
idea that he had spoken of them with unbecoming insult,
the right honourable gentleman might be described as having
acted wisely thus far, at least, as such a procedure could fulfil
his purpose: but, unluckily for such views, his words had
been " the Board of Control screened public delinquents in
" that House from investigation and inquiry," in making
which charge he meant that the pretence on which the right
honourable gentleman, opposite to him, had refused papers
which were called for, he in his conscience did not believe
were founded in reality. Mr. Fox stated Mr. Eden's Report,
as Chairman of the Committee of last session, on the East-
India Company's accounts, in support of the statement which
he had given in that House of the Company's affairs, and
declared that he was ready to meet the right honourable gentleman upon that ground whenever he should think proper.

The numbers on the second division, on the question to
omit the oath to be taken by the Governor General, were
125 for the oath's standing part of the bill, and 36 for omitting the oath.

The House adjourned.

Thursday, 23d March.

No business took place.

Friday, 24th March.

Major Scott   Major *Scott* begged leave to trouble the House with three
papers moved for by a right honourable gentleman (Mr.
Burke) relative to Benares. His first motion was, " That
" the Directors of the East-India Company do lay before this
" House, a copy of any proceedings they may have held at
" the India House in the year 1779, in consequence of a re-
" solution taken by the Government General of Bengal, on
" the 9th of July, 1778, to demand from Cheyt Sing five
" lacks of rupees, as his proportion of the expence incurred
" by the war with France, that they do also specify at what
" time they received the account of this demand, and at
                                          " what

" what time they received the fecret confultations of the
" Bengal Government of the 28th of September, 1778; and
" alfo, a copy of any orders fent to Bengal, or proceedings,
" obfervations, or protefts, of the Court of Directors, or of
" any of the Directors, that may appear upon the minutes
" of the Court either upon the receipt of the fecret letter
" from Bengal, of the 17th of Auguft, 1778, or in confe-
" quence of Mr. Haftings having recorded it as his opinion
" on the fecret confulations of the 28th September, 1778,
" that ' Mr. Fowke's inftructions related only to the fixed
" and annual revenus, but could never be underftood to pre-
" clude that right which every government inherently pof-
" feffes, to compel all its dependencies to contribute by extra-
" ordinary fupplies to the relief of extraordinary emergencies.''

Mr. *Francis* obferved, that he could not difcover what
were the views of the honourable gentleman in making fuch
a motion, unlefs, indeed, that he defigned to crimmate the
Directors for neglect. If that was the motive, he would
heartily join with the honourable gentlemen, who, he thought,
very well knew that the anfwer would be, *Non eft inventus;*
becaufe no inftructions relative to this fubject were at any
time difpatched to the Eaft Indies.

Mr. Fran-
cis.

Major *Scott* anfwered, that he did not entertain the leaft
doubt but that the reply would prove a *Non eft inventus,* yet
it appeared to him very material that the Houfe fhould know
it for a certainty, and he would ftate his reafon. In fome
obfervations publifhed by the Directors, in October, 1783,
when an honourable member (Sir Henry Fletcher) was the
Chairman, they feverely cenfured Mr. Haftings and his
Council, for demanding five lacks of rupees from Cheyt Sing.
Now if he could prove that Mr. Haftings folemnly and deliberately recorded the principle upon which he acted, in September, 1778, and that it was received in England in May,
1779, and never noticed by the Directors, furely it would
be fair to fay, that the filence was acquiefcence and approbation, and that the criminality, (if criminality exifted) refted not with Mr. Haftings, but with the Directors.

Major Scott.

Mr. *Sheridan* faid, that it might perhaps tend to prove
how unfit the Directors were for their ftations, but could
not exculpate Mr. Haftings, and that the right honourable
and learned gentleman (Mr. Dundas) was to blame for chufing fuch Directors. In fact he faw not any neceffity for
the motion; but, motions from different fides of the Houfe,
were fated to recieve far different encouragements.

Mr. Sheri-
dan.

Mr. *Dundas* expreffed his willingnefs to give every paper
for which either fide might call for, provided that they could
be granted without danger. With refpect to the Directors,
he had not the electing of them, and therefore was not refponfible;

Mr. Dun-
das.

sponsible; but the paper moved for by the honourable gentleman (Major Scott) referred to transactions which happened long before the establishment of the Board of Control.

Major Scott   Major *Scott* said, that the argument respecting the Directors being unfit for their offices, when not making the demand on Cheyt Sing till nine years after they heard it, would apply to both sides of the House. For, an honourable gentleman, not now a member (Mr. Gregory) and an honourable member, Sir Henry Fletcher, were in the direction at the time when the account was received relative to Cheyt Sing, and every year after, except when they were out by rotation, yet the right honourable gentleman (Mr. Fox) had fixed upon them to be two of the seven Directors under his bill, and of the nine Assistant Directors, seven at least were in the same situation. He never heard that any one of the number had protested against the demand made upon Cheyt Sing for three years successively, and enforced by military execution, until the subject was brought forward after the insurrection of Benares was canvassed in 1782.

The motion passed; and

Major Scott   Major *Scott* observing that his next proposition was meant to prove that, although the second demand was enforced by military execution, it had passed unnoticed by either the Minister or the Directors, moved, " That the Directors of " the East-India Company do lay before this House a copy " of any proceedings they may have held at the India House, " in consequence of a resolution taken by the Government " General of Bengal, on the 19th of July 1779, to require " from Cheyt Sing five lacks of rupees, as his proportion of " the expence incurred by the war with France, for that " year, that they do also specify at what period they received " the secret Bengal consultations upon the subject of the " above Demand, and when they received the secret letter " from Bengal of the 13th of March, 1780, which informed " them that the demand had been enforced by the march of " two battalions of sepoys to Benares, and that the Rajah " had been compelled to defray the expence of this detach- " ment; that the Directors be farther required to lay before " this House, a copy of any orders that were sent to Bengal " on this subject in 1780 or 1781, or of the observations or " protests of the Court of Directors, or of any of the Direc- " tors in consequence of these proceedings in Bengal."

Mr. Chancellor Pitt.   Mr. Chancellor *Pitt* observed, that though it could be no justification for Mr. Hastings (if he had done an act originally wrong) for that act; yet, if it appeared that he transmitted the earliest intelligence of what he had done, accompanied by his motives for doing it, and if the power which had a right to control him, did acquiesce in it, that such
acquiescence

acquiefcence was approbation. He did not know what the anfwer would be to the motion; but, it appeared to him that the motion itfelf might pafs.

The motion paffed.

Major *Scott* then moved, " That the Directors of the **Major Scott** " Eaſt-India Company do lay before this Houfe, a copy of " any proceedings they may have held at the India Houfe, " in confequence of a demand made by the Government Ge- " neral of Bengal, upon Cheyt Sing, on the 22d of June, " 1780, for five lacks of rupees, as his fhare of the expence " of the war for that year, that they be directed to inform " the Houfe at what period the advices relative to this fub- " ject were received by them, and what orders were fent to " Bengal in the year 1781, in confequence of the informa- " tion contained in the fecret letter from Bengal, of the fteps " taken in that year to enforce Cheyt Sing to pay the five " lacks of rupees; alfo copies of obfervations and protefts " of the Court of Directors, or of any of the Directors, made " in confequence of the information tranfmitted from Bengal " relative to Cheyt Sing in 1780."

After the reading of the order of the day for the Houfe to refolve itfelf into a Committee on the bill to explain and amend the bill of 1784,

Mr. *Sheridan* remarked that he had a propofition to offer **Mr. Sheri-** previous to their refolving themfelves into a Committee, **dan.** which he hoped would not be objected to. The bill confift- ed of two parts. The firft part related to the regulations of the government in India, the fecond to the new Court of Judicature to be inftituted at home, for the trial of perfons charged with having been guilty of acts of delinquency and mifdemeanor in India. As thefe were feparate and diftinct objects, he wifhed them to be feparately confidered, and, as probably Adminiftration had made it a condition with Earl Cornwallis, that he fhould go out to Bengal invefted with certain powers; it might be their defire to pafs fo much of the bill as related to the fyftem of government, to be adopted in India as foon as poffible. The fame neceffity for difpatch certainly did not apply to the judicature part of the bill, and as that part had been but little confidered when the bill of 1784 paffed, he could wifh that the learned and right ho- nourable gentleman oppofite to him would confent to divide the bill, and feparate the two fubjects. In that cafe Admi- niftration would have it in their power to make good any pro- mifes which they might have made to Earl Cornwallis, and time might be taken for fuch a deliberate difcuffion of the judicature part of the bill, as the importance of it required. Mr. Sheridan concluded with moving, " That it be an in- " ftruction to the faid Committee to divide the bill in two."

Mr.

Mr. *Dundas* obferved, that although not objecting to the motion, he muft beg leave to make a fhort reply to that part of the honourable gentleman's fpeech, in which he had fuggefted, that probably Adminiftration might have made certain promifes to Earl Cornwallis : he thought it due to that nobleman's character, to have it clearly underftood, that every regulation for the future government of India, and all the powers which the bill would give to the Governor General, were determined upon long before Earl Cornwallis was thought of for the fituation of Governor General ; and it was but juftice in him to declare moft folemnly, that there never was a man who acted in a more fair and honourable way than Earl Cornwalls had done relative to his acceptance of the office. He had taken it without making any condition or ftipulation whatfoever, and when he went out, the Public would be able to judge from the people whom Earl Cornwallis might take with him, whether any thing could be more praifeworthy than his conduct. With regard to the propofition of the honourable gentleman, he was always happy when he had it in his power to coincide with him, and could not but lament, that he had fo often differed with him in opinion, and moft probably fhould fo often differ with him in future ; on the prefent occafion he had not the fmalleft objection to his propofition.

Mr. Chancellor *Pitt* declared, he would not prefs what he had to offer, if the gentlemen on the other fide objected ; but as the part of the bill which referred to the mode of ballot for the Jury or Court of Judicature to try Eaft-India delinquents, he prefumed, would not meet the fmalleft oppofition, he might venture to afk, whether any gentleman defigned ferioufly to except againft the claufes ?

Mr. *Fox* remarked, that as the queftion to be difcuffed in future referred to the whole of the new judicature, he fhould conceive the whole confideration of it had better be referved for fubfequent difcuffion together, and therefore, as it would be neceffary to determine whether the new judicature fhould be inftituted or not before they proceeded to fettle the mode of ballot for its members, he fhould conceive, that it would be more prudent to poftpone the whole of the bill which referred to it for confideration hereafter.

Mr. Chancellor, Pitt acquiefced in this reafoning, and the inftructions paffed.

The Houfe then went into a Committee, and Mr. Dundas proceeded to propofe words to fill up the blanks of fuch of the remaining claufes as referred to the conduct of the Company's fervants in India, in regard to gradual rife to fuperior offices, &c.

The Committee went through the bill, and upon motion made, " That the report be now received ;" an amendment was

was propofed to infert the words " Monday next," inftead thereof.

After a fhort debate the Houfe divided on the queftion, that the word " now," ftand part of the queftion;

Ayes - - - - - 89
Noes - - - - - 24
                              ———
Majority - - - - 65

The main queftion was then put and agreed to, and the bill ordered to be read a third time on Monday next if engroffed.

The Houfe adjourned.

Monday, 27th March.

The Houfe having refolved itfelf into a Committee of the whole Houfe,

Mr. *Jenkinfon* made a propofition relative to the New-foundland trade and fifhery. refpecting which a bill had been brought in during the courfe of the preceding feffion, and gone as far as the fecond reading, but if the Committee were difpofed to hear him, he would explain to them the principles on which his opinion was founded, and ftate the general fyftem of regulations which appeared to him neceffary to be laid down and eftablifhed for the prefervation of the New-foundland trade and fifhery.—Firft, the high importance of the trade to this country—Next, the means moft likely to encourage and fupport it—And laftly, the fituation of it, compared with that of thofe foreign powers with whom we had to conteft in refpect to the fifheries, were thoroughly entitled to the moft ferious attention of the Houfe. The meafures purfued laft year in refpect to the Weft Indies, had proved, that under due regulations, our commerce with that quarter of the world had grown and increafed confiderably fince the feparation between Great Britain and the United States of America, and there was every reafon to believe, that our Newfoundland trade and fifhery, when properly conducted, would prove equally fuccefsful. The accounts of laft year evinced, that the gain upon that trade to this country amounted at leaft to 50,000l. annually; and that we fent out Britifh commodities and brought home fpecie or bills for the fifh which we fold to the Mediterranean, Portuguefe, and other foreign markets. The number of fhips and veffels employed in carrying on the trade were upwards of 450, in the manning of which 10,000 feamen were engaged: this, therefore proved, that the Newfoundland trade was not only a moft valuable branch of our commerce, but a confiderable fource of naval ftrength, fince it kept 10,000 men always

Mr. Jenkin-
fon.

ready whenever the exigency of public affairs should require their service.

Ireland also, he was persuaded, proved a considerable gainer, as she supplied Newfoundland with all her salted provisions, the intercourse with the United States having been entirely cut off. In order to manifest the great importance of the object, he would just state the principles on which he thought it most adviseable to regulate the Newfoundland fishery in future, the most essential of which was, to preserve it entirely a British fishery; and this could only be done by confining it to British ships, navigated from Great Britain, and by no means permitting any stationary settlement to be made on the island of Newfoundland. If a colony were to be settled there, courts of judicature must be instituted, and a civil government established, the obvious consequences of which would be, the loss of the fisheries to this country, as had been the case with respect to the New-England fisheries. No sooner was New England colonized, than the colony took the fisheries on their own coasts into their own hands, and we lost the fisheries. The old policy of this country in respect to Newfoundland, had always been, to put the fishery on such a footing as should avert this evil; and in order to do so the more effectually, it had been the practice to contract with the seamen, that they should be paid one part of the wages due to them for their service on the voyage outward and home again, in Great Britain, after their return home again: to this he should propose rigidly to adhere, and to such other regulations respecting the fisheries as were most likely to preserve the British fisheries; to the attainment of which end, it would materially conduce, to make all stands, stages, flakes, and curing houses on the island, no longer the property of those who might have erected them, than while they employed them in the business of the fishery, but if left, they should become liable to be occupied by those first arriving at the time of the ensuing fishing season. As emulation, and the spirit of adventure, were the source and vital spring of this trade, he should propose to hold out as many temptations for more to join in it as possible; and as it was perfectly free and open, and in which, of course, any person who chose it might embark, he should, by various ways, encourage men even of small fortunes and slender property to undertake it. This might be done by giving small bounties to every new adventurer, and by letting it be carried on by ships and vessels in which different people had shares. As to our situation in respect to the Newfoundland fishery, relatively to that of those foreign powers with whom we had to contest it, it was with no small satisfaction that he could say, that we enjoyed a manifest advantage over every competitor.

titor. France had endeavoured, by the moſt extravagant bounties, to encourage her fiſhery trade; ſhe granted ten livres per quintal on all fiſh caught by her fiſhermen and brought either into her iſlands or into Old France. She alſo laid a high duty of five livres per quintal, on all fiſh brought either into her colonies or into her kingdom by foreign veſ-ſels; this was manifeſtly levelled at the United States of America, and at the ſame time it ſhewed the debility of the ſtate of the French fiſheries, by evincing, that the fiſh which they catch did not amount to a ſufficient ſupply for them-ſelves at home and in their Weſt-India iſlands; if it had, France would have done as we did, have laid an actual pro-hibition on the importation of all fiſh into her colonies in foreign veſſels. France, beſides theſe two bounties, gave a third of ten livres per quintal upon all fiſh caught by their fiſhermen and exported to foreign countries. The bounties were extravagant almoſt to abſurdity; becauſe not only the fiſheries of France were much impoveriſhed, but ſhe was aware of the great importance of encouraging them as greatly as poſſible, and ſet no limits to the expence of accompliſhing ſuch views. It would prove our own faults if we ſuffered our fiſheries to dwindle and thoſe of France to outrival us: and as one of our veſſels, from the ſuperior excellence of the utenſils employed in the fiſhery, and the ſuperior addreſs and intrepidity of our ſeamen, could catch twice as many fiſh as a French fiſhing boat, he knew of no way for them to cope with us unleſs they debauched and enticed away our men, or got poſſeſſion of our fiſhing veſſels and the utenſils uſed by us in the trade. He meant, therefore, to impoſe certain pe-nalties, and to provide certain regulations, to prevent the ſale of any of our fiſhing veſſels except to Britiſh fiſhers. The bounties which he ſhould propoſe, would not amount to more than ſix or ſeven thouſand pounds; nor would he attempt to follow France in giving bounties on the export of our fiſh to foreign markets, becauſe to do that muſt coſt the nation 120,000l.; a ſum ſo large, that no perſon, he believed, would think it prudent to expend it in that manner.

He now moved, " That bounties be allowed to a certain " number of veſſels employed in the Britiſh fiſhery on the " banks of the iſland of Newfoundland, in manner follow- " ing; that is to ſay, to the firſt one hundred veſſels which " ſhall arrive in each year, in the ports of the ſaid iſland, " with a cargo of fiſh, not leſs than 10,000 by tale, " catched on the banks thereof, and ſhall, after landing the " ſame, proceed for, and return with one cargo of fiſh more " at leaſt, catched upon the ſaid banks, if carrying not leſs " than twelve men, forty pounds each; but if ſuch men " are carried upon ſhares, fifty pounds each. If carrying

" lefs than twelve men, and not lefs than feven, twenty-five
" pounds each; but if fuch men are carried upon fhares,
" thirty-five pounds each. And to the next one hundred
" veffels that fhall arrive in the faid ports with a like cargo,
" and fhall, after landing the fame, proceed again to the faid
" banks, and return from thence with one or more cargoes
" of fifh, in manner aforefaid, if carrying twelve men,
" twenty-five pounds each; but if fuch men are carried
" upon fhares, thirty-five pounds each. If carrying lefs
" than twelve men, and not lefs than feven men, eighteen
" pounds each; but if fuch men are carried upon fhares,
" twenty-one pounds each."

    When Mr. Gilbert, chairman of the Committee, had read the refolution,

Grey
oper.

    Sir *Grey Cooper* remarked, that far from meaning to oppofe the refolution, he felt it but an act of common juftice to declare his perfect concurrence in what the right honourable gentleman had ftated, with all that precifion and accuracy which was the conftant characteriftic of a thorough knowledge of the fubject. The bill of 1775 was near expiring, and therefore he had expected that a new bill would be brought in. The right honourable gentleman had taken a principal fhare in preparing and conducting the exifting bill through the Houfe, and at that time he had the benefit of the affiftance of an honourable Admiral, no longer a member of Parliament; who, from a long refidence at Newfoundland, and a fedulous inveftigation into the nature of the fifheries, was fully enabled to give advice upon the fubject. Undoubtedly the fifheries were great and important national concerns; they deferved every poffible encouragement and fupport, but moft of all, that ancient ftaple fifhery of this kingdom, the Newfoundland fifhery. It was to be confidered not merely as a fource of riches and commerce, but of naval power and maritime ftrength. He admired the magnificent queftion lately put by a right honourable gentleman in that Houfe, of " who fhould fet limits to the naval ftrength " of Great Britain?" The queftion however was eafily anfwered; the point fet its own limits, for it muft be obvious to every man, that it was to no purpofe to expend vaft fums in building large fhips of war, and increafing the number of our fleets, if we did not get men to man the fhips with after they were built. Every means therefore for providing nurferies for feamen ought to be carefully attended to by Government and by that Houfe, and furely none could prove more effectual for that purpofe than the encouraging of our fifheries.

Hop-
h.

    Mr. *Hopkins* trufted that when the bill to be founded on the refolution fhould be brought in, thofe who were chiefly con-

concerned in the Newfoundland trade would have proper time allowed them to make themselves masters of it, and to consider how far it would or would not prove injurious to their interests.

Captain *Berkeley* expressed his hopes that the right honourable gentleman did not carry his ideas so far as to mean to enact, that those who had expended ten or fifteen thousand pounds in erecting houses, flakes, and stages, on the island of Newfoundland, were to be deprived of their property, and the buildings made common property, and free to the possession of the first comers. If so, what man would venture to embark in a trade so manifestly injurious to his fortune? Captain Berkeley produced a clause, which he begged to submit to the right honourable gentleman, and if he approved it, he said, he would move it when the bill should be in a Committee. *[margin: Captain Berkeley.]*

Mr. *Jenkinson* answered, the present moment was by no means seasonable to the discussion of clauses for a bill which was not yet before the House; but he owned that he had no conception of any houses or stages, used in the fishery, costing any thing like ten or fifteen thousand pounds. He signified his determination, as far as his own opinion went, that all buildings not actually employed in the fishery at the time should be free to the first comers. *[margin: Mr. Jenkinson.]*

The resolution passed.

Mr. *Sheridan* remarked, that when he considered that scarcely many minutes had elapsed subsequently to the delivery of the Report of the Committee to inquire concerning the state of the national finances into the hands of the several members of that House, he could not avoid intimating to a right honourable gentleman (Mr. Pitt) his earnest wishes that he would consent to postpone the consideration of the Report until either the ensuing Monday or Friday. Great was the importance of the subject, and consequently it must make every gentleman desire that it should be considered and discussed in as full a House as possible; and therefore as the call of the House stood for the next Tuesday, he should conceive it would be right to let the subject be discussed as near the day of the call as possible. He had looked with accuracy enough in the Report to observe, that it would not give the satisfaction expected from it. He was aware that another business stood for Monday, but the deferring of that for one or two days, he presumed, would make no difference; yet if the consideration of the Report was postponed only till Friday, even that slight procrastination would give gentleman more time to examine and understand it. *[margin: Mr. Sheridan.]*

Mr. Chancellor *Pitt* answered, that the arguments of the honourable gentleman were by no means sufficient to warrant *[margin: Mr. Chancellor Pitt.]*

a delay

a delay in a bufinefs of fuch importance, and one to which
the objection of furprize could by no means be made, as it
had been fo long a fubject of anxious expectation, both to
that Houfe and the Public, and as fuch fteps had been taken
to bring it forward in a well-digefted and methodical manner,
by the Report of the Select Committee. It was rather fingular that the honourable gentleman fhould complain that he
had received a copy of the Report fufficiently early, and yet
fhould himfelf have ftated that he had read the whole of it
fo very accurately as to be able to enter into the detail of it,
and to ftate fo fully the objections which he intended to make.
The Report, he was perfuaded, would afford ample information to gentlemen who really wifhed to obtain information
from it, and it was fo clearly and precifely drawn up as to
require but little ftudy to underftand it completely. As to
waiting until the call of the Houfe to bring forward the firft
motion in the bufinefs, he thought that was by no means the
method to fecure it a complete and full attendance. On the
contrary, the better way would be to open it previous to the
call, fo as to have it in a ftate of forwardnefs at the time
when the operation of the call fhould be moft ftrong, that fo
a full confideration in a crouded Houfe might be infured in
the moft important ftate of the bufinefs — the introduction of
the bill. He indeed, even if he had not been called up by the
honourable gentleman, intended to have made a motion relative to the bufinefs, and as an introduction to it, he fhould
move, " That His Majefty's moft gracious fpeech to both
" Houfes of Parliament, upon the 24th of January laft,
" might be read." The clerk accordingly read, and Mr. Pitt
concluded with moving,

" That this Houfe will, upon Wednefday morning next,
" refolve itfelf into a Committee of the whole Houfe, to con-
" fider of fo much of His Majefty's faid moft gracious
" fpeech to both Houfes of Parliament as recommends to
" this Houfe the eftablifhment of a fixed plan for the reduc-
" tion of the national debt."

Mr. Pitt next moved,

" That the Report which, upon Tuefday laft, was made
" from the Select Committee, to whom it was referred to
" examine and ftate the feveral accounts and other papers
" prefented to the Houfe in this feffion of Parliament re-
" lating to the public income and expenditure, and to report
" to the Houfe what may be expected to be the annual
" amount of the faid income and expenditure in future, be
" referred to the faid Committee."

Sheri-   Mr. *Sheridan* begged leave to remind the right honourable
gentleman of his error, for the purpofe of rectifying which
he fhould not hefitate to affert, that he by no means ftated
that

that he had read the whole of the Report; he only faid, he had looked at the Report with fufficient accuracy to fee that it would not afford the Public the fatisfaction expected. However he certainly would not prefs the matter; but he hoped that the right honourable gentleman, by his eagernefs for an early day, looked forward to a day of triumph, and not to a day of difappointment to the Public, and of difgrace to himfelf. As far as he had feen, fo far from the exiftence of a confiderable furplus, at prefent there was not any, and therefore the Report completely difproved all that the right honourable gentleman had advanced relative to the matter.

Mr. Pitt's motions paffed.

The Eaft-India bill having been, on the motion of Mr. Dundas, read a third time, Mr. *Dempfter* propofed to annex a claufe by way of rider, for the purpofe of limiting the duration of the act of three or five years. Mr. Dempfter juftified the claufe on the ground, that as the bill was to veft a new and unheard-of difcretionary power in the Governor General to enable him to act in oppofition to the advice of his Council, it was neceffary to limit the duration of the exercife of fuch an extraordinary power.

Mr. *Dundas* oppofed the bringing up any fuch claufe, as a matter repugnant to the principle of his bill, which was to eftablifh a permanent government.

The Houfe divided; Ayes, for bringing up the claufe, 37; Noes, 108.

Sir James Erfkine moved to bring up three other claufes, but they were all rejected without a divifion.

The bill then paffed, and Mr. Dundas was ordered to carry it to the Lords.

The order of the day being read for the fecond reading of Stourbridge canal bill, a fhort converfation took place between Mr. Minchin, Lord Weftcote, Sir Richard Sutton, and others. Mr. Minchin moved to poftpone the fecond reading for three months, but afterwards gave up his motion.

The bill was then read a fecond time, and the Houfe proceeded to hear counfel and examine witneffes.

The Houfe adjourned.

Tuefday, 28th *March*.

No bufinefs took place.

END OF THE NINETEENTH VOLUME.

NEW PUBLICATIONS,

Printed for J. DEBRETT, oppofite Burlington Houfe, Piccadilly.

ARTICLES of CHARGE of HIGH CRIMES and MISDEMEANORS againft WARREN HASTINGS, Efq. late Governor General of Bengal: prefented to the HOUSE of COMMONS in 1786, by the Right Honourable EDMUND BURKE. Second Edition.

MINUTES of what was offered by WARREN HASTINGS, Efq. late Governor General of Bengal, at the Bar of the Houfe of Commons, upon the matter of Charge of High Crimes and Mifdemeanors, prefented againft him in 1786. Second Edition.

MINUTES of the EVIDENCE taken before a Committee of the whole Houfe of Commons, on the Articles of Charge of High Crimes and Mifdemeanors, prefented to the Houfe againft WARREN HASTINGS, Efq. late Governor General of Bengal—Containing the Evidence of Sir Robert Barker, Colonel Champion, Major Marfack, Captain Jacques, Majors Balfour, Gardner, and Gilpin; Mr. Middleton, and Captain Williams; with the feveral Papers which were read.

⁎ The above interefting Publications being all uniformly printed in 8vo, may be had complete, in two Volumes, price 15s. in boards.

Mr. HASTINGS's NARRATIVE of the INSURRECTION at BENARES, with an APPENDIX of AUTHENTIC PAPERS and AFFIDAVITS, elegantly printed in Quarto.

COPY of a LETTER from WARREN HASTINGS, Efq. to the Court of Directors, relative to their Cenfure on his Conduct at Benares; and alfo the ANSWER of the Court of Directors thereto; prefented to the Houfe of Commons upon the 2d Day of March, 1786.

To which is added,

Mr. HASTINGS's LETTER to William Devaynes, Efq. Chairman of the India Company, from Cheltenham, July 11, 1785; on the Subject of Money privately received. Price 1s. 6d.

A LETTER from WARREN HASTINGS, Efq. to the Hon. the Court of Directors of the Eaft-India Company, dated from Lucknow, April 30, with a Poftfcript, dated May 13, 1784. Price 1s. 6d.

OBSERVATIONS on the COMMUTATION PROJECT, by THOMAS BATES ROUS, Efq. Second Edition, with an Appendix. Price 1s.

TRANSACTIONS in INDIA, from the Commencement of the French War in 1756, to the Conclufion of the late Peace in 1783; containing a HISTORY of the BRITISH INTERESTS in INDOSTAN, during a period of near thirty years; diftinguifhed by two Wars with France, feveral Revolutions and Treaties of Alliance, the Acquifition of an extenfive Territory, and the Adminiftration of Governor Haftings. Price 6s. in Boards.

SPEECH of GEORGE DALLAS, Efq. Member of the Committee appointed by the Britifh Inhabitants refiding in Bengal, for the purpofe of preparing Petitions to His Majefty, and both Houfes of Parliament, praying Redrefs againft an Act of Parliament, &c. as delivered by him at a Meeting held at the Theatre, in Calcutta, on the 25th of July, 1785. A new Edition, with Additions. Price 1s. 6d.

PROCEEDINGS of the Britifh Inhabitants of Madras, on the fubject of Mr. PITT's Eaft-India Bill, at a Meeting held at the Town Hall of Fort St. George, on Monday the 19th Day of September 1785, in confequence of a Summons, by John Snow, Efq. Sheriff of Madras.

Mr. FRANCIS's Speech in the Houfe of Commons, March 7, 1786. Price 2s.

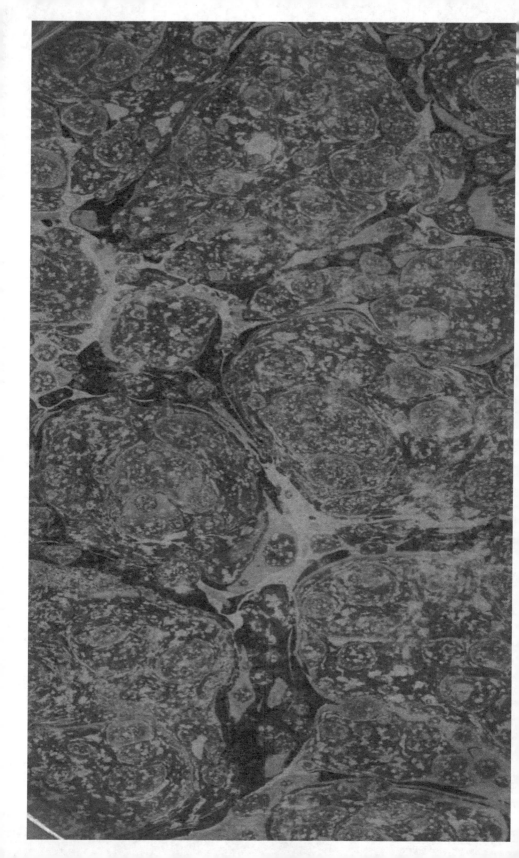

Check Out More Titles From HardPress Classics Series In this collection we are offering thousands of classic and hard to find books. This series spans a vast array of subjects – so you are bound to find something of interest to enjoy reading and learning about.

Subjects:
Architecture
Art
Biography & Autobiography
Body, Mind &Spirit
Children & Young Adult
Dramas
Education
Fiction
History
Language Arts & Disciplines
Law
Literary Collections
Music
Poetry
Psychology
Science
…and many more.

Visit us at www.hardpress.net

CPSIA information can be obtained
at www.ICGtesting.com
Printed in the USA
BVHW062213270819
556849BV00014B/1910/P

9 780371 043455